KANDINSKY

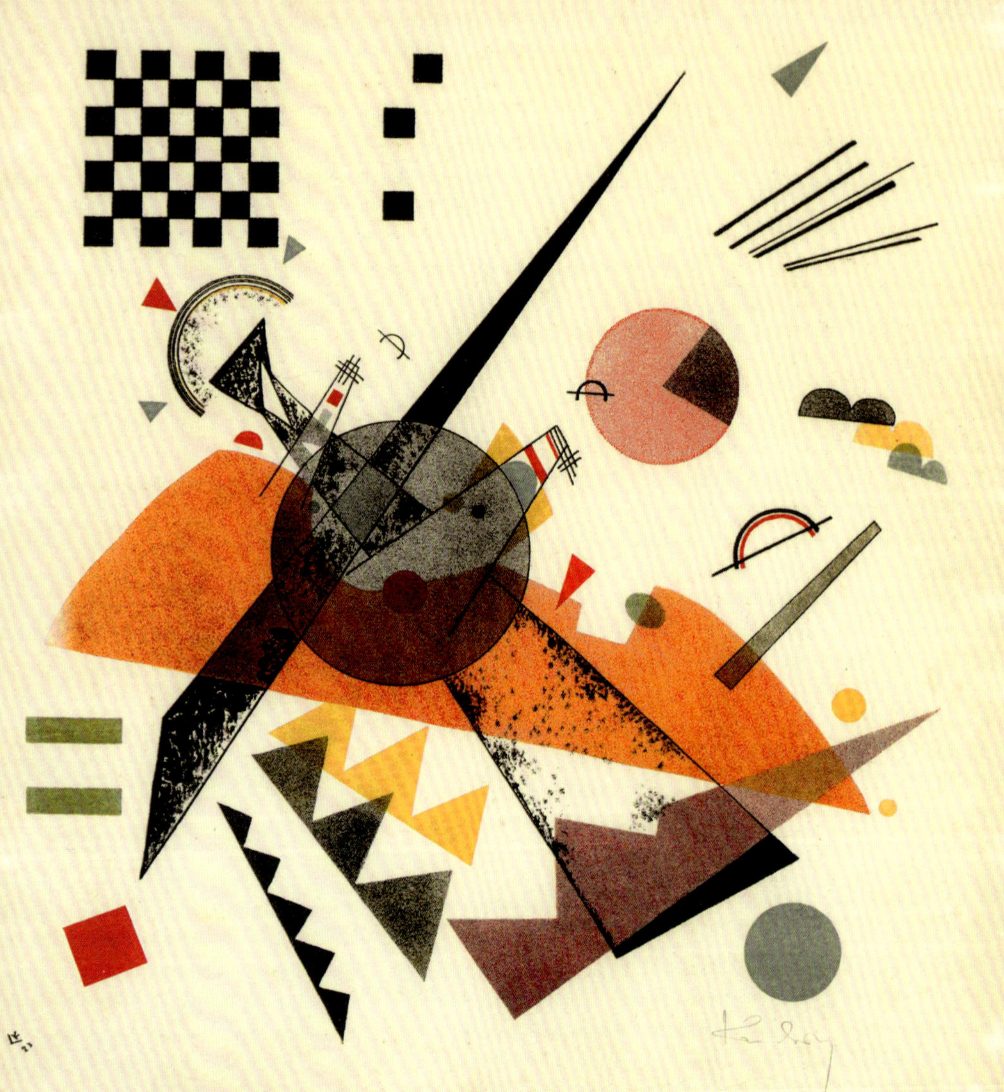

KANDINSKY

HAJO DÜCHTING

p. 2

Orange (R. 180)

Orange (R. 180)

Orange (R. 180)

Naranja

Arancia

Oranje

*Colour lithograph/Lithographie couleur,
48.1 × 44,3 cm, Private collection*

KÖNEMANN

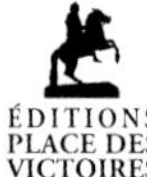

ÉDITIONS
PLACE DES
VICTOIRES

© Éditions Place des Victoires
6, rue du Mail – 75002 Paris
www.victoires.com
ISBN: 978-2-8099-1428-3
Dépôt légal: 2ᵉ trimestre 2023

Concept, Project Management: koenemann.com GmbH
Text: Dr. Hajo Düchting
Editing: Kathrin Jurgenowski

Translations: David Nash (GB), Denis-Armand Canal (F text), Virginie de Bermond-Gettle (F captions),
Patricia Jiménez (E), Francesca Magistro (I)

Translation NL:

TEXTCASE
Translation Agency

info@textcase.nl
Textcase.de   textcase.eu

Art Direction: Oliver Hessmann
Layout: Nora Hein, Holy Design
Picture credits: Bridgeman Images

ISBN: 978-3-95588-105-4 (international)

Printed in China by Shyft Publishing / Hunan Tianwen Xinhua Printing Co., Ltd

Contents
Sommaire
Inhalt
Índice
Indice
Inhoud

À propos

"He is an Asian who paints pictures which are indecent, very interesting and completely incomprehensible to other people."

«C'est un Asiate, qui peint des tableaux inconvenants, très intéressants, mais totalement incompréhensibles pour d'autres personnes.»

„Er ist Asiate, der unanständige, sehr interessante, anderen Leuten aber gänzlich schleierhafte Bilder malt."

"Es un asiático que pinta obras indecentes, muy interesantes y completamente incomprensibles para los demás."

"È un asiatico che dipinge quadri indecenti, molto interessanti e del tutto incomprensibili per altre persone."

"Hij is een Aziaat die onfatsoenlijke, zeer interessante maar voor andere mensen volstrekt ontoegankelijke schilderijen maakt."

AUGUST MACKE

Artist, Teacher, Cosmospolitan
Wassily Kandinsky was born in Moscow on 04.12.1866, growing up in an upper middle-class family where, already in his childhood, his talent for drawing avnd painting was recognised and encouraged. In 1871 the family moved to Odessa where Wassily's father became the manager of a tea-merchandising company. That same year saw the parents divorce, after which however, they remained on friendly terms. Despite Kandinsky's love of art he elected to study law and economics, earning his diploma in 1893, followed by a doctorate. With the offer of a professorship at the University of Dorpat (today in Estonia) in 1896, an academic career beckoned, and in the same year he married his cousin Anja Tschimiakin.

Artiste, enseignant, cosmopolite
Né le 4 décembre 1866 à Moscou, Vassily Kandinsky grandit dans un milieu aisé de grande bourgeoisie. Ses talents pour le dessin et la peinture sont découverts et encouragés dès son enfance. En 1871, la famille déménage à Odessa où le père reprend la direction d'une société de commerce du thé. La même année intervient la séparation des parents – qui restent toutefois en relations d'amitié. Malgré tout son amour pour l'art, Kandinsky étudie d'abord le droit et l'économie nationale, disciplines dans lesquelles il est diplômé en 1893, avant d'obtenir le titre de docteur. En 1896, l'offre d'un poste de professeur à l'université de Dorpat (aujourd'hui en Estonie) le met à portée d'une belle carrière académique. Il épouse la même année sa cousine, Anja Tchimiakine.

Künstler, Lehrer, Kosmopolit
Der am 4.12.1866 in Moskau geborene Wassily Kandinsky wächst in großbürgerlichen Verhältnissen auf. Schon in seiner Kindheit wird sein zeichnerisches und malerisches Talent entdeckt und gefördert. 1871 übersiedelt die Familie nach Odessa, wo der Vater die Direktion einer Teehandelsfirma übernimmt. Ins gleiche Jahr fällt die Scheidung der Eltern, die einander jedoch freundschaftlich verbunden bleiben. Trotz aller Liebe zur Kunst studiert Kandinsky zunächst Jura und Nationalökonomie, erwirbt 1893 ein Diplom und anschließend den Doktortitel. Mit dem Angebot einer Dozentur an der Universität von Dorpat (heute Estland) 1896 rückt eine akademische Karriere in greifbare

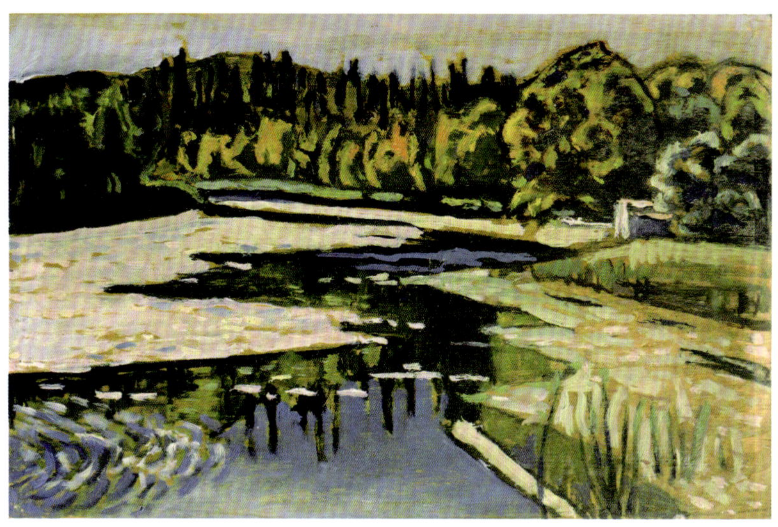

*1900, Oil on cardboard/Huile sur carton,
20 × 30,5 cm, State Russian Museum,
St. Petersburg*

Artista, maestro, cosmopolita

Wassily Kandinsky nació en Moscú
el 4 de diciembre de 1866; creció
en el seno de una familia de clase
media alta donde, ya desde su niñez,
su talento por el dibujo y la pintura
fueron reconocidos y fomentados. En
1871, la familia se muda a Odessa,
donde el padre de Wassily había sido
nombrado director de una empresa
de comercialización de té. Ese mismo
año se produjo el divorcio de sus
padres, que sin embargo mantuvieron
una relación de amistad. A pesar
del amor de Kandinsky por el arte,
decidió estudiar derecho y economía,
obteniendo su título en 1893,
seguido de un doctorado. Su carrera
académica despertó con la oferta
de una cátedra en la Universidad
de Dorpat (actualmente en Estonia)
en 1896, mismo año en que contrajo

Artista, insegnante, cosmopolita

Wassily Kandinsky nacque a Mosca
il 4 dicembre 1866 e crebbe in una
famiglia dell'alta borghesia che, sin
dalla sua infanzia, ne riconobbe e
incoraggiò il talento per il disegno e la
pittura. Nel 1871 la famiglia si trasferì
a Odessa, dove il padre di Wassily
divenne il direttore di un'azienda
che commercializzava tè. Nello
stesso anno i genitori divorziarono,
pur restando in buoni rapporti.
Nonostante il suo amore per l'arte,
Kandinsky decise di studiare diritto
ed economia, disciplina in cui ottiene
la laurea nel 1893, seguita da un
dottorato. Nel 1896 gli viene offerta
una cattedra presso l'Università di
Dorpat (oggi in Estonia), aprendogli la
strada per una carriera accademica,
e, nello stesso anno, sposò la cugina
Anja Tschimiakin.

Kunstenaar, leraar, reiziger

De op 4 december 1866 in Moskou
geboren Wassily Kandinsky groeit op
in welgestelde burgerlijke kringen.
Al in zijn kindertijd wordt zijn
talent voor tekenen en schilderen
ontdekt en gestimuleerd. In 1871
verhuist het gezin Kandinsky naar
Odessa, waar de vader directeur
van een theehandelsfirma wordt. In
hetzelfde jaar scheiden de ouders,
hoewel ze goede vrienden blijven.
Ondanks zijn grote passie voor de
kunst gaat Kandinsky aanvankelijk
rechten en staatshuishoudkunde
studeren. Hij studeert in 1893 af en
behaalt daarna de doctorstitel. Met
het aanbod van een positie als docent
aan de Universiteit van Dorpat (het
tegenwoordige Tartu in Estland) in
1896, ligt een academische carrière
voor het grijpen. In hetzelfde jaar

Two events, however, thwarted Kandinsky's bourgeois career path, encouraging him in his privately-cherished desire to become an artist: firstly, in the exhibition of French art in Moscow, he was overwhelmed by one of Monet's haystack pictures, because he recognized that the visual effect of the painting was independent of the object portrayed. His second experience was prompted by a visit to the opera, where he saw Wagner's "Lohengrin": "I saw all my colors in spirit, before my eyes. Wild, almost crazy lines were sketched in front of me." This concept of synaesthesia fascinated him as an artist and led to his theory of sound and color.

The final impetus was the discovery of radioactivity by the French physicist Antoine-Henri Becquerel in 1896: "In my soul the decay of the

Mais deux événements vont contrarier cette trajectoire bourgeoise et renforcer Kandinsky dans son souhait intérieurement caressé de devenir artiste. Dans une exposition d'art français à Moscou, il est subjugué par une *Meule de foin* de Monet : il reconnaît là que l'objet n'a guère d'importance pour l'effet du tableau. L'autre expérience décisive est l'opéra *Lohengrin* de Wagner : « Je voyais mentalement toutes mes couleurs, elles étaient devant mes yeux. Des lignes sauvages, presque folles, se dessinaient devant moi. » Cette représentation synesthésique va le retenir encore davantage et le conduire à sa théorie des rapports entre les couleurs et les sons.

La dernière incitation vient de la découverte de la radioactivité par le physicien français

Nähe. Im gleichen Jahr heiratet er seine Cousine Anja Tschimiakin.

Doch zwei Ereignisse durchkreuzen die bürgerliche Laufbahn und bestärken Kandinsky in dem innerlich gehegten Wunsch, Künstler zu werden: In der Ausstellung französischer Kunst in Moskau ist er von einem Heuschober-Bild Monets überwältigt, weil er erkennt, dass der Gegenstand für die Bildwirkung gar nicht bedeutsam ist. Die andere Erfahrung stützt sich auf den Besuch einer Lohengrin-Oper: „Ich sah alle meine Farben im Geiste, sie standen vor meinen Augen. Wilde, fast tolle Linien zeichneten sich vor mir." Diese synästhetische Vorstellung wird ihn auch als Künstler weiter fesseln und zu seiner Klangfarben-Theorie führen.

Den letzten Anstoß gibt die Entdeckung der Radioaktivität durch

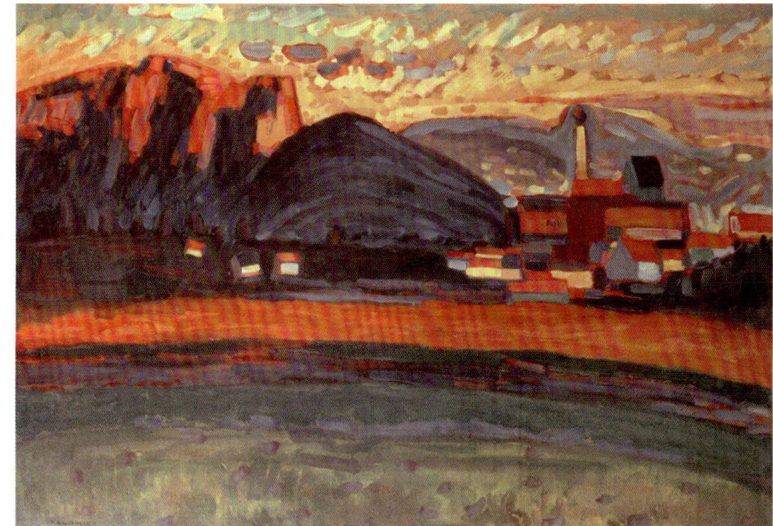

Landscape with Hills
Paysages avec collines
Landschaft mit Hügeln
Paisaje con colinas
Paesaggio con colline
Landschap met heuvels

*1908, Oil on cardboard/Huile sur carton,
70,5 × 96,5 cm, Private collection*

matrimonio con su prima Anja Tschimiakin.

Sin embargo, dos acontecimientos frustraron la carrera burguesa de Kandinsky, alentando su deseo interno de convertirse en artista: en primer lugar, la exposición de arte francés en Moscú, en la que quedó abrumado por uno de los Almiares de Monet, porque reconoció que el efecto visual de la pintura era independiente del objeto retratado. Su segunda experiencia fue fruto de su visita a la ópera, donde asistió a la obra "Lohengrin" de Wagner:"Vi todos mis colores en mi mente, estaban ante mis ojos. Líneas salvajes, casi enloquecidas se dibujaron frente a mí." Este concepto de sinestesia le fascinó como artista y le condujo a su teoría del sonido y el color.

Due eventi, però, mandarono all'aria la carriera borghese di Kandinsky e lo spinsero a perseguire il suo desiderio di diventare un artista: in primo luogo, la mostra di arte francese che ebbe luogo a Mosca, durante la quale fu profondamente colpito da uno dei quadri della serie Pagliai di Monet, che lo rese consapevole di come l'effetto visivo del dipinto fosse indipendente dall'oggetto rappresentato; in secondo luogo, una visita al teatro dell'opera, dove assistette al Lohengrin di Wagner: "Vidi nella mente tutti i miei colori, erano davanti ai miei occhi; linee tumultuose quasi folli si disegnavano davanti a me." Questo concetto di sinestesia lo affascinava come artista e lo portò a formulare la sua teoria del suono e del colore.

trouwt hij met zijn nicht Anja Sjemjakina.

Maar twee gebeurtenissen doorkruisen zijn burgerlijke loopbaan en versterken Kandinsky's innerlijk wens om kunstenaar te worden: op een tentoonstelling van Franse kunst in Moskou wordt hij overweldigd door een van de 'hooiberg-schilderijen' van Monet, omdat hij beseft dat de figuratieve inhoud van het schilderij niet belangrijk is voor de piturale uitwerking ervan. De andere ervaring is een bezoek aan een Lohengrin-opera: "Ik zag al mijn kleuren voor me, ze stonden me voor ogen. Wilde, bijna krankzinnige lijnen tekenden zich voor mij af." Dit synesthetische visioen zal hem ook als kunstenaar onveranderd fascineren en tot zijn theorie van kleurklanken leiden.

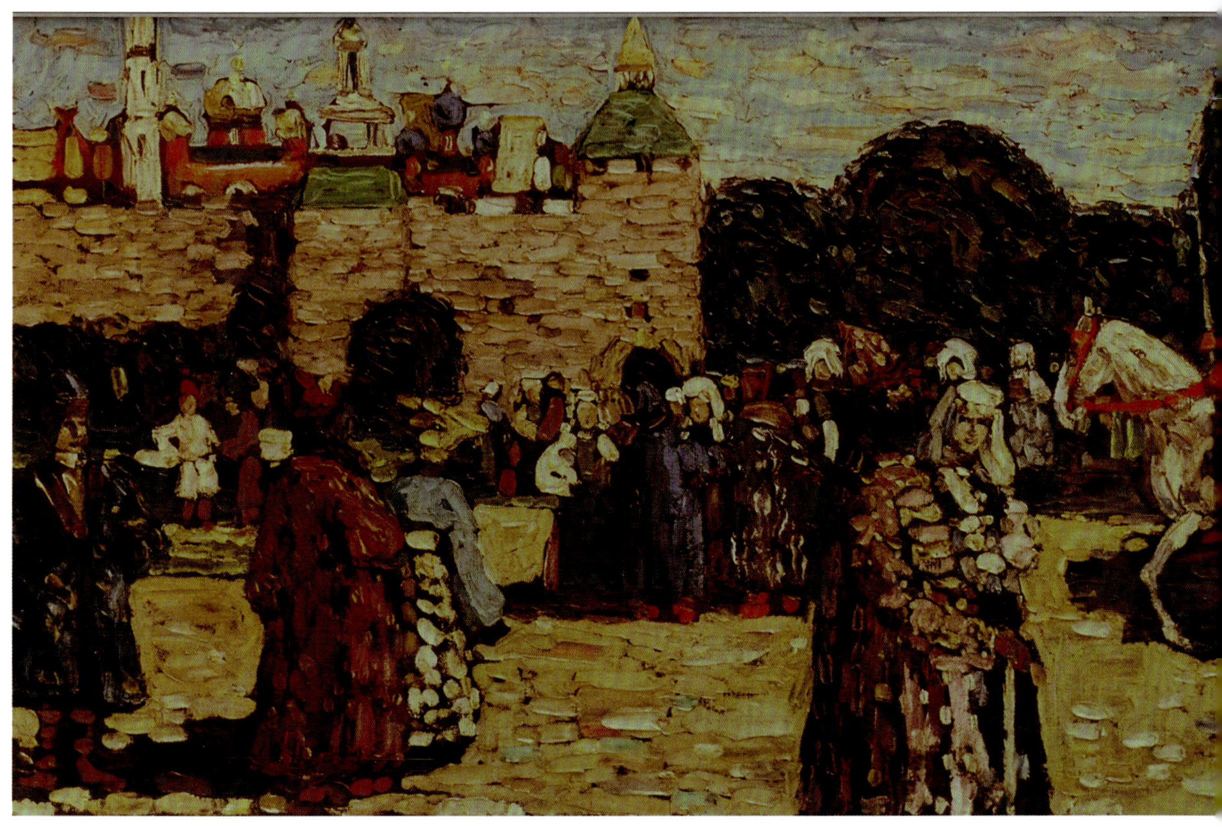

atom was the same as the decay of the whole world. Suddenly the sturdiest walls collapsed. Everything became uncertain, unsteady, and soft. It would not have amazed me if a stone had melted into the air before me and become invisible."

Antoine-Henri Becquerel, en 1896 : « La désintégration de l'atome était comparable dans mon âme à la désintégration du monde tout entier. Les murs les plus épais s'effondrèrent soudain. Tout devenait incertain, chancelant et mou. Je ne me serais pas étonné de voir une pierre fondre en l'air devant moi et devenir invisible. »

den französischen Physiker Antoine-Henri Becquerel im Jahre 1896: „Das Zerfallen des Atoms war in meiner Seele dem Zerfall der ganzen Welt gleich. Plötzlich fielen die dicksten Mauern. Alles wurde unsicher, wackelig und weich. Ich hätte mich nicht gewundert, wenn ein Stein vor mir in der Luft geschmolzen und unsichtbar geworden wäre."

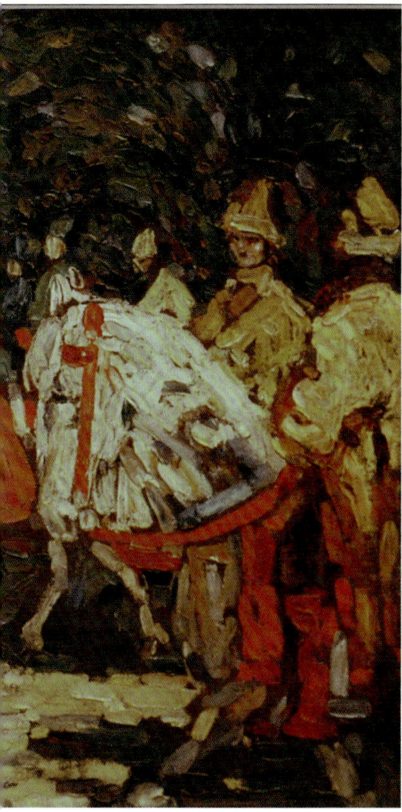

Sunday, Old Russia

Dimanche (Vieille Russie)

Sonntag (Altrussisch)

Domingo, Rusia viejo

Scena russa, domenica (Vecchia Russia)

Zondag (Oud-Russisch)

1904, Oil on canvas/Huile sur toile, 45 × 95 cm, Museum Boijmans Van Beuningen, Rotterdam

El impulso definitivo fue el descubrimiento de la radioactividad por parte del físico francés Antoine-Henri Becquerel en 1896: "En mi alma, la descomposición del átomo era lo mismo que la descomposición del mundo entero. De repente los muros más sólidos se derrumbaron. Todo se hizo precario, inestable, blando. No me hubiera asombrado ver una piedra fundirse en el aire frente a mí y hacerse invisible."

La spinta finale fu la scoperta della radioattività da parte del fisico francese Antoine-Henri Becquerel nel 1896: "La disintegrazione dell'atomo fu per me la disintegrazione del mondo. D'improvviso i muri più massicci crollarono. Tutto divenne incerto, malsicuro, mutevole. Non mi sarei stupito di vedere un sasso fondersi in aria e svanire."

De laatste aansporing krijgt Kandinsky door de ontdekking van de radioactiviteit, door de Franse natuurkundige Antoine-Henri Becquerel in 1896: "Het verval van het atoom stond in mijn ziel gelijk aan het verval van de ganse wereld. Plotseling stortten de dikste muren in. Alles werd onzeker, wankel en week. Het zou me niet hebben verbaasd als een steen voor mijn ogen in de lucht was gesmolten en onzichtbaar was geworden."

Bohemia and "Der Blaue Reiter"

Together with his young wife, Kandinsky left Moscow and settled in Munich which at that time was one of the most important European cities for art.

At first, Kandinsky visited the art school of Anton Ažbe (1862–1905) in order to hone his technical skills, producing a small number of impressionistic landscape scenes. A period of study under Franz von Stuck (1863–1928) from 1900–1901 was unable to satisfy him, so he decided to progress in an autodidactic manner. Two like-minded Russian painter colleagues, Marianne von Werefkin (1860–1938) and Alexej Jawlensky (1864/65–1941) supported him, exchanging artistic ideas and accompanying each other on painting expeditions in and around Munich.

In 1901 he founded the artistic and exhibiting association "Phalanx". In these exhibitions, he focused on art nouveau, which was still under-represented in Munich and which, with its possibilities for abstract forms, attracted Kandinsky. In

La bohème et le Blaue Reiter

Avec sa jeune épouse, Kandinsky quitte Moscou et s'installe à Munich – alors l'un des plus importants centres artistiques européens.

Il commence par fréquenter l'école d'art d'Anton Azbe (1862–1905), afin de s'exercer au dessin. Naissent alors, au passage, de petits paysages impressionnistes. Une étude du dessin chez Franz von Stück (1863–1928), de 1900 à 1901, ne le satisfait pas davantage à la longue, si bien qu'il se décide à continuer son développement en autodidacte. Il est soutenu dans cette démarche par deux collègues peintres russes, Marianne von Verefkine (1860–1938) et Alexeï Jawlensky (1864/65–1941), avec lesquels il échange régulièrement et part en tournées picturales dans les environs de Munich.

En 1901, il fonde « Phalanx », une association d'artistes et d'expositions. Ces dernières se concentrent sur le Jugendstil (« Art nouveau »), encore sous-représenté à Munich et qui attire l'attention de Kandinsky par ses potentialités de formes abstraites.

Bohème und „Der Blaue Reiter"

Zusammen mit seiner jungen Frau verlässt Kandinsky Moskau und lässt sich in München nieder, damals eine der wichtigsten europäischen Kunststädte.

Zunächst besucht Kandinsky die Kunstschule von Anton Ažbe (1862–1905), um sich im Zeichnen zu üben. Nebenbei entstehen kleine impressionistische Landschaftsszenen. Auch ein Zeichenstudium bei Franz von Stuck (1863–1928) von 1900–1901 kann ihn auf Dauer nicht befriedigen, sodass er beschließt sich autodidaktisch weiterzuentwickeln. Dabei unterstützen ihn zwei gleichgesinnte russische Malerkollegen: Marianne von Werefkin (1860–1938) und Alexej Jawlensky (1864/65–1941), mit denen er sich regelmäßig austauscht und gemeinsam auf Malausflüge in die Münchner Umgebung geht.

1901 gründet er den Künstler- und Ausstellungsverein „Phalanx". In den Ausstellungen konzentriert er sich auf den Jugendstil, der in München noch unterrepräsentiert ist und der

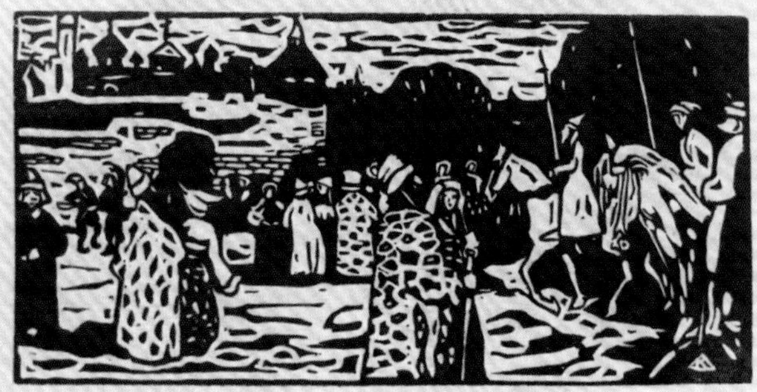

La bohemia y "Der Blaue Reiter"
Junto a su joven esposa, Kandinsky
abandona Moscú y se asienta en
Múnich, una de las ciudades más
importantes de Europa en materia de
arte de la época.

Al principio, Kandinsky visitó
la escuela de arte de Anton Ažbe
(1862–1905) para perfeccionar su
técnica, produciendo un pequeño
número de paisajes impresionistas.
Tampoco logró satisfacerle un periodo
de estudio bajo la tutela de Franz von
Stuck (1863–1928) durante 1900–1901,
por lo que decidió continuar adelante
de forma autodidacta. Dos pintores
rusos de ideas afines, Marianne
von Werefkin (1860–1938) y Alexej

La Bohème e Der Blaue Reiter
Insieme alla sua giovane moglie,
Kandinsky lasciò Mosca e si stabilì a
Monaco di Baviera, che a quel tempo
era una delle più importanti città
europee in campo artistico.

In un primo momento, Kandinsky
frequentò la scuola d'arte di Anton
Ažbe (1862–1905) per affinare le sue
capacità tecniche, e produsse un
esiguo numero di scene paesaggistiche
impressioniste. Il periodo di studio
dal 1900 al 1901 sotto la guida di
Franz von Stuck (1863–1928) fu poco
soddisfacente per l'artista russo,
che decise di progredire in maniera
autodidatta. Fu sostenuto da due
colleghi pittori, anch'essi russi e a lui

De bohémien en 'Der Blaue Reiter'
Samen met zijn jonge vrouw verhuist
Kandinsky van Moskou naar
München, destijds een belangrijk
centrum voor Europese kunst.

Allereerst neemt Kandinsky
tekenlessen aan de kunstschool van
Anton Ažbe (1862–1905). Daarnaast
schildert hij impressionistische
landschapjes. Ook de tekenlessen
in 1900 en 1901 bij Franz von Stuck
(1863–1928) kunnen hem op den duur
niet tevreden stellen, waarna hij
besluit zichzelf als autodidact verder
te scholen. Daarbij krijgt hij hulp van
twee gelijkgezinde Russische collega-
schilders: Marianne von Werefkin
(1860–1938) en Alexej Jawlensky

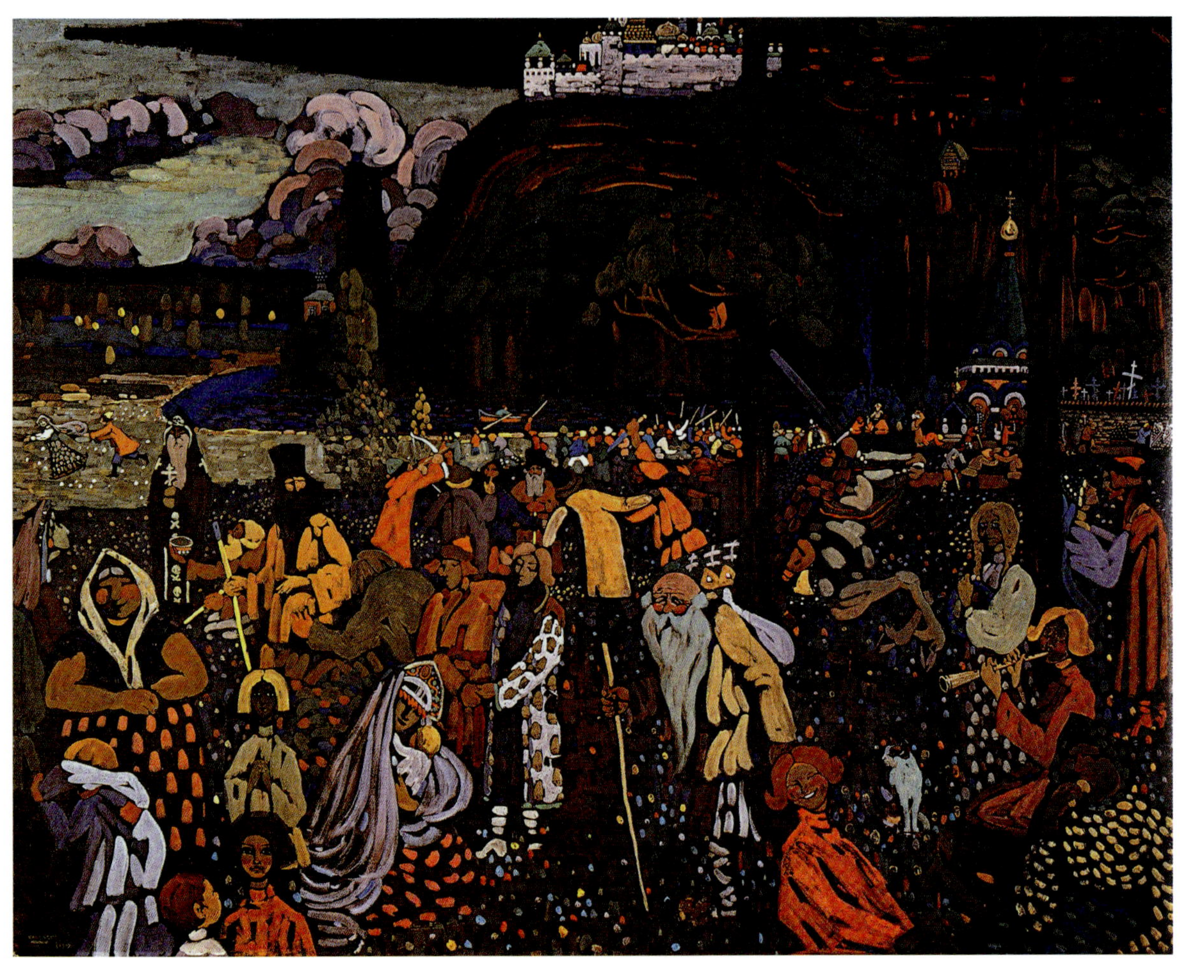

his so-called "fairy tale pictures", this influence is transformed into dreamlike scenes based upon German and Russian fairy tales.

Ses tableaux féériques élaborent cette influence en scènes rêveuses ayant pour bases des légendes russes et allemandes.

mit seinem Potential an abstrakten Formen die Aufmerksamkeit Kandinskys anzieht. In seinen sog. „Märchenbildern" wird dieser Einfluss in traumhaften Szenen verarbeitet, denen russische und deutsche Märchen zugrunde liegen.

The colourful life

La Vie mélangée

Das bunte Leben

La vida colorida

La vita colorata

Het bonte leven

1907, Tempera on canvas/ Tempéra sur toile, 130 × 162 cm, Städtische Galerie im Lenbachhaus, Munich

Kandinsky's attachment to his Russian homeland was expressed in a series of fairy tale pictures, in which he gathered together aspects of old Russian life as if on a colorful carpet.

Le lien de Kandinsky avec sa patrie russe s'exprime dans une série de tableaux de légendes, dans lesquels il rassemble des aspects de la vie "vieux-russe", comme sur une tapisserie bariolée.

Kandinskys Verbundenheit mit seiner russischen Heimat drückt sich in einer Serie von Märchenbildern aus, in denen er Aspekte des alt-russischen Lebens wie auf einem bunten Teppich versammelt.

Kandinsky expresó su apego a su Rusia natal en una serie de obras inspiradas en los cuentos de hadas, que reunía aspectos de la vieja vida rusa como si de una colorida alfombra se tratara.

Kandinsky espresse il suo attaccamento alla patria in una serie di quadri fiabeschi, in cui riunì diversi aspetti della vita della vecchia Russia come su un tappeto colorato.

Kandinsky's band met zijn Russische vaderland wordt in deze reeks 'sprookjesschilderijen' uitgedrukt, waarin hij aspecten van het traditionele Russische leven in een kleurrijk tapijt samenbrengt.

Jawlensky (1864/65–1941) apoyaron sus esfuerzos, intercambiando ideas artísticas y acompañándose en exposiciones de pintura en Múnich y alrededores.

En 1901 fundó Phalanx, una asociación artística para la organización de exposiciones. En estas exposiciones él se centraba en el art nouveau, aún con poca representación en Múnich y que, con sus posibilidades de abstracción de formas, atrajo a Kandinsky. En sus denominados "cuadros de cuentos de hadas", esta influencia se transformó en escenas oníricas basadas en los tradicionales cuentos de hadas alemanes y rusos.

intellettualmente affini: Marianne von Werefkin (1860–1938) e Alexej Jawlensky (1864/65–1941), con i quali scambiava idee artistiche e si recava in spedizioni pittoriche a Monaco e nei dintorni.

Nel 1901 fondò l'associazione artistica ed espositiva "Phalanx". In queste mostre, si concentrò sull'art nouveau, che era ancora sottorappresentata a Monaco di Baviera e che, con le sue possibilità di forme astratte, esercitava una grande attrazione su Kandinsky. Nei suoi cosiddetti "quadri fiabeschi", questa influenza si trasformò in scene oniriche basate su fiabe tedesche e russe.

(1864/65–1941), met wie hij veel optrekt en schilderkunstige uitstapjes in de omgeving van München onderneemt.

In 1901 richt hij de kunstenaars- en tentoonstellingsvereniging 'Phalanx' op. Bij de exposities richt hij zich op de Jugendstil, die in München relatief weinig aan bod is gekomen en die Kandinsky met haar potentieel aan abstracte vormen fascineert. In zijn zogenaamde 'sprookjesschilderijen' wordt deze invloed uitgewerkt in droomtaferelen die berusten op Russische en Duitse volksverhalen.

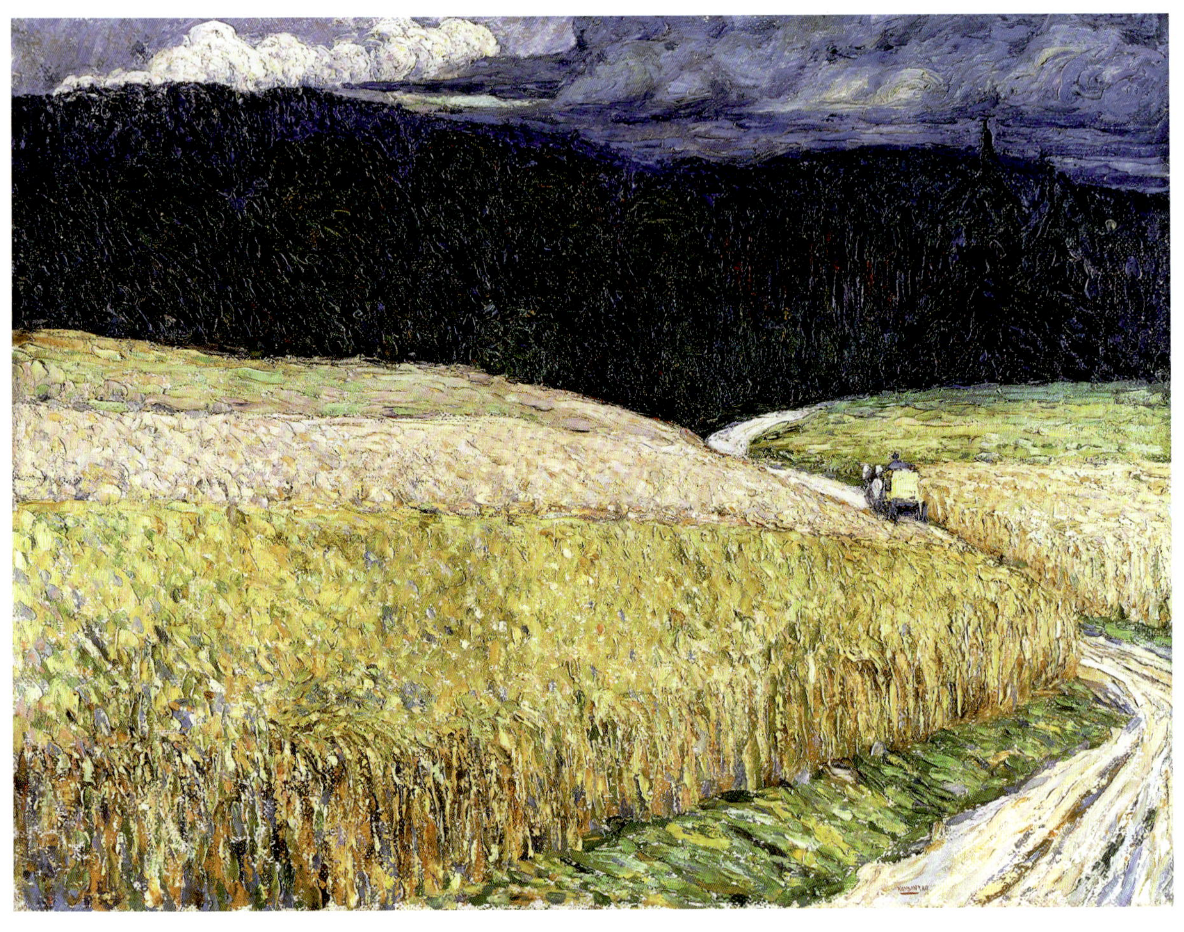

Kallmunz – Thunderstorm Atmosphere (The Stagecoach)

Kallmünz – Par temps d'orage (La diligence)

Kallmünz – Gewitterstimmung (Die Postkutsche)

Kallmünz – ambiente de tormenta (la diligencia)

Kallmünz – Aria di temporale (La diligenza)

Kallmünz – dreigend onweer (De postkoets)

1904, Oil on canvas/Huile sur toile, 76 × 99,5 cm, Private collection

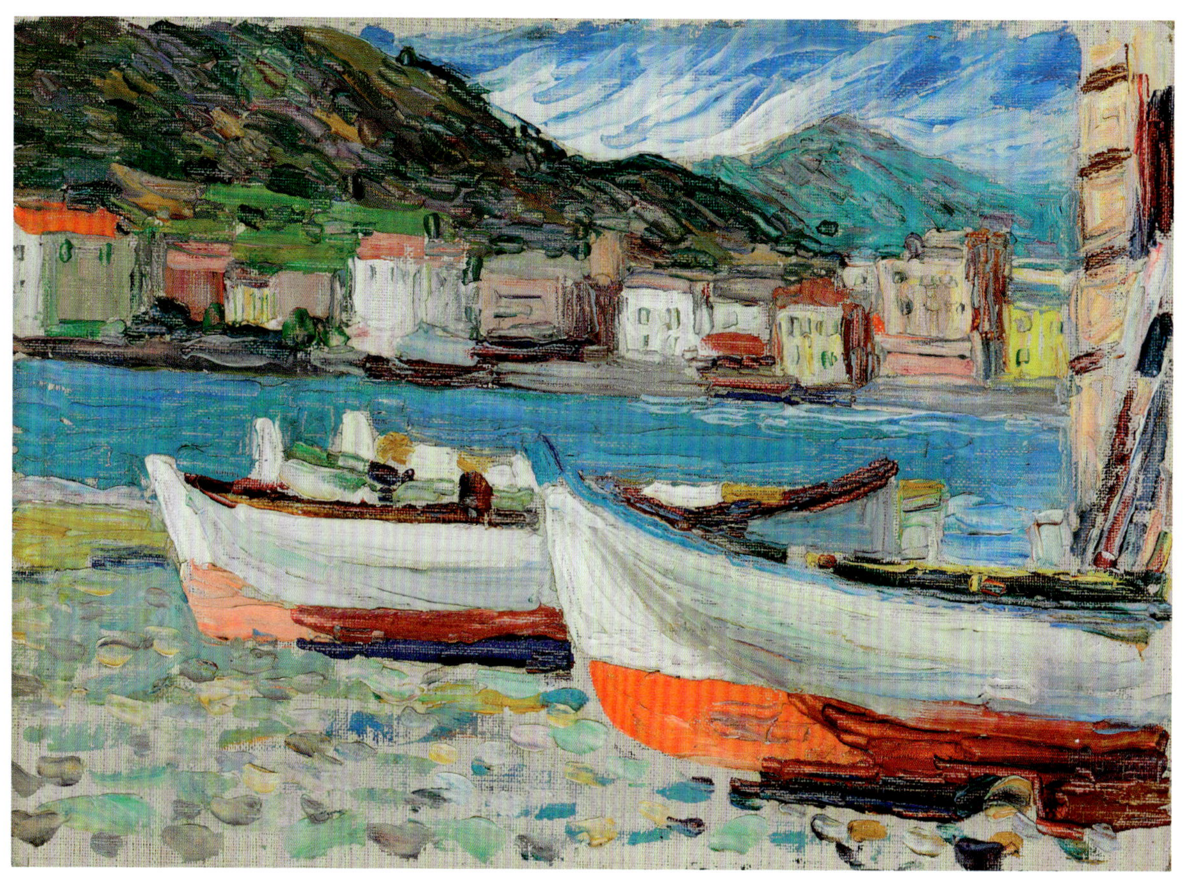

Rapallo, Boats   **Rapallo-Boote**   **Rapallo, barche**

Bateaux á Rapallo   **Rapallo, barcos**   **Rapallo-boten**

1905, Oil on cardboard/Huile sur carton, 24 × 32,9cm, Private collection

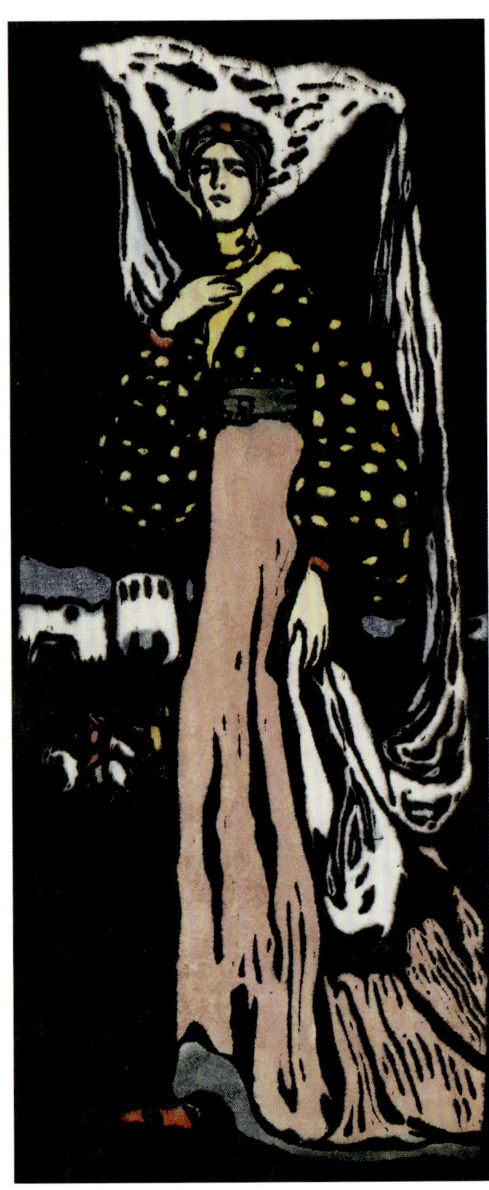

The Night (Large Version)
La Nuit (Grande version)
Die Nacht (Große Fassung)
La noche (Versión grande)
La notte (Versione grande)
De nacht (Grote uitvoering)

*1903, Woodcut printed in colors/Bois gravé en couleurs,
29,8 × 12,8 cm, Private collection*

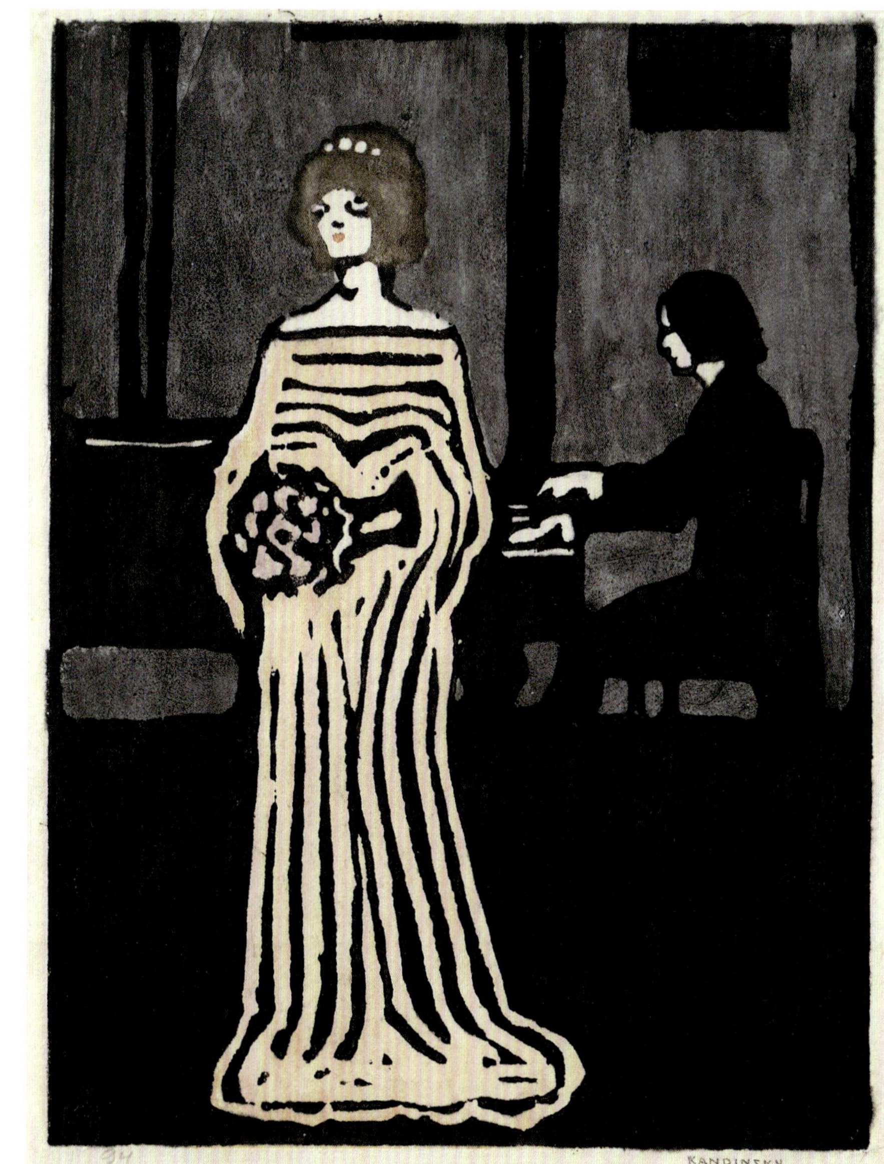

The Singer

La Chanteuse

Die Sängerin

El cantante

La cantante

De zangeres

1903, Woodcut printed in colors/
Bois gravé en couleurs,
20 × 14,8 cm,
Private collection

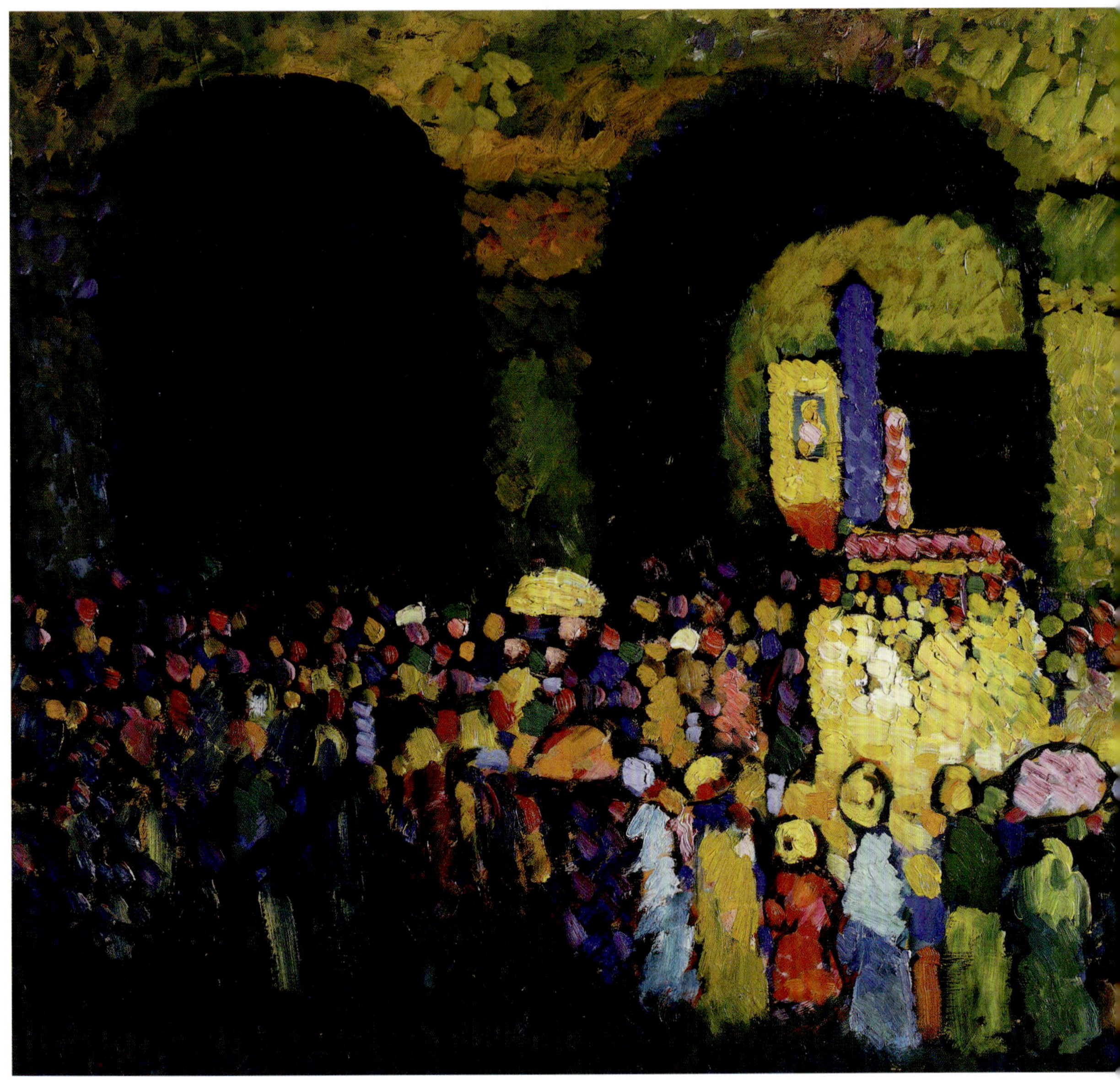

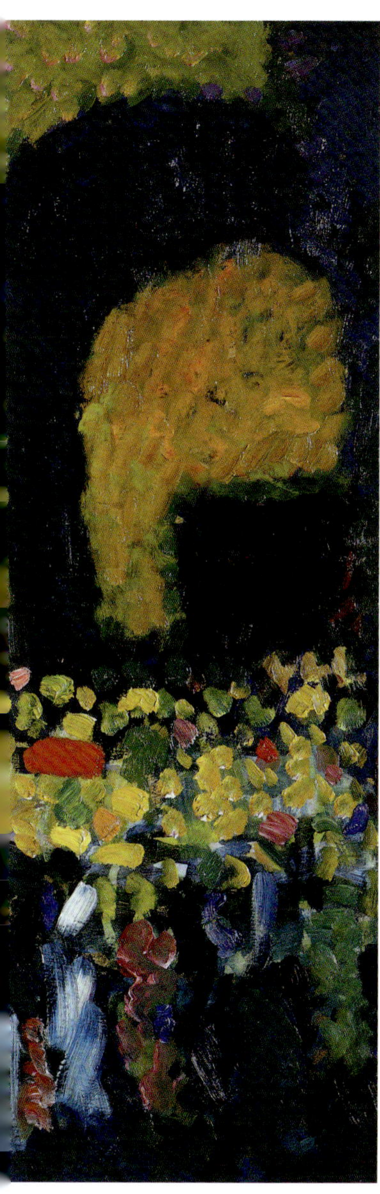

The Ludwigskirche in Munich
La Ludwigskirche à Munich
Ludwigskirche in München
La Ludwigskirche en Múnich
La Ludwigskirche a Monaco
De Ludwigskirche in München
1908, Oil on cardboard/Huile sur carton, 67,3 × 96 cm, Collection Museo Thyssen-Bornemisza, Madrid

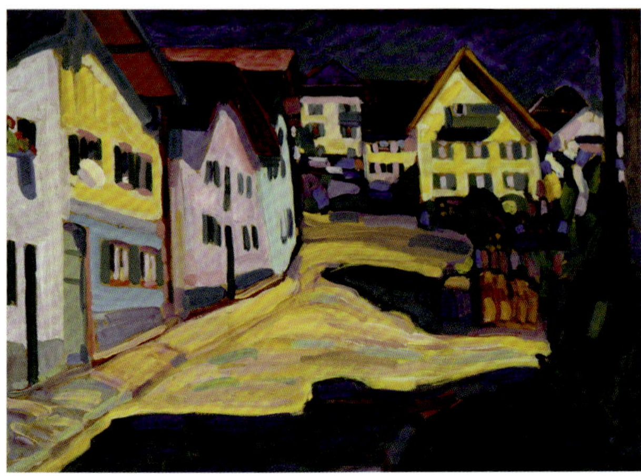

Through his attachment to "Phalanx", Kandinsky met the student Gabriele Münter (1877–1962) who soon became his companion and lover. Kandinsky took part in international exhibitions along with artists including Claude Monet, Paul Signac, Théo van Rysselberghe, Félix Vallotton and Henri de Toulouse-Lautrec, as well as painters of the "Berlin Secession", who included Lovis Corinth, Max Slevogt, Max Liebermann and Wilhelm Trübner. Kandinsky found incompatibility between his teaching work and the development of his own painting, which led to his decision to leave the "Phalanx". Over the next few years Kandinsky and Münter led a lavish lifestyle which took them to Tunisia, Italy, France, Switzerland and back again through German cities, traveling by train, by coach, by bicycle or on foot, and always interrupted by the artist's participation in important

Dans l'école de peinture de l'association « Phalanx », Kandinsky fait la connaissance de Gabriele Münter (1877–1962), une élève qui va devenir bientôt sa collègue et sa compagne. Il fréquente des expositions internationales où sont présentés des artistes comme Claude Monet, Paul Signac, Théo van Rysselberghe, Félix Vallotton et Henri de Toulouse-Lautrec, mais aussi des peintres de la « Sécession berlinoise » comme Lovis Corinth, Max Slevogt, Max Liebermann et Wilhelm Trübner. Toutefois, ces activités sont incompatibles avec l'enseignement comme avec sa propre peinture, si bien qu'il se résout à quitter l'association « Phalanx ». Au cours des années qui suivent, Kandinsky et Münter mènent une vie de voyages vagabonde qui les conduit en Tunisie, en Italie, en France, en Suisse et dans de nombreuses villes allemandes – en train, en diligence, à vélo ou

In der angeschlossenen Malschule des „Phalanx"-Vereins lernt Kandinsky die Schülerin Gabriele Münter (1877–1962) kennen, die bald zu seiner Weggefährtin und Geliebten wird. Kandinsky besetzt internationale Ausstellungen mit Künstlern wie Claude Monet, Paul Signac, Théo van Rysselberghe, Félix Vallotton, Henri de Toulouse-Lautrec, aber auch Malern der „Berliner Secession" wie Lovis Corinth, Max Slevogt, Max Liebermann und Wilhelm Trübner. Doch diese Vereinstätigkeit wird mit dem Unterricht und der eigenen Malerei unvereinbar, sodass er beschließt die „Phalanx" zu verlassen. Über die nächsten Jahre führen Kandinsky und Münter ein aufwendiges Reiseleben, das sie nach Tunesien, Italien, Frankreich, in die Schweiz und immer wieder durch deutsche Städte führt, teils mit der Bahn, mit der Kutsche, mit dem Rad oder auch zu Fuß, immer wieder

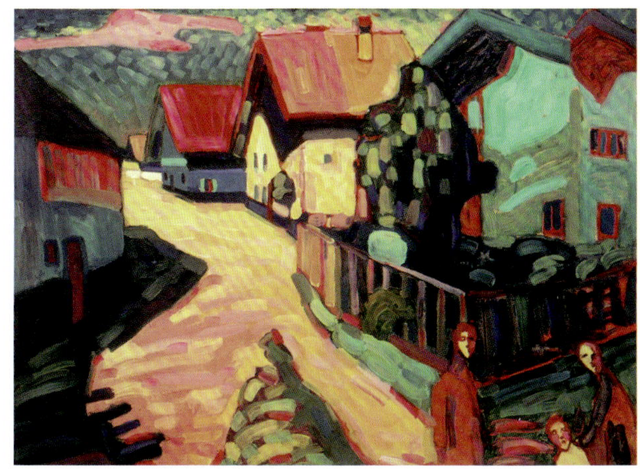

The Road to Murnau
Murnau: rue avec femmes
Straße nach Murnau
El camino a Murnau
La strada per Murnau
Weg naar Murnau
1908, Oil on canvas/Huile sur toile, 71 × 97 cm, Private collection

Gracias a su relación con "Phalanx", Kandinsky conoce a la estudiante Gabriele Münter (1877–1962) que pronto se convertirá en su compañera y amante. Kandinsky participó en exposiciones internacionales junto con artistas como Claude Monet, Paul Signac, Théo van Rysselberghe, Félix Vallotton y Henri de Toulouse-Lautrec, así como con pintores de la "Secesión de Berlín", como Lovis Corinth, Max Slevogt, Max Liebermann y Wilhelm Trübner. Kandinsky sufrió la incompatibilidad entre su trabajo como maestro y el avance de su propia pintura, que le impulsó a tomar la decisión de abandonar "Phalanx". En los años siguientes, Kandinsky y Münter mantuvieron un fastuoso estilo de vida que les llevó a Túnez, Italia, Francia, Suiza y de vuelta a las ciudades alemanas, viajando en tren, carruaje, bicicleta o a pie, interrumpido siempre

Attraverso la "Phalanx" Kandinsky conobbe la studentessa Gabriele Münter (1877–1962), che divenne ben presto la sua compagna e amante. Kandinsky partecipò a mostre internazionali insieme ad artisti come Claude Monet, Paul Signac, Théo van Rysselberghe, Félix Vallotton ed Henri de Toulouse-Lautrec, nonché a pittori della "Secessione di Berlino", tra cui Lovis Corinth, Max Slevogt, Max Liebermann e Wilhelm Trübner. Ad un certo punto, Kandinsky si rese conto che il suo lavoro come insegnate e lo sviluppo della sua carriera pittorica erano incompatibili, per cui decise di lasciare la "Phalanx". Nel corso dei primi anni a seguire, Kandinsky e Münter condussero uno stile di vita sfarzoso, che li portò in Tunisia, Italia, Francia, Svizzera e in varie città tedesche. Viaggiavano in treno, pullman, bicicletta o a piedi, e si fermavano di tanto in tanto affinché l'artista potesse partecipare

In de schilderschool van 'Phalanx' leert hij de kunststudente Gabriele Münter (1877–1962) kennen, die al snel zijn levensgezellin en geliefde wordt. Kandinsky toont zijn werk op internationale tentoonstellingen, samen met dat van schilders als Claude Monet, Paul Signac, Théo van Rysselberghe, Félix Vallotton en Henri de Toulouse-Lautrec, en met het werk van de kunstenaars van de 'Berliner Secession', onder wie Lovis Corinth, Max Slevogt, Max Liebermann en Wilhelm Trübner. Maar zijn activiteiten voor 'Phalanx' zijn niet langer te verenigen met zijn lessen en zijn eigen werk, dus besluit hij uit de vereniging te stappen. In de jaren daarna leiden Kandinsky en Münter een opwindend leven van reizen, deels per trein, deels in rijtuigen, op de fiets of ook te voet. Ze bezoeken Tunesië, Italië, Frankrijk en Zwitserland, en steeds opnieuw de Duitse steden, vaak onderbroken door deelnames

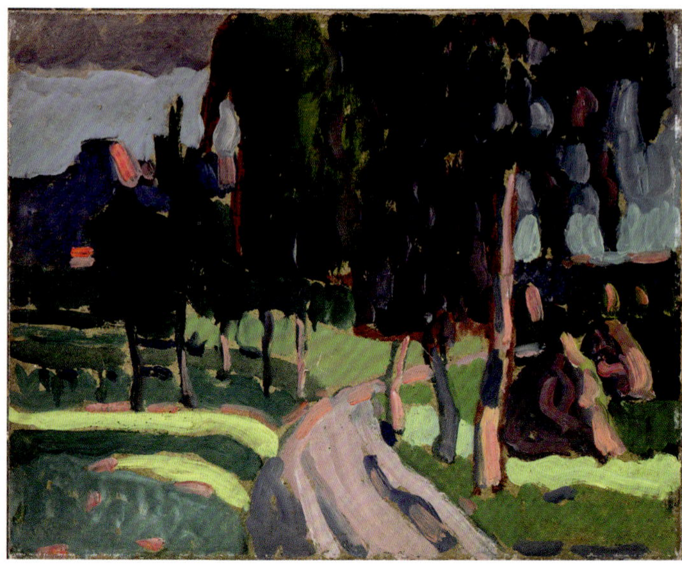

1908, Oil on cardboard/Huile sur carton,
32 × 40 cm, Private collection

exhibitions in Paris, Berlin and Moscow.

Only in 1908 did Kandinsky settle again in Munich, rooting himself more securely in the city's art scene by co-founding the Neue Künstlervereinigung München (Munich New Artists' Association) during the following year. Kandinsky found peace and perseverance in his painting, especially in Murnau, where Münter had bought a house, the so-called "Russian House", which they furnished lovingly with a potpourri of decoration. The road to abstraction began to emerge and this was already being pursued by Kandinsky in his Murnau landscapes.

même à pied – voyages entrecoupés de participations à d'importantes expositions à Paris, Berlin et Moscou.

C'est en 1908 seulement que Kandinsky est de nouveau « sédentarisé » à Munich. La fondation en 1909 de la Neue Künstlervereinigung München (« Nouvelle association d'artistes à Munich ») l'ancre de nouveau solidement sur la scène artistique munichoise. Kandinsky trouve le calme et la continuité dans le travail en peignant avant tout à Murnau am Staffelsee, petit village où Münter acquiert une maison vite baptisée localement le Russenhaus (« Maison du Russe ») ; les deux artistes l'aménagent et la décorent avec amour. La tendance à l'abstraction se cristallise de plus en plus chez Kandinsky, qui la développe dans les paysages de Murnau.

unterbrochen durch Beteiligungen an wichtigen Ausstellungen in Paris, Berlin und Moskau.

Erst 1908 wird Kandinsky wieder in München sesshaft. Durch die Gründung der „Neuen Künstlervereinigung München" im nächsten Jahr wird er wieder stärker in der Münchner Kunstszene verwurzelt. Kandinsky findet Ruhe und Beharrlichkeit beim Malen vor allem in Murnau, wo Münter ein Haus erwirbt, das sog. „Russenhaus", das sie liebevoll einrichten und mit allerlei Dekor ausschmücken. Immer stärker kristallisiert sich der Willen zur Abstraktion heraus, den Kandinsky bereits in den Murnauer Landschaften verfolgt.

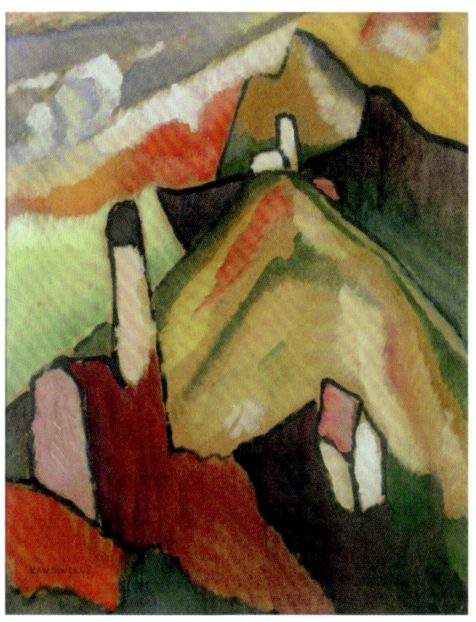

*1908, Mixed media on paper/Technique mixte sur papier,
34 × 28,6 cm, Private collection, Mayor Gallery, London*

por la participación del artista en importantes exposiciones en París, Berlín y Moscú.

Solo en 1908 Kandinsky se asienta de nuevo en Múnich, estableciéndose de forma más firme en la escena artística de la ciudad y cofundando la Neue Künstlervereinigung München (Asociación de nuevos artistas de Múnich) durante el siguiente año. Kandinsky encuentra la paz y la perseverancia en su pintura, especialmente en Murnau, donde Münter había adquirido una casa, la llamada "Casa rusa", que amueblaron con cariño y un sentido decorativo ecléctico. Comienza a emerger el camino a la abstracción, que ya buscaba Kandinsky en sus paisajes de Murnau.

ad importanti mostre a Parigi, Berlino e Mosca.

Fu solo nel 1908 che Kandinsky tornò a stabilirsi a Monaco di Baviera, rinsaldando la sua posizione nel panorama artistico della città mediante la co-fondazione, nel 1909, della Neue Künstlervereinigung München (Nuova associazione di artisti di Monaco). Kandinsky trovò pace e perseveranza nella sua pittura, soprattutto a Murnau, dove Münter aveva comprato una casa, nominata "Russenhaus" (La casa dei russi), che la coppia arredò con cura con un pot-pourri di elementi decorativi. Fu in questo momento che cominciò a materializzarsi il percorso dell'artista verso l'astrazione, già evidente nei suoi paesaggi di Murnau.

aan belangrijke tentoonstellingen in Parijs, Berlijn en Moskou.

Pas in 1908 vestigt Kandinsky zich weer in München. Door de oprichting van de 'Nieuwe Kunstenaarsvereniging München' in het jaar daarop, raakt hij weer nauw betrokken bij de kunstscene in de Beierse hoofdstad. Rust en concentratie vindt Kandinsky vooral tijdens het schilderen in Murnau, waar hij een huis koopt – het zogenaamde 'Russenhuis', dat het paar liefdevol inricht en met talloze decorstukken uitrust. Steeds sterker ontvouwt zich nu de wil tot abstractie, die Kandinsky al in zijn Murnause landschappen nastreeft.

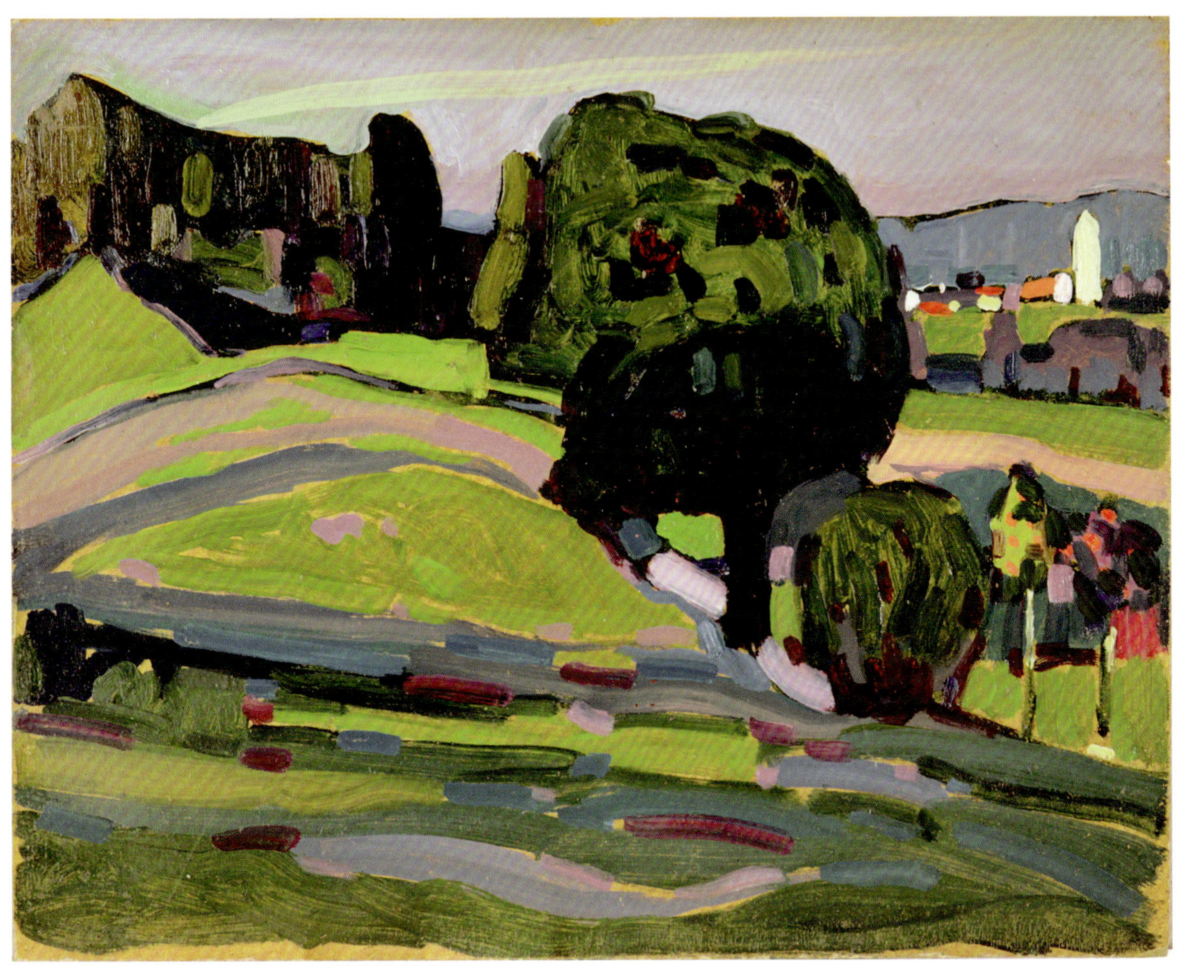

Landscape near Murnau   ***Landschaft bei Murnau***   ***Paesaggio vicino a Murnau***
Paysage près de Murnau   ***Paisaje cerca de Murnau***   ***Landschap bij Murnau***

1908, Oil on cardboard/Huile sur carton, 32,8 × 41 cm, Private collection

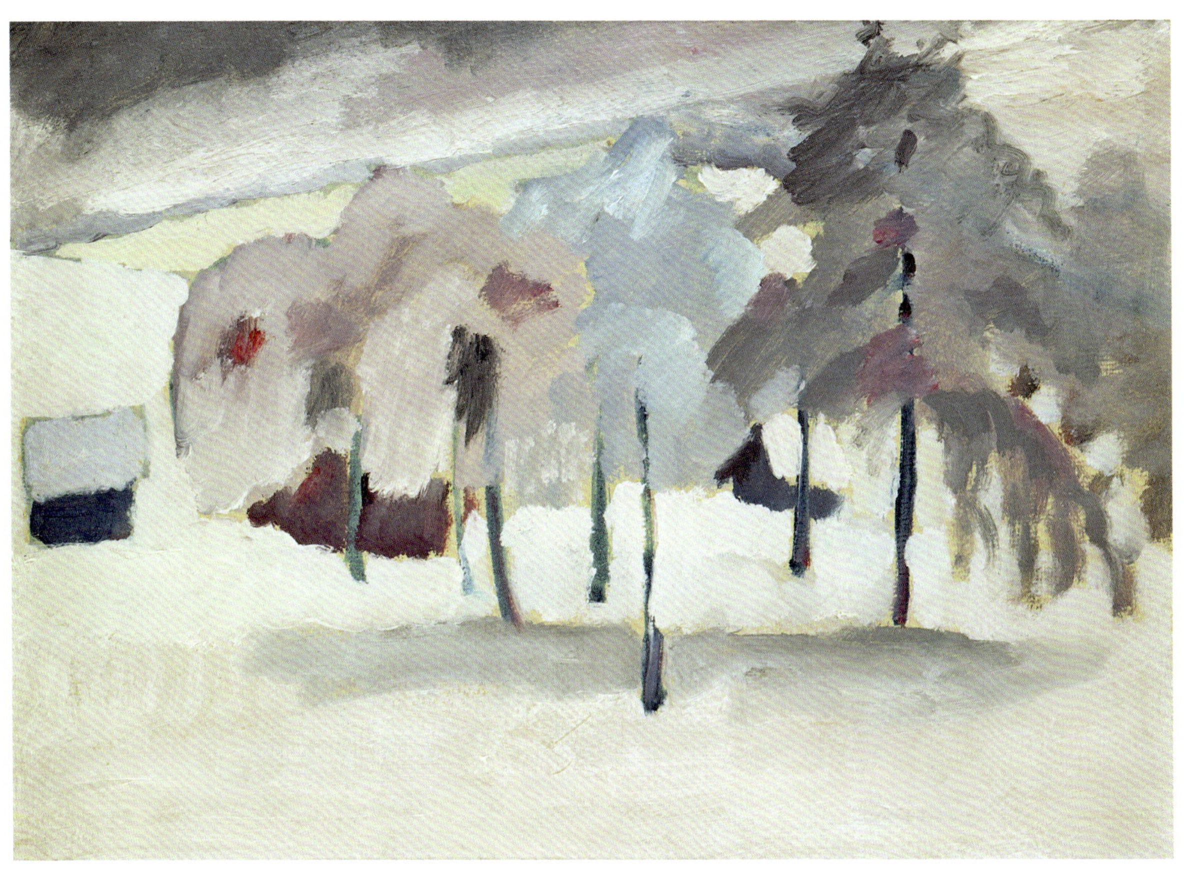

Study of Murnau V

Etude de Murnau V

Studie von Murnau V

Estudio de Murnau V

Studio di Murnau V

Studie van Murnau V

c. 1910, Oil on canvas/Huile sur toile, Städtische Galerie im Lenbachhaus, Munich

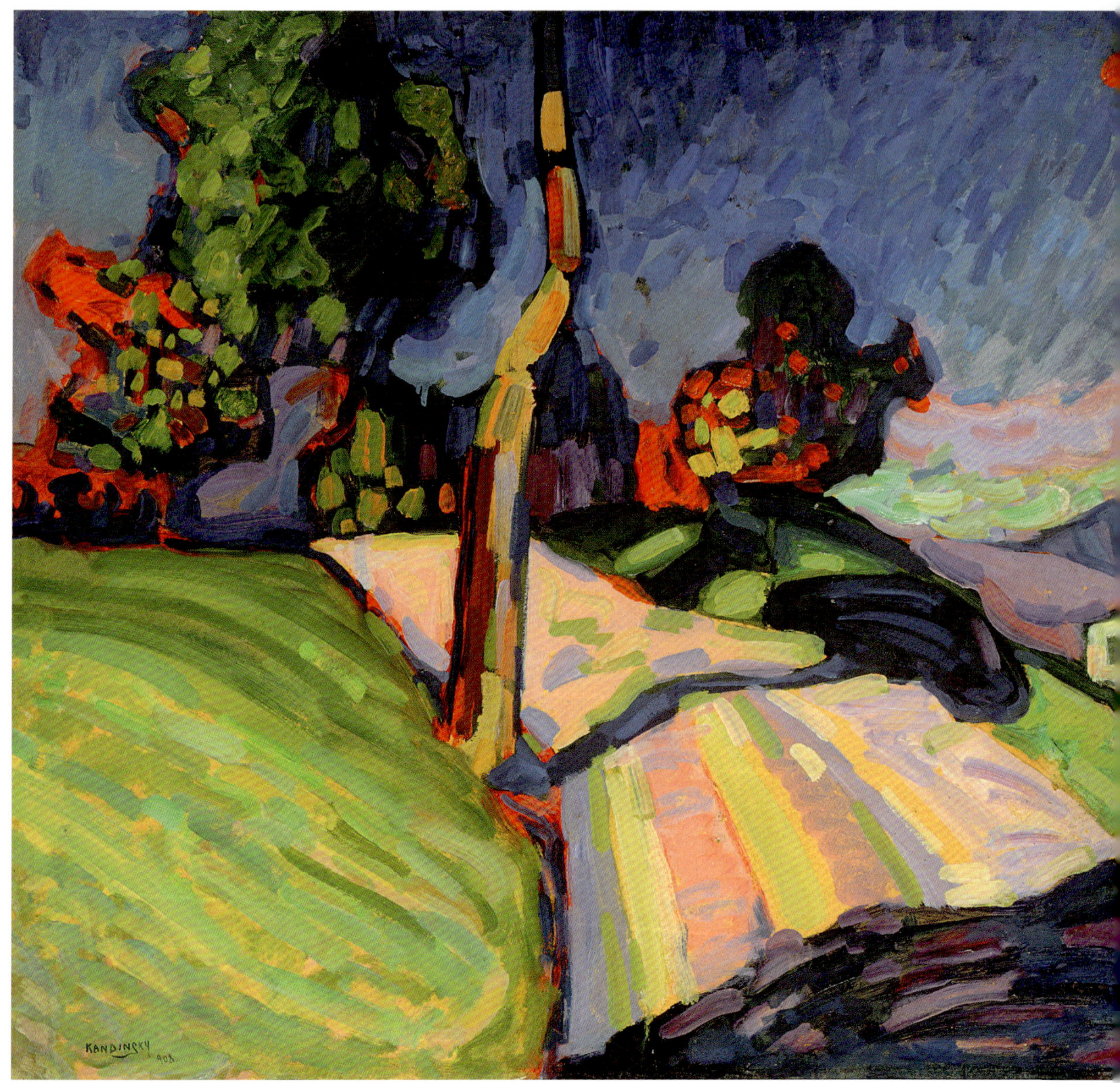

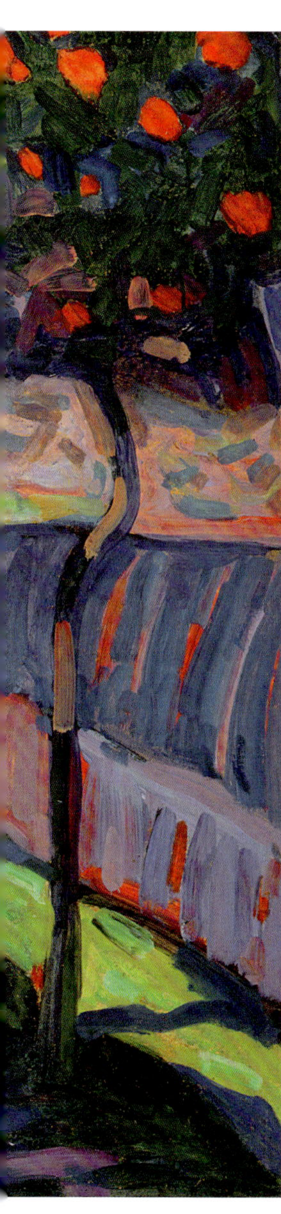

Autumn Landscape, Murnau

Paysage d'automne à Murnau

Herbstlandschaft Murnau

Paisaje de otoño, Murnau

Paesaggio autunnale, Murnau

Herfstlandschap bij Murnau

1908, Oil on cardboard/Huile sur carton, 69,2 × 94,6 cm, Museum of Modern Art, New York

The objective motif almost disappears behind the intense flood of colors. Colors and shapes become increasingly independent.

Le motif figuratif disparaît presque derrière l'intensité du flot de couleurs. Formes et couleurs deviennent de plus en plus autonomes.

Das gegenständliche Motiv verschwindet fast hinter der intensiven Farbenflut. Farben und Formen werden zunehmend eigenständiger.

El tema objetivo casi desaparece detrás de la intensa avalancha de colores. Los colores y formas son cada vez más independientes..

Il motivo obiettivo scompare quasi completamente dietro l'intensa marea cromatica. I colori e le forme diventano sempre più indipendenti.

Het figuratieve onderwerp verdwijnt bijna achter de intense kleurenvloed. De vormen en kleuren worden steeds autonomer.

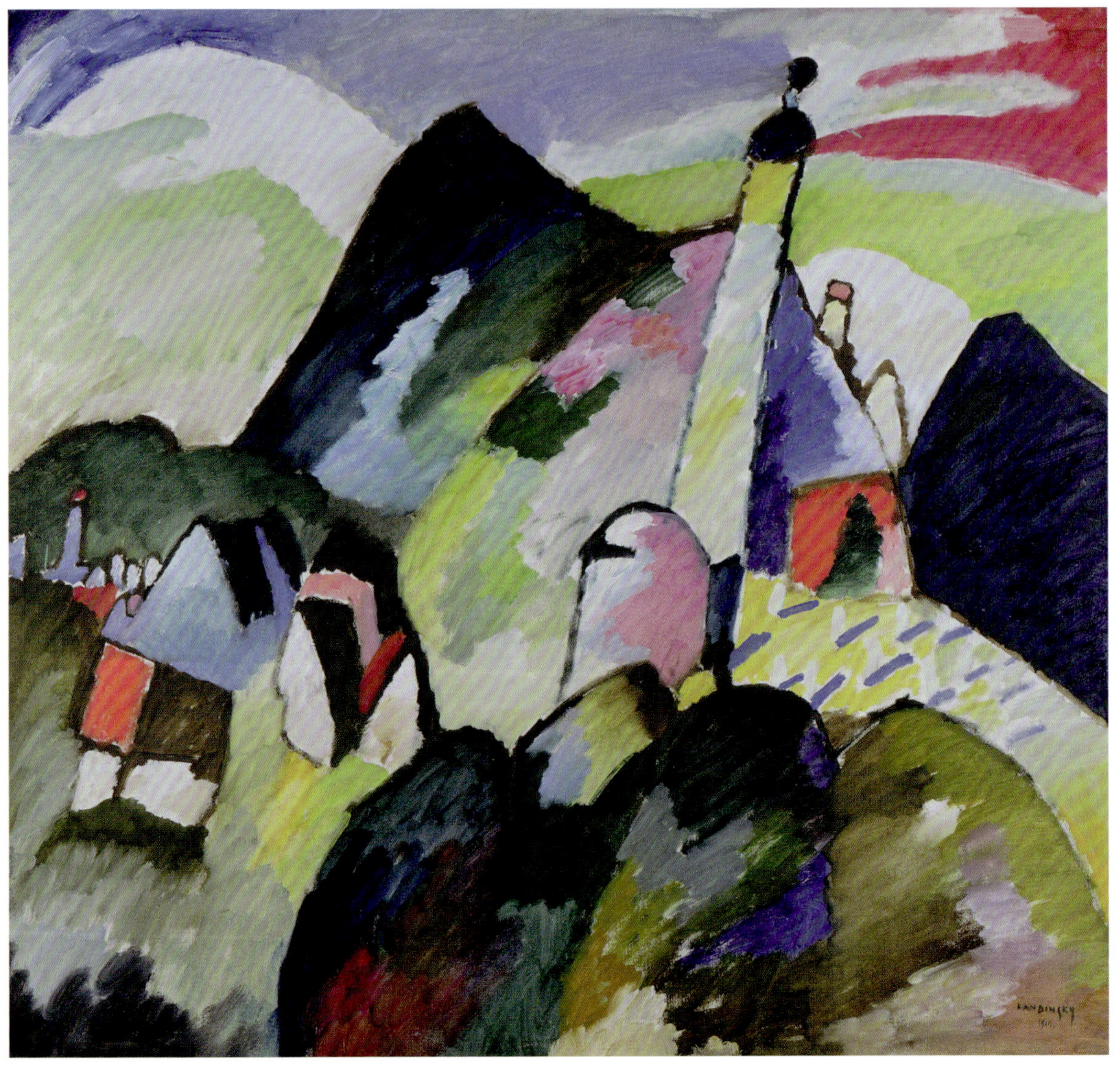

Murnau with Church II

Vue de Murnau avec église II

Blick auf Murnau mit Kirche II

Murnau con iglesia II

Murnau con chiesa II

Blik op Murnau met kerk II

1910, Oil on canvas/Huile sur toile, Stedelijk van Abbe Museum, Eindhoven

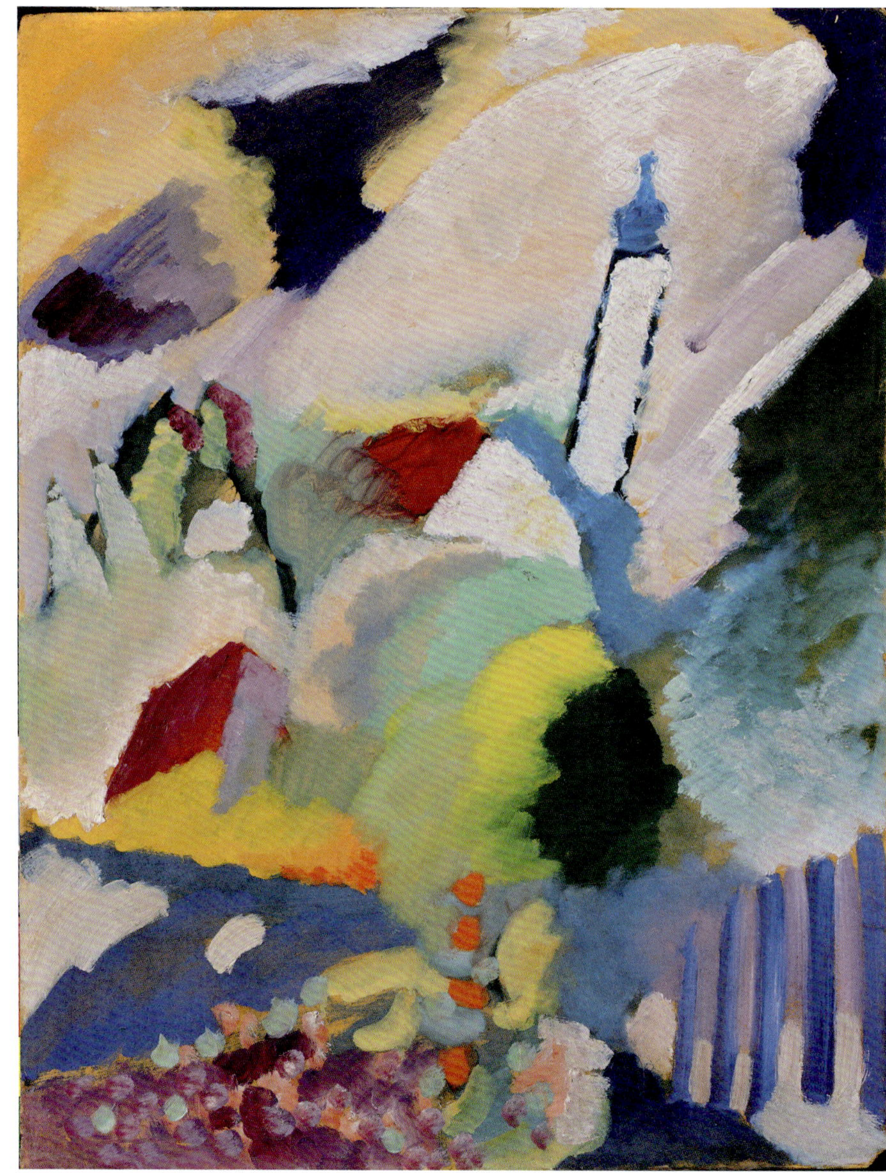

Murnau with Church I

Vue de Murnau avec église I

Blick auf Murnau mit Kirche I

Murnau con iglesia I

Murnau con chiesa I

Blik op Murnau met kerk I

1910, Oil on cardboard/Huile sur carton, 64 × 50 cm, Staatsgalerie Moderner Kunst, Munich

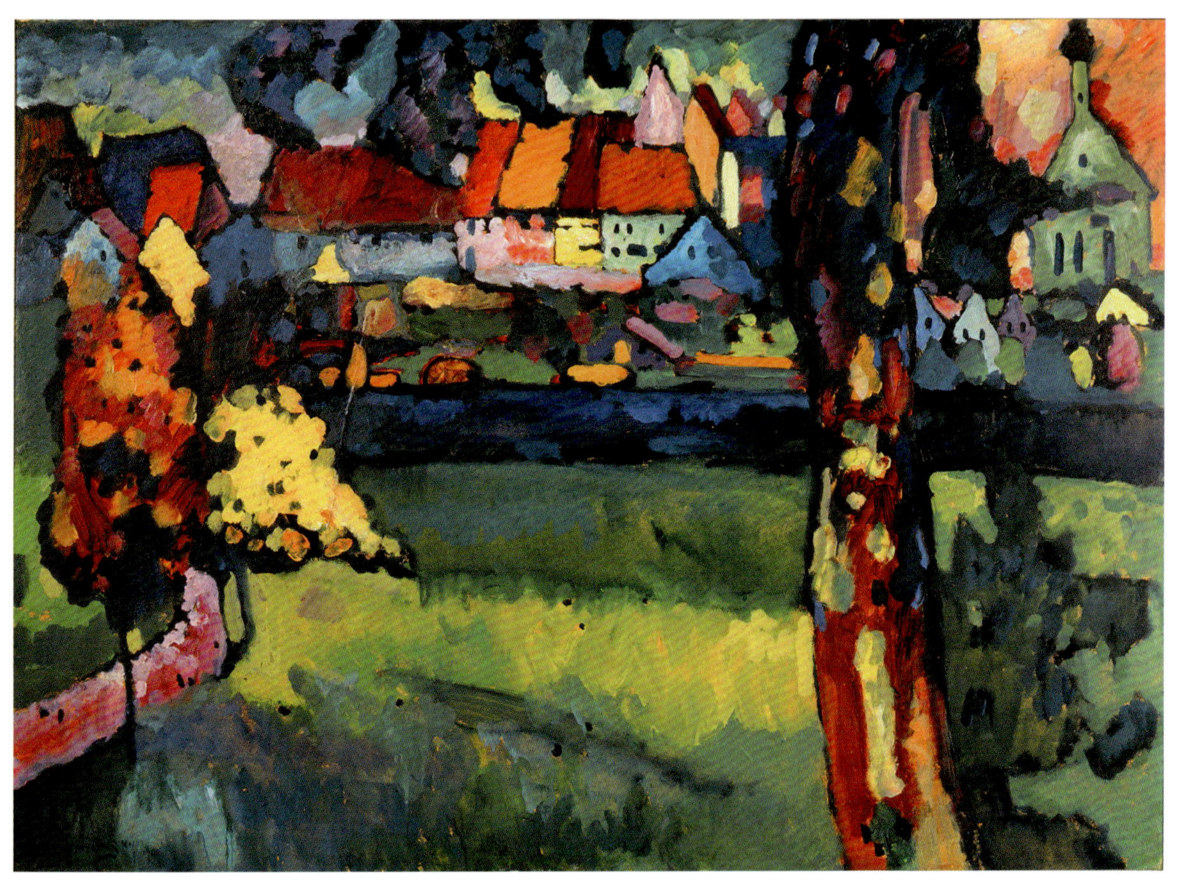

Murnau, Landscape with Tree Trunks   ***Murnau-Landschaft mit Baumstämmen***   ***Murnau, paesaggio con tronchi***

Paysage à Murnau avec troncs d'arbres   ***Murnau, paisaje con troncos de árboles***   ***Murnau – landschap met boomstammen***

1909, Oil on cardboard/Huile sur carton, 71,5 × 97,5 cm, Museum Kunstpalast, Düsseldorf

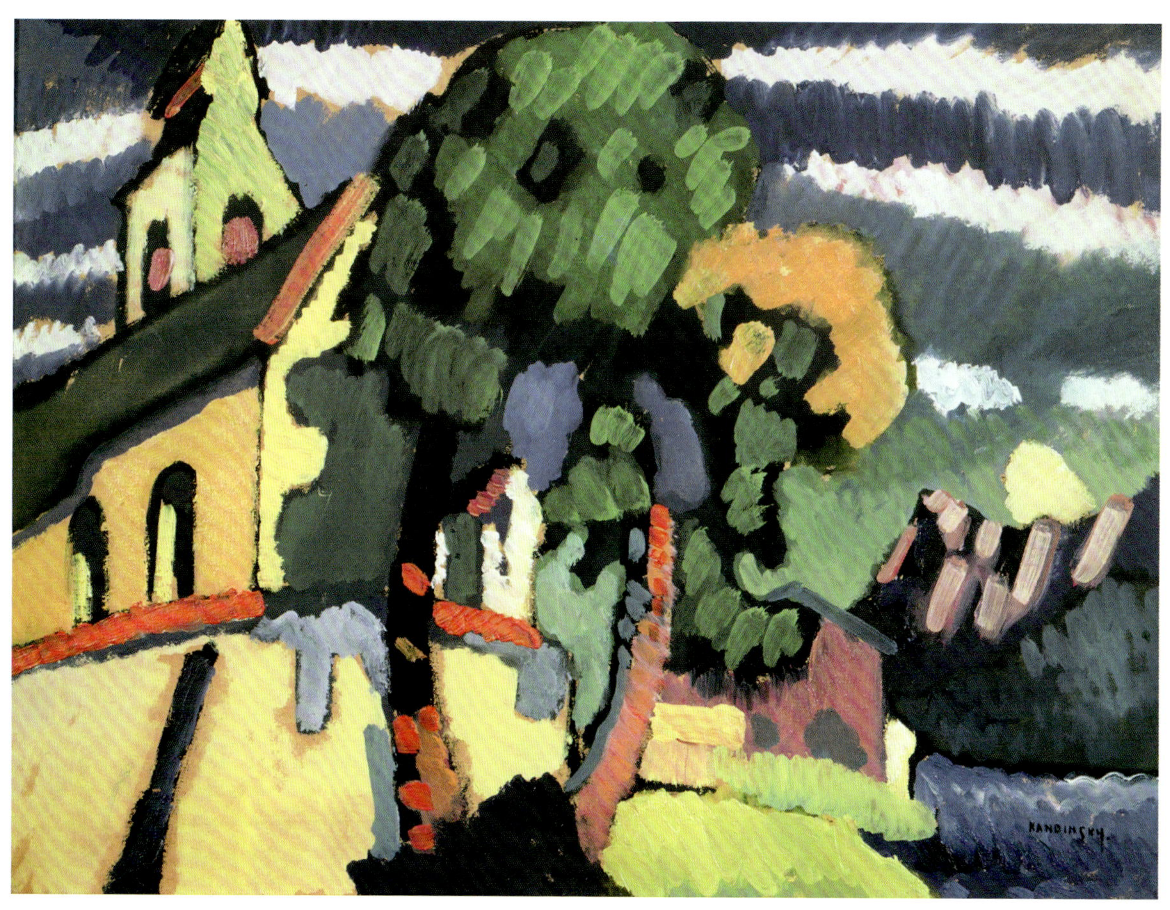

Riegsee Village Church

L'Église du village de Riegsee

Riegsee-Dorfkirche

Iglesia de la aldea de Riegsee

Chiesa di villaggio a Riegsee

Dorpskerk van Riegsee

1908, Oil on cardboard/Huile sur carton, 33 × 45 cm, Van der Heydt Museum, Wuppertal

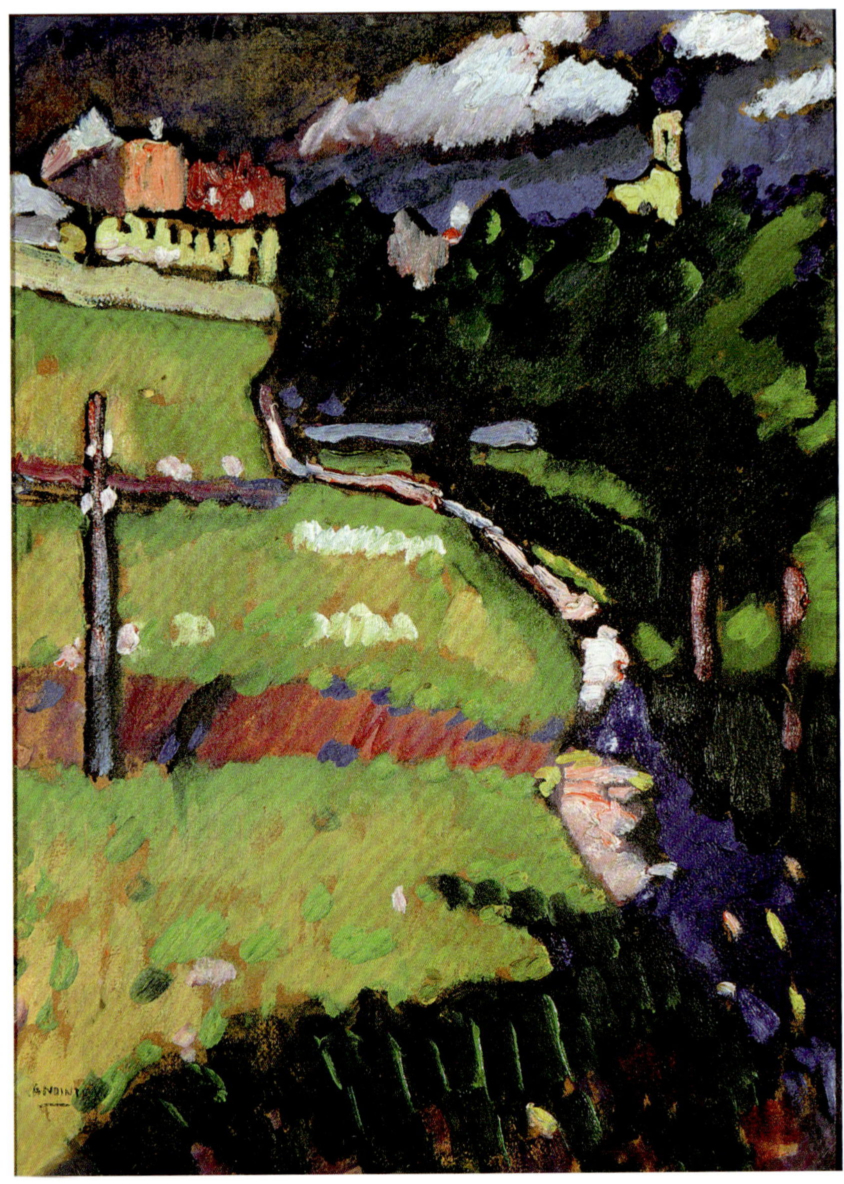

The Church in Murnau
L'Église à Murnau
Die Kirche in Murnau
La iglesia en Murnau
La chiesa a Murnau
De kerk van Murnau

1908/09, Oil on canvas/Huile sur toile, 44,5 × 32,8 cm, Regional M. Vrubel Art Museum, Omsk

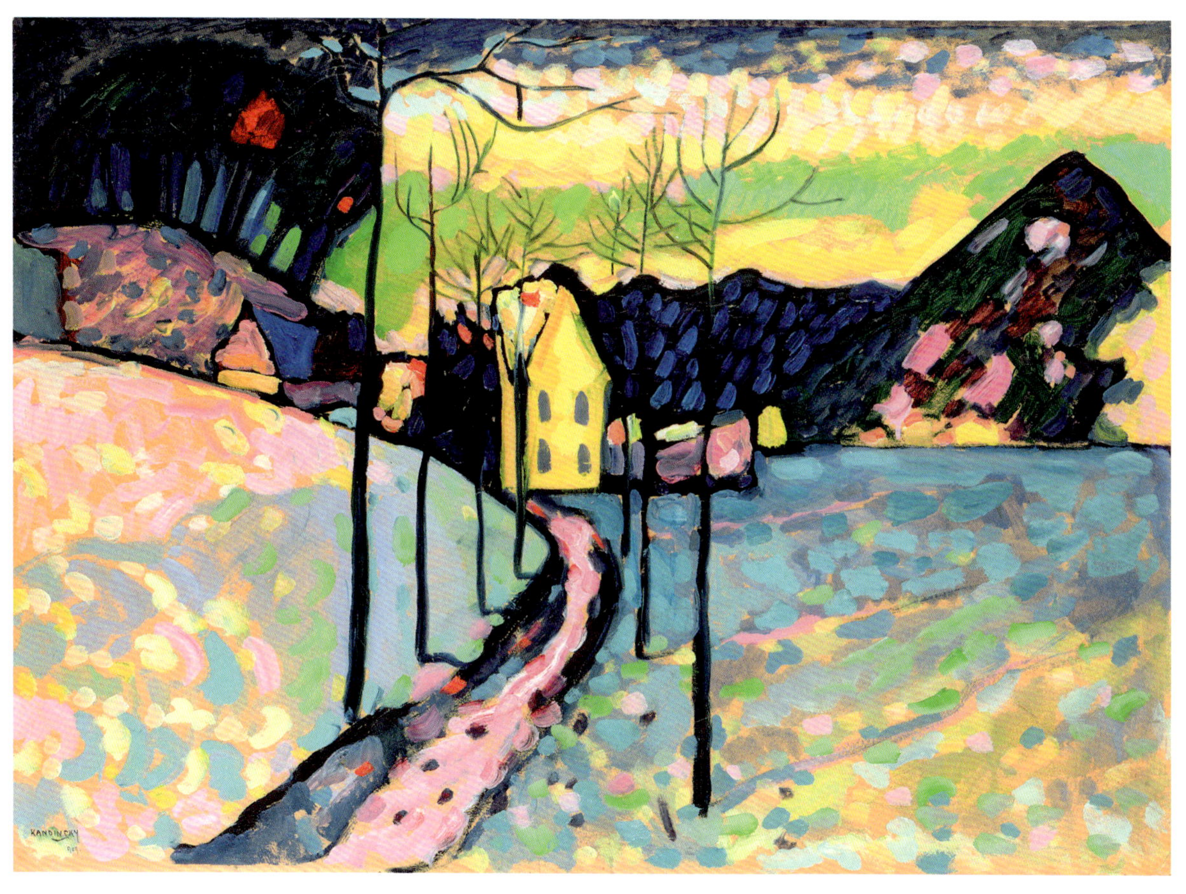

Winter Landscape

Paysage d'hiver

Winterlandschaft

Paisaje de invierno

Paesaggio invernale

Winterlandschap

1909, Oil on canvas/Huile sur toile, 70 × 97 cm,
State Hermitage Museum, St. Petersburg

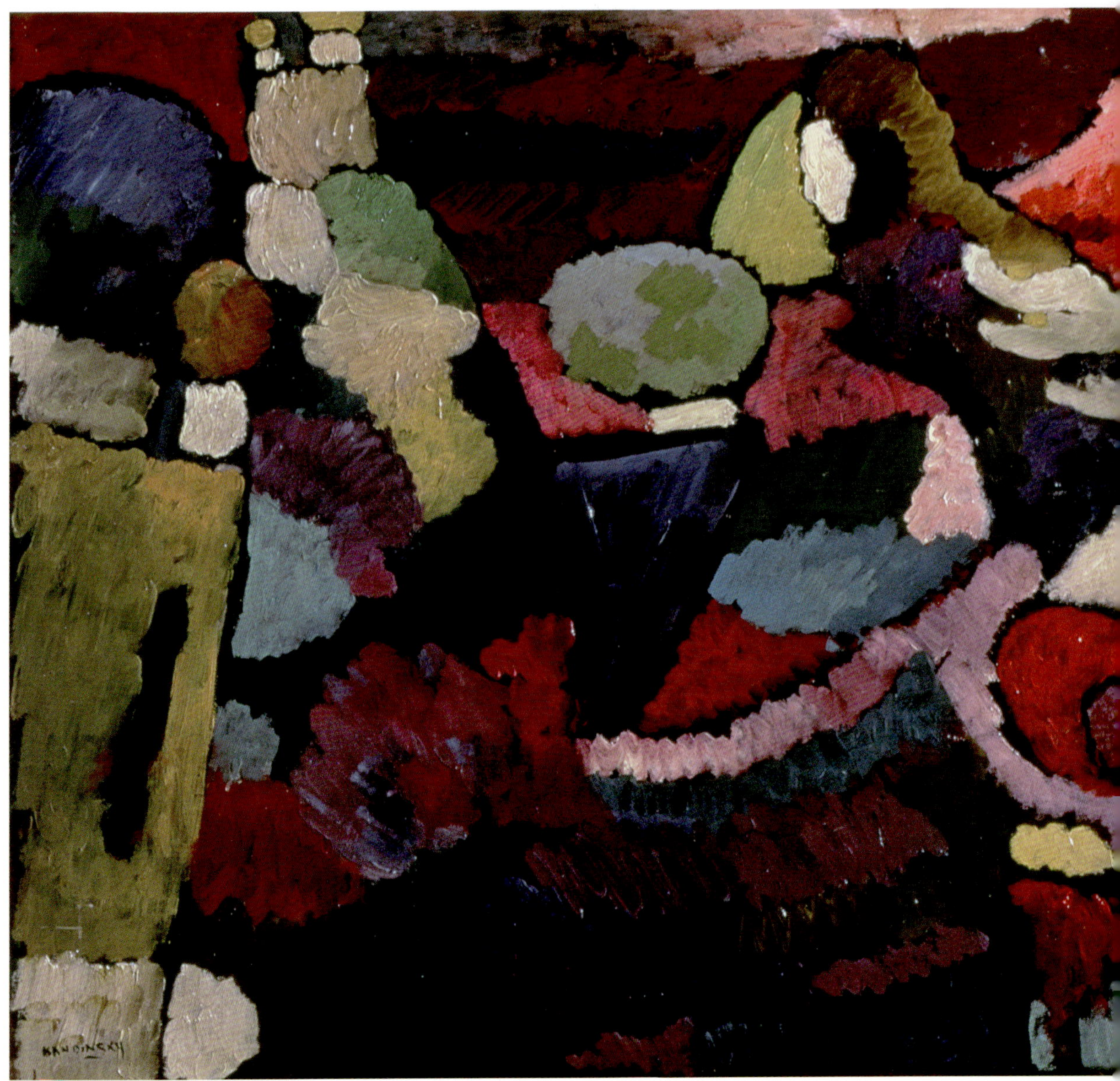

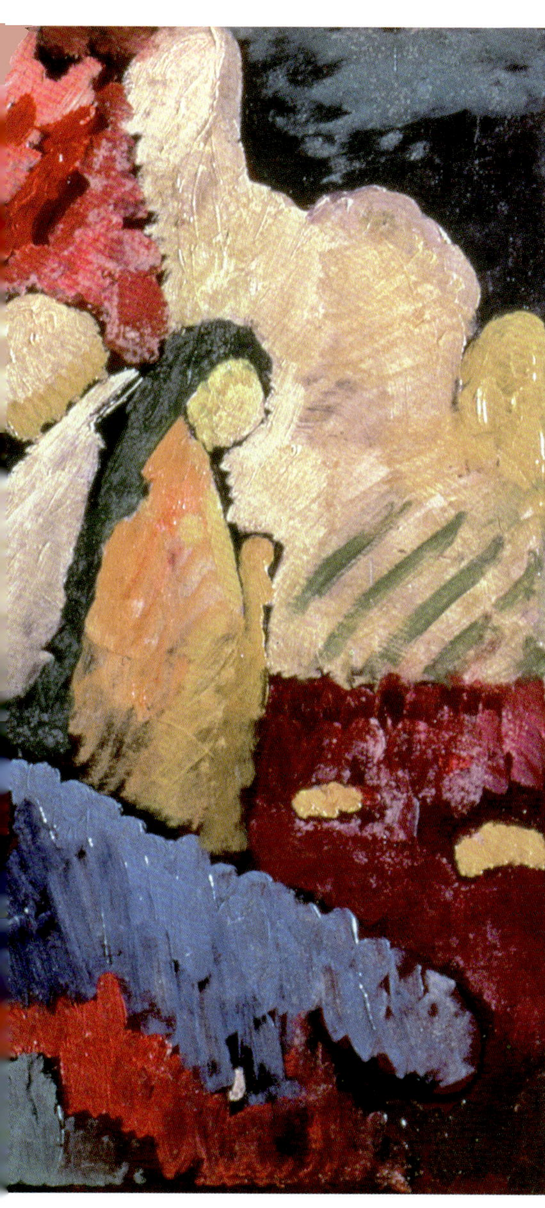

Improvisation

Improvisation

Improvisation

Improvisación

Improvvisazione

Improvisatie

1910, Oil on panel/Huile sur bois, 63,5 × 99 cm, Musee National d'Art Moderne,
Centre Pompidou, Paris

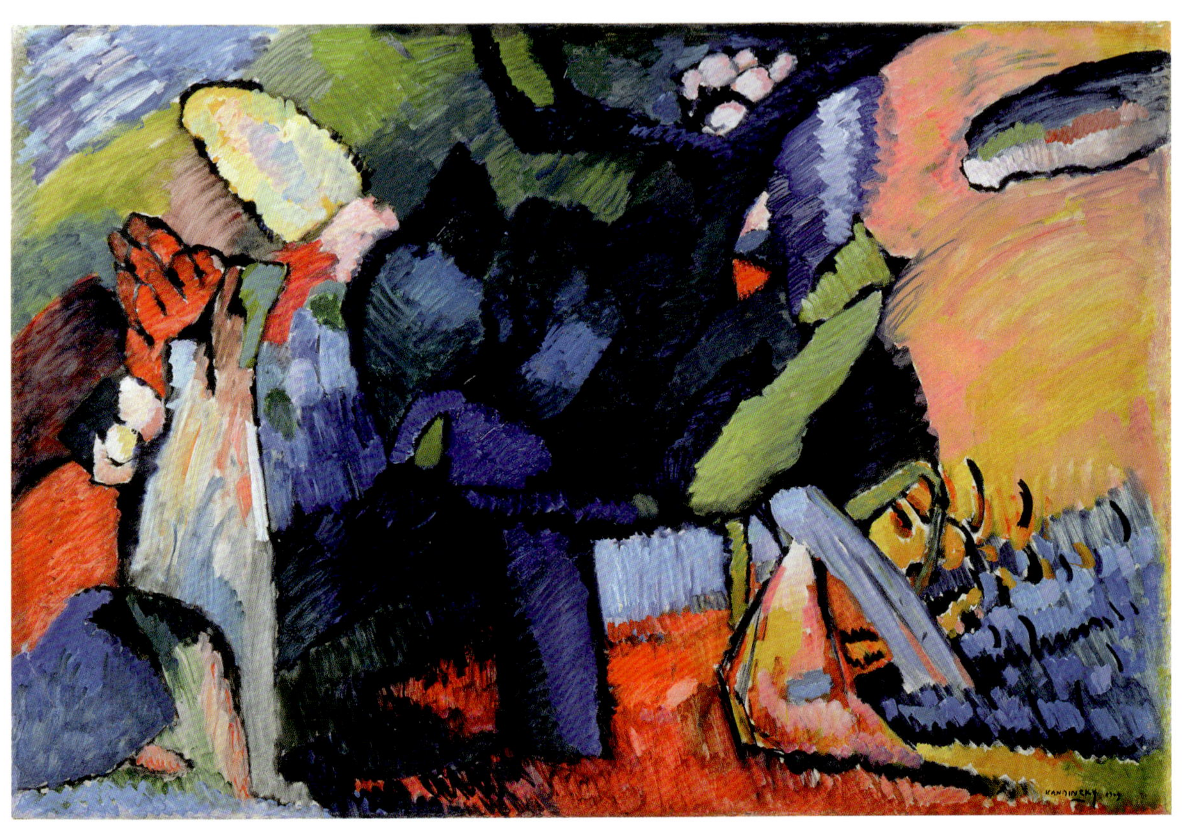

Improvisation 4

Improvisation 4

Improvvisazione 4

Improvisation 4

Improvisación 4

Improvisatie 4

1909, Oil on canvas/Huile sur toile, 107 × 158,8 cm, State Art Museum, Nizhny Novgorod

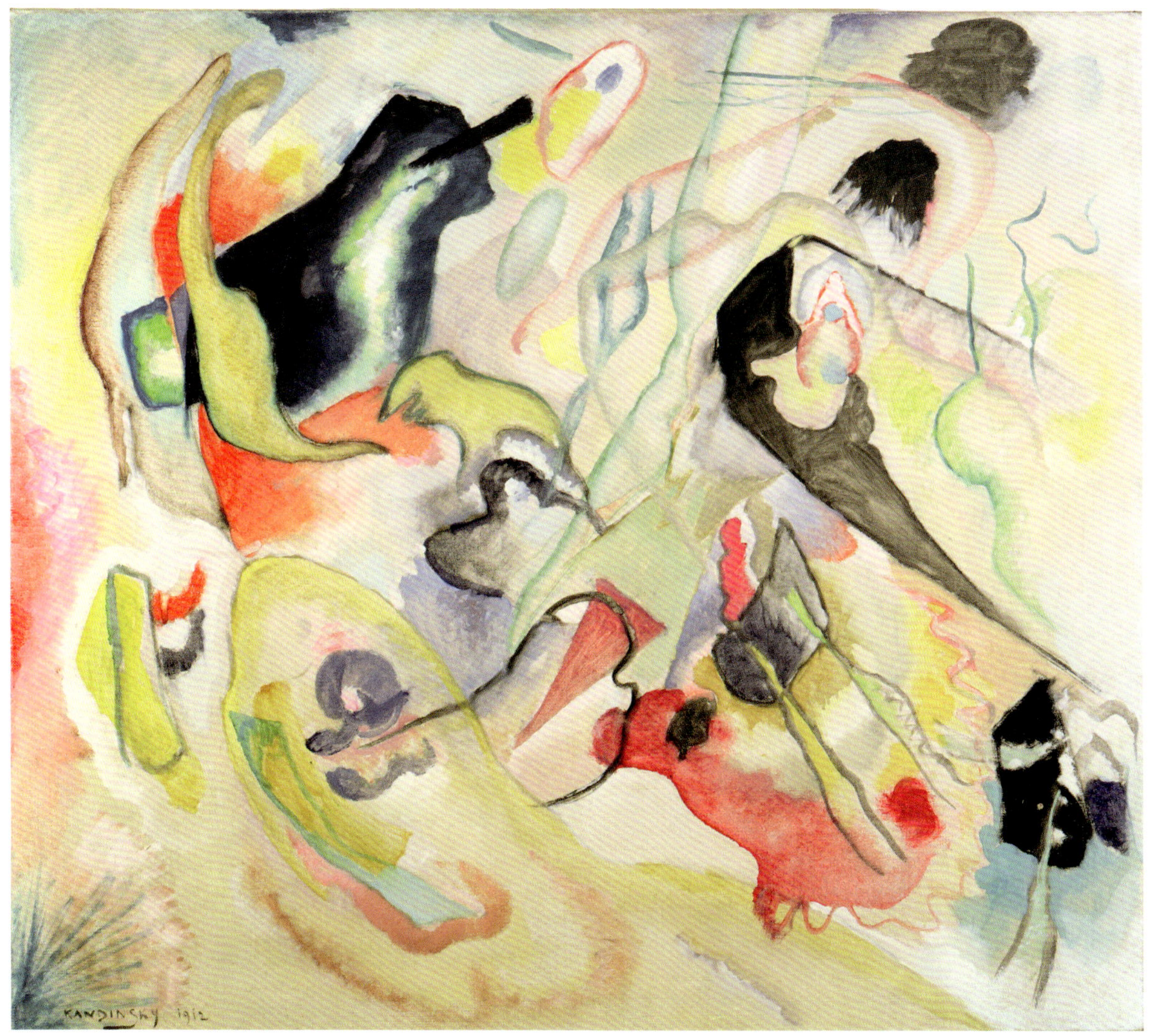

Deluge II   **Sintflut II**   **Diluvio II**

Déluge II   **Diluvio II**   **Zondvloed II**

1912, Watercolor/Aquarelle, Private collection

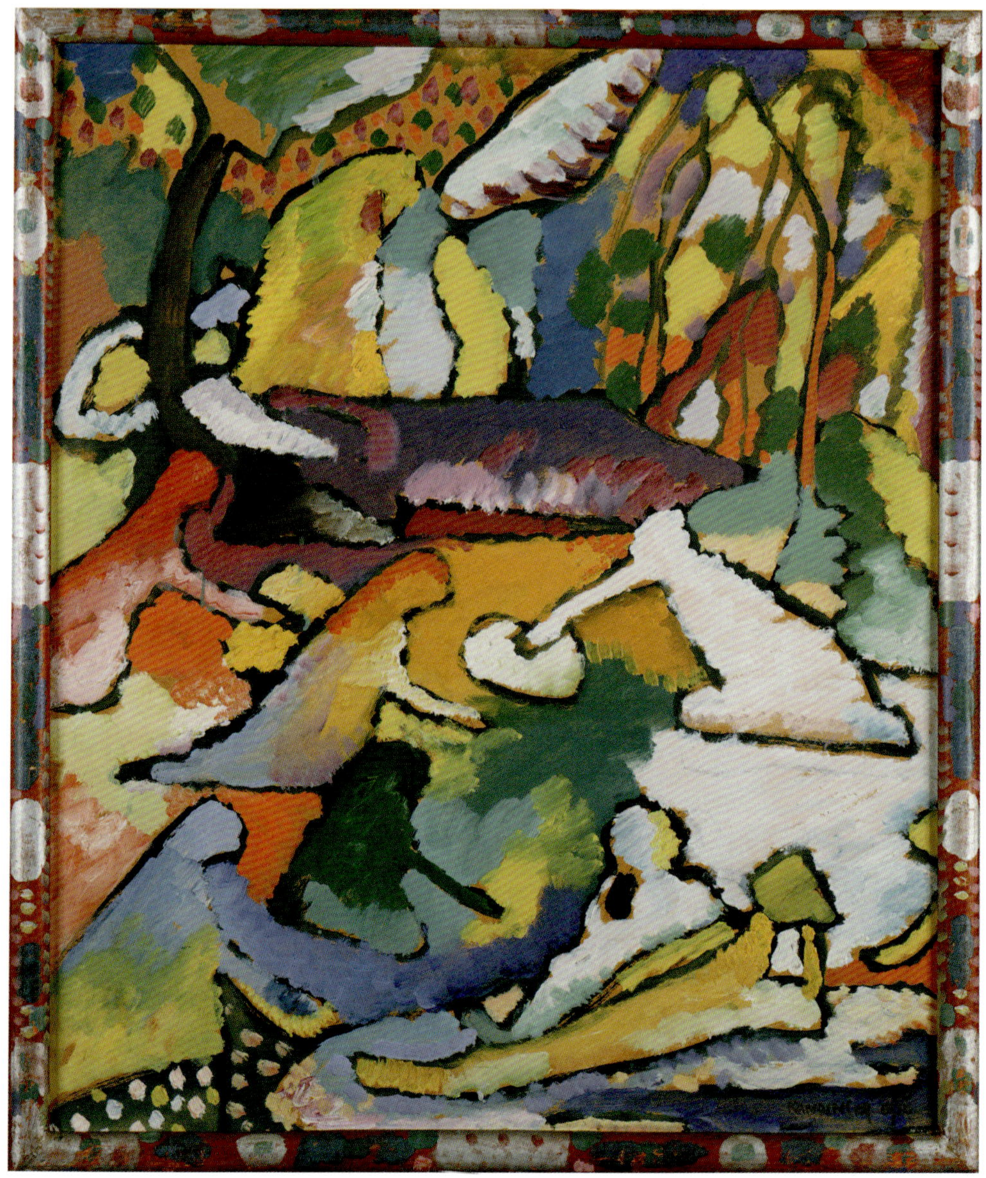

Sketch for **Composition II**

Étude pour **Composition II**

Skizze für **Komposition II**

Boceto para **Composición II**

Schizzo per **Composizione II**

Schets voor **Compositie II**

1910, Oil on cardboard/Huile sur carton, Private collection

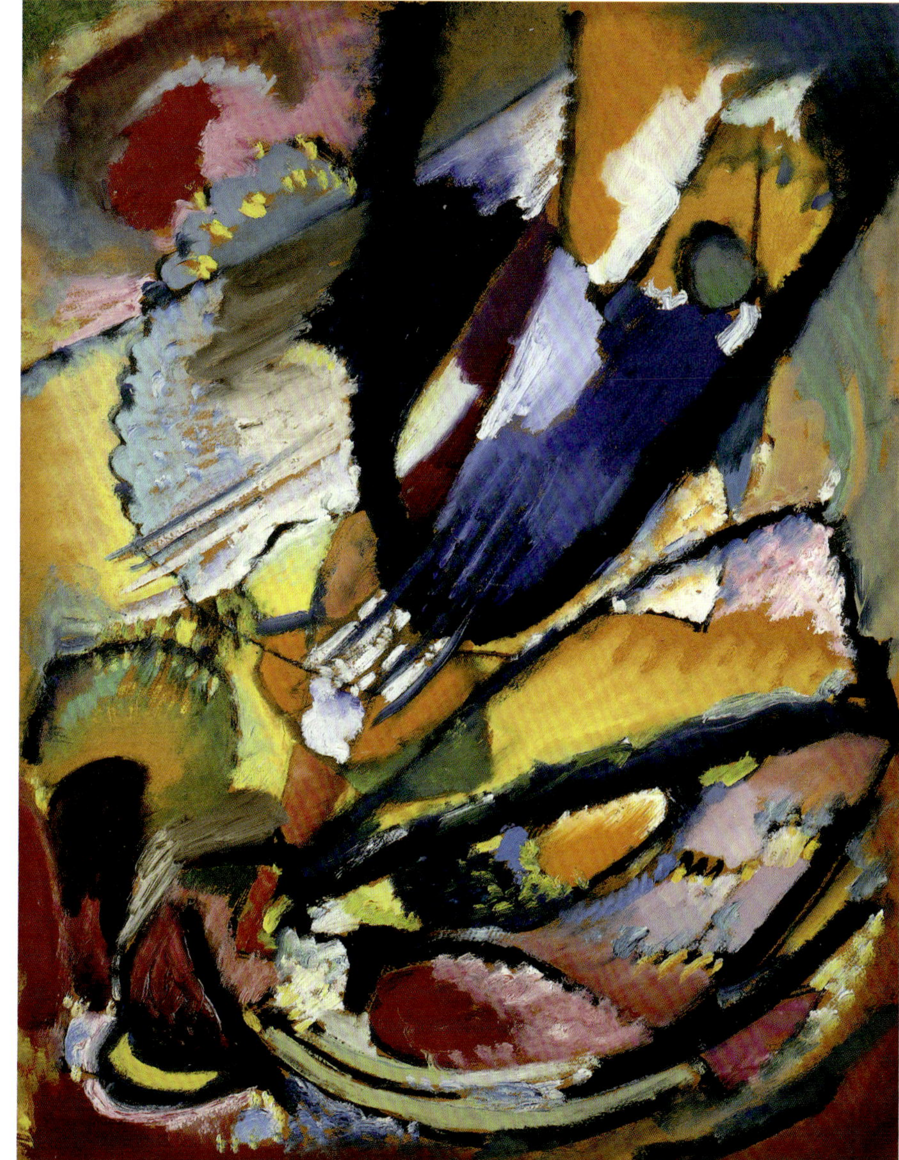

Angel of Judgment

Ange du Jugement dernier

Engel des Jüngsten Gerichts

Ángel del juicio

Angelo del giudizio

Engel van het Laatste Oordeel

c. 1911, Oil on paper on panel/ Huile sur papier marouflé sur bois, 64,7 × 50,5 cm, Private collection

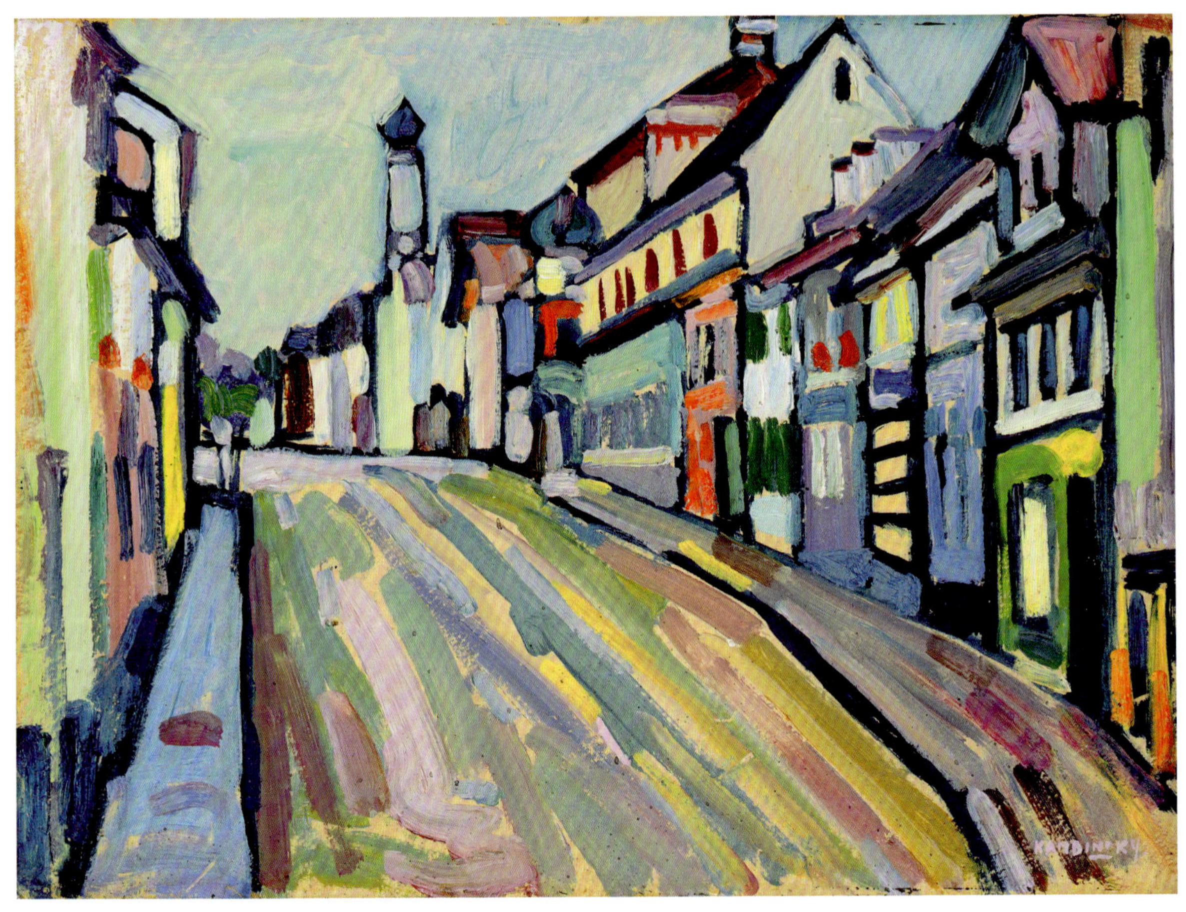

Murnau - Lower Market Street **Murnau – Untermarkt** *Murnau - Mercato inferiore*

Murnau - Bas de la rue du Marché **Murnau - calle más baja del mercado** **Murnau – Untermarkt**

1908, Oil on cardboard/Huile sur carton, 33 × 44,5 cm, Private collection

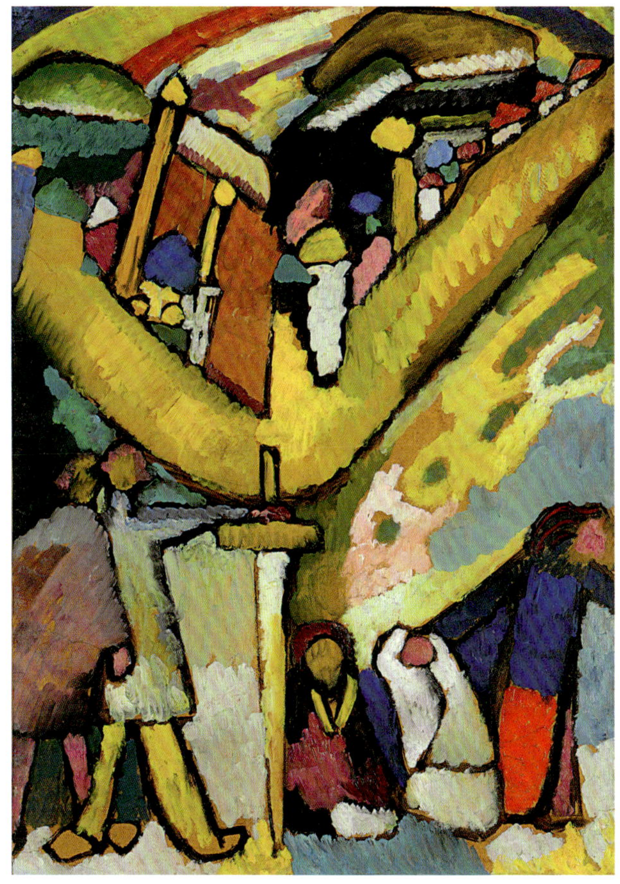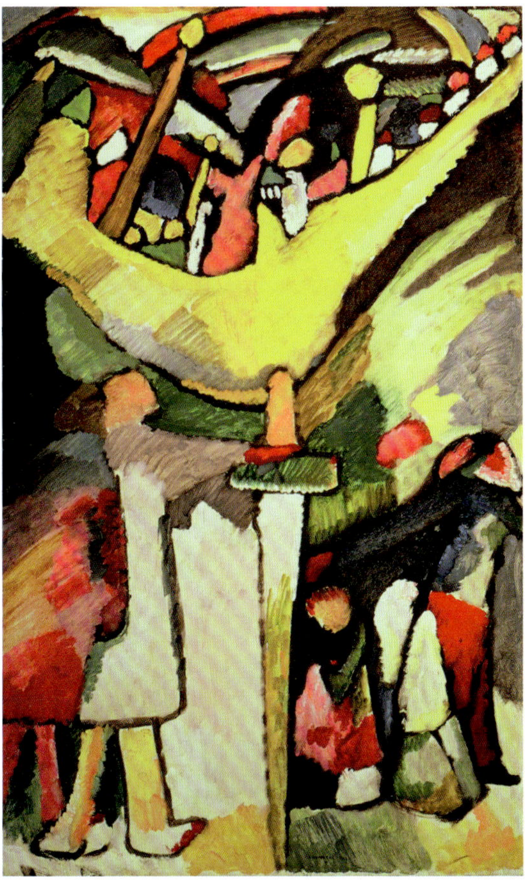

Study for **Improvisation 8**

Etude pour **Improvisation 8**

Studie für **Improvisation 8**

Estudio para la **improvisación 8**

Studio per **Improvvisazione 8**

Studie voor **Improvisatie 8**

1909, Oil on cardboard on canvas/Huile sur papier marouflé sur toile, 98 × 70 cm, Private collection

Improvisation 8

Improvisation 8

Improvisation 8

Improvisación 8

Improvvisazione 8

Improvisatie 8

1909, Oil on canvas/Huile sur toile, 125 × 73 cm, Herbert Rothschild Collection, New York

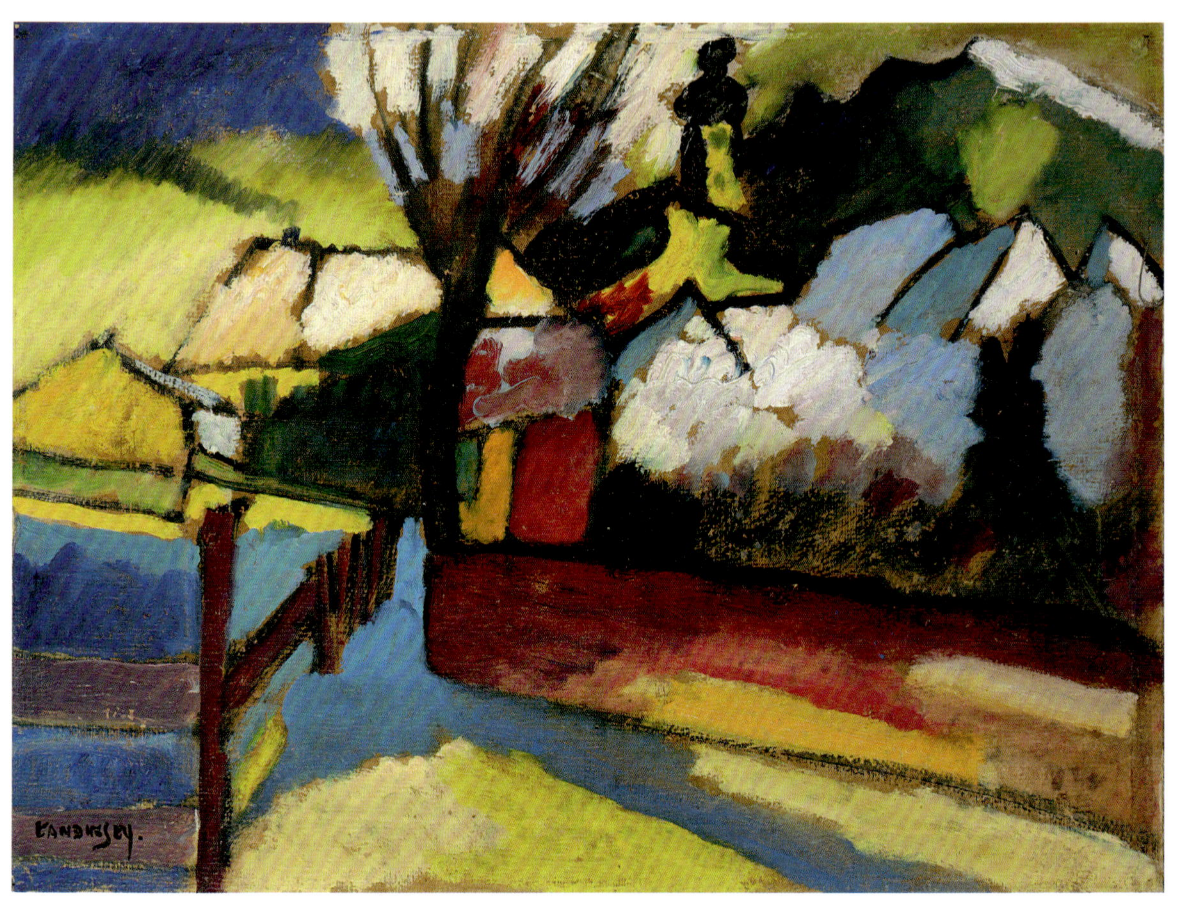

Autumn Landscape with Tree   **Herbstlandschaft mit Baum**   **Paesaggio autunnale con albero**

Paysage d'automne avec arbre   **Paisaje de otoño con árbol**   **Herfstlandschap met boom**

1910, Oil on cardboard/Huile sur carton, 32,9 × 44,2 cm, Private collection

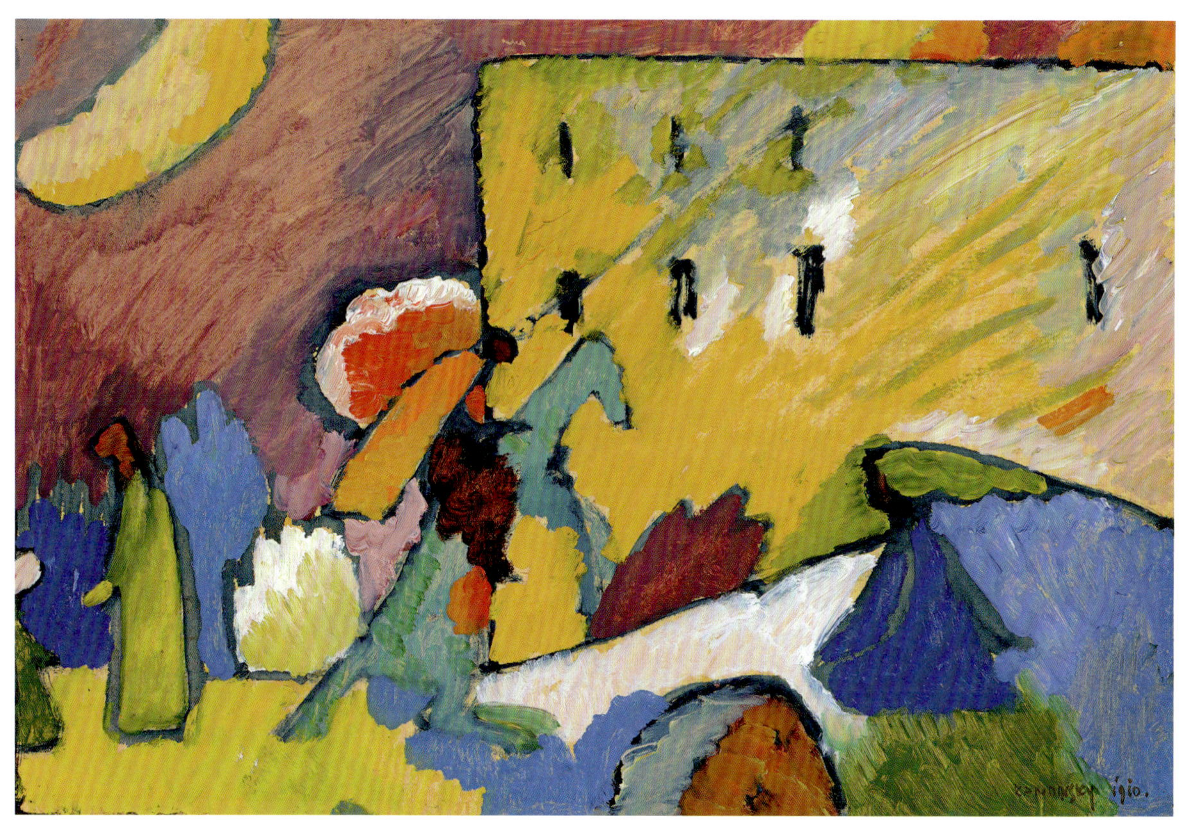

Study for **Improvisation 3**   Studie für **Improvisation 3**   Studio per **Improvvisazione 3**

Étude pour **Improvisation 3**   Estudio para la **improvisación 3**   Studie voor **Improvisatie 3**

1909, Oil and gouache on board/Huile et gouache sur carton, 44,5 × 64,7 cm, Private collection

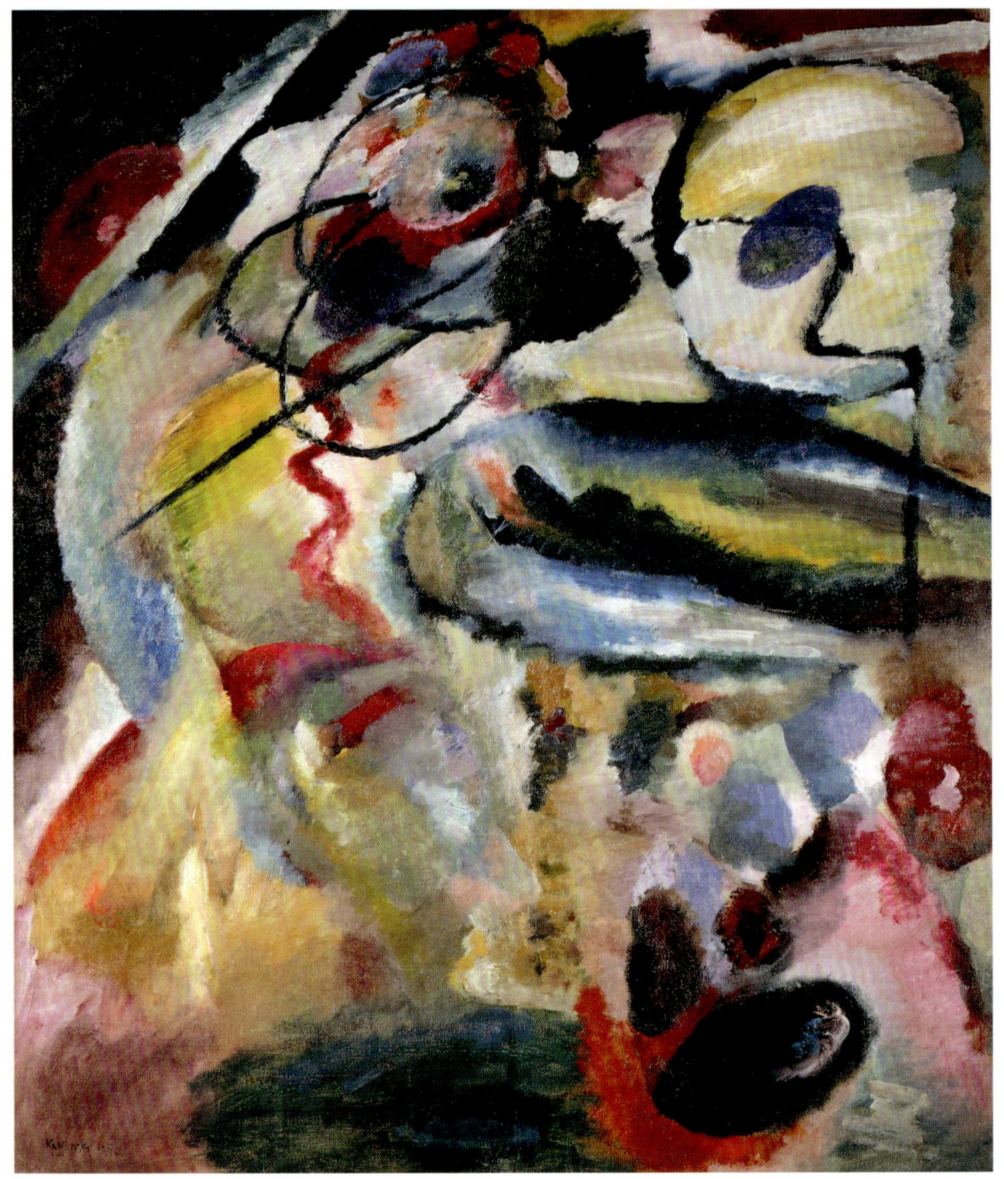

**Painting with
a circle**

*Tableau avec
cercle*

Bild mit Kreis

**Pintura con
circuli**

**Dipinto con
cerchio**

Beeld met cirkel

*1911, Oil on
canvas/Huile sur
toile, 139 × 111 cm,
Georgian National
Museum, Tbilissi*

**Painting with
red spot**

*Tableau à la
tache rouge*

**Bild mit
rotem Fleck**

**Cuadro con
mancha roja**

**Quadro con
macchia rossa**

**Schilderij met
rode vlek**

*1914, Oil on
canvas/Huile sur
toile, 130 × 130 cm,
Musee National
d'Art Moderne
Centre Pompidou,
Paris*

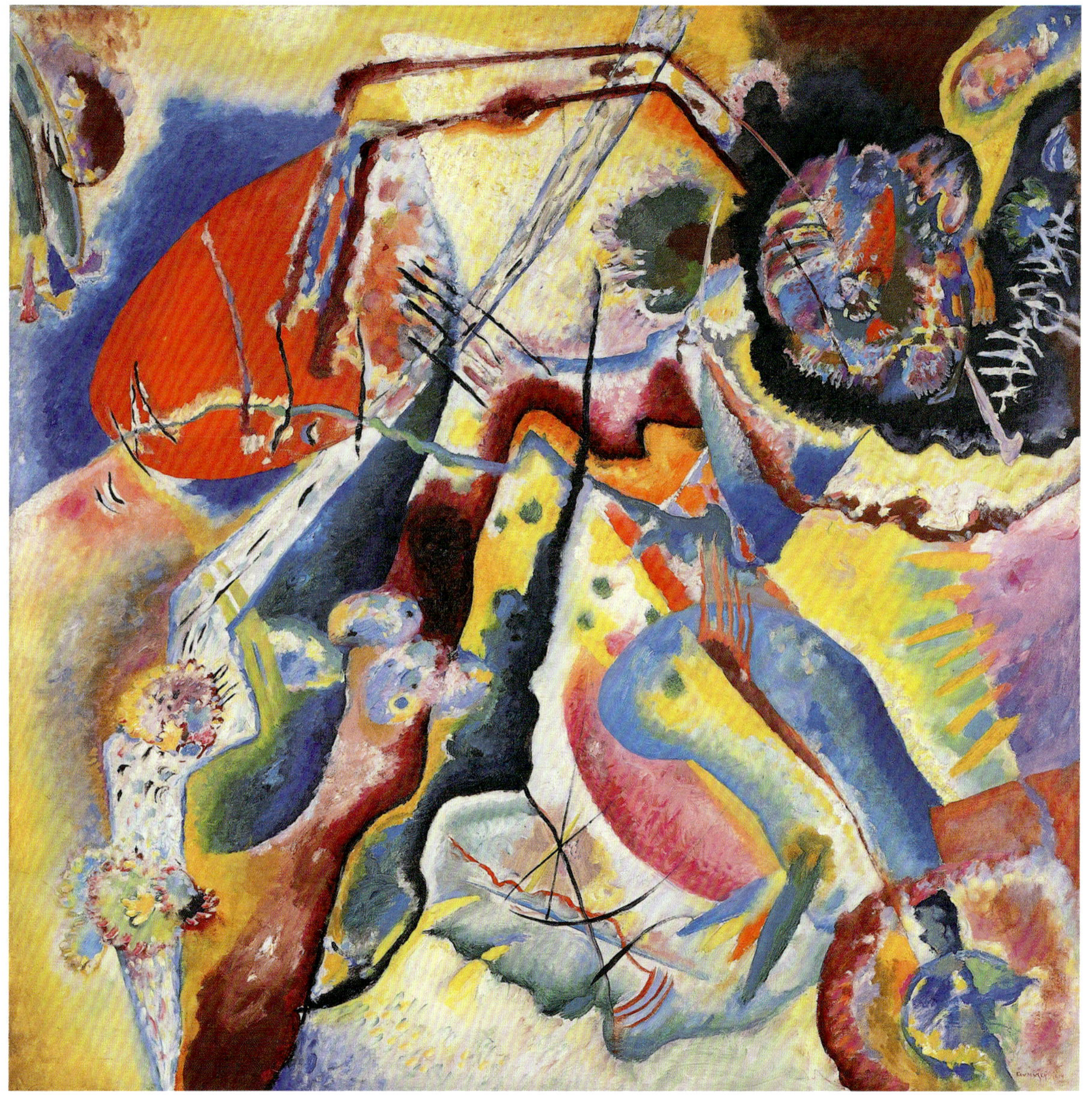

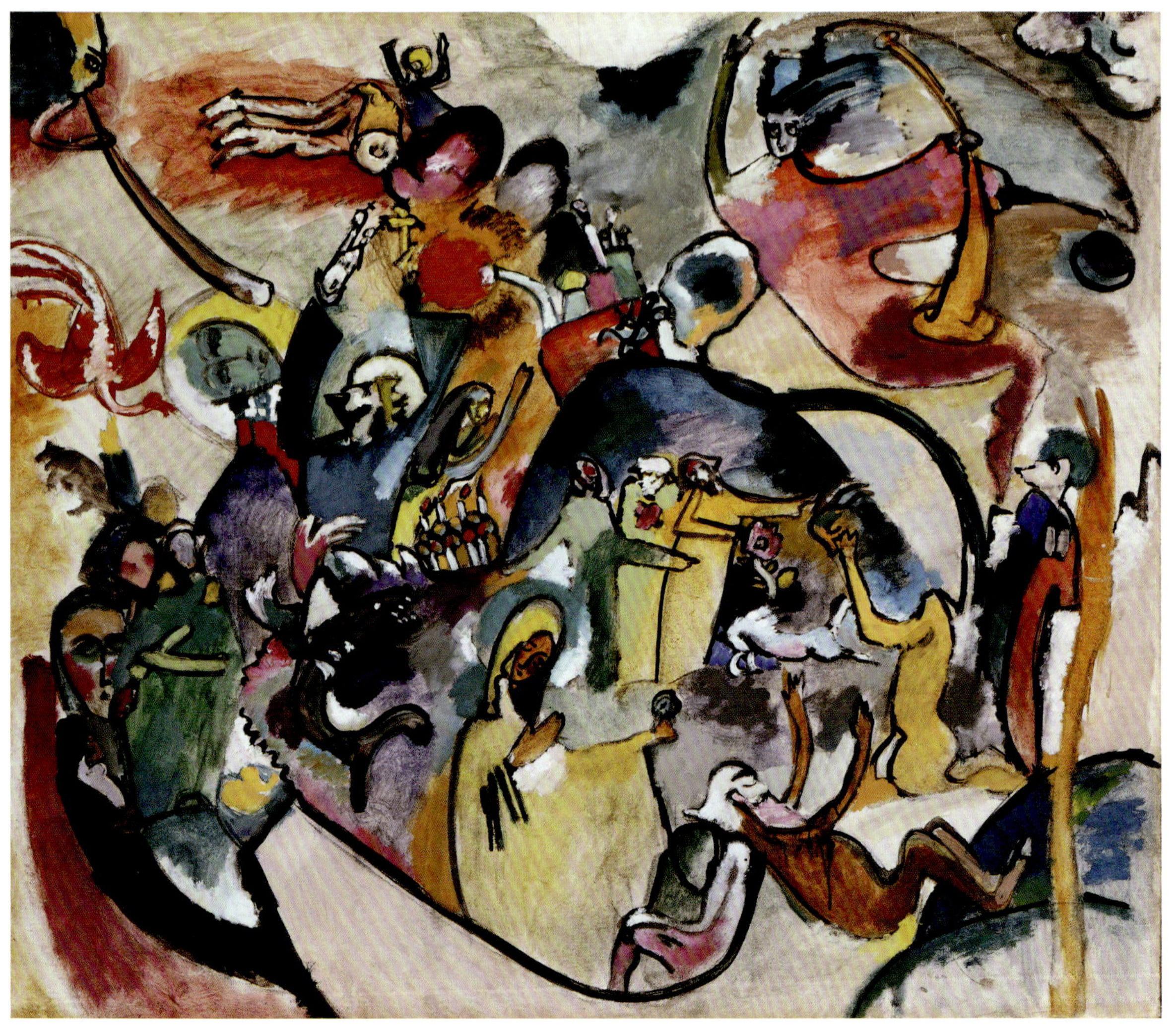

Couples in the castle park II — *Paare im Schlosspark II* — *Coppie nel parco del castello II*

Couples dans le parc du château II — *Parejas en el parque del castillo II* — *Stellen in het Slotpark II*

1911, Oil on canvas/Huile sur toile, 86 × 99 cm, Städtische Galerie im Lenbachhaus, Munich

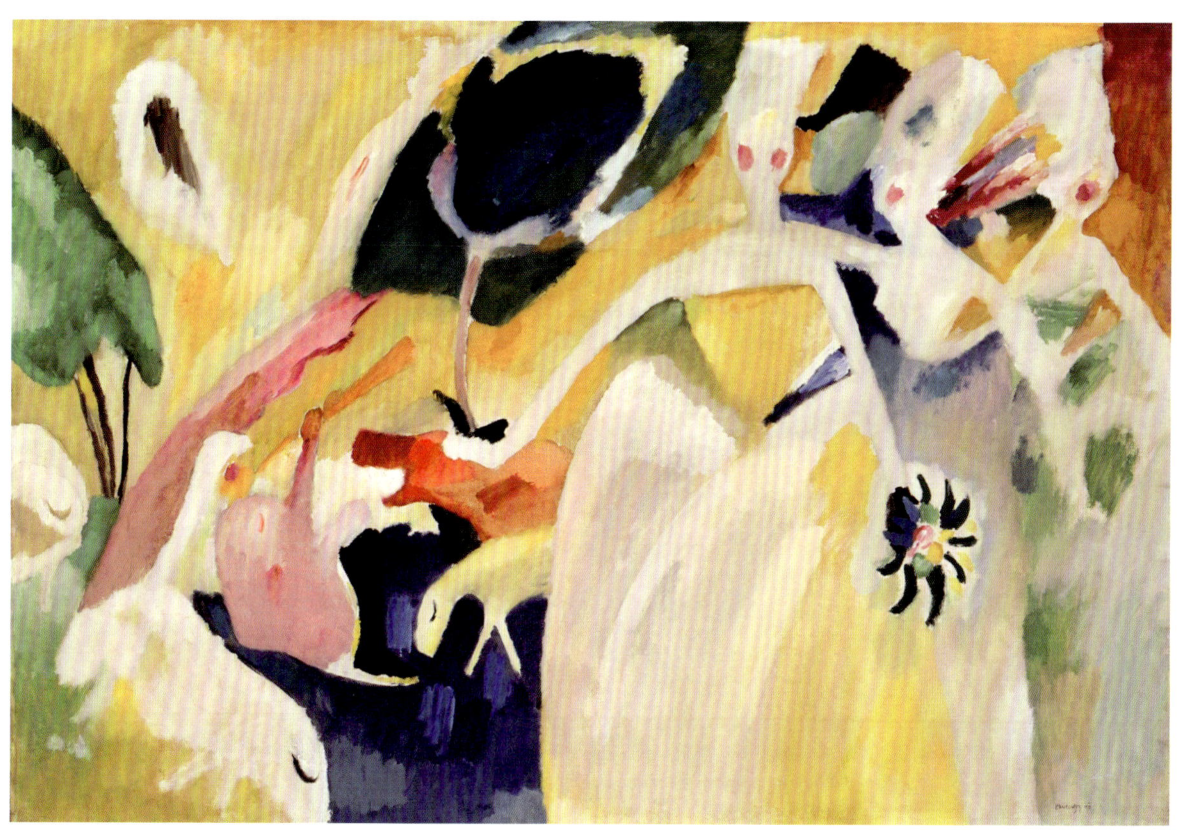

Pastoral   **Pastorale**   **Pastorale**

Pastorale   **Pastoral**   **Pastorale**

1911, Oil on canvas/Huile sur toile, 106 × 156 cm,
Solomon R. Guggenheim Museum, New York

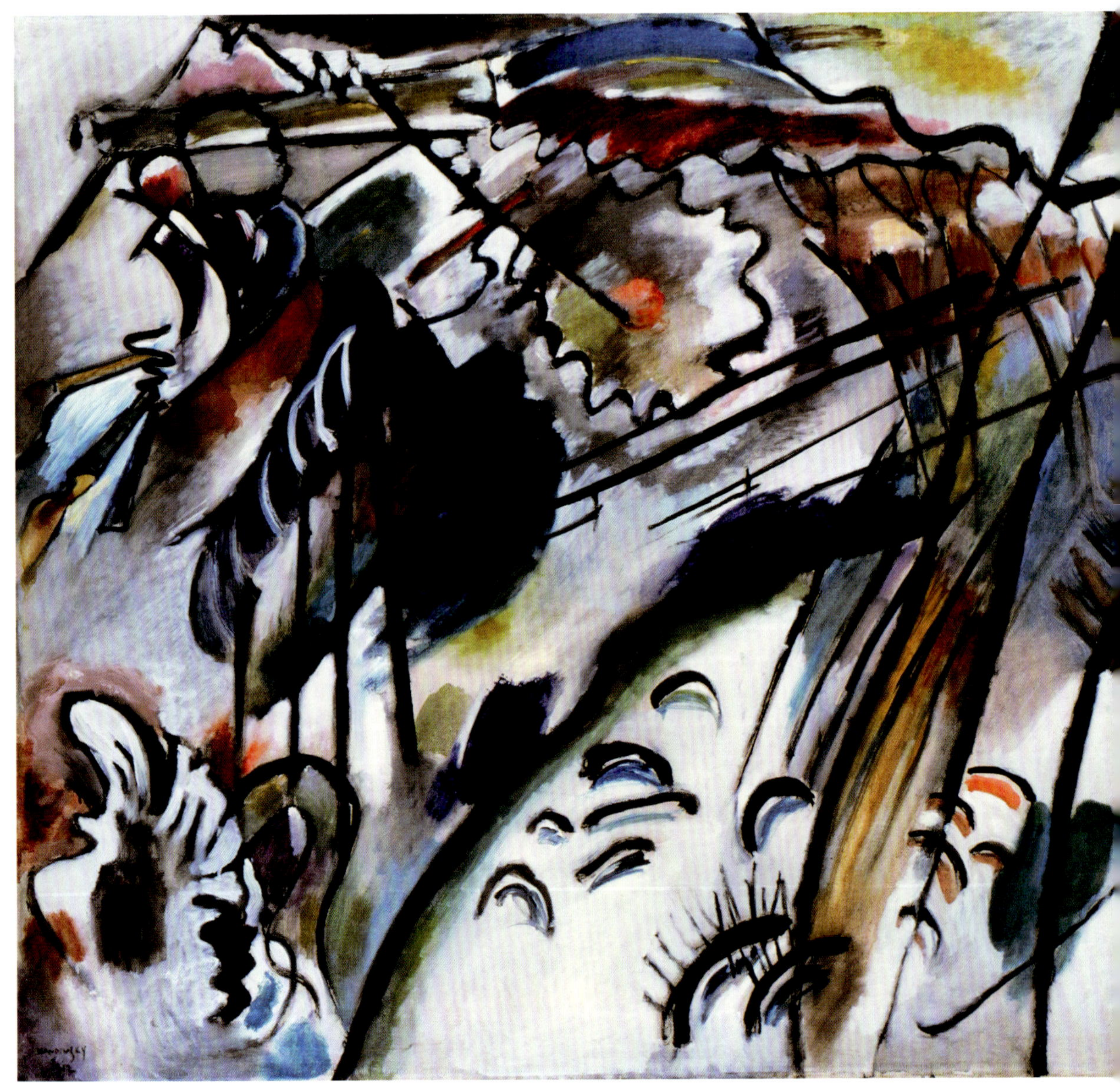

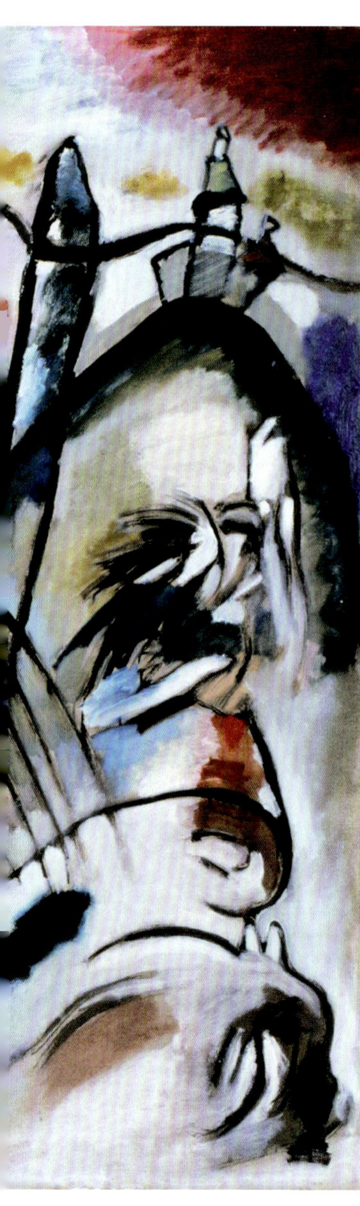

Improvisation 28 (second version)

***Improvisation 28**,* 2e version

***Improvisation 28**,* 2. Fassung

Improvisación 28 (segunda versión)

Improvvisazione 28 (seconda versione)

***Improvisatie 28**,* 2de versie

1912, Oil on canvas/Huile sur toile, 111 × 162 cm, Solomon R. Guggenheim Museum, New York

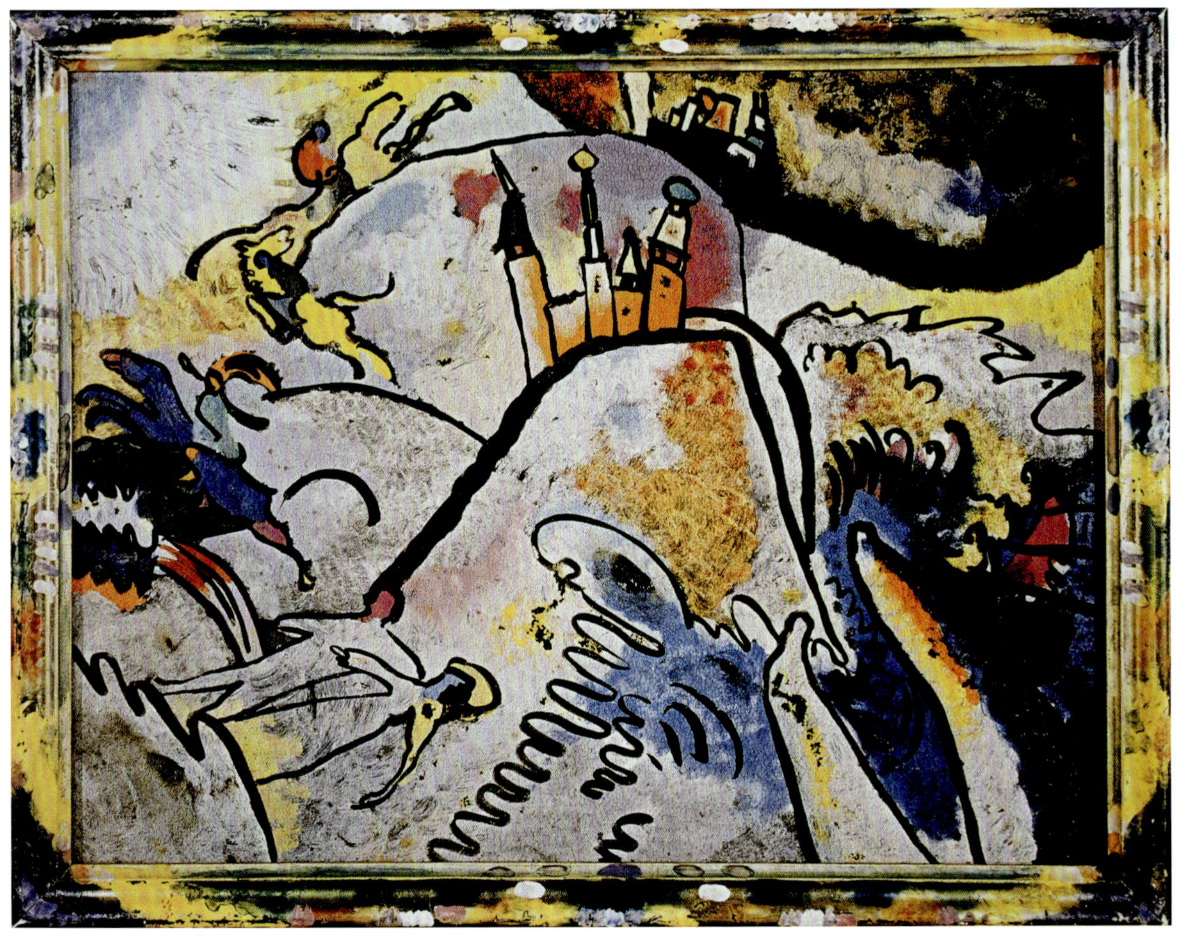

Glass painting with the Sun (Small pleasures)

Peinture sous verre au soleil

Glasbild mit Sonne (Kleine Freuden)

Pintura de cristal con el sol (pequeños placeres)

Pittura su vetro con il sole (Piccoli piaceri)

Glasschilderij met zon (Kleine geneugten)

1910, Reverse glass painting/Peinture sur verre, 31 × 40 cm, Städtische Galerie im Lenbachhaus, Munich

Improvisation 6 (African)

Improvisation 6 (africaine)

Improvisation 6 (Afrikanisches)

Improvisación 6 (africano)

Improvvisazione 6 (africana)

Improvisatie 6 ('Afrikanisches')

1909, Oil on canvas/Huile sur toile, 107 × 99,5 cm, Städtische Galerie im Lenbachhaus, Munich

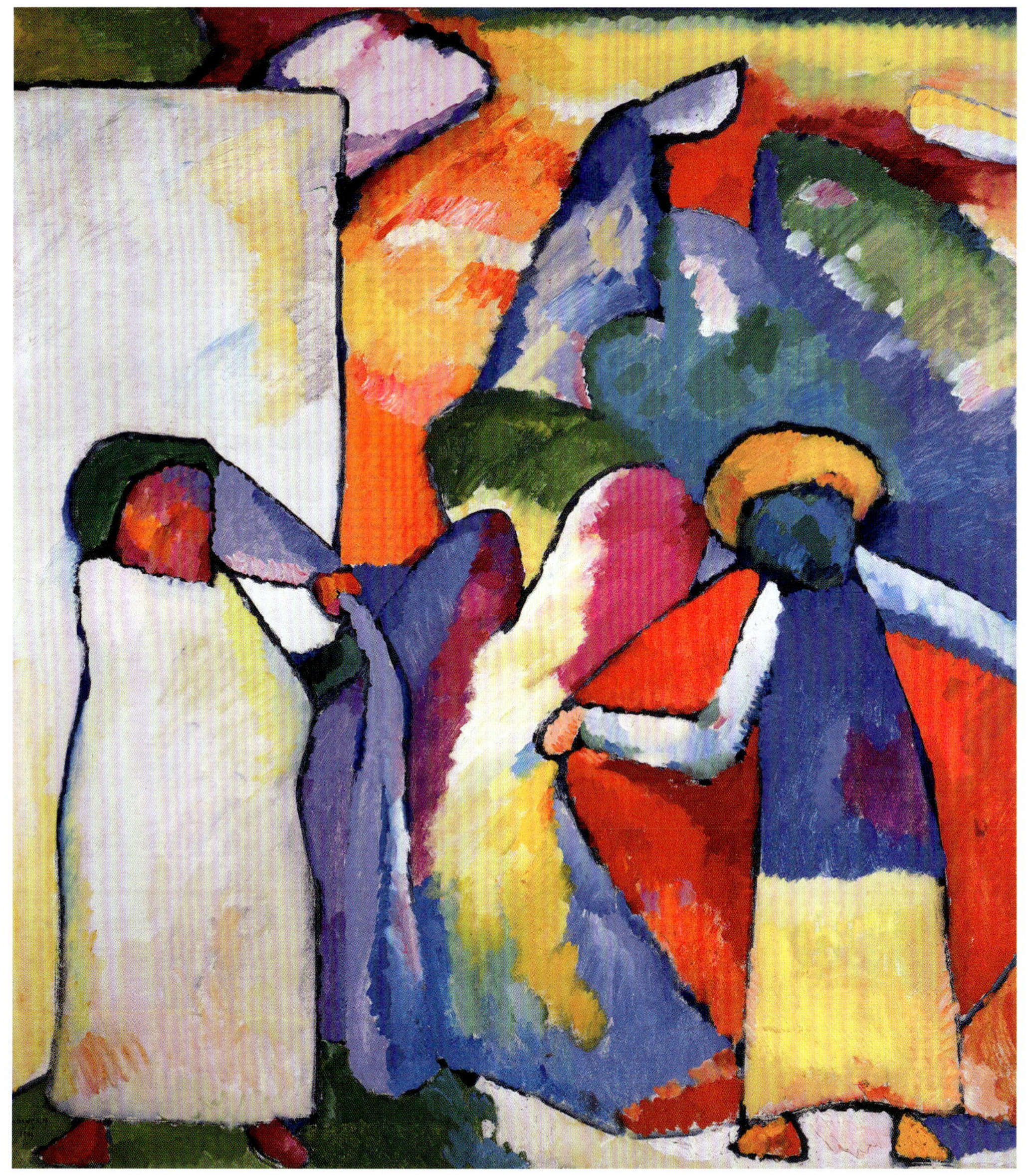

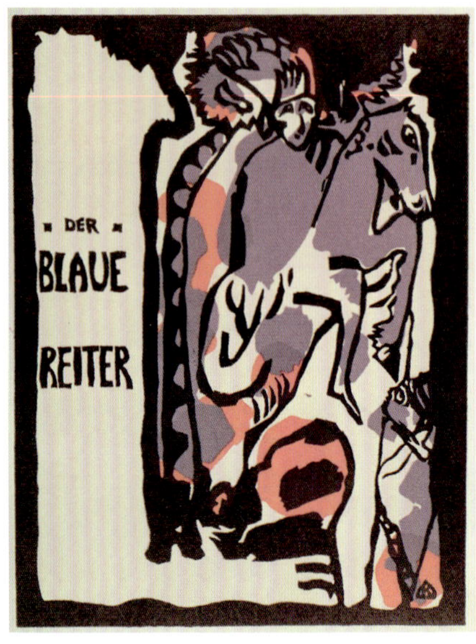

Cover for **Der Blaue Reiter**

Couverture de l'almanach du **Blaue Reiter**

Umschlag für **Der Blaue Reiter**

Cubierta para **Der Blaue Reiter**

Copertina per **Der Blaue Reiter**

Omslag van **Der Blaue Reiter**

*1911, Lithograph/Lithographie,
Städtische Galerie im Lenbachhaus, Munich*

The decision to exclude a large painting of Kandinsky's from the 3rd exhibition of the "Munich New Artists' Association" presented an opportunity for the artist to leave the association in December 1911, along with Münter, Franz Marc and Alfred Kubin. Together with Franz Marc (1880–1916), he was already drafting an entirely new book, which was to be named "Der Blaue Reiter" and present all the important art movements. By December 1911 they had organized their first exhibition in Heinrich Thannhauser's "Modern Gallery" and a short time later Kandinsky's treatise "Concerning the Spiritual in Art" was published by the Piper Verlag. The almanac, however, was not published until May 1912 after the 2nd exhibition of "Der Blaue Reiter"

Le refus d'un grand tableau de Kandinsky à la troisième exposition de la Neue Künstlervereinigung München est l'occasion pour lui de quitter l'association en décembre 1911, en compagnie de Münter, Franz Marc et Alfred Kubin. Il travaille alors déjà avec Franz Marc (1880–1916) à la rédaction d'un tout nouvel ouvrage qui doit s'appeler Der Blaue Reiter (« Le Cavalier bleu ») et présenter tous les courants importants de l'art moderne. En décembre 1911 encore, ils organisent leur première exposition dans la Moderne Galerie de Heinrich Thanhauser. Peu après paraît aux Éditions Piper le livre de Kandinsky, *Über das Geistige in der Kunst, insbesondere in der Malerei (Du Spirituel dans l'art et dans la peinture en particulier).* L'almanach

Die Ausjurierung eines großen Gemäldes von Kandinsky aus der 3. Ausstellung der „Neuen Künstlervereinigung München" nimmt dieser zum Anlass, den Verein im Dezember 1911 zusammen mit Münter, Franz Marc und Alfred Kubin zu verlassen. Zusammen mit Franz Marc (1880–1916) sitzt er bereits an der Redaktion eines ganz neuen Buchs, das „Der Blaue Reiter" heißen und alle wichtigen modernen Kunstströmungen vorstellen soll. Noch im Dezember 1911 organisieren sie die erste Ausstellung in der „Modernen Galerie" von Heinrich Thannhauser. Wenig später erscheint im Piper-Verlag Kandinskys Schrift „Über das Geistige in der Kunst". Der Almanach erscheint dagegen erst im Mai 1912, nach der 2. Ausstellung

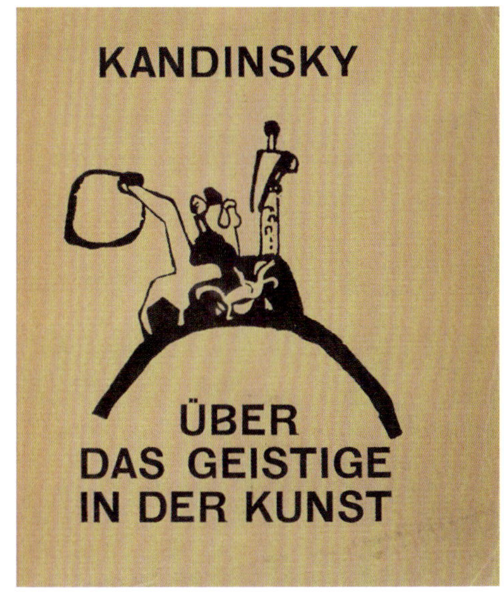

Title page of Kandinsky's *Über das Geistige in der Kunst*

Page titre du livre *Über das Geistige in der Kunst ("Du spirituel dans l'art")*

Titelseite des Buches *Über das Geistige in der Kunst*

Página de título de Kandinsky *Über das Geistige in der Kunst*

Pagina del titolo dell'opera di Kandinsky *Lo spirituale nell'arte (Über das Geistige in der Kunst)*

Titelpagina van *Über das Geistige in der Kunst*

1912, Lithograph/Lithographie, Private collection

La decisión de excluir una gran pintura de Kandinsky de la 3ª exposición de la "Asociación de nuevos artistas de Múnich", demostró ser oportunidad de abandonar la asociación en diciembre de 1911, junto a Münter, Franz Marc y Alfred Kubin. Junto con Franz Marc (1880–1916), ya había elaborado una nueva colección completa, que se denominaría "Der Blaue Reiter" y presentaría todos los movimientos artísticos importantes. En diciembre de 1911 organizaron su primera exposición en la "Modern Gallery" de Heinrich Thannhauser y poco tiempo después Piper Verlag publicó el tratado de Kandisky "Sobre lo espiritual en el arte". El almanaque, sin embargo, no se publicó hasta mayo de 1912, tras la 2ª exposición del "Der Blaue Reiter" en la Galerie Goltz

La decisione di escludere un grande dipinto di Kandinsky dalla 3ª mostra della Nuova associazione di artisti di Monaco rappresentò l'occasione ideale per l'artista per abbandonare l'associazione nel dicembre 1911, insieme a Münter, Alfred Kubin e Franz Marc (1880–1916). Insieme a quest'ultimo aveva già iniziato a scrivere un libro del tutto nuovo, che si sarebbe chiamato Der Blaue Reiter e avrebbe presentato tutti i più importanti movimenti artistici. A dicembre 1911 organizzarono la loro prima mostra presso la "Galleria Moderna" di Heinrich Thannhauser, e poco tempo dopo fu pubblicato dalla casa editrice Piper Verlag il trattato di Kandinsky Lo spirituale nell'arte. L'almanacco, però, non fu pubblicato fino a maggio 1912, dopo

Wanneer een groot schilderij van Kandinsky door de jury van de derde tentoonstelling van de 'Neue Künstlervereinigung München' wordt geweigerd, besluit de kunstenaar de vereniging in december 1911 samen met Münter, Franz Marc en Alfred Kubin vaarwel te zeggen. Samen met Franz Marc (1880–1916) zit hij al in de redactie van een nieuw boek, met de beoogde titel Der Blaue Reiter ('De blauwe ruiter'), waarin alle belangrijke moderne kunststromingen zullen worden voorgesteld. In december 1911 organiseren ze de eerste tentoonstelling in de 'Moderne Galerie' van Heinrich Thannhauser. Kort daarna verschijnt Kandinsky's verhandeling Über das Geistige in der Kunst bij uitgeverij Piper (in

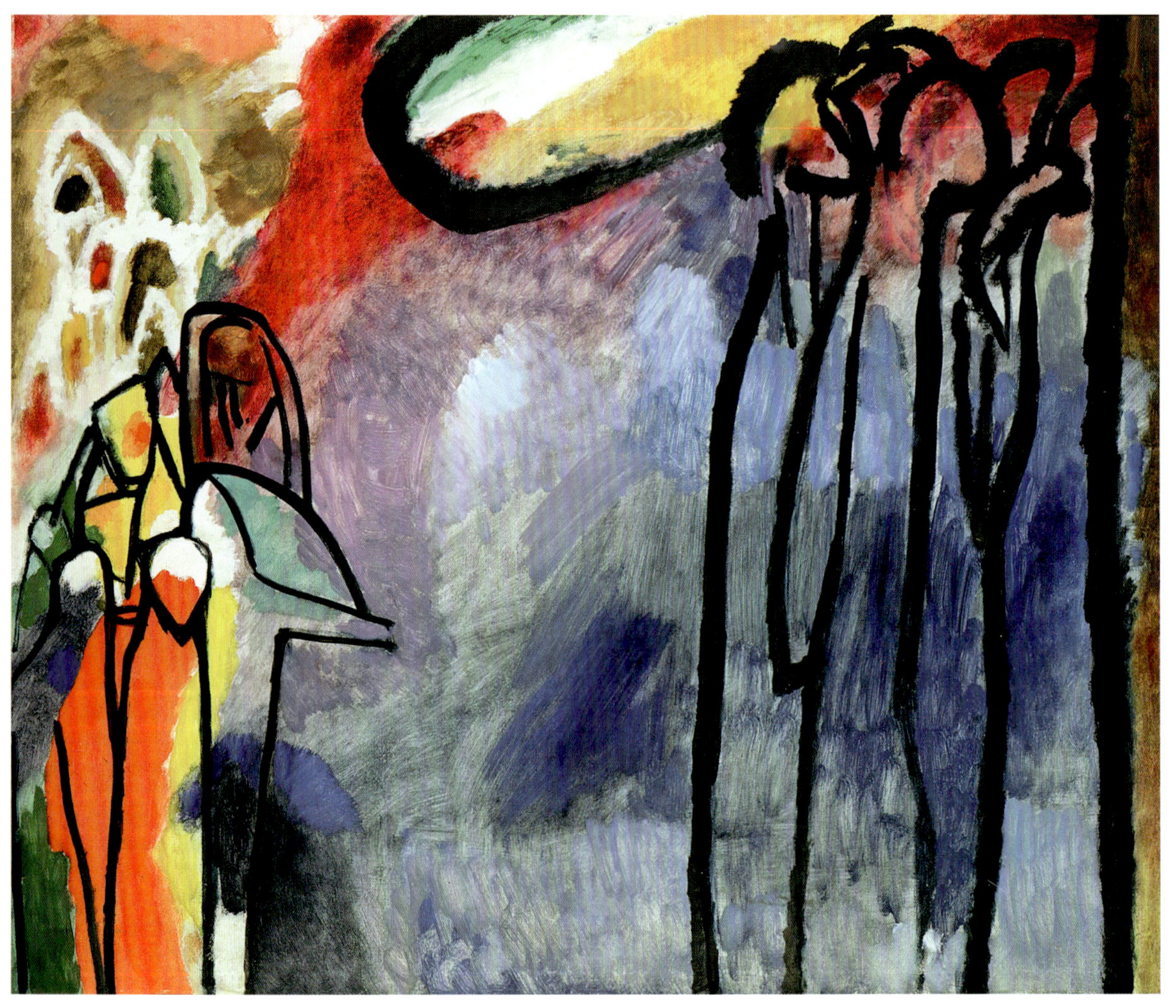

Improvisation 19

Improvisation 19

1911, Oil on canvas/Huile sur toile, 120 × 141,5 cm, Städtische Galerie im Lenbachhaus, Munich

A crowd flows into the image from the left. To the right, gigantic figures move over a blue field and out of the picture, signalling the spiritual transformation of humanity through the "spiritual in art".

Une foule d'hommes afflue par la gauche dans le tableau. Des silhouettes gigantesques se déplacent vers la droite sur un espace bleu, pour sortir du champ iconographique – emblème de la métamorphose spirituelle de l'humanité à travers « le spirituel dans l'art ».

Improvisation 19

Improvisación 19

Eine Menschenmenge strömt von links ins Bild. Nach rechts bewegen sich riesenhafte Gestalten über ein blaues Feld aus dem Bild hinaus, Zeichen für die spirituelle Verwandlung der Menschheit durch das „Geistige in der Kunst".

Un grupo de gente entra en la imagen desde la izquierda. A la derecha, figuras gigantes se mueven sobre un campo azul y salen de la imagen, indicando la transformación espiritual de la humanidad a través de lo "espiritual en el arte".

Improvvisazione 19

Improvisatie 19

Una folla scorre nell'immagine da sinistra. A destra, figure gigantesche si muovono su un campo blu verso l'esterno del quadro, simboleggiando la trasformazione spirituale dell'umanità attraverso lo "spirituale nell'arte".

Een mensenmenigte dringt van links het schilderij binnen terwijl reusachtige gestalten zich op een blauw veld naar rechts uit het beeldvlak begeven, als teken van de spirituele transformatie van de mensheid door het 'abstracte in de kunst'.

de Múnich. Kandinsky se encontraba ahora bajo los focos de la escena de arte internacional. Sus imágenes abstractas causaron sensación y recorrieron las las principales exposiciones, así como su primera exposición en solitario en la berlinesa galería "Der Sturm", donde estableció una estrecha relación con Herwarth Walden (1878–1941) y su círculo.

la seconda mostra del gruppo "Der Blaue Reiter" presso la Galleria Goltz di Monaco di Baviera. Kandinsky era ormai sotto i riflettori della scena artistica internazionale. I suoi quadri astratti suscitarono scalpore e furono esposti in importanti mostre e nella sua prima mostra personale presso la galleria "Der Sturm" di Berlino, durante la quale l'artista strinse uno stretto rapporto con Herwarth Walden (1878–1941) e la sua cerchia.

het Nederlands uitgebracht als Het abstracte in de kunst en later ook als Spiritualiteit en abstractie in de kunst). De almanak Der Blaue Reiter ziet echter pas in mei 1912 het licht, na de tweede tentoonstelling van de gelijknamige groep in Galerie Goltz in München. Kandinsky staat nu in de belangstelling van de internationale kunstwereld. Zijn abstracte werken baren opzien en worden op belangrijke exposities getoond, zoals op zijn eerste solotentoonstelling in Galerie 'Der Sturm' in Berlijn, waaruit een nauw contact met Herwarth Walden (1878–1941) en diens kunstenaarskring voortkomt.

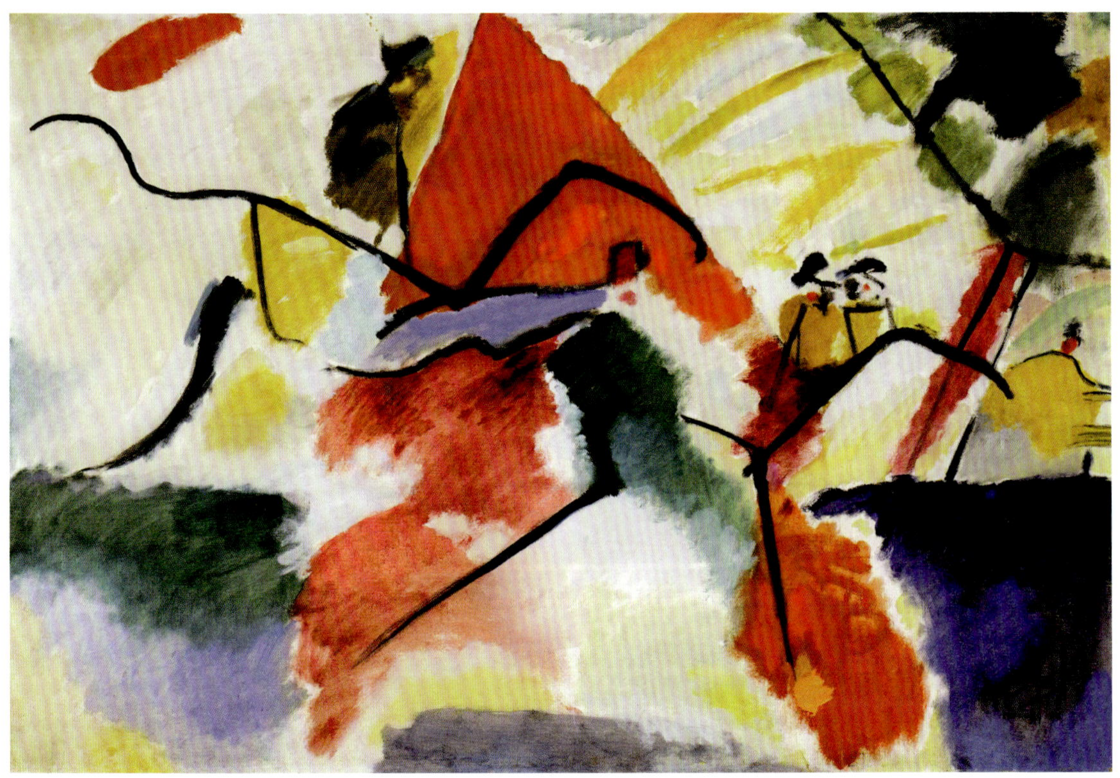

at Galerie Goltz in Munich. Kandinsky was now in the spotlight of the international art scene. His abstract images caused a sensation and were shown in major exhibitions, as well as in his first solo show in the Berlin gallery "Der Sturm", during which he established a close relationship with Herwarth Walden (1878–1941) and his circle.

paraît en revanche en mai 1912, après la deuxième exposition du Blaue Reiter, dans la galerie Goltz à Munich. Kandinsky est désormais au premier plan de la scène artistique internationale. Ses tableaux abstraits font sensation et sont présentés dans des expositions importantes – par exemple dans sa première exposition personnelle à la galerie Der Sturm de Berlin, grâce à laquelle il entre en contact étroit avec Herwarth Walden (1878–1941) et son cercle.

„Der Blaue Reiter" in der Galerie Goltz in München. Kandinsky steht nun im Rampenlicht der internationalen Kunstszene. Seine abstrakten Bilder erregen Aufsehen und werden in wichtigen Ausstellungen gezeigt, wie in seiner ersten Einzelausstellung in der Galerie „Der Sturm" in Berlin, wodurch ein enger Kontakt zu Herwarth Walden (1878–1941) und seinem Kreis entsteht.

Impression V (Park)

Impression V (Parc)

Impression V (Park)

Impresión V (Parque)

Impressione V (Parco)

Impressie V (Park)

1911, Oil on canvas/Huile sur toile, 106 × 157,5 cm, Musée National d'Art Moderne, Centre Pompidou, Paris

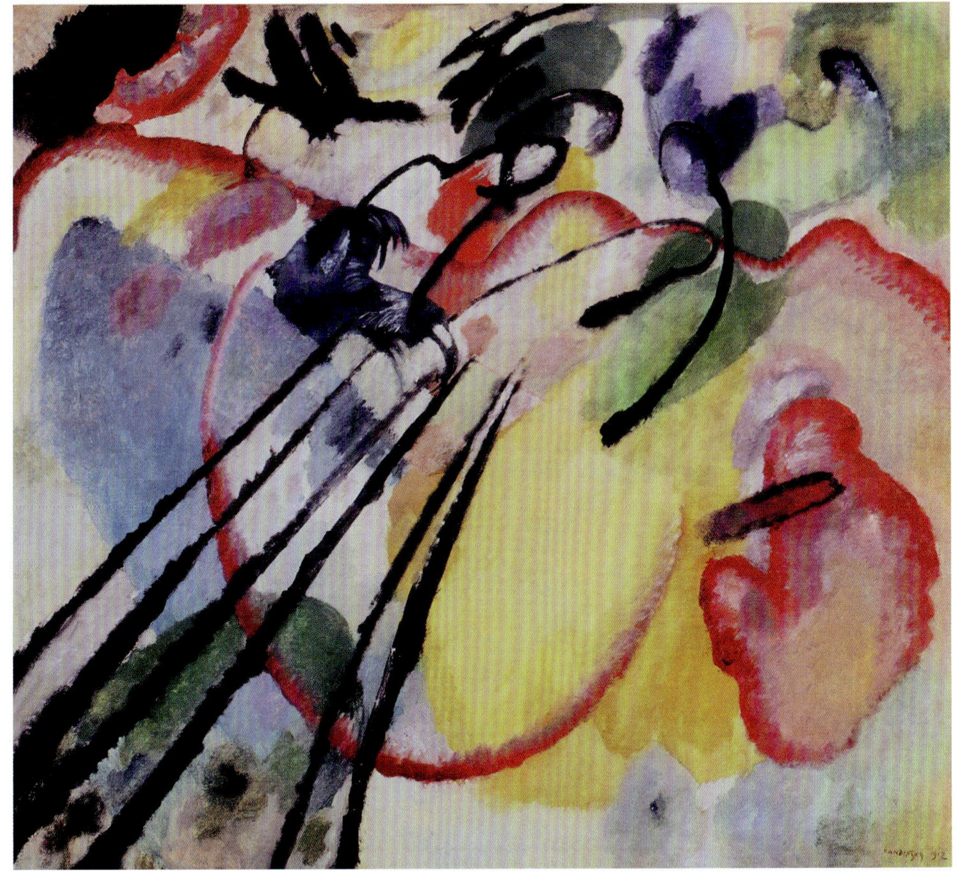

Improvisation No. 26 (Rowing)

Improvisation 26 (Rudern)

Improvvisazione 26 (Remi)

Improvisation 26 (En ramant)

Improvisación Nº 26 (remo)

Improvisatie 26 (Roeien)

1912, Oil on canvas/Huile sur toile, 97 × 107,5 cm, Städtische Galerie im Lenbachhaus, Munich

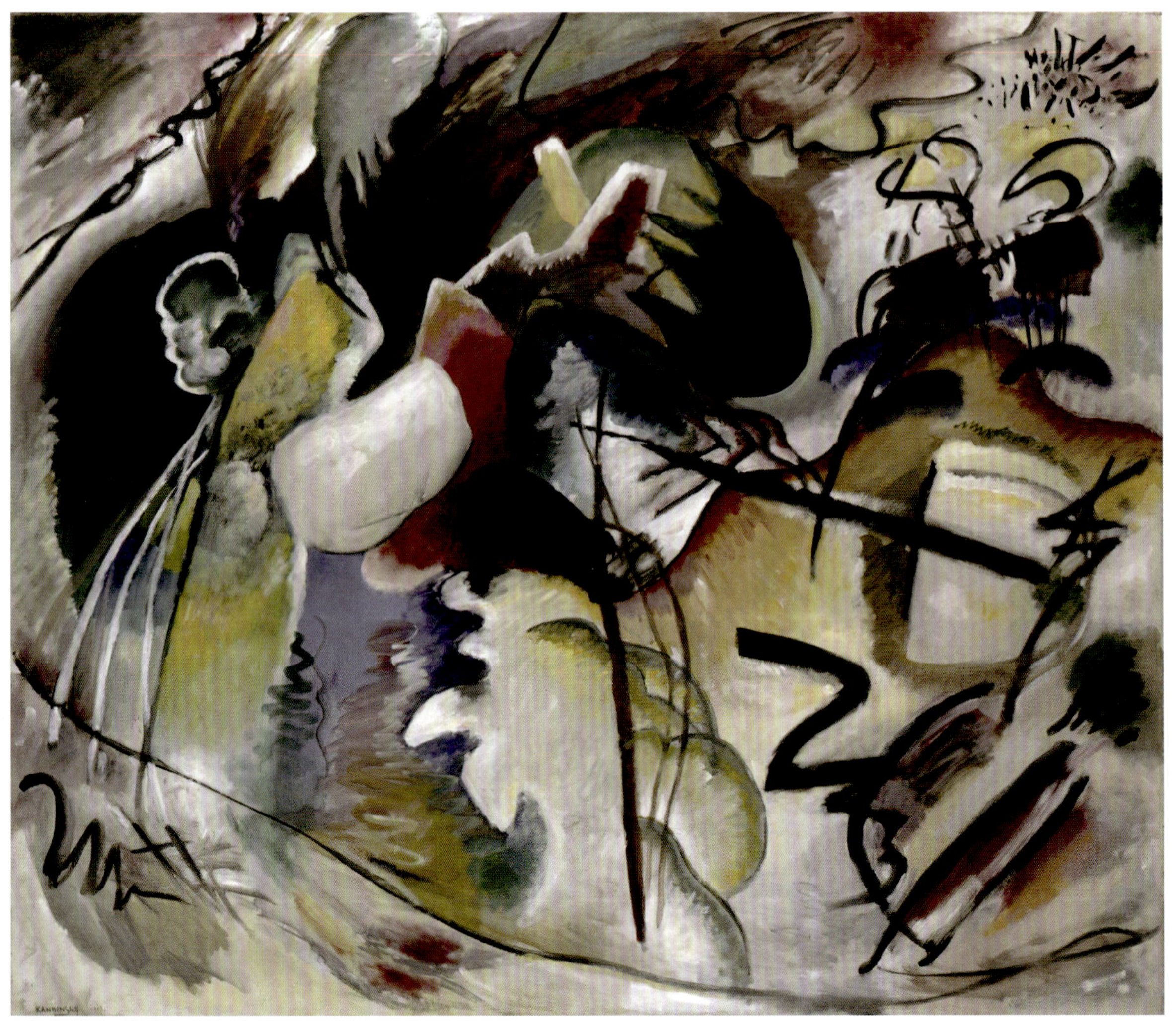

Painting with white form   **Bild mit weißer Form**   **Dipinto con forma bianca**

Peinture avec forme blanche   **Pintura blanca del formulario**   **Schilderij met witte vorm**

1913, Oil on canvas/Huile sur toile, 120,3 × 139,6 cm, Haags Gemeentemuseum, The Hague

60

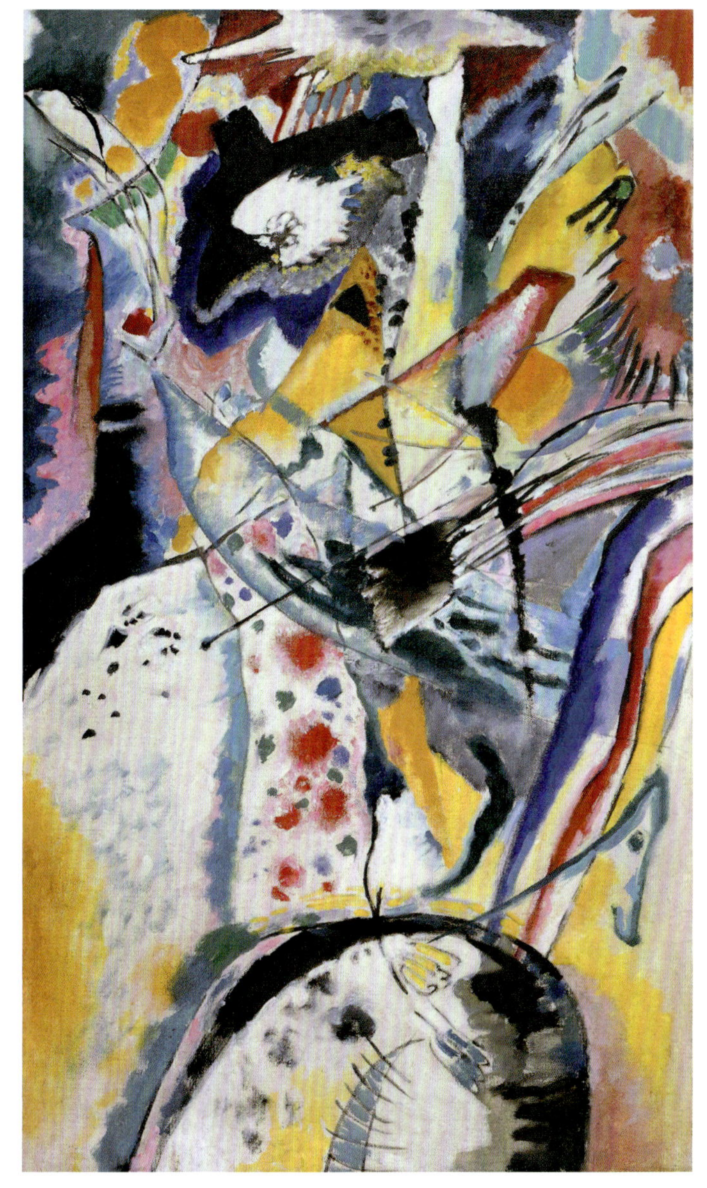

Panel for Edwin R Campbell (Summer)

Grande étude de peinture murale pour Edwin R. Campbell (L'Été)

Große Studie zu einem Wandbild für Edwin R. Campbell (Sommer)

Panel de Edwin R Campbell (verano)

Pannello per Edwin R. Campbell (Estate)

Grote studie voor een muurschildering voor Edwin R. Campbell (Zomer)

1914, Oil on canvas/Huile sur toile, Städtische Galerie im Lenbachhaus, Munich

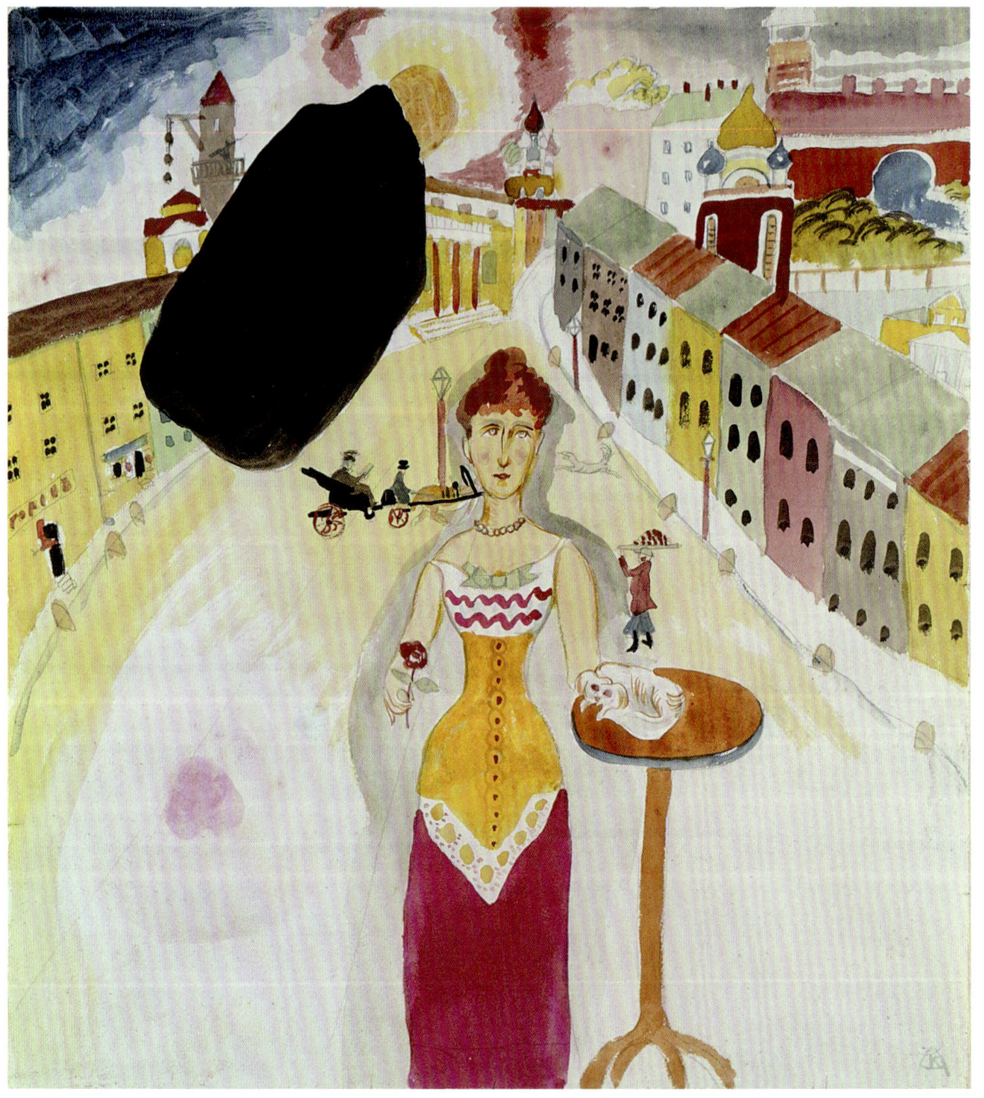

Woman in Moscow

Dame à Moscou

Dame in Moskau

Mujer en Moscú

Donna a Mosca

Dame in Moskou

1912, Watercolor on
paper/Aquarelle sur
papier, 31,5 × 28 cm,
Private collection

View of Moscow

Vue de Moscou

Blick auf Moskau

Vista de Moscú

Vista di Mosca

Gezicht op Moskou

1914, Oil on canvas/
Huile sur toile,
39 × 36 cm, Haags
Gemeentemuseum,
The Hague

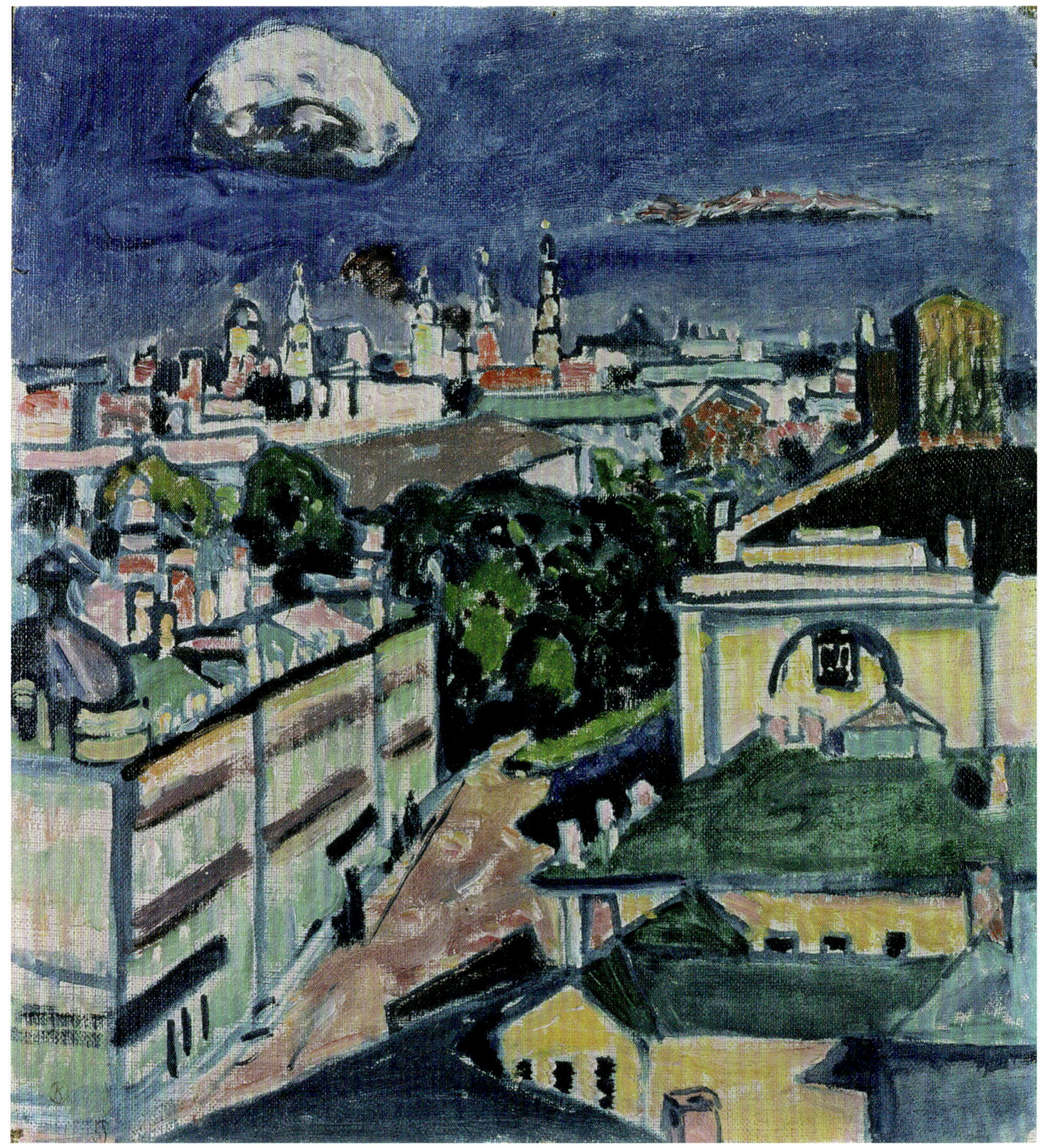

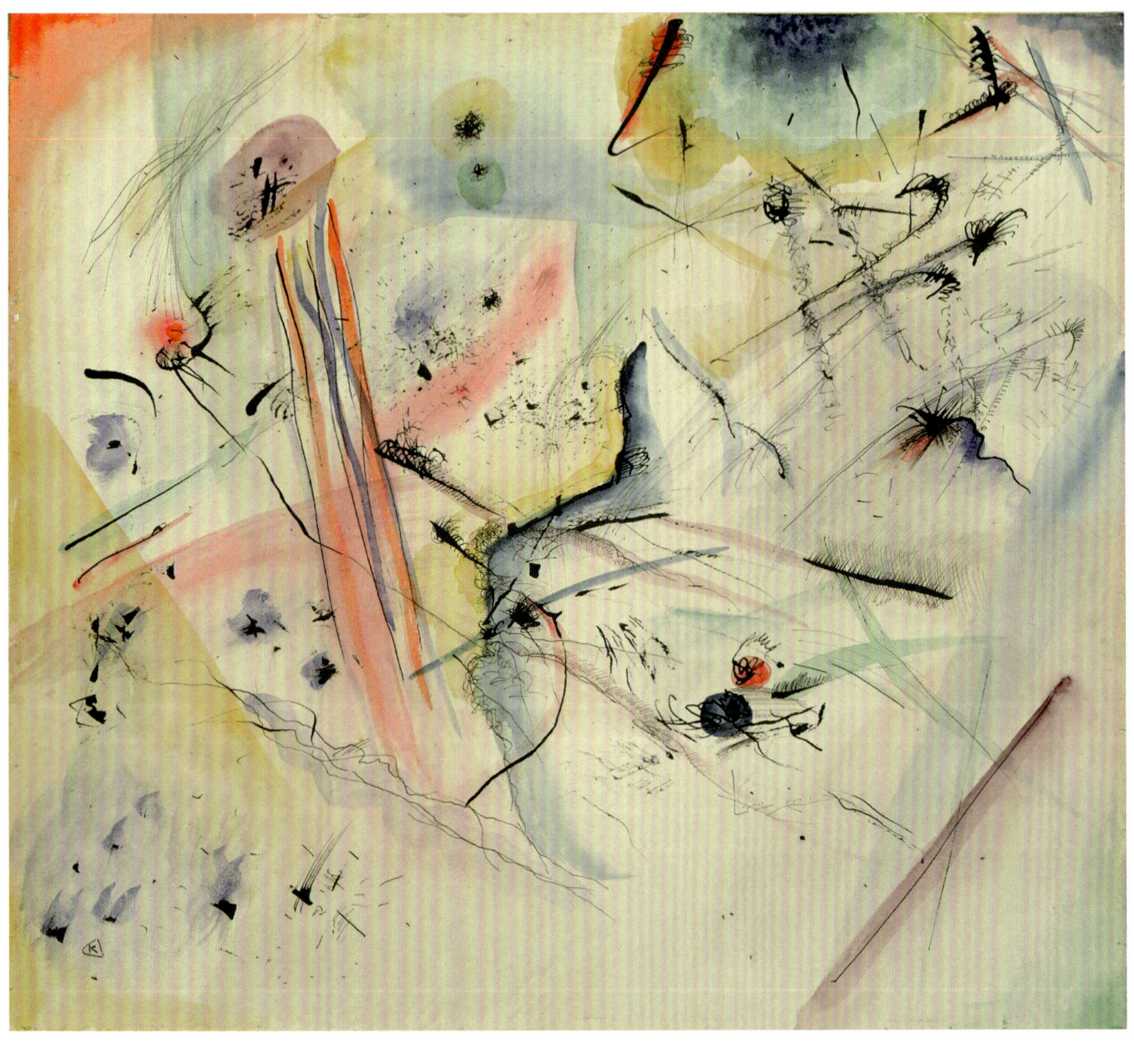

Composition with Red and Blue Stripes
Composition à bandes rouges et bleues

Komposition mit roten und blauen Streifen
Composición con rayas rojas y azules.

Composizione con righe rosse e blu
Compositie met rode en blauwe strepen

1913, Watercolor/Aquarelle, 36 × 40 cm, Private collection

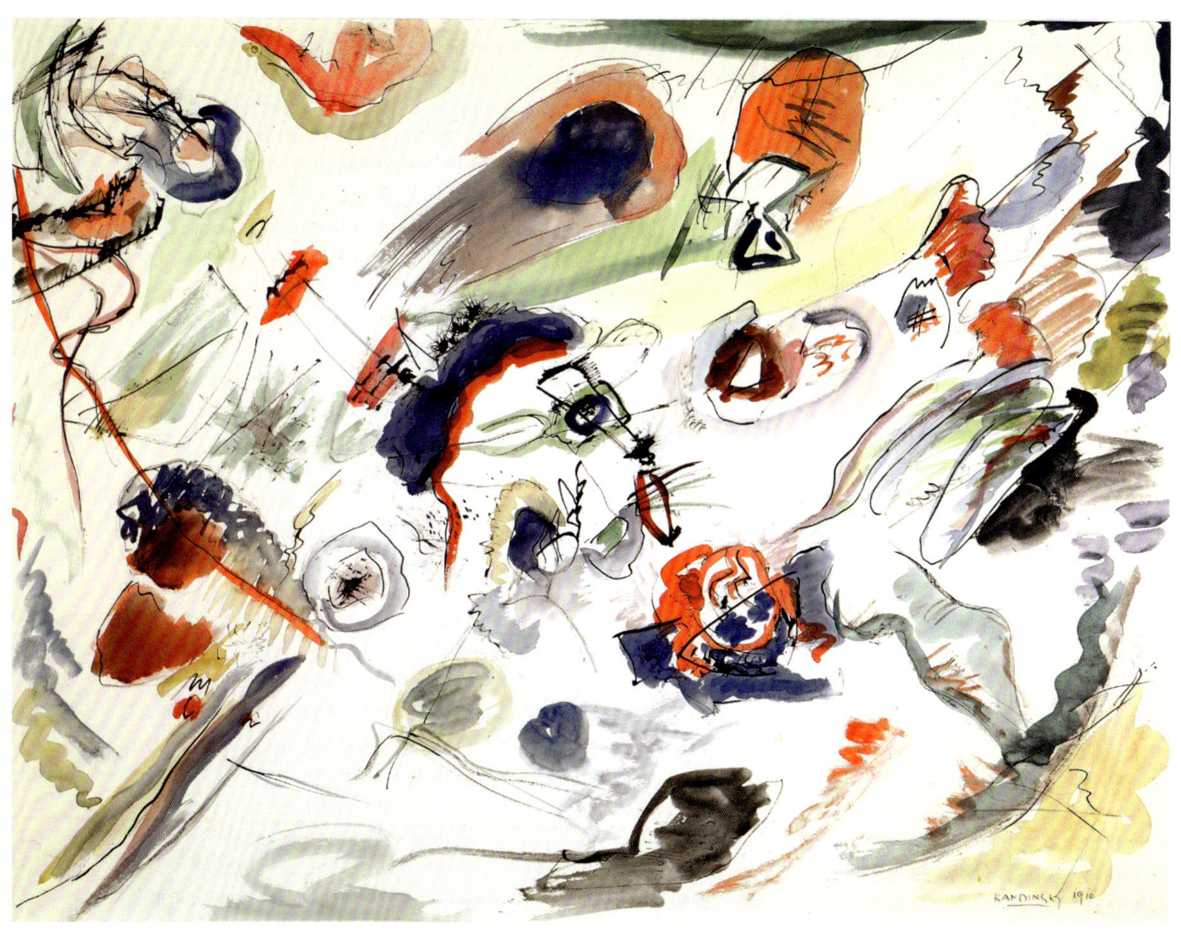

Untitled - First Abstraction

Sans titre (première aquarelle abstraite)

Ohne Titel (Erstes Abstraktes Aquarell)

Sin título - primera abstracción

Senza titolo - Prima astrazione

Senza titolo - Prima astrazione

1910, Pencil, watercolor and ink on paper/Mine de plomb, aquarelle et encre de Chine sur papier, 49 × 64 cm, Musée National d'Art Moderne, Centre Pompidou, Paris

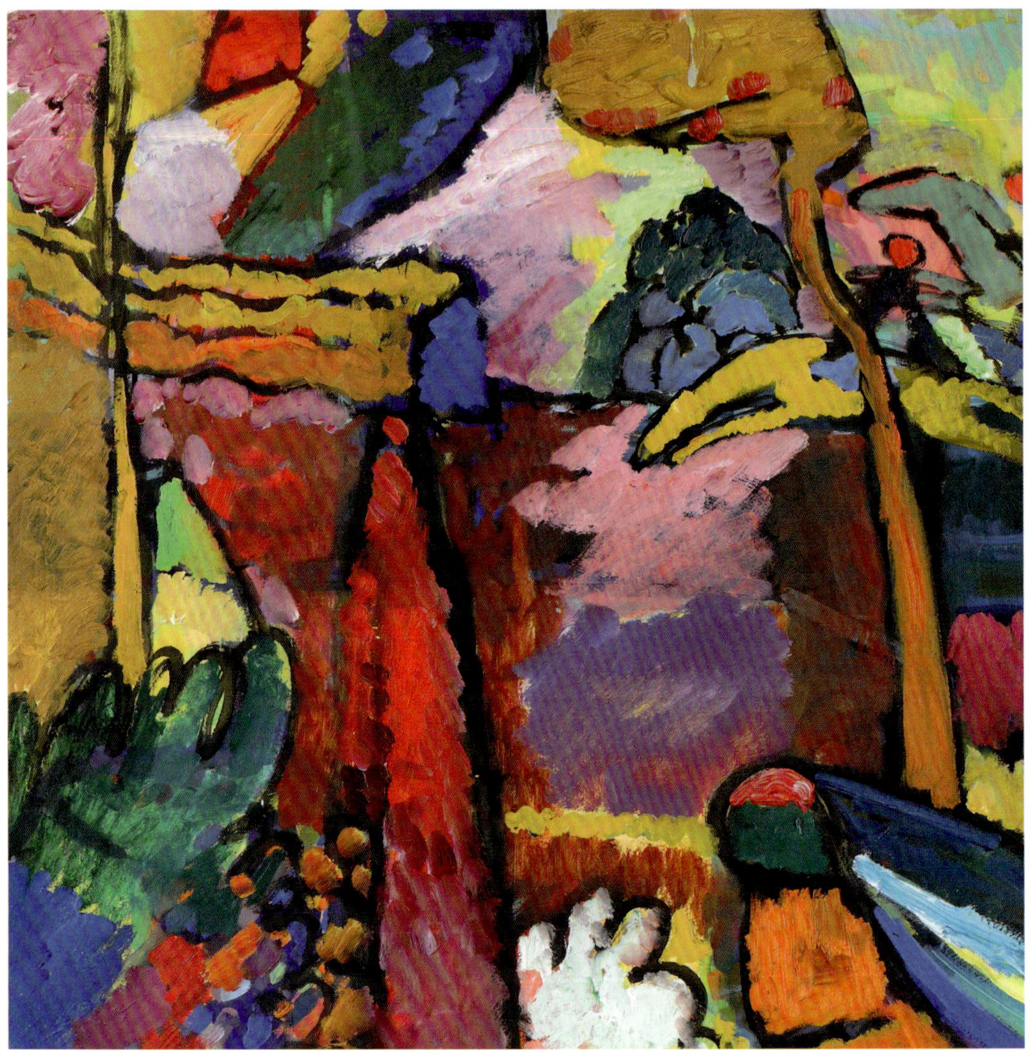

Study for Improvisation V **Studie zu Improvisation V** **Studio per Improvvisazione V**

Étude pour Improvisation V **Estudio para la improvisación V** **Studie voor Improvisatie V**

1910, Oil on cardboard/Huile sur carton, 70,2 × 69,9 cm, Minneapolis Institute of Arts, MN

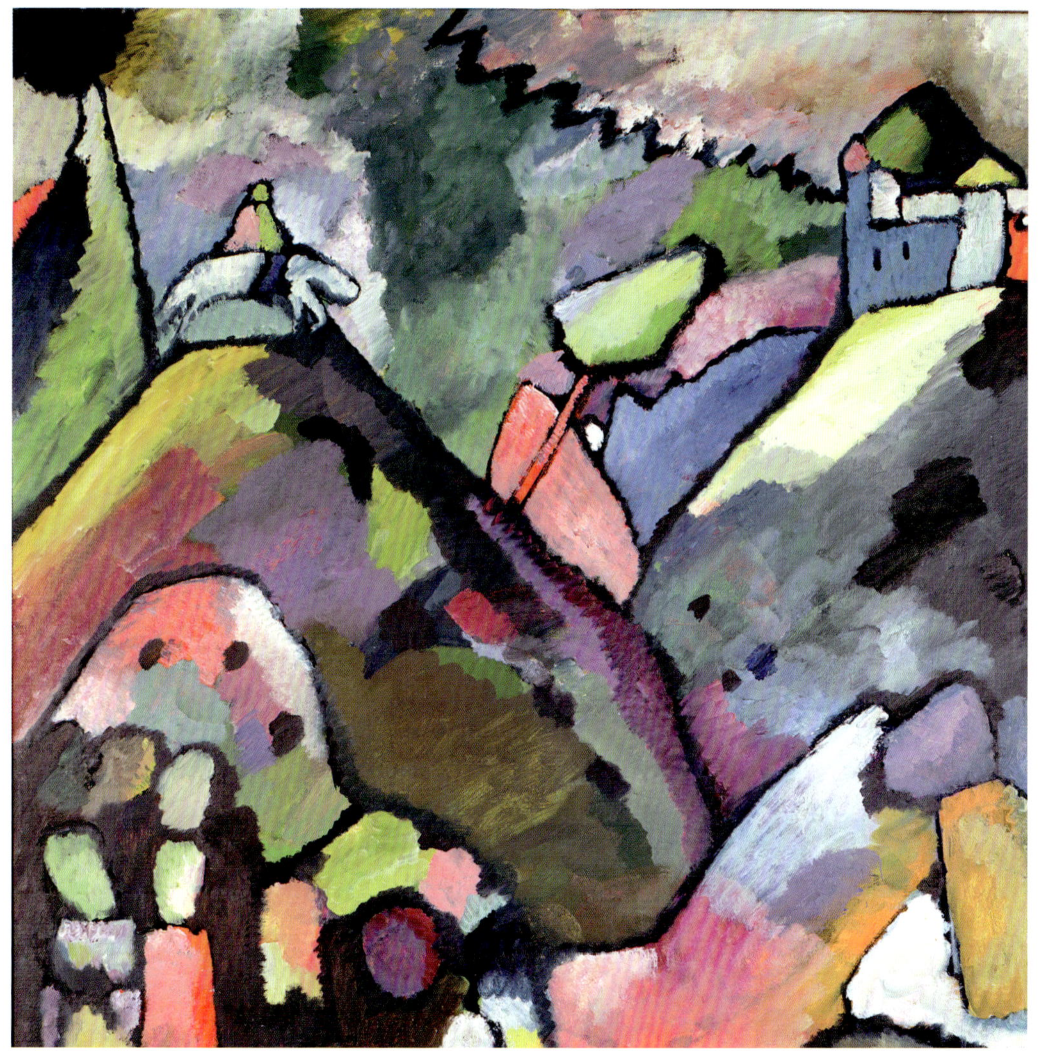

Improvisation 9 **Improvisation 9** **Improvvisazione 9**

Improvisation 9 **Improvisación 9** **Improvisatie 9**

1910, Oil on canvas/Huile sur toile, 110 × 110 cm, Private collection

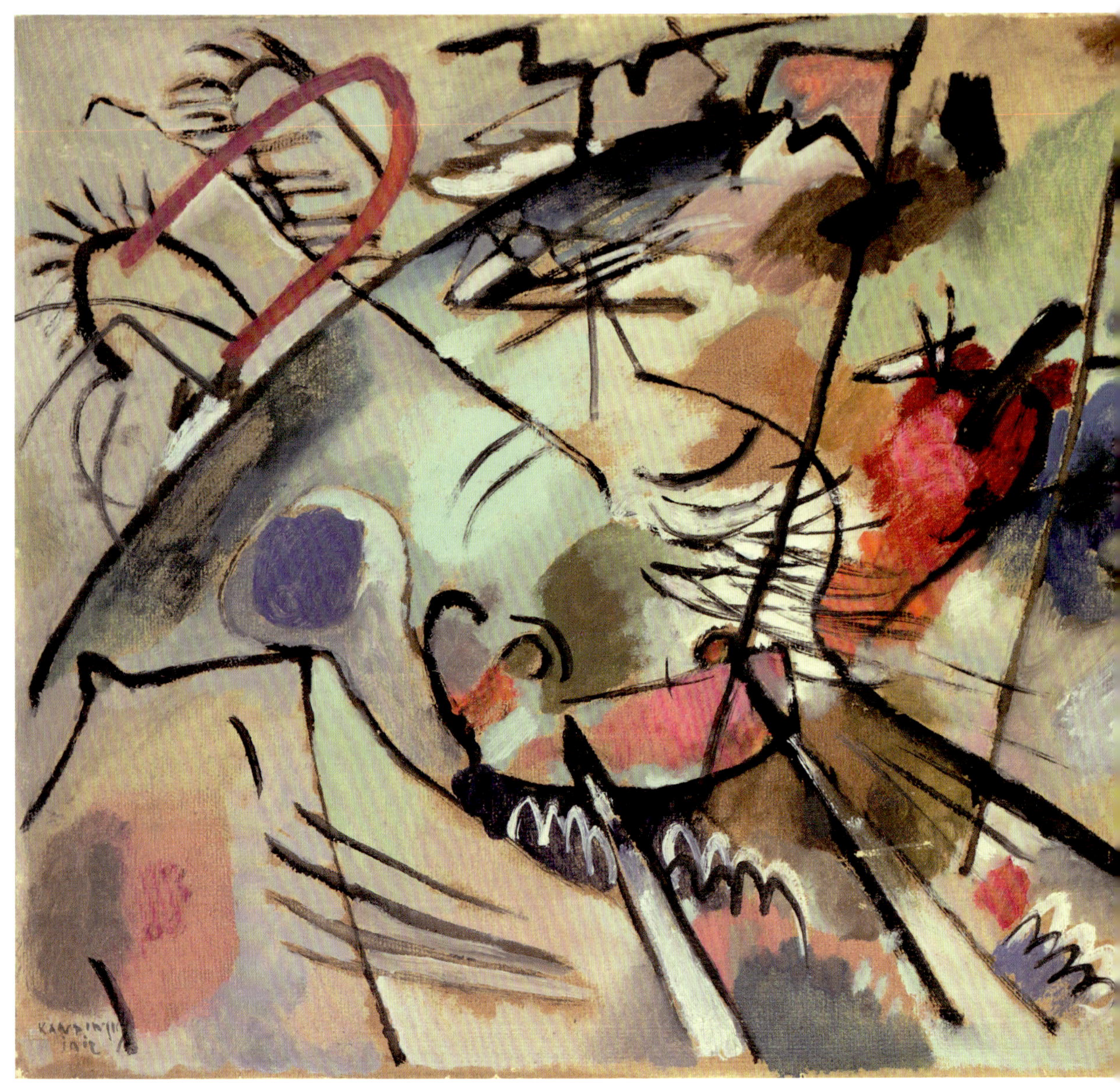

Study for **Improvisation 24**

Etude pour **Improvisation 24**

Studie für **Improvisation 24**

Estudio para la **improvisación 24**

Studio per **Improvvisazione 24**

Studie voor **Improvisatie 24**

1912, Oil on canvas/Huile sur toile, 49 × 67,5 cm, Private collection

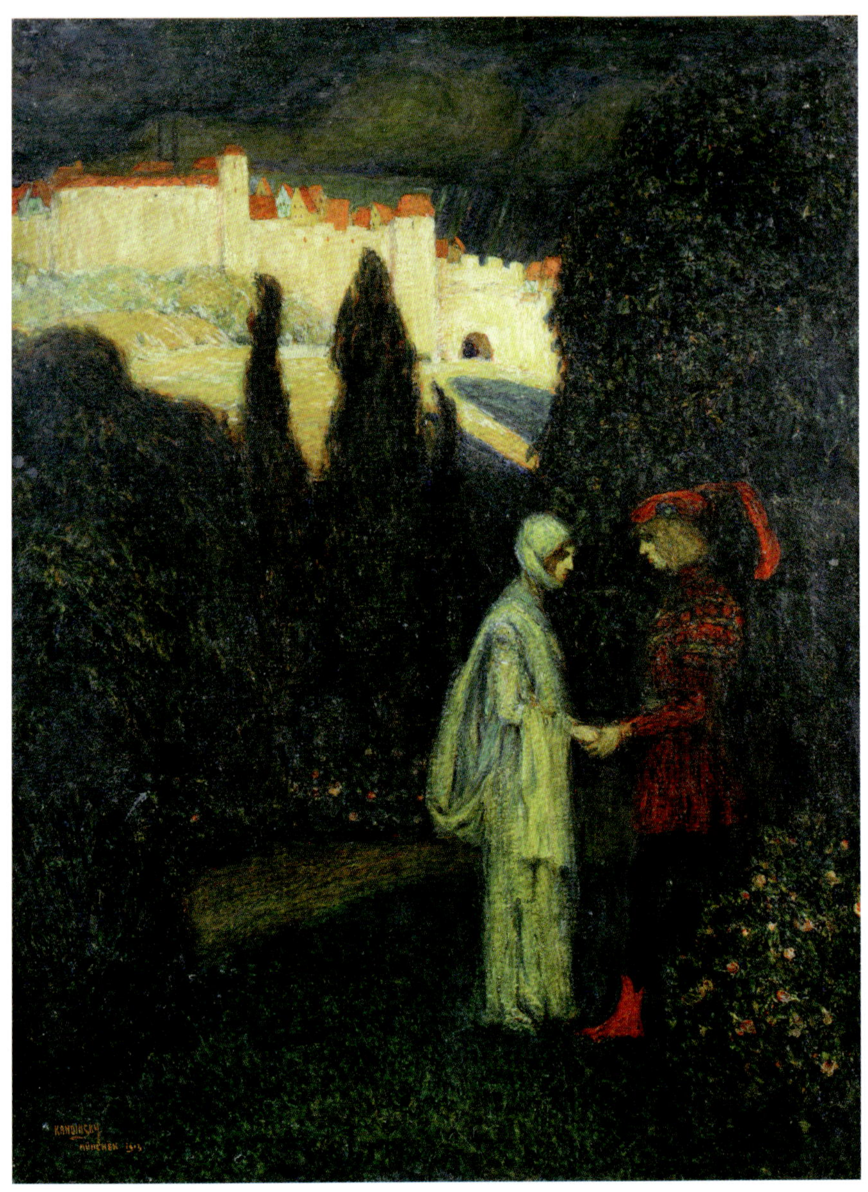

Tryst

La Rencontre

Stelldichein I

Apuntamiento

Apuntamento

Rendez-vous I

1901, Oil on canvas/Détrempe sur toile, 100 × 175 cm, Private collection

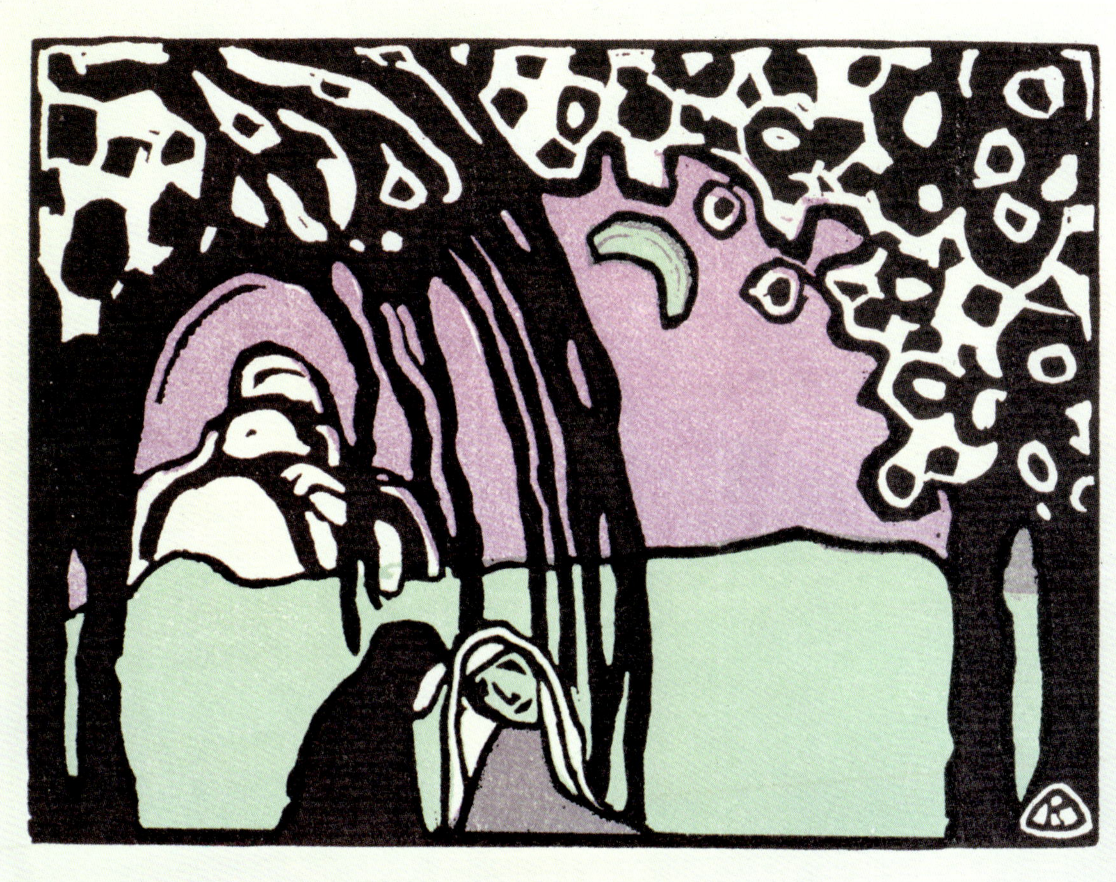

Two Women in the Moonlight
Deux femmes dans un paysage au clair de lune

Zwei Frauen in Mondlandschaft
Dos mujeres de la luna

Due donne in un paesaggio al chiaro di luna
Twee vrouwen in maanlandschap

1911, Woodcut/Bois gravé, 9,3 × 12,4 cm, Städtische Galerie im Lenbachhaus, Munich

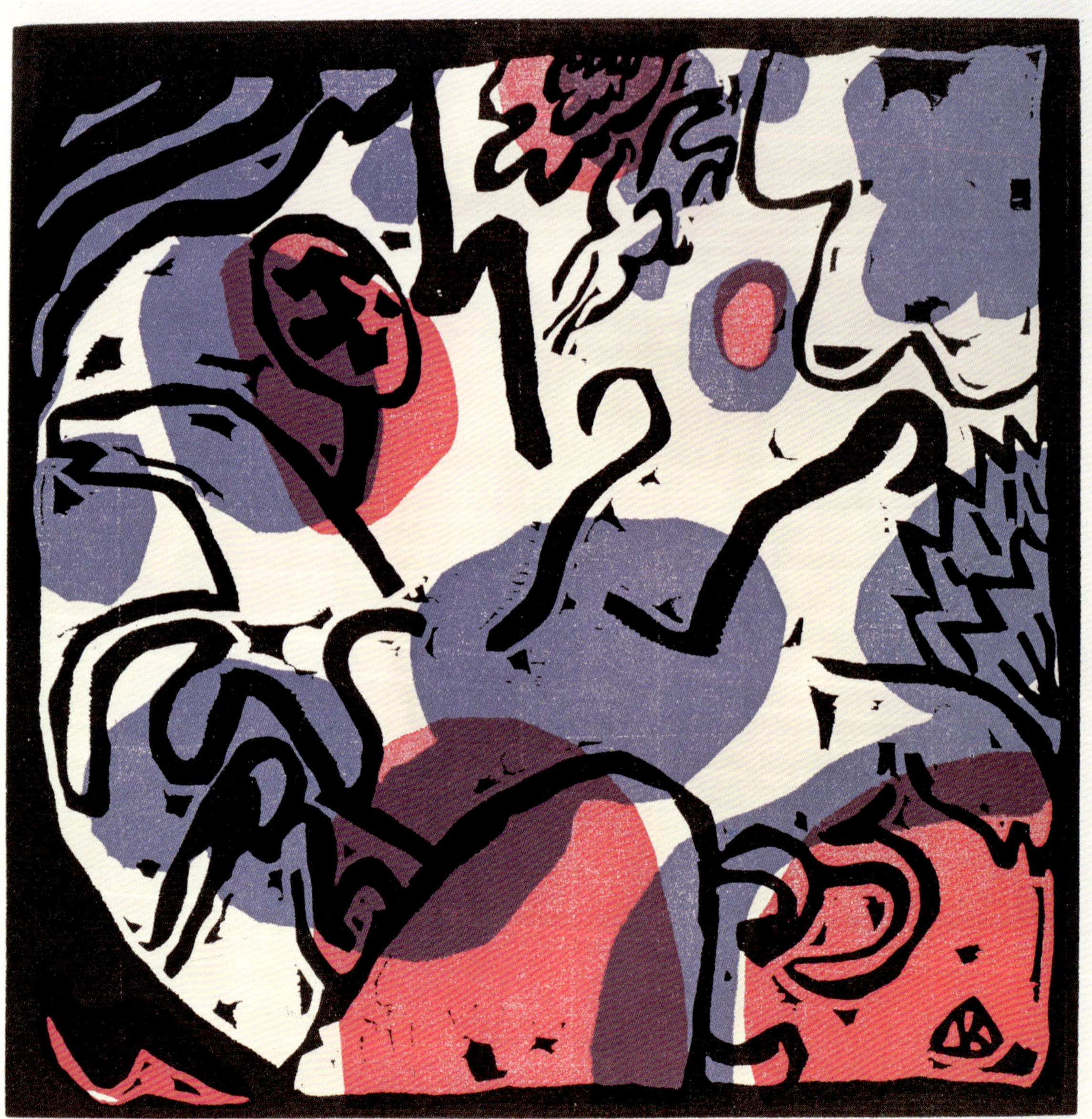

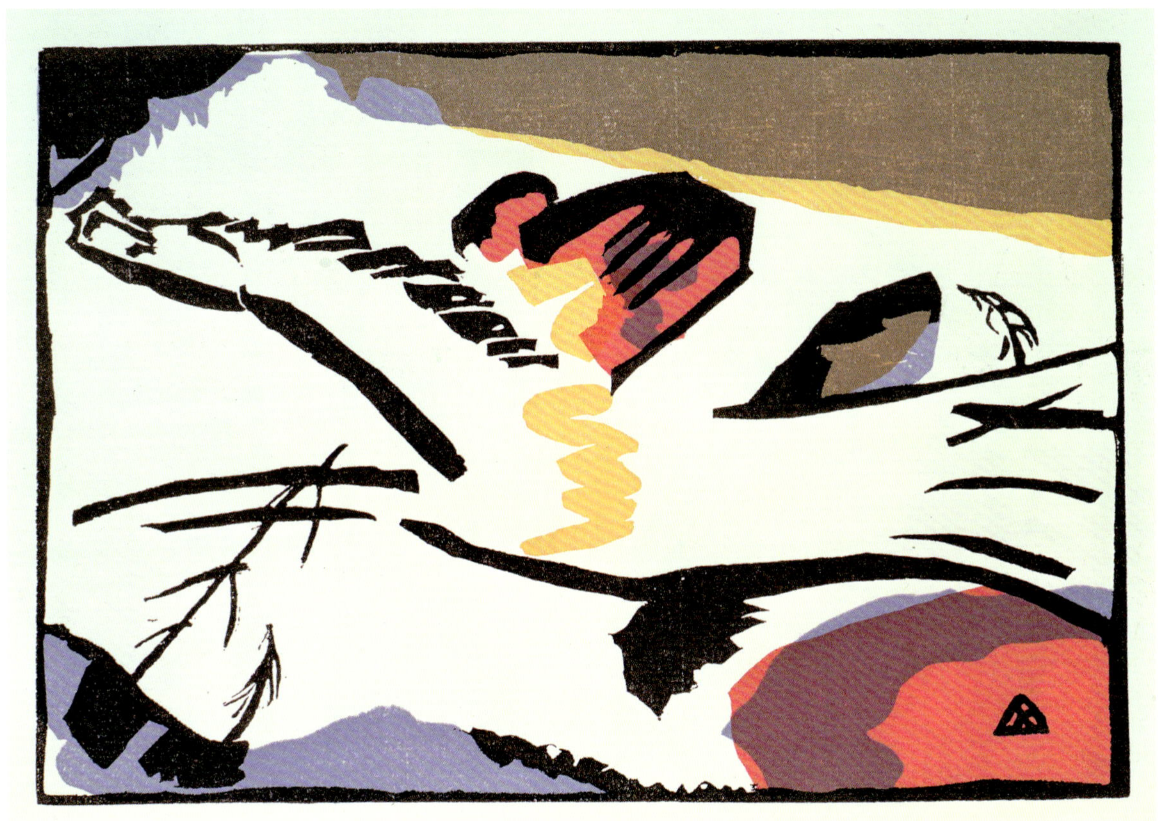

Three Riders in Red, Blue and Black

Composition du Blaue Reiter

Drei Reiter in Rot, Blau und Schwarz

Tres jinetes en rojo, azul y negro

Tre cavalieri in rosso, blu e nero

Drie ruiters in rood, blauw en zwart

1911, Woodcut/Bois gravé, 21,9 × 22,2 cm,
Städtische Galerie im Lenbachhaus, Munich

Lyrical

Lyrique

Lyrisches

Lírico

Lirica

'Lyrisches'

1911, Woodcut/Bois gravé, 14,5 × 21,7 cm,
Städtische Galerie im Lenbachhaus, Munich

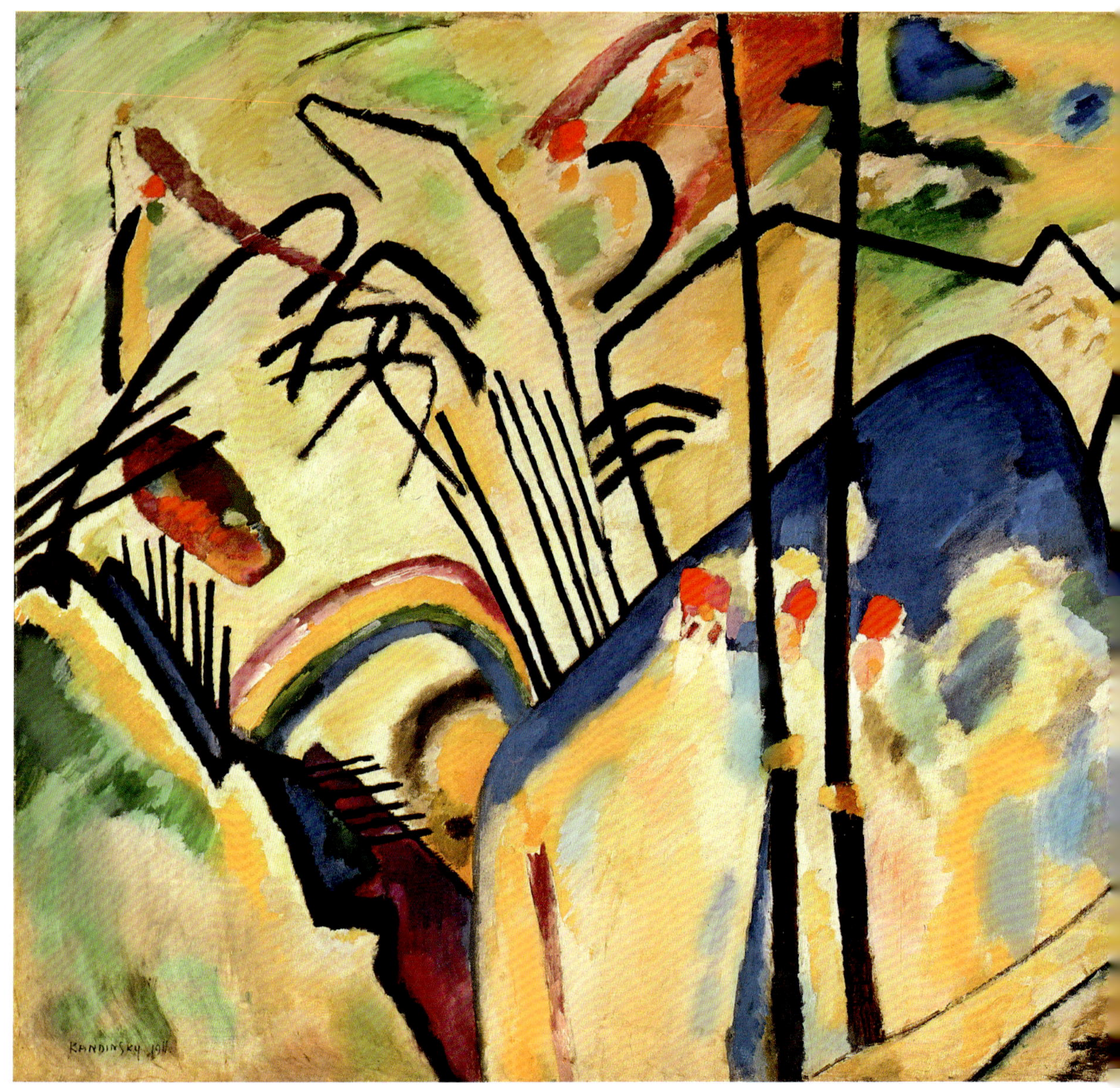
KANDINSKY 1911

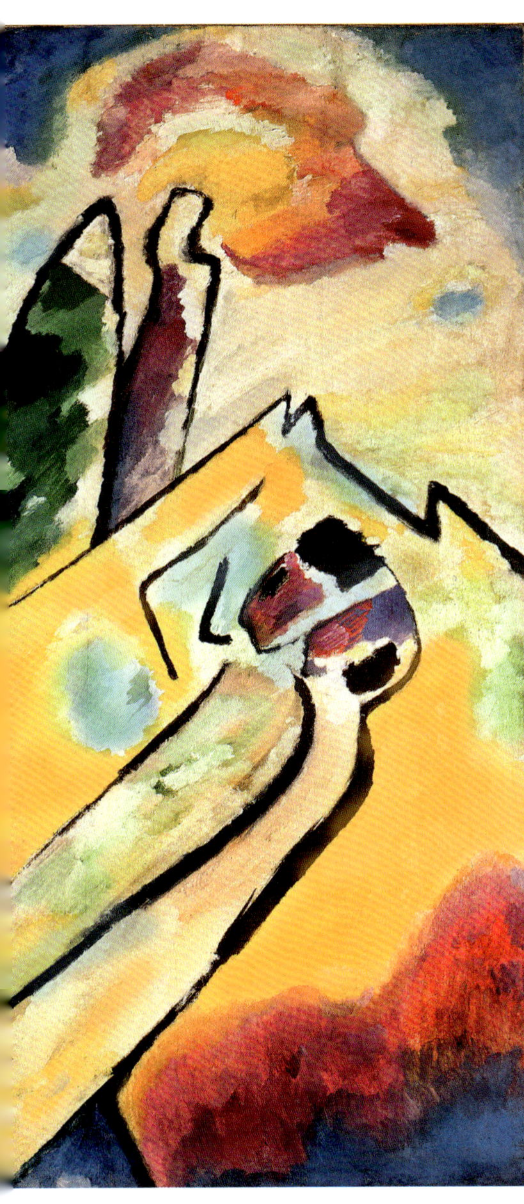

Composition IV

Composition IV

Komposition IV

Composición IV

Composizione IV

Compositie IV

1911, Oil on canvas/Huile sur toile, 159,5 × 250,5 cm, Kunstsammlung Nordrhein-Westfalen, Dusseldorf

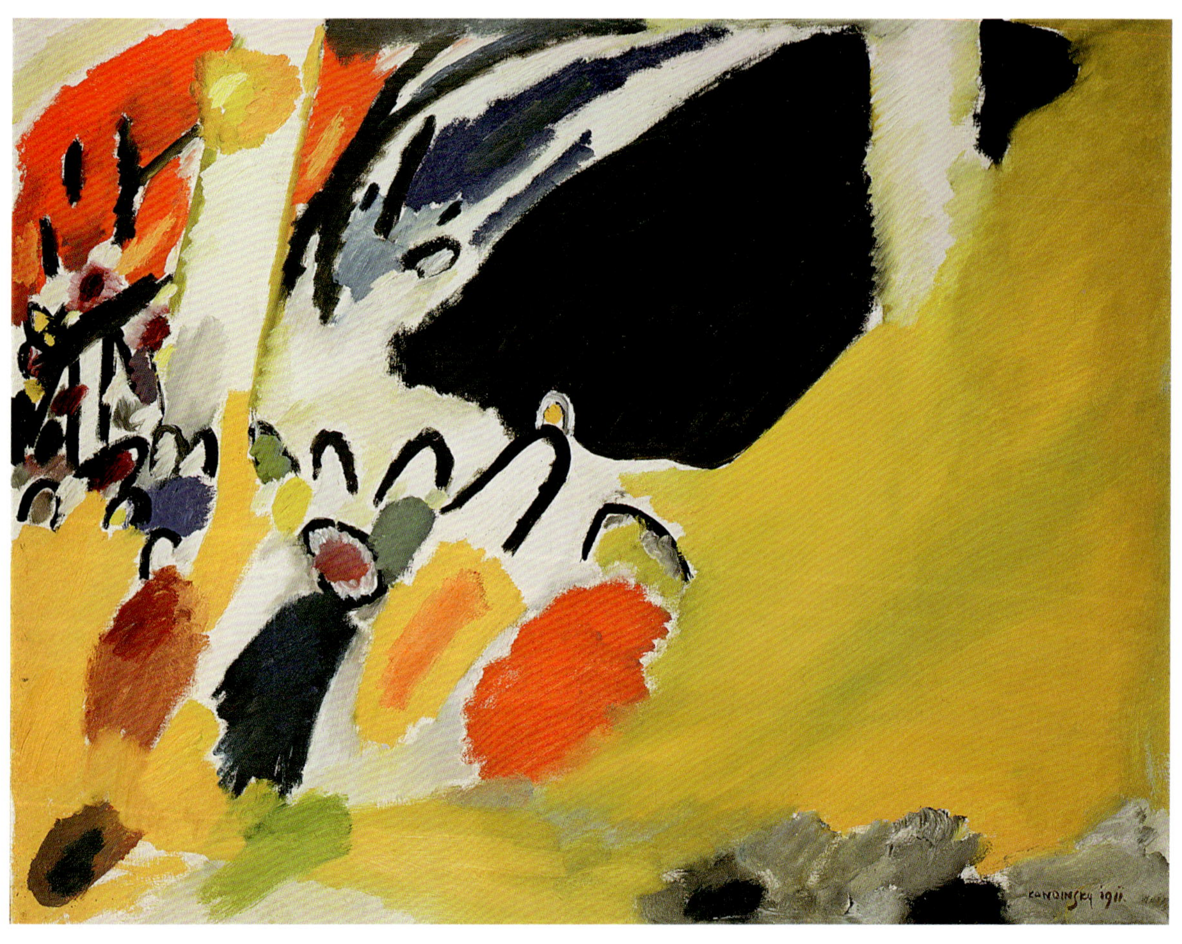

Impression no. 3 (Concert)   **Impression III (Konzert)**   **Impressione 3 (Concerto)**

Impression III (concert)   **Impresión N° 3 (concierto)**   **Impressie III (Concert)**

1911, Oil on canvas/Huile sur toile, 77,5 × 100 cm, Städtische Galerie im Lenbachhaus, Munich

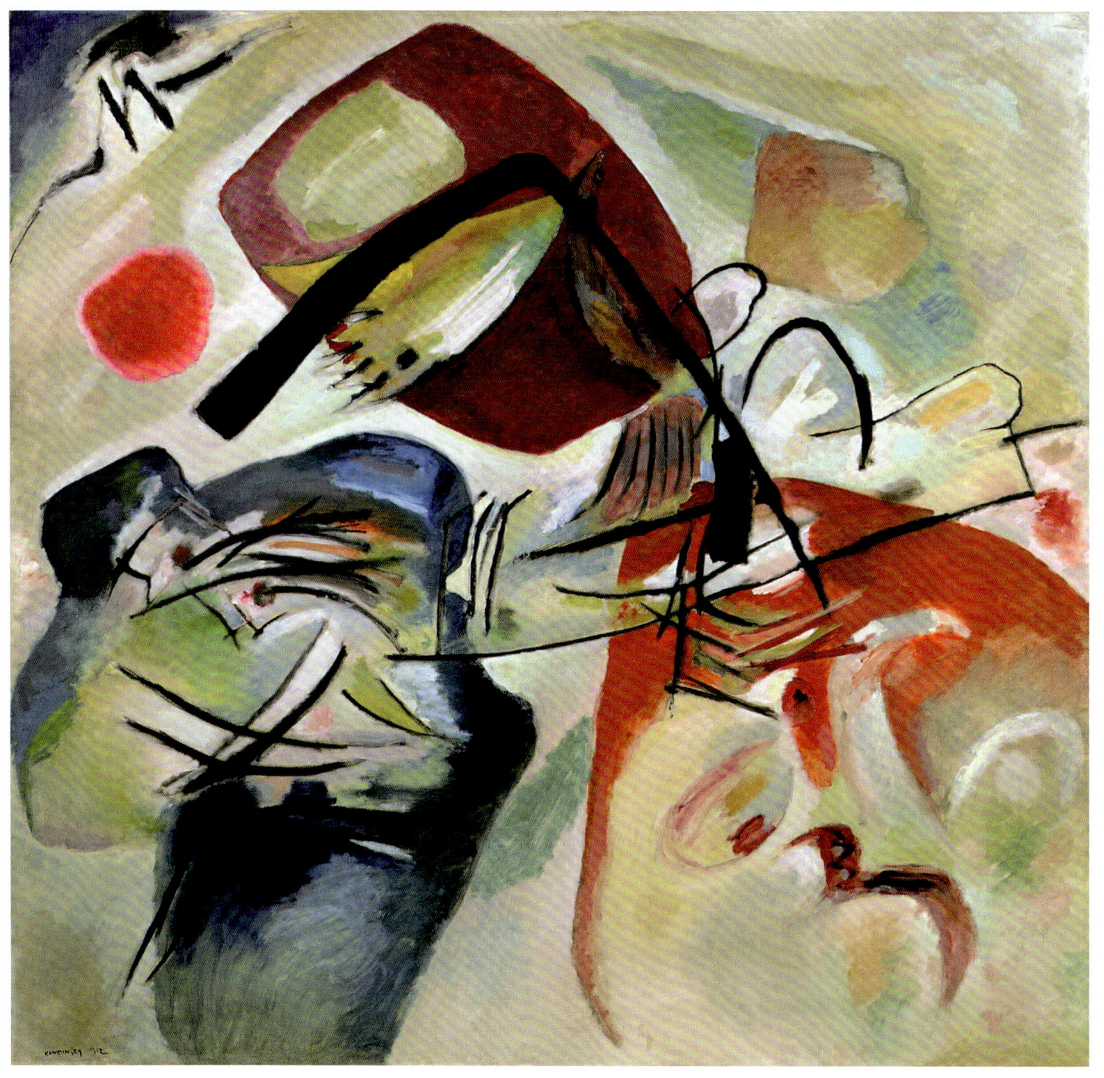

With the Black Arch

Avec l'arc noir

Bild mit schwarzem Bogen

Con el arco negro

Con l'arco nero

Schilderij met zwarte boog

1912, Oil on canvas/Huile sur toile, 189 × 198 cm, Musée National d'Art Moderne, Centre Pompidou, Paris

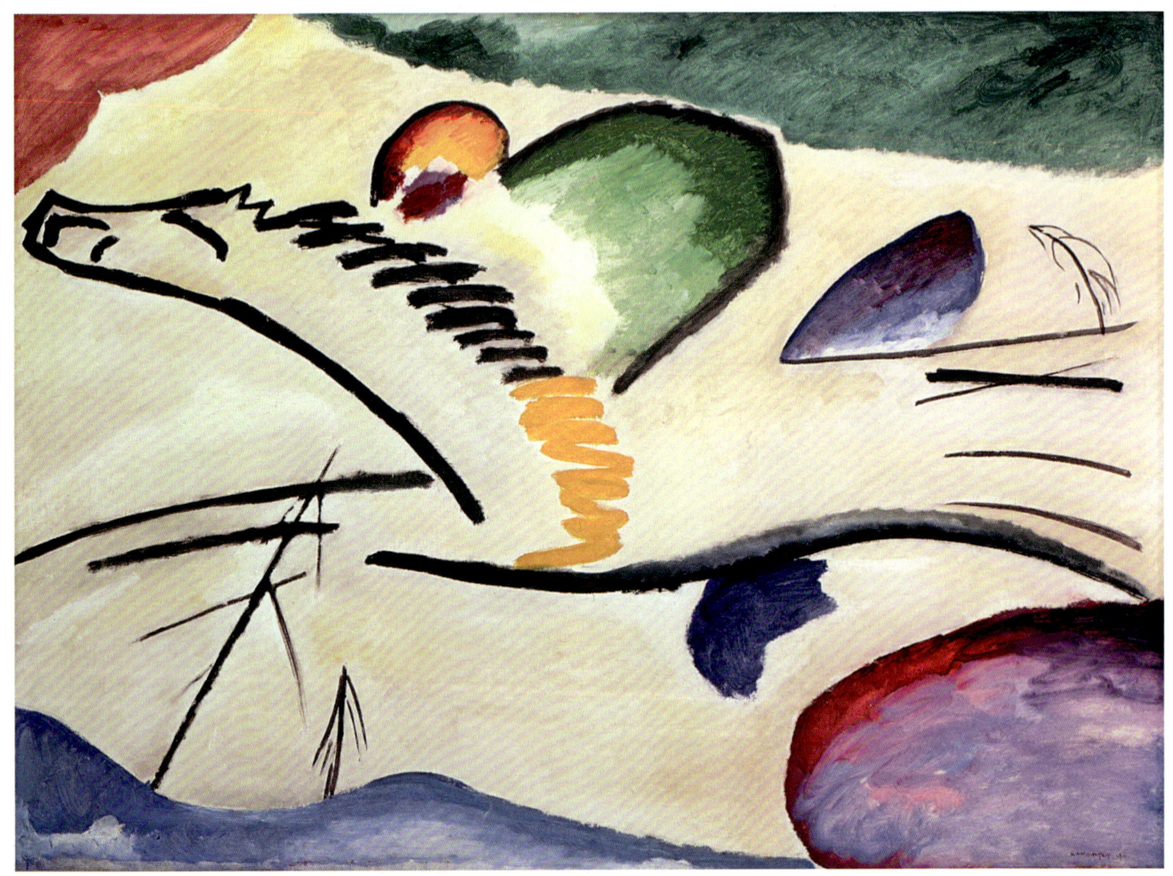

Lyrical

Lyrique

Lyrisches

Lírico

Lirica

'Lyrisches'

1911, Oil on canvas/Huile sur toile, 94 × 130 cm,
Museum Boymans van Beuningen, Rotterdam

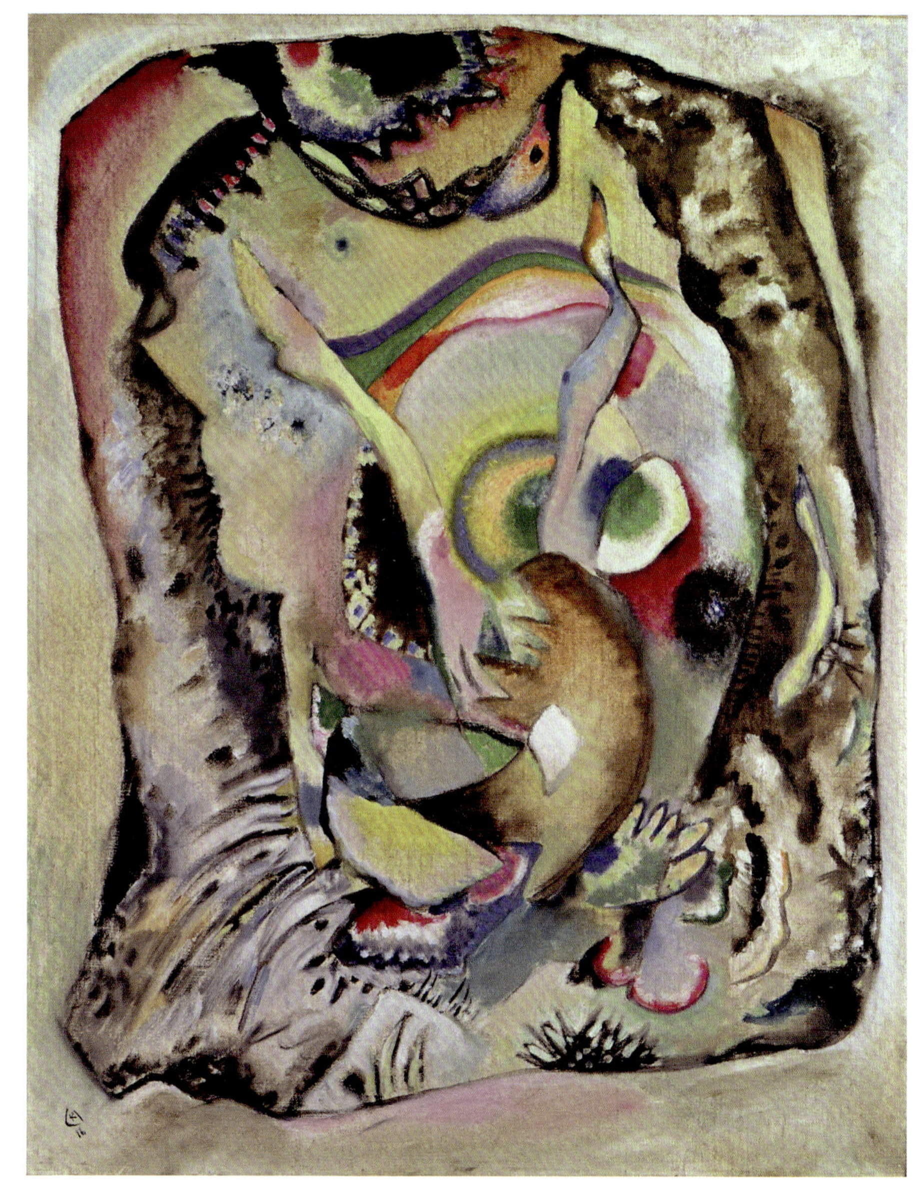

Painting on a Light Ground

Tableau sur fond clair

Bild auf hellem Grund

Pintura en un campo de luz

Dipinto su sfondo chiaro

Schilderij op heldere ondergrond

1916, Oil on canvas/Huile sur toile, 100 × 78 cm, Musée National d'Art Moderne, Centre Pompidou, Paris

Together with the artists of "Der Blaue Reiter", Kandinsky participated in one of the most important artistic undertakings of the pre-war period, the "Erster Deutscher Herbstsalon" (First German Autumn Salon) of autumn 1913, located in Berlin.

At the invitation of Herwarth Walden, Kandinsky and Marc organized the "First German Autumn Salon", inspired by Parisian exhibitions and gathering together all the important modern artists. In addition to pictures from the Futurists and cubists, excepting Picasso, new works by Robert (1885–1941) and Sonia Delaunay (1885–1979) were the exhibition's focus. Franz Marc and August Macke (1887–1914) showed their major works, such as "The Tower of Blue Horses" or "Zoological Garden I". Kandinsky also sent his most important pictures such as the large "Composition VI", which he elaborately described in his publication "Rückblicke". The "First German Autumn Salon" lacked only the expressionist artists, who were concurrently showing at the "Free Secession" exhibition. Nevertheless, the amazing number of high-quality artists made the "First German Autumn Salon" the most important manifestation of modernity before the war.

Et c'est avec le cercle du Cavalier bleu que Kandinsky participe à l'une des plus grandes entreprises artistiques de l'avant-guerre, l'Erster Deutscher Herbstsalon (« Premier Salon d'automne allemand ») à Berlin, en 1913.

À l'invitation de Herwarth Walden, Kandinsky et Marc organisent ce salon, qui rassemble – sur le modèle parisien – tous les artistes modernes importants. À côté des tableaux des futuristes et des cubistes (Picasso excepté), les nouvelles œuvres de Robert Delaunay (1885–1941) et de Sonia (1885–1979) sont au centre de l'attention. Franz Marc et August Macke (1887–1914) y présentent leurs chefs-d'œuvre – respectivement *Turm der blauen Pferde* (« Tour des chevaux bleus »), et *Zoologischer Garten I* (« Jardin zoologique I »). Kandinsky expose ses tableaux les plus importants, comme la grande *Composition VI* qu'il a décrite en détail dans ses Rückblicke (« Regards sur le passé »). Il ne manque que les artistes expressionnistes, qui se sont joints à l'exposition concomitante de la Freie Secession
(« sécession libre »). Reste que le nombre étonnant d'artistes exceptionnels fait du « Premier Salon d'automne » allemand la manifestation artistique la plus importante du modernisme avant la Première Guerre mondiale.

Zusammen mit dem Künstlerkreis des „Blauen Reiters" beteiligt sich Kandinsky an einer der größten künstlerischen Unternehmungen der Vorkriegszeit, dem „Ersten Deutschen Herbstsalon" im Herbst 1913 in Berlin.

Auf Einladung von Herwarth Walden organisieren Kandinsky und Marc den „Ersten Deutschen Herbstsalon", der nach Pariser Vorbild alle wichtigen Künstler der Moderne versammelt. Neben den Bildern der Futuristen und Kubisten (außer Picasso) stehen die neuen Werke von Robert (1885–1941) und Sonia Delaunay (1885–1979) im Mittelpunkt. Franz Marc und August Macke (1887–1914) zeigen ihre Hauptwerke, z. B „Turm der Blauen Pferde" bzw. „Zoologischer Garten I". Kandinsky schickt ebenfalls seine wichtigsten Bilder wie die große „Komposition VI", die er ausführlich in „Rückblicke" beschrieben hat. Es fehlen nur die expressionistischen Künstler, die sich der gleichzeitig stattfindenden Ausstellung in der „Freien Secession" angeschlossen haben. Trotzdem macht die erstaunliche Vielzahl von qualitätsvollen Künstlern den „Ersten Deutschen Herbstsalon" zur wichtigsten Manifestation der Moderne vor dem Krieg.

Junto a los artistas de "Der Blaue Reiter", Kandinsky participó en uno de los proyectos artísticos más importantes del periodo pre-bélico, el "Erster Deutscher Herbstsalon" (Primer salón de otoño alemán) en el otoño de 1913, ubicado en Berlín.

Por invitación de Herwarth Walden, Kandinsky y Marc organizan el "Primer salón de otoño alemán", inspirado en las exposiciones parisinas y que reuniría a todos los artistas modernos importantes del momento. Además de las imágenes de los futuristas y cubistas, exceptuando a Picasso, el foco central de las exposiciones fueron los nuevos trabajos de Robert (1885–1941) y Sonia Delaunay (1885–1979). Franz Marc y August Macke (1887–1914) expusieron sus trabajos más importantes, como "La torre de caballos azules" o "Jardín zoológico I". Kandinsky también envió sus obras más importantes, como la gran "Composición VI", que describió elaboradamente en su publicación "Rückblicke". En el "Primer salón del otoño alemán" solo faltaron los expresionistas, presentes en las mismas fechas en la exposición "Free Secession". No obstante, el increíble número de artistas de alta calidad convirtió al "Primer salón de otoño alemán" en la manifestación artística más importante de la modernidad antes de la guerra.

Insieme agli artisti del gruppo "Der Blaue Reiter", Kandinsky partecipò a una delle più importanti iniziative artistiche del periodo pre-bellico, l'Erster Deutscher Herbstsalon (Primo salone tedesco d'autunno), che ebbe luogo a Berlino nell'autunno 1913.

Su invito di Herwarth Walden, Kandinsky e Marc organizzarono, ispirandosi alle mostre parigine, il Primo salone tedesco d'autunno, che riunì tutti i più importanti artisti moderni. Oltre ai quadri dei futuristi e dei cubisti, ad eccezione di Picasso, dominarono la scena le nuove opere di Robert (1885–1941) e Sonia Delaunay (1885–1979). Franz Marc e August Macke (1887–1914) esposero le loro opere più importanti, quali La Torre dei cavalli azzurri o Giardino zoologico I. Anche Kandinsky inviò i suoi quadri principali, come la grande Composizione VI, descritta dall'artista stesso in modo elaborato nella sua pubblicazione Rückblicke. Al Primo salone tedesco d'autunno mancarono solo gli espressionisti, occupati in quel momento con la mostra della "Secessione Libera". Ciò nonostante, l'incredibile numero di artisti di alta qualità che vi parteciparono ha fatto del Primo salone tedesco d'autunno la manifestazione più importante della modernità dell'anteguerra.

Samen met de kunstenaarskring 'Der Blaue Reiter' neemt Kandinsky deel aan een van de grootste artistieke projecten in de periode voorafgaande aan de Eerste Wereldoorlog, de 'Eerste Duitse Herfstsalon', in de herfst van 1913 te Berlijn.

Op uitnodiging van Herwarth Walden organiseren Kandinsky en Marc naar het voorbeeld van Parijs de 'Eerste Duitse Herfstsalon', waar het werk van alle belangrijke kunstenaars van het modernisme gezamenlijk wordt getoond. Naast schilderijen van de futuristen en kubisten (maar zonder Picasso) staat het vernieuwende werk van Robert (1885–1941) en Sonia Delaunay (1885–1979) centraal. Franz Marc en August Macke (1887–1914) tonen hun belangrijkste werken, waaronder De toren der blauwe paarden of Zoologischer Garten I. Ook Kandinsky stuurt zijn belangrijkste schilderijen, waaronder de grote Compositie VI, die hij later uitvoerig in zijn memoires (Rückblicke) zal beschrijven. Alleen de expressionisten ontbreken, omdat deze hun werk op de gelijktijdig plaatsvindende tentoonstelling van de 'Freie Secession' exposeren. Toch maakt de aanwezigheid van zo'n opmerkelijk aantal hoogwaardige kunstenaars de Eerste Duitse Herfstsalon tot een van de belangrijkste kunstmanifestaties in de periode vóór de Eerste Wereldoorlog.

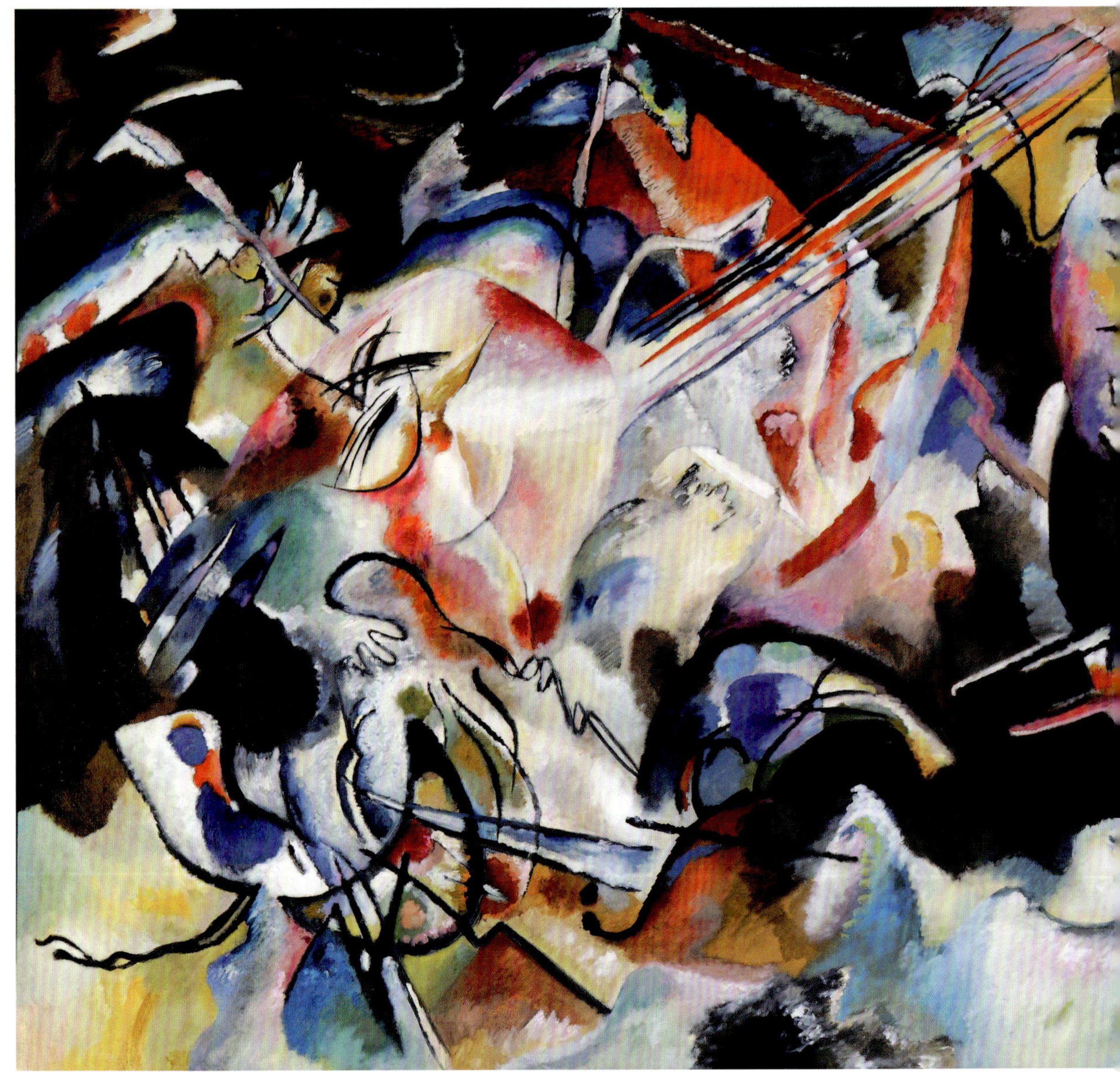

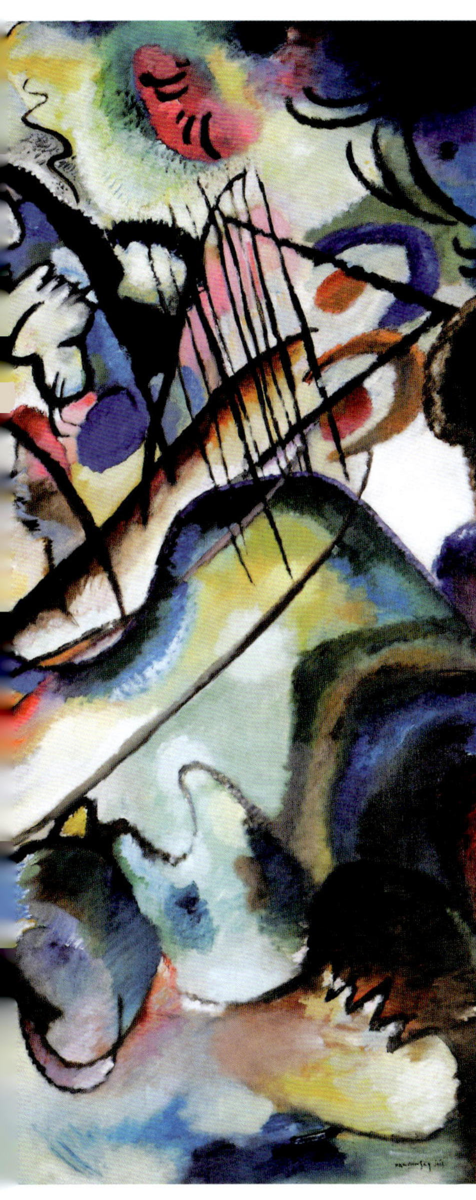

Composition VI
Composition VI
Komposition VI
Composición VI
Composizione VI
Compositie VI

1913, Oil on canvas/Huile sur toile, 195 × 300 cm, State Hermitage Museum, St Petersburg

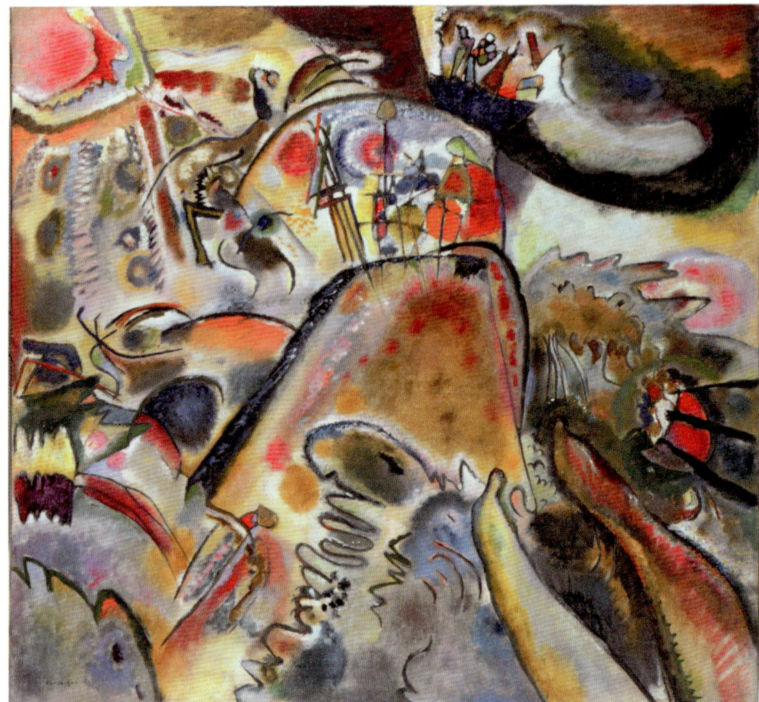

*1913, Oil on canvas/Huile sur toile,
109,9 × 119,9 cm, Solomon R. Guggenheim
Museum, New York*

Kandinsky's lively artistic, political and organizational activity ended abruptly with the outbreak of the First World War. The circle of friends was broken and Kandinsky had to leave Munich, living initially in Switzerland together with Gabriele Münter. This relationship ended, however, after a final meeting in Stockholm in December 1915. On 25 November, he traveled through the Balkans to Odessa, where he stayed for one week, before continuing to Moscow on 20 December.

L'intense activité de Kandinsky – dans les domaines de l'art, de la politique culturelle et de l'organisation – se termine brutalement avec l'éclatement de la Première Guerre mondiale. Le cercle des amis se défait, Kandinsky doit quitter Munich pour aller d'abord vivre en Suisse avec Gabriele Münter (qu'il finira par quitter définitivement après une ultime rencontre à Stockholm, en décembre 1915). Le 25 novembre, il traverse les Balkans jusqu'à Odessa, où il s'arrête une semaine, avant de partir pour Moscou le 20 décembre.

Kandinskys rege künstlerische, kunstpolitische und organisatorische Tätigkeit endet jäh durch den Ausbruch des Ersten Weltkrieges. Der Freundeskreis zerbricht, Kandinsky muss München verlassen und lebt zunächst in der Schweiz, zusammen mit Gabriele Münter, die er jedoch nach einem letzten Treffen in Stockholm im Dezember 1915 endgültig verlässt. Am 25. November reist er über den Balkan nach Odessa, wo er sich eine Woche aufhält, bevor er am 20. Dezember nach Moskau fährt.

La entusiasta actividad organizadora, política y artística de Kandinsky cesó bruscamente con el comienzo de la Primera Guerra Mundial. El círculo de amigos se había roto y Kandinsky se vio obligado a abandonar Múnich, recalando inicialmente en Suiza junto a Gabriele Münter. Esta relación terminó, sin embargo, tras una reunión final en Estocolmo en diciembre de 1915. El 25 de noviembre viajó a través de los Balcanes hasta Odessa, donde permaneció una semana antes de continuar hacia Moscú el 20 de diciembre.

La vivace attività artistica, politica e organizzativa di Kandinsky si concluse bruscamente con lo scoppio della Prima guerra mondiale. La cerchia di amici si disgregò e Kandinsky dovette lasciare Monaco di Baviera per andare a vivere inizialmente in Svizzera insieme a Gabriele Münter. La relazione giunse tuttavia al termine dopo un ultimo incontro a Stoccolma nel dicembre 1915. Il 25 novembre, Kandinsky attraversò i Balcani fino a Odessa, dove rimase per una settimana prima di proseguire il suo viaggio verso Mosca il 20 dicembre.

Aan Kandinsky's drukke activiteiten op artistiek, cultuurpolitiek en organisatorisch gebied komt pas met het uitbreken van de Eerste Wereldoorlog een einde. De vriendenkring valt uiteen, Kandinsky moet München verlaten en verhuist samen met Gabriele Münter naar Zwitserland. Na een laatste ontmoeting in december 1915 in Stockholm verlaat hij haar echter definitief. Op 25 november reist hij via de Balkan naar Odessa, waar hij een week verblijft; op 20 december vertrekt hij naar Moskou.

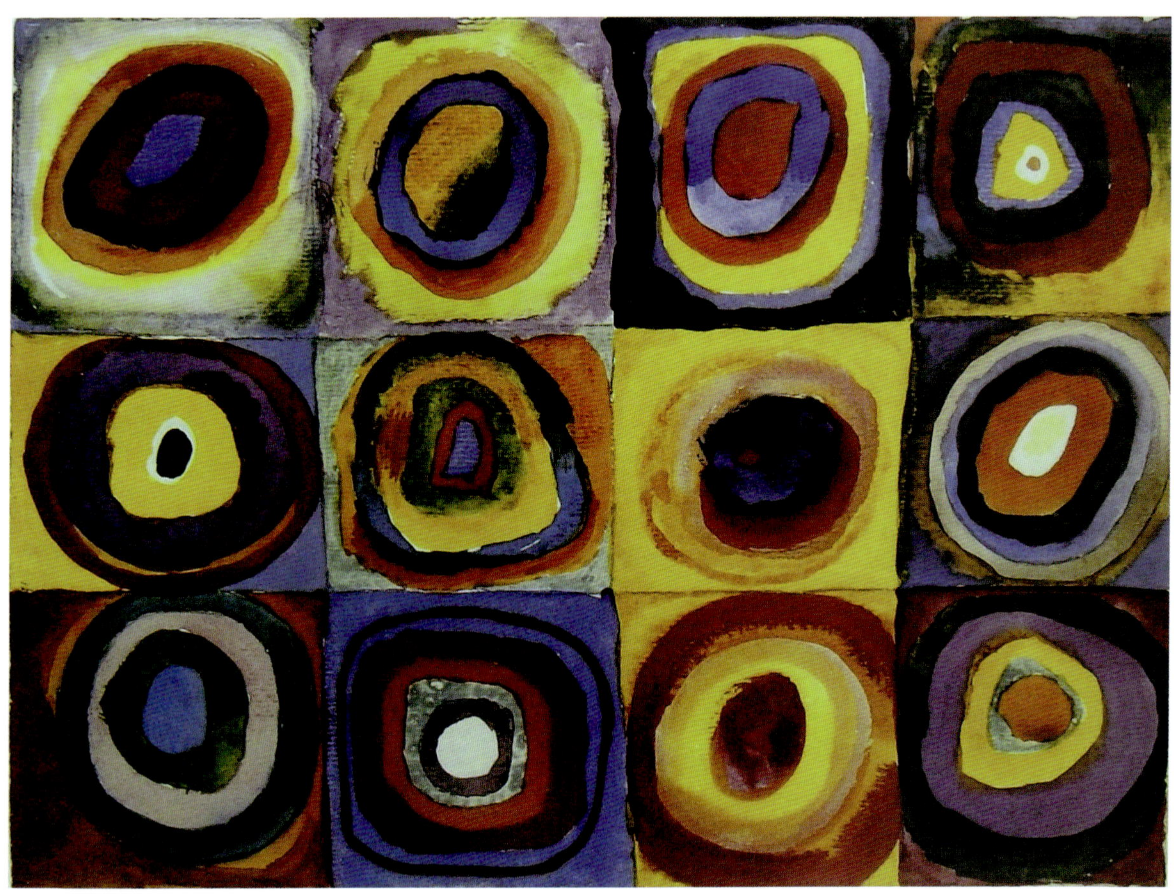

Concentric Circles
Cercles concentriques

Konzentrische Kreise
Círculos concéntricos

Cerchi concentrici
Concentrische cirkels'

1913, Gouache on paper/Gouache sur papier, Private collection

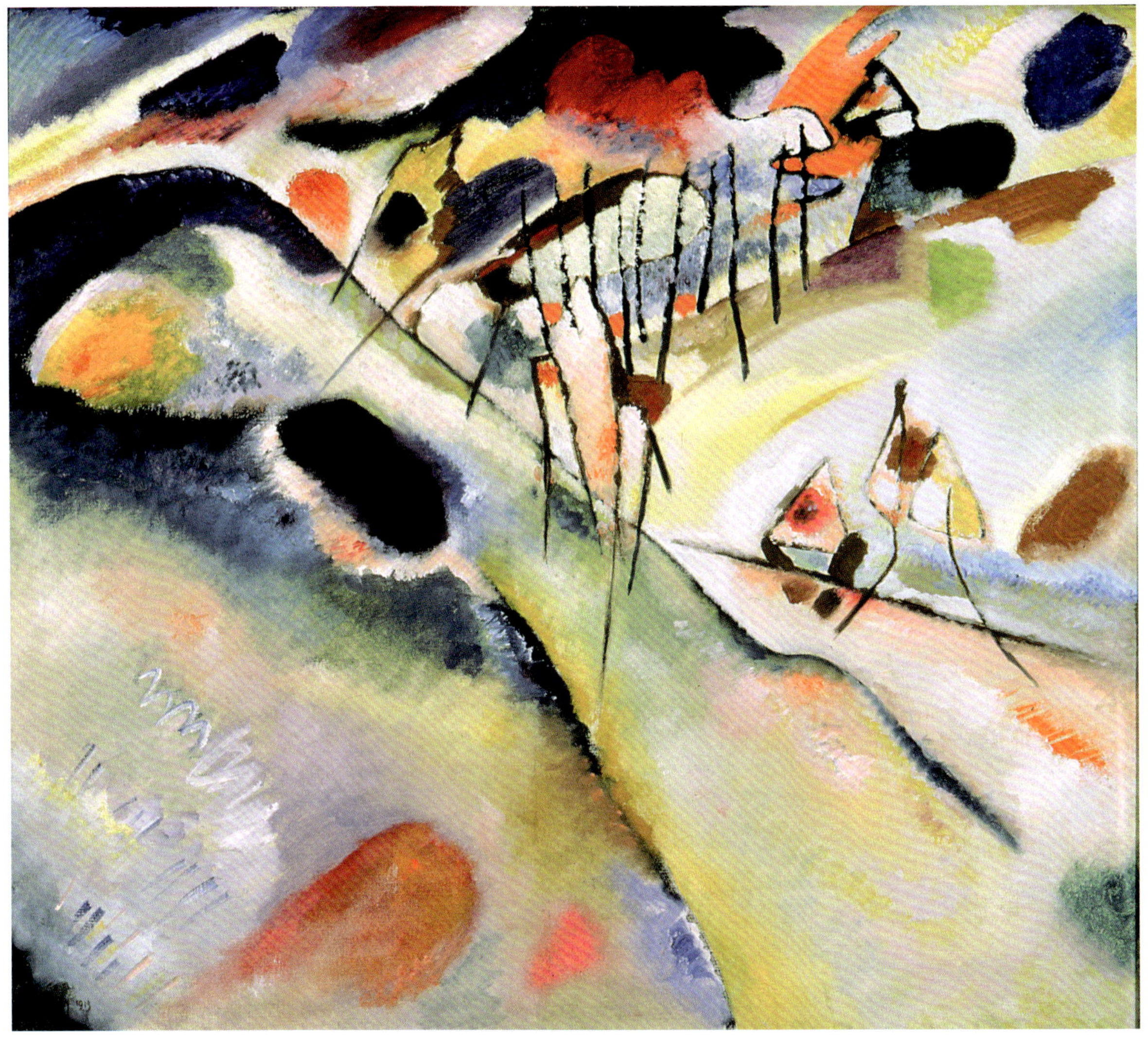

Landscape   **Landschaft**   **Paesaggio**

Paysage   **Paisaje**   **Landschap**

1913, Oil on canvas/Huile sur toile, 88 × 100 cm, State Hermitage Museum, St. Petersburg

Intermezzo in Russia

The Russian translation of "Concerning the Spiritual in Art", published in 1914, made Kandinsky's art theory accessible to a wider circle. In the Russian edition, the geometric diagram is already depicted, showing the interrelationship of basic forms with primary colors. Kandinsky had big plans. Now wealthy from his inheritance, he wanted to build a house with a studio for himself and his new wife, Nina von Andreewsky (1893–1980). The 1918 November Revolution, however, wrecked these plans and robbed Kandinsky of his assets. Due to his great experience, Kandinsky became immediately involved in the cultural and political developments following the revolution. He became a member of the department of visual arts (IZO) in the People's Commissariat for Education (Narkompros). From autumn 1918, he held several professorships in the newly established cultural institutions of Moscow. Kandinsky's curriculum was based on his observations concerning the interrelationship between painting and music, and on his analysis of elementary colors and shapes. Additionally, he was the head of the State purchasing committee and had responsibility for the establishment of new museums in the provinces. Nevertheless, the calls from within the Soviet art committees for the artist to work more in the service of their Marxist-Leninist policy became increasingly loud.

Intermezzo en Russie

La traduction russe du spirituel dans l´art, en 1914, a donné au programme artistique de Kandinsky une audience élargie. Dans l'édition russe figure déjà le diagramme géométrique qui montre les rapports mutuels entre formes de base et tons fondamentaux. Le peintre a de grands projets. Enrichi par son héritage, il veut aménager pour lui et sa nouvelle épouse Nina von Andreevsky (1893–1980) une résidence avec un atelier.
La Révolution d'Octobre anéantit ces plans en le dépouillant de son héritage – mais en raison de sa grande expérience, il est aussitôt impliqué dans le développement de la politique culturelle qui suit cette révolution. Il devient membre de la Section des arts plastiques (IZO) et au Commissariat du Peuple à l'éducation (NARKOMPROS). À compter de l'automne 1918, il occupe plusieurs chaires professorales dans les nouvelles institutions culturelles créées à Moscou. Le programme d'enseignement de Kandinsky repose sur les idées qu'il a développées : rapports entre peinture et musique, analyse des formes et des couleurs élémentaires. Il est en outre directeur de la Commission d'État des achats, et chargé d'activités pour l'installation de nouveaux musées en province. Reste que dans l'ensemble de la politique culturelle soviétique, l'exilgence de mettre plus fortement l'artiste au service du marxisme-léninime se fait de plus en plus pesante.

Intermezzo in Russland

Die 1914 publizierte russische Übersetzung von „Über das Geistige in der Kunst" machte auch Kandinskys Kunstprogramm einem weiten Kreis zugänglich. In der russischen Ausgabe ist bereits das geometrische Diagramm abgebildet, das die Wechselbeziehung der Grundformen zu den Grundfarben zeigt. Kandinsky hat große Pläne. Durch sein Erbe vermögend, will er für sich und seine neue Frau Nina von Andreewsky (1893–1980) ein Wohnhaus mit Atelier errichten lassen. Die Novemberrevolution 1918 macht diese Pläne zunichte und beraubt Kandinsky seines Vermögens. Wegen seiner großen Erfahrung wird Kandinsky aber sofort in die kulturpolitische Entwicklung nach der Revolution einbezogen. Er wird Mitglied der Abteilung für Bildende Künste (IZO) im Kommissariat für kulturelle Bildung (NARKOMPROS). Ab Herbst 1918 hält er mehrere Professuren an den neu eingerichteten Kulturinstitutionen Moskaus. Kandinskys Lehrplan beruht auf seinen Ausführungen zur Wechselbeziehung zwischen Malerei und Musik und auf der Analyse der elementaren Farben und Formen. Schließlich wird er noch Leiter der Staatlichen Ankaufskommission und ist für die Einrichtung neuer Museen in der Provinz tätig. Die Forderung innerhalb der gesamten sowjetischen Kunstpolitik, den Künstler stärker in den Dienst der marxistisch-leninistischen Politik zu stellen, wird aber immer lauter.

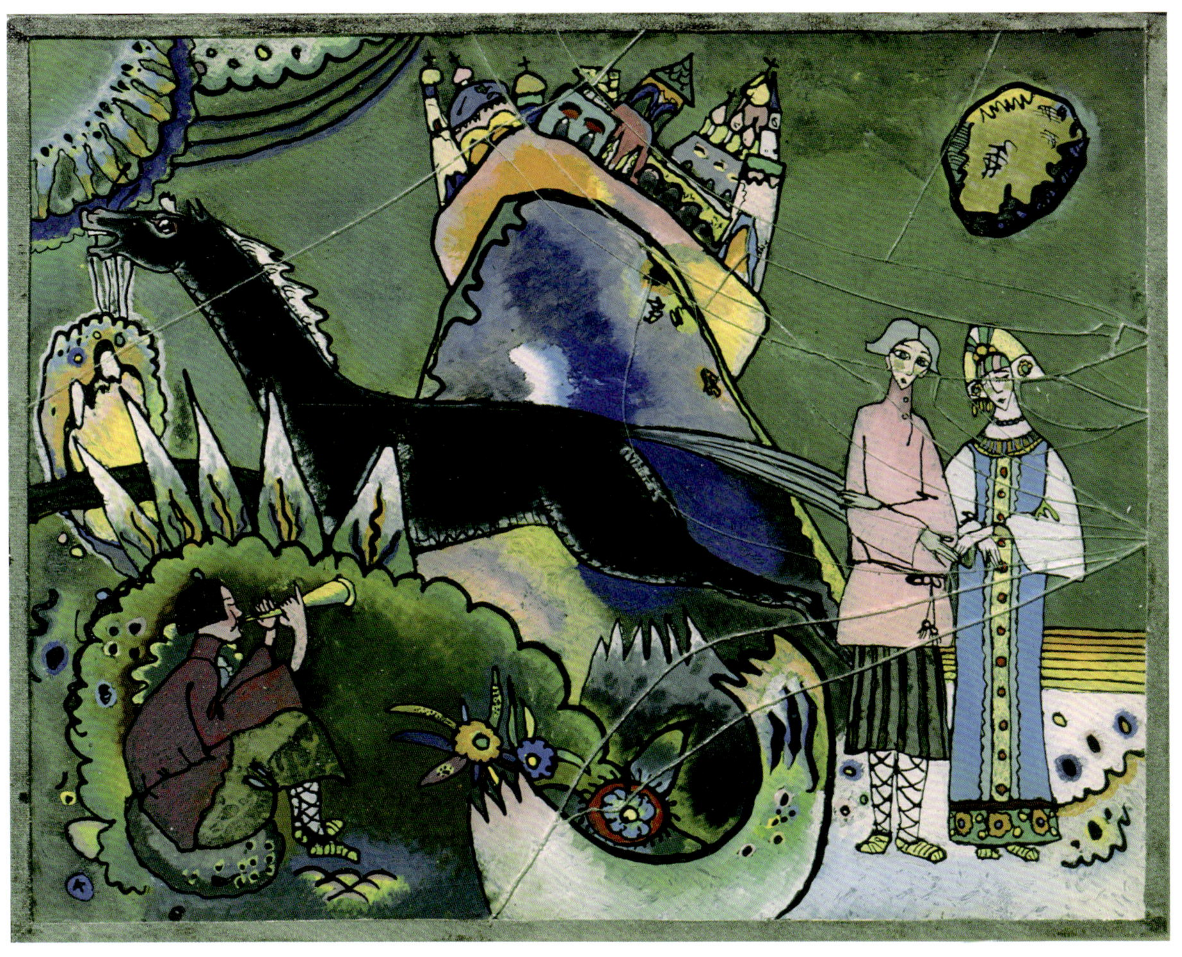

Golden Cloud

Le Nuage d'or

Goldene Wolke

Nube de oro

Nuvola dorata

Gouden wolk

1918, Oil on canvas/Huile sur toile, 24 × 31 cm, State Russian Museum, St. Petersburg

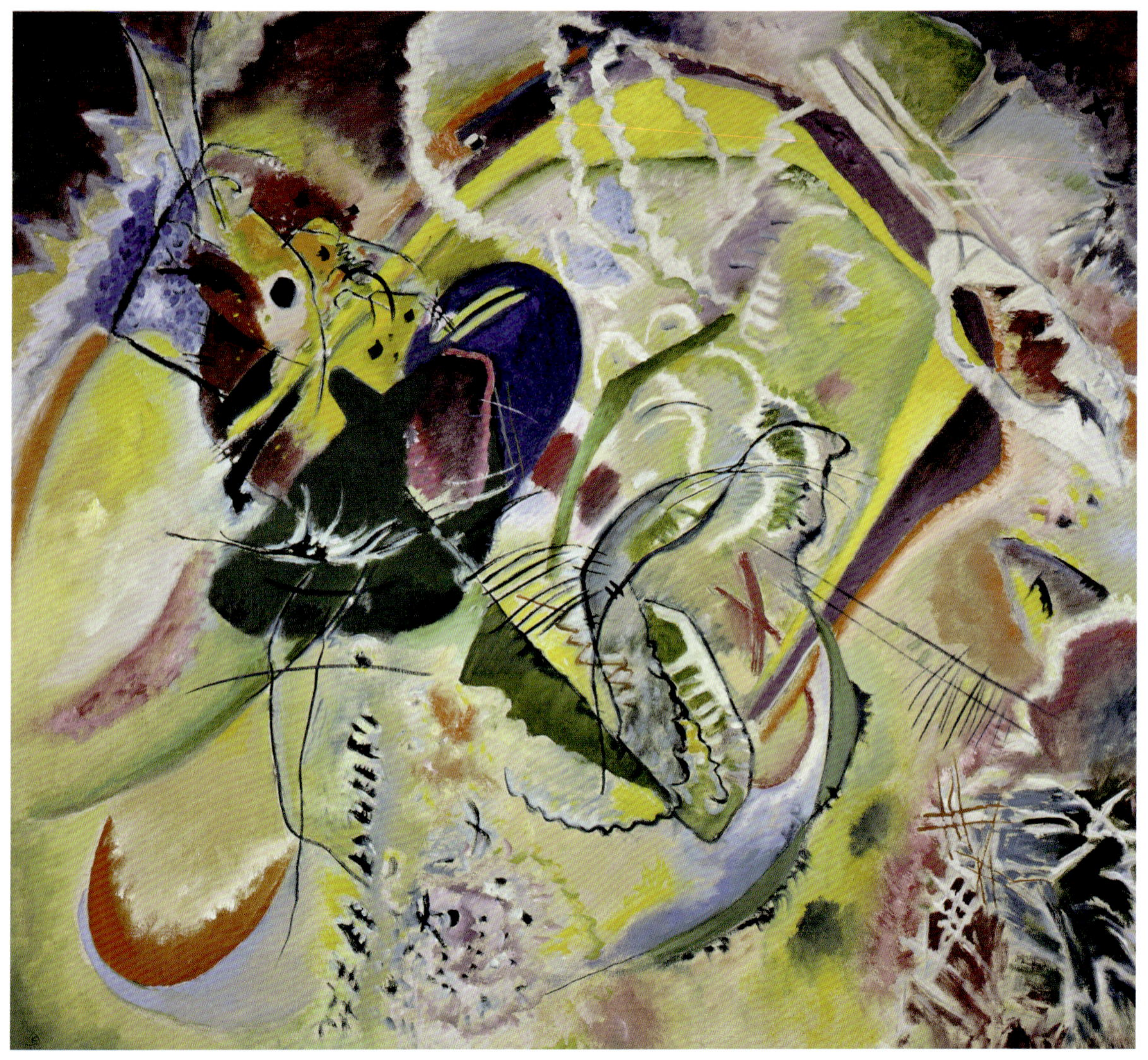

Improvisation 35   **Improvisation 35**   **Improvvisazione 35**

Improvisation 35   **Improvisación 35**   **Improvisatie 35**

1914, Oil on canvas/Huile sur toile, 110,3 × 120,3 cm, Kunstmuseum, Basel

Intermezzo en Rusia

La traducción al ruso del tratado
"Sobre lo espiritual en el arte",
publicada en 1914, logró que la teoría
del arte de Kandinsky resultara
accesible a un círculo más amplio.
En la edición rusa se retrata ya el
diagrama geométrico, mostrando
la interrelación de las formas
básicas con los colores primarios.
Kandinsky tenía grandes planes.
En una posición acomodada tras
recibir su herencia, quería construir
una casa con estudio para él y su
nueva esposa, Nina von Andreewsky
(1893–1980). La revolución de
noviembre de 1918, sin embargo,
destruye todos estos planes y despoja
a Kandinsky de sus bienes. Gracias
a su gran experiencia, Kandinsky
vuelve a implicarse de inmediato
en los avances políticos y culturales
tras la revolución. Se convierte en
miembro del departamento de artes
visuales (IZO) en el Comisariado
Popular de Educación (Narkompros).
A partir del otoño de 1918, ostentó
diversas cátedras en las recién
establecidas instituciones culturales
de Moscú. El currículo de Kandinsky
se basaba en las observaciones
relativas a la interrelación entre
la pintura y la música, así como en
su análisis de las formas y colores
elementales. Además, era el líder
del Comité estatal de Adquisiciones,
con la responsabilidad de establecer
nuevos museos en las provincias.
No obstante, las peticiones desde los
comité de ate soviéticos para que
el artista trabajase más al servicio
de su política marxista-leninista
eran cada vez más acuciantes.

Intermezzo in Russia

La traduzione russa del saggio Lo
spirituale nell'arte, pubblicata
nel 1914, rese la teoria dell'arte di
Kandinsky accessibile a una cerchia
più ampia. In questa edizione è già
raffigurato lo schema geometrico
che mostra l'interrelazione delle
forme di base con i colori primari.
Kandinsky aveva grandi progetti.
Ricco grazie all'eredità ricevuta,
voleva costruire una casa con uno
studio per sé stesso e la sua nuova
moglie, Nina von Andreewsky
(1893–1980). La Rivoluzione di
novembre del 1918, però, mandò a
monte i suoi piani e derubò Kandinsky
dei suoi beni. Grazie alla sua vasta
esperienza, Kandinsky fu subito
coinvolto negli sviluppi culturali e
politici che seguirono alla rivoluzione.
Divenne membro del Dipartimento di
arti visive (IZO) del Commissariato del
popolo per l'istruzione (Narkompros)
e, a partire dall'autunno 1918, ricoprì
diverse cattedre nelle istituzioni
culturali di nuova costituzione di
Mosca. Il curriculum di Kandinsky
si basava sulle sue osservazioni
riguardanti l'interrelazione tra
la pittura e la musica e sulla sua
analisi delle forme e dei colori
elementari. Inoltre, fu il direttore
del Comitato di Stato per gli acquisti
e fu incaricato della creazione di
nuovi musei nelle province.
Tuttavia, le richieste da parte
dei comitati di arte sovietica di
lavorare di più al servizio della
loro politica marxista-leninista
divennero sempre più insistenti.

Intermezzo in Rusland

Door de Russische vertaling van
Über das Geistige in der Kunst, die in
1914 verschijnt, wordt Kandinsky's
artistieke programma in brede kring
bekend. In de Russische uitgave
is ook het geometrische diagram
afgedrukt dat de wisselwerking tussen
basisvormen en -kleuren weergeeft.
Kandinsky heeft grootse plannen.
Door zijn erfenis is hij een welvarend
man en hij wil voor hemzelf en zijn
nieuwe vrouw Nina von Andrejevsky
(1893–1980) een huis met een atelier
laten bouwen. Maar de Russische
Revolutie van 1918 doorkruist deze
plannen en berooft Kandinsky van zijn
vermogen. Wegens zijn grote ervaring
wordt Kandinsky meteen na de
Revolutie bij de nieuwe cultuurpolitiek
betrokken. Hij wordt lid van de
Afdeling Beeldende Kunsten (Izo) van
het Volkscommissariaat voor Culturele
Vorming (Narkompros). Vanaf de
herfst van 1918 bekleedt hij meerdere
posten in de op revolutionaire leest
gestoelde cultuurinstellingen van
Moskou. Kandinsky's leerplan
berust op zijn verhandelingen over
het verband tussen schilderkunst
en muziek en op de analyse
van basiskleuren en -vormen.
Uiteindelijk wordt hij ook leider van
de Staatsaankoopcommissie en is hij
verantwoordelijk voor de inrichting
van nieuwe musea in de provincie.
Maar de eis binnen de Sovjetcultuur
dat de kunstenaar meer in dienst moet
staan van de marxistisch-leninistische
politiek, wordt steeds luider.

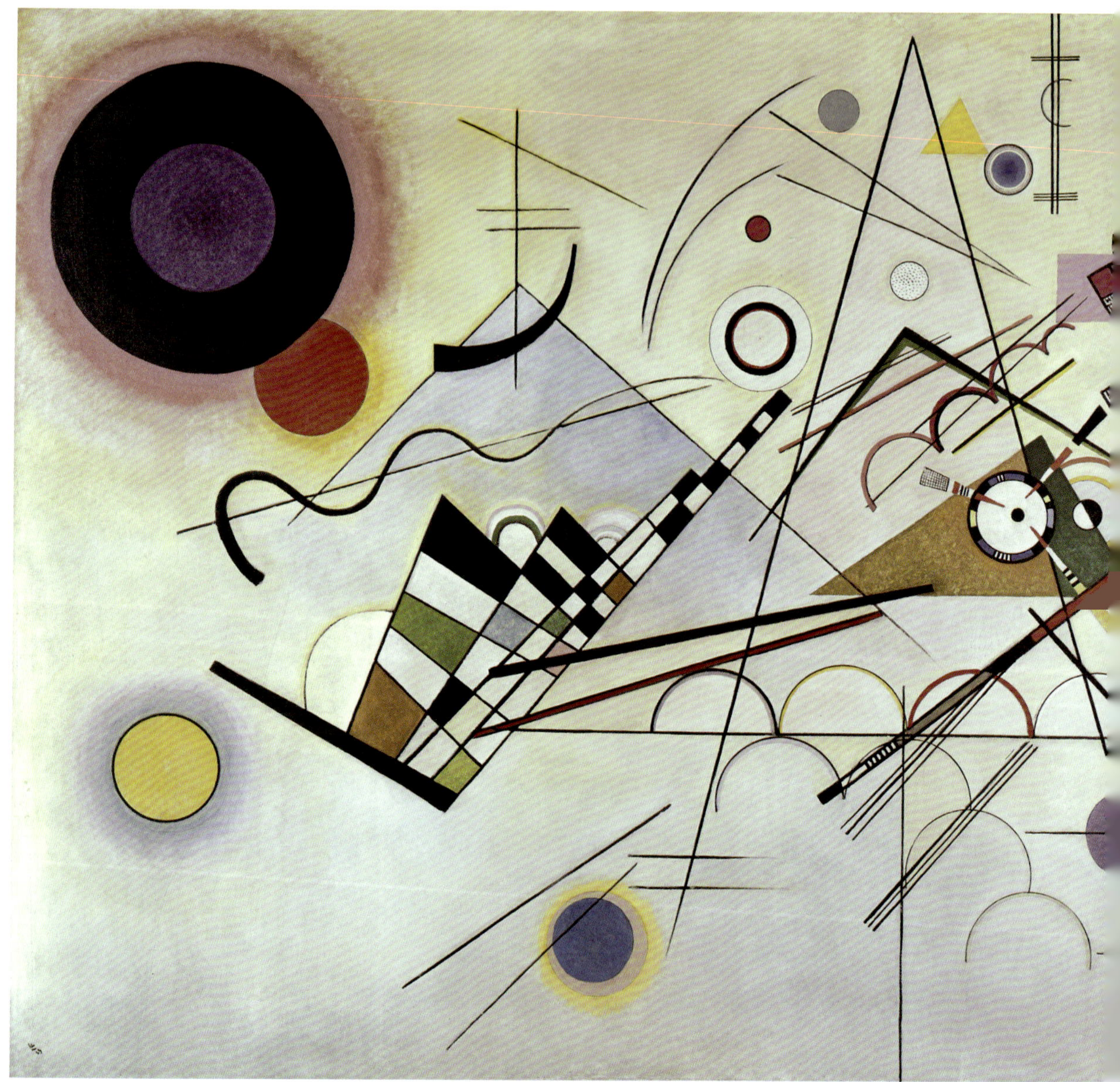

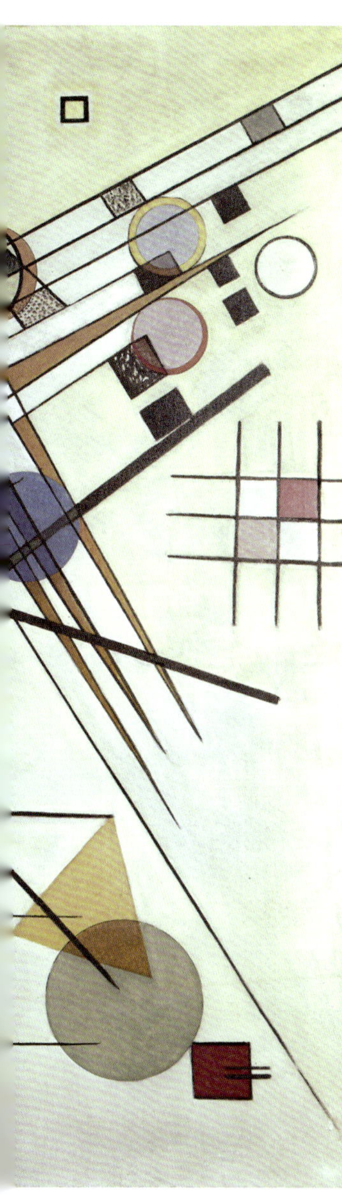

Composition VIII

Composition VIII

Komposition VIII

Composición VIII

Composizione VIII

Compositie VIII

1923, Oil on canvas/Huile sur toile, 140 × 201 cm, Solomon R. Guggenheim Museum, New York

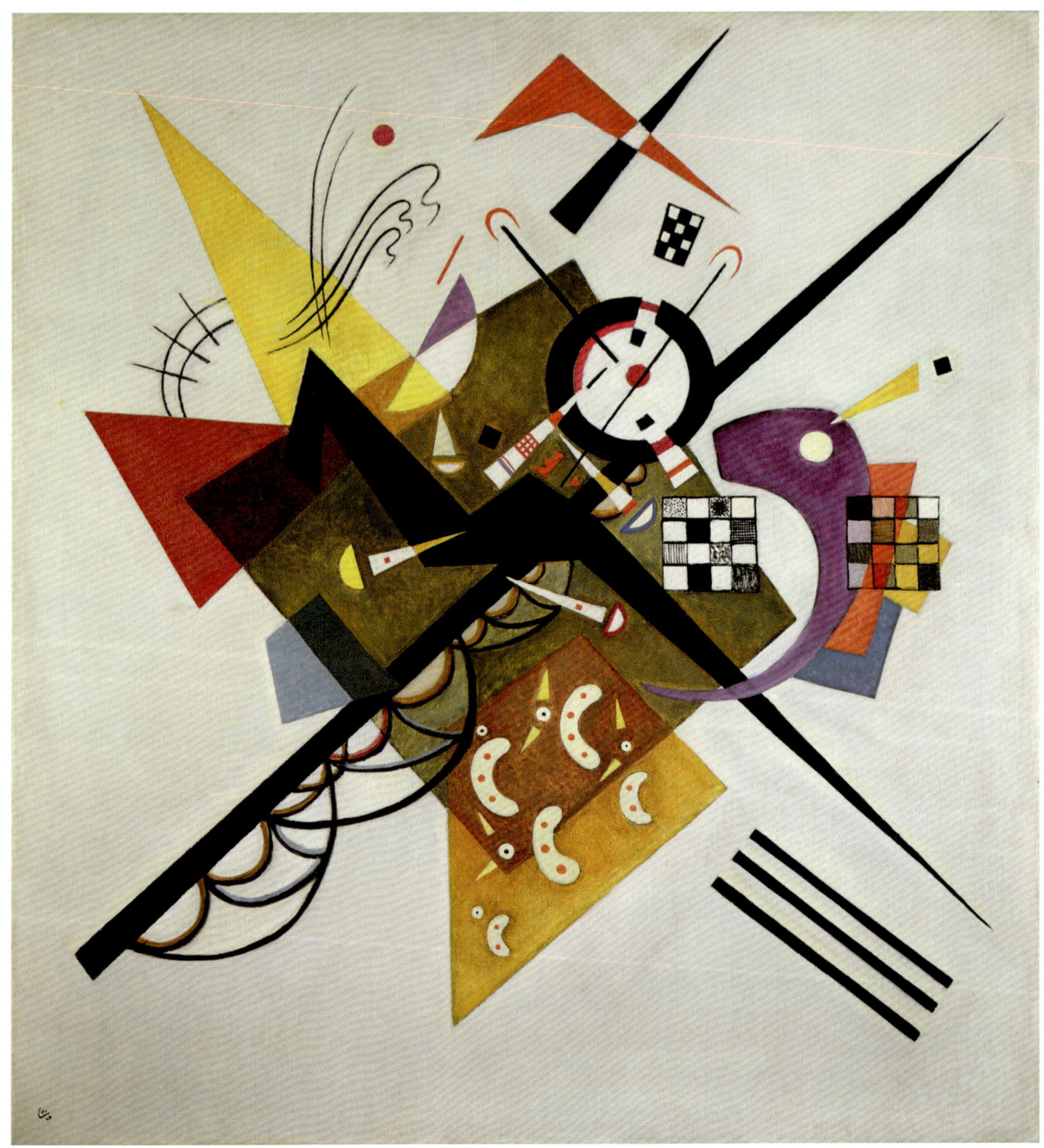

On White II

Sur blanc II

Auf Weiß II

En blanco II

Su bianco II

Op wit II

1923, Oil on canvas/Huile sur toile, 105 × 98 cm, Musée National d'Art Moderne, Centre Pompidou, Paris

In the Bright Oval

Dans l´ovale lumineux

Im hellen Oval

El óvalo luminoso

Nell'ovale luminoso

In de heldere ovaal

1925, Oil on cardboard/ Huile sur carton, 73 × 59 cm, Thyssen-Bornemisza Collection, Madrid

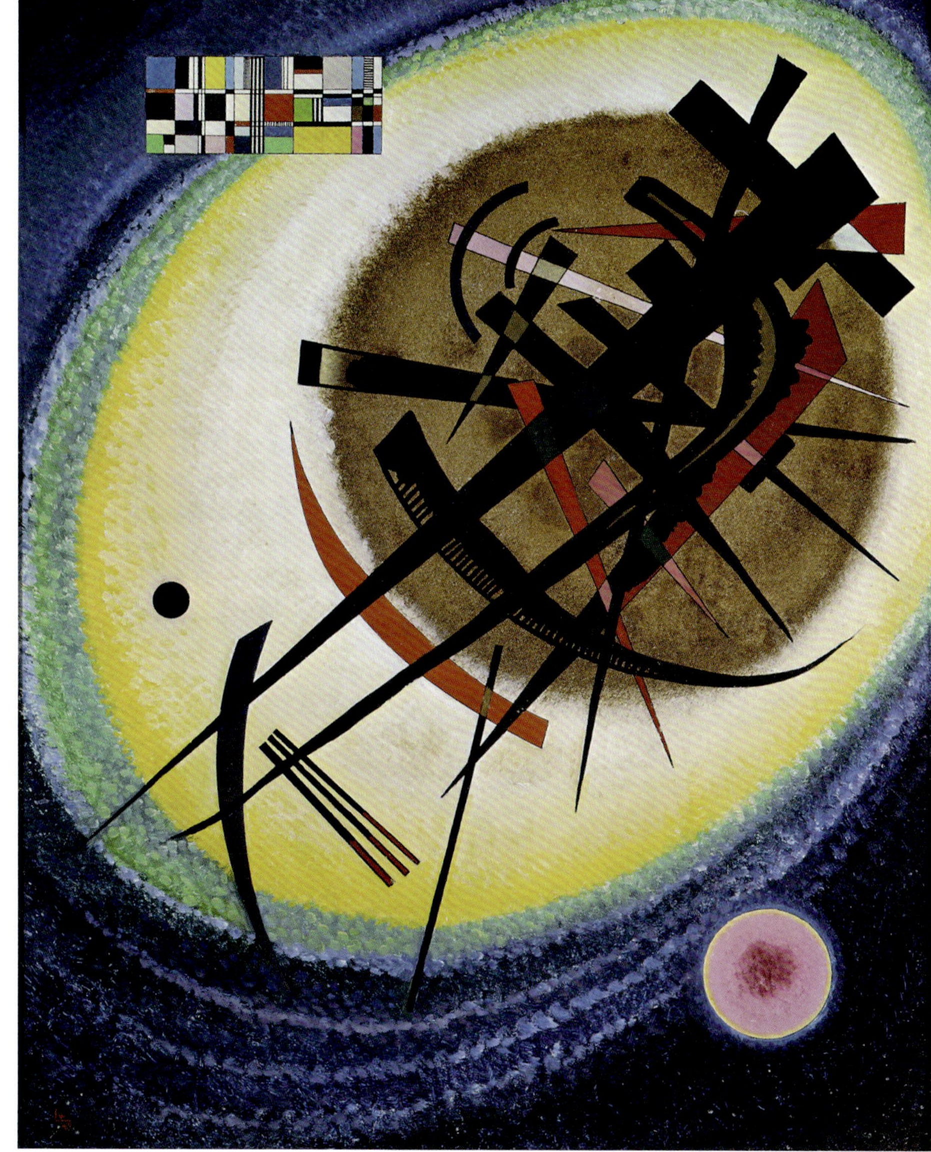

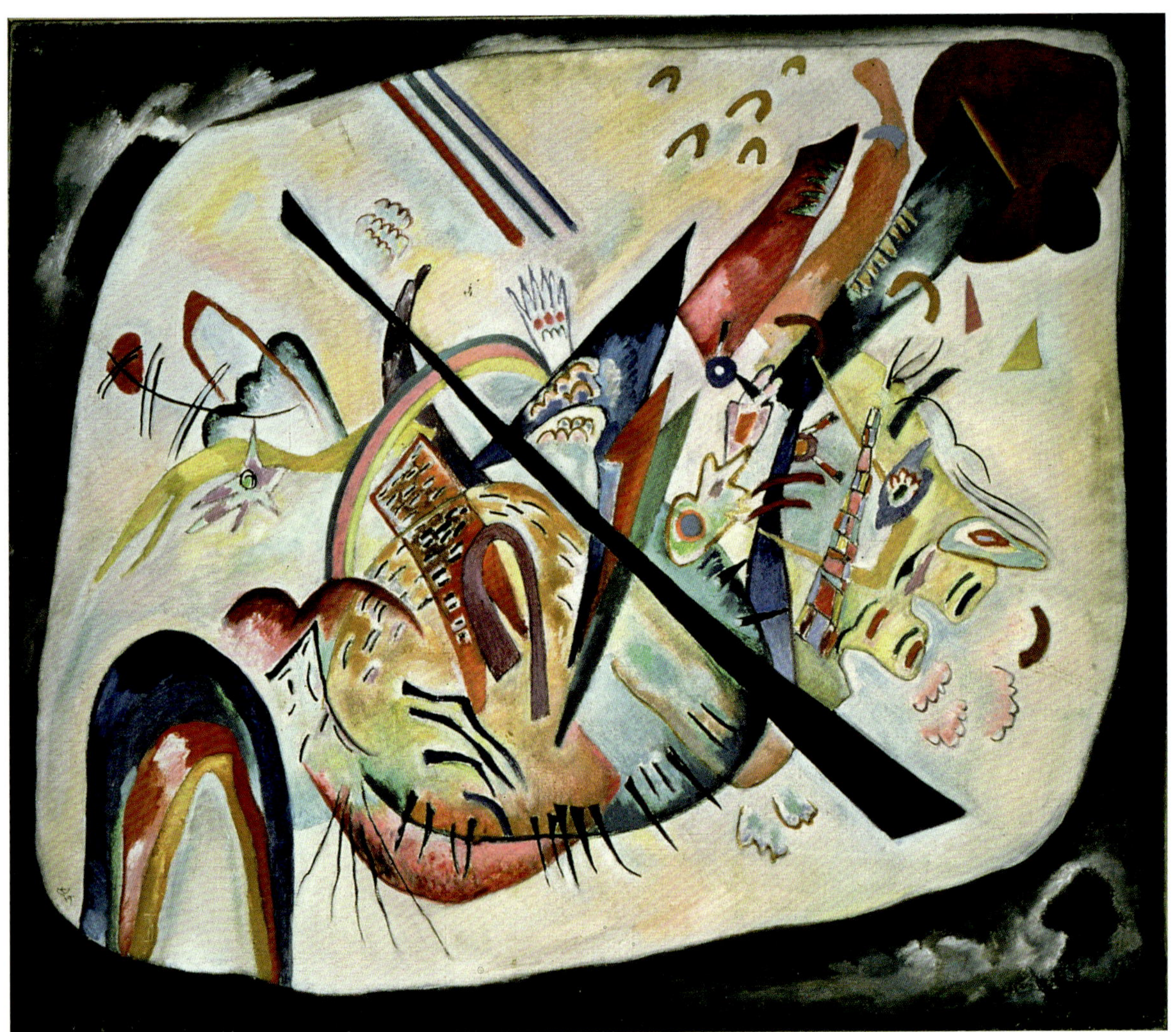

White Oval

Ovale blanc

1919, Oil on canvas/Huile sur toile, 79,5 × 92 cm, Tretyakov Gallery, Moscow

His differences with Russian constructivism brought about a clarification of colors and shapes, even though once again rudimentary symbolic elements appear.

Le contact avec le constructivisme russe produit une clarification des couleurs et des formes – au risque, une fois encore, de l'apparition d'éléments symboliques sommaires.

Weißes Oval

Óvalo blanco

Die Auseinandersetzung mit dem russischen Konstruktivismus bewirkt eine Klärung der Farben und Formen, auch wenn hier noch einmal rudimentäre symbolische Elemente auftauchen.

Sus diferencias con el constructivismo ruso dieron lugar a una clarificación de los colores y las formas, incluso cuando vuelven a aparecer elementos simbólicos rudimentarios.

Ovale bianco

Witte ovaal

Le sue differenze con il costruttivismo russo resero i colori e le forme più chiari, sebbene comparissero ancora elementi simbolici rudimentali.

Kandinsky's kennismaking met het constructivisme leidt tot een verheldering van zijn kleuren en vormen, ook al duiken her en der in zijn werk nog rudimentaire symbolische elementen op.

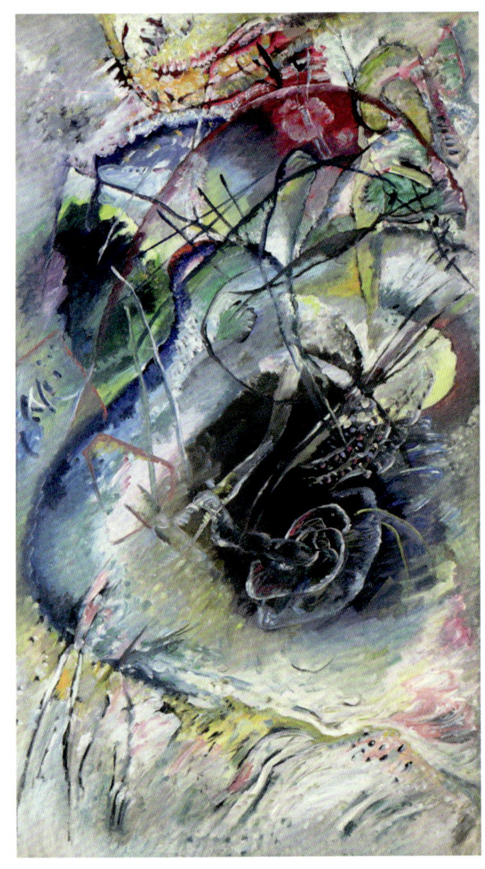

Untitled Improvisation

Improvisation sans titre

Improvisation ohne Titel

Improvisación sin título

Improvvisazione senza titolo

Improvisatie zonder titel

1914, Oil on canvas/Huile sur toile,
Städtische Galerie im Lenbachhaus, Munich

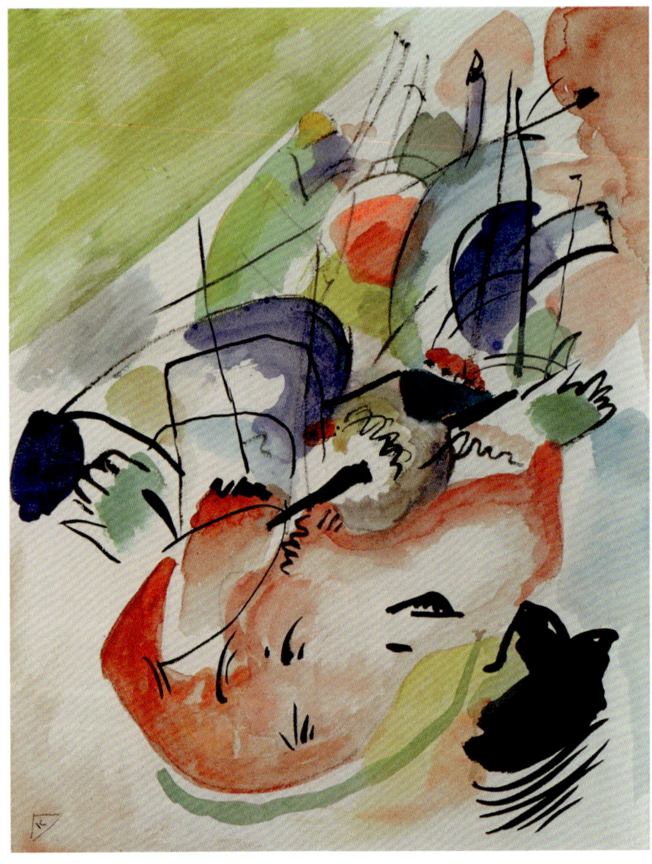

Sketch for Improvisation 31 (Naval Battle)

Etude pour Improvisation 31 (Bataille navale)

Skizze zu Improvisation 31 (Seeschlacht)

Boceto para la improvisación 31 (Batalla Naval)

Schizzo per Improvvisazione 31 (Battaglia navale)

Schets voor Improvisatie 31 (Zeeslag)

1913, Pencil, watercolor and ink on paper/Mine de plomb, aquarelle et encre de Chine sur
papier, 34 × 23,7 cm, Musée National d'Art Moderne, Centre Pompidou, Paris

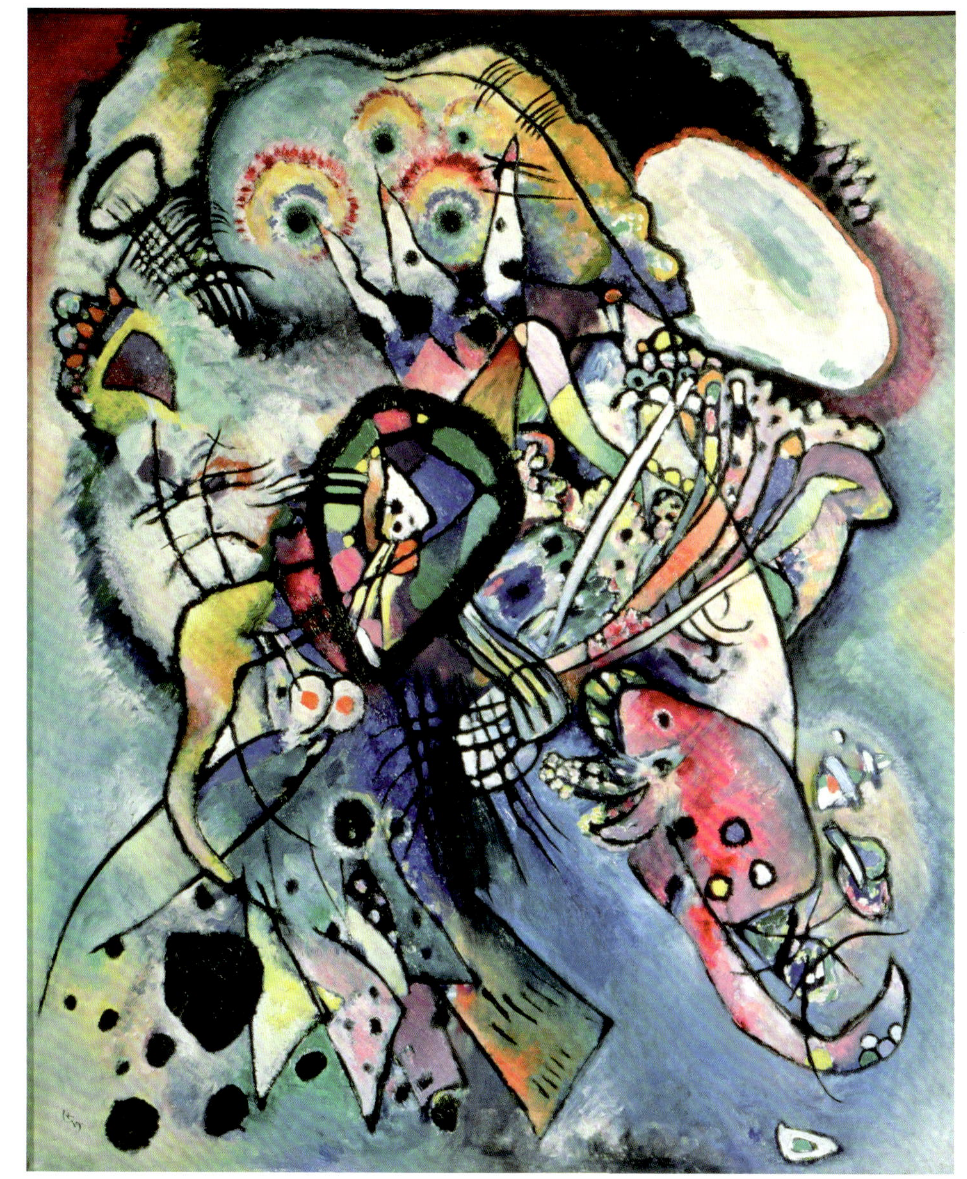

Composition 218

Composition 218

Komposition 218

Composición 218

Composizione 218

Compositie 218

1919, Oil on canvas/Huile sur toile, 107 × 89,5 cm, State Russian Museum, St. Petersburg

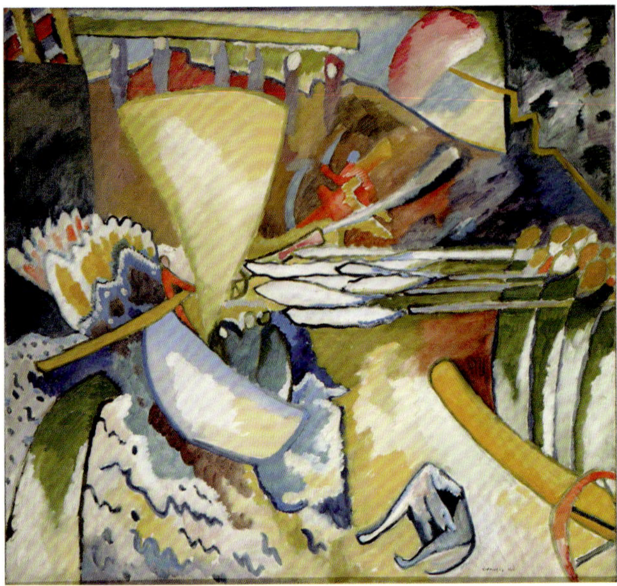

Improvisation 11

Improvisation 11

Improvisation 11

Improvisación 11

Improvvisazione 11

Improvisatie 11

*1910, Oil on canvas/Huile sur toile, 97,5 × 106,5 cm,
State Russian Museum, St. Petersburg*

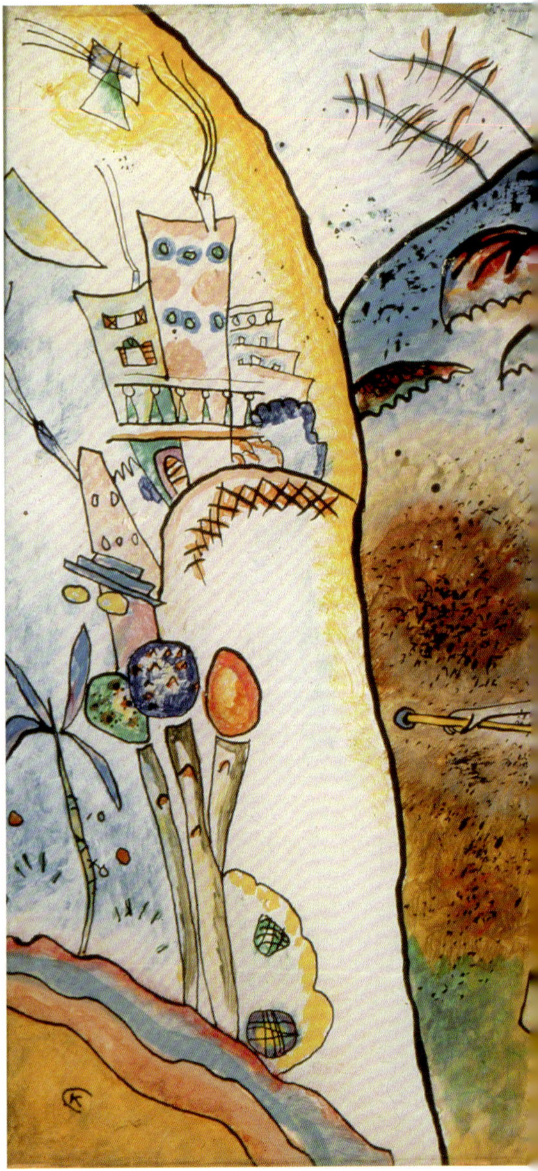

Ladies in a Landscape

Dames dans un paysage

Damen in Landschaft

Señoras en un paisaje

Donne in un paesaggio

Dames in een landschap

*1918, Gouache on paper/Gouache sur papier,
Tretyakov Gallery, Moscow*

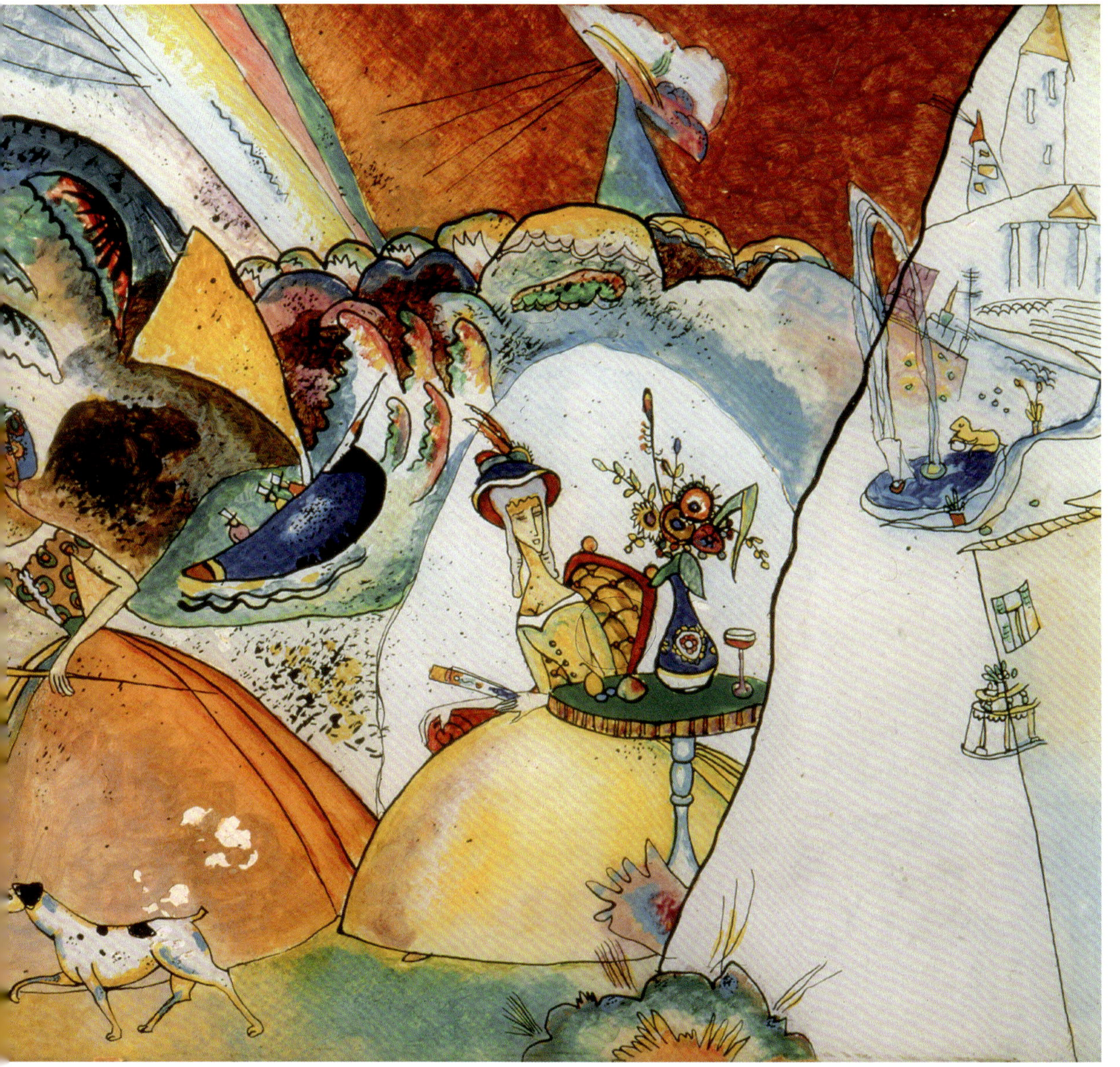

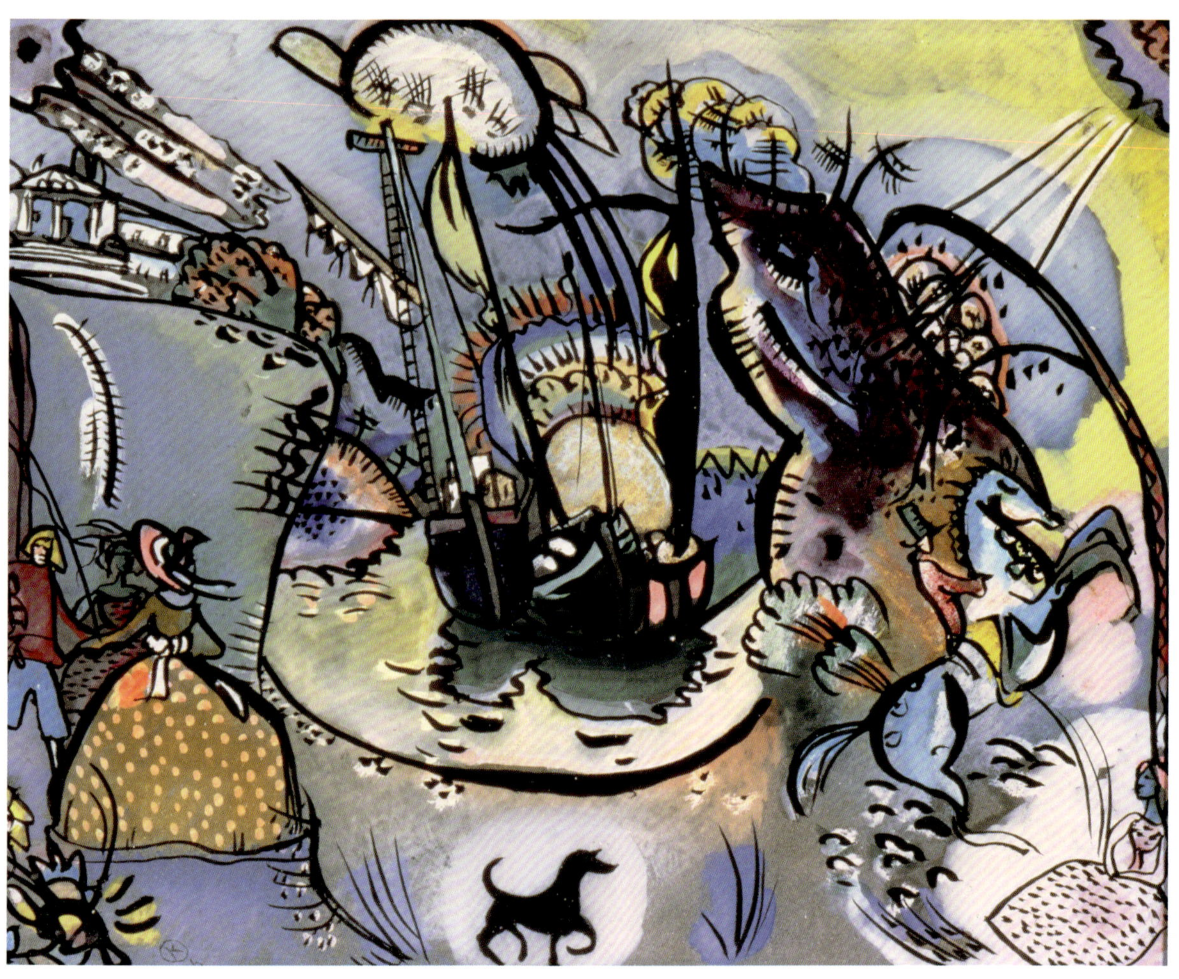

The Harbor **Der Hafen** **Il porto**

Le Port **El puerto de** **De haven**

1916, Gouache on paper/Gouache sur papier,
21,5 × 26,5 cm, Tretyakov Gallery, Moscow

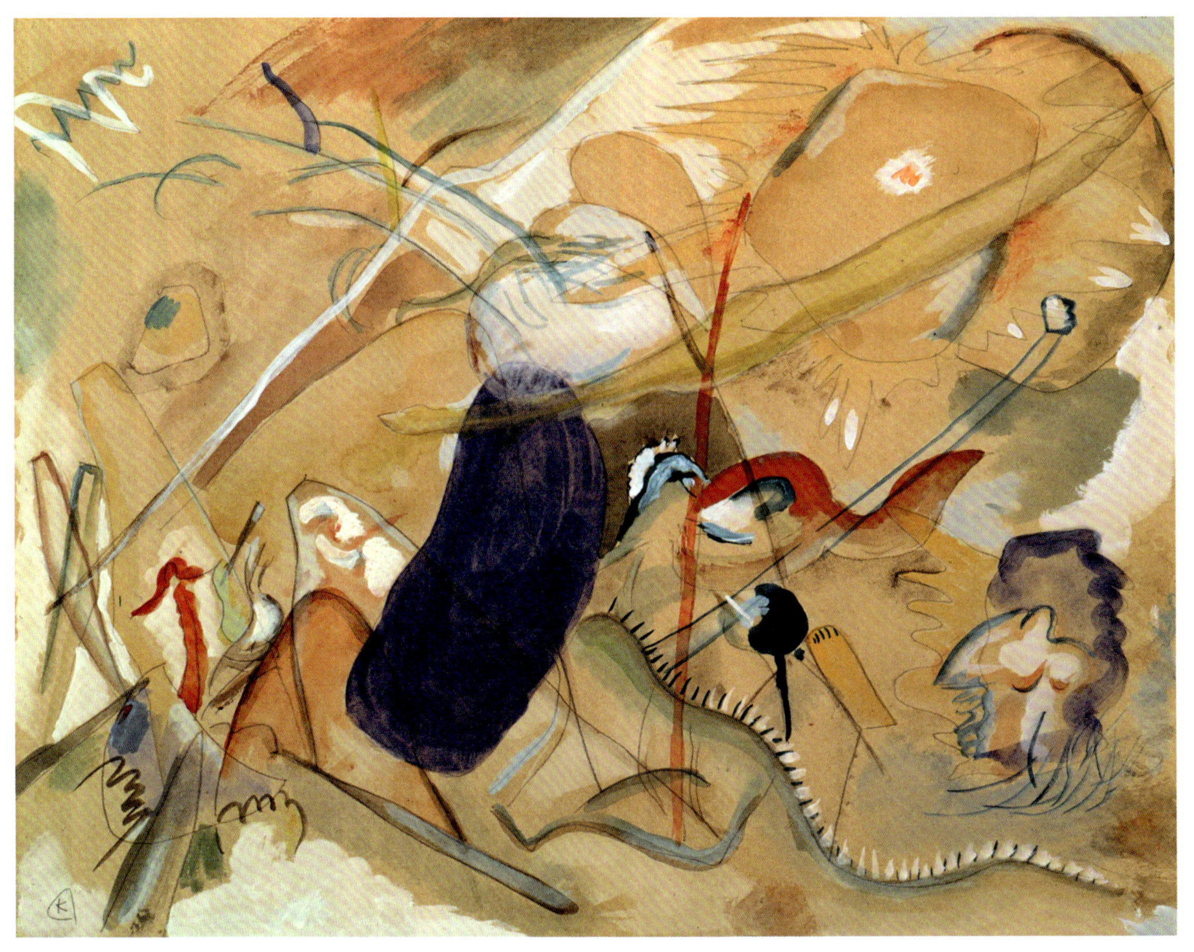

Blaricum

1920, Oil on canvas/Huile sur toile,
Private collection

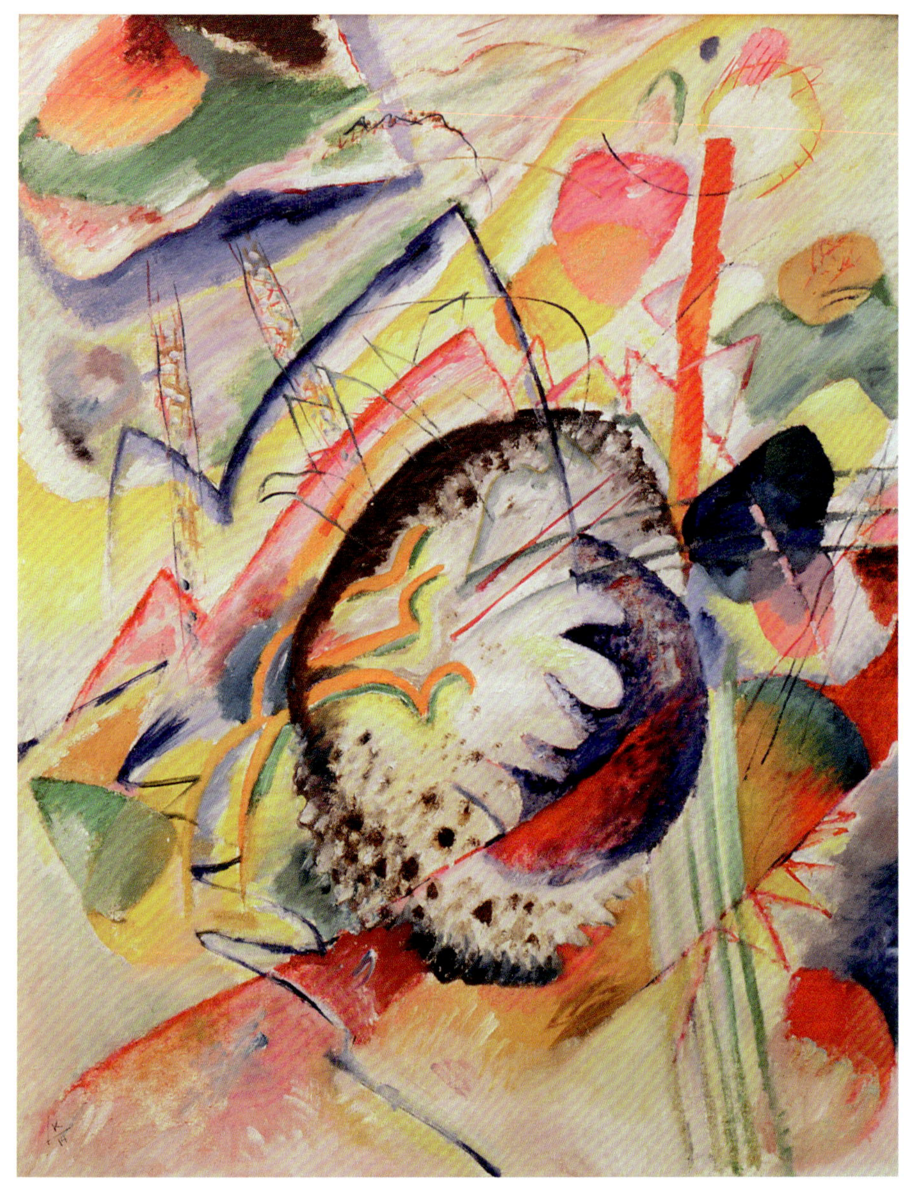

Large Study

Grande Étude

Große Studie

Estudio grande

Grande studio

Grote studie

1914, Oil on canvas/
Huile sur toile, 78 × 100 cm,
Museum Boymans van
Beuningen, Rotterdam

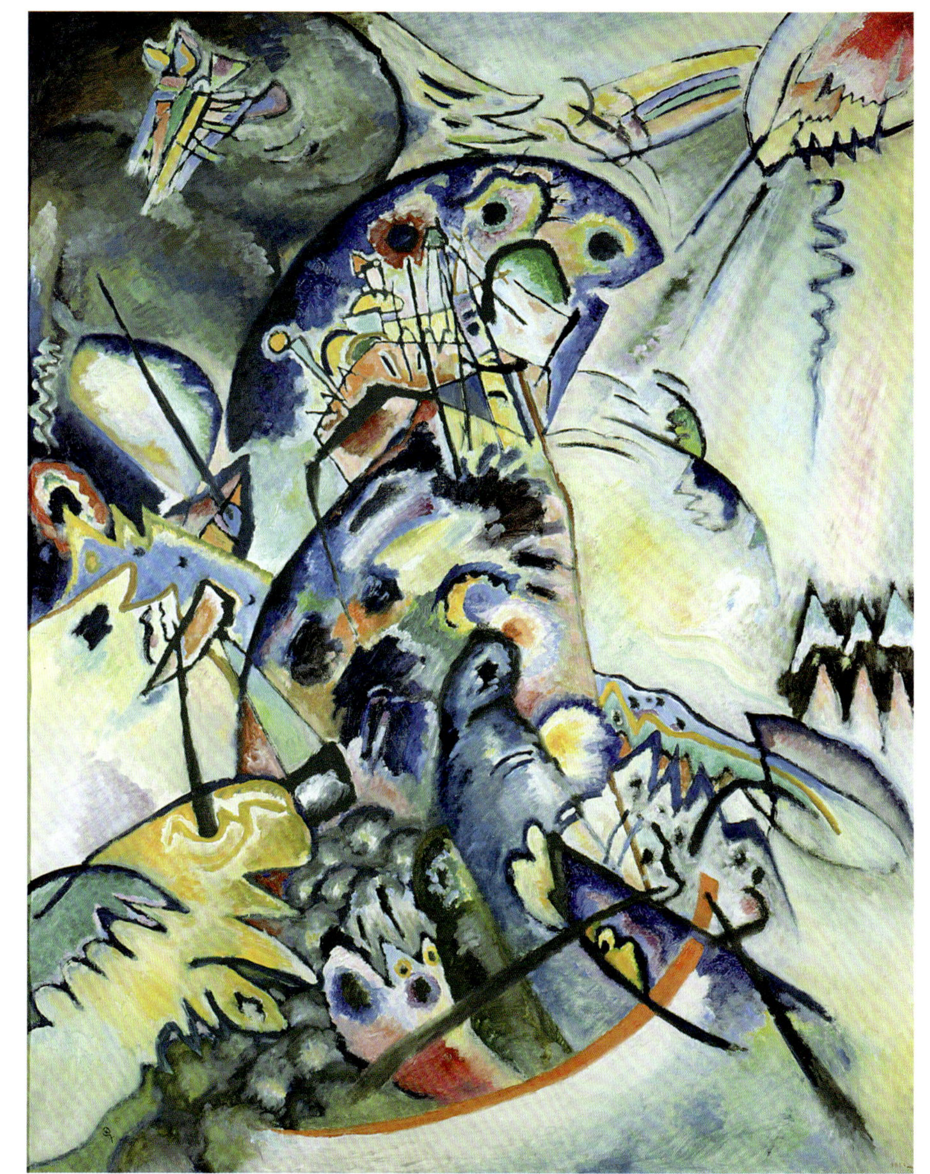

Blue Comb
La Crête bleue
Blauer Kamm
Peine azul
Pettine blu
Blauwe kam

*1917, Oil on canvas/
Huile sur toile, 133 × 104 cm,
State Russian Museum,
St. Petersburg*

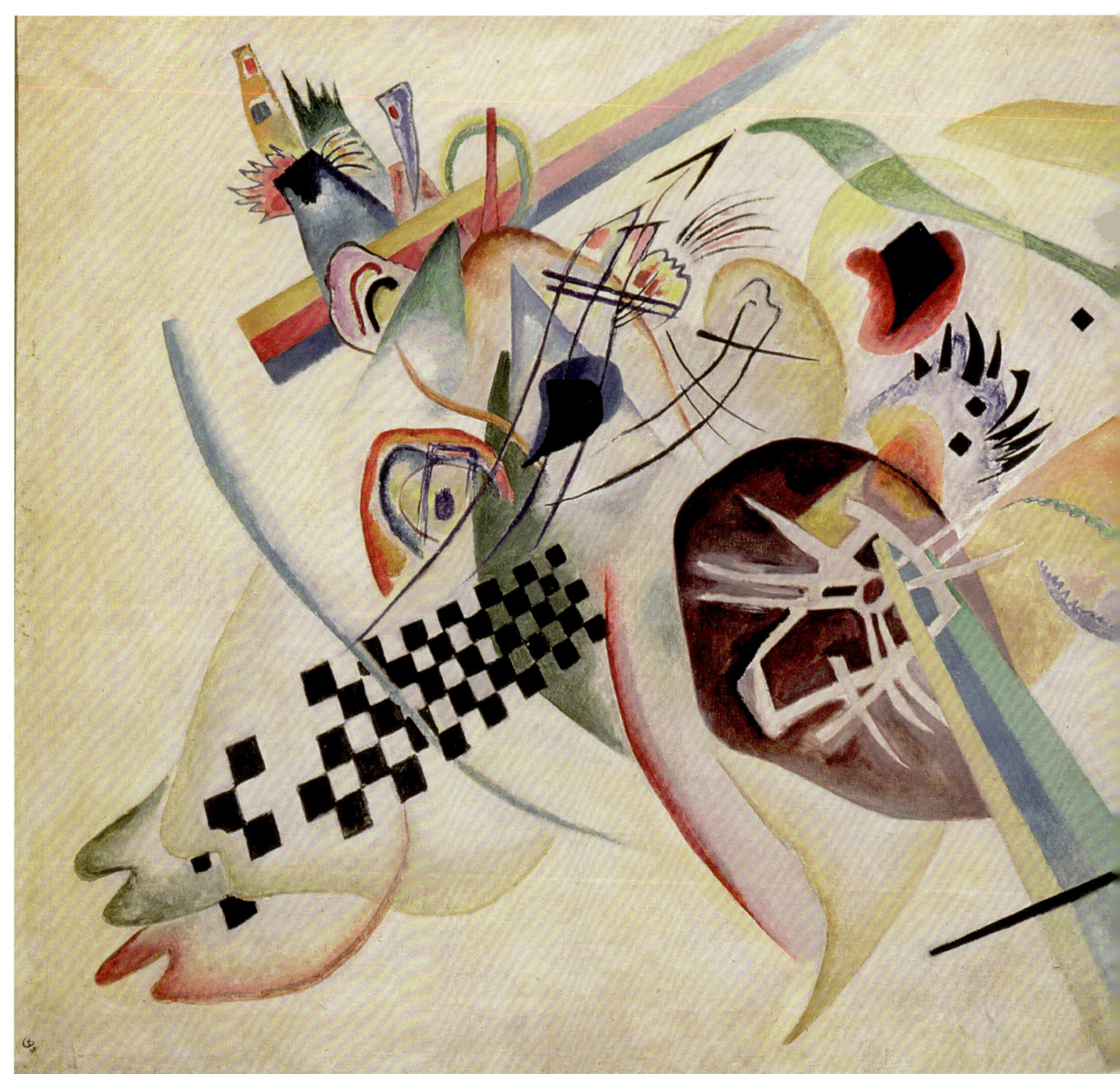

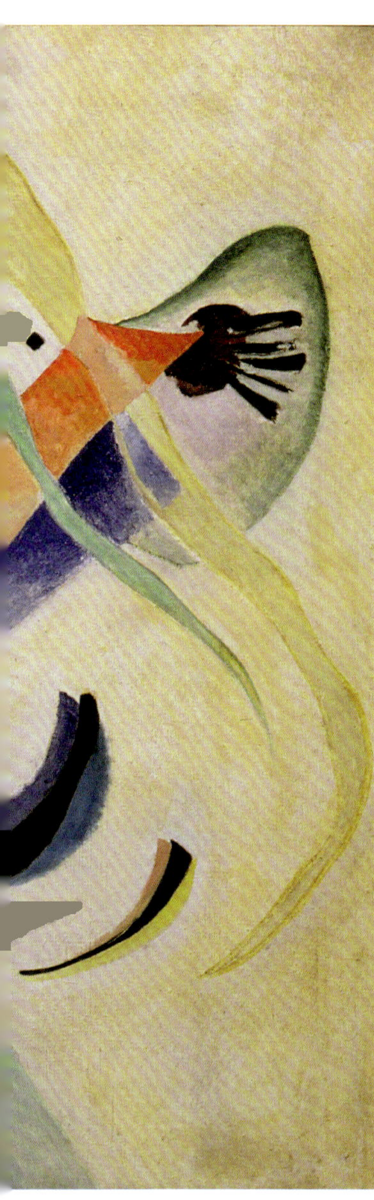

Composition 224

Composition 224 - Sur fond blanc

Komposition 224

Composición 224

Composizione 224

Compositie 224

1920, Oil on canvas/Huile sur toile, 95 × 138 cm,
State Russian Museum, St. Petersburg

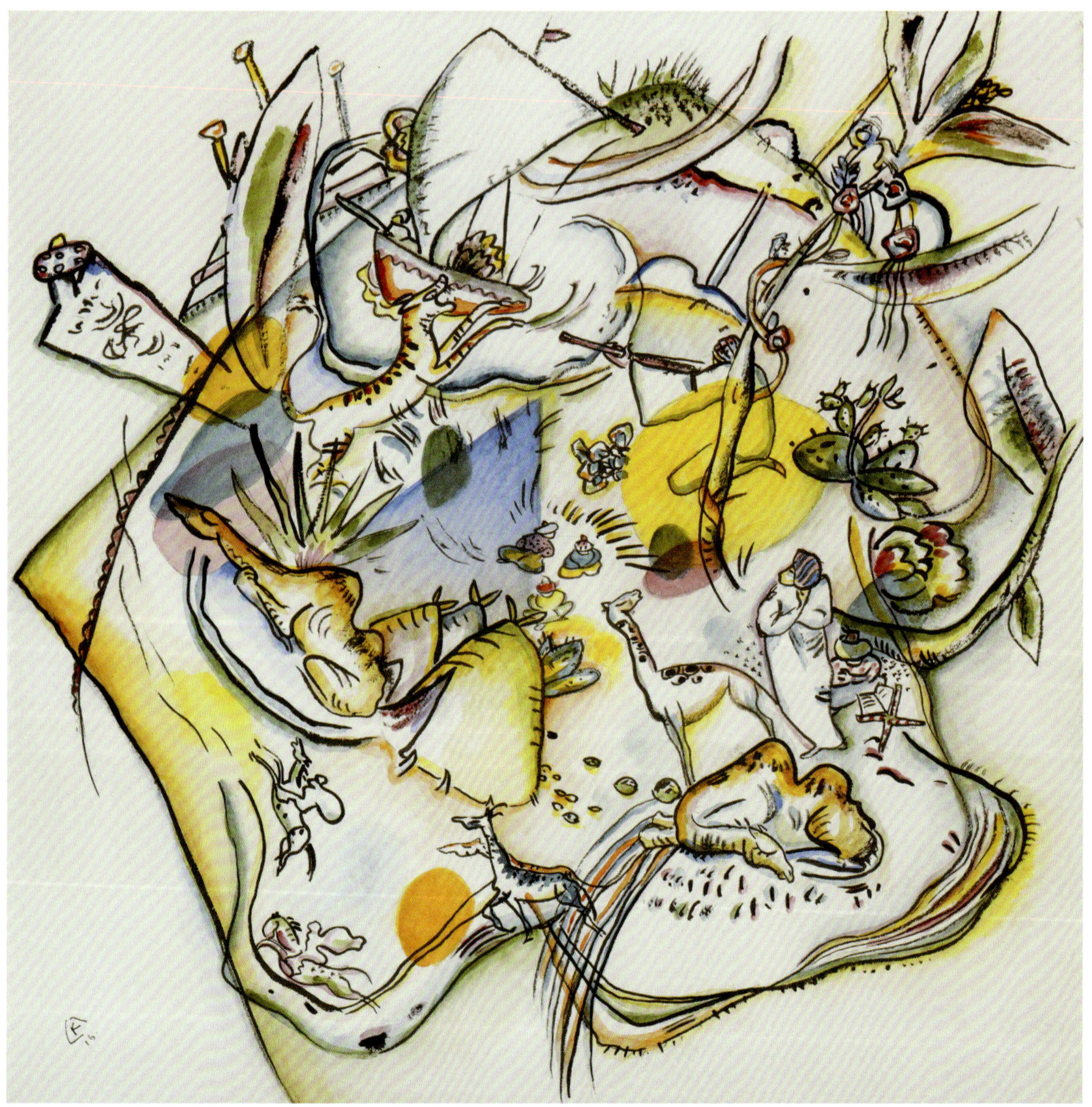

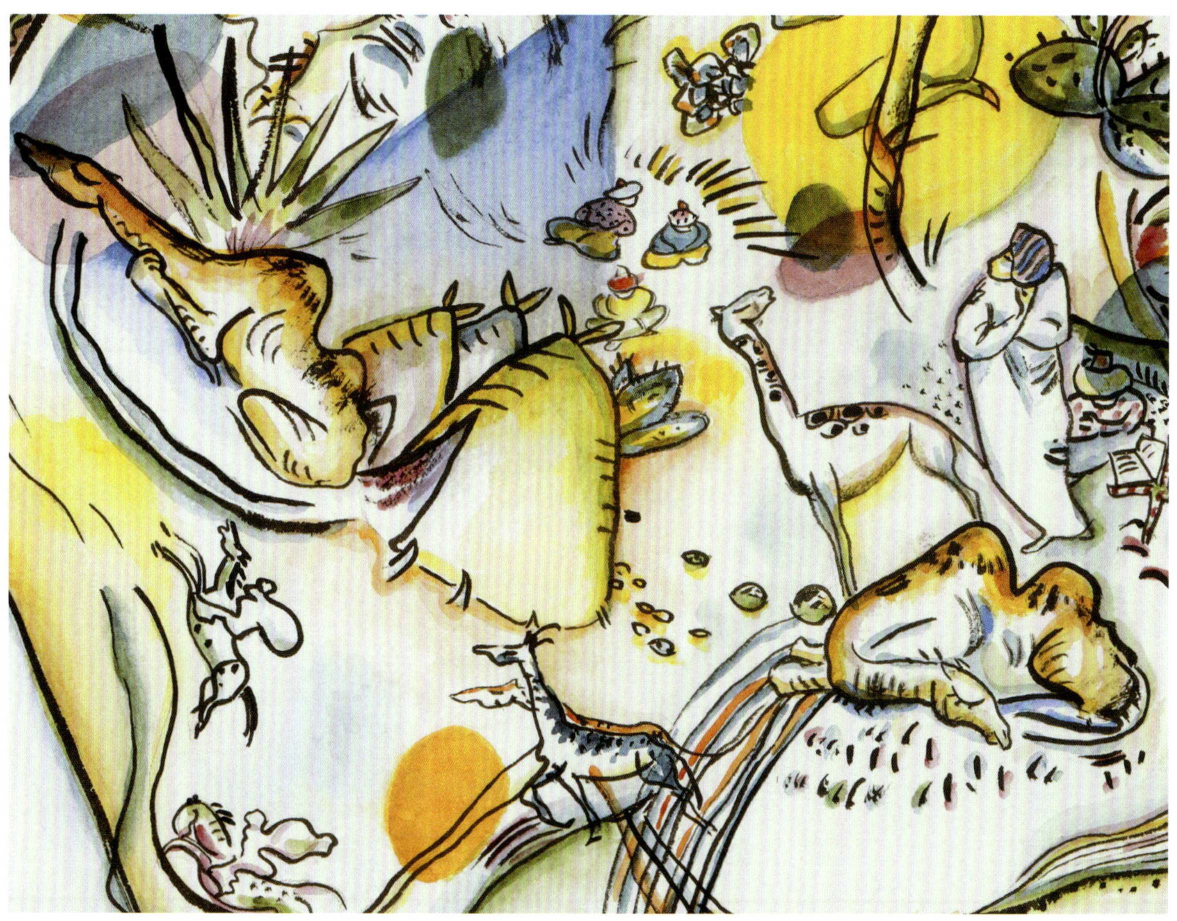

Africa

Afrique

Afrika

África

Africa

Afrika

*1916, Watercolor and ink on paper/Aquarelle et encre de Chine sur papier,
34,2 × 34,2 cm, Private collection*

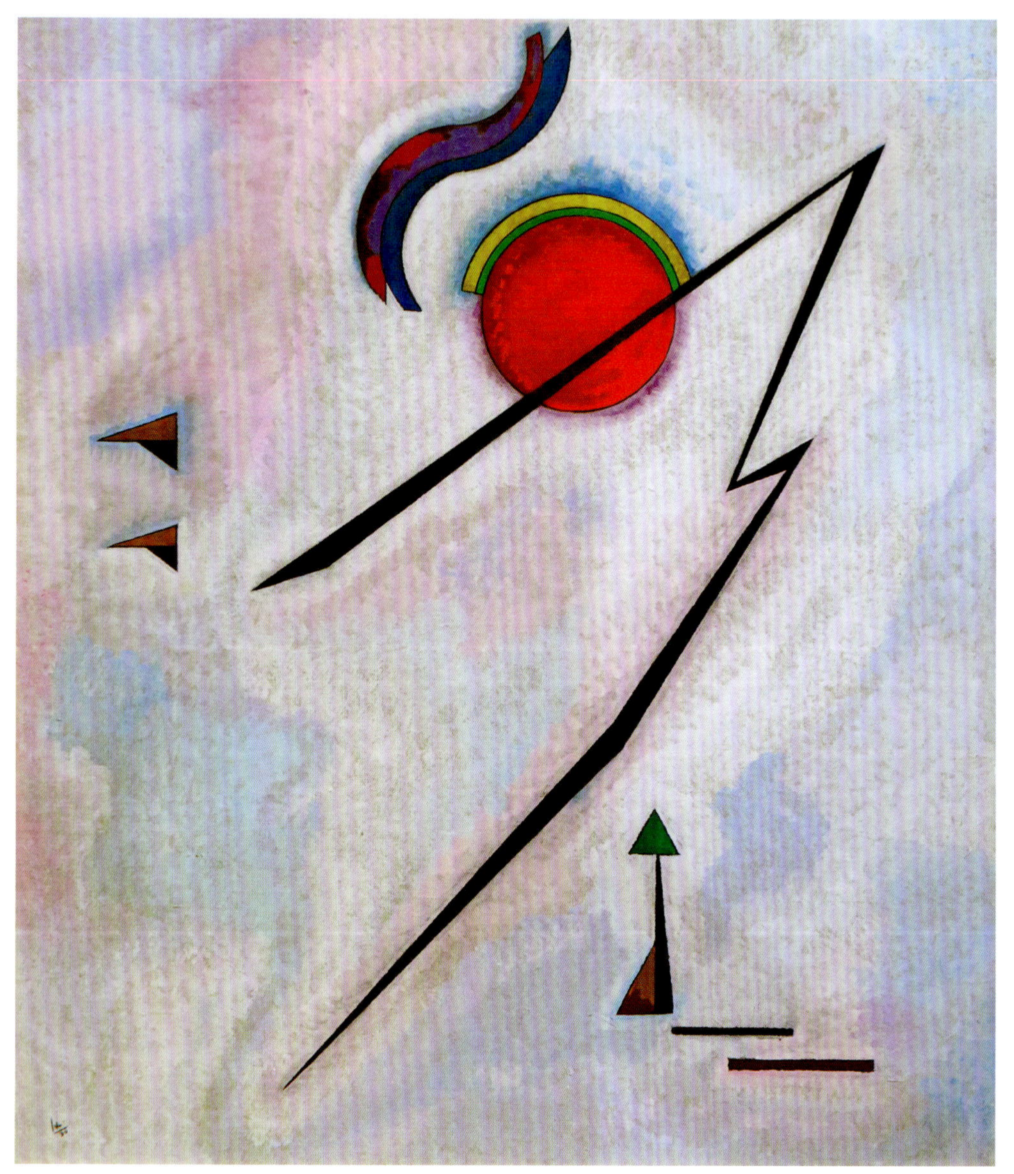

Angular Line
Ligne anguleuse
Gewinkelte Linie
Línea angular
Linea angolare
Gehoekte lijn

1930, Oil on canvas/
Huile sur toile,
70 × 60 cm,
Galleria Nazionale
d'Arte Moderna,
Rome

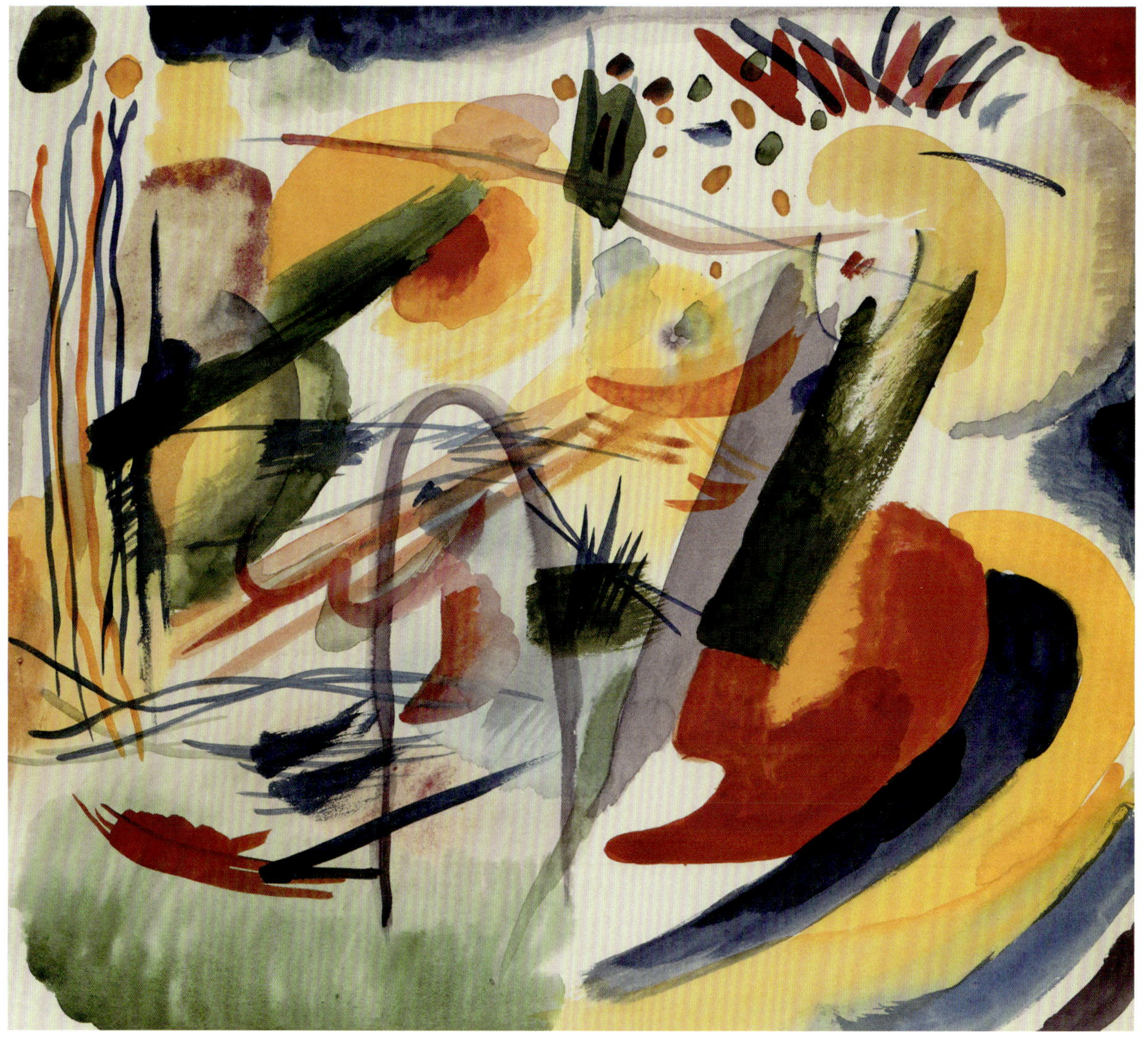

Untitled   **Ohne Titel**   **Senza titolo**

Sans titre   **Sin título**   **Zonder titel**

1912 – 13, Watercolor on paper/Aquarelle sur papier, 35,7 × 39,7 cm, Private collection

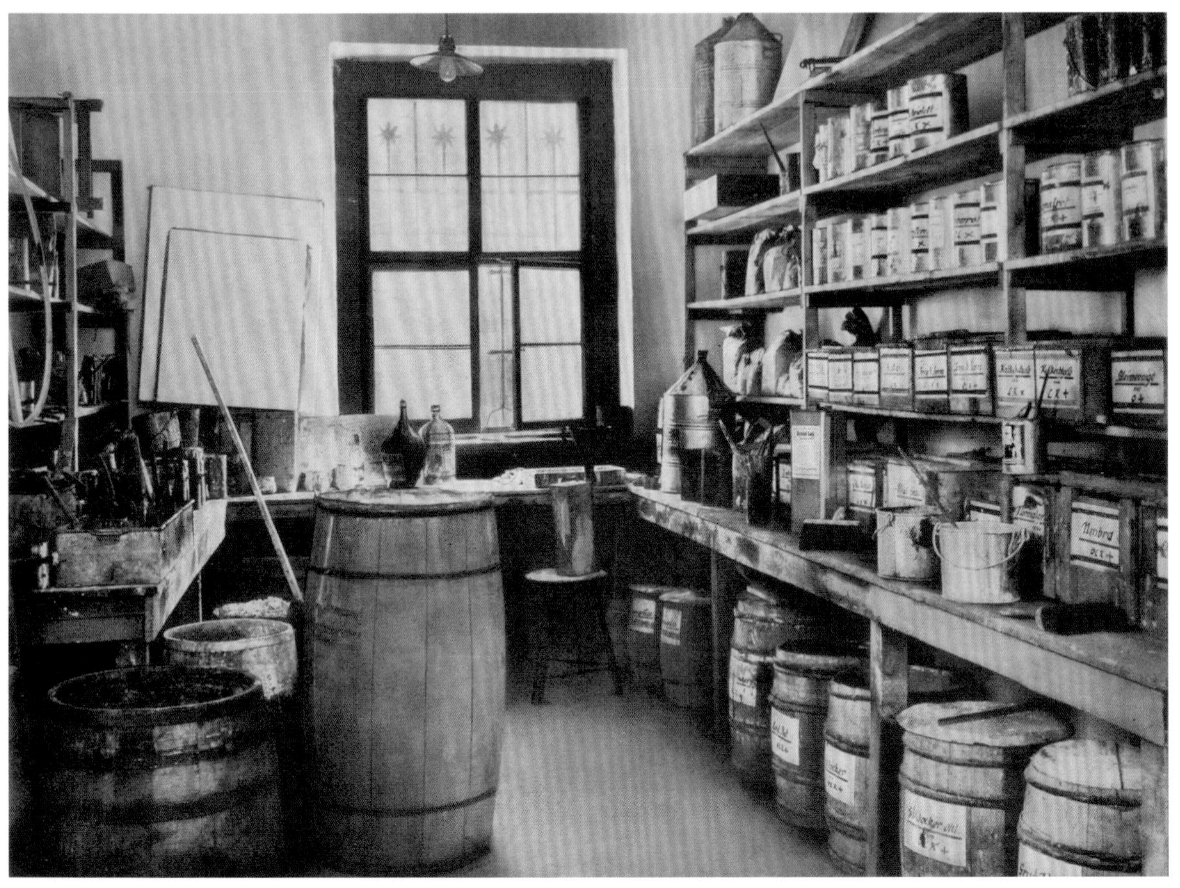

Kandinsky decided to return to Germany where he had to start again, almost from scratch, in Berlin. He was happy, therefore, to take up the offer from Walter Gropius (1883–1969), founder of the Bauhaus Weimar, to head the mural workshop in Weimar from 1922.

Kandinsky décide finalement de retourner en Allemagne – où il doit presque repartir de zéro à Berlin. Il n'en est que plus enclin à accepter l'offre de Walter Gropius (1883–1969), fondateur de l'école d'État du Bauhaus à Weimar, dans laquelle il va diriger l'atelier de fresque murale à partir de 1922.

Kandinsky beschließt nach Deutschland zurückzukehren, wo er in Berlin fast wieder bei Null anfangen muss. Nur zu gerne folgt er daher dem Angebot von Walter Gropius (1883–1969), dem Gründer des Staatlichen Bauhauses Weimar, und leitet ab 1922 die dortige Werkstatt für Wandmalerei.

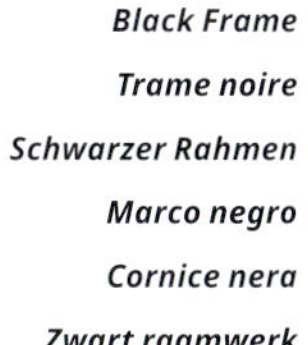

Kandinsky decide regresar a Alemania, donde tuvo que volver a empezar prácticamente desde cero, en Berlín. Le alegró por lo tanto aceptar la oferta de Walter Gropius (1883–1969), fundador de la Bauhaus Weimar, para encabezar el taller mural en Weimar a partir de 1922.

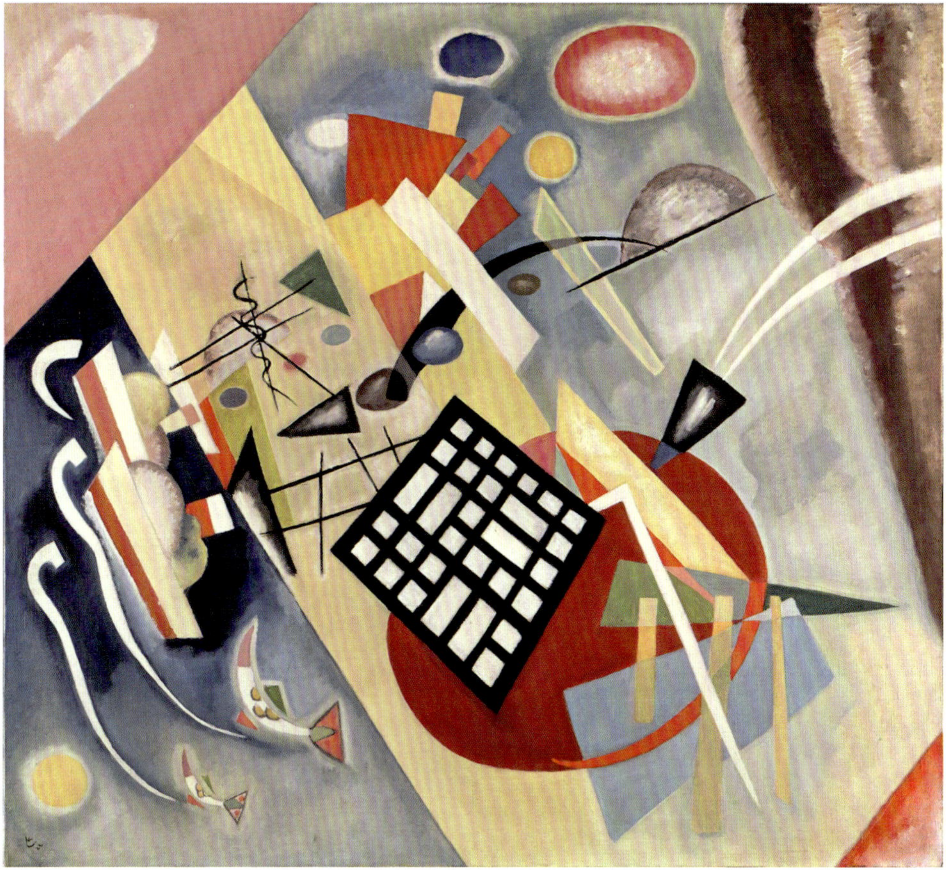

Kandinsky decise infine di tornare in Germania, dove dovette ricominciare, quasi da zero, a Berlino. Fu dunque felice di accettare l'offerta di Walter Gropius (1883–1969), fondatore del Bauhaus di Weimar, di dirigere il laboratorio murale di questa città tedesca dal 1922.

Kandinsky besluit naar Duitsland terug te keren, waar hij in Berlijn vrijwel helemaal opnieuw moet beginnen. Hij gaat daarom maar al te graag in op het aanbod van Walter Gropius (1883–1969), grondlegger van het Staatliche Bauhaus in Weimar, en leidt vanaf 1922 het Bauhaus-atelier voor muurschilderkunst.

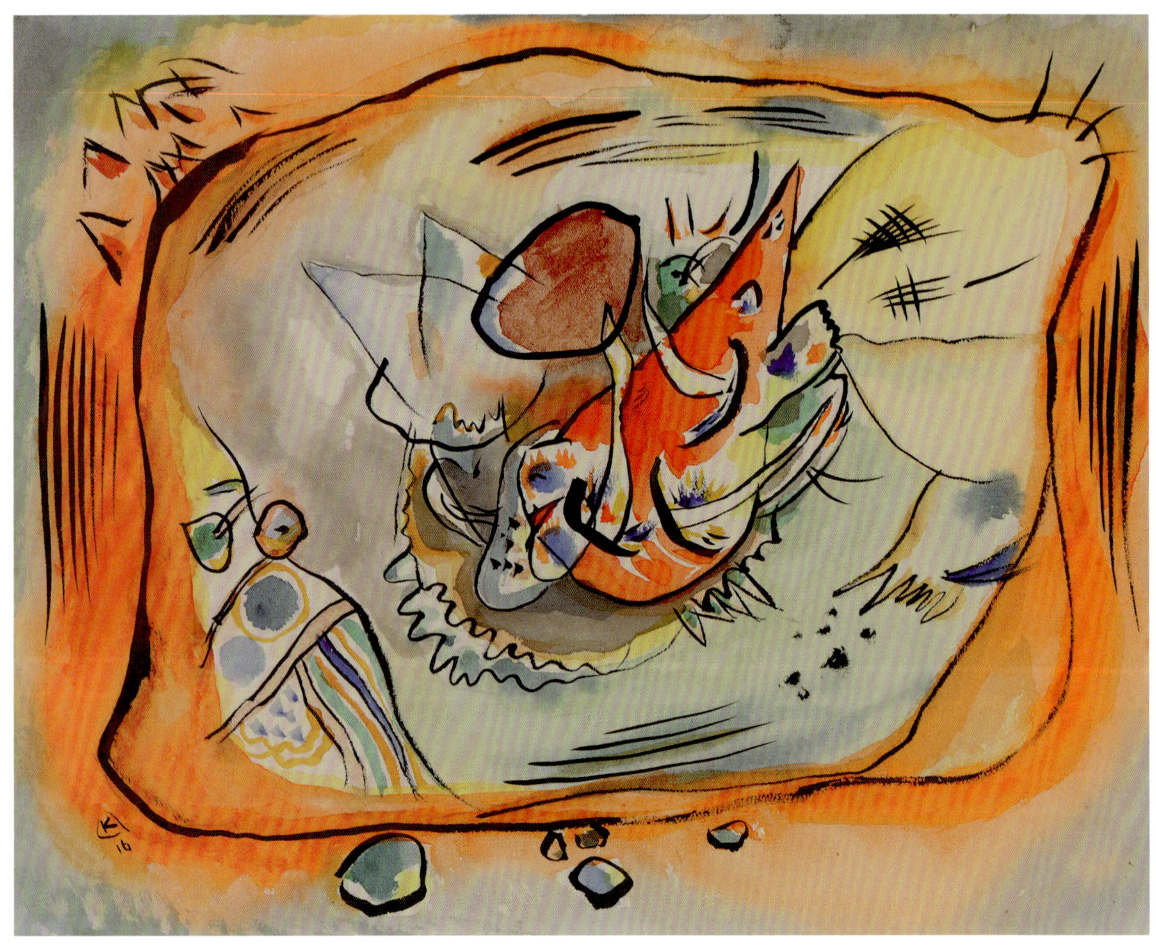

Sketch for **Painting with Orange Border**

Etude pour **Peinture au bord orange**

Skizze für **Bild mit orangenem Rand**

Boceto para **la pintura con borde naranja**

Schizzo per **Dipinto con bordo arancione**

Schets voor **Schilderij met oranje rand**

1916, Watercolor and ink on paper/Aquarelle et encre de Chine sur papier, 23 × 28,6 cm, Private collection

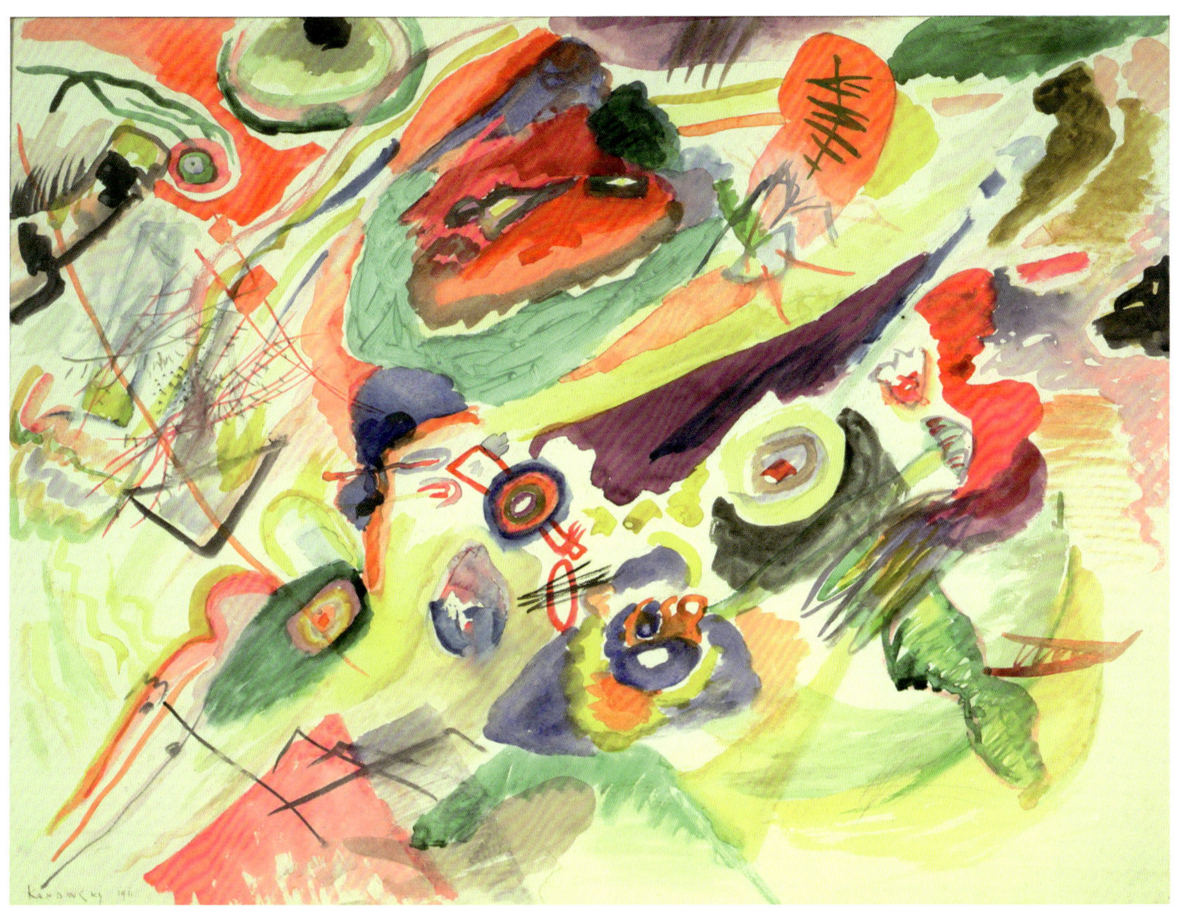

Watercolor with a Red Stain   **Aquarell mit rotem Fleck**   **Acquerello con macchia rossa**

Aquarelle avec tache rouge   **Acuarela con una mancha roja**   **Aquarel met rode vlek**

1911, Watercolor/Aquarelle, 48,3 × 63,5 cm, Private collection

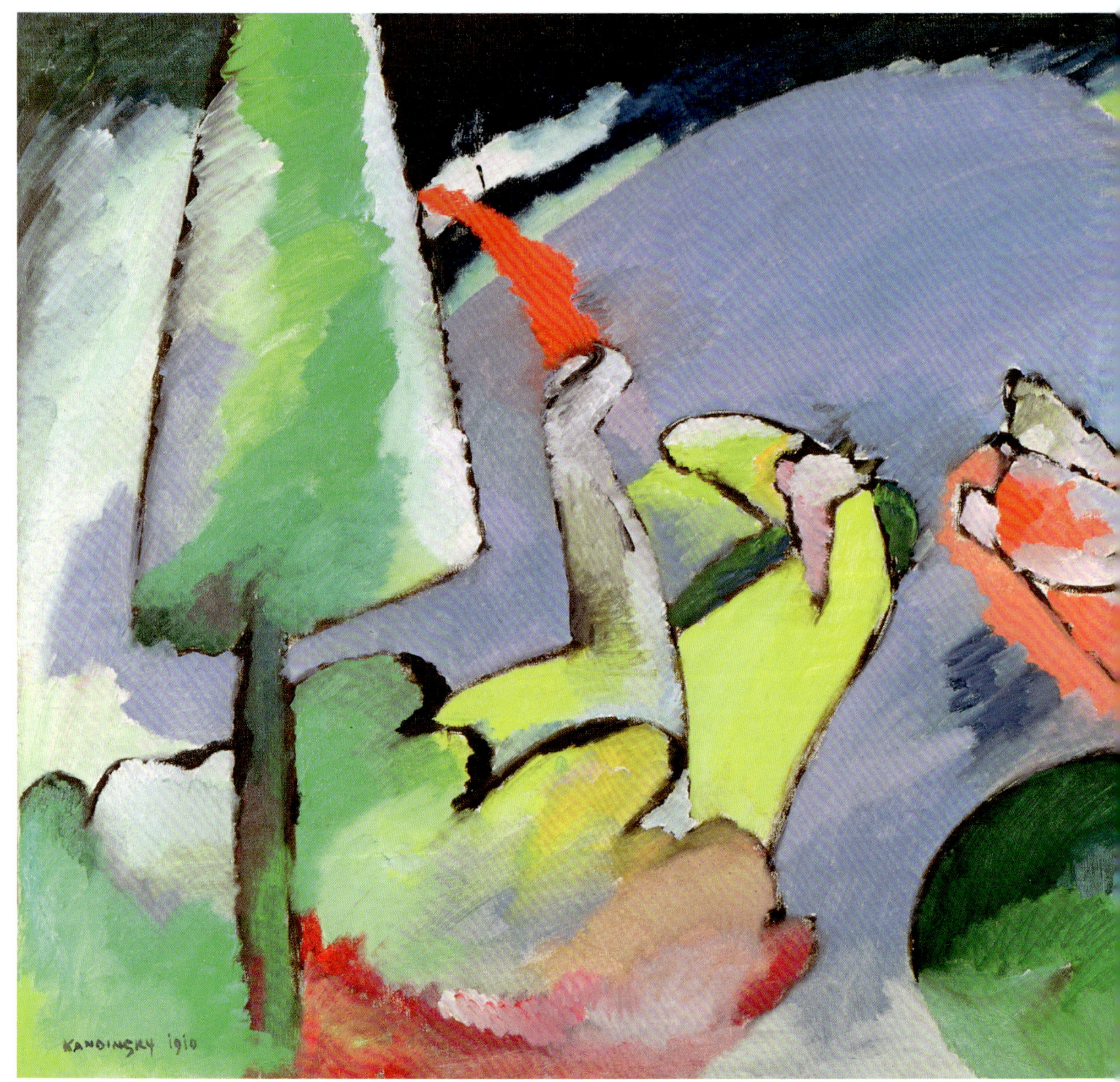

KANDINSKY 1910

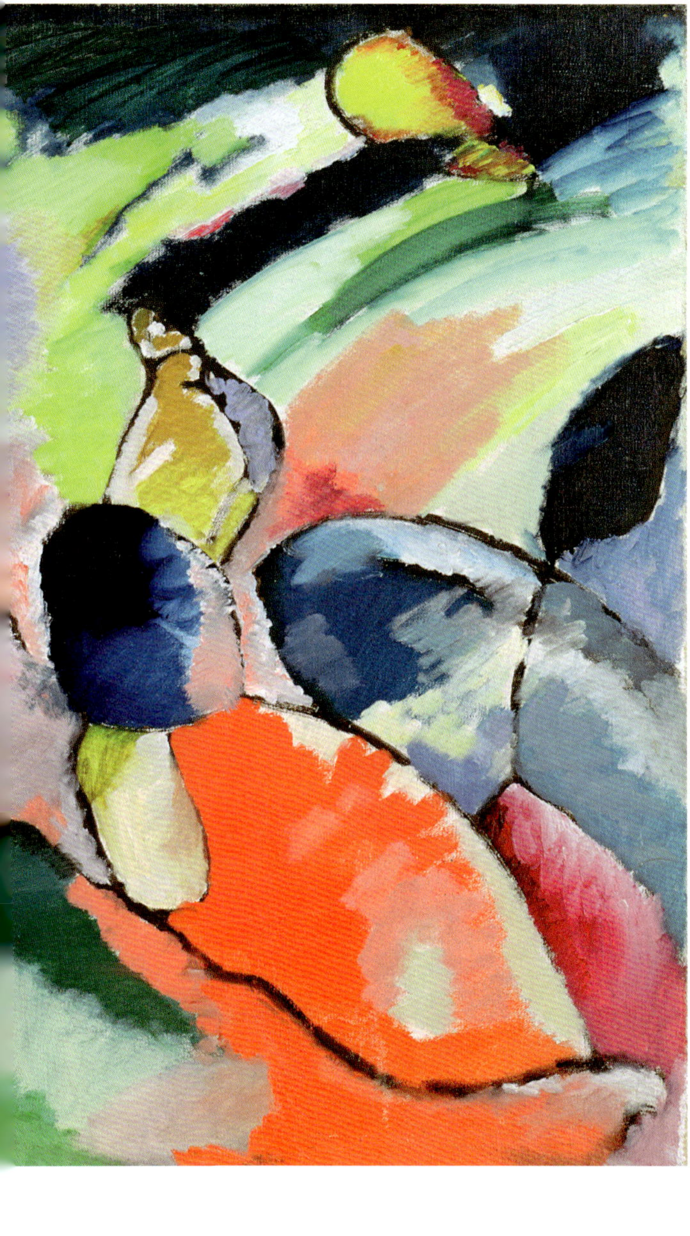

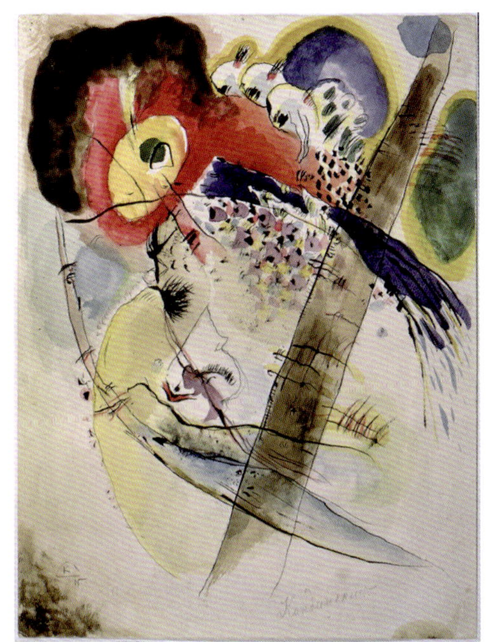

Birds of Paradise

Oiseaux exotiques

Exotische Vögel

Aves del paraíso

Uccelli del Paradiso

Exotische vogels

*1915, Watercolor on paper/Aquarelle sur papier,
Pushkin Museum, Moscow*

Improvisation 14

Improvisation 14

Improvisation 14

Improvisación 14

Improvvisazione 14

Improvisatie 14

*1910, Oil on canvas/Huile sur toile, 74 × 125,5 cm,
Musée National d'Art Moderne, Centre Pompidou, Paris*

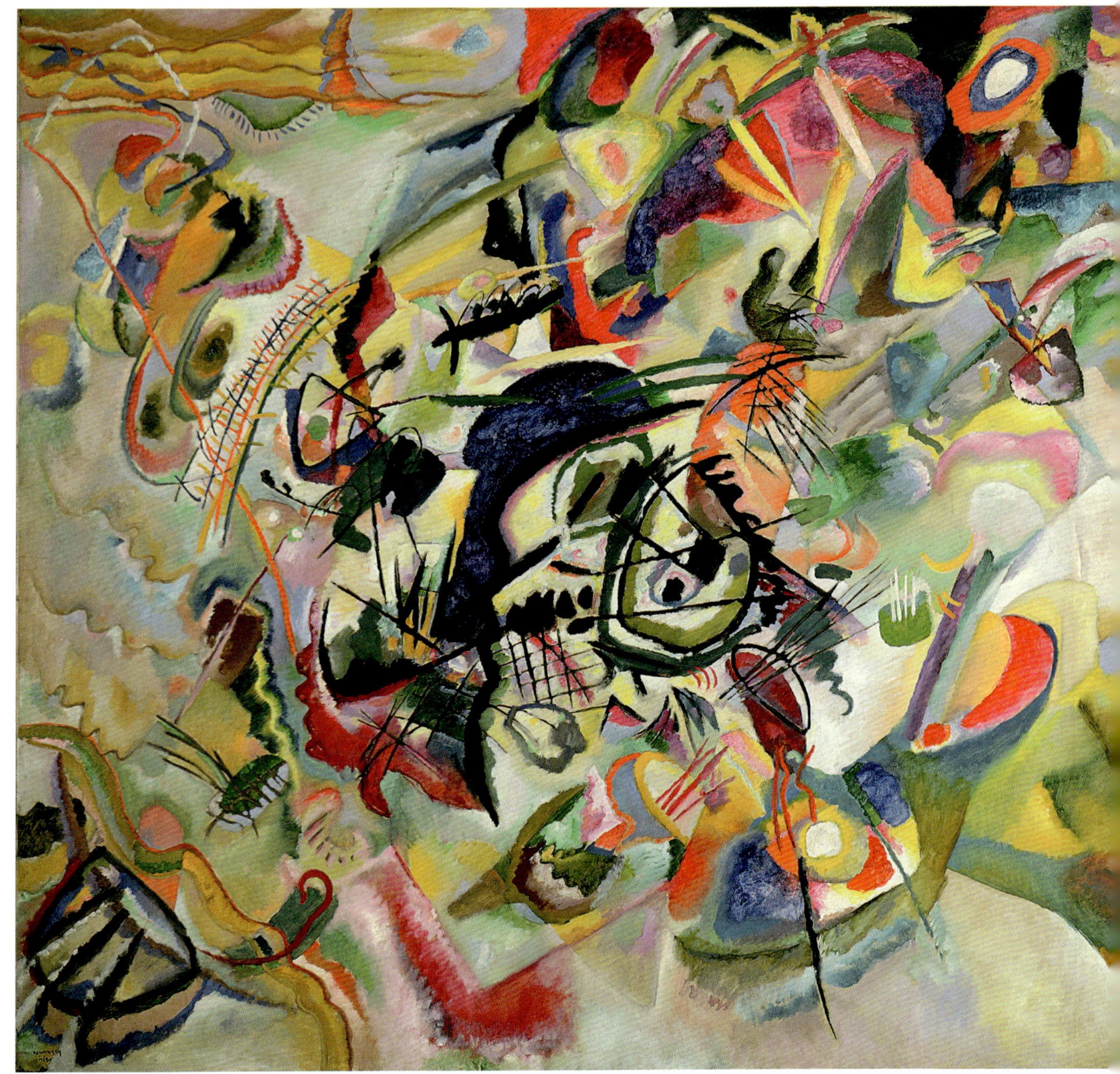

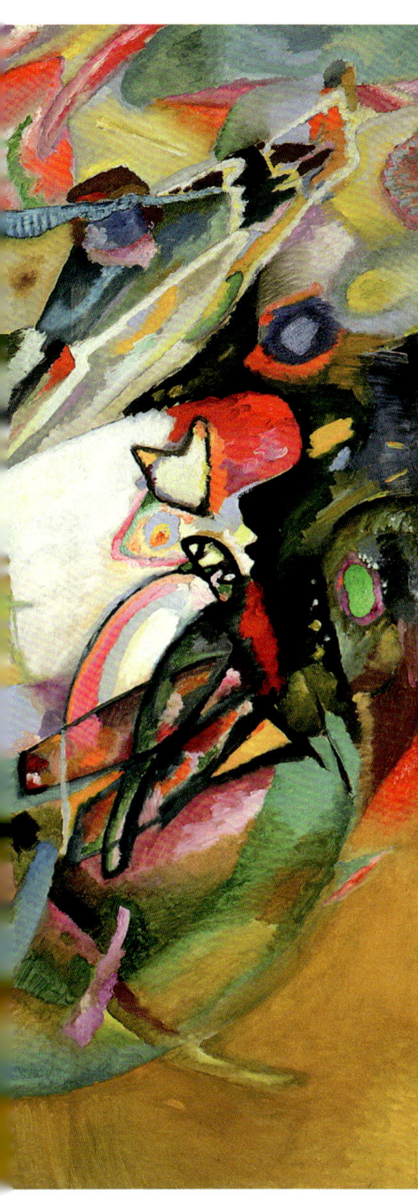

Composition 7

Composition 7

Komposition 7

Composición 7

Composizione 7

Compositie 7

1913, Oil on canvas/Huile sur toile, 200 × 300 cm, Tretyakov Gallery, Moscow

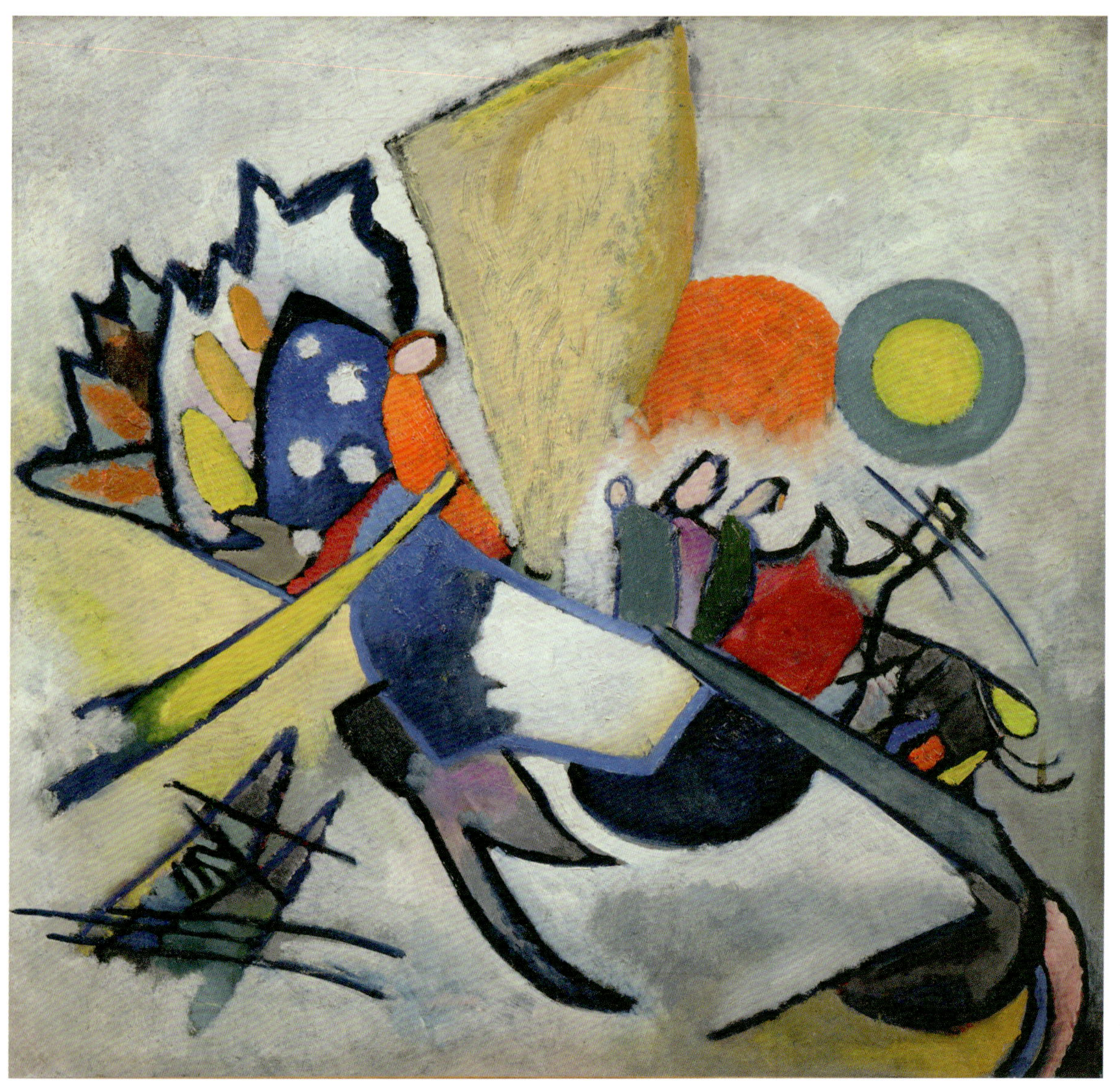

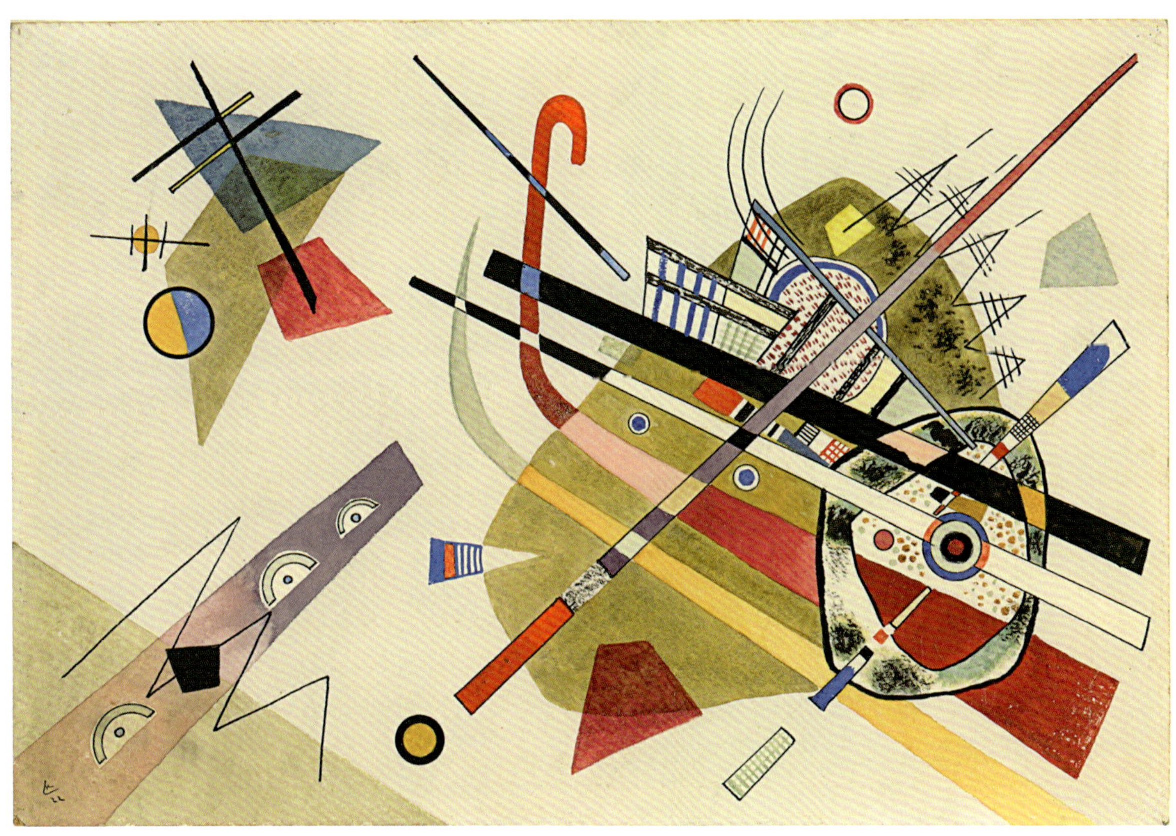

Improvisation 209

Improvisation 209

Improvisatlon 209

Improvisación 209

Improvvisazione 209

Improvisatie 209

Untitled

Sans titre

Ohne Titel

Sin título

Senza titolo

Zonder titel

1917, Oil on canvas/Huile sur toile,
State V.I Surikov Art Museum, Krasnoyarsk

1922, Watercolor and ink on paper/Aquarelle et encre de Chine sur papier,
33 × 46,9 cm, Private collection

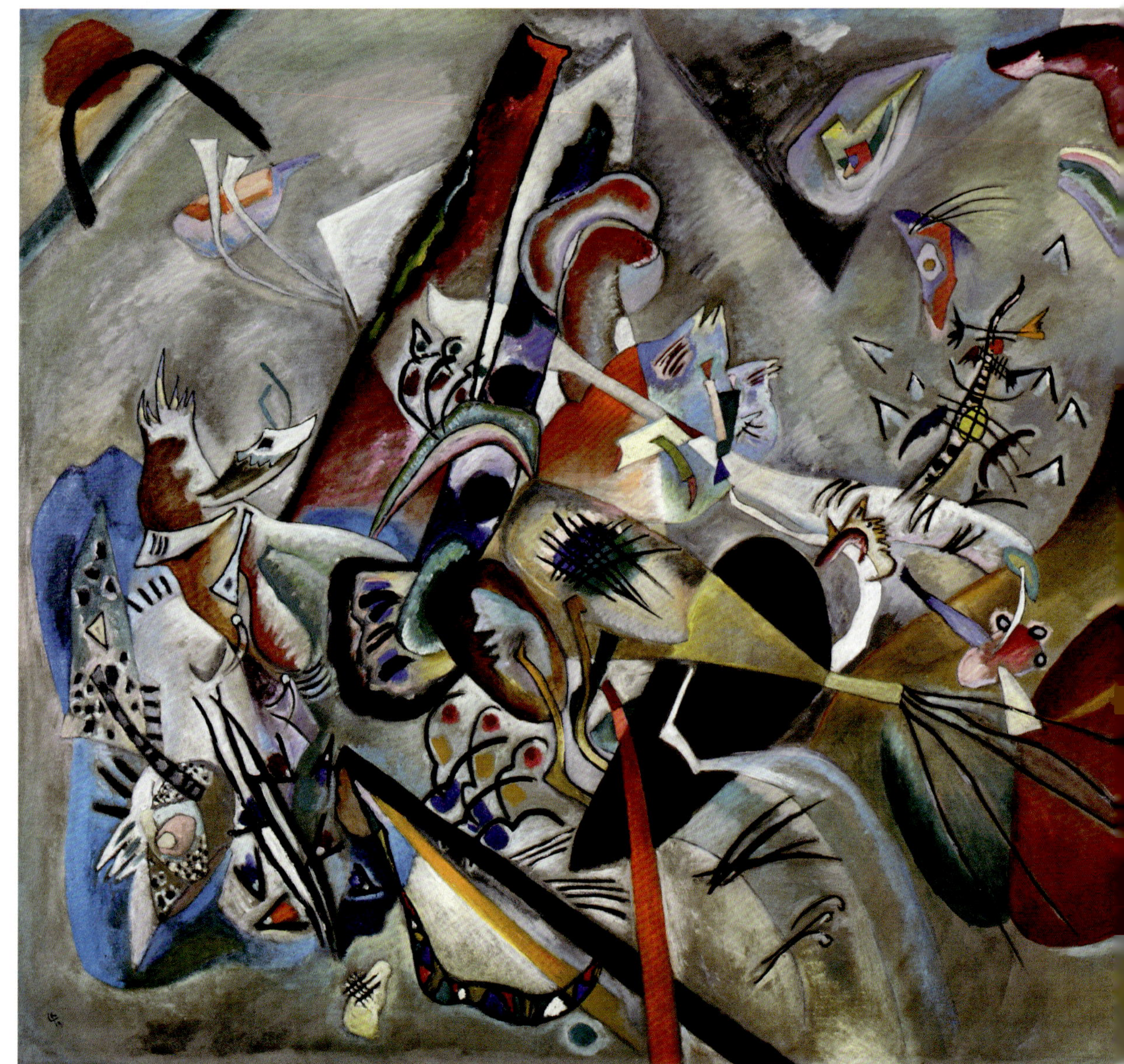

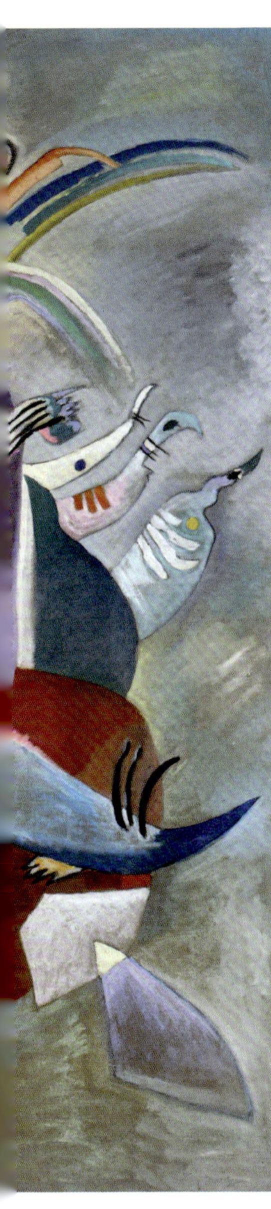

In Gray

Dans le gris

Im Grau

En gris

Nel grigio

In grijs

1919, Oil on canvas/Huile sur toile, 129 × 176 cm, Musee National d'Art Moderne, Centre Pompidou, Paris

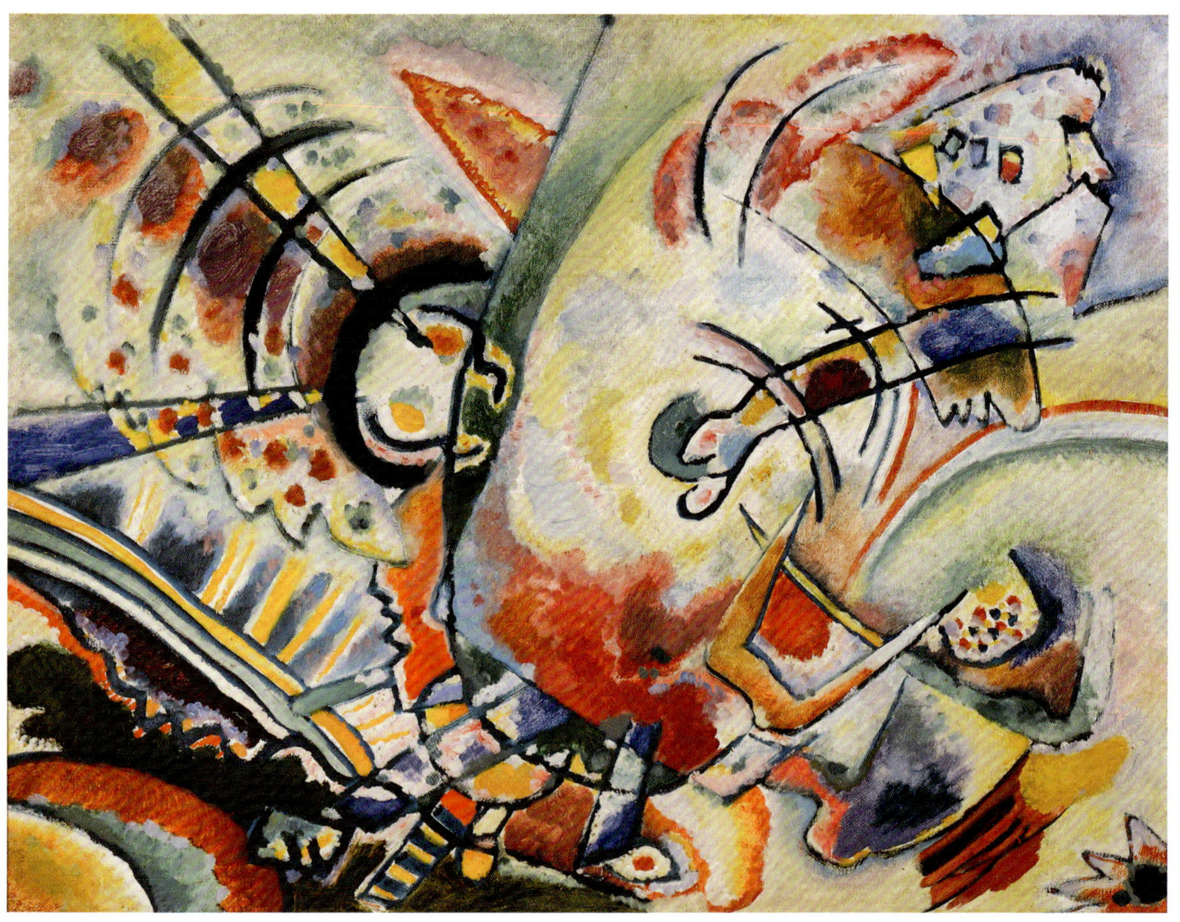

Non-objective

Non-objectif

Ungegenständlich

No-objetivo

Non obiettivo

Niet-figuratief

1910, Oil on canvas/Huile sur toile, 65 × 81 cm, Art Museum A.W.Lunascharski, Krasnodar

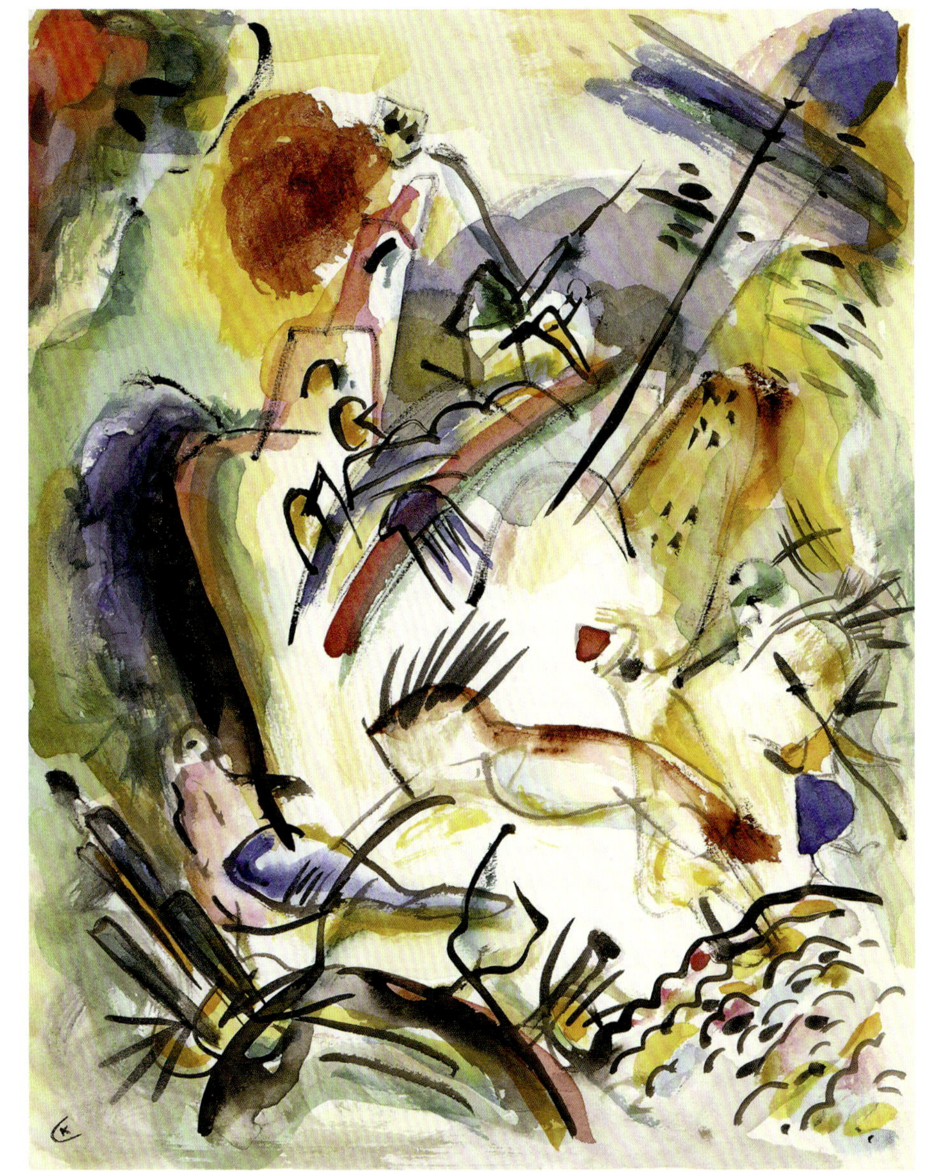

Untitled

Sans titre

Ohne Titel

Sin título

Senza titolo

Zonder titel

1915-17, Watercolor and ink on paper/Aquarelle et encre de Chine sur papier, 29 × 22,8 cm, Private collection

c. 1920, b/w photograph/Photographie, Private collection

(L-R : Josef Albers, Hinnerk Scheper, Georg Muche, Laslo Moholy Nagy, Herbert Bayer, Joost Schmidt, Walter Gropius, Marcel Breuer, Wassily Kandinsky, Paul Klee, Lyonel Feininger, Gunta Stozl and Oskar Schlemmer on the roof of the Bauhaus in Weimar)

Point and Line to Plane: Kandinsky at the Bauhaus
The first few years at the Bauhaus were characterized by the post-war conditions of student poverty and the lack of materials, which required a high degree of improvisation and with the shortages being compensated for by lofty idealism. A particularly good example of this would be Johannes Itten (1888–1967), who led the famous "Preliminary Course".

Point et ligne sur plan : Kandinsky au Bauhaus
Les premières années du Bauhaus sont encore marquées par les difficultés de l'après-guerre : pauvreté des étudiants, manque de matériels, talents d'improvisation indispensables. Ces pénuries sont toutefois compensées par la force de l'idéalisme. L'exemple archétypique en est avant tout le Suisse Johannes Itten (1888-1967), directeur du Cours préparatoire (Vorkurs).

Punkt und Linie zu Fläche: Kandinsky am Bauhaus
Die ersten Jahre am Bauhaus sind noch sehr von der nachkriegsbedingten Armut der Studenten, dem fehlenden Material und dem daher geforderten Improvisationstalent geprägt. Der Mangel wird aber durch einen hohen Idealismus wieder wettgemacht. Beispielhaftes Vorbild ist vor allem Johannes Itten (1888–1967), der den berühmten „Vorkurs" leitete.

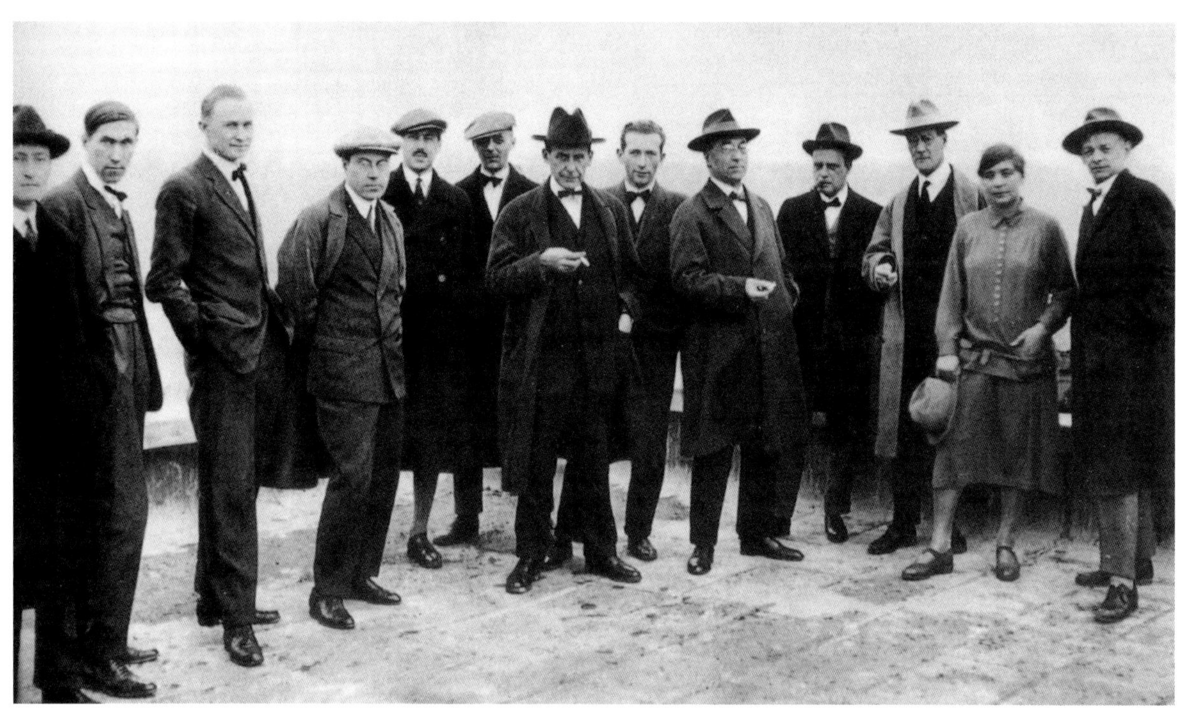

Punto y línea a plano: Kandinsky en la Bauhaus

Los primeros años de la Bauhaus se caracterizaron por las condiciones de postguerra, la pobreza de los estudiantes y la falta de materiales, que exigían un alto grado de improvisación y la necesidad de compensar la escasez con altas dosis de idealismo. Un ejemplo especialmente bueno sería Johannes Itten (1888–1967), quien dirigió el famoso "Curso preliminar".

Punto, linea, superficie: Kandinsky al Bauhaus

I primi anni al Bauhaus furono caratterizzati dalla scarsità di studenti e di materiali dovuta al dopoguerra, che richiese un elevato grado di improvvisazione e la compensazione della penuria mediante un nobile idealismo. Un ottimo esempio è rappresentato da Johannes Itten (1888-1967), che teneva il famoso «Corso preliminare».

Punt en lijn tot vlak: Kandinsky aan het Bauhaus

De eerste jaren aan het Bauhaus worden, zo kort na de Eerste Wereldoorlog, bepaald door de armoedige situatie waarin de studenten verkeren, het gebrek aan kunstenaarsbenodigdheden en het daardoor vereiste improvisatievermogen van alle betrokkenen. De tekorten worden echter gecompenseerd door een grote dosis idealisme. Een goed voorbeeld daarvan is Johannes Itten (1888–1967), leider van de befaamde 'Inleidingscursus'.

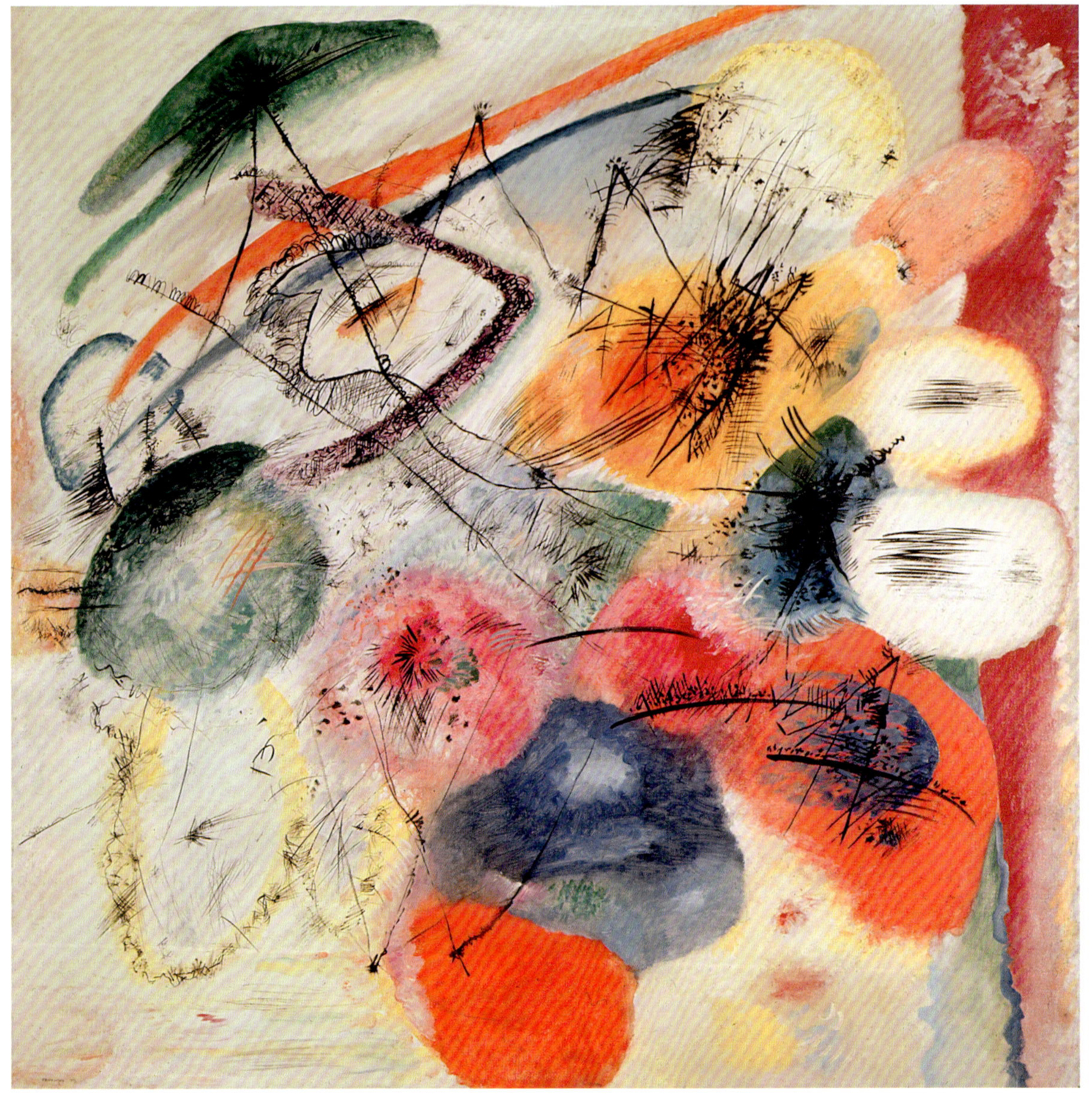

Black Lines I

Lignes noirs I

Schwarze Striche I

Líneas de negro I

Linee nere I

Zwarte strepen I

*1913, Oil on canvas/Huile sur toile, 129,4 × 131 cm,
Solomon R. Guggenheim Museum, New York*

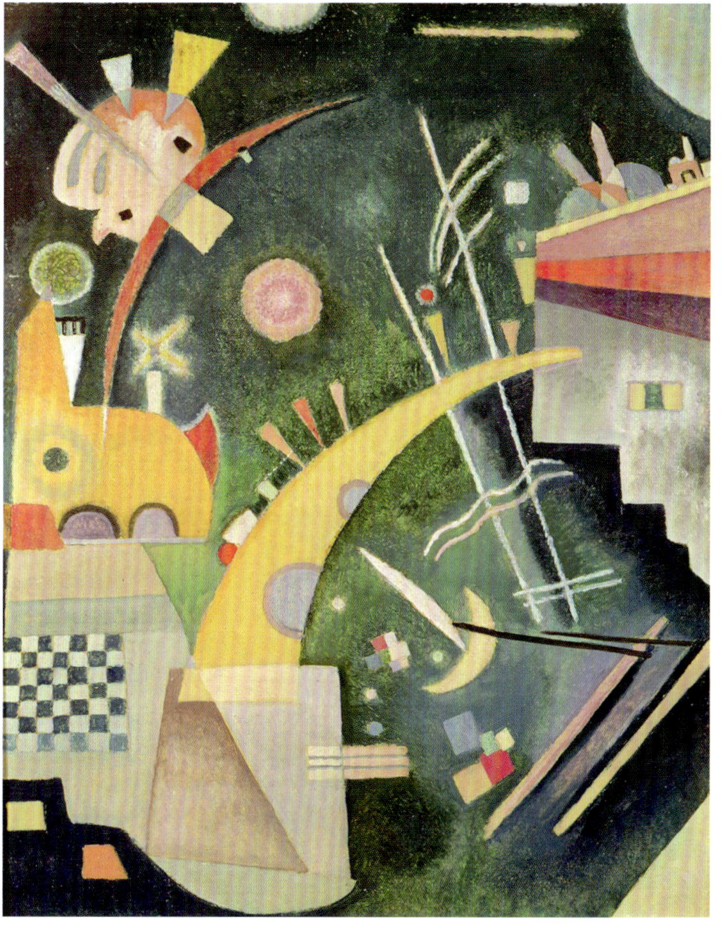

Hornform

Hornform (Forme de corne)

Hornform

Hornform

Forma di corno

Hoornvorm

1924, Oil on canvas/Huile sur toile, 57,5 × 49,5 cm, Nationalgalerie, Berlin

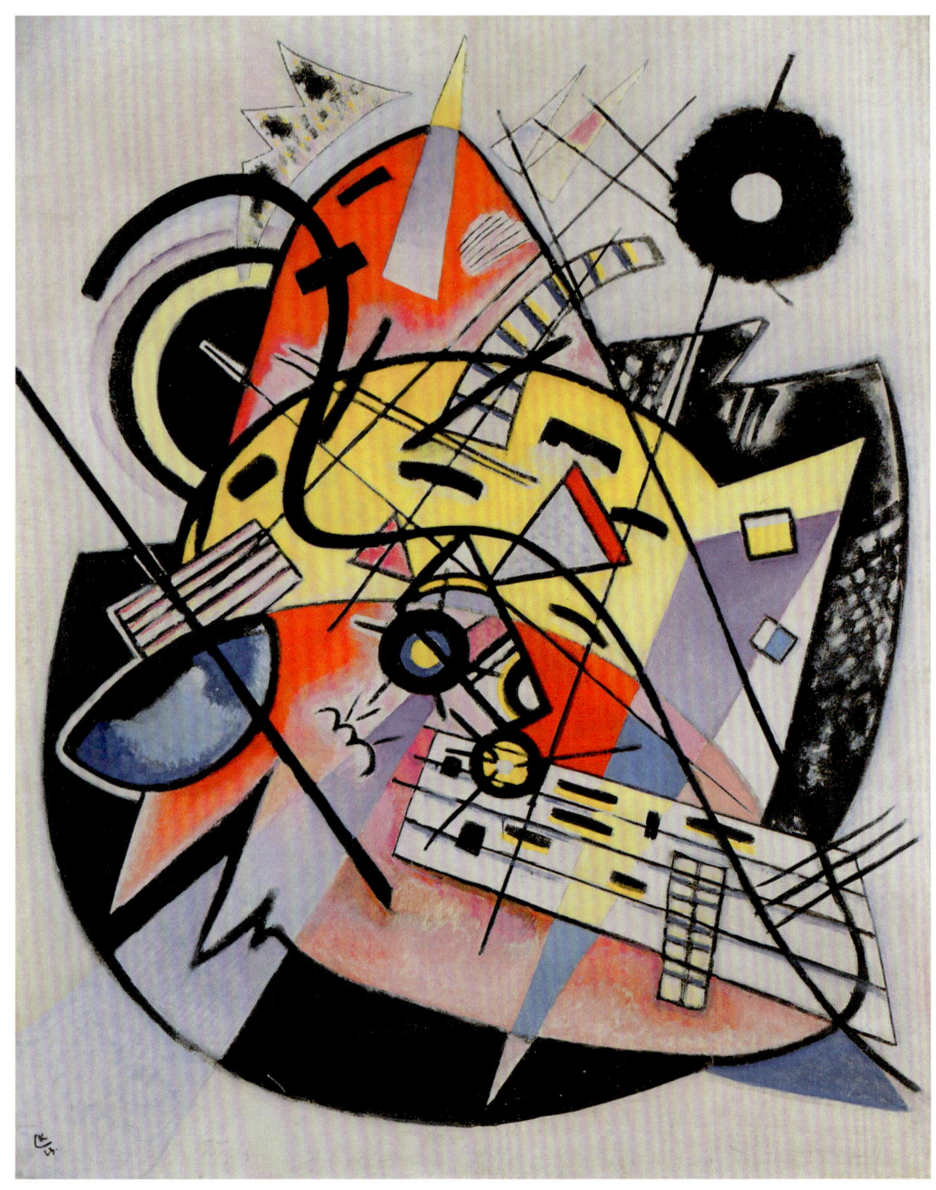

White Point

**Point blanc
(Composition 248)**

Weißer Punkt

Punto blanco

Punto bianco

Witte punt

*1923, Oil on canvas/Huile
sur toile, 91,5 × 73,3 cm,
Hamburger Kunsthalle,
Hamburg*

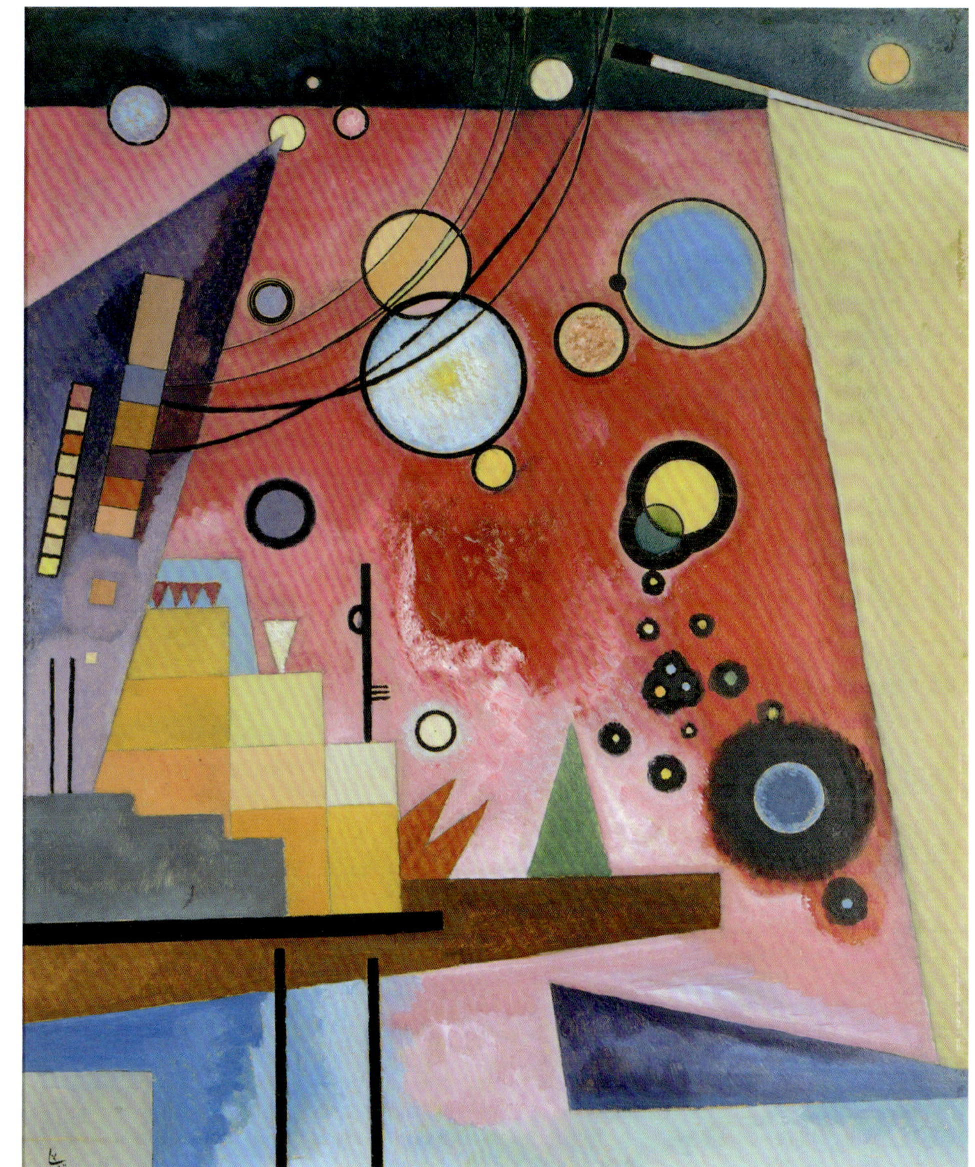

Heavy Red
Rouge pesant
Schweres Rot
Rojo pesado
Rosso pesante
Zwaar rood

1924, Oil on canvas/
Huile sur carton,
58,7 × 48,7 cm
Kunstmuseum, Basel

Preliminary Course

In the Preliminary Course conceived by Johannes Itten, the students did not acquire any drawing skills but took a foundation course in which they made creative experiments with different materials. In this way, they could assess their abilities and talents, allowing them to subsequently enter a suitable workshop. This preliminary course was later partially adopted by academies and colleges.

Kandinsky's teaching consisted of lectures on color and morphology, in which the basic forms were presented along with their fundamental psychological effects.

Cours préparatoire

Dans ce Vorkurs organisé par Johannes Itten, les étudiants n'acquéraient aucune capacité en dessin, mais suivaient une sorte de formation de base à l'aide d'expériences créatrices à partir des matériaux les plus divers. Ils devaient ainsi tester leurs talents et leurs capacités, avant d'intégrer les ateliers qui leur conviendraient le mieux. (Ce « Cours préparatoire » fut ensuite partiellement repris dans les universités et les écoles professionnelles supérieures.)

L'enseignement de Kandinsky comporte une doctrine des formes et des couleurs, dans laquelle les formes élémentaires sont également présentées dans leurs effets psychologiques fondamentaux.

Vorkurs

In dem von Johannes Itten eingerichteten Vorkurs erwarben die Studenten keine zeichnerischen Fähigkeiten, sondern machten in einer Art Grundlagenausbildung gestalterische Experimente mit unterschiedlichsten Materialien. So sollten sie ihre Fähigkeiten und Talente erproben, um dann in die ihnen passende Werkstätte einzutreten. Dieser Vorkurs wurde später in Teilen auch an Akademien und Fachhochschulen übernommen.

Kandinskys Unterricht besteht aus einer Farb- und Formlehre, in der auch die Grundformen in ihren grundlegenden psychologischen Wirkungen vorgestellt werden.

Curso Preliminar

En el curso preliminar, concebido por Johannes Itten, los estudiantes no adquirían ninguna técnica de dibujo, sino que asistían a un curso básico en el que realizaban experimentos creativos con distintos materiales. De este modo, podían evaluar sus capacidades y talento, permitiéndoles acceder posteriormente al taller más adecuado. Este curso preliminar fue adoptado parcialmente más tarde por diversas academias y universidades.

Las enseñanzas de Kandinsky consistían en ponencias sobre el color y la morfología donde presentaba las formas básicas junto a sus efectos psicológicos fundamentales.

Il Corso preliminare

Nel Corso preliminare ideato da Johannes Itten, gli studenti non acquisivano alcuna abilità di disegno, ma avevano la possibilità di eseguire esperimenti creativi con materiali diversi. In questo modo, potevano valutare le proprie capacità e il proprio talento per scegliere successivamente il laboratorio più adatto a loro. Questo corso preliminare fu in seguito parzialmente adottato da accademie e università.

Kandinsky teneva lezioni incentrate sul colore e sulla morfologia, in cui le forme di base venivano presentate insieme ai loro effetti psicologici fondamentali.

Inleidingscursus

In de door Johannes Itten gegeven Inleidingscursus kregen de studenten geen tekenles, maar volgden een soort basisopleiding aan de hand van vormgevingsexperimenten met de meest uiteenlopende materialen. Daarmee moesten ze hun vaardigheden en talenten verkennen, om pas daarna in het voor hen passende atelier aan de slag te gaan. De Inleidingscursus werd later deels overgenomen door kunstacademies en vakopleidingen.

Kandinsky's lessen bestaan uit een kleuren- en vormenleer waarin ook de fundamentele psychologische effecten van basisvormen worden geanalyseerd.

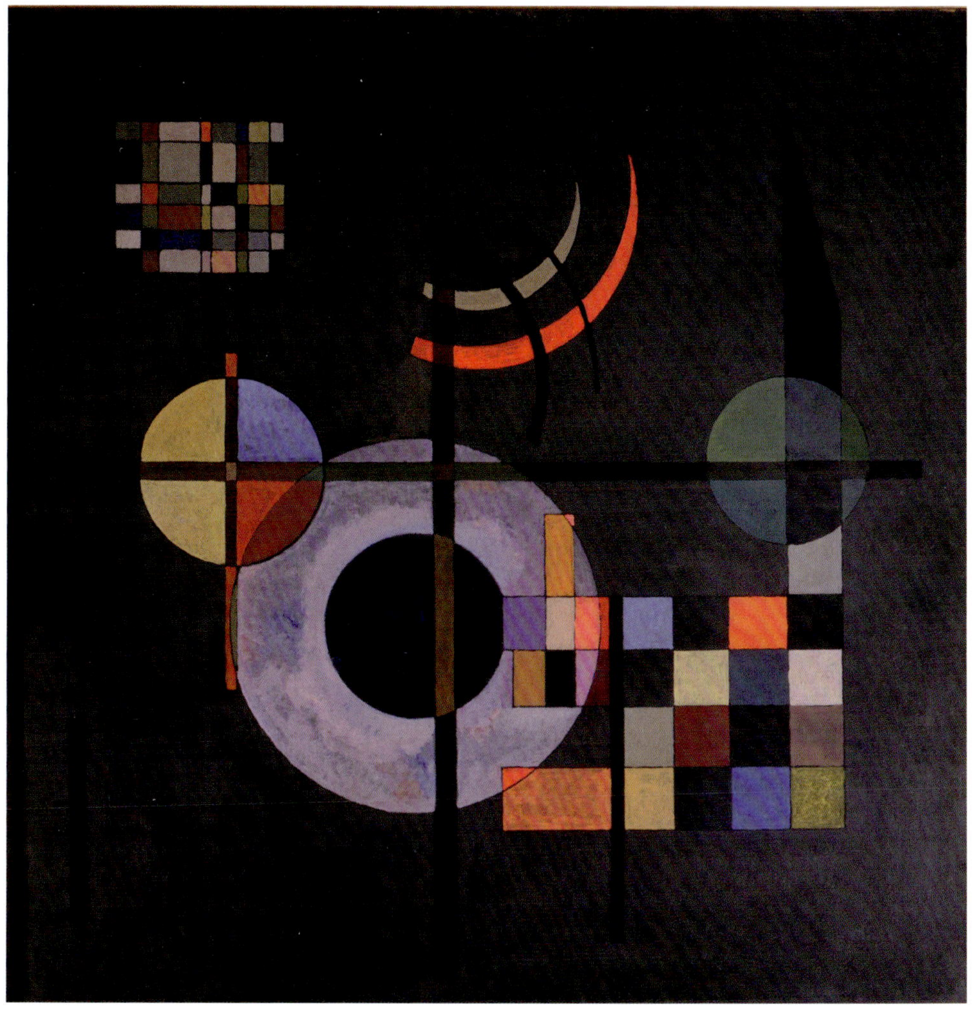

Counterweights **Gegengewichte** **Contrappesi**

Contrepoids **Contrapesos** **Tegenwichten**

1926, Oil on canvas/Huile sur toile, 49,5 × 49,5 cm, Städtisches Museum, Mühlheim

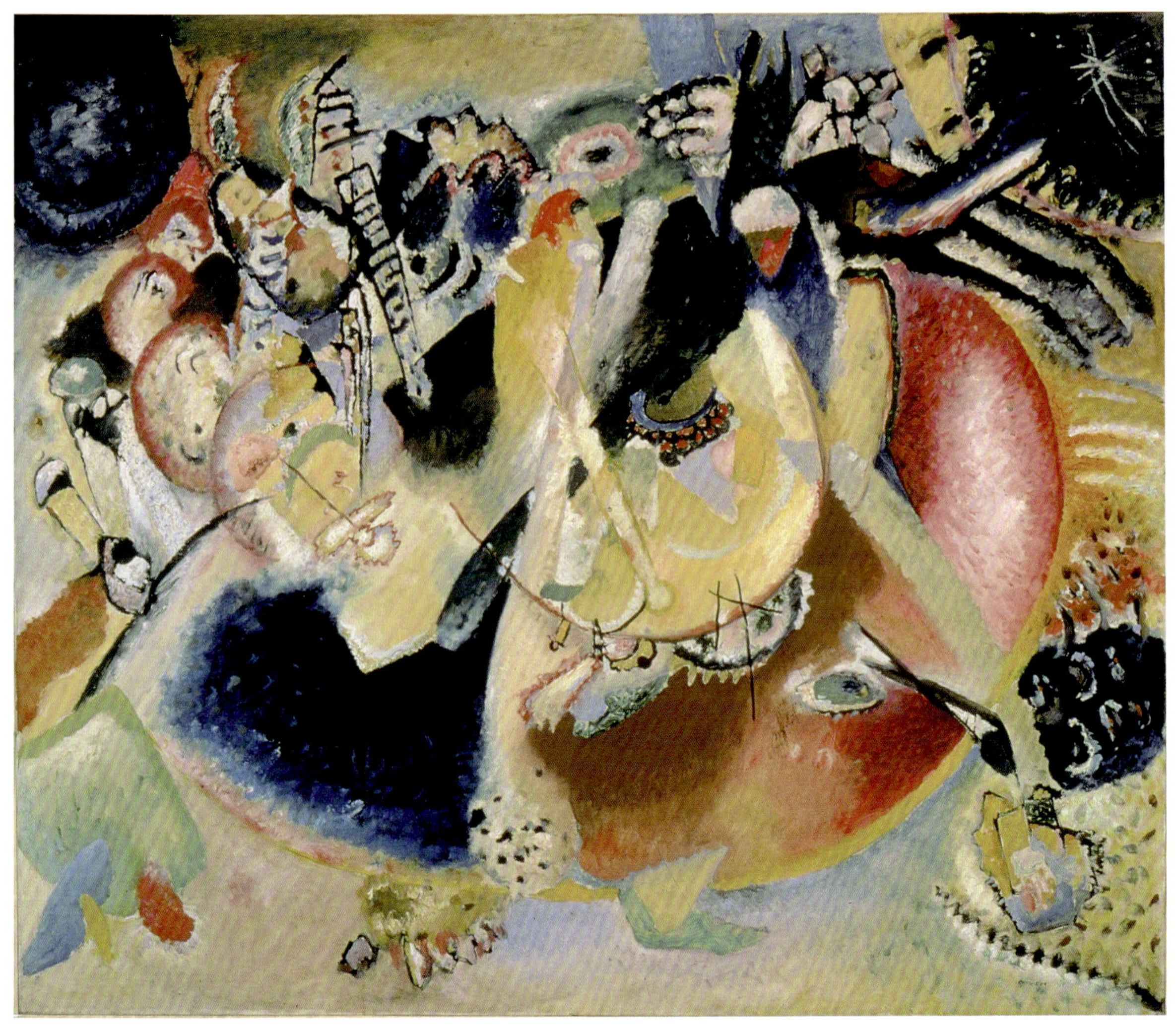

Improvisation of Cold Forms

Improvisation aux formes froides

Improvisation mit kalten Formen

Improvisación de formas frías

Improvvisazione con forme fredde

Improvisatie met koude vormen

1914, Oil on canvas/Huile sur toile, 104 × 133,5 cm, Art Museum, Ekaterinburg

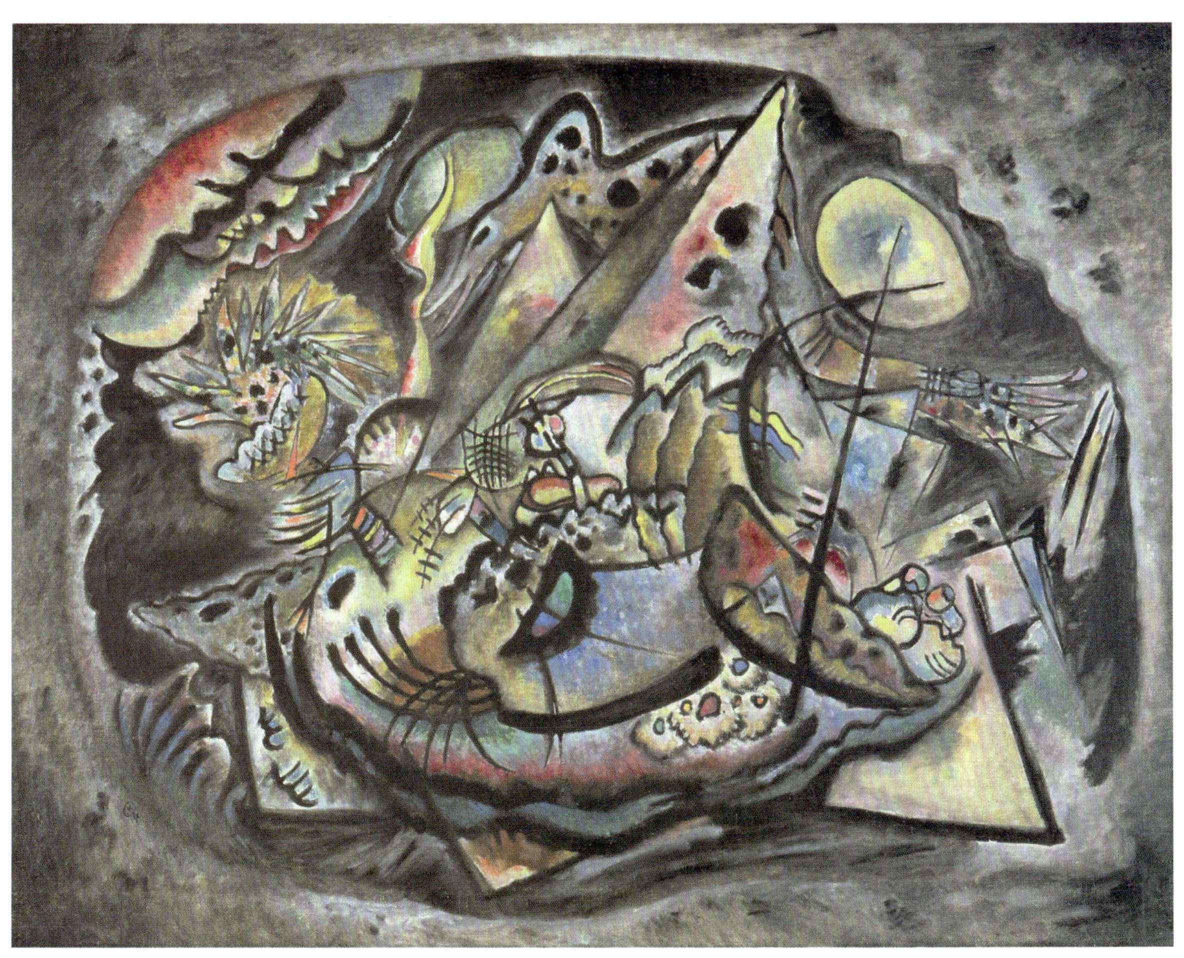

Composition: The Grey Oval   *Komposition im grauen Oval*   *Composizione: l'ovale grigio*

Composition dans l'ovale gris   *Composición: El óvalo gris*   *Compositie in grijze ovaal*

1917, Oil on canvas/Huile sur toile, 70.1× 70,1 cm, NOMA New Orleans Museum of Art

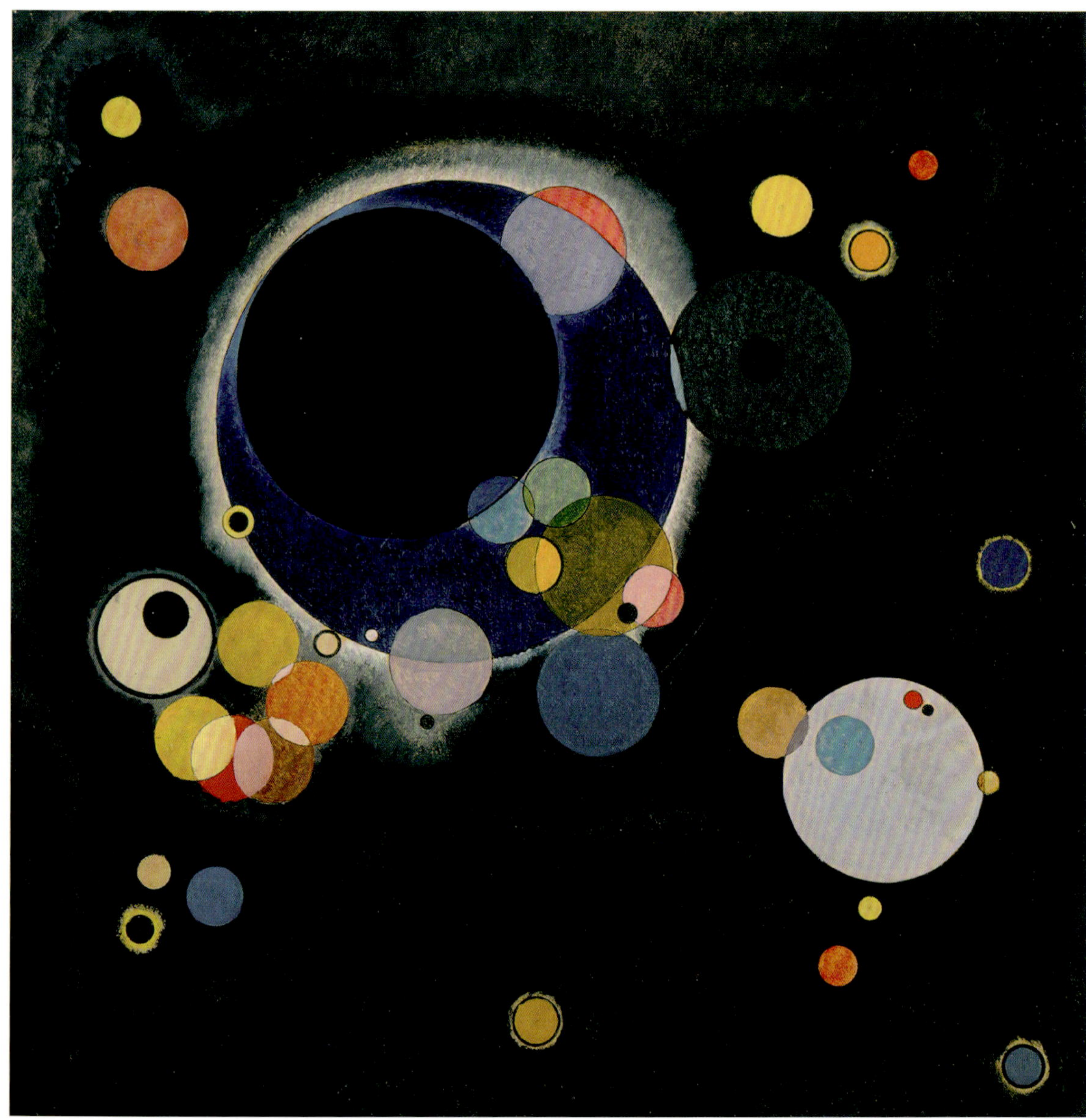

Sketch for **Several Circles**

Esquisse pour **Quelques cercles**

Skizze für **Einige Kreise**

Boceto para **Varios círculos**

Schizzo per **Vari cerchi**

Schets voor **Enkele cirkels**

1925, Oil on paper on canvas/Huile sur papier sur toile, 70,1 × 70,1 cm, NOMA New Orleans Museum OF Art

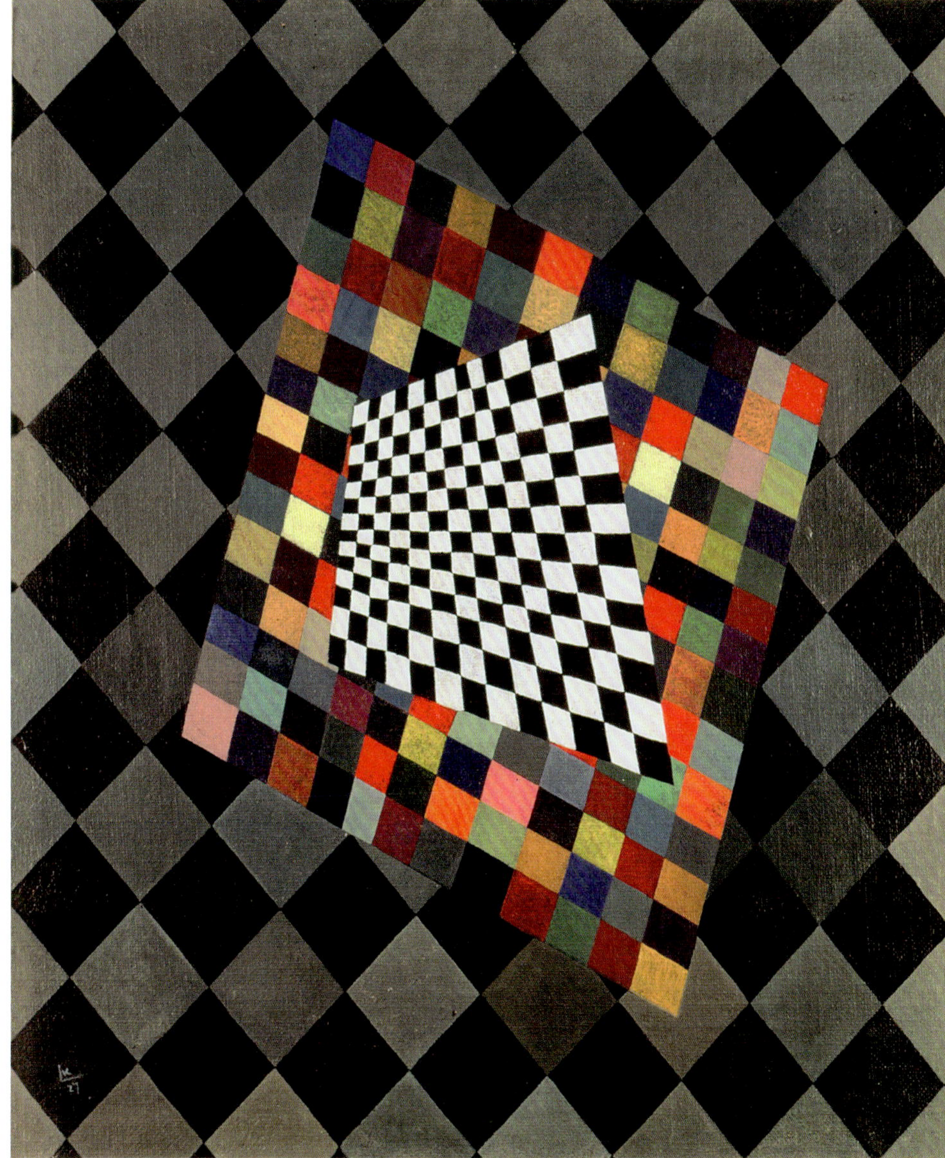

Square

Carrés

Quadrat

Plaza

Quadrato

Vierkant

1927, Oil on panel/Huile sur bois, 73 × 60 cm, Galerie Maeght, Paris

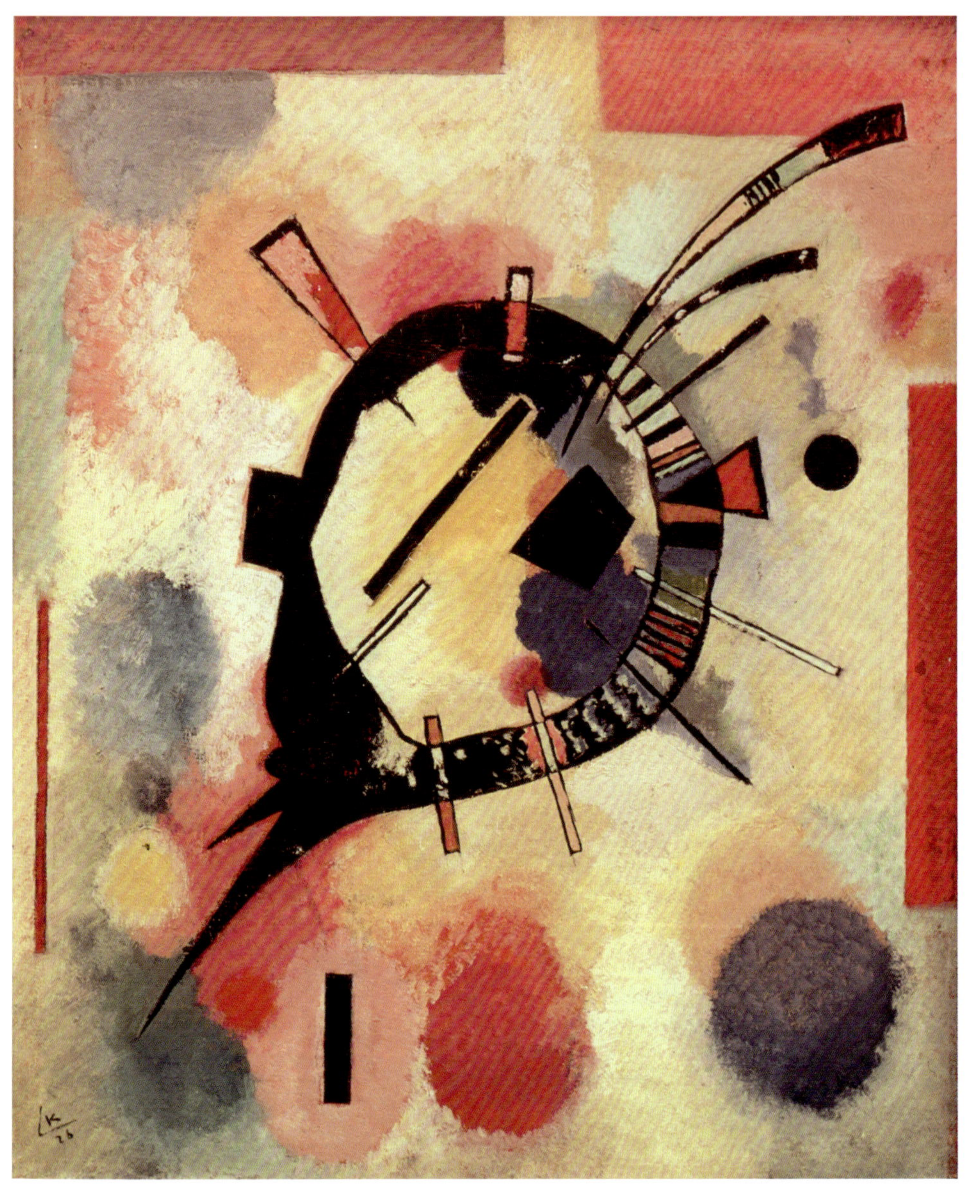

Yellow Center

Centre jaune

Gelbes Zentrum

Centro amarillo

Centro giallo

Geel centrum

*1926, Oil on cardboard/
Huile sur carton,
45 × 37 cm,
Museum Boymans van
Beuningen, Rotterdam*

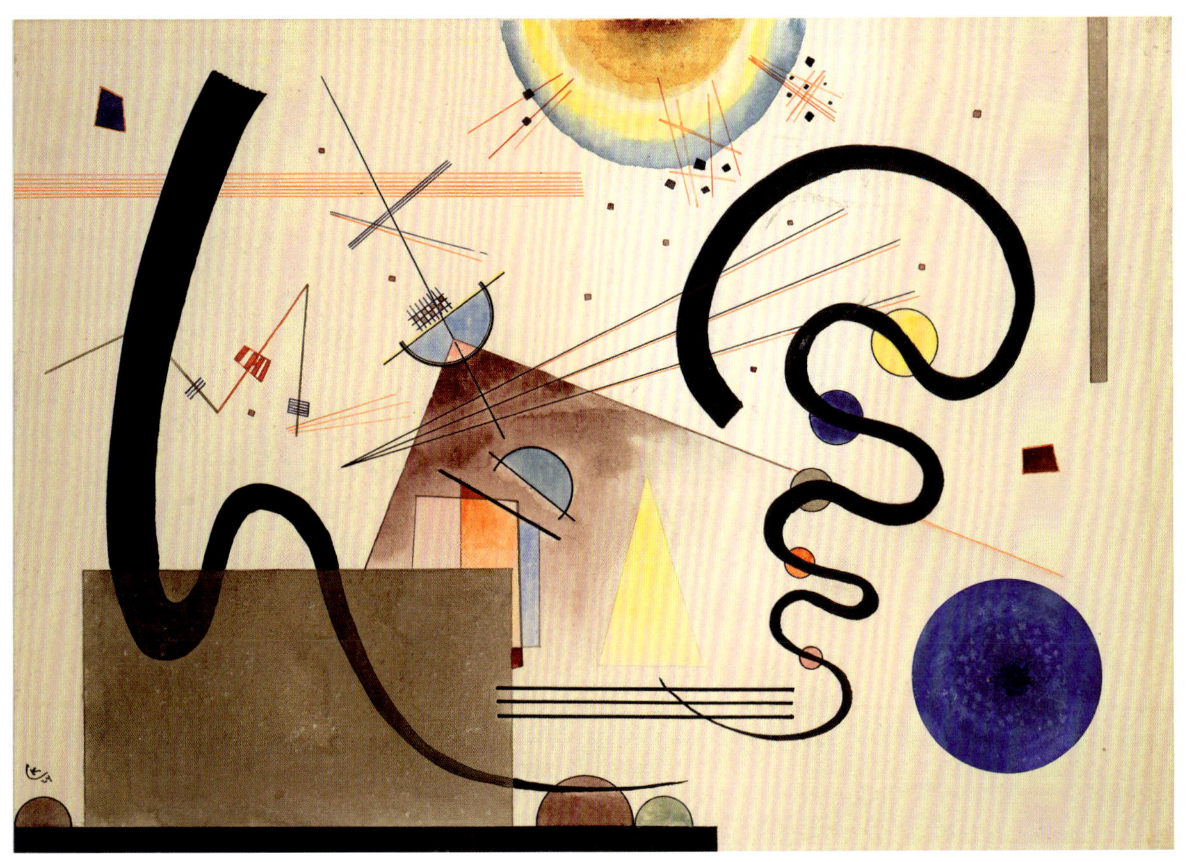

Two Motions   **Zwei Bewegungen**   **Due movimenti**

Deux Mouvements   **Dos mociones**   **Twee bewegingen**

1924, Watercolor, black and colored inks on paper/Aquarelle et encre de Chine sur papier,
33,7× 47,3 cm, Private collection

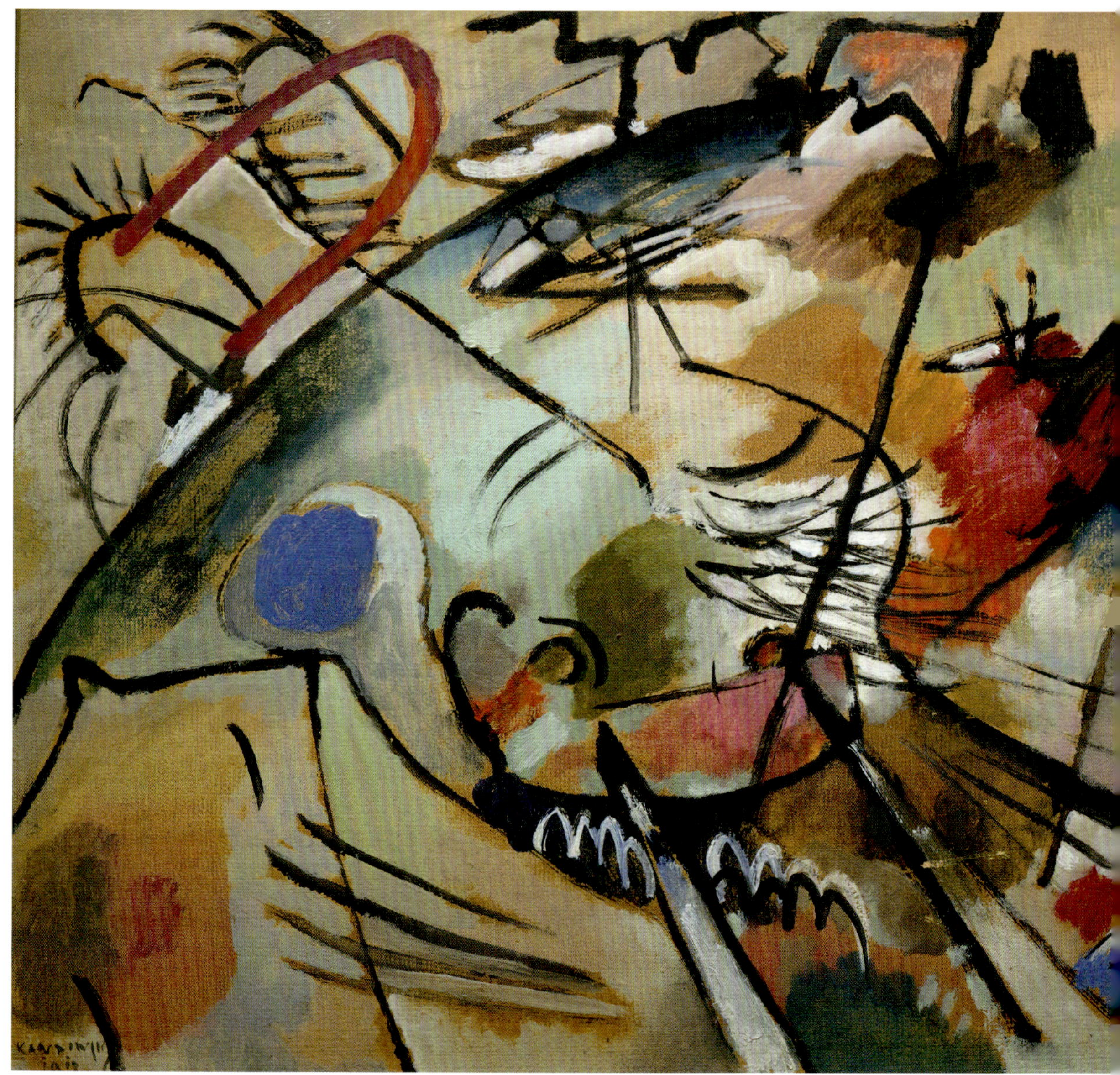

KANDINSKY
1910

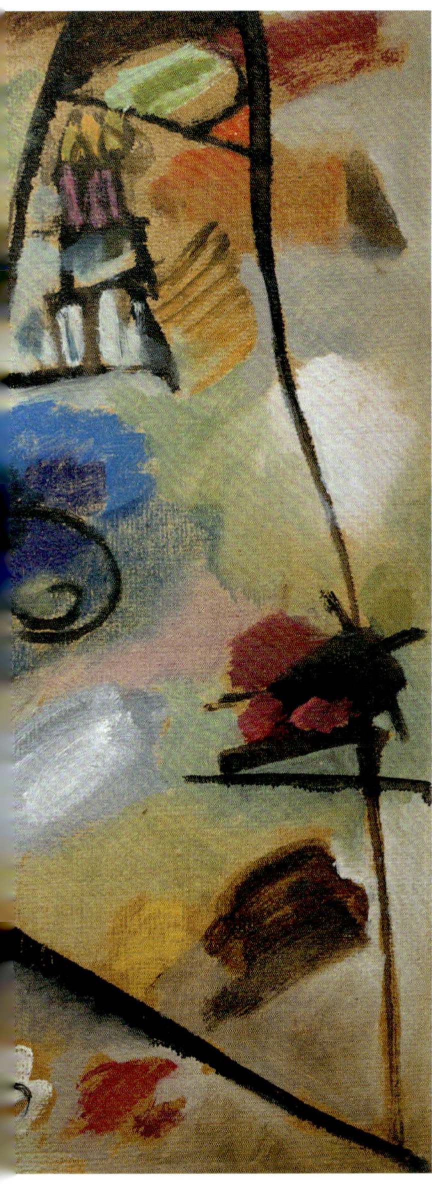

Study for **Improvisation 24 (Trioka III)**

Etude pour **Improvisation 24 (Troïka III)**

Studie für **Improvisation 24 (Troika III)**

Estudio para la **improvisación
24 (Trioka III)**

Studio per **Improvvisazione 24 (Troika III)**

Studie voor **Improvisatie 24 (Trojka III)**

*1924, Oil on board/Huile sur carton,
49 × 67,5 cm, Private collection*

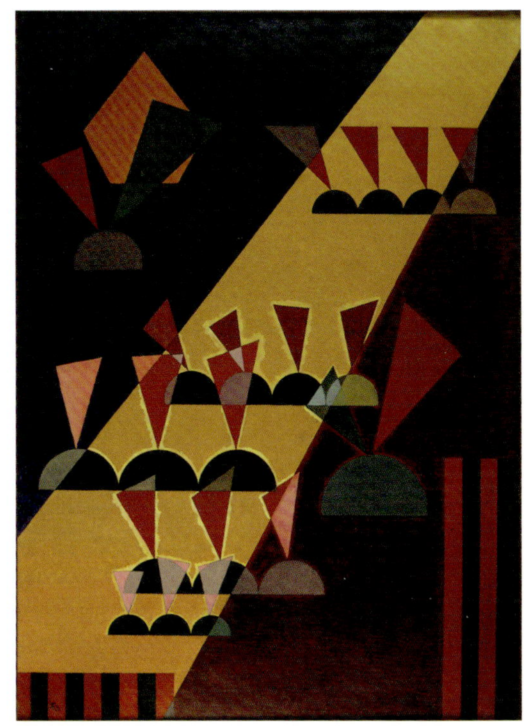

Sharp Ideas

Idées pénétrantes

Scharfe Ideen

Ideas de Sharp

Idee affilate

Scherpe ideeën

*1927, Oil on canvas/Huile sur toile,
Private collection*

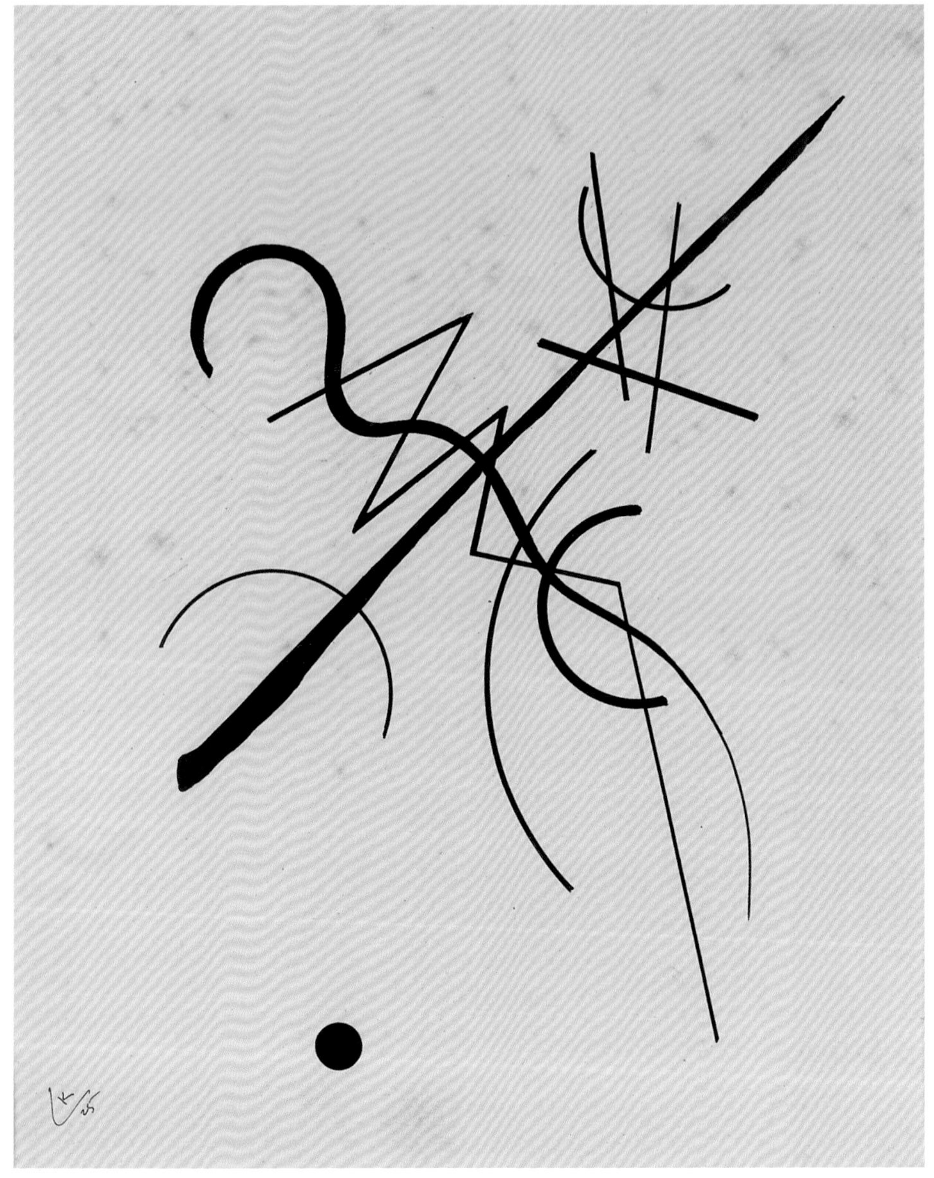

Drawing for book **Punkt und Linie zu Fläche**

Dessin pour le livre **Point, ligne, surface**

Zeichnung für das Buch **Punkt und Linie zu Fläche**

Dibujo para el libro **Punkt und Linie zu Fläche**

Disegno per il libro **Punto, linea, superficie**

Tekening voor het boek **Punkt und Linie zu Fläche**

1925, Brush and ink on paper/Pinceau et encre de Chine sur papier, 38,4 × 30,8 cm, Private collection

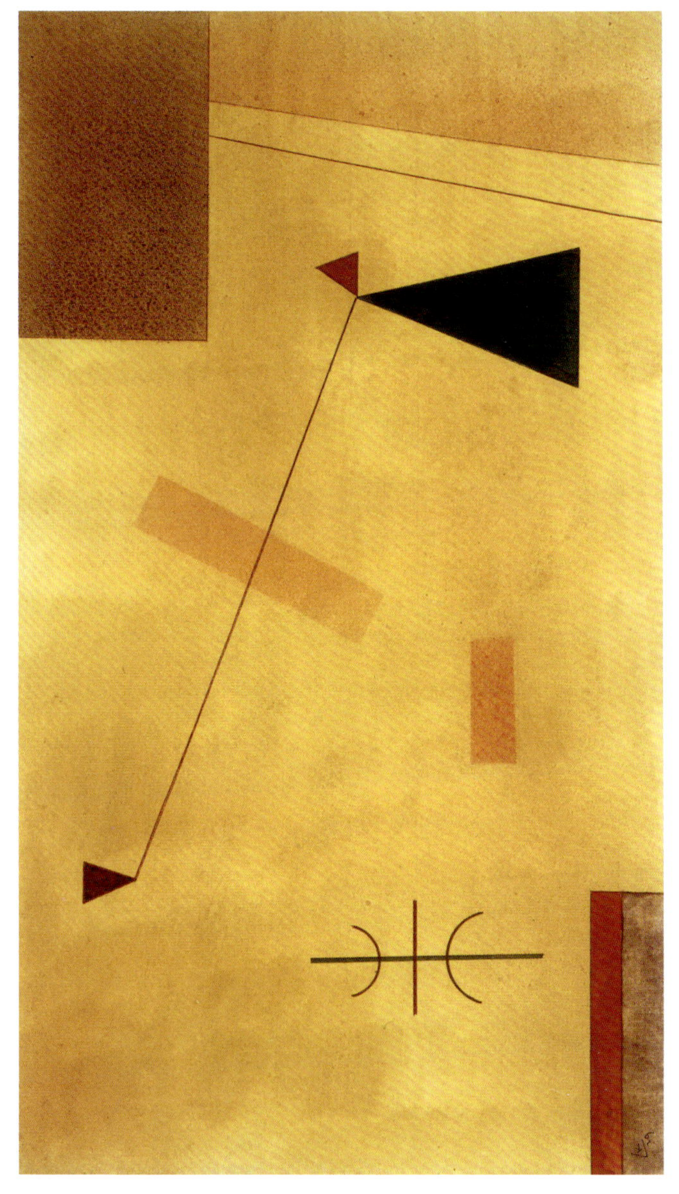

Without Weight

Sans poids

Ohne Gewicht

Sin peso

Senza peso

Zonder gewicht

1929, Watercolor, black and colored inks on paper/Aquarelle et encre de Chine sur papier, 26,7 × 47,6 cm, Private collection

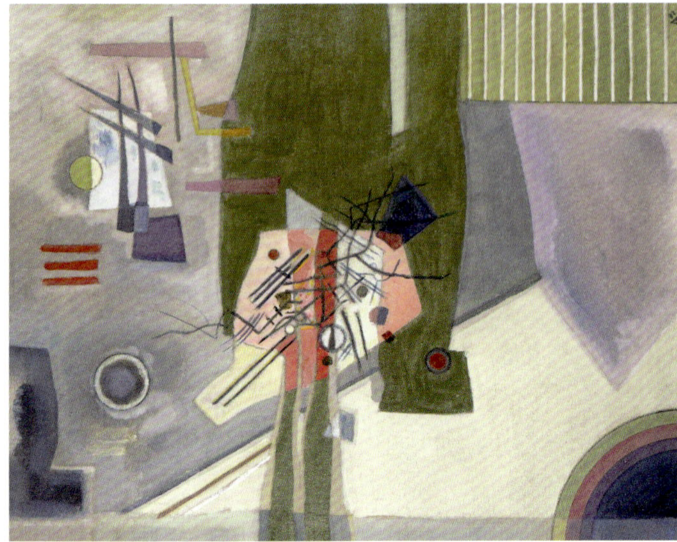

Pink in Gray
Rose dans le gris
Rosa in Grau
Rosa en gris
Rosa nel grigio
Roze in grijs

1926, Oil on canvas/Huile sur toile,
41 × 52,5 cm, Private collection

A move to Dessau in 1925 began a new phase of the Bauhaus. A new spacious building housed the classrooms, workshops and an administrative wing, along with other rooms having a social function, such as an auditorium, cafeteria and stage.

Alongside the main building were the Masters' houses, including a semi-detached house for Kandinsky and Paul Klee (1879–1940), who had shared a close friendship since their appointment to the Bauhaus.

The creative atmosphere in Dessau became overshadowed in 1928 following the appointment of Hannes Meyer (1889–1954) as the successor to Gropius. This resulted in an uneasy polarization which was reinforced by a new functional orientation under Meyer.

Une nouvelle phase du Bauhaus commence avec le déménagement à Dessau, en 1925. Le nouveau bâtiment grandiose accueille les salles de cours, les ateliers, une aile administrative et des espaces à fonction sociale officielle : salle des Fêtes (Aula), réfectoire (Mensa) et théâtre.

Dans le même temps que le bâtiment principal sont édifiées les « maisons des Maîtres » (Meisterhäuser), comme le double pavillon pour Kandinsky et Paul Klee (1879-1940) – étroitement liés depuis leur engagement au Bauhaus.

L'ambiance d'émulation créatrice s'assombrit à Dessau en 1928, avec la nomination de Hannes Meyer (1889-1954) comme successeur de Gropius. Une orientation négative se fait bientôt jour, aggravée par le nouvel organigramme fonctionnel imaginé

Mit dem Umzug nach Dessau 1925 beginnt eine neue Phase des Bauhauses. In dem neuen großzügigen Bau sind die Unterrichtsräume, Werkstätten, ein Verwaltungstrakt und Räume mit sozialer Funktion wie Aula, Mensa und Bühne zusammen untergebracht.

Gleichzeitig mit dem Hauptgebäude entstehen die Meisterhäuser, unter anderem auch das Doppelhaus für Kandinsky und Paul Klee (1879–1940), die seit ihrer Berufung ans Bauhaus eng befreundet sind.

Die kreative Atmosphäre in Dessau wird 1928 durch die Berufung von Hannes Meyer (1889–1954) als Nachfolger von Gropius überschattet. Schon bald zeigt sich eine ungute Polarisierung, die durch die neue funktionale Ausrichtung Meyers verstärkt wird.

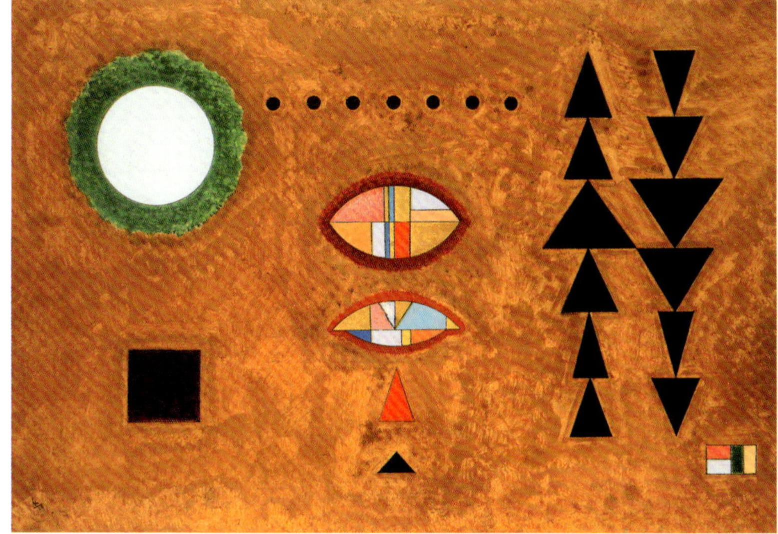

White-White
Blanc-blanc
Weiß-Weiß
Blanco-blanco
Bianco-Bianco
Wit-wit

*1929, Oil on board/Huile sur carton,
49,5 × 71 cm, Private collection*

Un traslado a Dessau en 1925 daría comienzo a una nueva fase de la Bauhaus. Un nuevo y espacioso edificio alojaba las aulas, talleres y un ala administrativa, junto con otras estancias con una función social, como el auditorio, la cafetería y el escenario.

Junto al edificio principal se encontraban las viviendas de los maestros, incluyendo una casa pareada para Kandinsky y Paul Klee (1879–1940), que habían compartido una estrecha amistad desde su unión a la Bauhaus.

La atmósfera creativa en Dessau quedó oscurecida en 1928 tras el nombramiento de Hannes Meyer (1889–1954) como sucesor de Gropius. Esto derivó en una molesta polarización reforzada por una nueva orientación funcional liderada por Meyer.

Il trasferimento a Dessau nel 1925 diede inizio ad una nuova fase del Bauhaus. Un nuovo e spazioso edificio ospitava le aule, i laboratori e gli uffici amministrativi, oltre ad altre stanze con una funzione sociale, come l'auditorio, la caffetteria e il palco.

Accanto all'edificio principale si trovavano le case dei Maestri, tra cui la casa semi-indipendente di Kandinsky e Paul Klee (1879-1940), che strinsero amicizia fin dal loro arrivo al Bauhaus.

L'atmosfera creativa di Dessau fu incupita nel 1928 dalla nomina di Hannes Meyer (1889-1954) come successore di Gropius, sotto la cui direzione fu istituito un nuovo orientamento funzionale che rafforzò la polarizzazione del disagio creatasi.

Kandinsky fu coinvolto in una trama che portò all'allontanamento

Met de verhuizing naar Dessau in 1925 begint het Bauhaus aan een nieuwe fase. Het nieuwe en ruime gebouw biedt onderdak aan leslokalen, ateliers, de administratie en sociale ruimten als de aula, de mensa en een podium.

Tegelijkertijd met het hoofdgebouw ontstaan ook de 'meesterwoningen', waaronder de dubbele woning voor Kandinsky en Paul Klee (1879–1940), die sinds hun kennismaking aan het Bauhaus goede vrienden zijn geworden.

De creatieve sfeer in Dessau wordt in 1928 door de aanstelling van Hannes Meyer (1889–1954) als opvolger van Gropius overschaduwd. Al snel ontstaat een onverkwikkelijke polarisatie, die door de nieuwe functionele aanpak van Meyer wordt verscherpt.

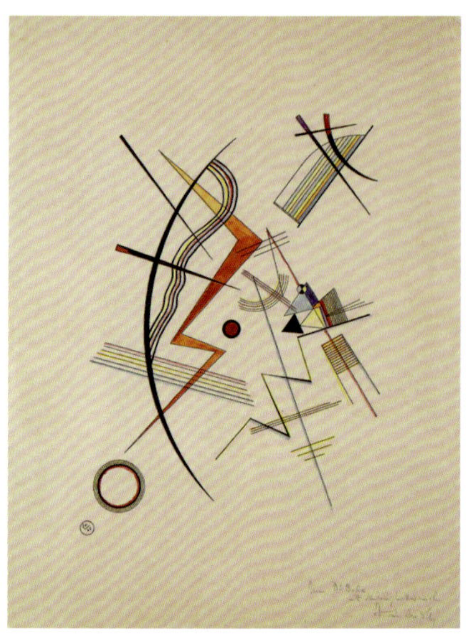

1925, Lithograph/Lithographie, 35,5 × 25,5 cm, Private collection

Kandinsky was involved in an intrigue, the consequence of which was that Hannes Meyer was dismissed in 1930 for political reasons, to be succeeded by the architect Ludwig Mies van der Rohe (1886–1969), who was able to steer the Bauhaus into calmer waters by focusing on architectural education.

After the dissolution of the Bauhaus in Dessau during 1932 due to the Nazis, classes were continued for a while in Berlin in a disused telephone factory. Kandinsky accompanied them and for a while continued his teaching, but the political circumstances of the time forced a self-dissolution following a police raid on 11 March 1933, thus ending the era of the Bauhaus.

par Meyer. À la suite de manœuvres auxquelles Kandinsky n'est pas étranger, Meyer est écarté pour des raisons politiques. Son successeur est l'architecte Ludwig Mies van der Rohe (1886-1969), qui réussit à ramener le Bauhaus dans des eaux plus calmes, par une concentration sur l'enseignement de l'architecture.

Les cercles nazis ayant fait fermer le Bauhaus à Dessau en 1932, les cours continuent encore un peu à Berlin, dans une ancienne usine de téléphones désaffectée. Kandinsky y poursuit son enseignement. Mais les circonstances politiques entraînent finalement le sabordage. Le 11 mars 1933, une descente de police met fin aux activités d'enseignement – et du même coup à l'ère du Bauhaus.

Infolge einer auch von Kandinsky mitgetragenen Intrige wird Hannes Meyer 1930 aus politischen Gründen entlassen, Nachfolger wird der Architekt Ludwig Mies van der Rohe (1886–1969), dem es gelingt, das Bauhaus durch die Konzentration auf die Architekturlehre in ruhigere Gewässer zu lenken.

Nach der Auflösung des Bauhauses in Dessau durch die nationalsozialistischen Kreise 1932 wird der Unterricht noch eine Weile in Berlin in einer stillgelegten Telefonfabrik weitergeführt. Auch Kandinsky ist mitgegangen und hält seinen Unterricht weiter ab. Doch die politischen Umstände zwingen zur Selbstauflösung. Eine Polizeirazzia beendet am 11.März 1933 den Lehrbetrieb und damit die Ära des Bauhauses.

Kandinsky se vio implicado en una intriga cuya consecuencia fue el despido de Hannes Meyer en 1930 por motivos políticos, a quien sustituiría el arquitecto Ludwig Mies van der Rohe (1886–1969), que fue capaz de conducir la Bauhaus hacia aguas más tranquilas centrándose en la educación arquitectónica.

Tras la disolución de la Bauhaus en Dessau durante 1932 debido a los nazis, las clases continuaron durante algún tiempo en Berlín, en una fábrica de teléfonos abandonada. Kandinsky les acompañó y continuó enseñando durante algún tiempo, pero las circunstancias políticas del momento forzaron una auto-disolución tras una redada policial el 11 de marzo de 1933, que puso fin a la era Bauhaus.

di Hannes Meyer nel 1930 per motivi politici. Gli successe l'architetto Ludwig Mies van der Rohe (1886-1969), che riuscì a riportare la tranquillità al Bauhaus concentrandosi sulla formazione in architettura.

Dopo lo scioglimento del Bauhaus di Dessau nel 1932 a causa dei nazisti, le lezioni proseguirono per un breve lasso di tempo a Berlino in una fabbrica di telefoni in disuso. Kandinsky si trasferì nella capitale tedesca e continuò ad insegnare per un po', ma le circostanze politiche del tempo forzarono l'auto-dissoluzione del gruppo a seguito di un raid della polizia l'11 marzo 1933, che pose fine all'era del Bauhaus.

Na een intrige waarbij ook Kandinsky betrokken is, wordt Hannes Meyer in 1930 op politieke gronden ontslagen; zijn opvolger wordt de architect Ludwig Mies van der Rohe (1886–1969), die zich op de architectuurtheorie richt en daarmee het Bauhaus naar rustiger vaarwater weet te sturen.

Nadat het Bauhaus in Dessau op instigatie van de nazi's in 1932 wordt gesloten, worden de lessen nog enige tijd in Berlijn voortgezet in een stilgelegde telefoonfabriek. Ook Kandinsky gaat mee en geeft daar les. Maar door de politieke verhoudingen moet de school zijn deuren sluiten. Na een razzia door de politie op 11 maart 1933 worden de lessen afgebroken en eindigt het Bauhaus-tijdperk

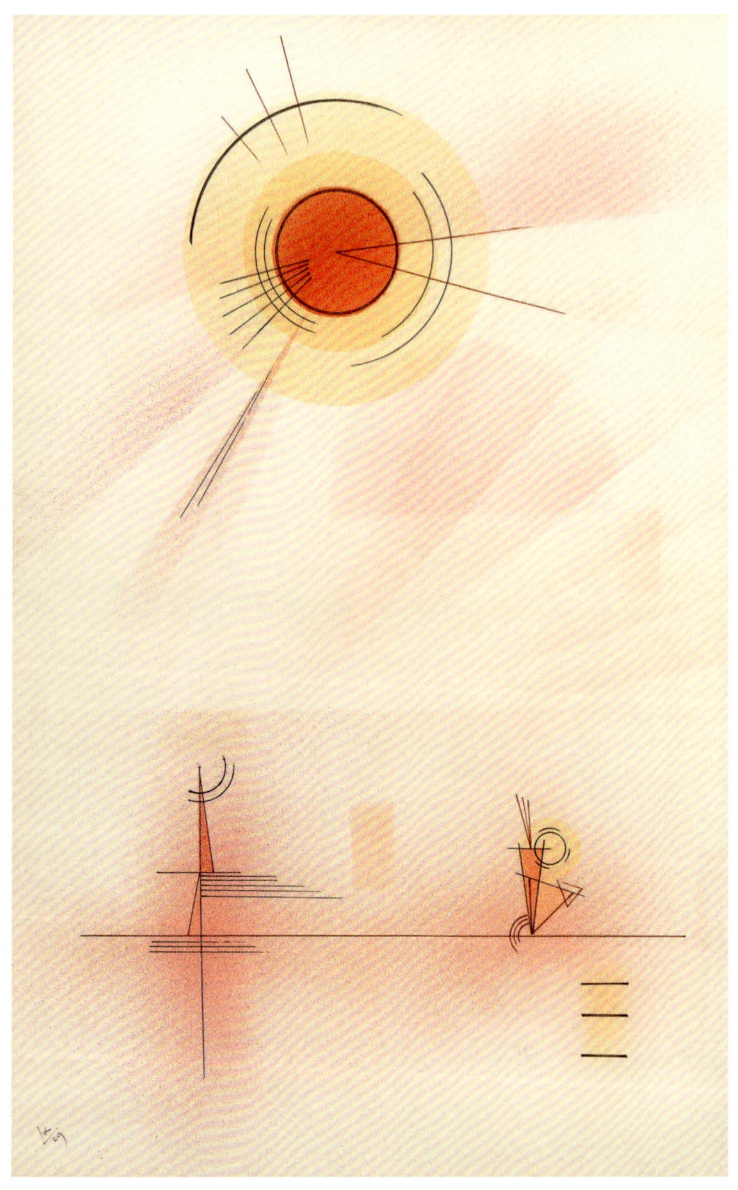

Sunshine

Soleil

Sonnenschein

Sol

Luce solare

Zonneschijn

1929,Watercolor, black and colored inks on paper/
Aquarelle et encre de Chine sur papier, 53 × 33,8 cm,
Private collection

Varied Rectangles

Rectangles variés

Verschiedene Rechtecke

Rectángulos variadas

Rettangoli vari

Verschillende rechthoeken

1929, Watercolor and ink on paper/Aquarelle et encre de
Chine sur papier, 39,7 × 38,3 cm, Private collection

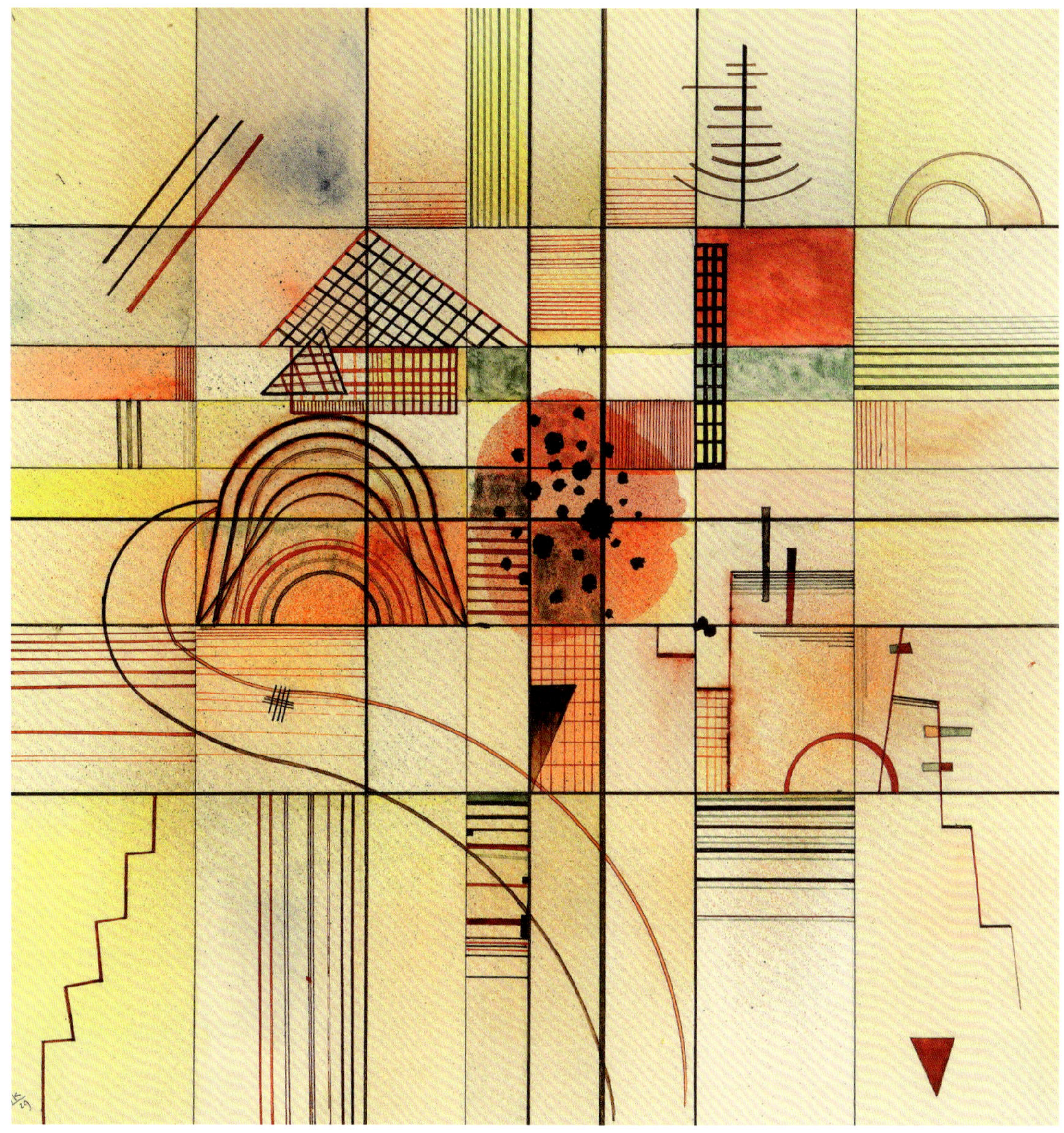

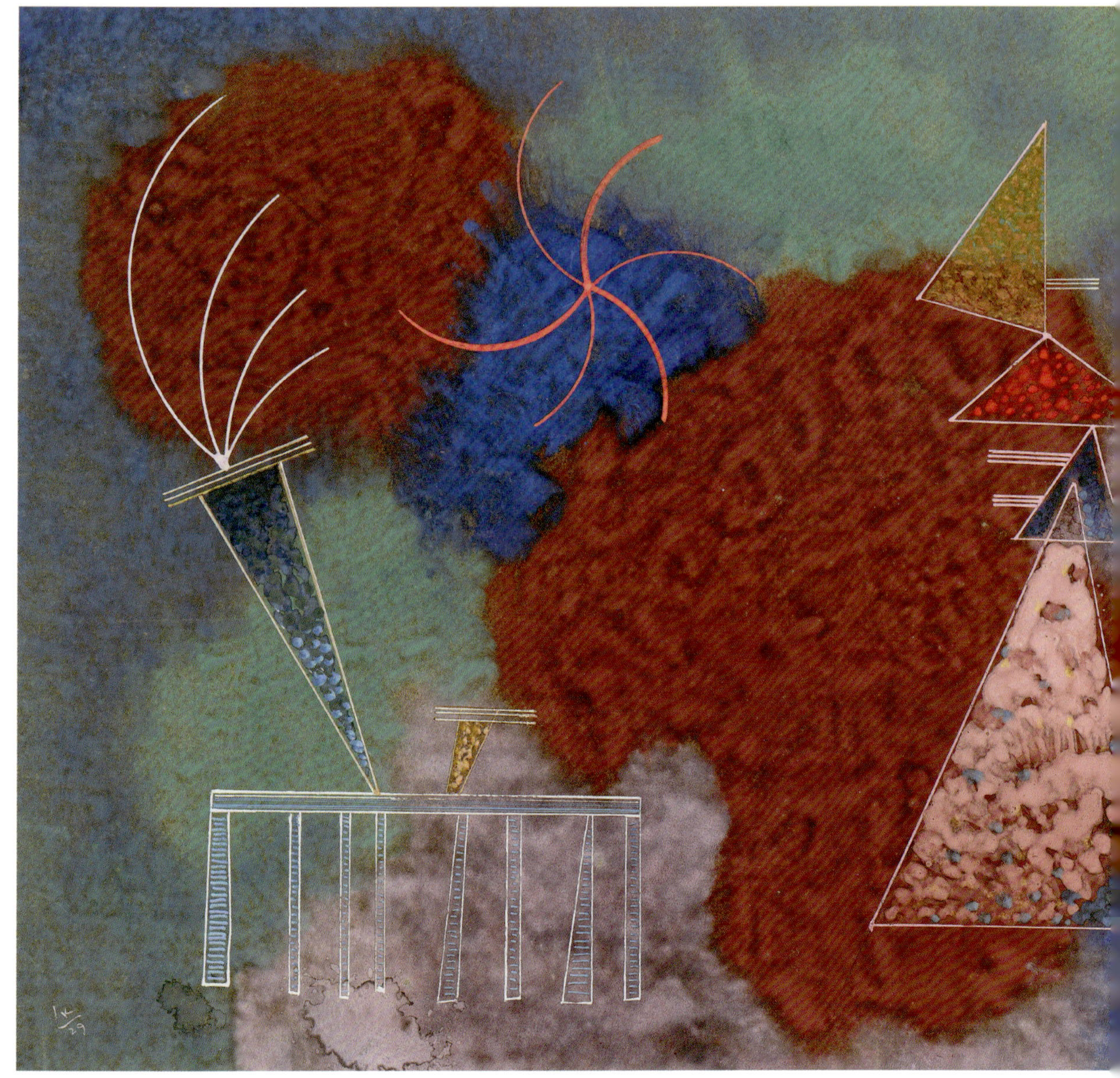

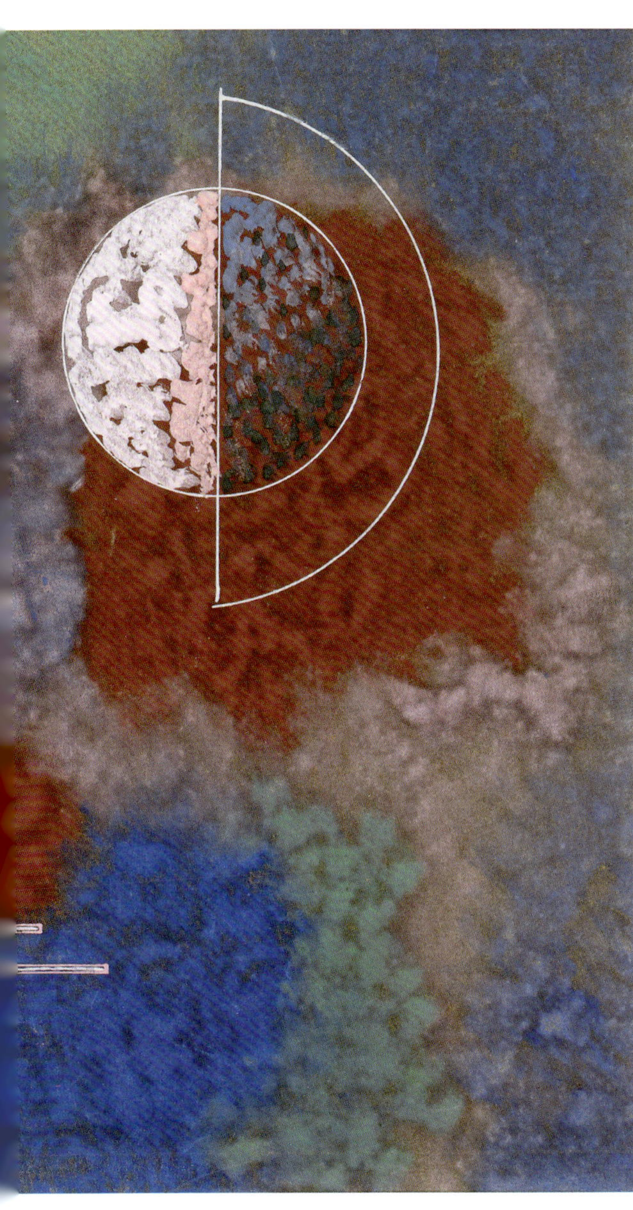

Stains on the Rich

Sur des taches saturées

Auf satten Flecken

Manchas a los ricos

Su macchie intense

Op zatte vlekken

1929, Gouache on paper on cardboard/Gouache sur papier sur carton, 31,8 × 52 cm, Private collection

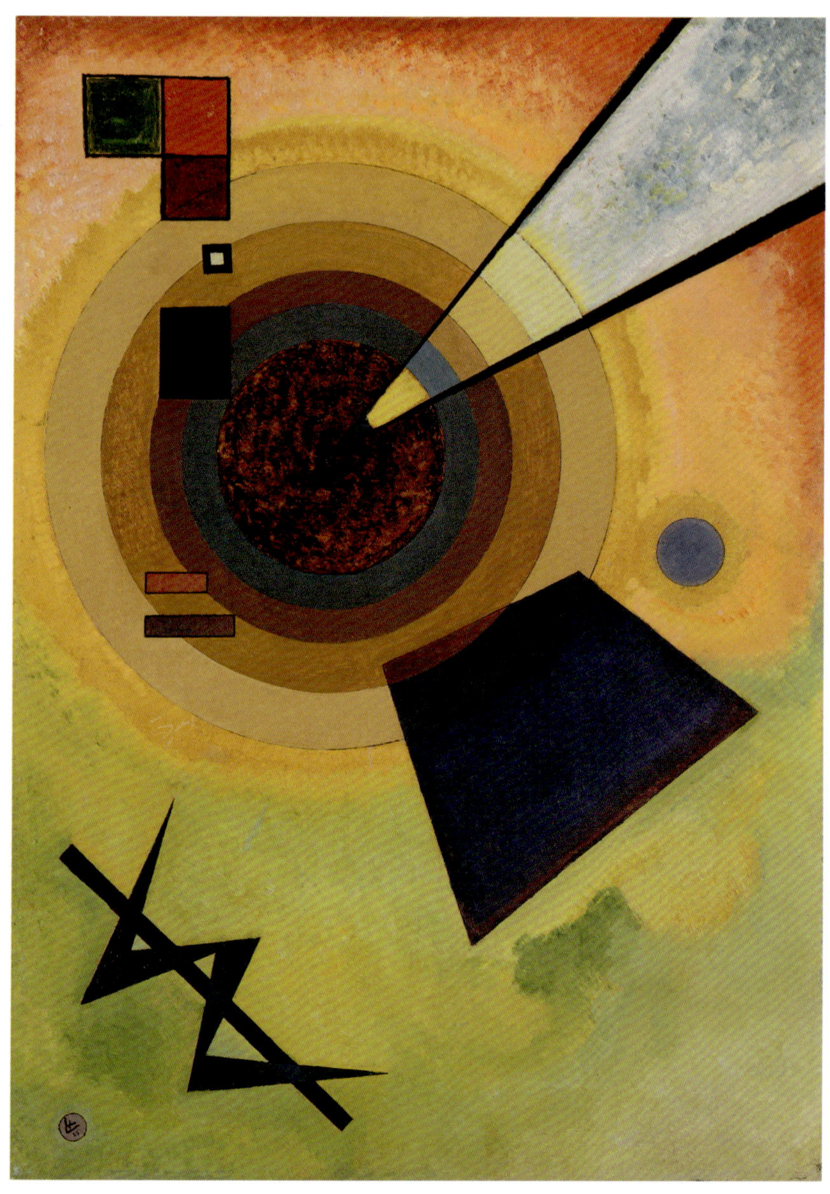

Green and Red

Vert et rouge

Grün und Rot

Verde y rojo

Verde e rosso

Groen en rood

*1925, Oil on board/Huile sur carton,
69,2 × 49,5 cm, Private collection*

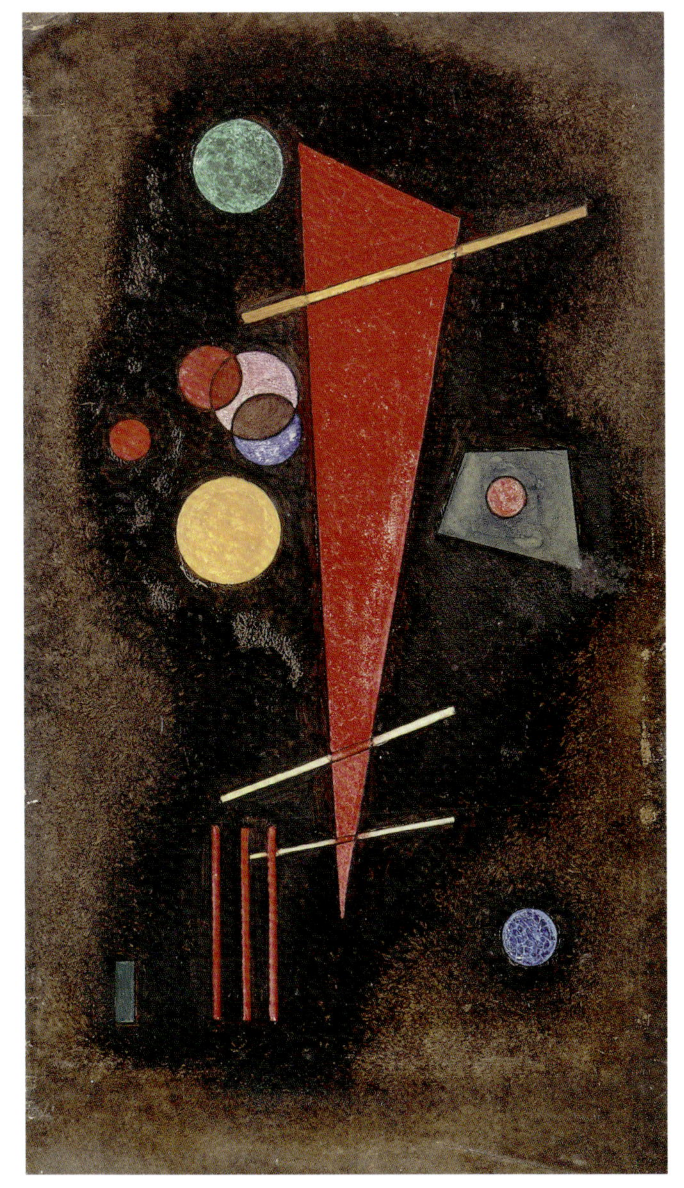

*1928, Oil and tempera on board/Huile et tempéra sur carton,
35 × 20 cm Private collection*

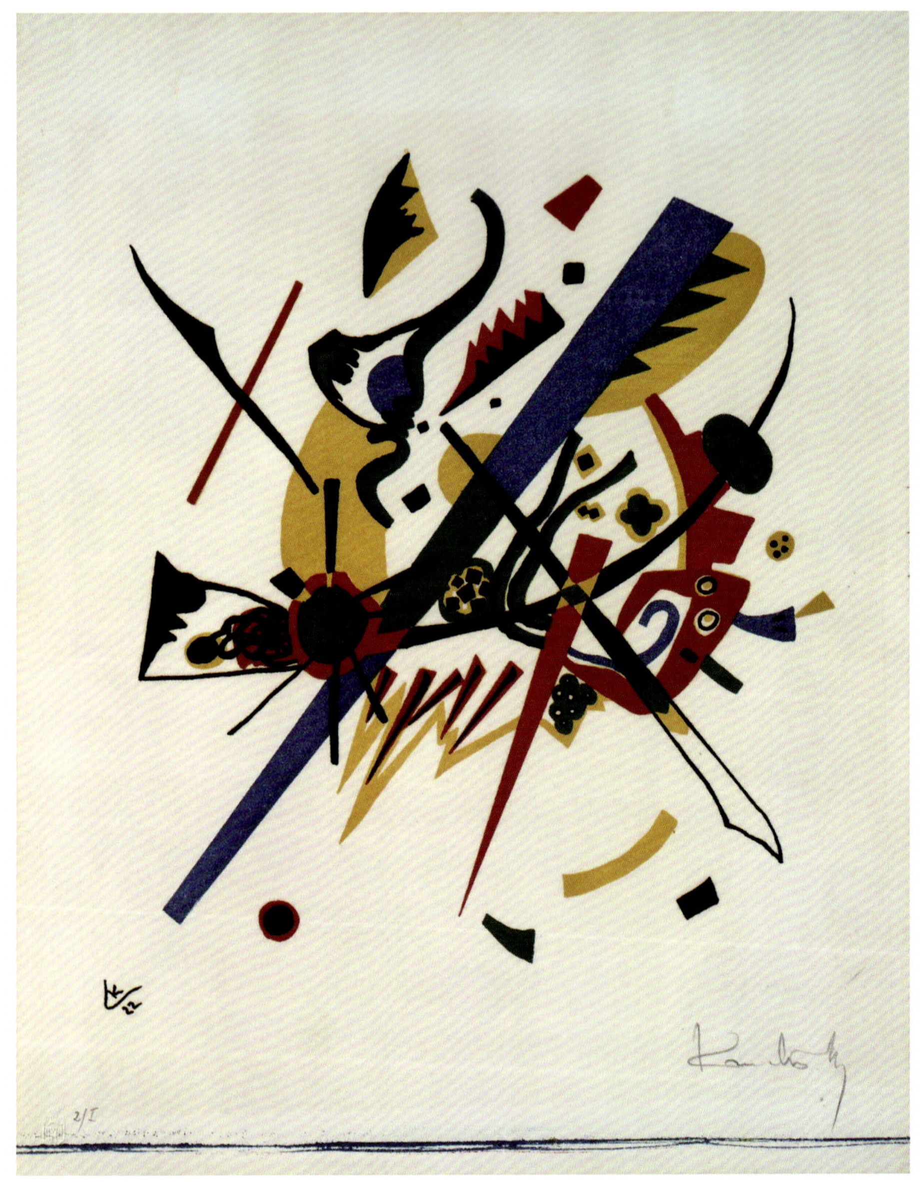

Small Worlds I

Petits Mondes I

Kleine Welten I

Pequeños mundos

Piccoli mondi I

Kleine werelden I

*1922, Color lithograph/
Lithographie en couleur,
46,5 × 35,5 cm,
Private collection*

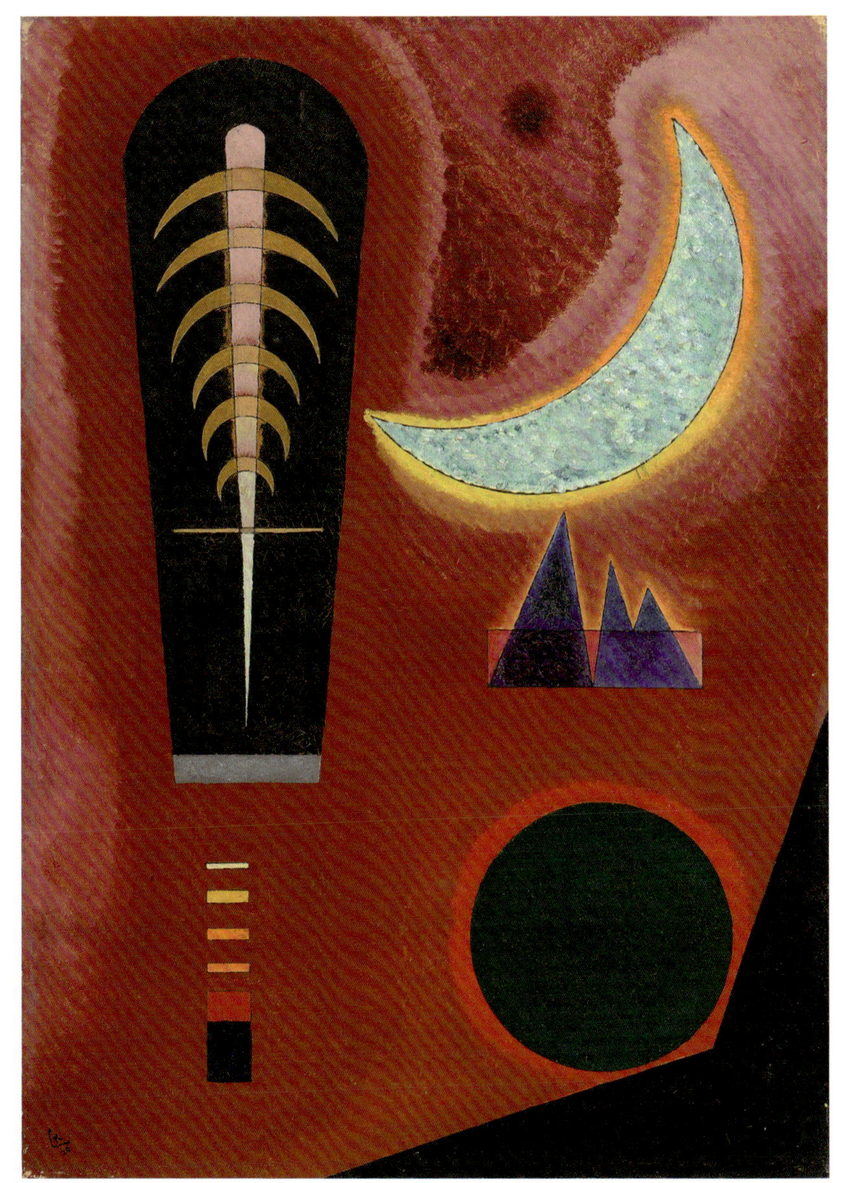

Loosely in Red
Vrac en rouge
Lose in Rot
Losely en rojo
Liberamente in rosso
Los in rood
1925, Oil on cardboard/Huile sur carton,
69,3 × 49,5 cm, Private collection

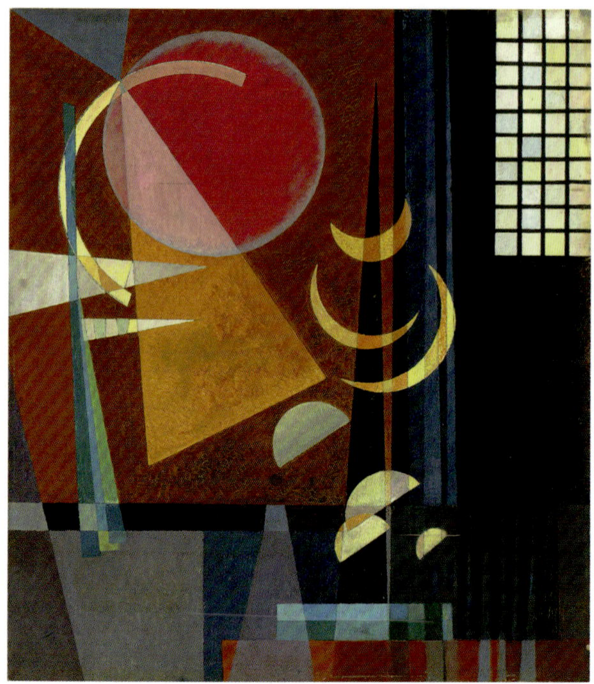

Scharf-Ruhig

Coupant-calme

Scharf-Ruhig

Tranquilidad de Sharp

Scharf-Ruhig

Scherp-rustig

1927, Oil on cardboard/Huile sur carton,
 42,5 × 37,5 cm, Private collection

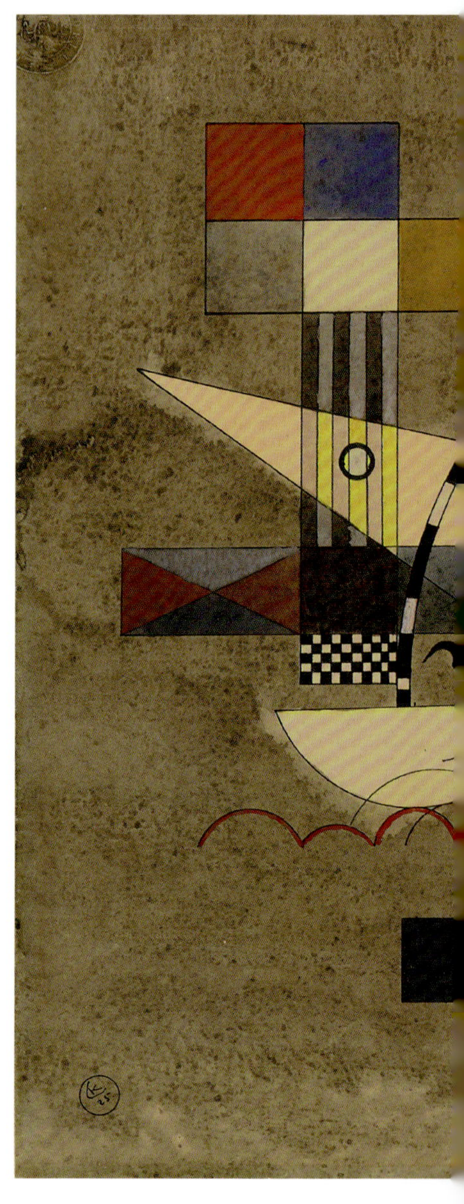

Solid III

Solide III

Festes III

III sólido

Solido III

Vast III

1925, Gouache, watercolor and ink on paper/
Gouache, aquarelle et encre de Chine sur
papier, 31 × 48 cm
Private collection

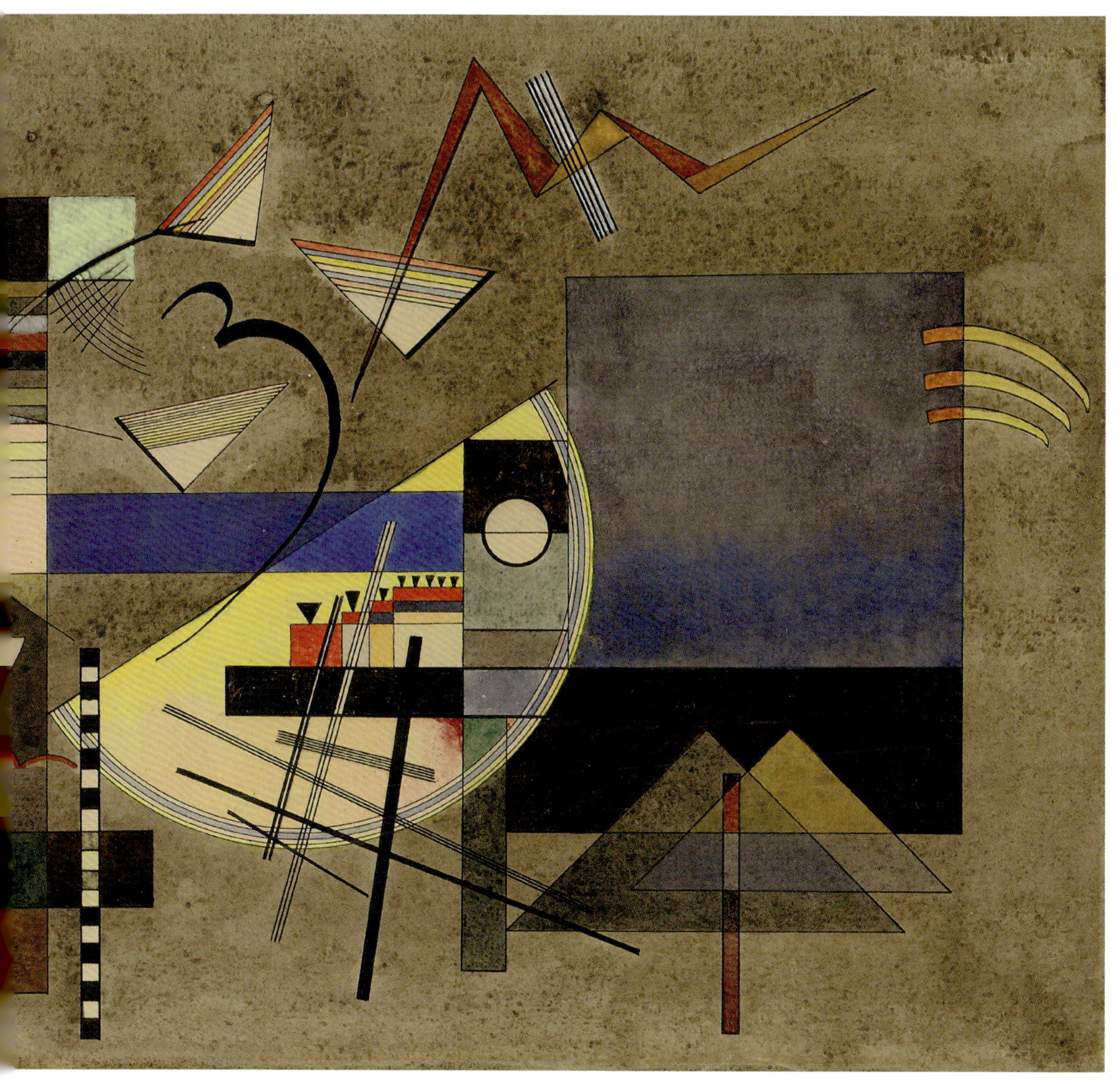

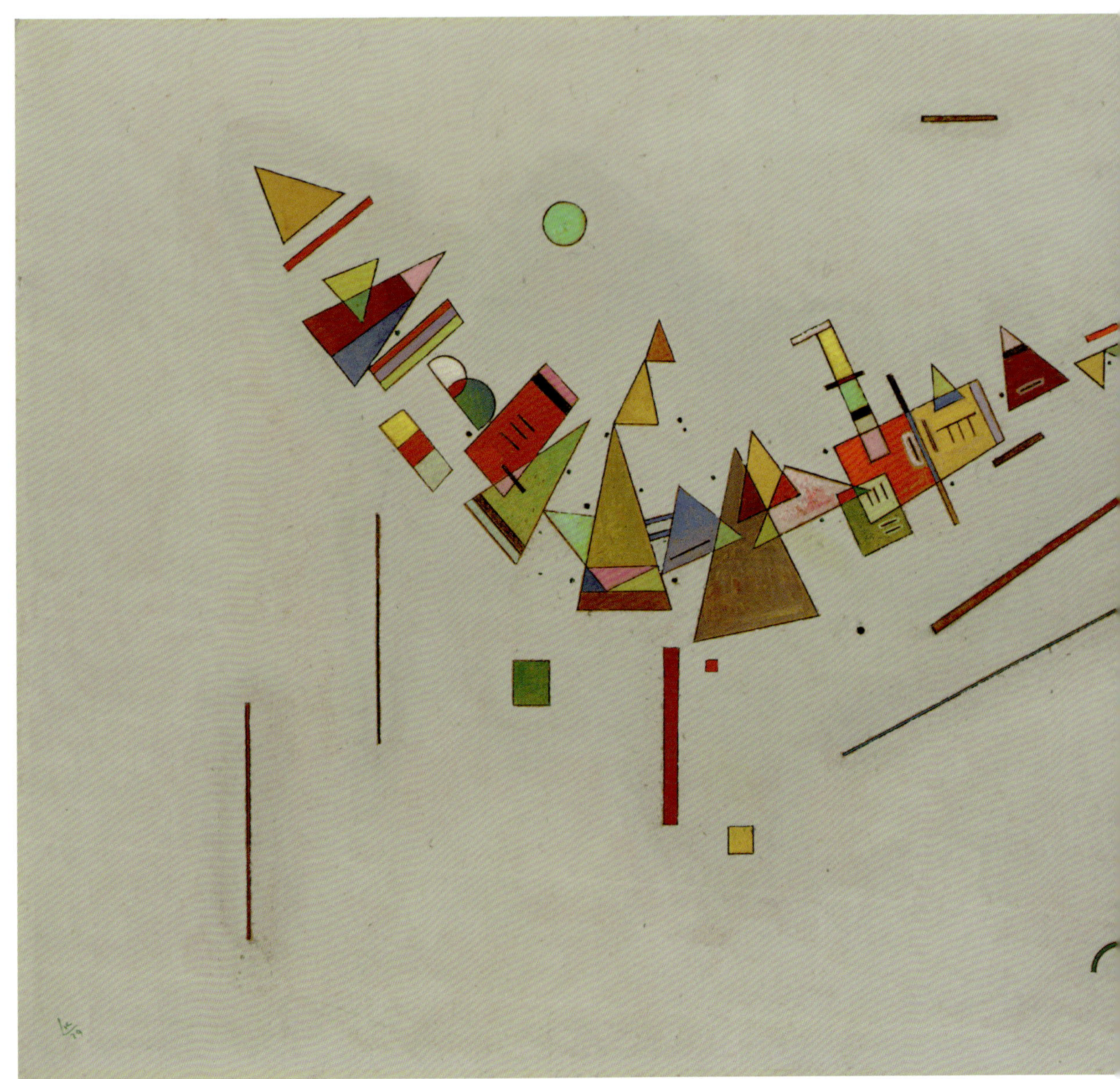

Angular Swing

Triangles

Winkelschwung

Giro angular

Oscillazione angolare

Hoekige zwaai

1929, Oil on board/Huile sur carton, 48,5 × 70 cm, Private collection

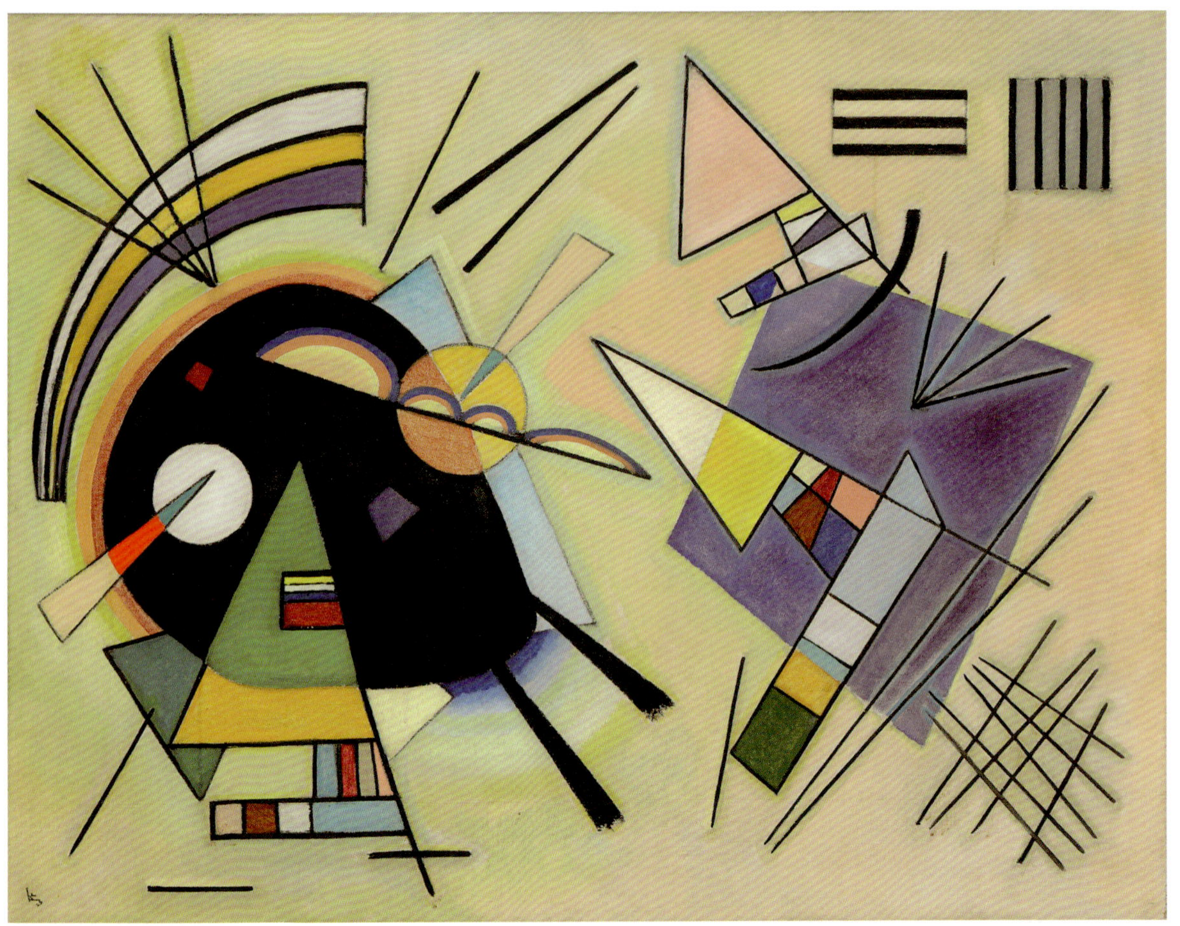

Black and Violet

Noir et violet

Schwarz und Violett

Negro y violeta

Nero e viola

Zwart en paars

1923, Oil on canvas/Huile sur toile, 77,8 × 100,4 cm, Private collection

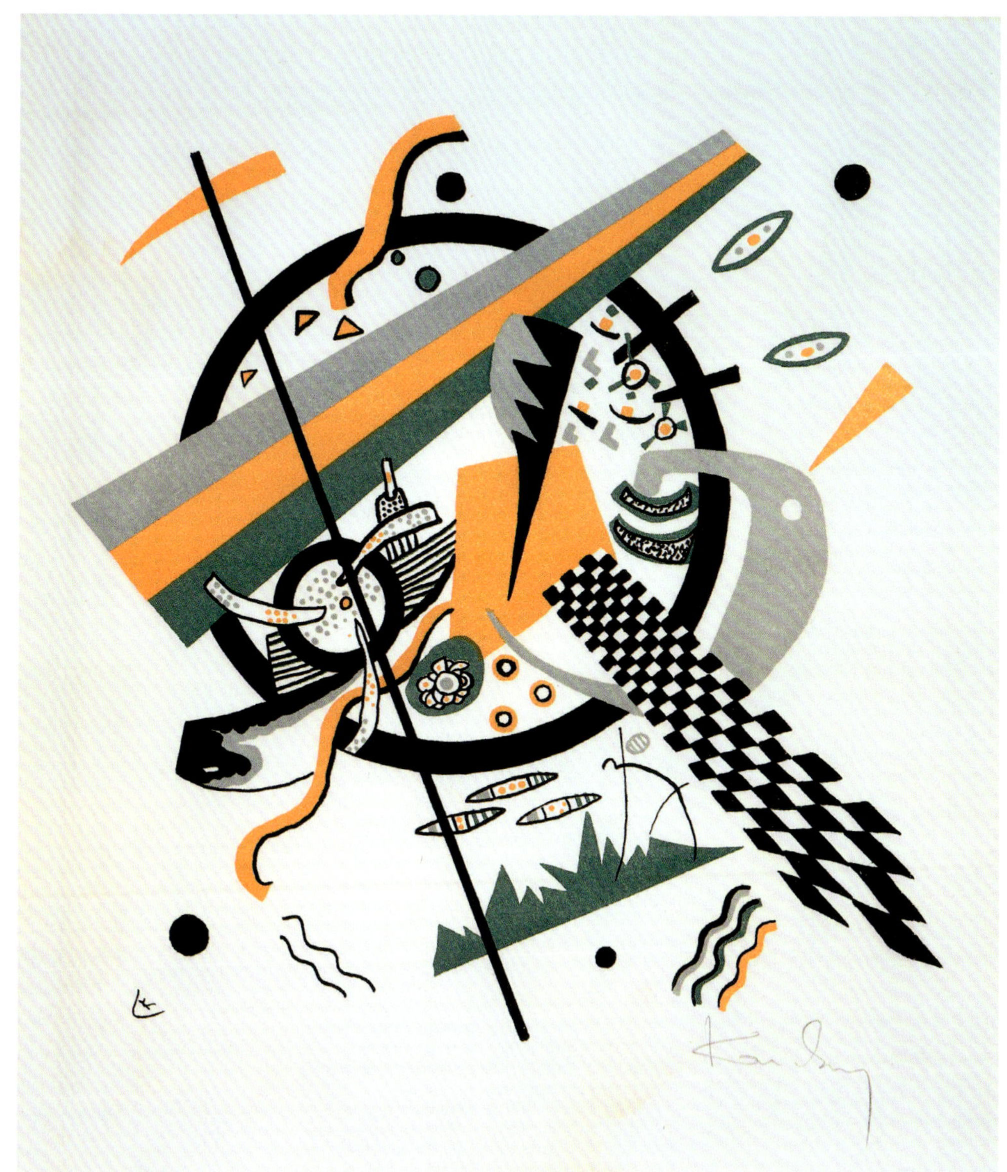

Small Worlds IV

Petits Mondes IV

Kleine Welten IV

Pequeños mundos IV

Piccoli mondi IV

Kleine werelden IV

1922, Color lithograph/ Lithographie en couleur, 26,6 × 25,5 cm, Cincinnati Art Museum, Cincinnati

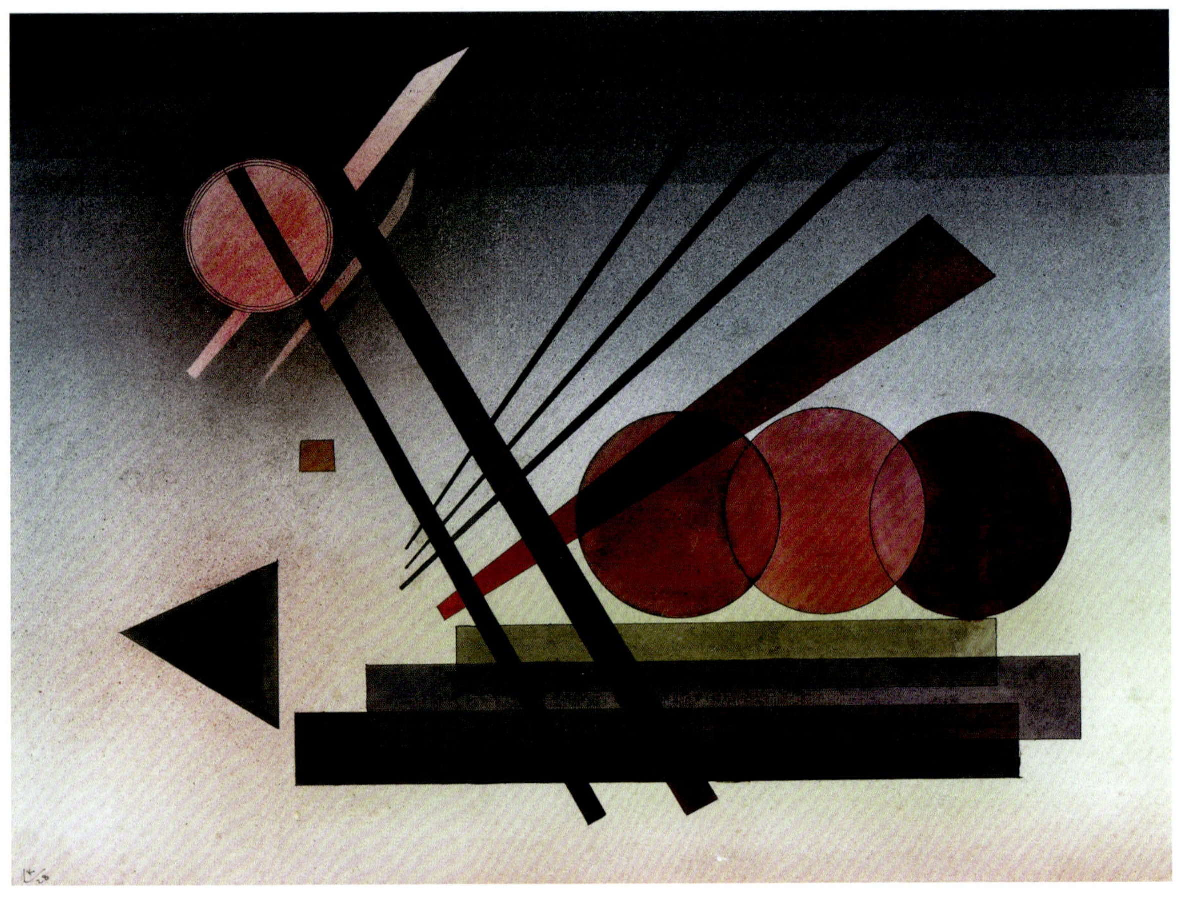

Floating Strength

Force en suspension

Schwebende Kraft

Fuerza de flotación

Forza galleggiante

Zwevende kracht

*1928, Watercolor on paper/Aquarelle sur papier,
34 × 47 cm, Private collection*

Orange – Composition with Chessboard

Composition orange avec échiquier

Orange – Komposition mit Schachbrett

Naranja – composición con tablero de ajedrez

Composizione arancio con scacchiera

Oranje – compositie met schaakbord

*1923, Color lithograph/Lithographie en couleur,
48,3 × 44,5 cm, Dallas Museum of Art, Dallas*

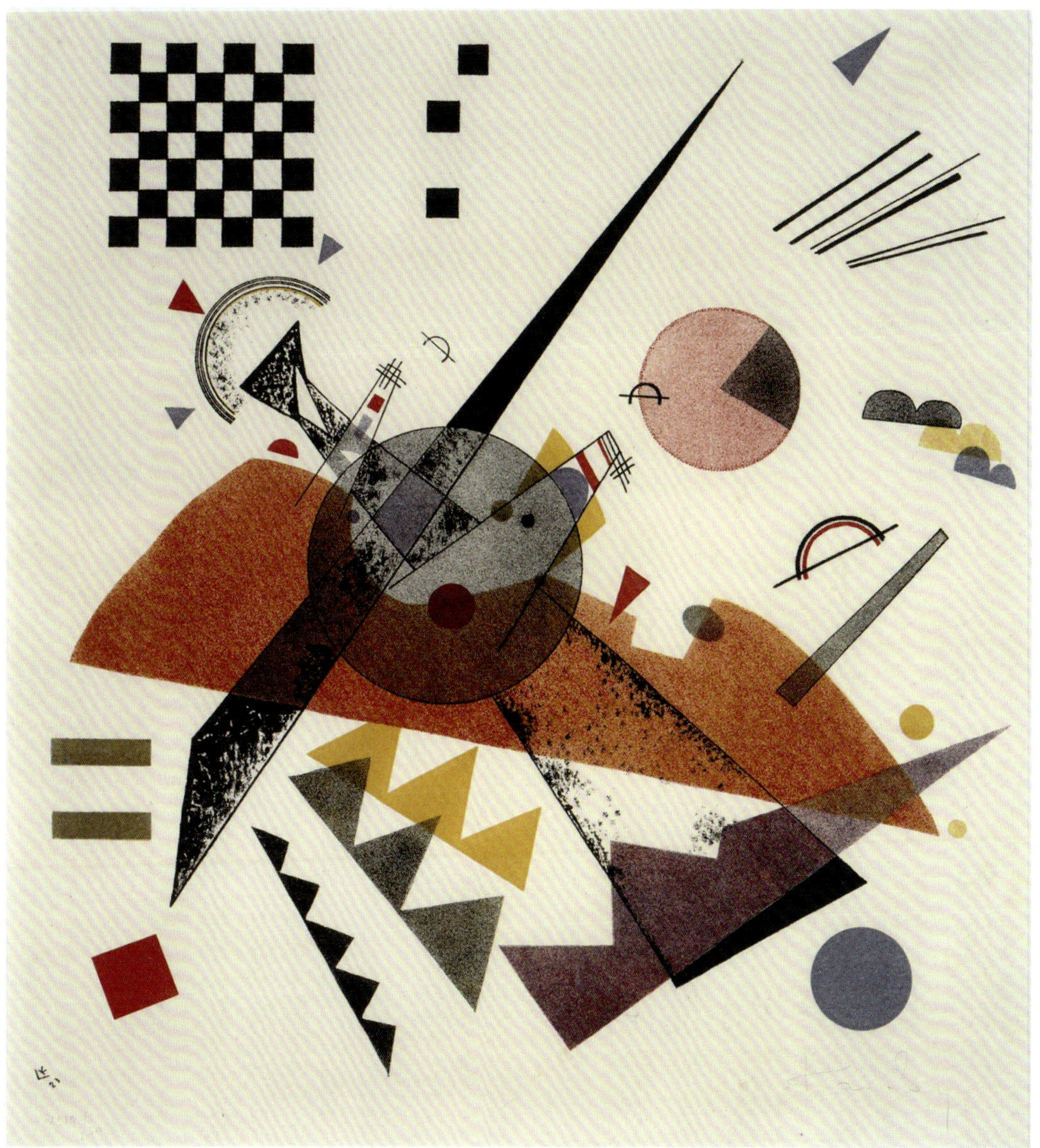

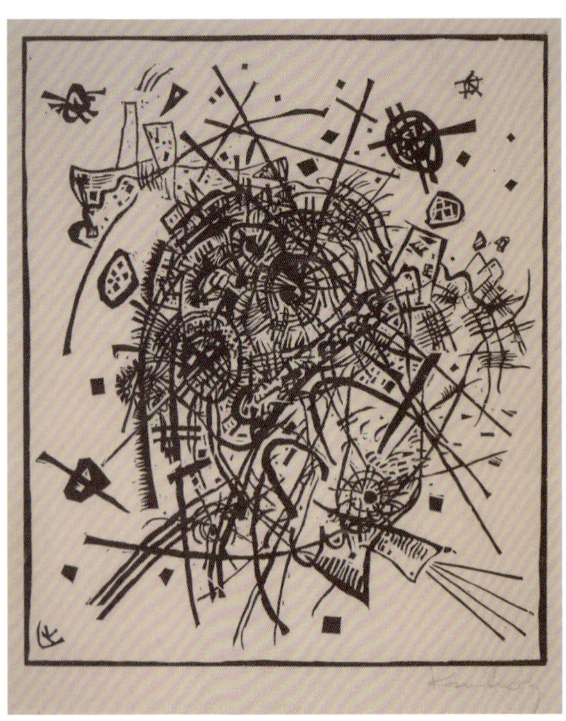

Small Worlds VIII

Petits Mondes VIII

Kleine Welten VIII

Pequeños mundos VIII

Piccoli mondi VIII

Kleine werelden VIII

1922, Woodcut/Bois gravé, 27,3 × 23,3 cm, Dallas Museum of Art, Dallas

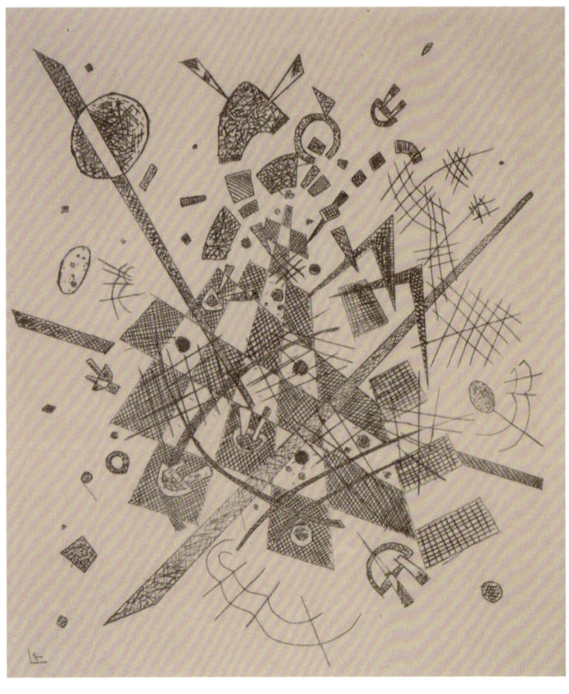

Small Worlds IX

Petits Mondes IX

Kleine Welten IX

Pequeños mundos IX

Piccoli mondi IX

Kleine werelden IX

1922, Etching/Eau forte, 23,8 × 19,7 cm, Dallas Museum of Art, Dallas

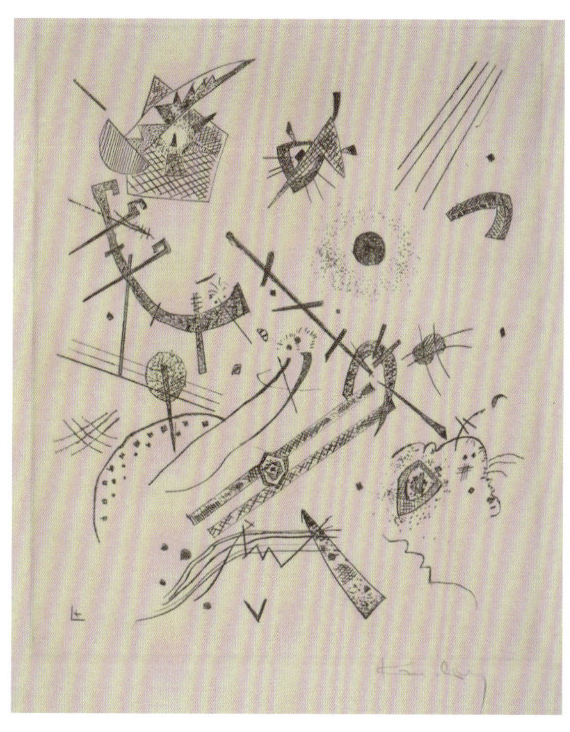

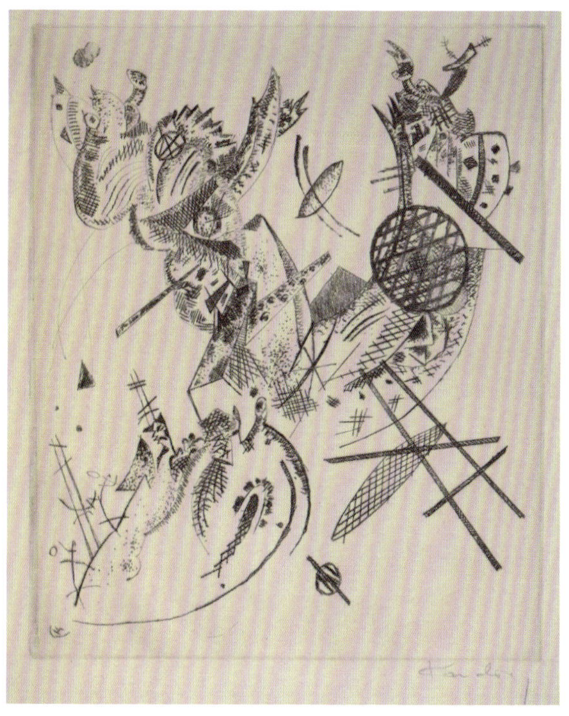

Small Worlds XI

Petits Mondes XI

Kleine Welten XI

Pequeños mundos XI

Piccoli mondi XI

Kleine werelden XI

1922, Etching/Eau forte, 23,8 × 19,5 cm, Dallas Museum of Art, Dallas

Small Worlds XII

Petits Mondes XII

Kleine Welten XII

Pequeños mundos XII

Piccoli mondi XII

Kleine werelden XII

1922, Etching/Eau forte, 24,6 × 19,7 cm, Dallas Museum of Art, Dallas

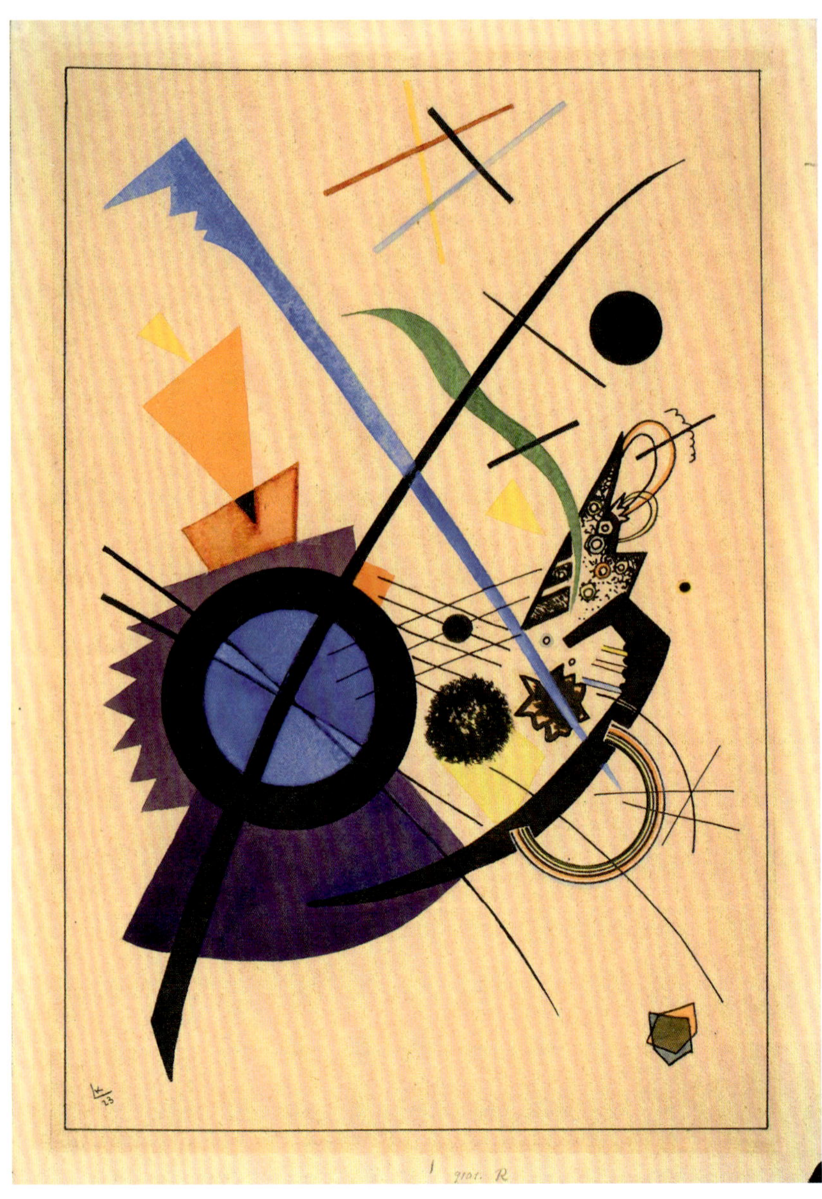

Blue in Violet

Bleu dans violet

Blau in Violett

Azul violeta

Blu nel viola

Blauw in paars

1923, Watercolor, gouache and ink on paper/Aquarelle, gouache et encre de Chine sur papier, 34 × 24,1 cm, Davis Museum and Cultural Center, Wellesley College, MA

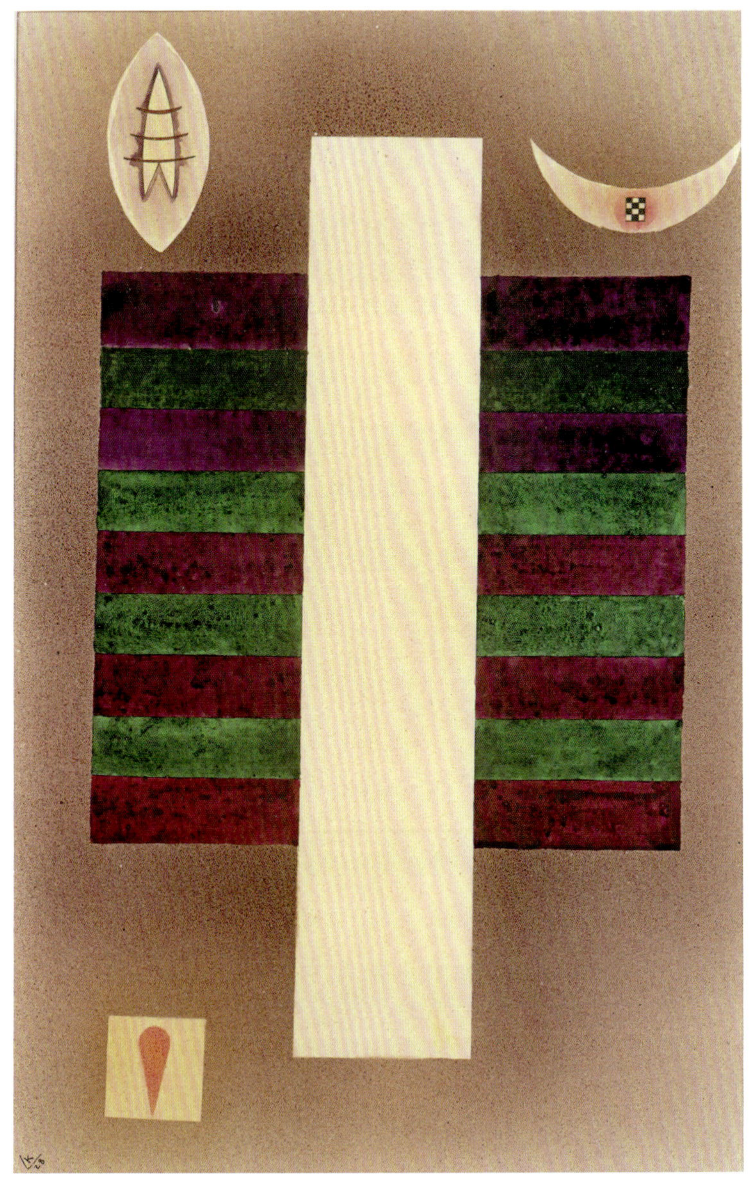

Vertical

Vertical

Vertikal

Vertical

Verticale

Verticaal

1928, Gouache and watercolor on paper/Gouache et
aquarelle sur papier, 47 × 30,5 cm,
Private collection

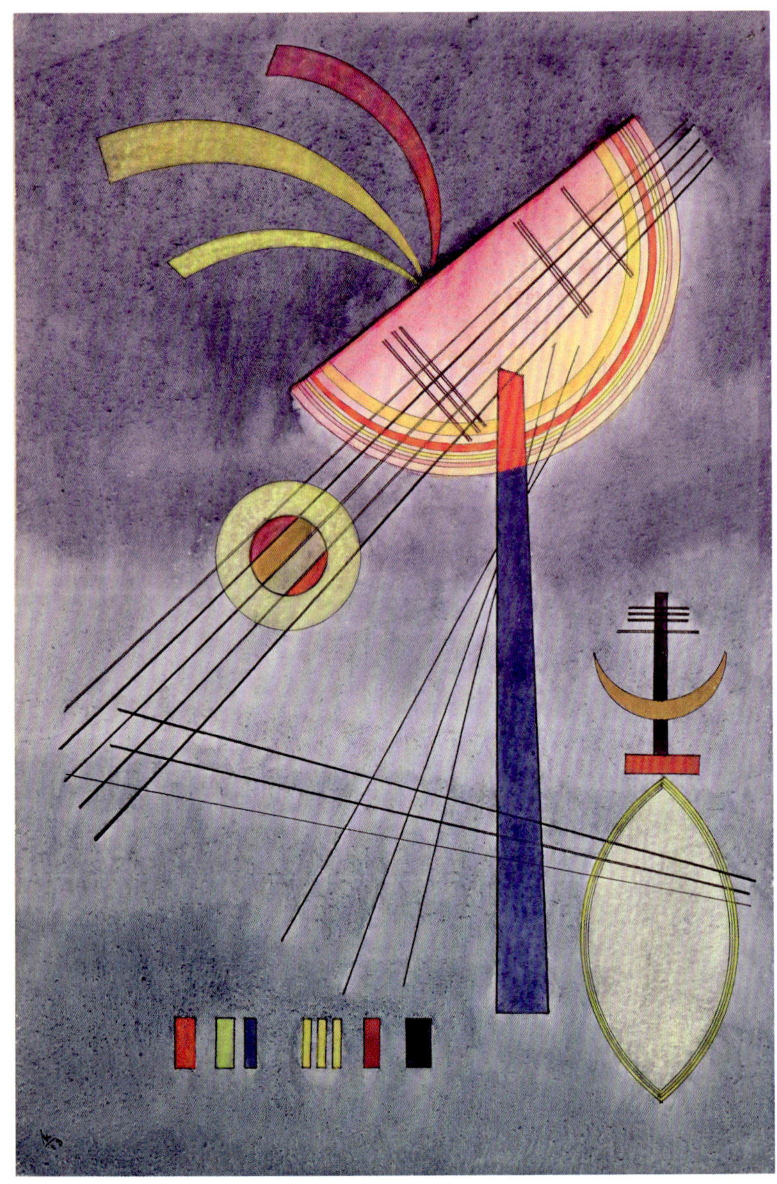

Leaning Semicircle

Demi-cercle incliné

Aufgestützter Halbkreis

Semicírculo que se inclina

Semicerchio pendente

Ondersteunde halve cirkel

1928, Watercolor, pen and ink on paper/Aquarelle,
plume et encre de Chine sur papier,
45,9 × 30,5 cm, Private collection

Gray Square

Carré gris

Graues Quadrat

Gris cuadrado

Quadrato grigio

Grijs vierkant

1923, Watercolor, pen and ink on paper/Aquarelle,
plume et encre de Chine sur papier,
45,1 × 40 cm, Private collection

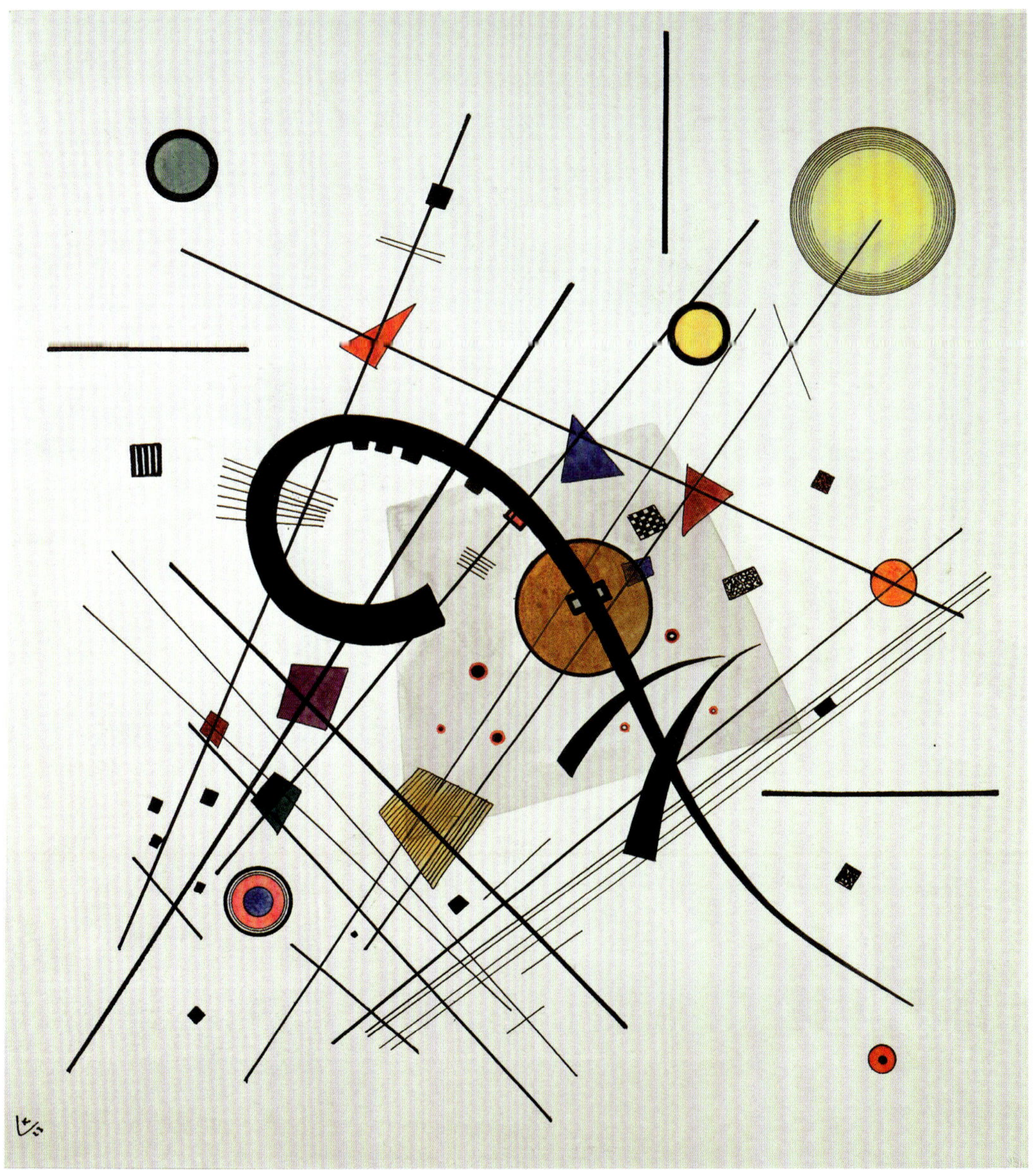

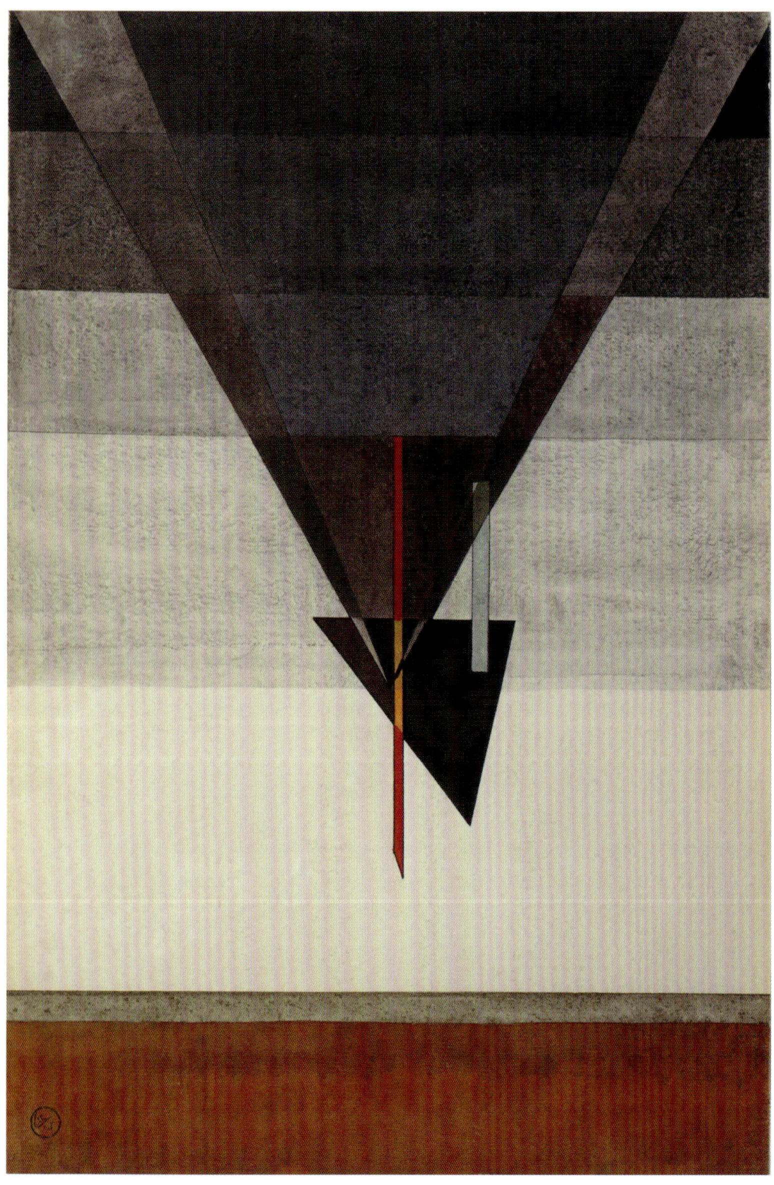

Descent

Descendant

Absteigend

Pendiente

Discendente

Afdalend

1925, Gouache and mixed media on paper/
Gouache et technique mixte sur papier,
48 × 32 cm, Private collection

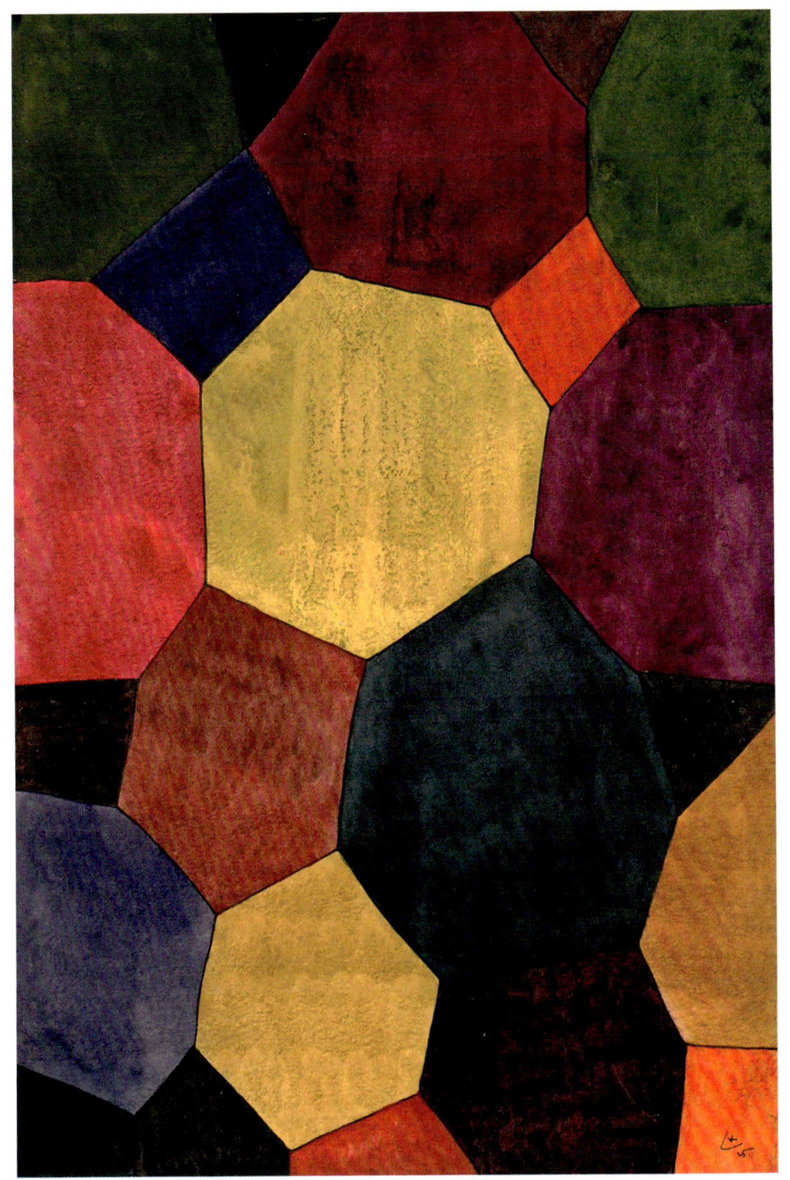

Colored Hexagons
Hexagones colorés
Farbige Hexagone
Hexágonos de colores
Esagoni colorati
Kleurige hexagonalen

1925, Gouache on paper/Gouache sur papier,
48,7 × 32,5 cm, Private collection

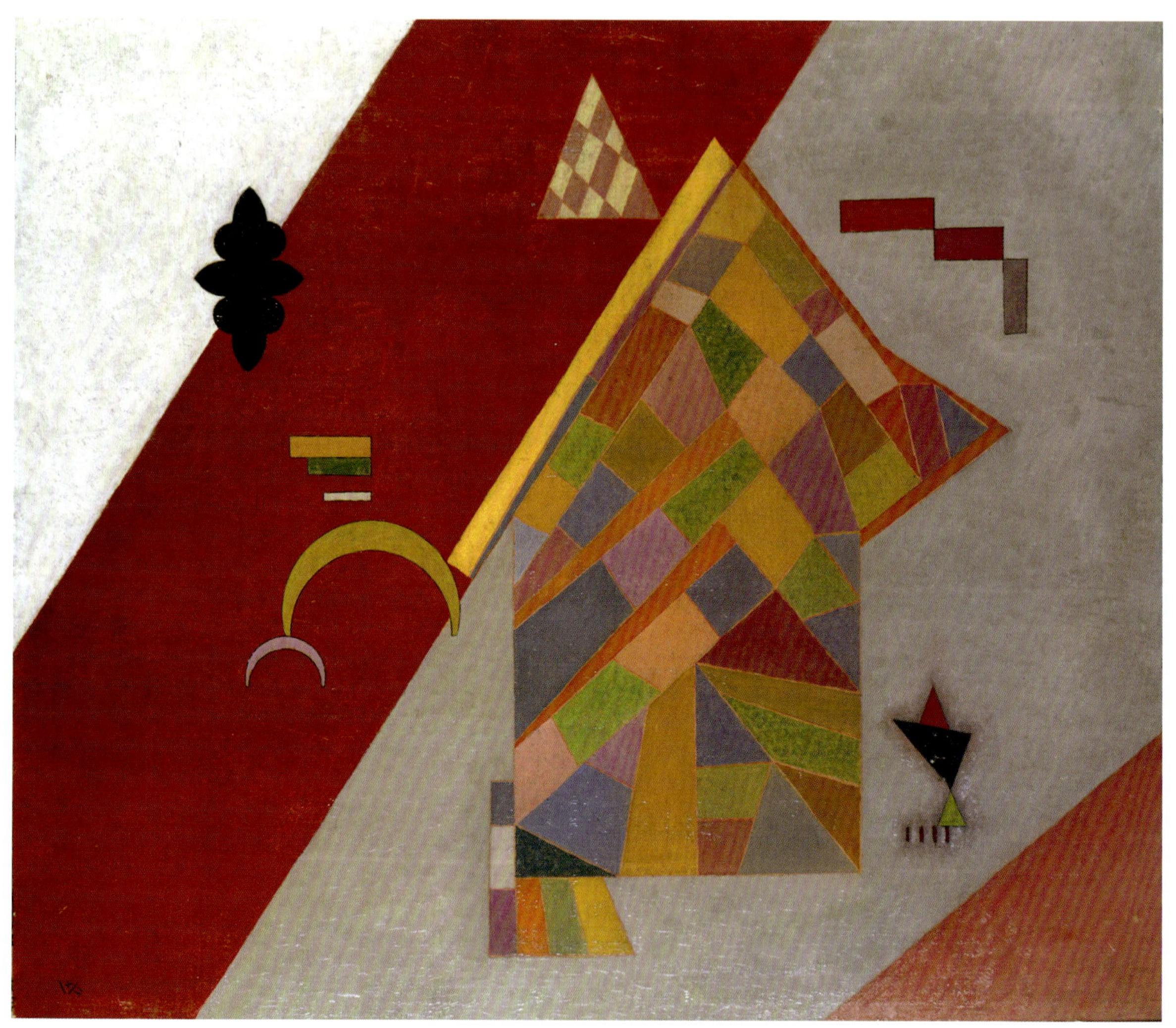

Red Across **Diagonales Rot** **Rosso diagonale**

Rouge diagonal **Rojo a través de** **Diagonaal rood**

1931, Oil and tempera on cardboard/Huile et tempéra sur carton, 70 × 80 cm, Private collection

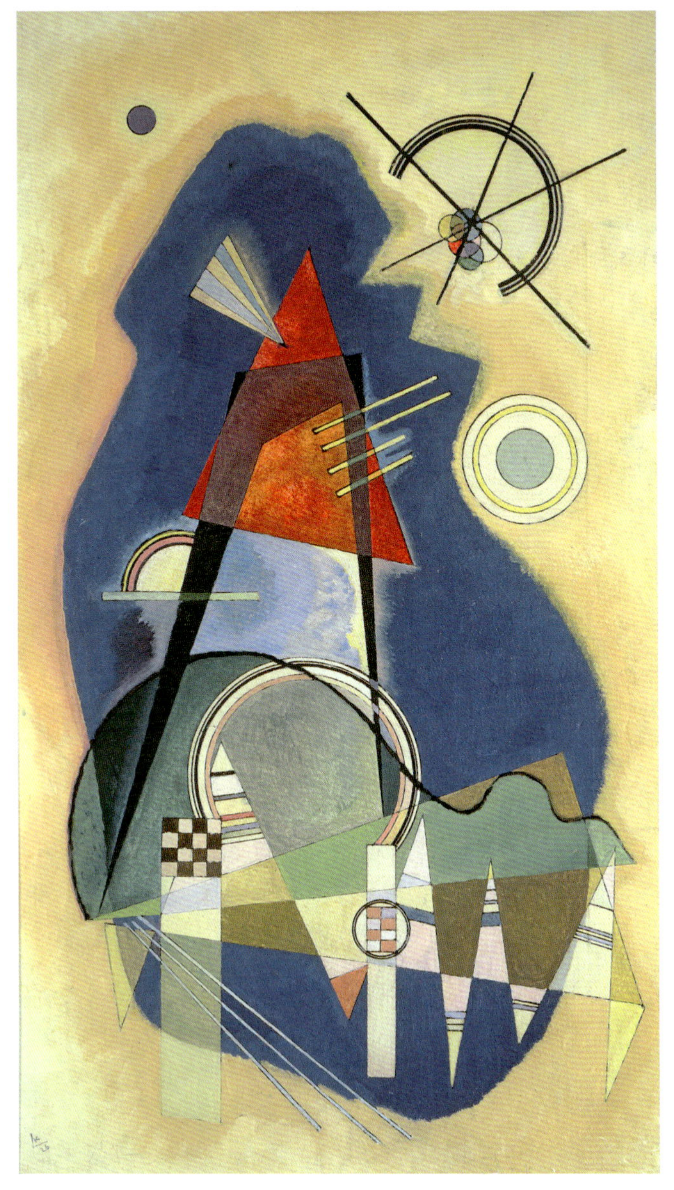

Discreet Blue
Bleu discret
Diskretes Blau
Blue discreta
Blu discreto
Discreet blauw

*1926, Oil on canvas/Huile sur toile,
60 × 35 cm, Private collection*

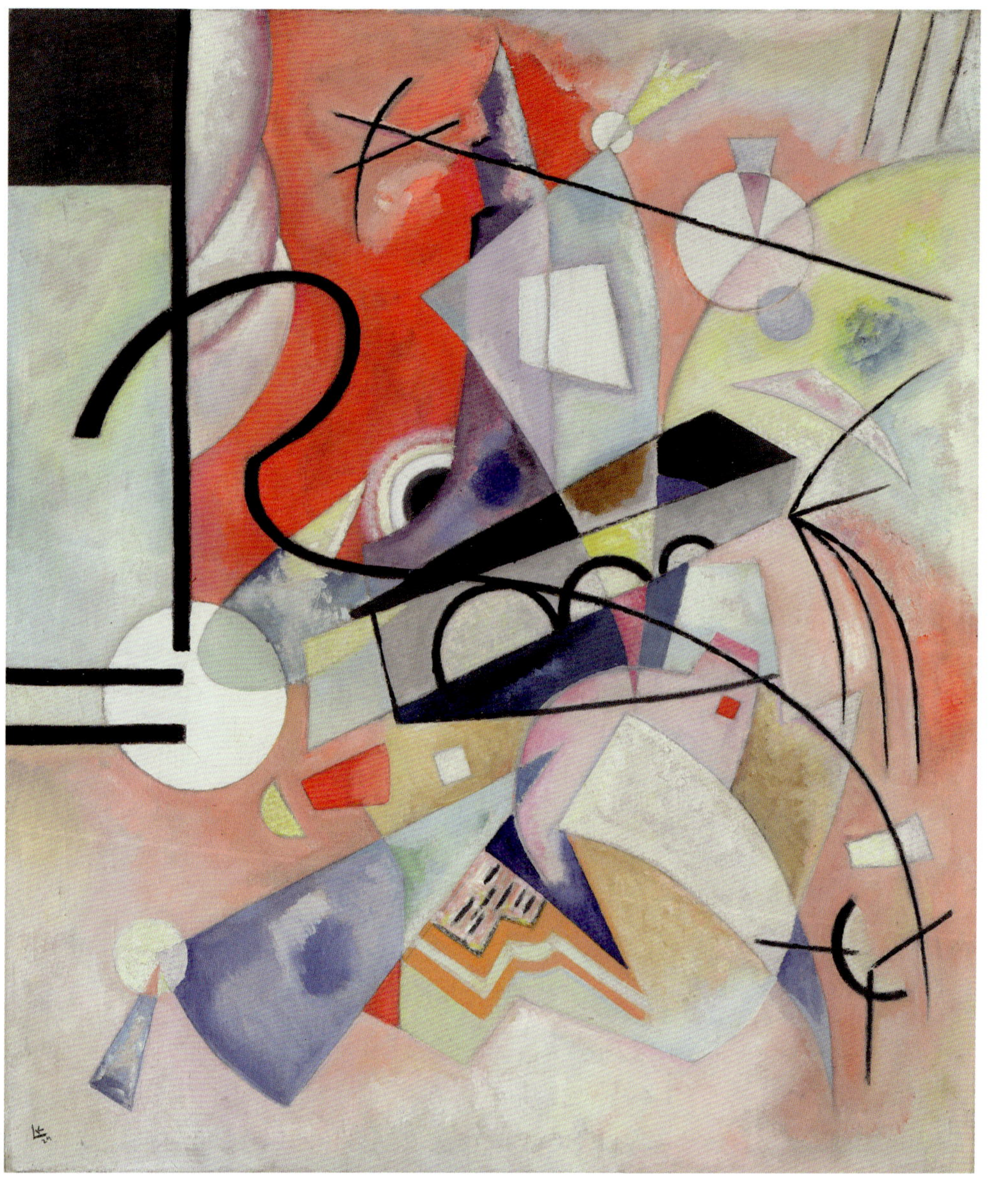

Self-illuminating
Auto-éclairant
Selbstleuchtend
Uno mismo-iluminación
Autoilluminante
Zelfverlichtend
1924, Oil on canvas/
Huile sur toile,
69,5 × 59,5 cm,
Private collection

Green Composition
*Composition
en vert*
*Komposition
in Grün*
Composición verde
*Composizione
verde*
*Compositie
in groen*
1923, Oil on canvas/
Huile sur toile,
Private collection

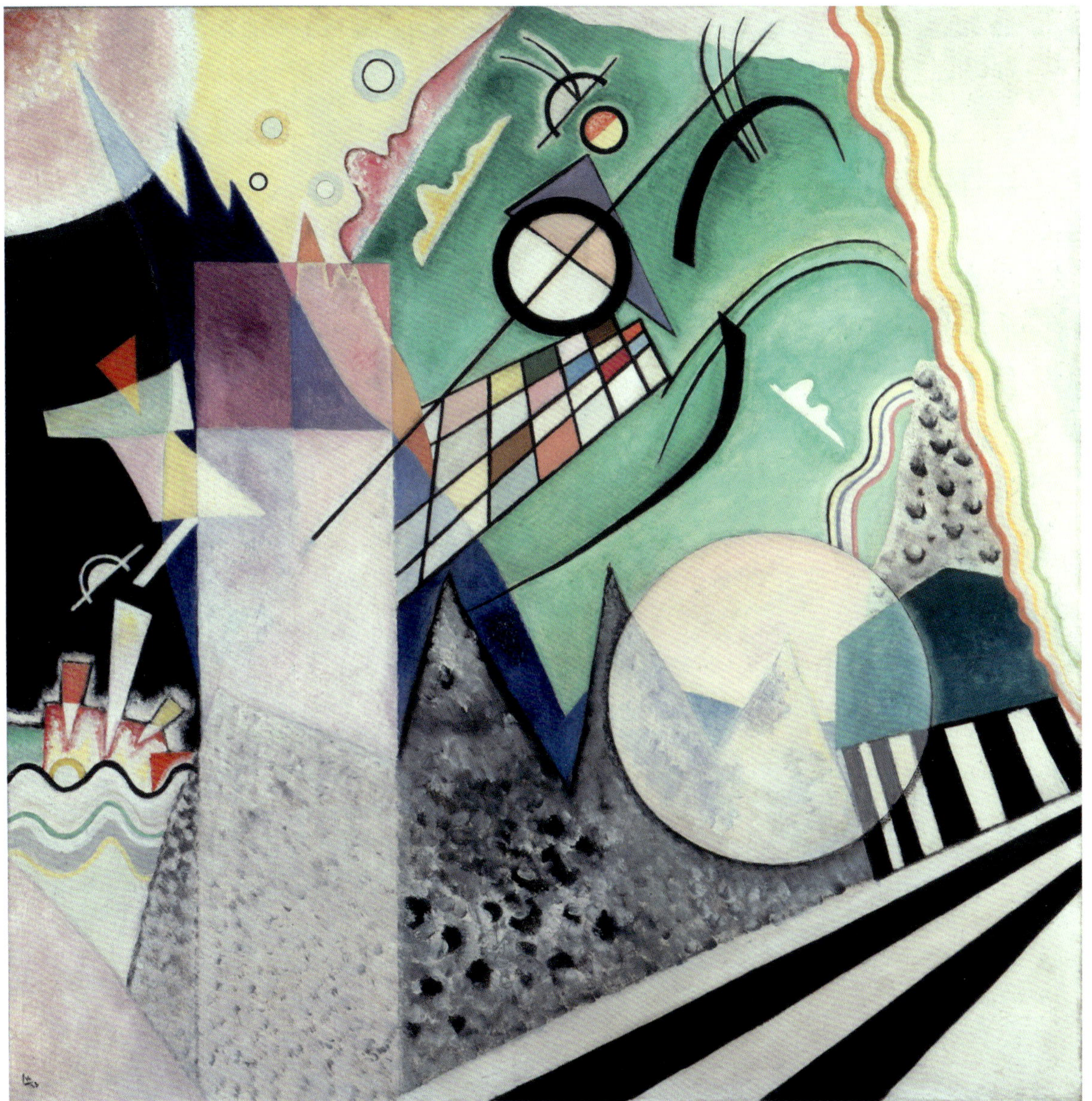

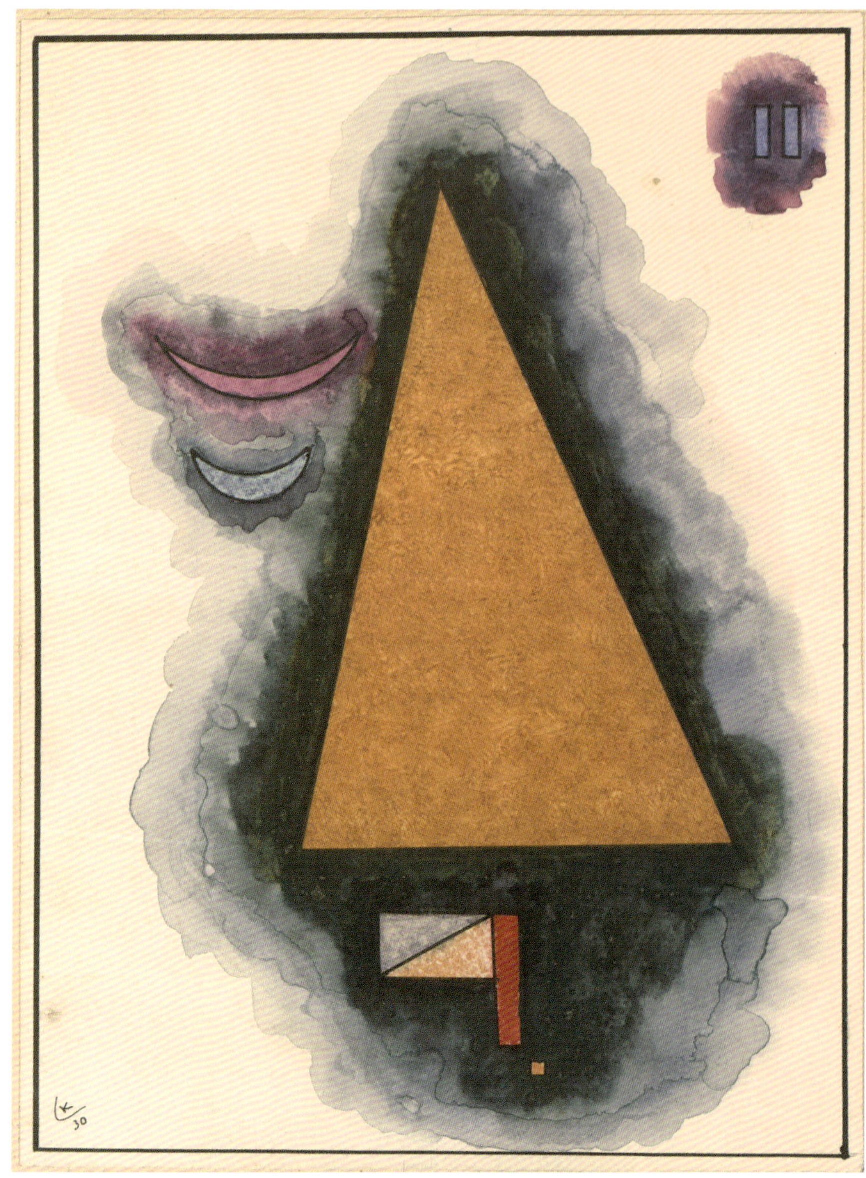

Composition

Composition

Komposition

Composición

Composizione

Compositie

*1930, Watercolor, pencil and ink
on paper/Aquarelle, mine de plomb
et encre de Chine sur papier,
23,6 × 17,5 cm, Private collection*

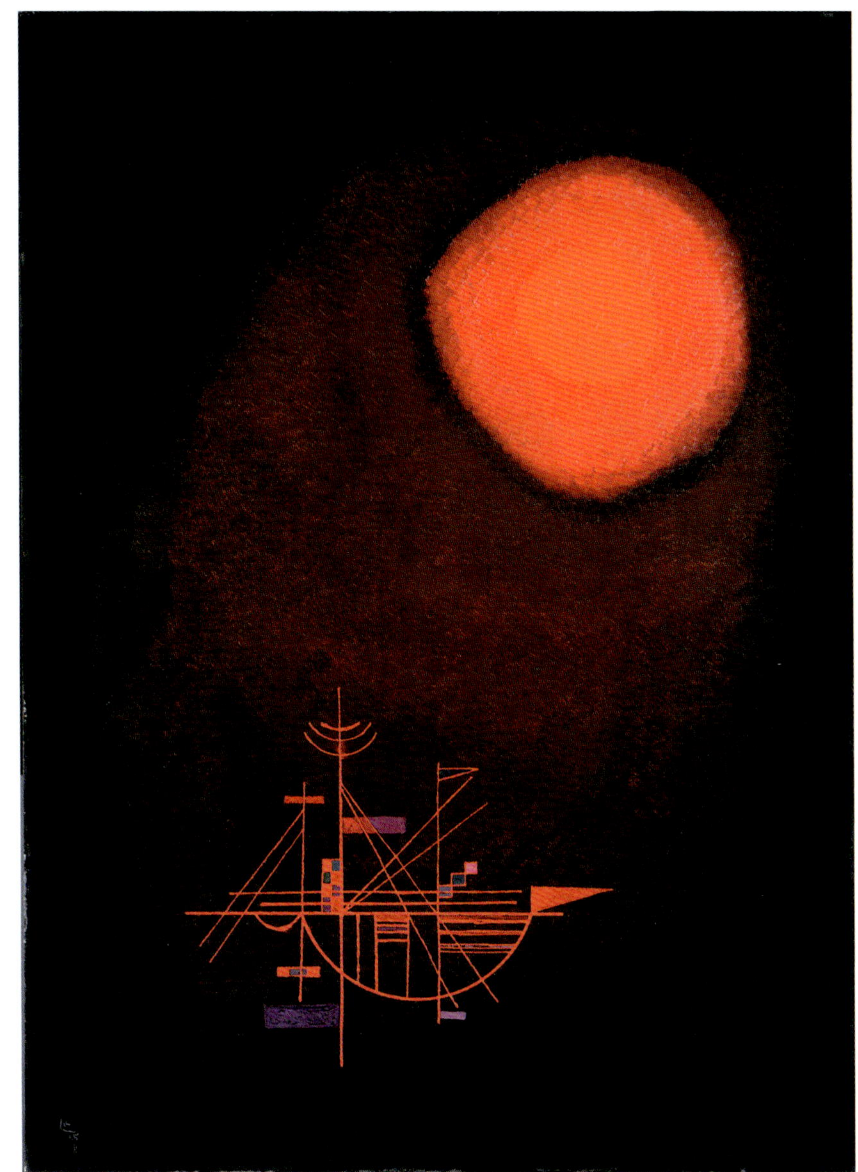

One Spit
Une Tache
Ein Fleck
Un asador
Una macchia
Een vlek
1925, Oil on cardboard/Huile sur carton, Private collection

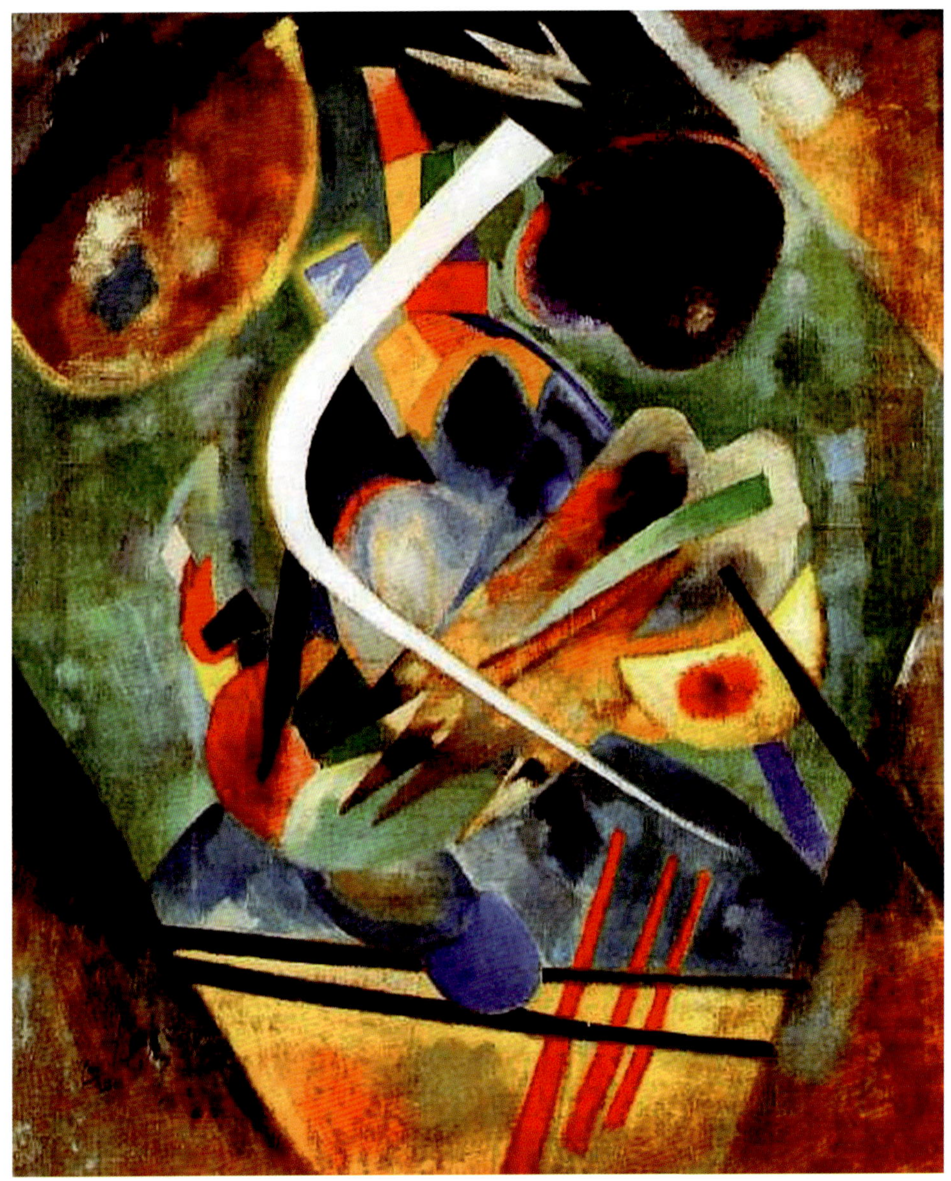

White Line

Trait blanc

Weißer Strich

Línea blanca

Linea bianca

Witte streep

1920, Oil on canvas/Huile sur toile, 80 × 98 cm, Museum Ludwig, Köln

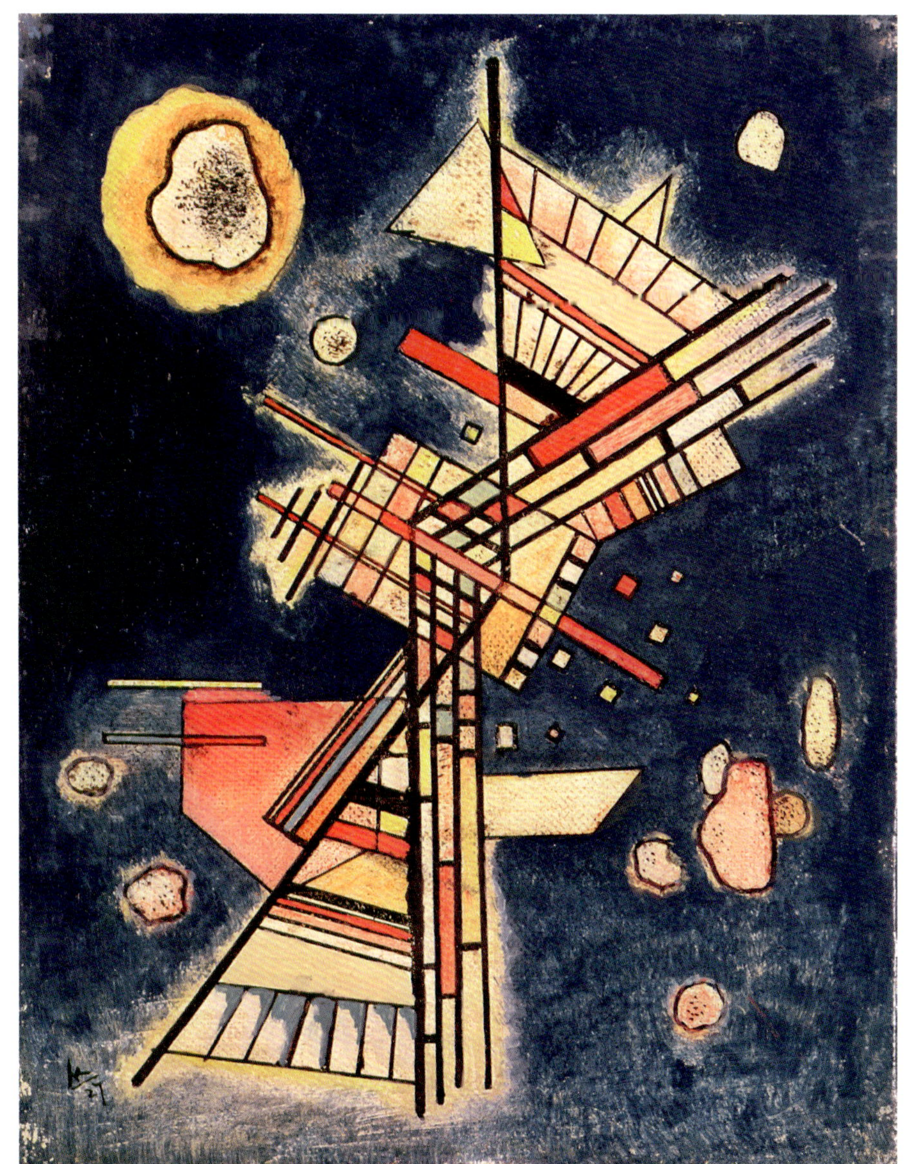

*Composition with a
Blue Background*

Composition avec fond bleu

*Komposition mit blauem
Hintergrund*

Composición con fondo azul

Composizione con sfondo blu

*Compositie met blauwe
achtergrond*

1927, Oil on canvas/Huile sur
toile, Private collection

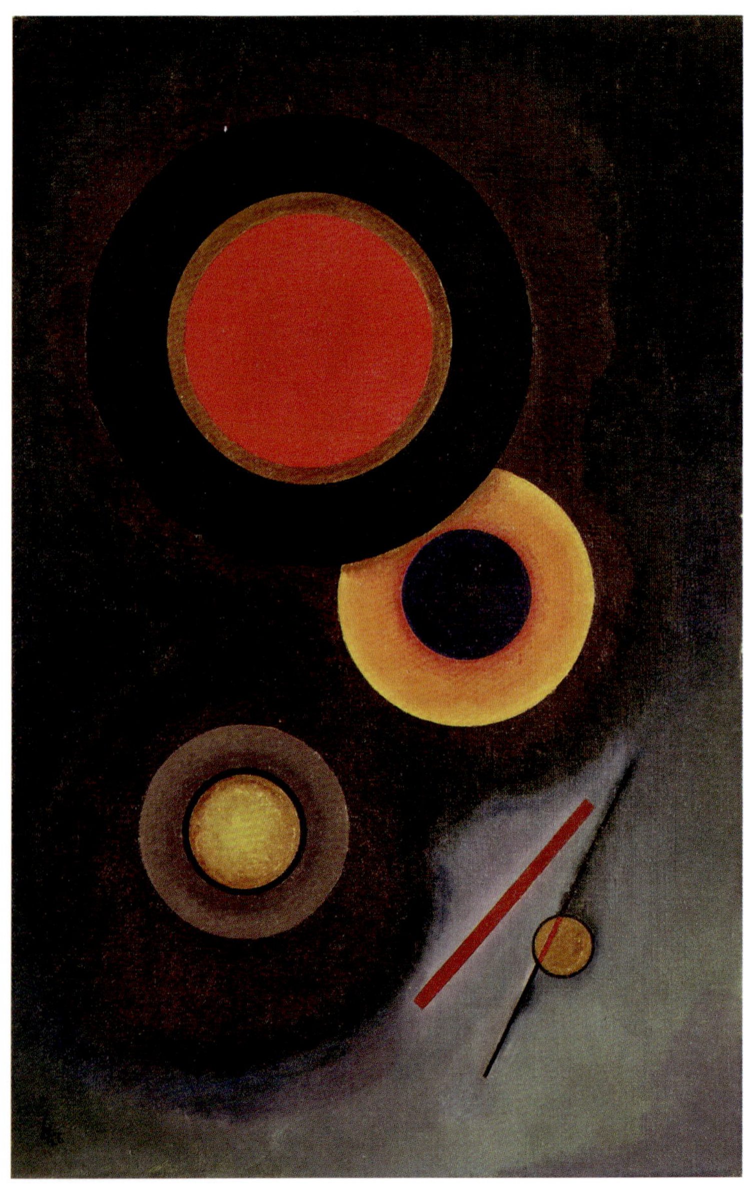

Composition with Circles and Lines
Composition avec cercles et lignes
Komposition mit Kreisen und Linien
Composición con círculos y líneas
Composizione con cerchi e linee
Compositie met cirkels en lijnen

*1926, Oil on canvas/Huile sur toile, 100 × 64 cm,
Museum Ludwig, Köln*

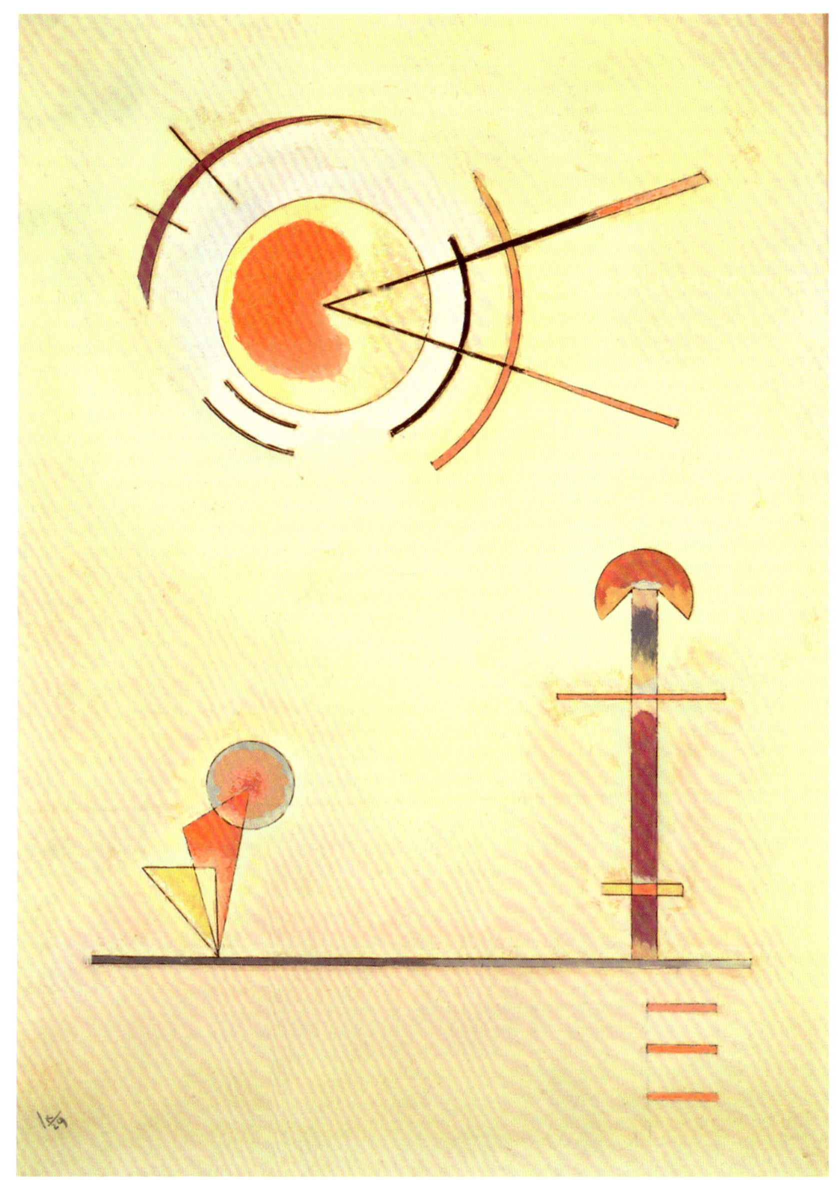

Composition

Composition

Komposition

Composición

Composizione

Compositie

1929, Oil on canvas/Huile sur toile,
Fondation Maeght, St. Paul de Vence

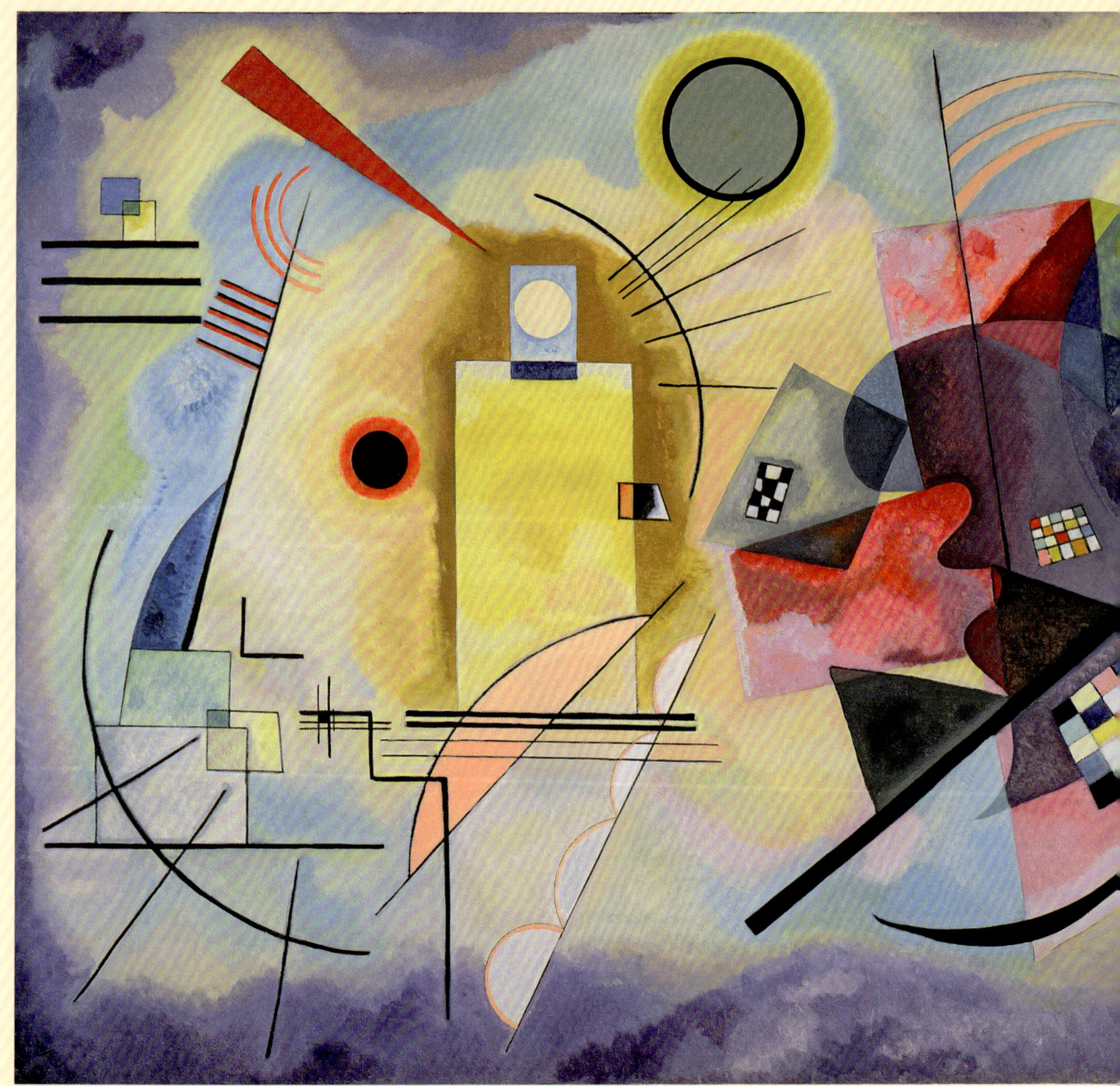

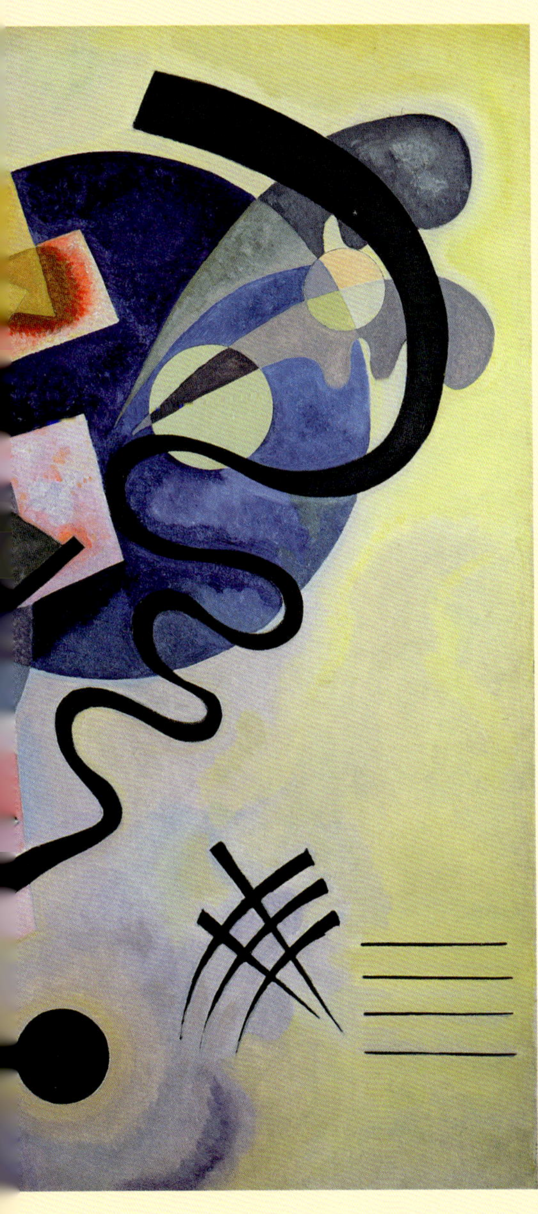

Yellow-Red-Blue

Jaune-Rouge-Bleu

Gelb-Rot-Blau

Amarillo-rojo-azul

Giallo, rosso, blu

Geel-rood-blauw

1925, Oil on canvas/Huile sur toile, 127 × 200 cm,
Musée National d'Art Moderne, Centre Pompidou, Paris

Yellow-Red-Blue, 1925

The painting "Yellow-Red-Blue" is the most important work of Kandinsky's Weimar phase of the Bauhaus period in both its size and its significance.

The left half of the image is bright and easy, graphical and linear; the right side is darker and heavier, but with rather more pictorial ideas like the dark blue circle and the curving black line. The "earthly" Yellow stands for strength, "heavenly" Blue wants to float up to the right. This contrast of form and color is reminiscent of Kandinsky's earlier motif, the struggle between the holy knight, St. George, and the dragon, representing the materialism which must be overcome. He seems to reappear here, completely formalized.

In addition to the main event, more graphical elements were added to the image, for example, linear radiating patterns or overlaps and color filled checkerboard patterns, which hint at Kandinsky's knowledge of the emerging perceptual psychology.

Jaune-Rouge-Bleu, 1925

Autant par sa taille que par sa signification, le tableau *Jaune-Rouge-Bleu* est l'œuvre principale de Kandinsky pendant la phase weimarienne du Bauhaus.

La partie gauche du tableau est claire et légère, conçue linéairement et graphiquement, alors que sa partie droite est plus sombre et plus lourde, avec des intrusions plutôt picturales comme le cercle bleu et les sinuosités de la puissante ligne noire. Le jaune "terrestre" signifie la fête, tandis que le bleu "céleste" tend à s'échapper vers le haut, à droite. Dans sa constellation formelle et colorée, ce couple antithétique rappelle un ancien leitmotiv de Kandinsky : le combat entre le chevalier saint (saint Georges) et le dragon (symbolisant le matérialisme triomphant). Ce thème semble réapparaître ici, totalement formalisé.

En outre, plusieurs éléments graphiques ont été intégrés dans le tableau, à côté de l'événement principal : par exemple, des motifs linéaires rayonnants ou des superpositions de motifs d'échiquier remplis de couleurs, qui renvoient à la connaissance qu'avait Kandinsky des théories de la psychologie perceptive qui commençaient à se répandre.

Gelb-Rot-Blau, 1925

Das Gemälde „Gelb-Rot-Blau" ist sowohl in seiner Größe wie seiner Bedeutung Kandinskys Hauptwerk aus der Weimarer Phase der Bauhauszeit.

Die linke Hälfte des Bildes ist hell und leicht, graphisch und geradlinig gestaltet, die rechte dunkler und schwerer, mit eher malerischen Einfällen wie dem dunkelblauen Kreis und der kräftigen, gebogenen schwarzen Linie. Das „irdische" Gelb bedeutet Festigkeit, das „himmlische" Blau will nach rechts oben entschweben. Dieses Gegensatzpaar erinnert in seiner formalen und farbigen Konstellation an Kandinskys früheres Leitmotiv, den Kampf zwischen dem heiligen Ritter (hl. Georg) und dem Drachen (stellvertretend für den zu überwindenden Materialismus). Er scheint hier gänzlich formalisiert wieder aufzutauchen.

Zusätzlich zum Hauptgeschehen wurden mehrere graphische Elemente ins Bild aufgenommen, z. B. lineare Strahlenmuster oder Überschneidungen und farbig ausgefüllte Schachbrettmuster, die auf Kandinskys Kenntnis der damals aufkommenden Wahrnehmungspsychologie hinweisen.

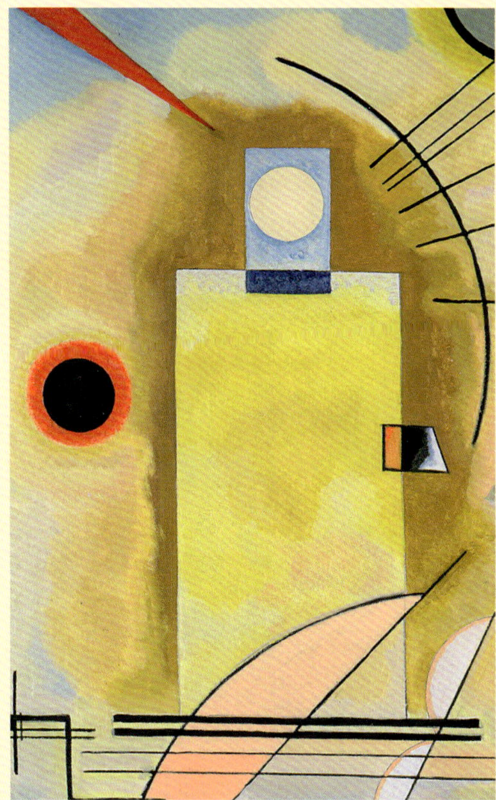 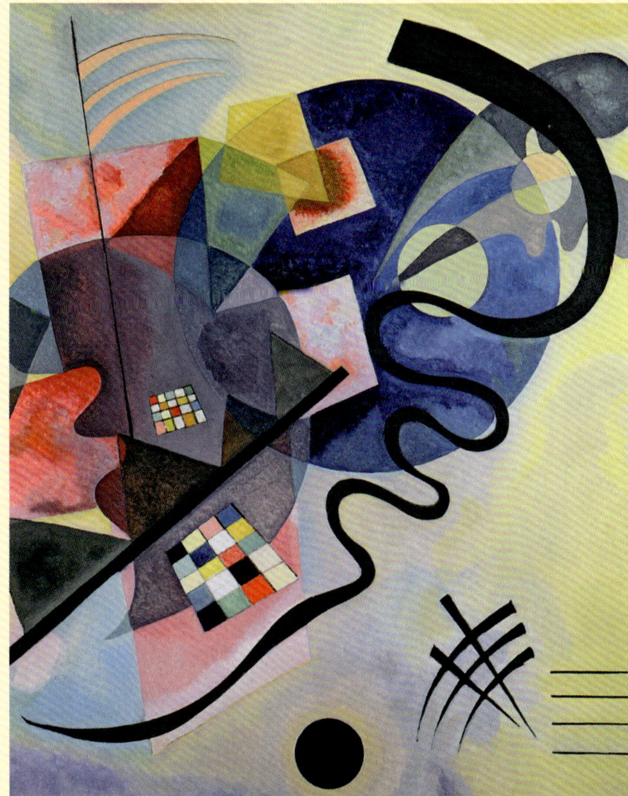

Amarillo-Rojo-Azul, 1925

La pintura "Amarillo-Rojo-Azul" es el trabajo más importante de la fase Weimar de Kandinsky durante su periodo en la Bauhaus, tanto en tamaño como en importancia.

La mitad izquierda de la imagen es brillante y sencilla, gráfica y lineal; el lado derecho es más oscuro y pesado, pero con ideas notablemente más pictóricas, como el círculo azul oscuro y la línea negra curvada. El amarillo

Giallo, Rosso, Blu, 1925

Il quadro Giallo, rosso, blu è l'opera più importante del periodo che Kandinsky trascorse a Weimar come insegnante presso il Bauhaus, sia per le sue dimensioni sia per il suo significato.

La metà sinistra dell'immagine è luminosa e semplice, grafica e lineare; il lato destro è più scuro e più pesante, ma con idee più pittoriche, come il cerchio blu scuro e la linea nera

Geel-Rood-Blauw, 1925

Het schilderij Geel-rood-blauw is zowel wat betreft zijn omvang als zijn betekenis een hoofdwerk uit Kandinsky's Bauhaus-periode in Weimar.

De linkerhelft van het beeldvlak is helder en licht, en grafisch en rechtlijnig vormgegeven, terwijl de rechterhelft donkerder en zwaarder is en meer schilderkunstige motieven toont, zoals de donkerblauwe cirkel

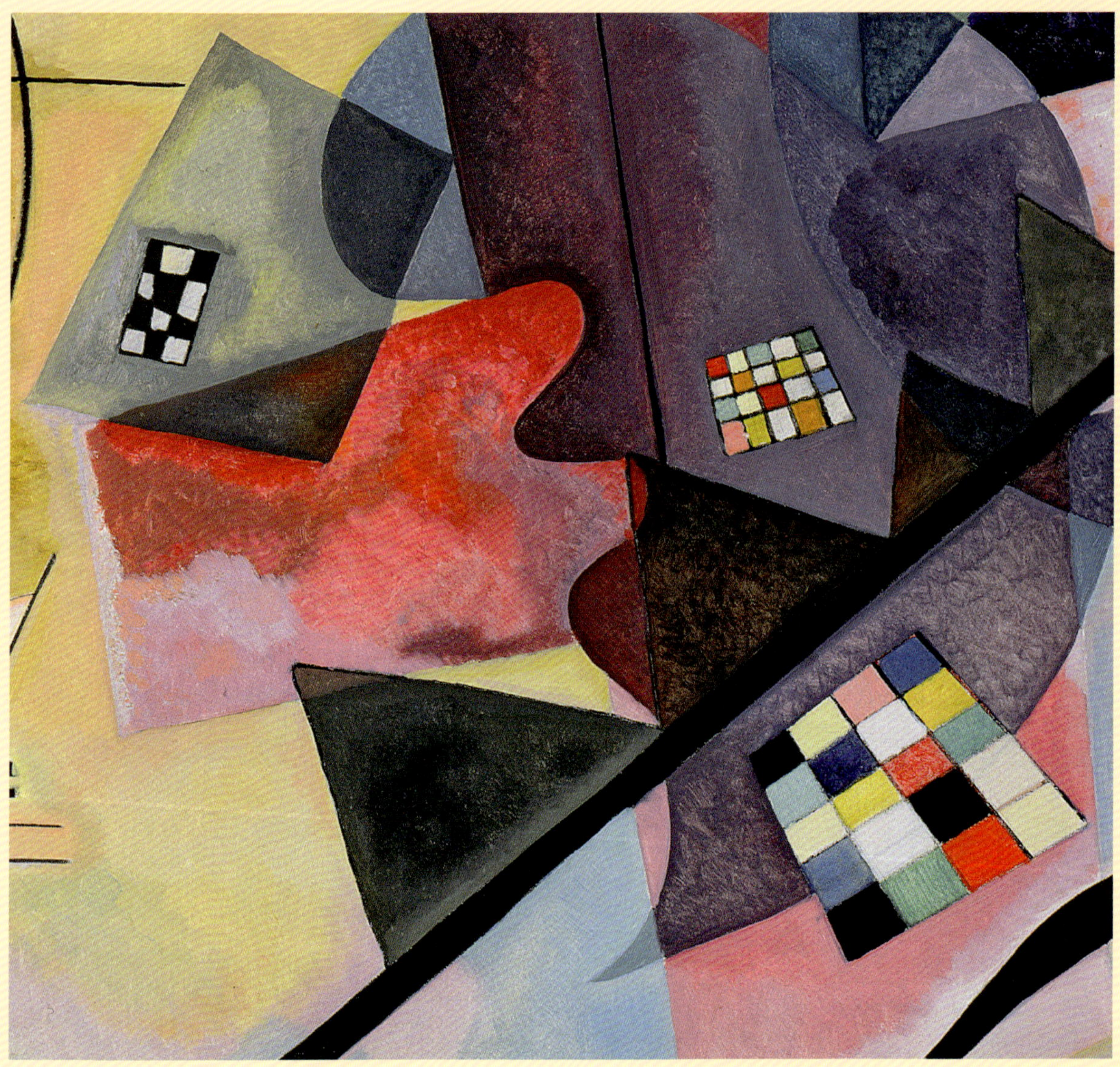

"terrenal" representa la fuerza, el azul lo "divino" que desea flotar arriba a la derecha. Este contraste de forma y color es reminiscente de un tema anterior de Kandinsky, la lucha entre el caballero sagrado, San Jorge, y el dragón, que representa el materialismo a dominar. Este parece reaparecer aquí, plenamente formalizado.

Además del tema principal, se han añadido más elementos gráficos a la imagen, como patrones lineales o solapados en estructuras radiales o patrones de tablero de ajedrez llenos de color, que dejan entrever el conocimiento de Kandinsky de la psicología perceptual emergente.

curva. Il giallo «terrestre» simboleggia la forza, mentre il blu «celestiale» sembra voler galleggiare in alto a destra. Questo contrasto di forme e colori ricorda il motivo precedente di Kandinsky, la lotta tra il santo cavaliere, San Giorgio, e il drago, che rappresenta il materialismo da superare, il quale sembra riapparire in quest'opera completamente formalizzato.

Oltre all'evento principale, sono stati aggiunti all'immagine altri elementi grafici, quali ad esempio le rette irradianti o le sovrapposizioni e le scacchiere colorate, che alludono alle conoscenze di Kandinsky in materia di psicologia percettiva emergente.

en de opvallende, gebogen zwarte lijn. Het 'aardse' geel staat voor stabiliteit, terwijl het 'hemelse' blauw naar rechtsboven wil wegzweven. Dit stel tegenstellingen doet in zijn formele en kleurrijke constellatie denken aan een eerder leidmotief van Kandinsky, de strijd tussen de heilige ridder Sint Joris en de draak (die staat voor het materialisme dat moet worden overwonnen). Dit motief schijnt hier, nu in geheel formele zin, weer op te duiken.

Naast het centrale thema zijn meerdere grafische elementen in het schilderij opgenomen, waaronder lineaire stralenpatronen of overlappingen en met kleur ingevulde schaakbordpatronen, die verwijzen naar de nog nieuwe waarnemingspsychologie waarin Kandinsky zich destijds begon te verdiepen.

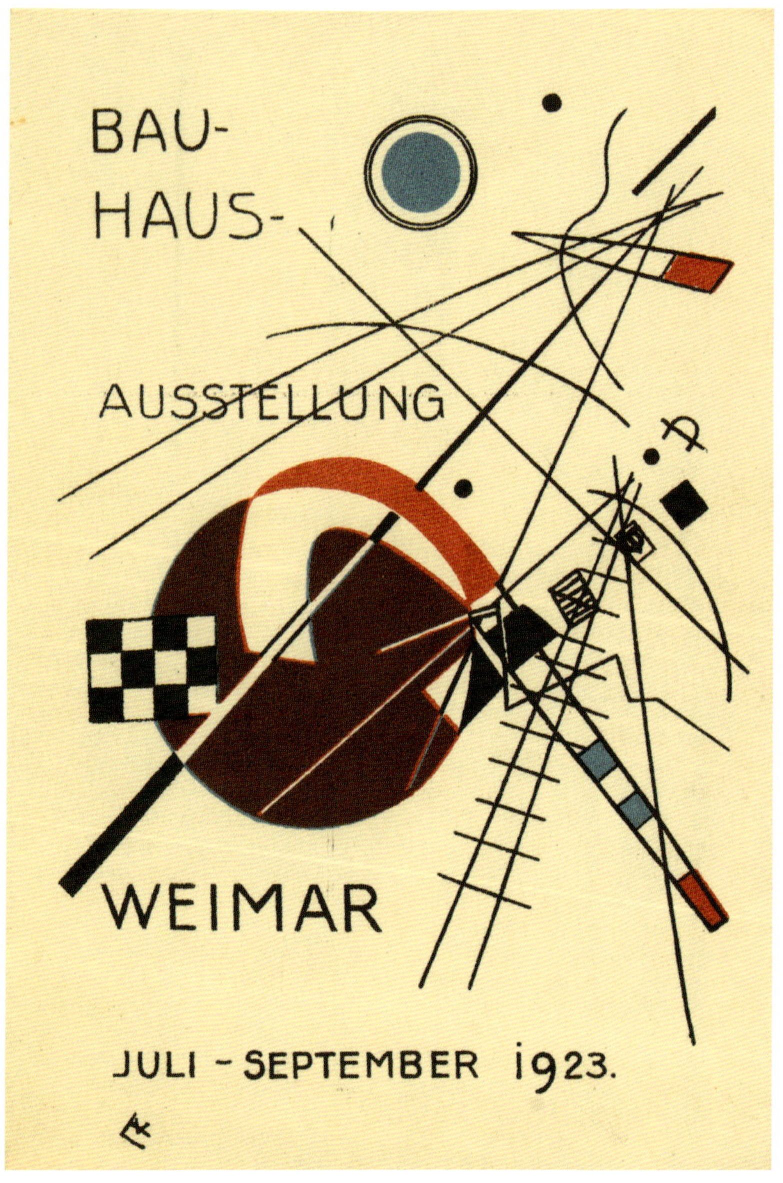

Postcard for the Bauhaus Exhibition

Carte postale pour l'exposition du Bauhaus

Postkarte für die Bauhaus-Ausstellung

Postal para la exposición Bauhaus

Cartolina per l'Esposizione del Bauhaus

Ansichtkaart voor Bauhaus-tentoonstelling

1923, Color lithograph/Lithographie en couleur, 15 × 10,2 cm, Private collection

In the Black Circle

Dans le cercle noir

Im schwarzen Kreis

En el círculo negro

Nel cerchio nero

In de zwarte cirkel

1923, Oil on canvas/Huile sur toile, 130 × 130 cm, Private collection

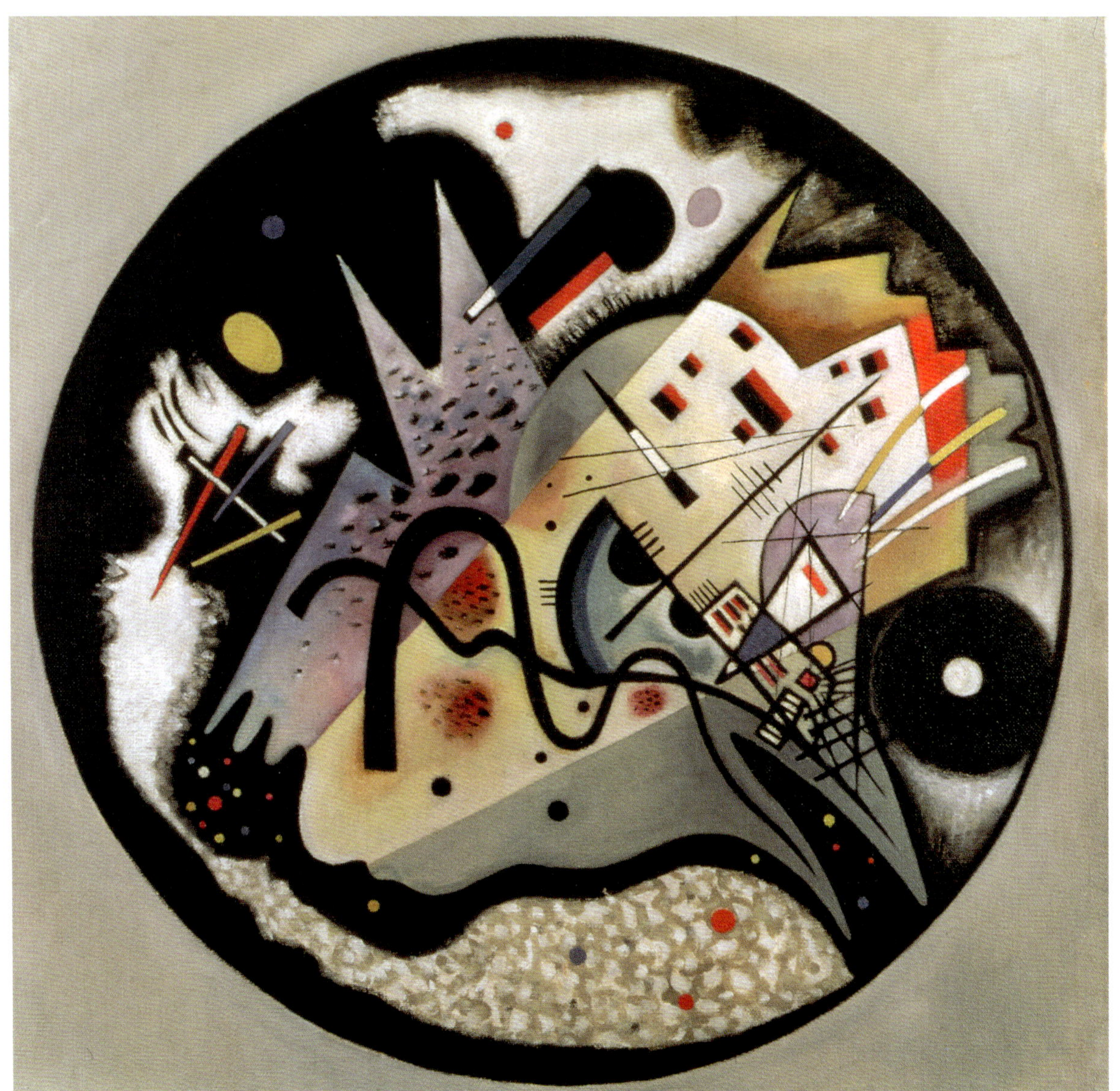

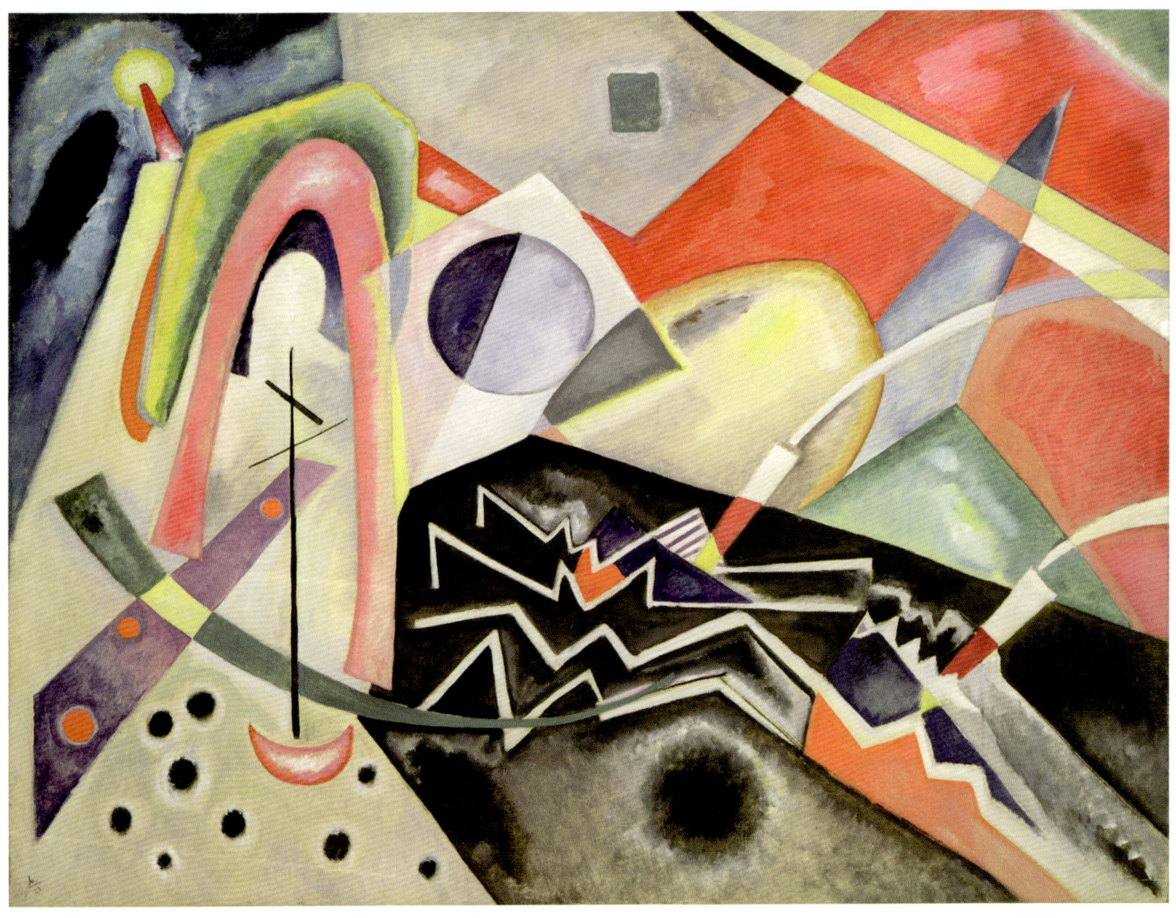

White Zig-Zags

Zigzags blancs

Weiße Zickzack-Linien

Blanco Zig-Zags

Zig-zag bianchi

Witte zigzaglijnen

1922, Oil on canvas/Huile sur toile, 95 × 125 cm, Galleria d'Arte Moderna, Venice

Cat

Chat

Katze

Gato

Gatto

Kat

1926, Oil on canvas/Huile sur toile, 51,4 × 46,4 cm, Private collection

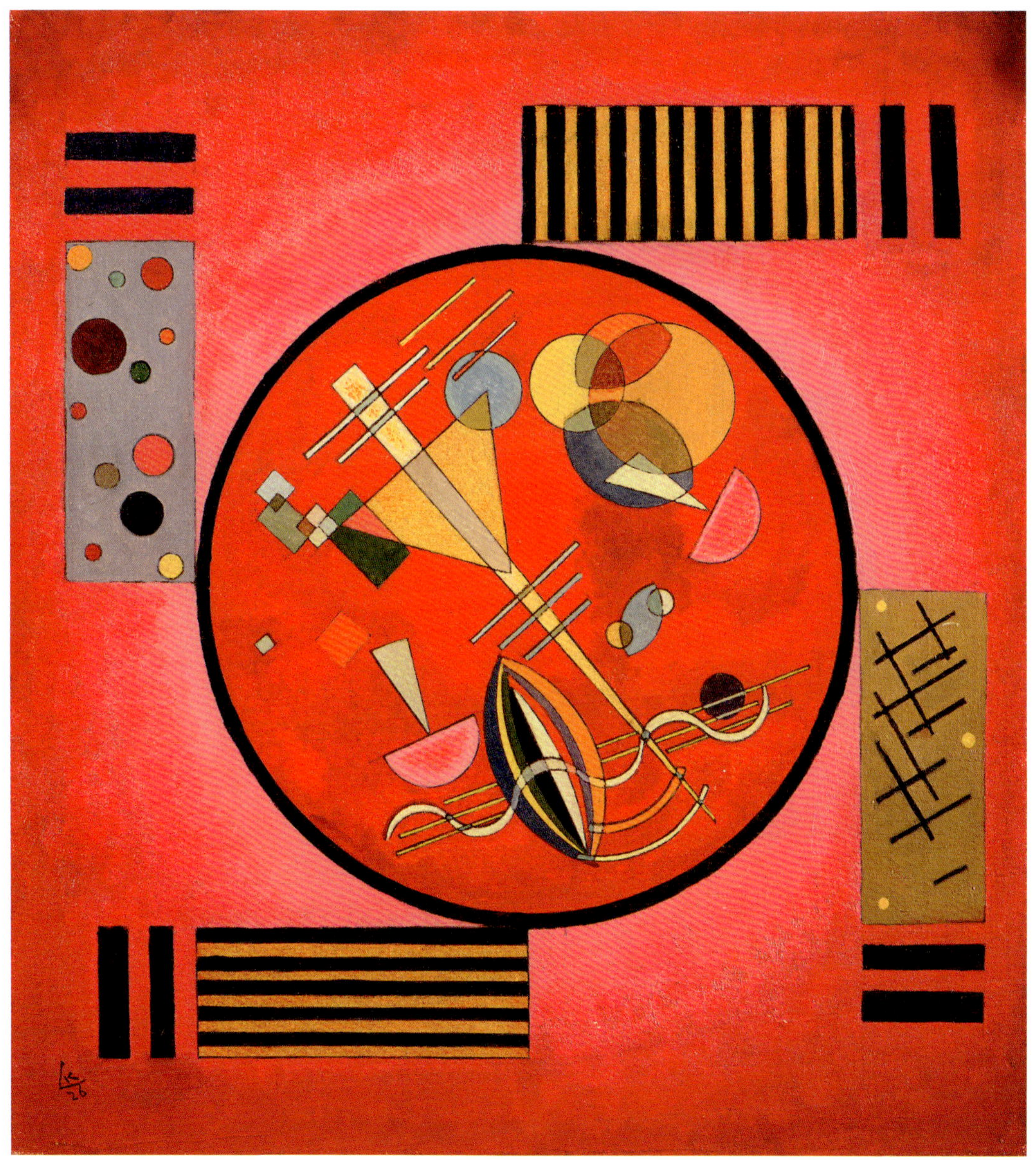

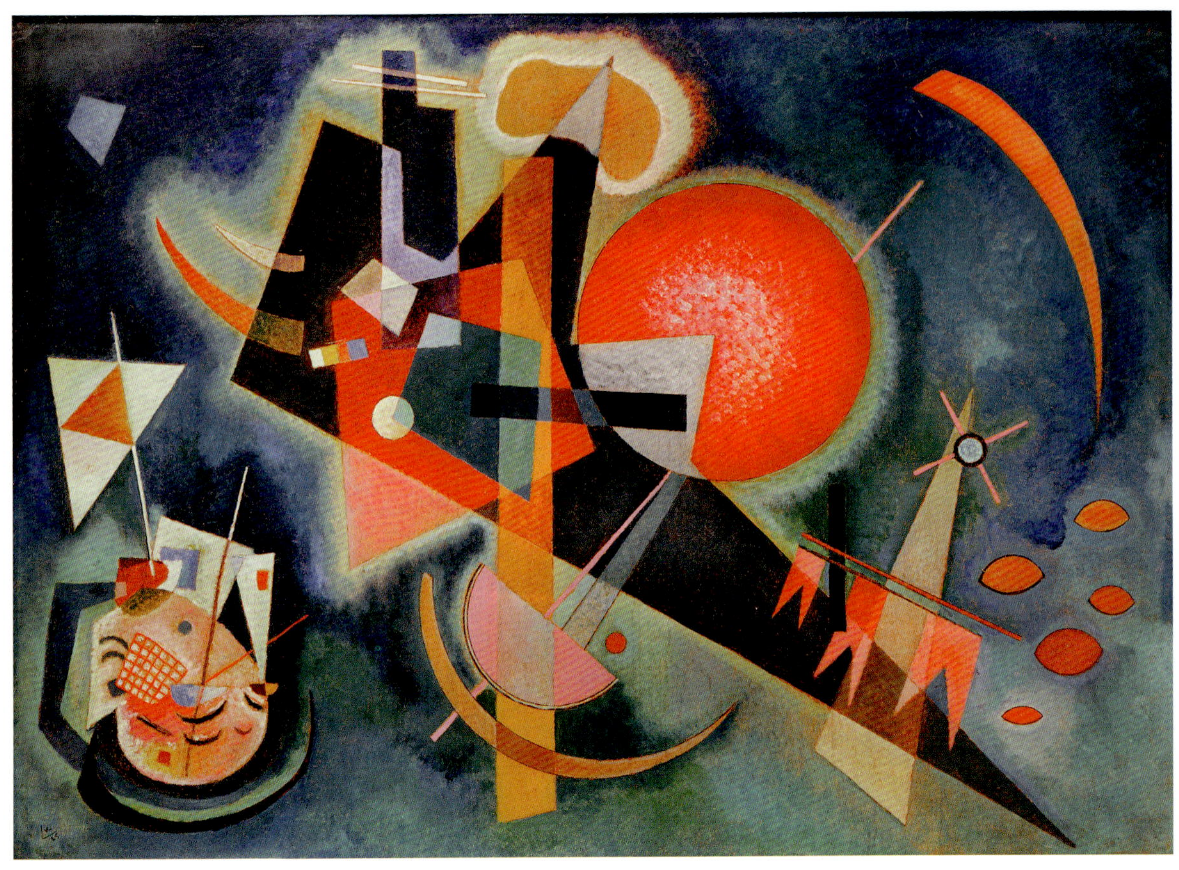

In Blue

Dans le bleu

Im Blau

En azul

Nel blu

In het blauw

1925, Oil on canvas/Huile sur toile,
Kunstsammlung Nordrhein-Westfalen, Dusseldorf

On the Points

Sur les pointes

Auf Spitzen

En los puntos

Sui punti

Op spitsen

1928, Oil on canvas/Huile sur toile, 140 × 140 cm,
Musee National d'Art Moderne, Centre Pompidou, Paris

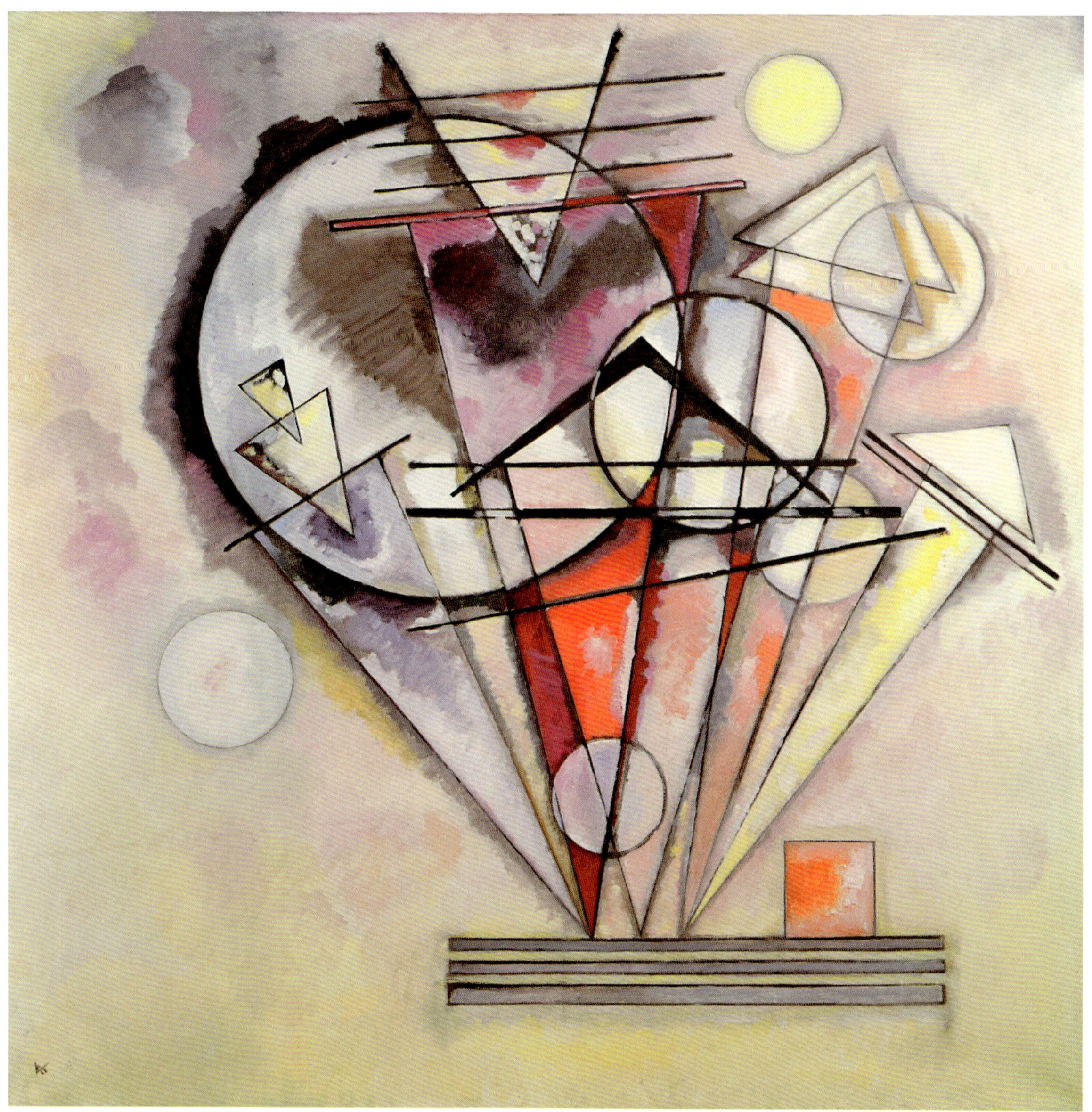

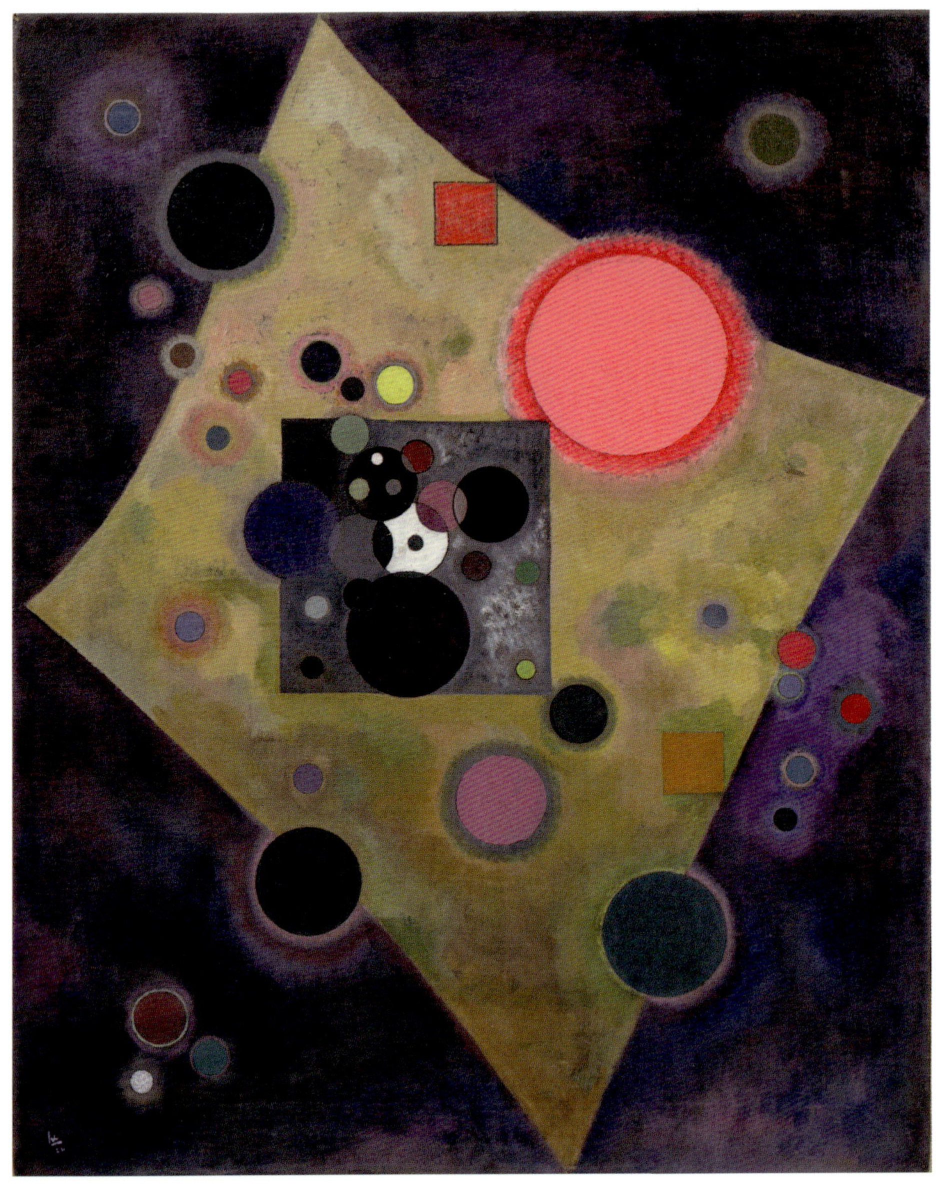

Accent en Rose

Accent en rose

Akzent in Rosa

Acento en rosa

Accento in rosa

Accent in roze

*1926, Oil on canvas/
Huile sur toile,
100,5 × 80,5 cm, Musée
National d'Art Moderne,
Centre Pompidou, Paris*

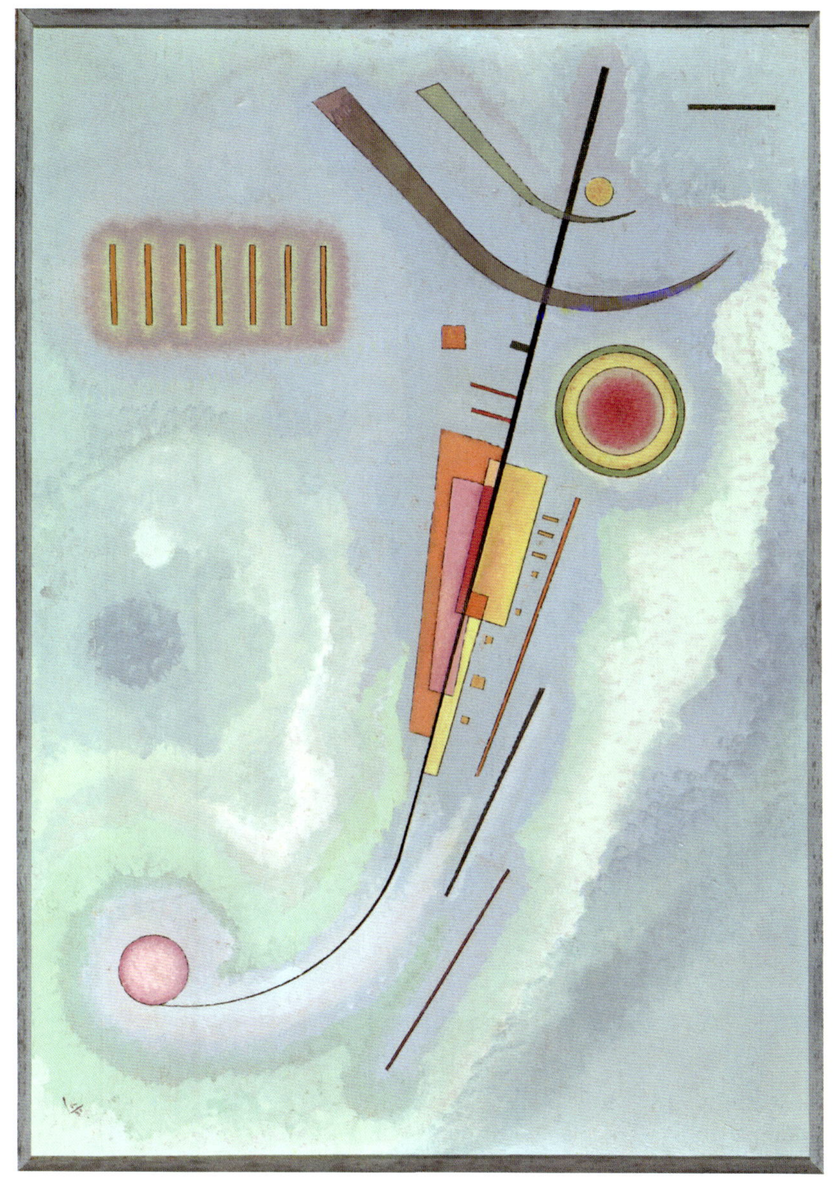

Light
Léger
Leichtes
Luz
Leggero
Licht

1930, Oil on cardboard/Huile sur carton,
69 × 48 cm, Musée National d'Art Moderne,
Centre Pompidou, Paris

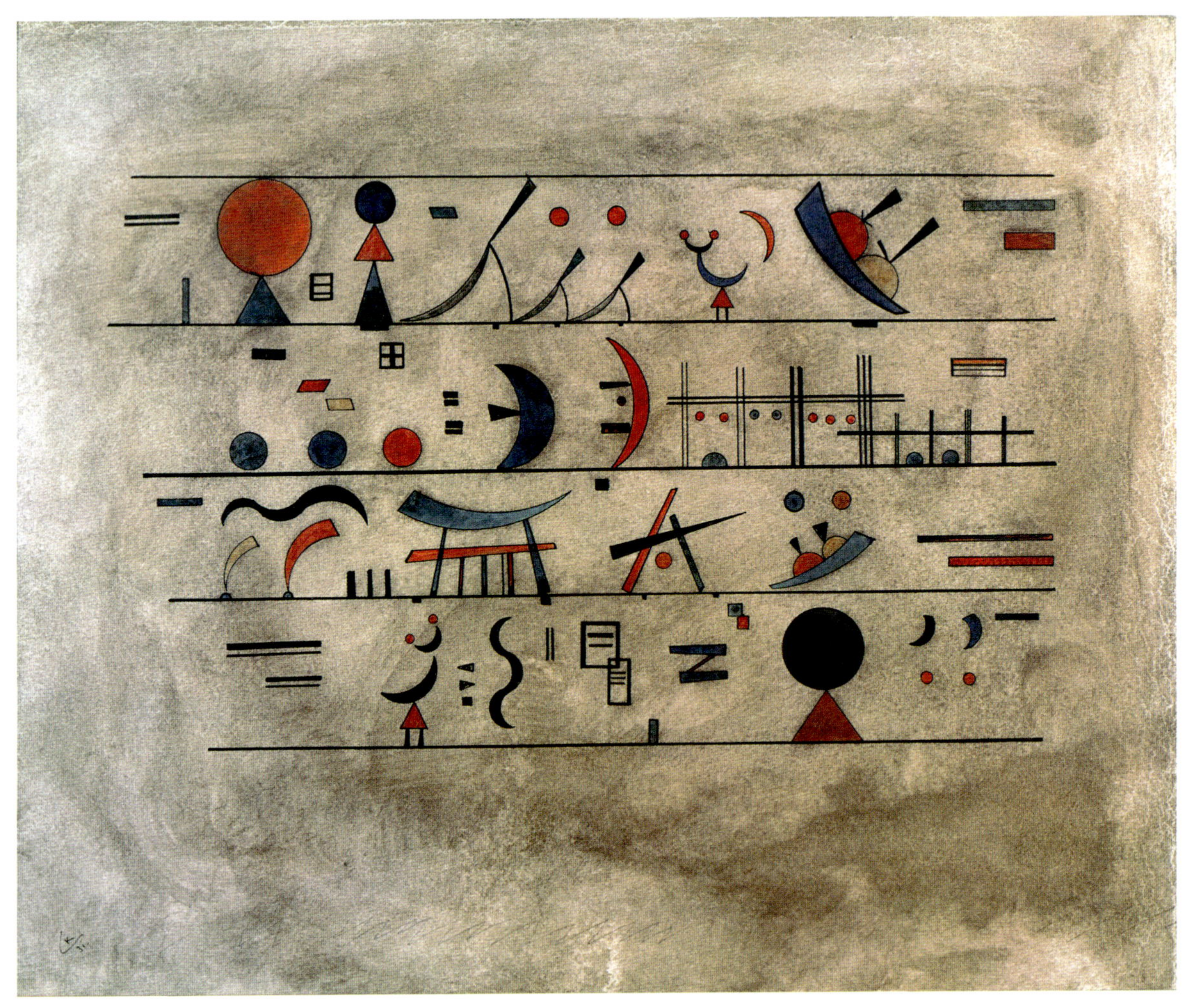

Rows of Signs   **Zeichenreihen**   **Righe di segni**

Lignes de signes   **Filas de signos**   **Tekenrijen**

1931, Oil on canvas/Huile sur toile, 41,5 × 50,5 cm, Kunstmuseum, Basel

196

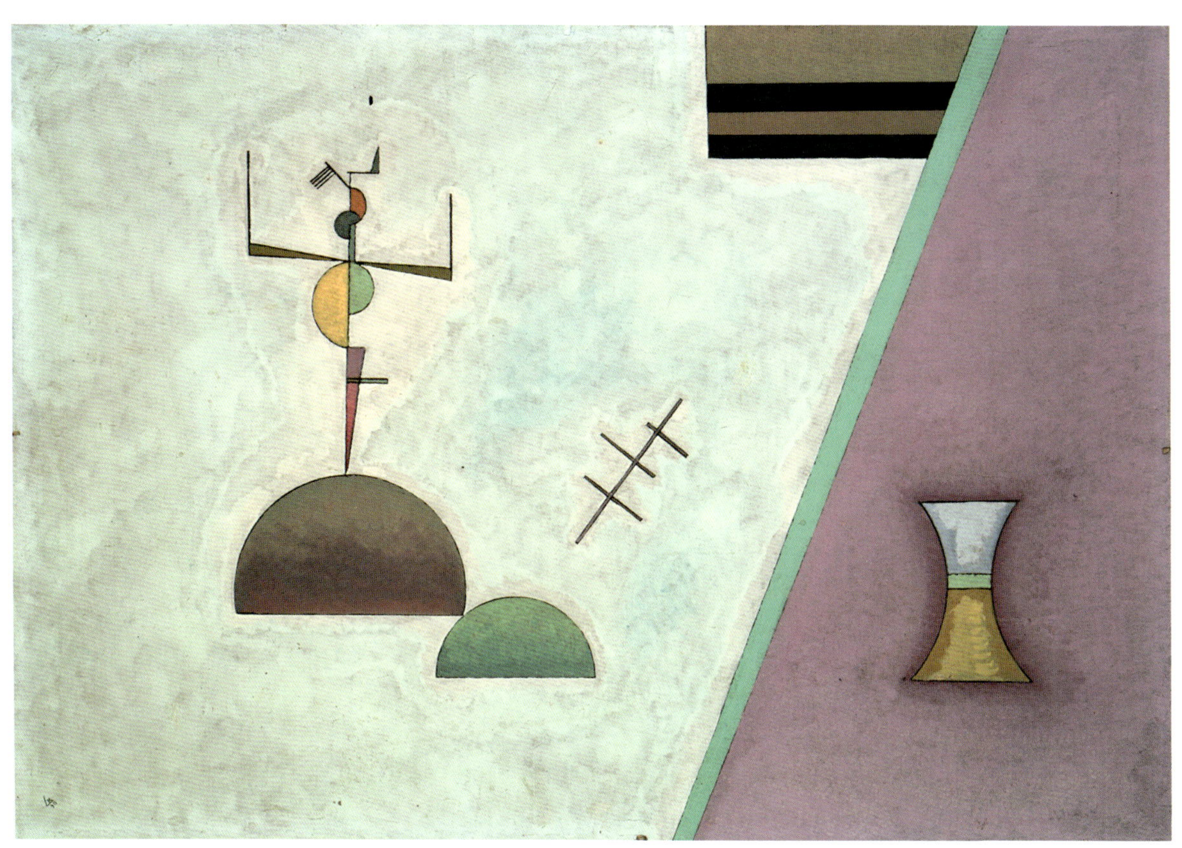

Two Black Lines   **Zwei schwarze Linien**   **Due linee nere**

Deux lignes noirs   **Dos líneas negras**   **Twee zwarte lijnen**

1930, Oil on panel/Huile sur bois, 49 × 71 cm, Private collection

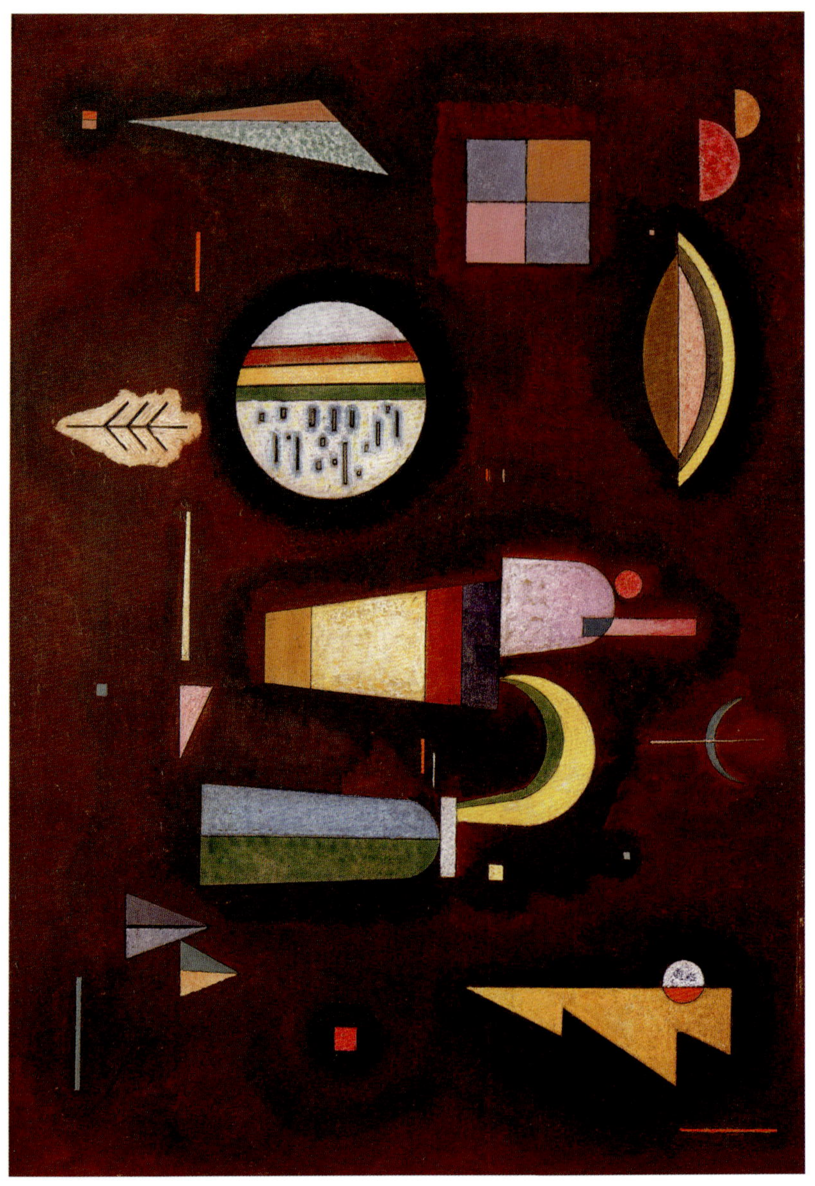

1930, Oil on canvas/Huile sur toile,
49 × 69,5 cm, Private collection

1931, Oil and watercolor on paper/
Huile et aquarelle sur papier,
36,5 × 38 cm, Private collection

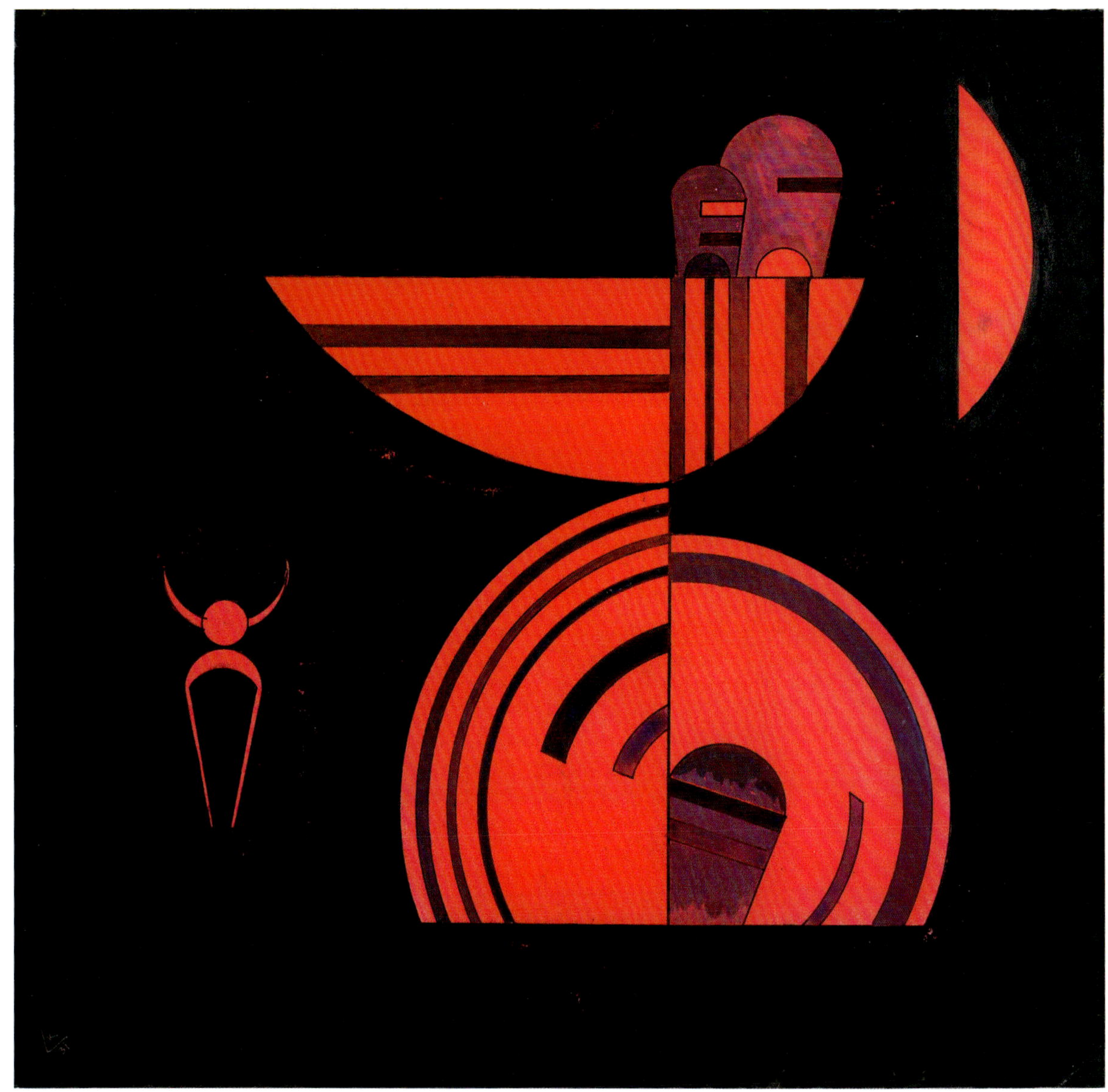

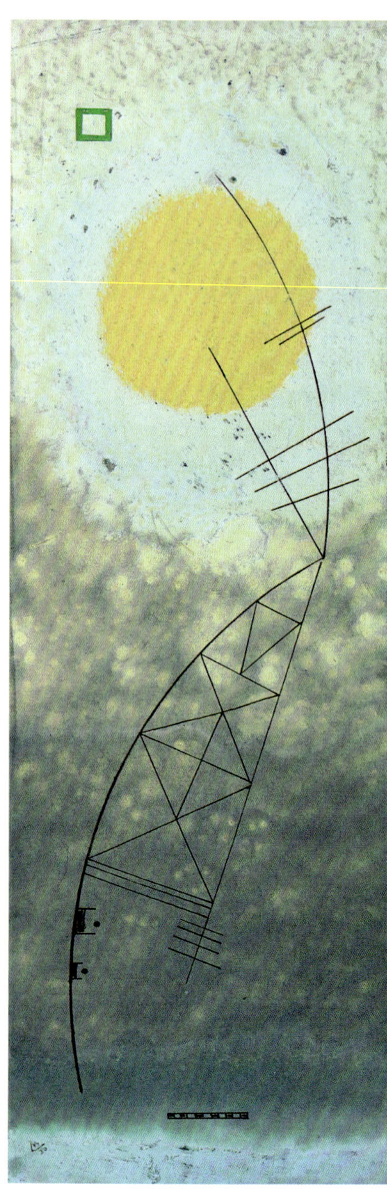

Dünn gebogen

Fines lignes courtres

Dünn gebogen

Dünn curvos

Dünn gebogen

Dun gebogen

1930, Gouache on paper/Gouache sur papier, 50 × 17 cm, Private collection

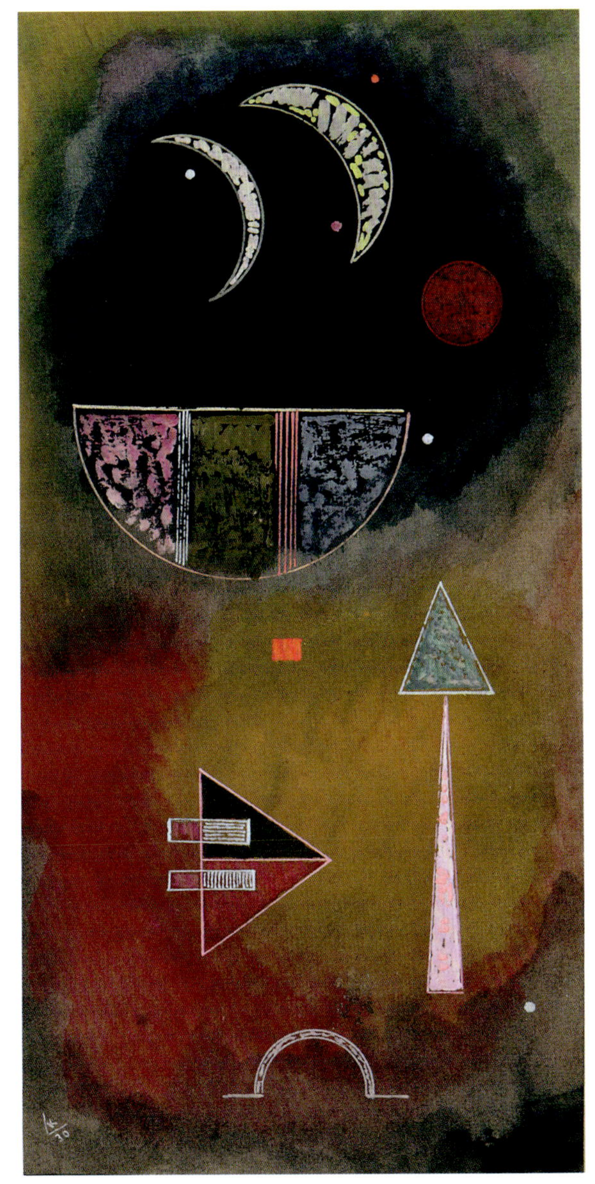

From Light into Dark
De la clarté à l'obscurité
Von Hell zu Dunkel
De la luz en la oscuridad
Dalla luce al buio
Van licht naar donker

1930, Watercolor and gouache on paper/Aquarelle et gouache sur papier,
Private collection

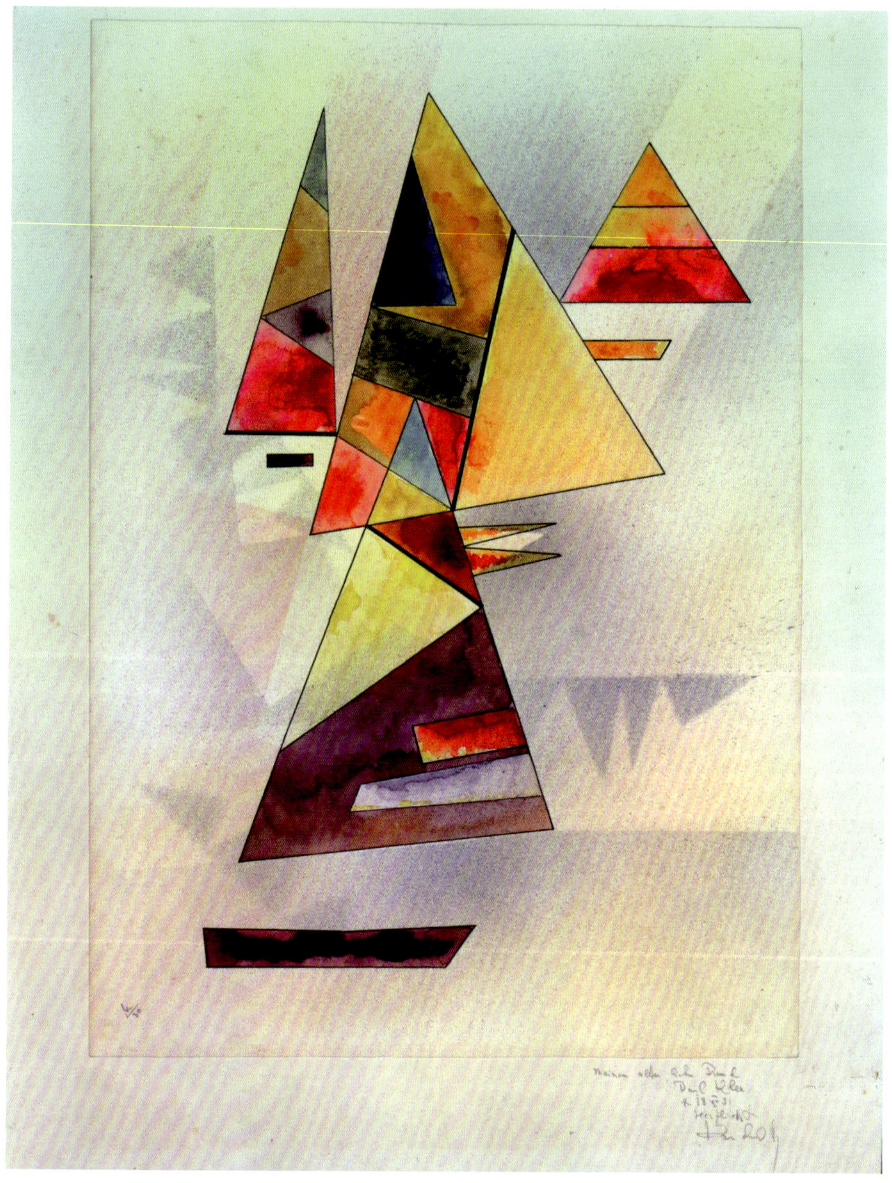

Composition

Composition

Komposition

Composición

Composizione

Compositie

1930, Watercolor and gouache on paper/Aquarelle et gouache sur papier, 48 × 33,1 cm, Private collection

Calm

Tranquillisé

Beruhigt

Calma

Calma

Gerustgesteld

1930, Oil on board/Huile sur carton, 48,9 × 48,6 cm, Private collection

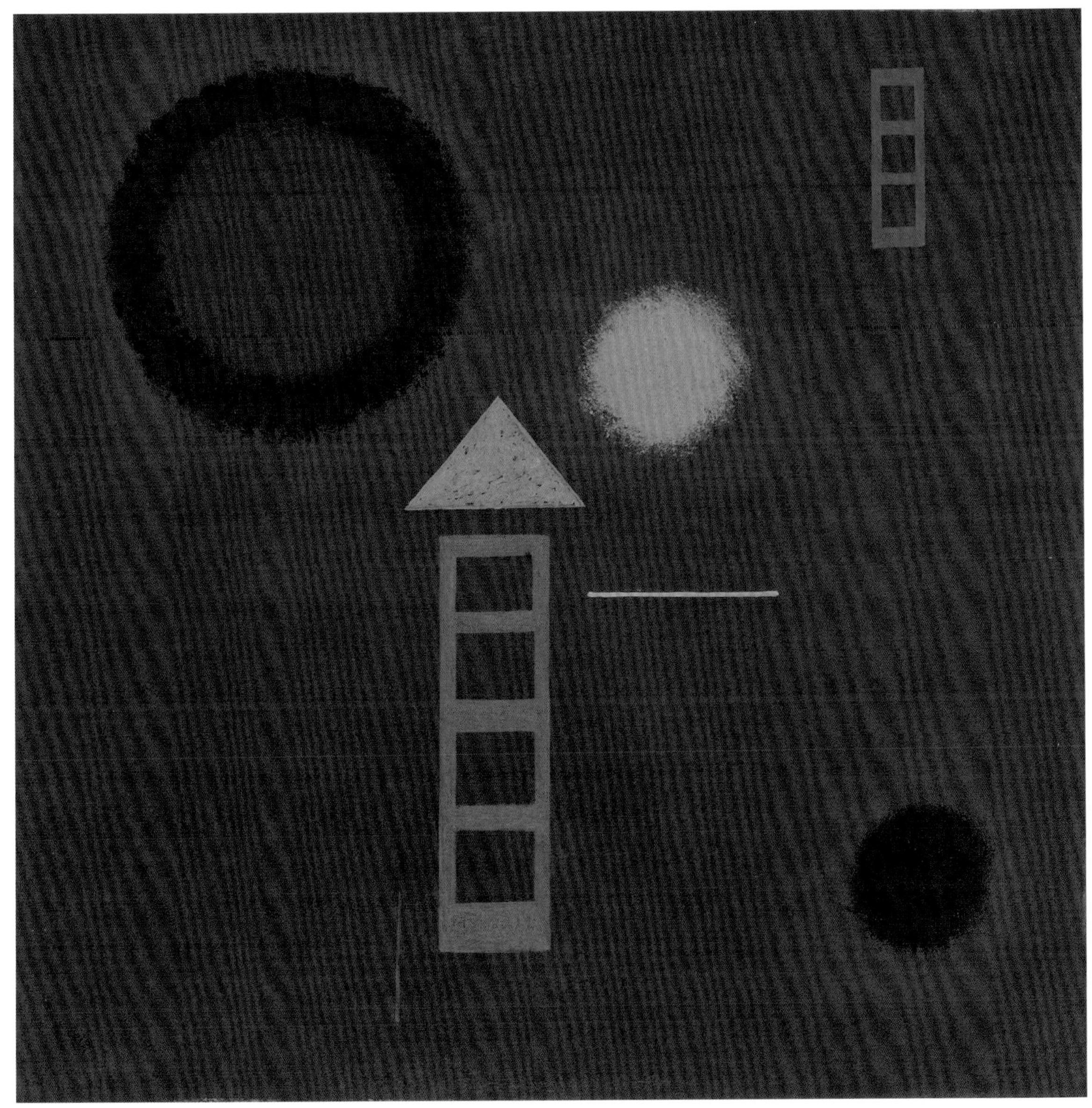

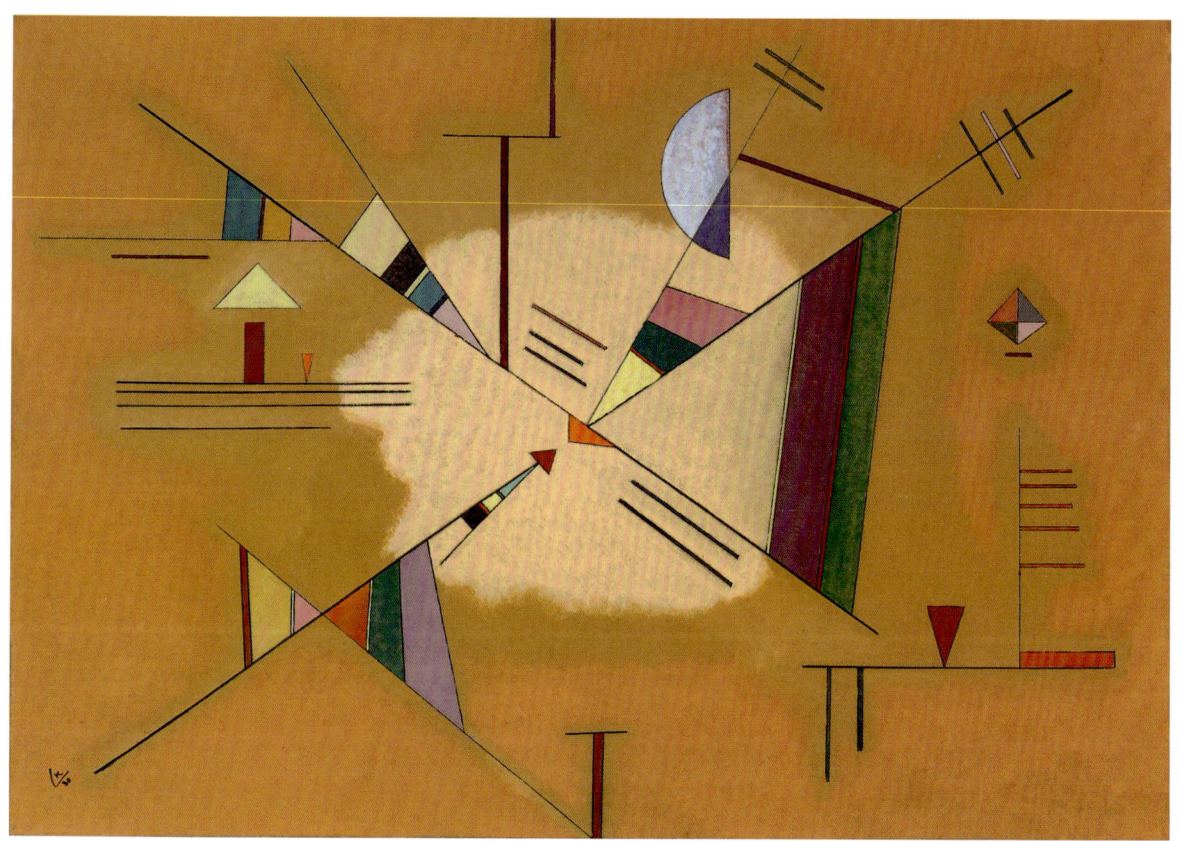

Diagonal

Diagonal

Diagonal

Diagonal

Diagonale

Diagonaal

1930, Oil on cardboard/Huile sur carton, 49 × 70 cm, Private collection

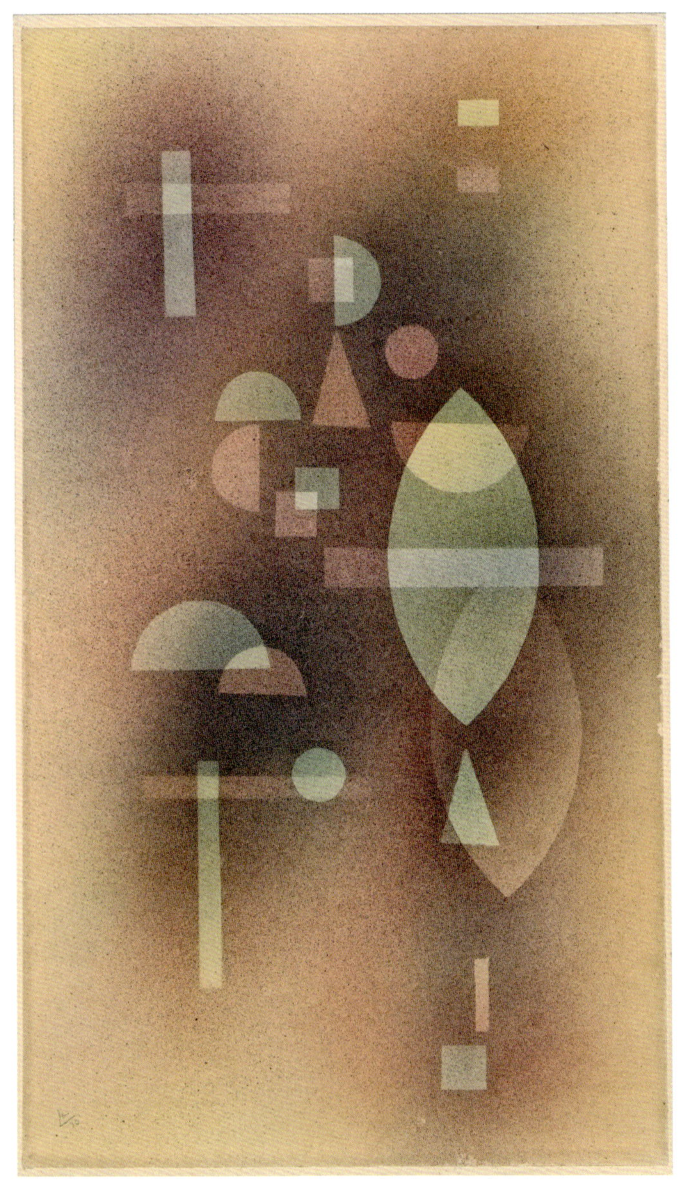

Transparency
Transparence
Durchsicht
Transparencia
Trasparenza
Transparantie

*1930, Watercolor on paper on cardboard/
Aquarelle sur papier marouflé sur carton,
49,8 × 28,3 cm, Private collection*

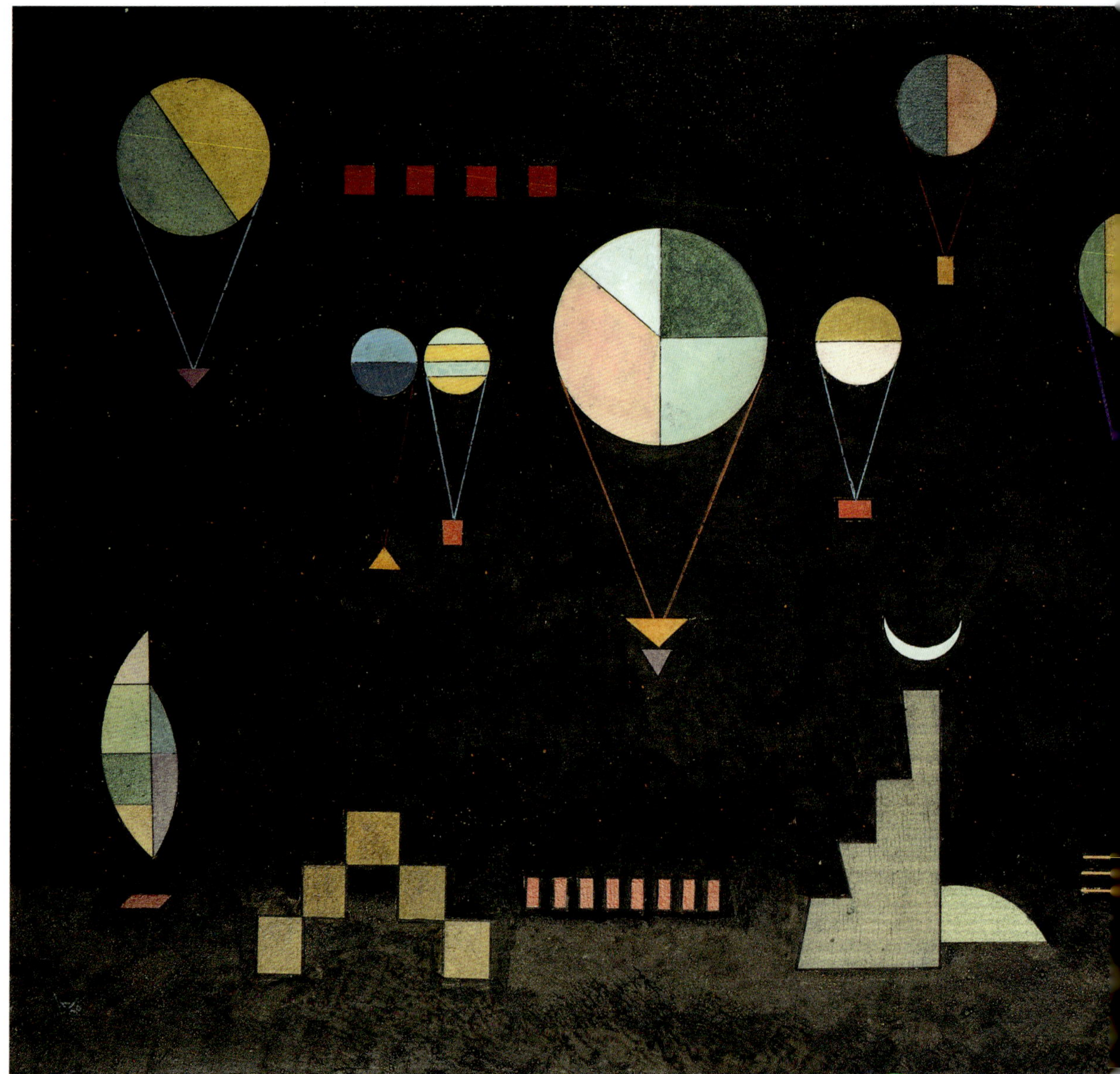

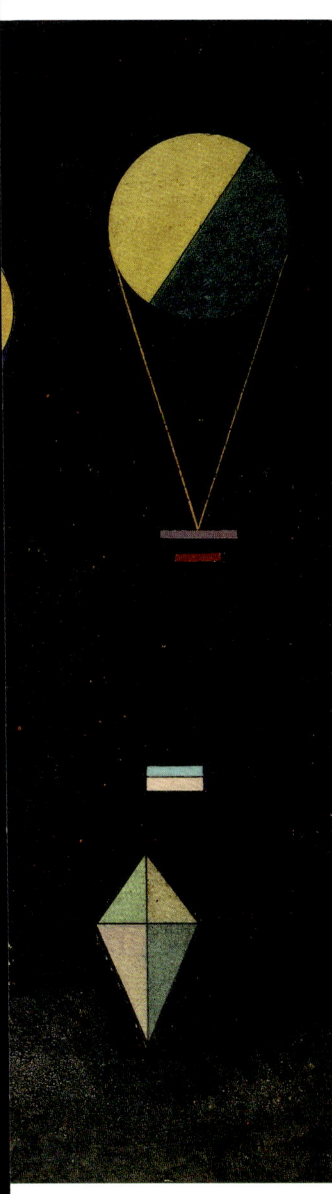

Flach-Tief

Plat-profond

Flach-Tief

Plana baja

Flach-Tief

Plat-diep

1930, Oil on cardboard/Huile sur carton, 48,6 × 69,6 cm, Private collection

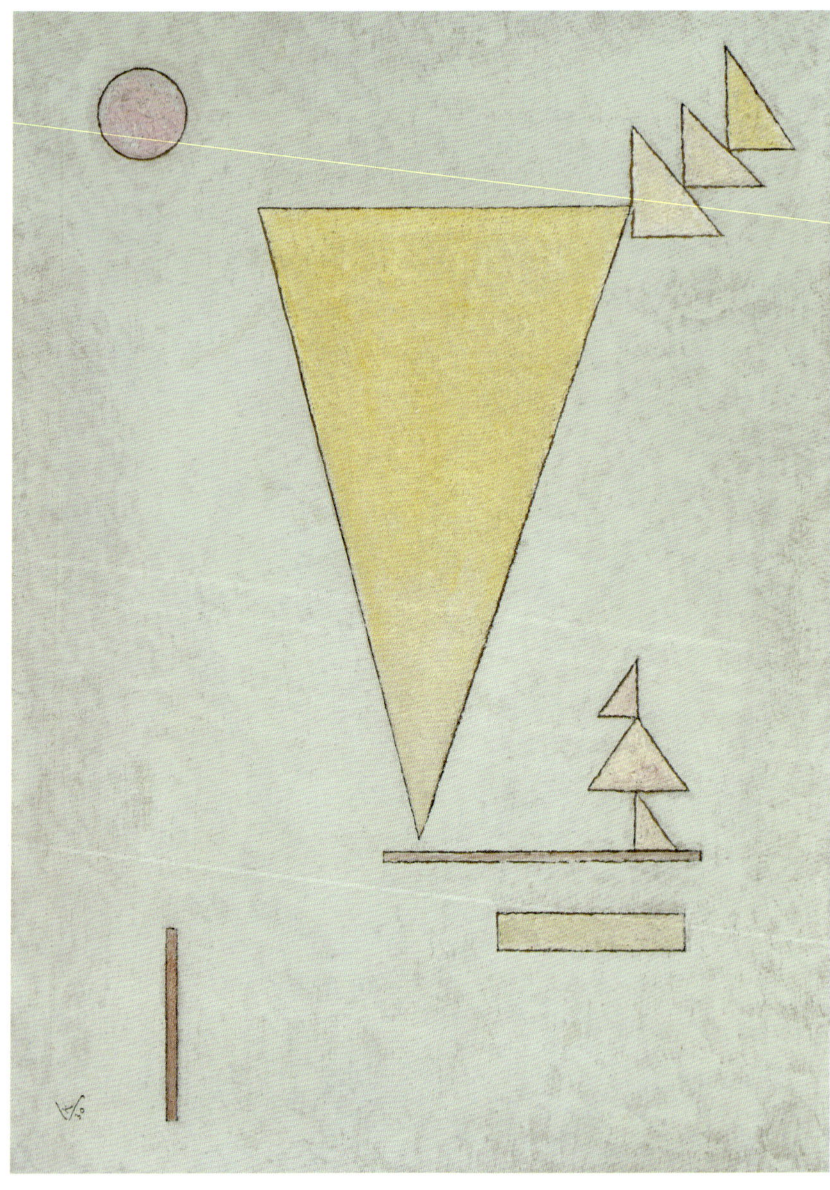

White

Blanc

Weiß

Blanco

Bianco

Wit

1930, Oil on cardboard/Huile sur carton,
49 × 35 cm, Private collection

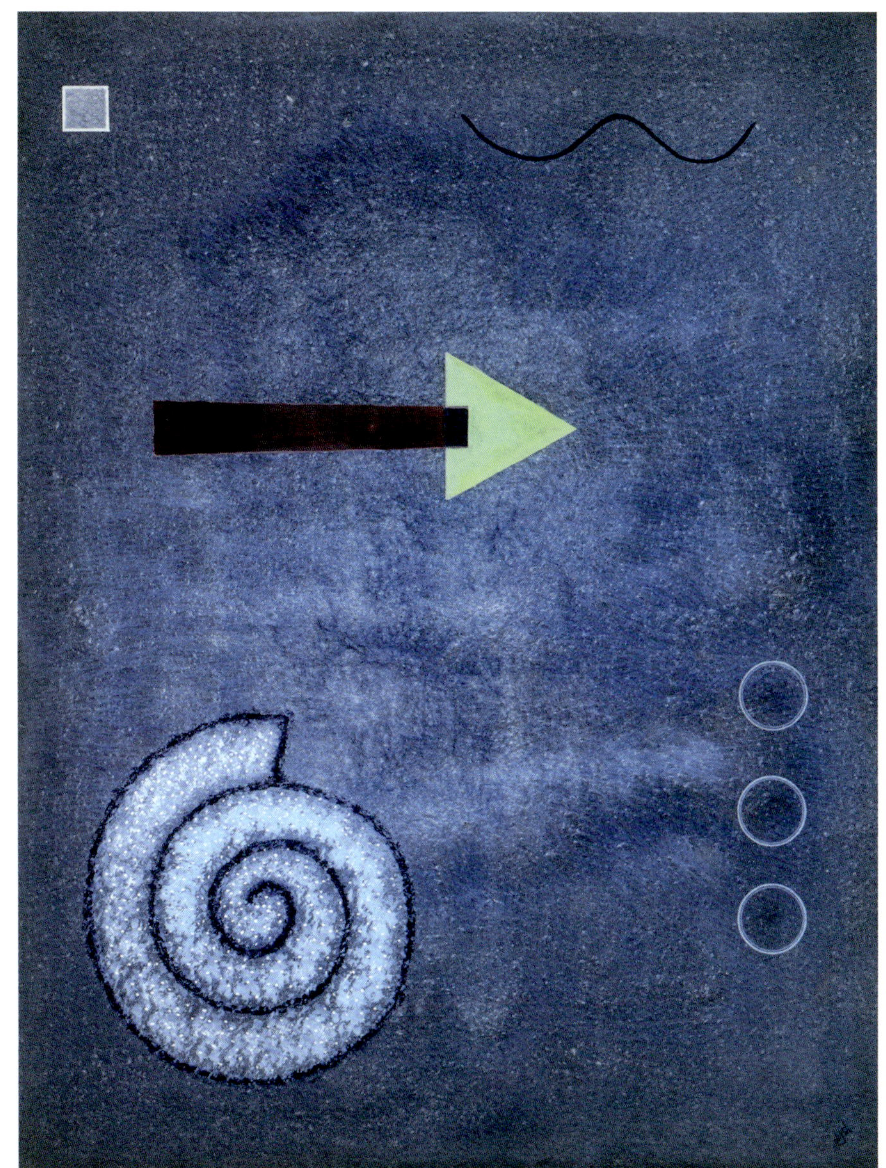

Green Points
Pointe verte
Grüne Spitze
Verde points
Punta verde
Groene spitsen

1932, Gouache on paper on board/
Gouache sur papier marouflé sur
carton, 31,8 × 42,5 cm,
Private collection

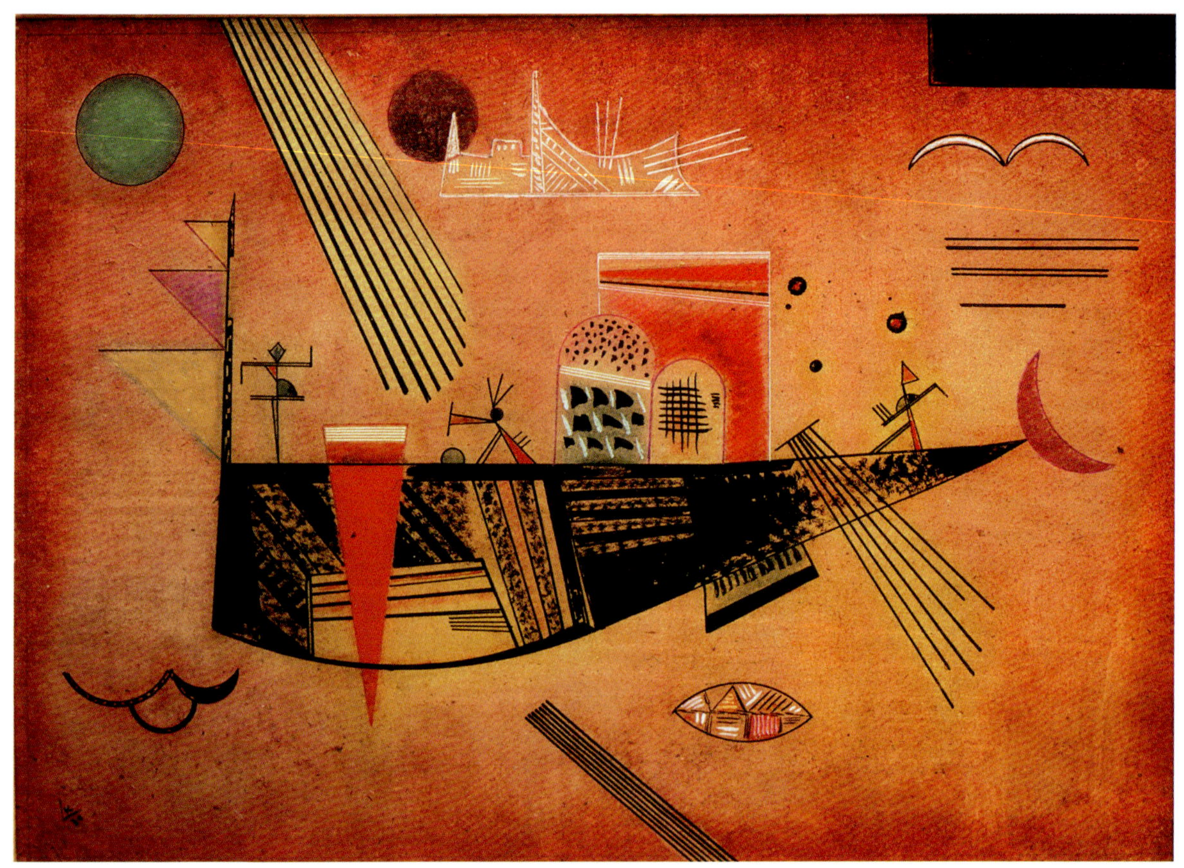

Whimsical

Capricieux

Launisches

Whimsical

Capriccioso

Grillig

1930, Oil on cardboard/Huile sur carton, 40,5 × 56 cm, Museum Boymans van Beuningen, Rotterdam

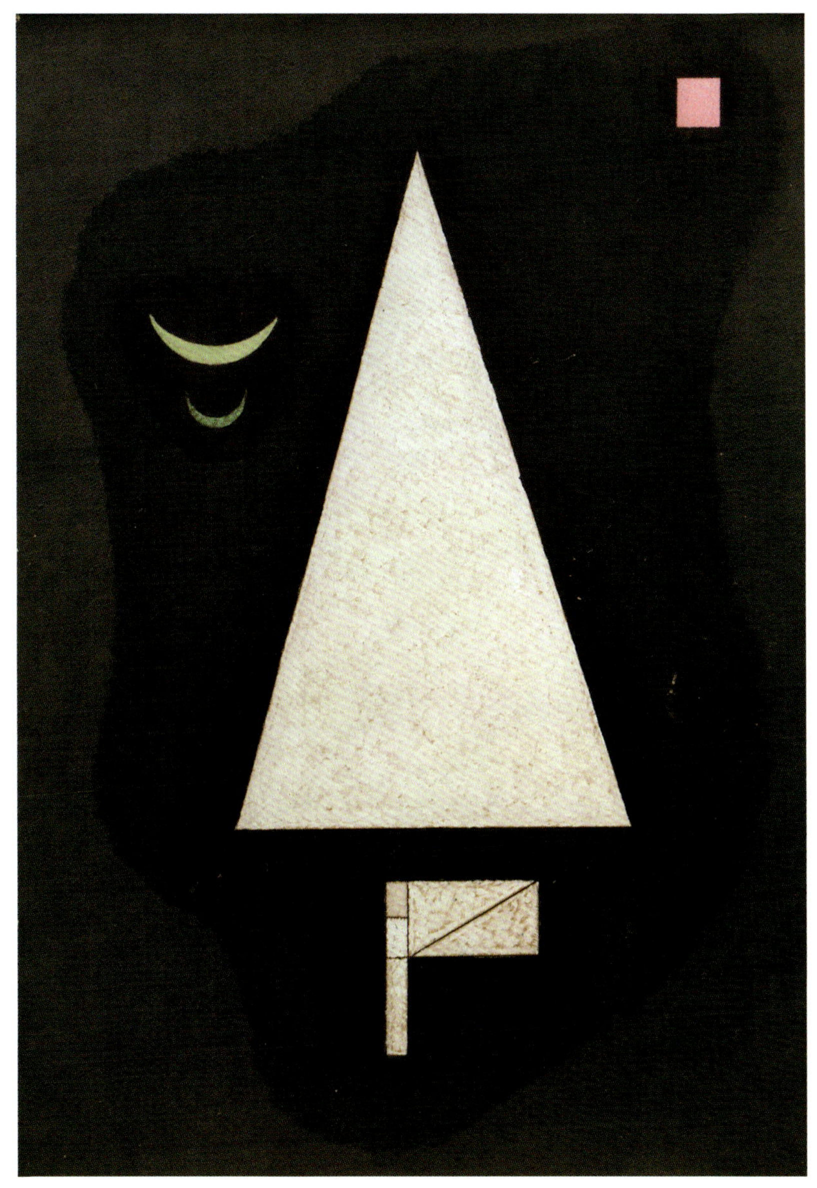

White Sharpness
Blanc net
Weiße Schärfe
Nitidez blanco
Acutezza bianca
Witte scherpte

1930, Oil on canvas/Huile sur toile, 70 × 49 cm, Museum Boymans van Beuningen, Rotterdam

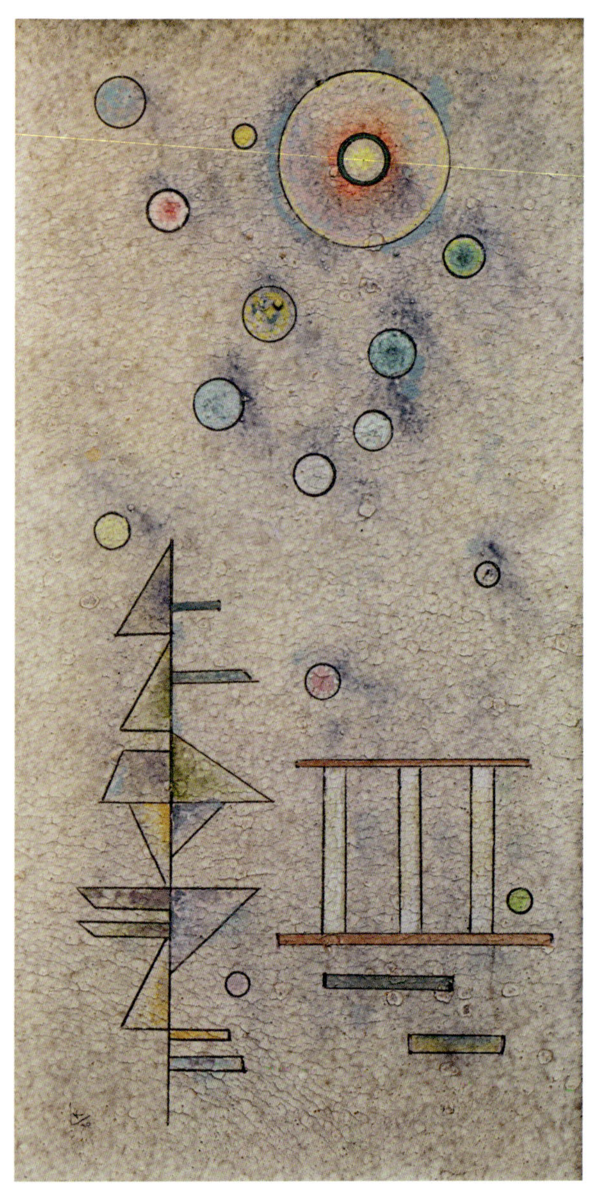

Scarcely

Timidement

Zaghaft

Apenas

Scarsamente

Aarzelend

*1930, Tempera on gesso/Tempera sur gesso sur toile,
35 × 16 cm, Museum Boymans van Beuningen, Rotterdam*

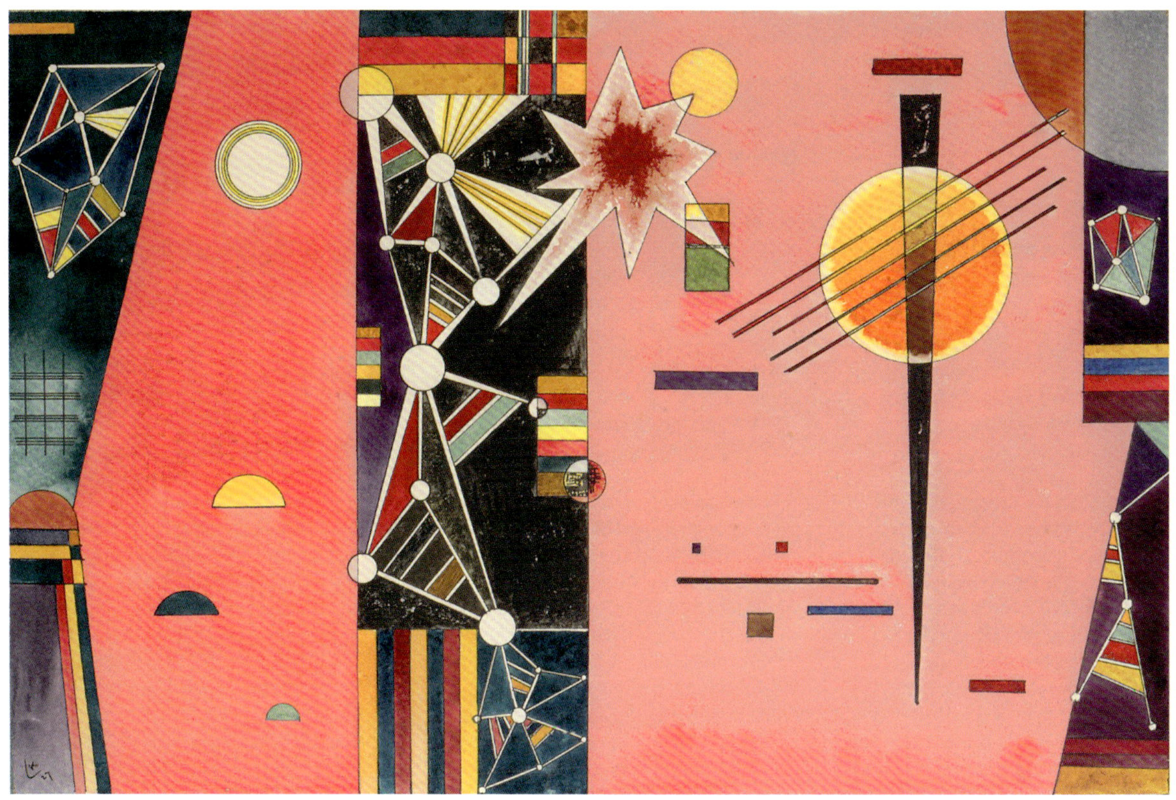

Rose Red

Rose rouge

Rosa Rot

Rosa roja

Rosa

Roze rood

1927, Watercolor and gouache on paper/Aquarelle et gouache sur papier, 32,2 × 48,6 cm, Private collection

Kandinsky's painting technique

Using the term "Improvisation", borrowed from music, Kandinsky meant images which portray expressions or instances of internal state of being, mainly involuntary, many happening suddenly, as "impressions of inner nature". With its influence from Bavarian reverse glass painting, this picture acts like a colorful fairytale carpet, without having a clearly defined subject. One can make out in the foreground a horse with red saddle cloth which bears a rider wearing a green robe, with billowing white hair and red cap. The meaning of the scene, which takes place in front of a red and light-blue colored mountainside, remains nevertheless enigmatic. Colors and shapes give the picture a mysterious life of its own, and its associations with St. George as "Der Blaue Reiter" would recur a little later on the cover of the almanac.

La technique picturale de Kandinsky

Sous le concept d'« improvisation » emprunté à la musique, Kandinsky entendait représenter les « expressions ou les événements du caractère intérieur, essentiellement inconnus, survenant pour la plupart de façon soudaine », comme des « impressions de la nature intérieure ». À l'instar des peintures sur verre bavaroises, ce tableau fait l'effet d'un tapis féérique et bariolé, sans sujet évident. On identifie bien au premier plan un cheval à chabraque et un cavalier vêtu de vert, à chevelure blanche flottante et cape rouge. Mais le sens de la scène, sur fond de pente montagneuse rouge et bleu ciel, n'en reste pas moins mystérieux. Couleurs et formes mènent une vie propre et secrète – avec des associations à saint Georges qui apparaîtra un peu plus tard sur la couverture de l'almanach *Der Blaue Reiter*.

Kandinsky a choisi comme support une toile apprêtée en blanc.

Zu Kandinskys Maltechnik

Mit dem aus der Musik entlehnten Begriff „Improvisation" meinte Kandinsky Bilder, die „hauptsächlich ungewußte, größtenteils plötzlich entstandene Ausdrücke oder Vorgänge inneren Charakters" darstellen, als „Eindrücke innerer Natur". In Anlehnung an bayerische Hinterglasbilder wirkt dieses Bild daher wie ein bunter Märchenteppich ohne eindeutiges Sujet. Man erkennt zwar im Vordergrund ein Pferd mit roter Schabracke und einen Reiter mit grünem Gewand, wehendem weißen Haar und roter Kappe. Der Sinn der Szene vor einem rot und hellblau gefärbten Berghang bleibt gleichwohl rätselhaft. Farben und Formen führen ein geheimnisvolles Eigenleben, mit Assoziationen an den hl. Georg, wie er wenig später im Umschlag des Almanachs „Der Blaue Reiter" auftauchen wird.

Als Bildträger wählte Kandinsky ein weiß grundiertes Leinwandgewebe.

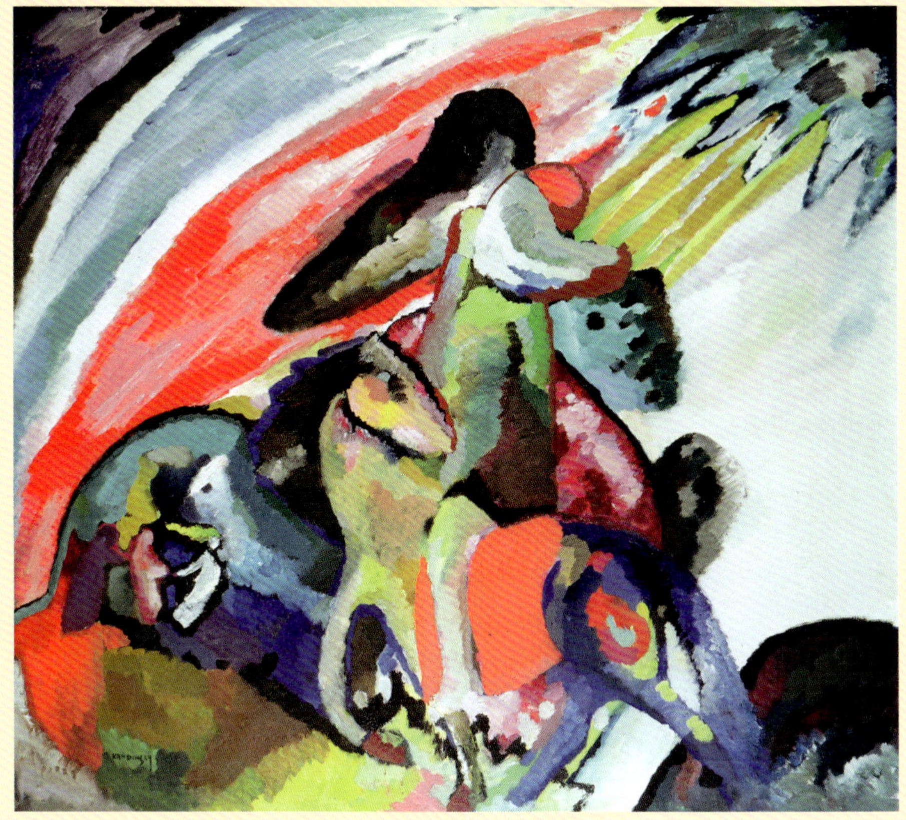

Improvisation 12 (Rider)

Improvisation 12 (Cavalier)

Improvisation 12 (Reiter)

Improvisación 12 (jinete)

Improvvisazione 12 (Cavaliere)

Improvisatie 12 (Ruiter)

1910, Oil on canvas/Huile sur toile, 97 × 106,5 cm, Staatsgalerie Moderner Kunst, Munich

Técnica de pintura de Kandinsky
Empleando el término "improvisación", tomado prestado de la música, Kandinsky hace referencia a imágenes que retratan expresiones o ejemplos de estados de ánimo interiores, principalmente involuntarios, muchos de los cuales aparecen de repente, como "impresiones de la naturaleza interior". Con su influencia de la pintura sobre cristal inversa bábara,

Tecnica pittorica di Kandinsky
Con il termine «improvvisazione», preso in prestito dalla musica, Kandinsky si riferiva a immagini che ritraggono espressioni o manifestazioni dello stato d'essere interiore, principalmente involontarie e nella maggior parte dei casi improvvise, come «impressioni della natura interiore». Influenzata dalla pittura sotto vetro bavarese, quest'opera funge da colorato tappeto

Over Kandinsky's schildertechniek
Met het aan de muziek ontleende begrip 'Improvisatie' duidde Kandinsky op die schilderijen die "voornamelijk onbewuste, hoofdzakelijk plotseling opkomende uitdrukkingen of processen van interne aard" uitbeelden, als "indrukken van een innerlijke natuur". Geïnspireerd door de Beierse achterglasschilderingen, doet dit werk dan ook aan als een

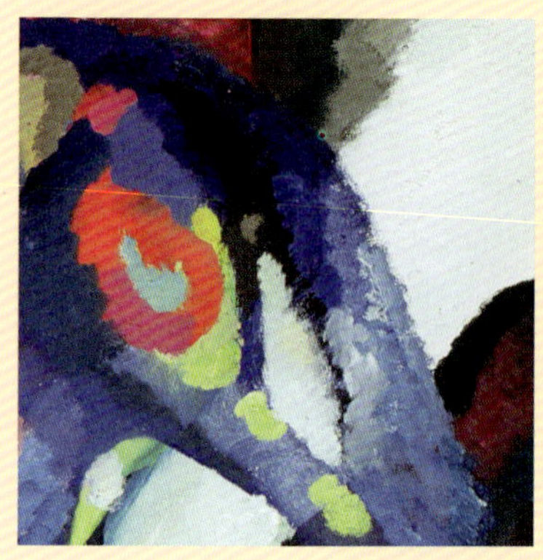 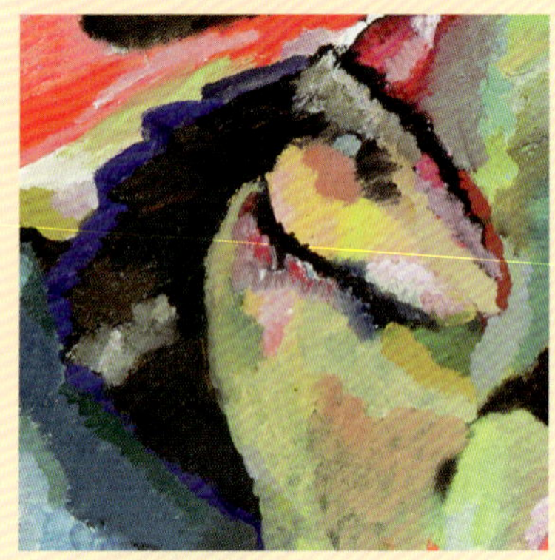 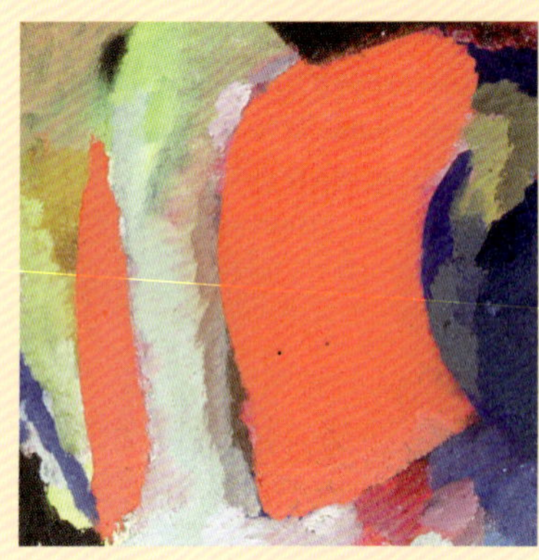

As medium, Kandinsky chose a white-primed canvas fabric. The first layer of the composition was carried out with a few dark blue outlines which defined the positions of the rider and the horse. Most areas of color were filled by Kandinsky with low-viscosity, opaque to semi-opaque colors. It is noteworthy that Kandinsky sometimes used different types of paint application and color mixtures, as well as working with varying surface textures and gloss levels. The blue horse is particularly varied in this respect: we may observe in a given small area that different blends of dark blue paint are colored with white and yellow. The color effect is also furthermore supported by the contrasting of "flat", thinly applied paint with thick, 'impasto' colored areas. With the help of an additive, Kandinsky was also able to enhance the surface gloss, for instance in the black mane of the horse and the red saddlecloth.

La première indication de composition est faite de contours bleu foncé peu nombreux, marquant la position du cheval et du cavalier. Le peintre a rempli ensuite la plupart des plages colorées de touches minces et fluides, totalement ou partiellement couvrantes. On remarque alors que Kandinsky travaillait avec différents types de touches et de mélanges de couleurs, mais aussi en variant les textures de surface et les degrés de brillance. Le cheval bleu est, à cet égard, particulièrement riche en variations : on peut observer sur une petite surface différents types de mélange de peinture bleu foncé avec du blanc et du jaune. L'effet chromatique est en outre renforcé par le contraste entre plages colorées « plates » traitées en couches minces, et plages « plastique » travaillées en touches pâteuses et chargées de matière. L'adjonction d'un additif à la peinture a permis à Kandinsky d'accentuer le brillant de certaines plages, par exemple la crinière noire du cheval et la chabraque rouge.

Die erste Anlage der Komposition erfolgte mit wenigen dunkelblauen Konturen, die die Position des Reiters und des Pferdes festlegten. Die meisten Farbflächen füllte Kandinsky mit dünnflüssigen, deckenden bis halbdeckenden Farbtönen aus. Dabei fällt auf, dass Kandinsky sowohl mitunterschiedlichen Arten des Farbauftrags und Farbmischungen als auch mithilfe variierender Oberflächentexturen und Glanzgrade arbeitete. Besonders variantenreich ist in dieser Hinsicht das blaue Pferd gestaltet: Auf einer kleinen Fläche sind verschiedene Mischungsarten von dunkelblauer Malfarbe mit Weiß und Gelb zu beobachten. Die Farbwirkung wird zudem durch den Kontrast von „flachen", dünn aufgetragenen, und „plastischen", pastos aufgetragenen Farbbereichen unterstützt. Durch Zugabe eines Malmittels konnte Kandinsky zudem den Oberflächenglanz z. B. bei der schwarzen Mähne des Pferds und der roten Satteldecke verstärken.

esta imagen actúa como una colorida alfombra de cuento de hadas, sin un tema claramente definido. Uno puede adivinar en el fondo un caballo con un faldón rojo que lleva a lomos un jinete vestido con una túnica verde, con gorro rojo y el pelo blanco ondeando al viento. El significado de la escena, que tiene lugar frente a la ladera de una montaña roja y azul claro, continúa siendo enigmático. Los colores y las formas confieren a la imagen una misteriosa vida en sí misma y sus asociaciones con San Jorge como "Der Blaue Reiter" se repetirán un poco más tarde en la portada del almanaque.

Como medio, Kandinsky escoge lienzo reforzada con imprimación en blanco. La primera capa de la composición se realiza con unos cuantos trazos en azul oscuro que definen las posiciones del jinete y el caballo. Kandinsky rellena la mayor parte de las áreas de color con tonos entre opacos y semi-opacos de baja viscosidad. Resulta digno de mención que Kandinsky empleara en ocasiones distintos tipos de aplicación de pintura y mezclas de colores, además de trabajar con distintos niveles de brillo y texturas superficiales. El caballo azul es particularmente variado en este aspecto: podemos observar, en un área reducida concreta, que distintas mezclas de pintura azul oscura se colorean con blanco y amarillo. El efecto del color también lo respalda el contraste "plano", de áreas apenas pintadas con zonas densamente coloreadas de "empaste". Con la ayuda de un aditivo, Kandinsky es también capaz de realzar el brillo de la superficie, por ejemplo, en las crines negras del caballo y el faldón rojo.

fiabesco privo di un soggetto ben definito. Si può distinguere in primo piano un cavallo con una gualdrappa rossa montato da un cavaliere con fluttuanti capelli bianchi che indossa una tunica verde e un berretto rosso. Il significato della scena, che si svolge davanti ad una montagna di colore rosso e celeste, rimane comunque enigmatico. Colori e forme fanno sì che il quadro abbia una misteriosa vita propria, e le sue associazioni con San Giorgio come «Der Blaue Reiter» riappariranno più tardi sulla copertina dell'almanacco.

Per quest'opera Kandinsky scelse un tessuto di tela con imprimitura bianca. Il primo strato della composizione è costituito da alcune linee blu scuro che definiscono la posizione del cavaliere e del cavallo. La maggior parte delle aree colorate è stata riempita da Kandinsky con colori a bassa viscosità da opachi a semi-opachi. È interessante notare che Kandinsky utilizzava a volte diverse modalità di applicazione della pittura e miscele di colori, e lavorava con superfici di diverse texture e livelli di brillantezza differenti. Il cavallo blu è un ottimo esempio in questo senso: possiamo osservare in una piccola area determinata che diverse miscele di pittura blu scuro sono colorate di bianco e giallo. L'effetto cromatico è inoltre sostenuto dalla contrapposizione di strati di pittura «piatti», applicati sottilmente, con aree colorate spesse, «tridimensionali». Inoltre, con l'aiuto di un additivo, Kandinsky risaltò la lucentezza delle superfici, ad esempio nella criniera nera del cavallo e nella gualdrappa rossa.

bont sprookjestapijt zonder duidelijk onderwerp. Weliswaar kan men op de voorgrond een paard met een rode sjabrak (zadelkleed) en een ruiter in een groen gewaad en met wuivend wit haar en een rode muts herkennen, maar de inhoud van dit tafereel tegen de achtergrond van een rood en felblauw gekleurde berghelling blijft geheimzinnig. De kleuren en vormen leven een raadselachtig eigen leven en verwijzen naar de Sint Joris die korte tijd later op de omslag van de almanak Der Blaue Reiter zal opduiken.

Als beelddrager koos Kandinsky voor canvas met een witte grondering. De eerste opzet van de compositie werd aangeduid met enkele spaarzame donkerblauwe contouren, waarmee hij de positie van ruiter en paard bepaalde. De meeste kleurvlakken vulde Kandinsky op met verwaterde, dekkende en half-dekkende kleurtonen, waarbij opvalt dat hij bij het opbrengen en mengen van de kleuren verschillende technieken gebruikte en ook met uiteenlopende oppervlaktetexturen en glansgraden werkte. In dat opzicht is het blauwe paard bijzonder gevarieerd uitgevoerd: op een klein vlak zijn de donkerblauwe kleuren in verschillende mengtechnieken met wit en geel opgebracht. Het kleureffect wordt bovendien versterkt door het contrast tussen 'vlakke', dun opgebrachte en 'plastische', dik opgebrachte kleurvelden. Door de toevoeging van een medium wist Kandinsky daarnaast de oppervlakteglans te verhogen, bijvoorbeeld in de zwarte manen van het paard en het rode zadelkleed.

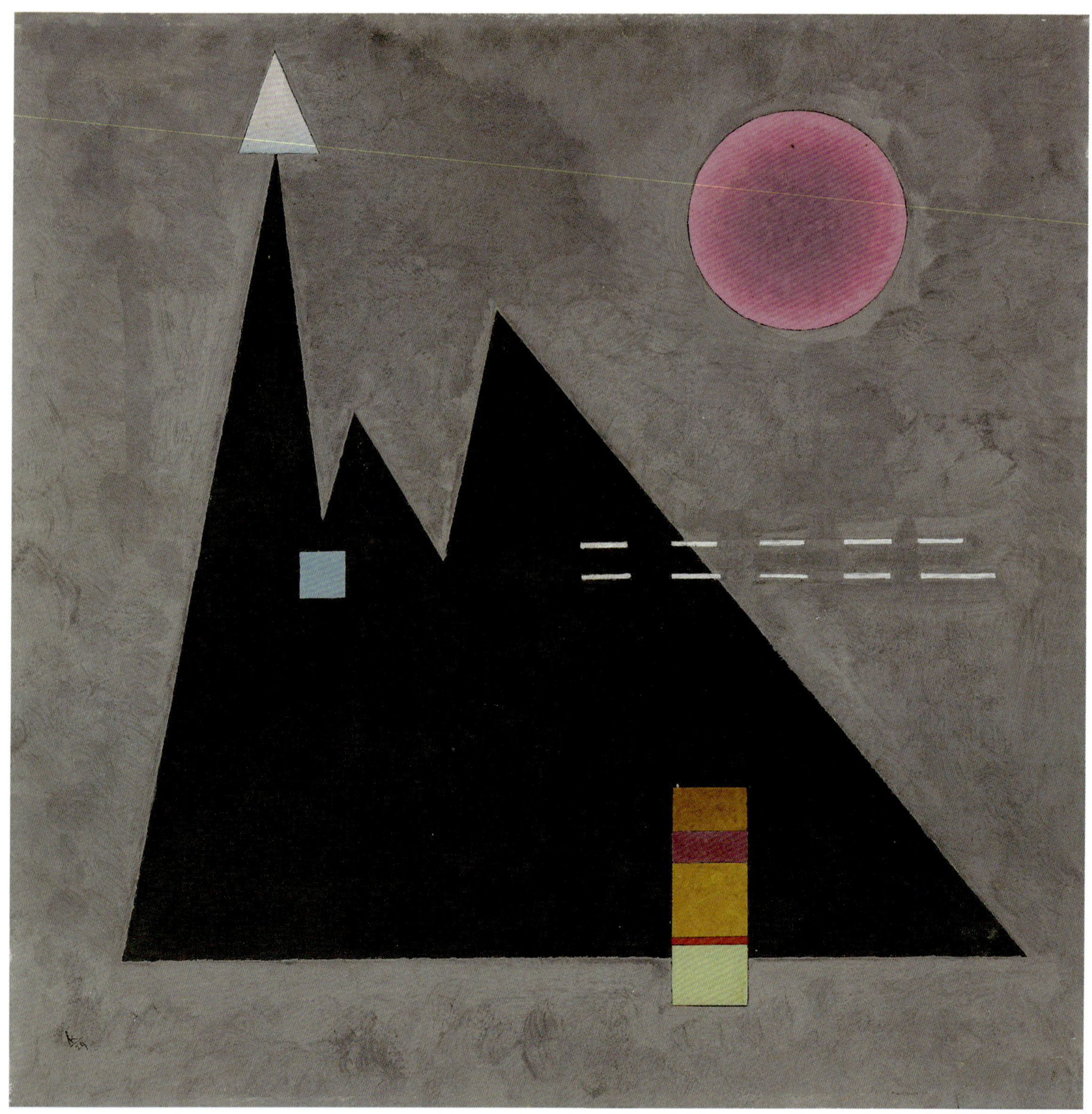

Sharp in Blunt

Tranchant dans le terne

Scharf im Dumpfen

Sostenido en Roma

Appuntito smussato

Scherp in bot

1929, Oil on board/Huile sur carton,
49 × 49 cm, Private collection

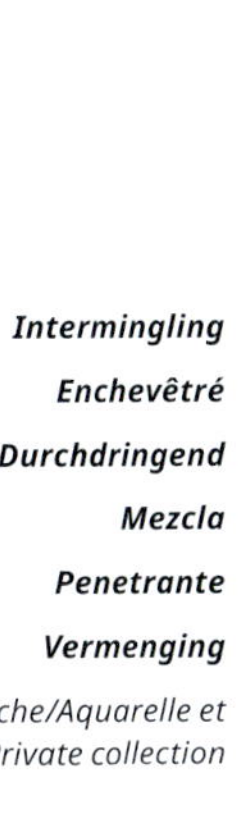

Intermingling

Enchevêtré

Durchdringend

Mezcla

Penetrante

Vermenging

1928, Watercolor and gouache/Aquarelle et
gouache, 48,5 × 32 cm, Private collection

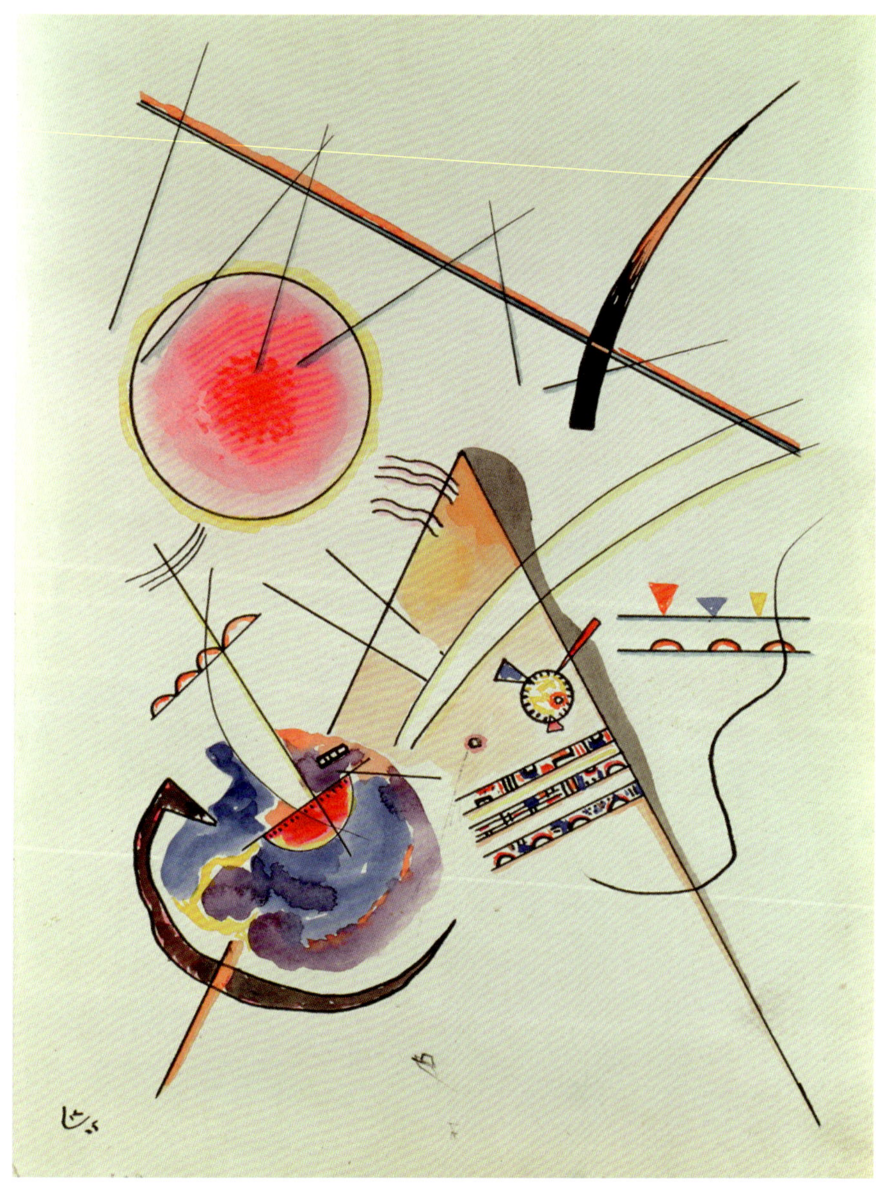

Untitled

Sans titre

Ohne Titel

Sin título

Senza titolo

Zonder titel

*1925, Watercolor on paper/
Aquarelle sur papier,
28 × 21,3 cm, Private collection*

220

Surfaces and Lines
Surfaces et lignes
Flächen und Linien
Superficies y líneas
Superfici e linee
Vlakken en lijnen
1930, Oil on cardboard/Huile sur carton, 49 × 70 cm, Private collection

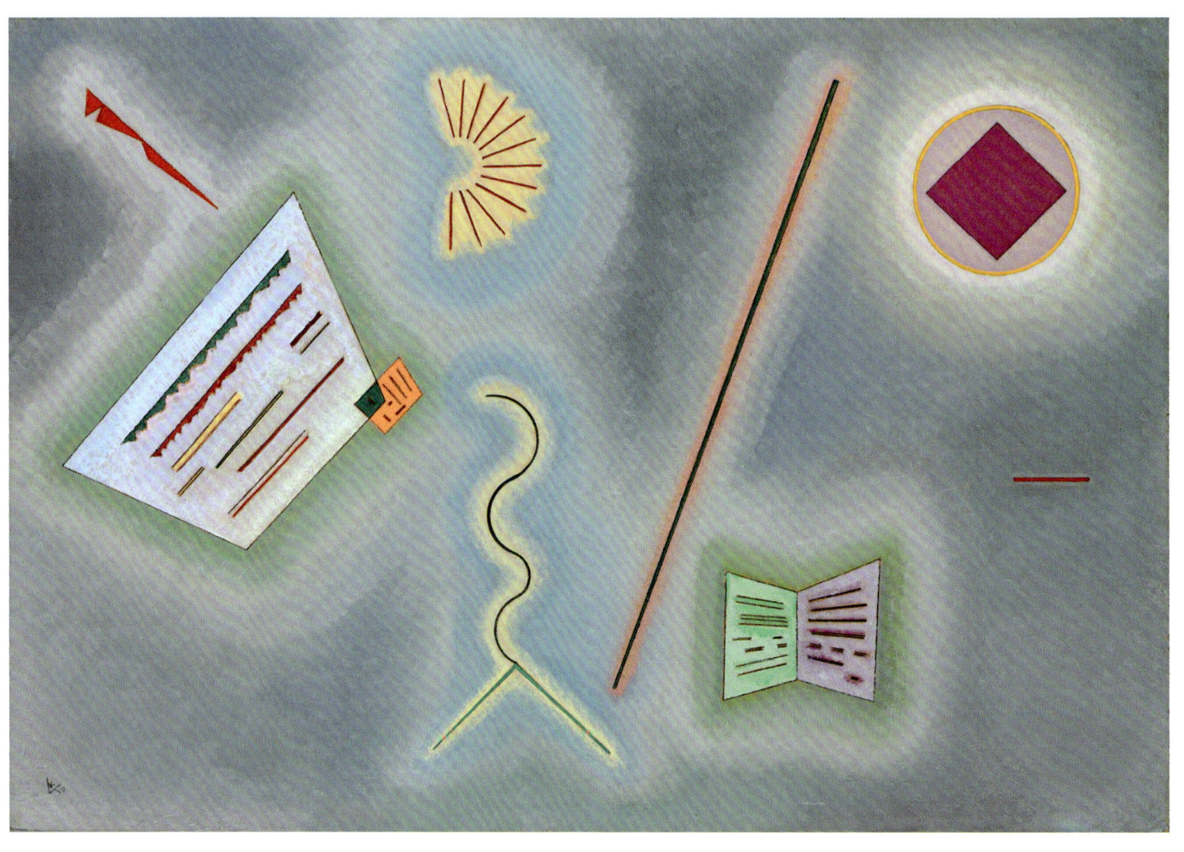

221

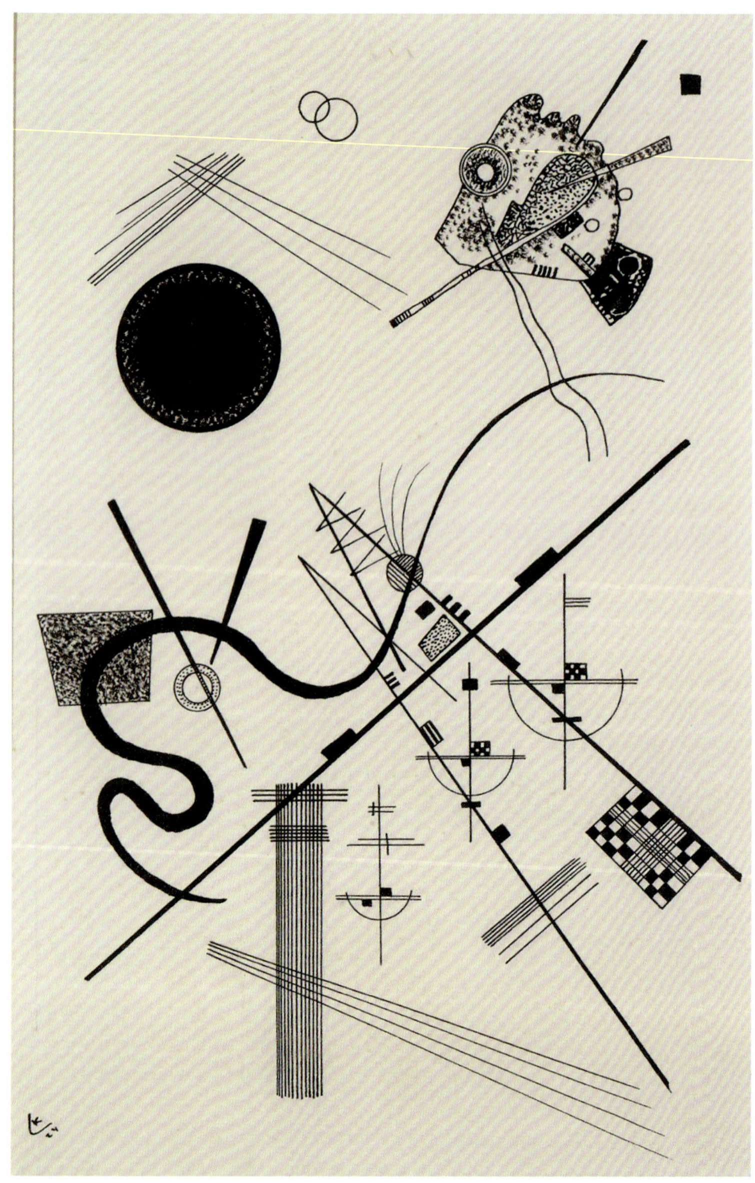

Drawing 4

Dessin 4

Zeichnung 4

Dibujo 4

Disegno 4

Tekening 4

1924, Ink on paper/Encre de Chine sur papier,
35 × 23 cm, Private collection

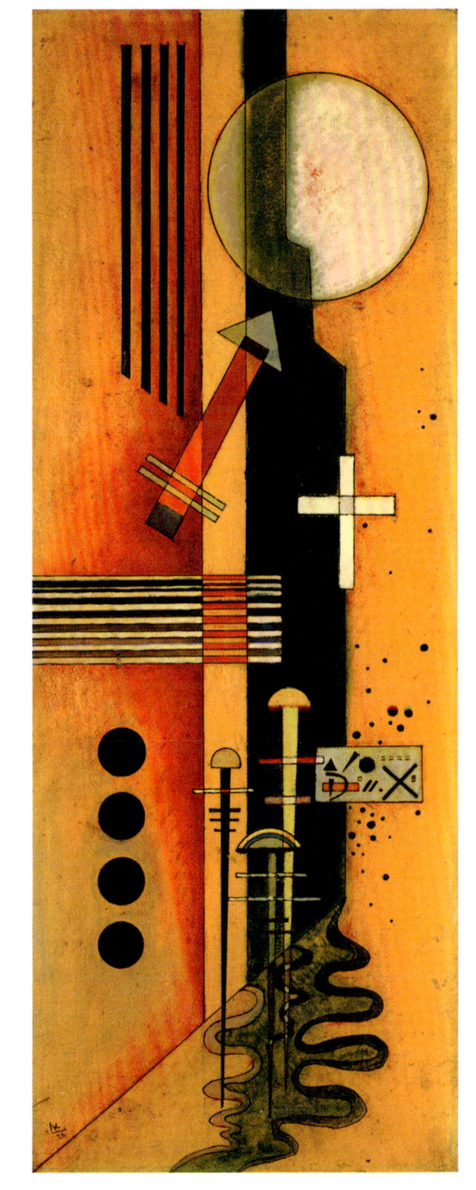

Toward Pink
Vers le rose
Zum Rosa
Hacia la rosa
Verso il rosa
Naar het roze

1926, Oil on cardboard/Huile sur carton, 71 × 27 cm, Private collection

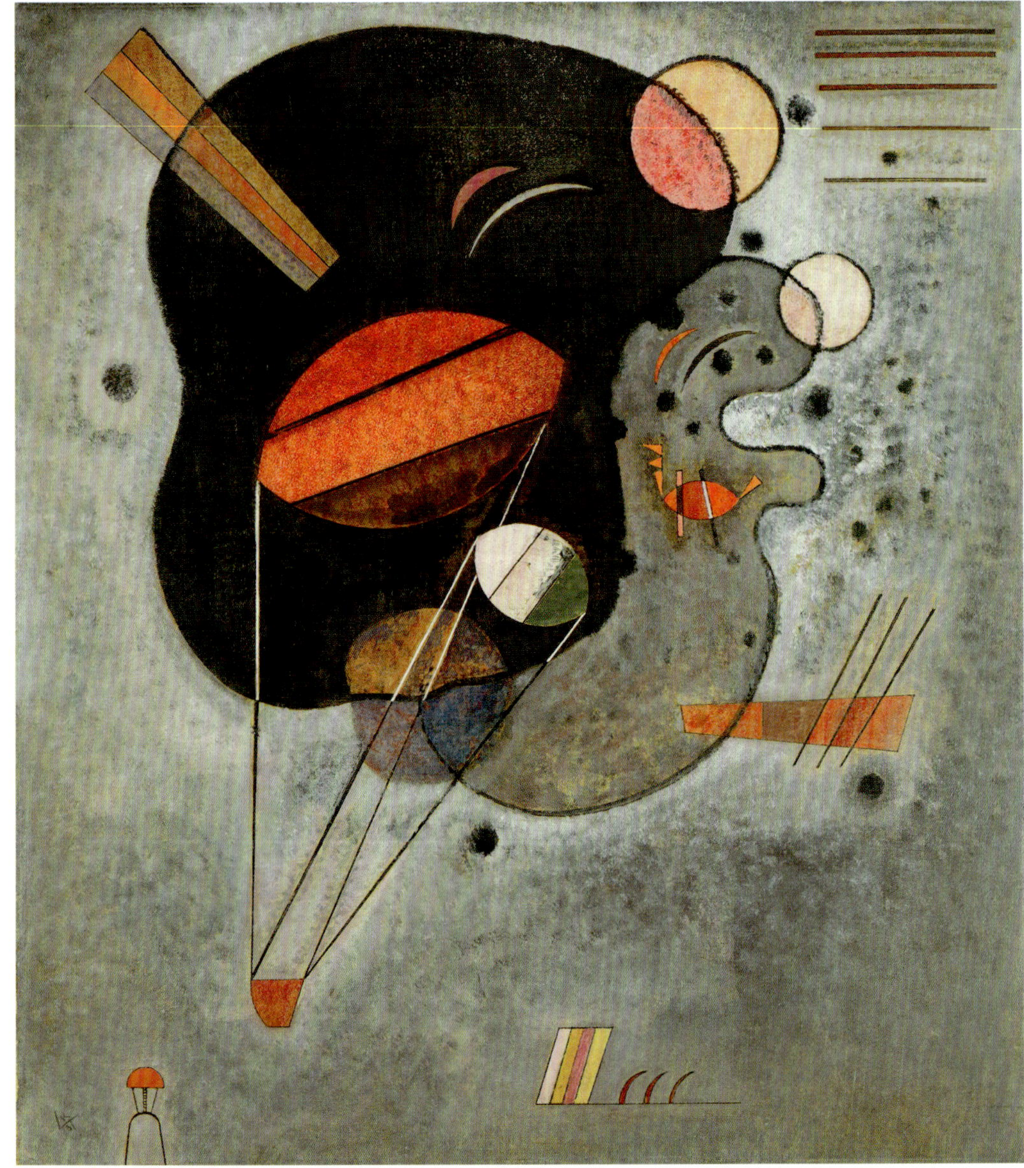

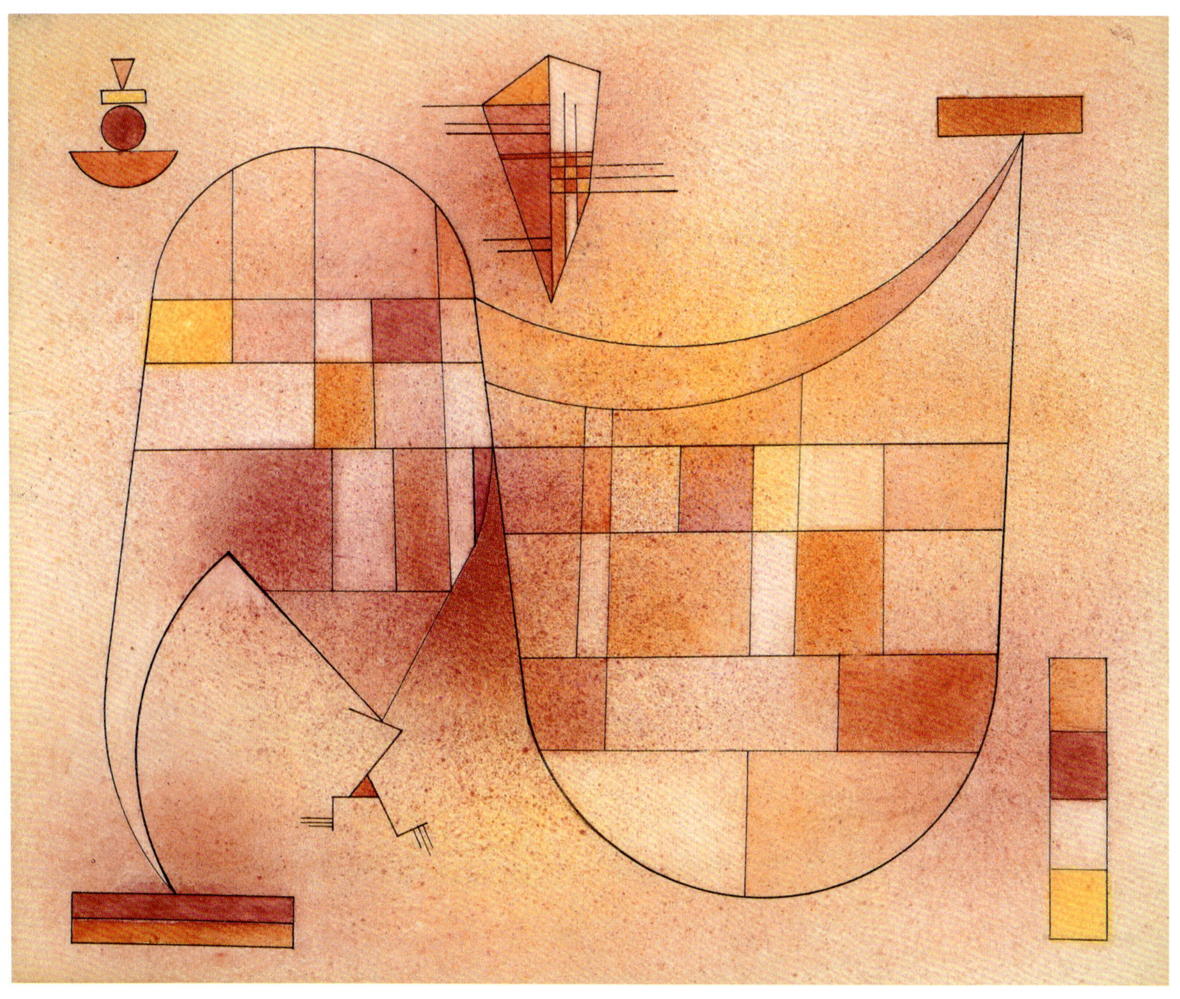

| *Hovering Print* | *Schwebender Druck* | *Stampa sospesa* | | *Yellow Pink* | *Gelb Rosa* | *Giallo rosa* |
| *Imprimé en suspension* | *Imprimir flotando* | *Zwevende druk* | | *Jaune rose* | *Amarillo Rosa* | *Geel roze* |

1931, Oil and tempera on board/Huile et tempéra sur carton, 79 × 69,2 cm, Private collection

1929, Watercolor and ink on paper on board/Aquarelle et encre de Chine sur papier marouflé sur carton, 40,5 ×48,1 cm, Private collection

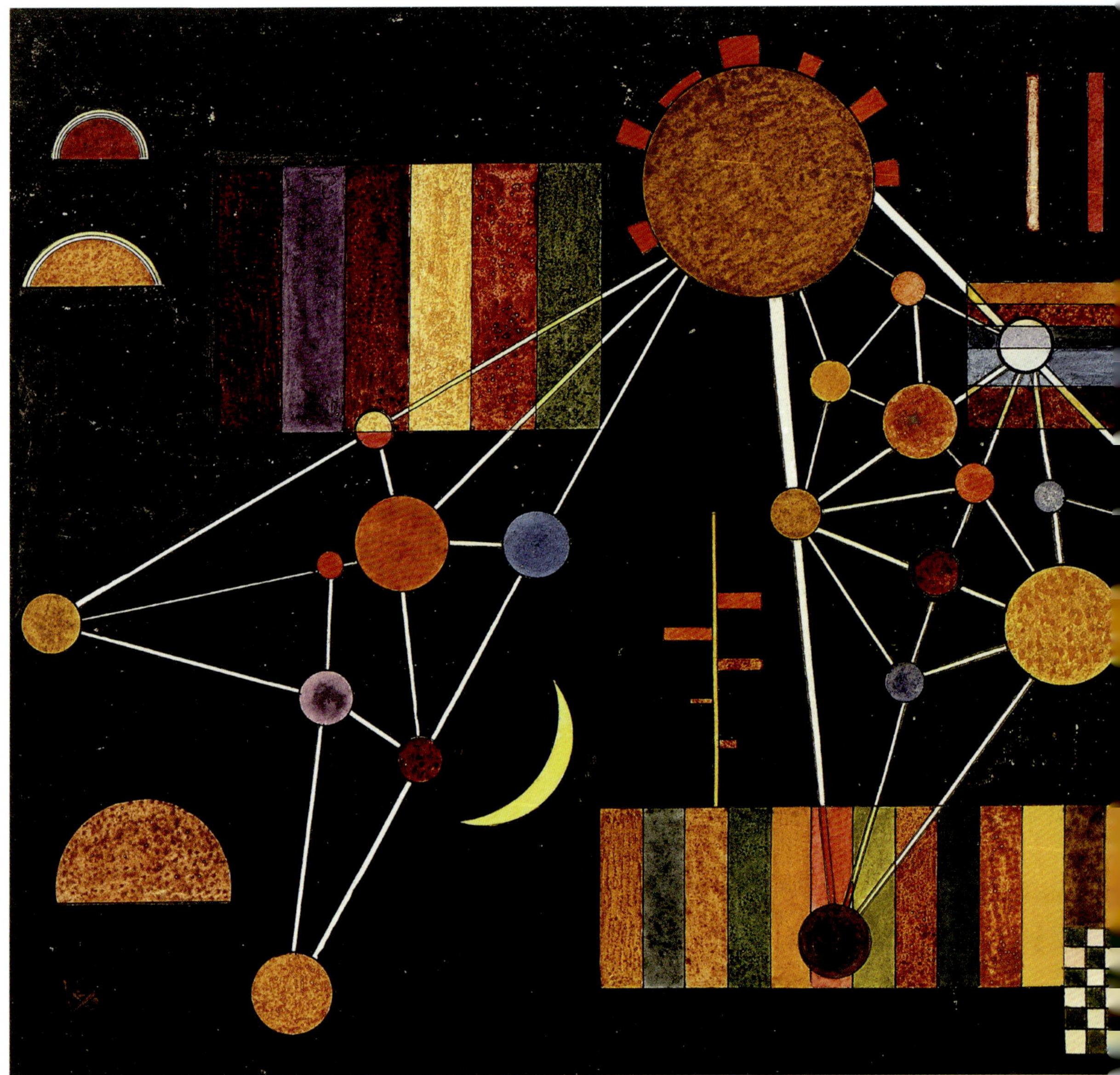

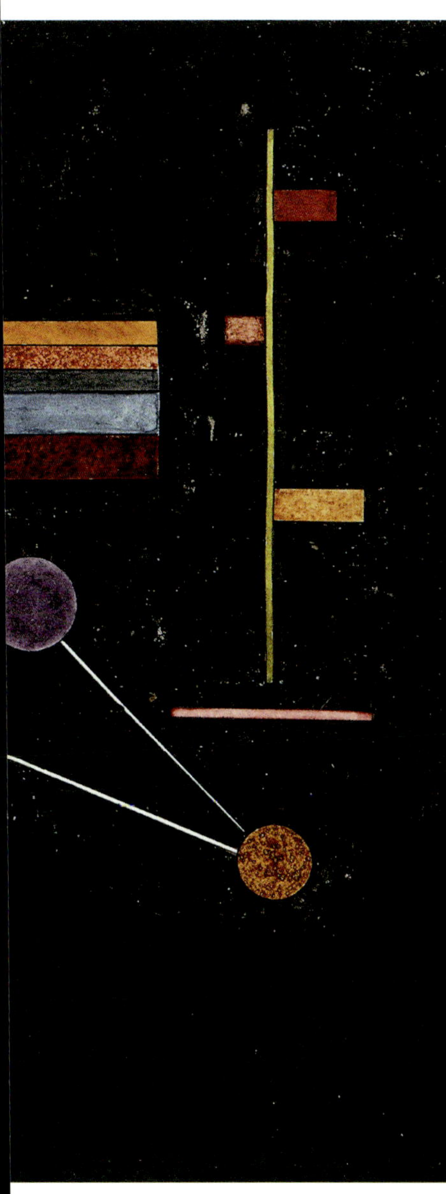

Network seen from Above No. 231

Entrelacs vus d'en haut n° 231

Geflecht von Oben Nr. 231

La red vista desde arriba no. 231

Intreccio dall'alto n. 231

Vlechtwerk van boven Nr. 231

1927, Gouache, watercolor, ink on paper/Gouache, aquarelle et encre de Chine sur papier, 32,1 × 48,3 cm, Private collection

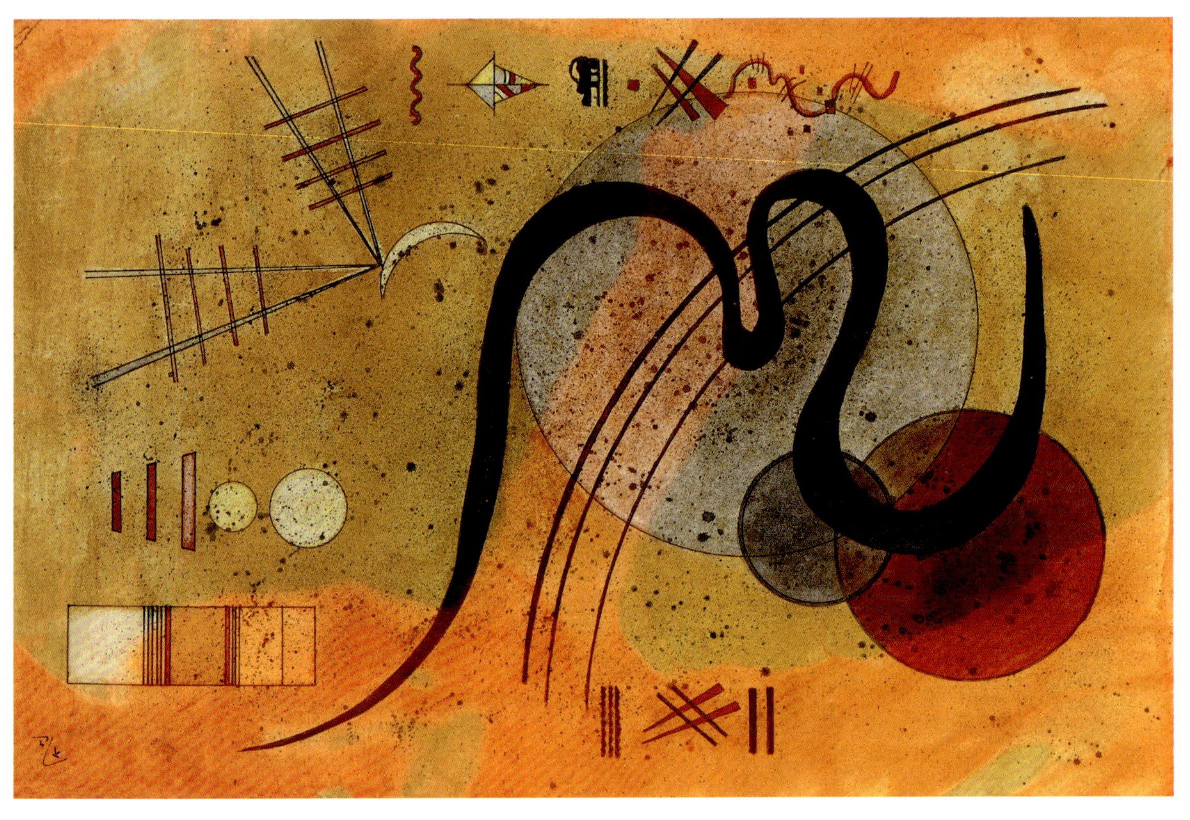

Launelinie

1927, Gouache, watercolor, ink on paper/Gouache, aquarelle
et encre de Chine sur papier, 48 × 32 cm, Private collection

Study for **Circles in Black**

Étude pour **Cercles en noir**

Studie für **Kreise in Schwarz**

Estudio para **Los círculos en negro**

Studio per **Cerchi su nero**

Studie voor **Cirkels in zwart**

1921, Watercolor and ink on paper/Aquarelle et encre de Chine sur papier,
25,5 × 25,5 cm, Private collection

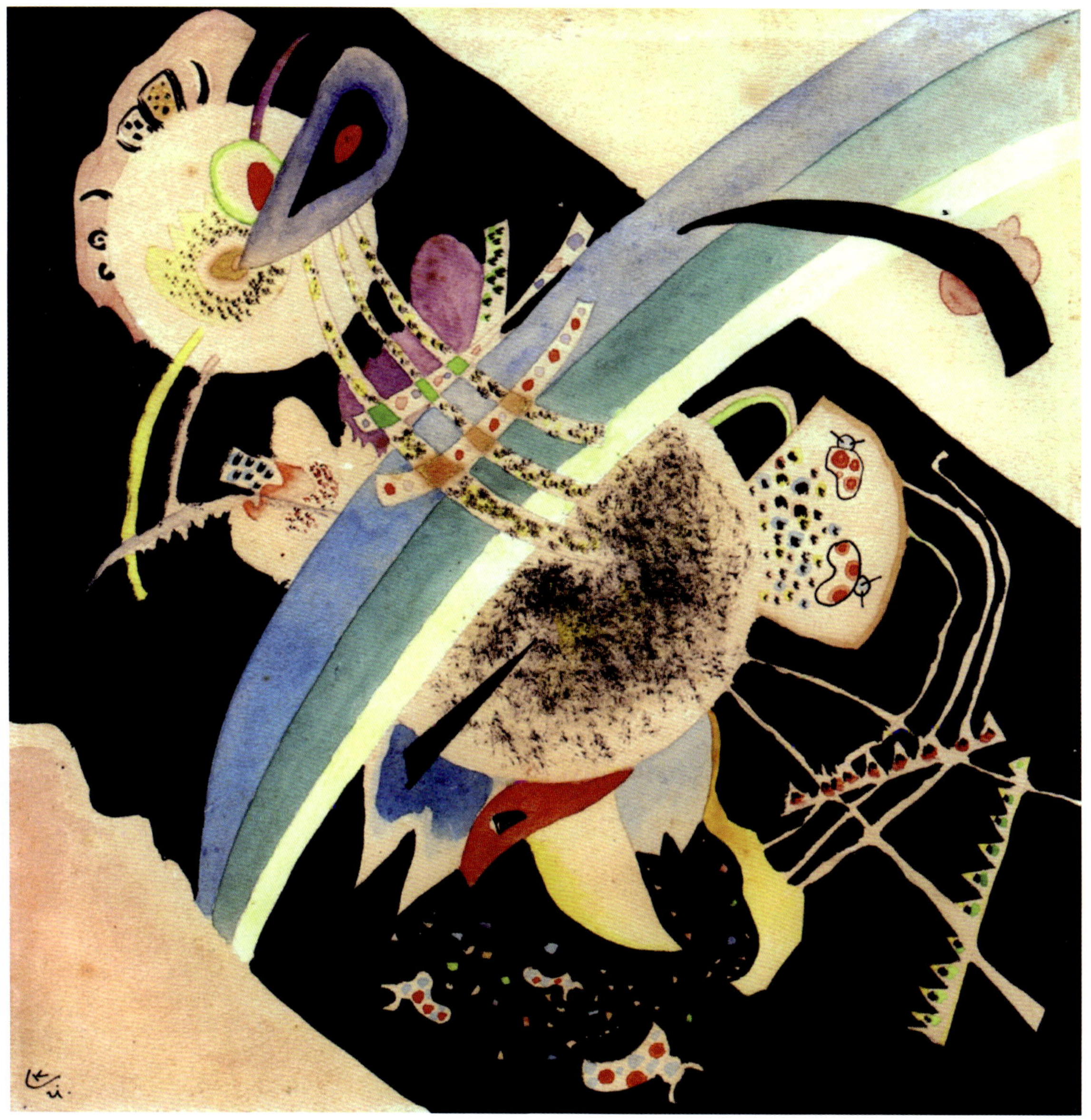

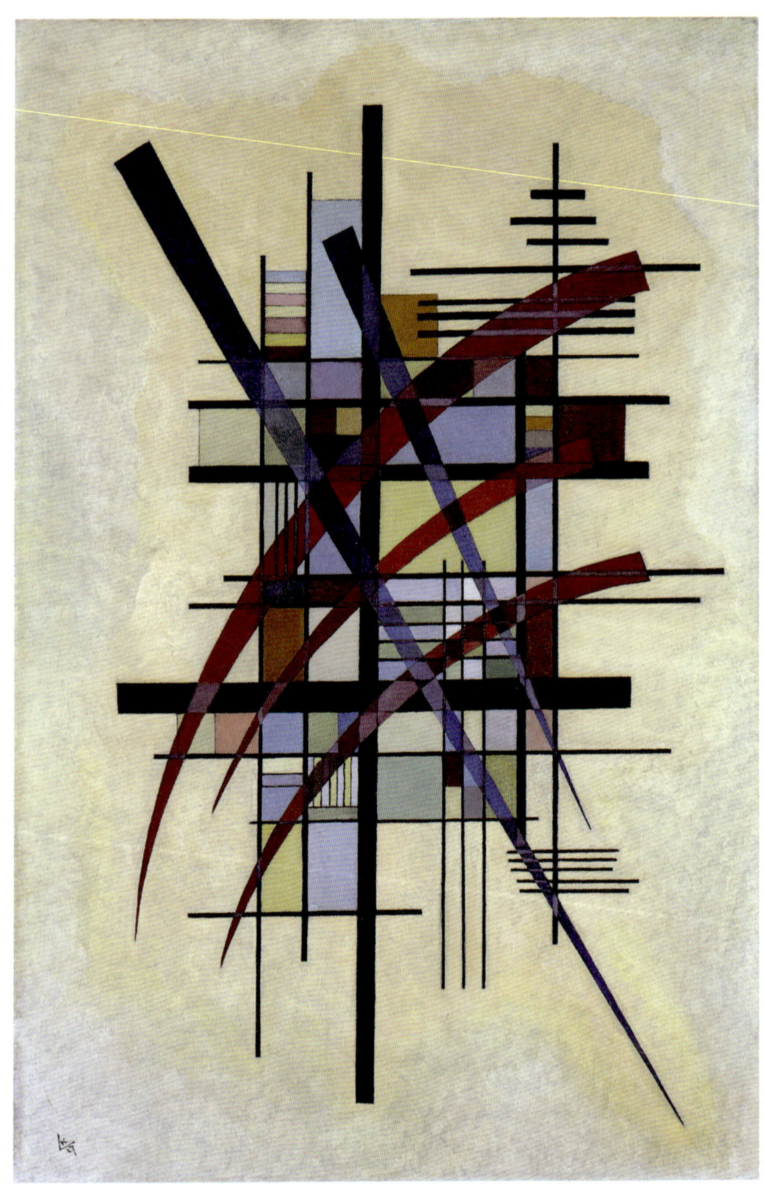

Sign with Accompaniment
Signe avec accompagnement
Zeichen mit Begleitung
Muestra con acompañamiento
Segno con accompagnamento
Teken met gevolg

1927, Oil on canvas/Huile sur toile, 81 × 52 cm,
Private collection

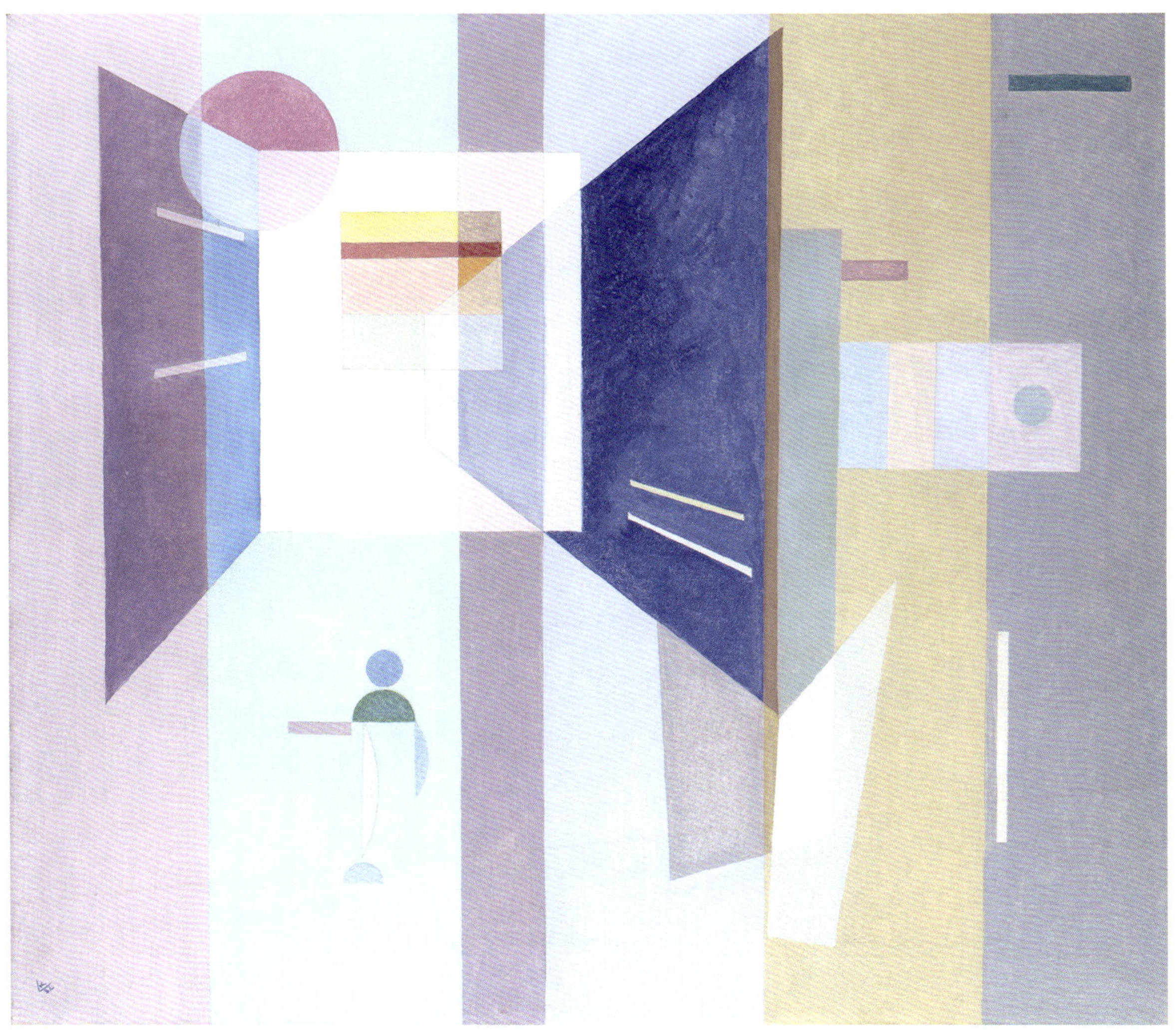

To the Right

Nach Rechts-Nach Links

Verso destra-Verso sinistra

Vers la droite - vers la gauche

A la derecha - a la izquierda

Naar rechts – naar links

1932, Oil on canvas/Huile sur toile, 60 × 70,5 cm, Private collection

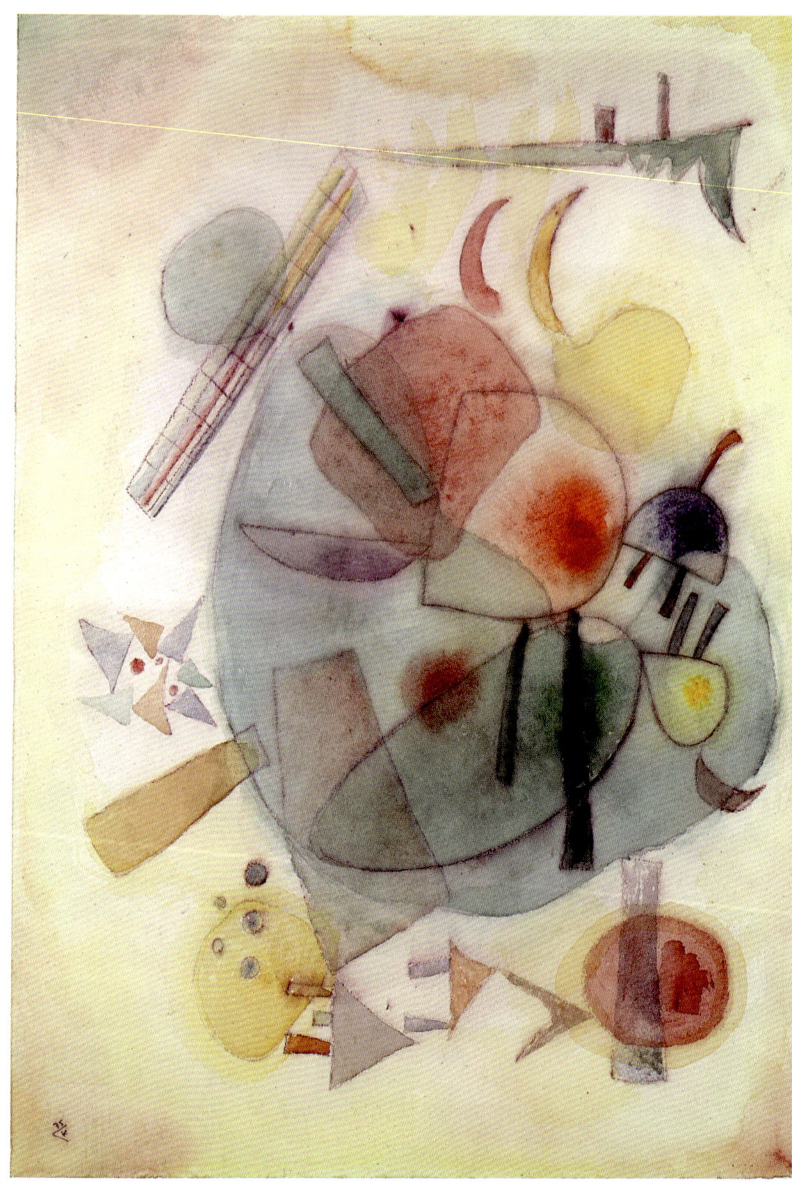

Blurred

Flouté

Verschwommen

Borrosa

Sfocato

Verwaterd

1932, Watercolor on paper/Aquarelle sur papier, 40 × 58 cm, Private collection

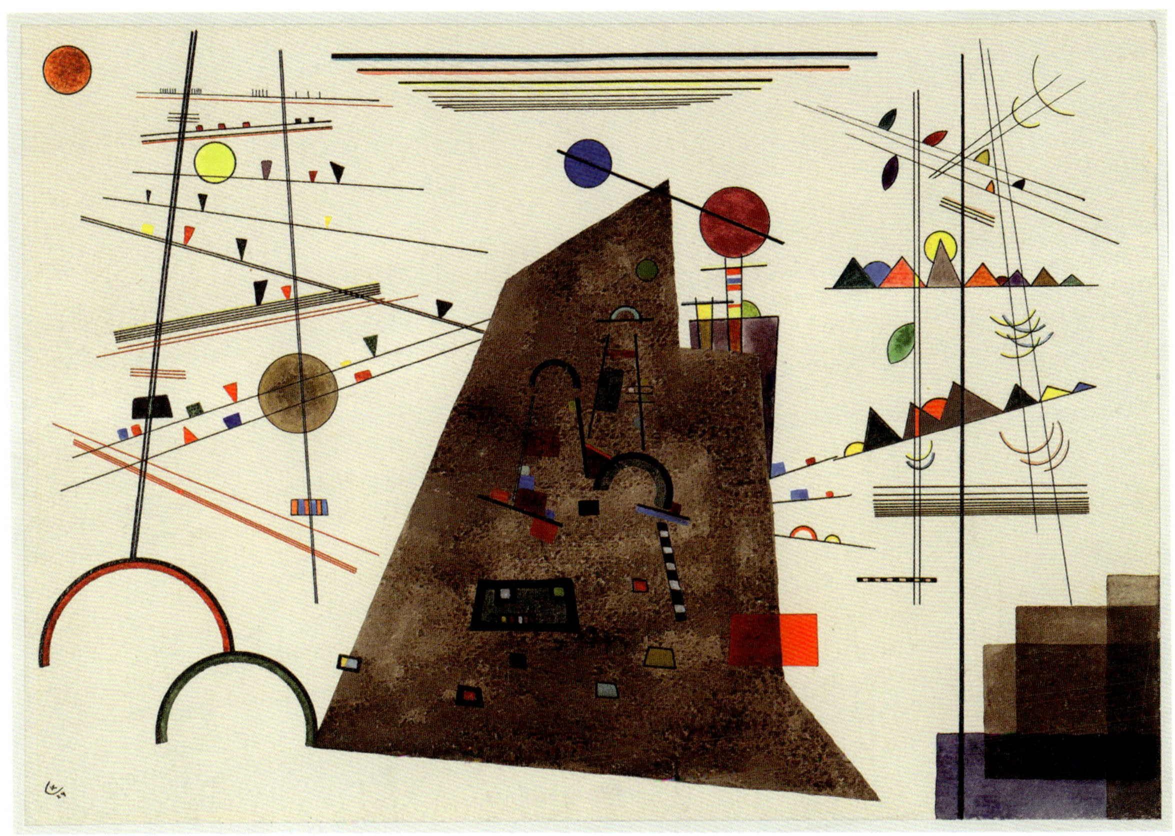

Heavy between Light

Lourd/léger

Schweres zwischen Leichtem

Pesado entre la luz

Pesante tra il leggero

Zwaar tussen licht

1924, Gouache, watercolor and ink on paper/Gouache, aquarelle et encre de Chine sur papier, 33,8 × 48,7 cm, Private collection

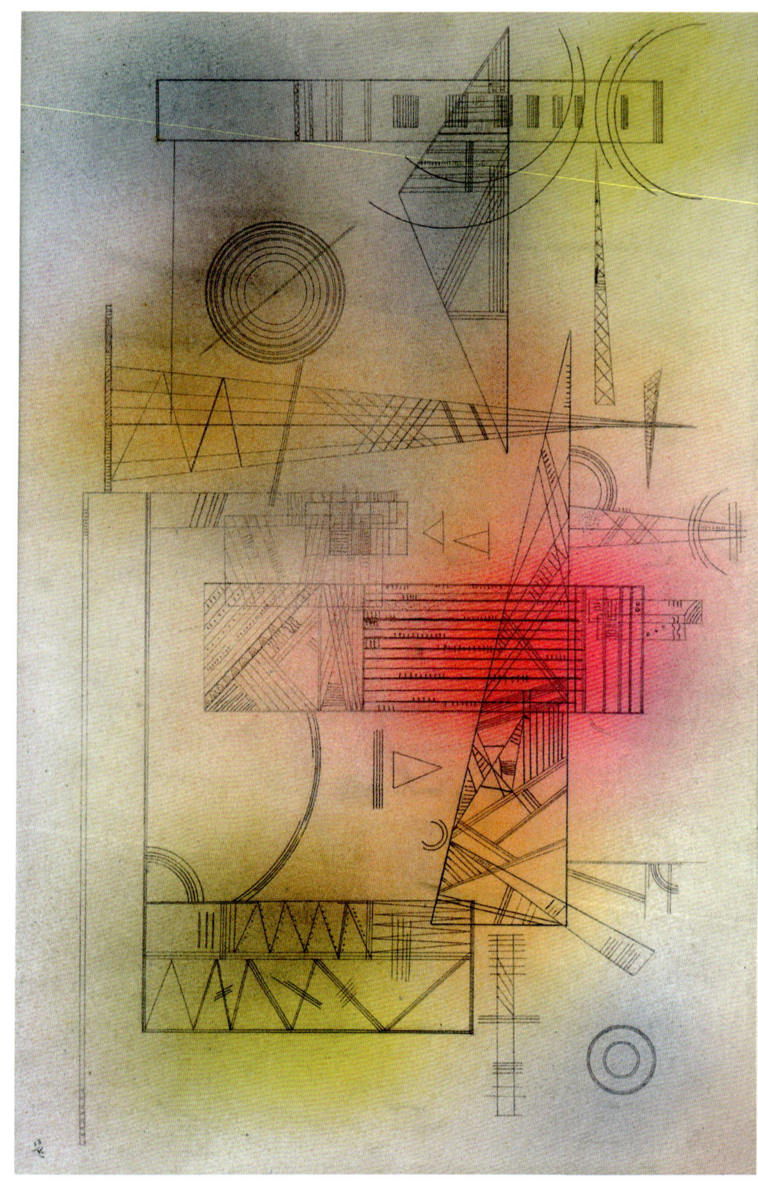

Composition 302

Composition n° 302

Komposition Nr. 302

Composición 302

Composizione 302

Compositie Nr. 302

1928, Watercolor and ink on paper/Aquarelle et encre de Chine sur papier, 38 × 58 cm, Private collection

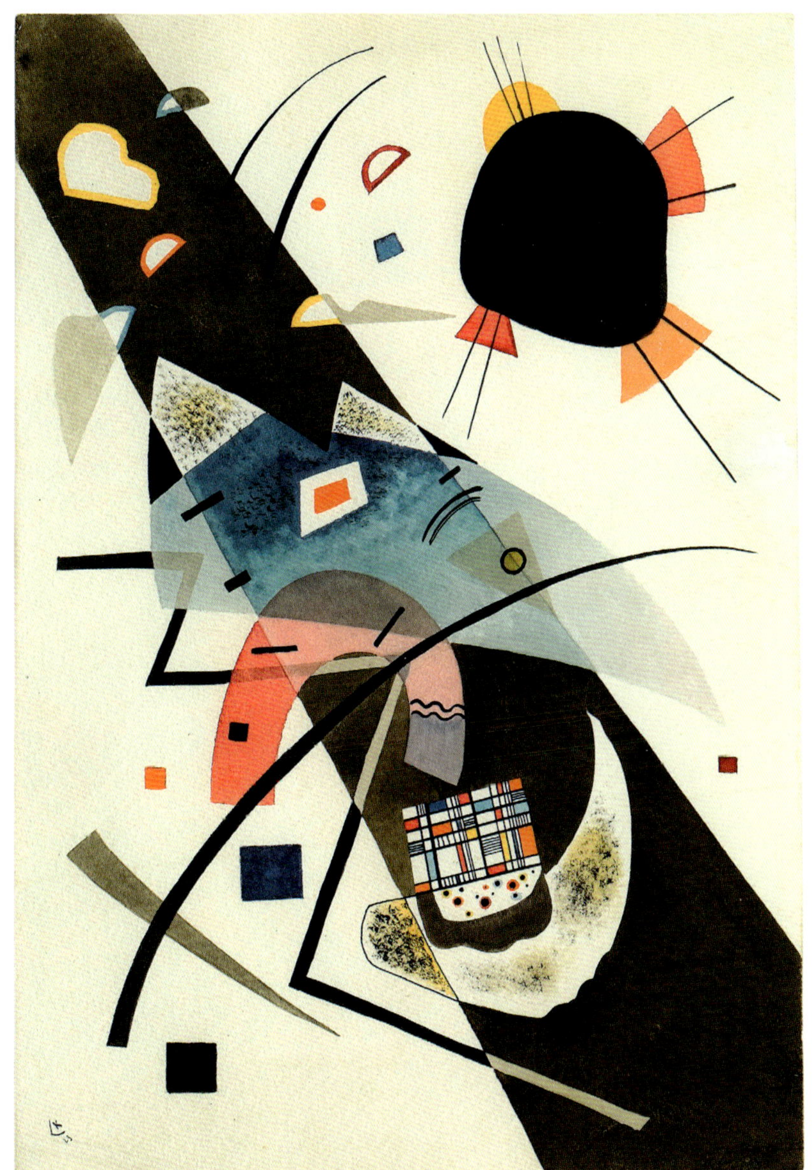

Two Black Spots

Deux taches noires

Zwei schwarze Flecken

Dos puntos negros

Due macchie nere

Twee zwarte vlekken

1923, Watercolor and ink on paper/Aquarelle
et encre de Chine sur papier, 47,5 × 32,7 cm,
Private collection

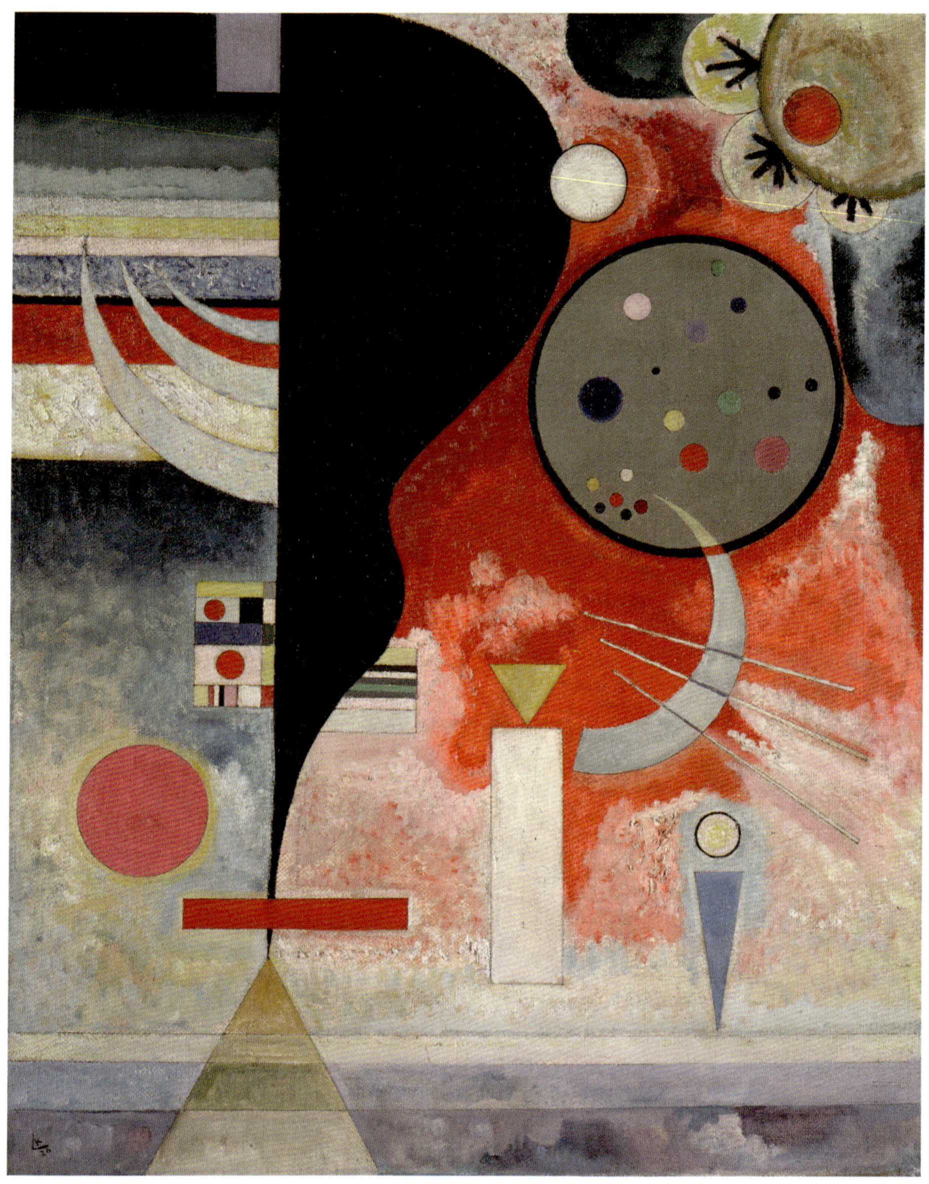

Rift
Fissure
Riss
Grieta
Fenditura
Scheur

1926, Oil on canvas/
Huile sur toile, 101 × 82 cm,
Private collection

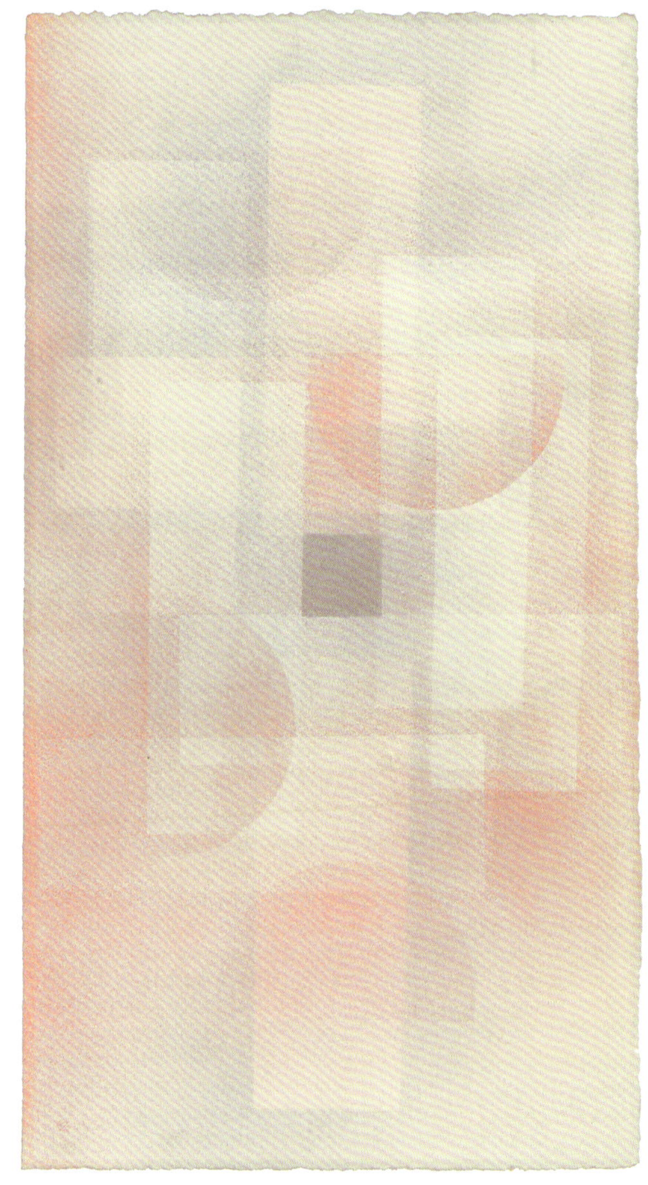

Square in the Fog
Carré dans le brouillard
Quadrat im Nebel
La plaza en la niebla
Quadrato nella nebbia
Vierkant in de mist

*1932, Watercolor on paper on card/Aquarelle sur papier sur carton,
57,7 × 32 cm, Private collection*

Kandinsky in Paris

In 1933 Kandinsky emigrated with Nina to Paris, taking a small apartment in Neuilly-sur-Seine.

The Parisian art scene responded rather reservedly to Kandinsky's arrival. After several failed attempts at establishing contact with the Russian émigré scene, Kandinsky limited his contacts to a few artists such as Sonia and Robert Delaunay, Joan Miró (1893–1983) and Hans Arp (1886–1966), or André Breton (1896–1966) and his circle of surrealists. The new direction of abstract painting displeased him due to their overly dogmatic focus on geometric abstraction. He withdrew to his studio apartment and created new biomorphic pictures, whose highly detailed teeming images actually seemed to fit more into the orbit of the surrealists than following in the steps of Mondrian and his purists. Kandinsky's world remained in abstraction, and now seemed to be reverting into the realm of fairy tale or fantasy once again, disengaged from any theory.

Kandinsky became once more caught up in the wake of political events following the infamous "Degenerate Art" exhibition of 1937, which was held in the Munich Hofgarten and in which Kandinsky images were defamed. Also at this time, the German passports held by the couple ran out, so they decided to take French citizenship. In 1940, they spent three summer months in the Pyrenees, during which time they learned of the death of their longtime friend Paul Klee. The occupation of France by German troops forced their

Kandinsky à Paris

En 1933, Kandinsky émigre à Paris où il emménage avec Nina dans un petit appartement de Neuilly-sur-Seine.

La scène artistique parisienne réagit à l'arrivée de Kandinsky de façon plutôt réservée. Après quelques tentatives avortées en direction de l'émigration russe, les contacts de Kandinsky se limitent à quelques artistes comme Robert et Sonia Delaunay, Joan Miró (1893-1983), Jean Arp (1886-1966) ou André Breton (1896-1966) et son cercle de surréalistes. La nouvelle tendance de la peinture abstraite lui déplaît en raison de sa tendance trop dogmatique à l'abstraction géométrique. Il se retire donc dans sa résidence-atelier et peint de nouveaux tableaux « biomorphes » dont le grouillement morcelé semble plus proche de l'atmosphère des surréalistes que de celle de Mondrian et de ses puristes. Le monde de Kandinsky reste l'abstraction, à présent libérée de toute théorie, et qui semble se développer en revenant au domaine du légendaire ou de l'imaginaire.

Kandinsky replonge toutefois bientôt dans le tourbillon des événements politiques. Ses tableaux sont vilipendés, eux aussi, dans le cadre de l'exposition de l'« Art dégénéré » en 1937, dans le Münchner Hofgarten. Les passeports allemands des Kandinsky étant périmés, ils décident de prendre la nationalité française. En 1940, ils passent les trois mois d'été dans les Pyrénées (où ils apprennent la mort de leur vieil ami Paul Klee). L'occupation de la France par les troupes allemandes les force à revenir.

Kandinsky in Paris

1933 emigriert Kandinsky mit Nina nach Paris, in ein kleines Appartement in Neuilly-sur-Seine.

Die Pariser Kunstszene reagiert auf Kandinskys Ankunft eher zurückhaltend. Nach einigen fehlgeschlagenen Anknüpfungsversuchen zur russischen Emigrantenszene beschränken sich Kandinskys Kontakte auf einige wenige Künstler wie Sonia und Robert Delaunay, Joan Miró (1893–1983), Hans Arp (1886–1966) oder André Breton (1896–1966) und dessen Surrealistenkreis. Die neue Richtung abstrakter Malerei missfällt ihm dagegen wegen ihrer allzu dogmatischen Ausrichtung auf die geometrische Abstraktion. So zieht er sich in seine Atelierwohnung zurück und malt neue biomorphe Bilder, deren kleinteiliges Gewimmel tatsächlich eher in den Dunstkreis der Surrealisten zu passen scheint als in die Gefolgschaft von Mondrian und seinen Puristen. Kandinskys Welt bleibt die Abstraktion, die sich nun ungebunden von jeder Theorie wieder zurück in märchenhafte oder phantastische Gefilde zu entwickeln scheint.

Doch Kandinsky gerät erneut in den Sog der politischen Ereignisse. Auf der Schmähausstellung „Entartete Kunst" 1937 im Münchner Hofgarten werden auch Kandinskys Bilder diffamiert. Außerdem läuft der deutsche Pass des Ehepaars ab, sodass sie beschließen, die französische Staatsbürgerschaft anzunehmen. 1940 verbringen sie drei Sommermonate in den Pyrenäen, wo sie vom Tod des langjährigen Freundes Paul Klee

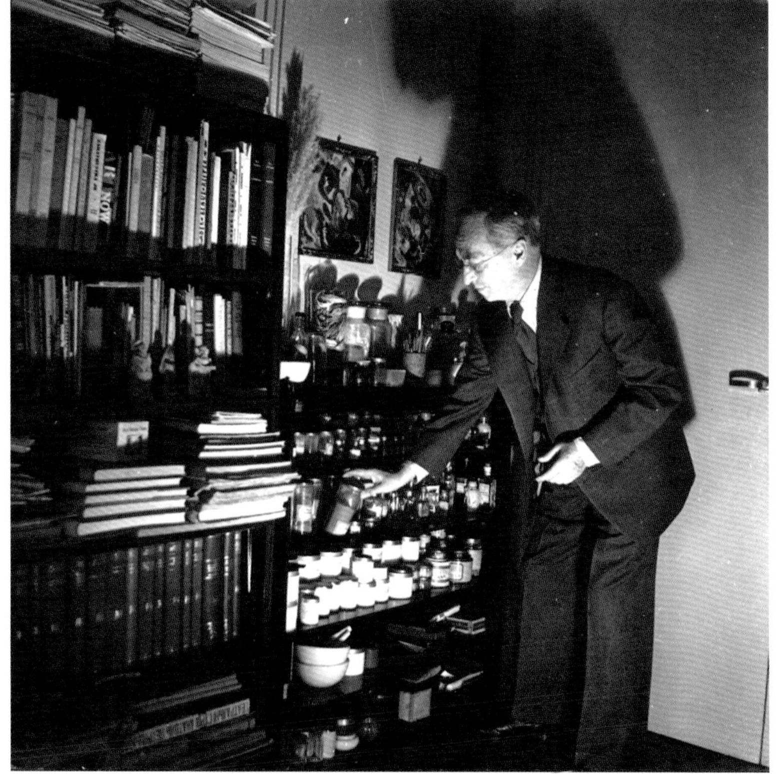

Kandinsky en París

En 1933, Kandinsky emigra con Nina a París, ocupando un pequeño apartamento en Neuilly-sur-Seine.

La escena artística parisina respondió de forma más bien reservada a la llegada de Kandinsky. Tras varios intentos fallidos de establecer contacto con la escena de los emigrados rusos, Kandinsky limitó sus contactos a unos pocos artistas como Sonia y Robert Delaunay, Joan Miró (1893–1983) y Hans Arp (1886–1966) o

Kandinsky a Parigi

Nel 1933 Kandinsky emigrò con Nina a Parigi, dove prese un piccolo appartamento a Neuilly-sur-Seine.

La scena artistica parigina rispose in modo piuttosto riservato all'arrivo di Kandinsky. Dopo diversi tentativi falliti di allacciare contatti con la comunità di emigrati russi, Kandinsky strinse rapporti con pochi artisti, tra cui Sonia e Robert Delaunay, Joan Miró (1893-1983), Hans Arp (1886-1966) e André

Kandinsky in Parijs

In 1933 emigreert Kandinsky samen met Nina naar Parijs en vestigt zich in een klein appartement in Neuilly-sur-Seine.

De Parijse kunstwereld reageert tamelijk terughoudend op zijn komst. Na enkele mislukte pogingen om contact te leggen met kringen van Russische emigranten beperken Kandinsky's relaties zich tot een handvol kunstenaars, onder wie Sonia en Robert Delaunay, Joan Miró (1893–

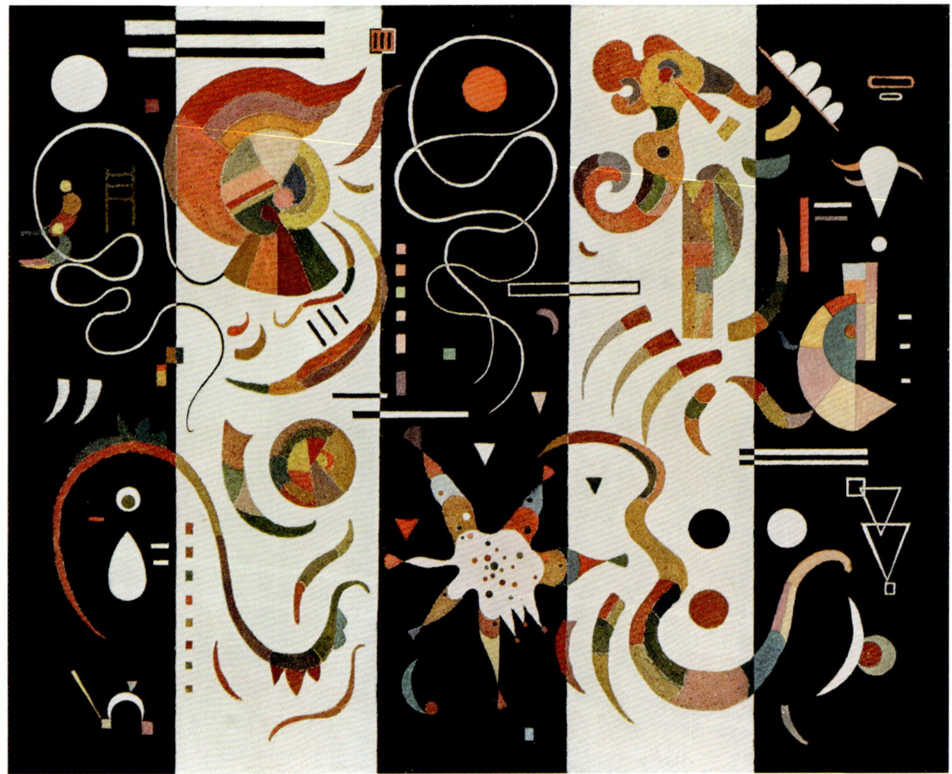

*1934, Oil on canvas/
Huile et sable sur toile,
83 × 100 cm,
Solomon R. Guggenheim
Museum, New York*

return to Paris. In his last few years during the war Kandinsky suffered from a shortage of materials and painted mainly on small cardboard boxes.

Kandinsky died on 13 December 1944 after suffering for a long time from arteriosclerosis and being weakened by the flu.

Dans les dernières années de guerre, le manque de matériel contraint le peintre à travailler sur des cartons de petit format. Depuis longtemps atteint d'artériosclérose et affaibli par une grippe, Kandinsky meurt à 78 ans, le 13 décembre 1944.

erfahren. Die Besetzung Frankreichs durch deutsche Truppen zwingt sie zur Rückkehr. Die letzten Jahre während des Krieges malt Kandinsky aus Materialmangel vorwiegend auf kleinen Kartons.

Schon lange an Arteriosklerose erkrankt und von einer Grippe geschwächt, stirbt Kandinsky am 13. Dezember 1944.

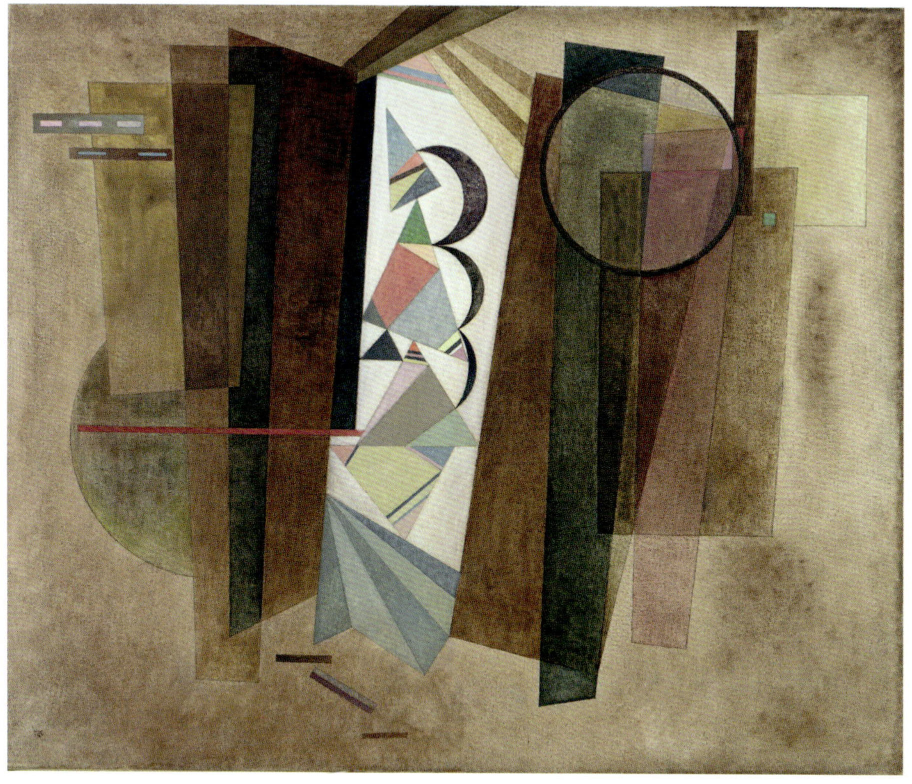

Development in Brown
Développement en brun
Entwicklung in Braun
Desarrollo en marrón
Sviluppo in marrone
Ontwikkeling in bruin

1933, Oil on canvas/
Huile sur toile, 100 × 120,5 cm,
Musée Cantini, Marseille

André Breton (1896–1966) y su círculo de surrealistas. La nueva dirección de la pintura abstracta le desagradaba debido a su excesivo dogmatismo centrado en la abstracción geométrica. Se retiró a su estudio-apartamento y creó nuevas obras biomórficas, cuyas imágenes altamente detalladas parecían encajar mejor en la órbita de los surrealistas que seguir los pasos de Mondrian y sus puristas. El mundo de Kandinsky permaneció en la abstracción y ahora parecía regresa

Breton (1896- 1966) e la sua cerchia di surrealisti. La nuova direzione della pittura astratta non era di suo gradimento a causa dell'orientamento eccessivamente dogmatico verso l'astrazione geometrica. Si ritirò nel suo appartamento e creò nuovi quadri biomorfi, le cui brulicanti immagini altamente dettagliate sembravano più rientrare nell'orbita dei surrealisti piuttosto che seguire le orme di Mondrian e dei suoi puristi. Il mondo di Kandinsky continuava a risiedere

1983), Hans Arp (1886–1966), André Breton (1896–1966) en diens kring van surrealisten. De nieuwe stroming van de abstracte schilderkunst bevalt Kandinsky niet, vanwege de al te dogmatische ontwikkeling naar geometrische abstractie. Hij trekt zich in zijn atelierwoning terug en schildert nieuwe, biomorfe werken, waarin het wemelt van creaturen die inderdaad meer tot de schemerwereld van de surrealisten lijken te behoren dan tot het puristische universum

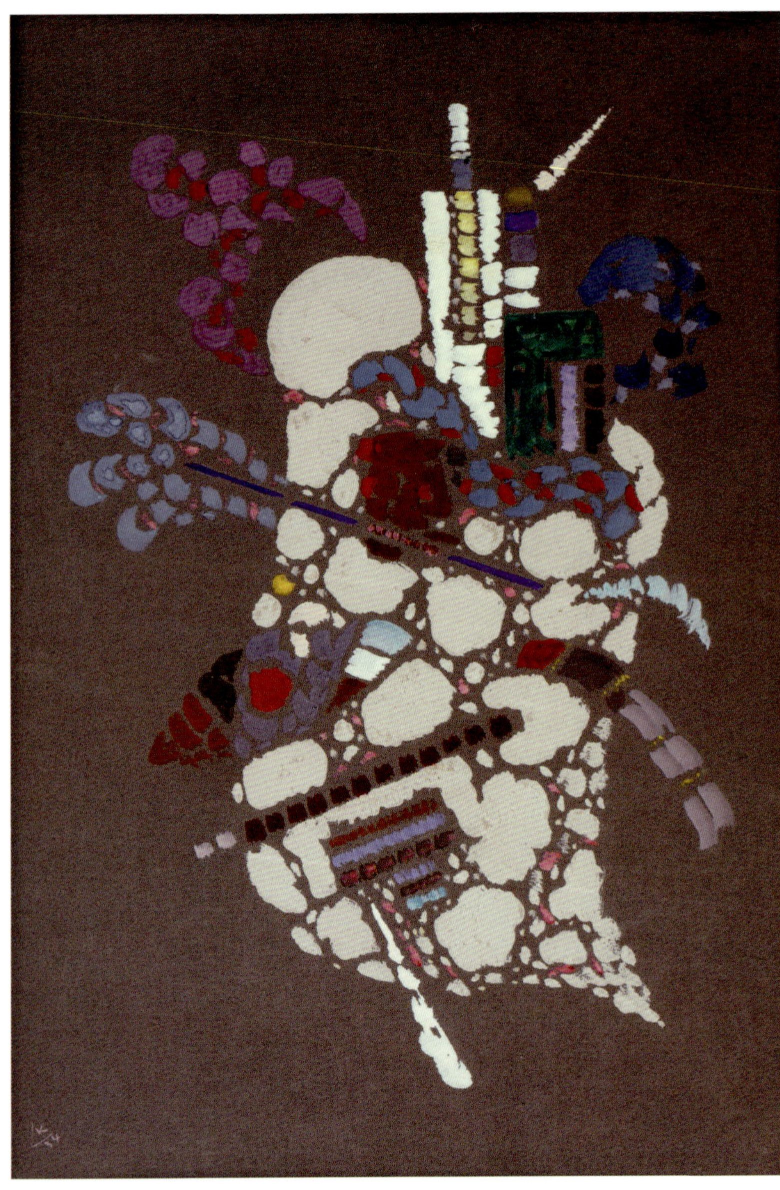

Composition X

Composition X

Komposition X

Composición X

Composizione X

Compositie X

1939, Oil on canvas/Huile sur toile,
130 × 195 cm, Kunstsammlung
Nordrhein-Westfalen, Dusseldorf

Taches Grises

Taches grises

Graue Flecken

Ganchos Grises

Macchie grigie

Grijze vlekken

1934, Tempera on grey paper/Tempera sur
papier gris, Private collection

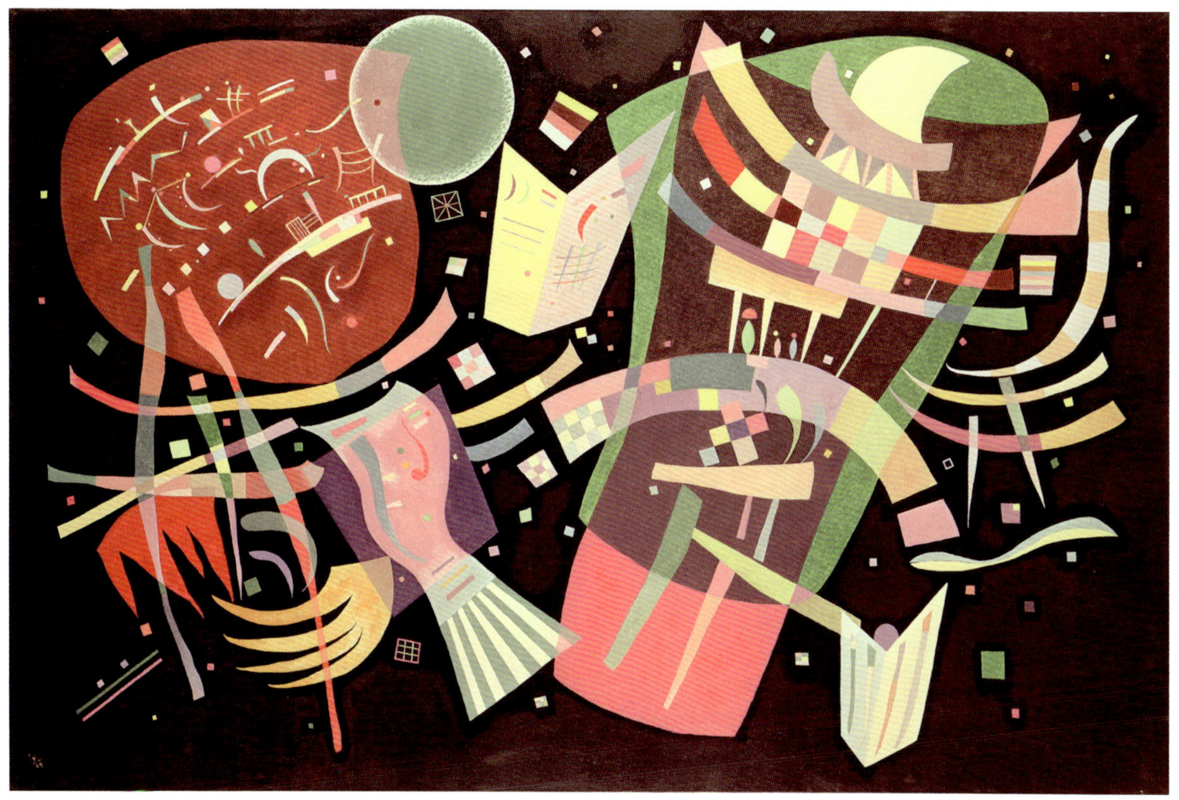

al reino de los cuentos de hadas o la fantasía, desprendiéndose de cualquier otra teoría.

Kandinsky quedó una vez más atrapado en la oleada de eventos políticos que siguieron a la tristemente conocida exposición "Arte Degenerado" de 1937, celebrada en el Hofgarten de Múnich y en la que los cuadros de Kandinsky fueron difamados. Al mismo tiempo caducaron los pasaportes alemanes de la pareja, que decidió adoptar

nell'astrazione, e ora sembrava tornare nel regno delle fiabe o della fantasia, svincolato da qualsiasi teoria.

Kandinsky si ritrovò nuovamente coinvolto nella scia degli eventi politici in seguito alla famigerata mostra „Arte degenerata" del 1937, che si tenne nell'Hofgarten di Monaco e in cui furono diffamati alcuni quadri di Kandinsky. Inoltre, in tale momento, i passaporti tedeschi detenuti dalla coppia scaddero, per cui Kandinsky

van Mondriaan. Kandinsky's wereld blijft de abstractie, die zich nu los van enige theorie in sprookjesachtige of fantasierijke tableaus lijkt te ontvouwen.

Opnieuw wordt Kandinsky meegezogen in de politieke gebeurtenissen van zijn tijd. Op de als aanklacht bedoelde tentoonstelling 'Entartete Kunst', in 1937 in de Münchense Hofgarten, worden ook de schilderijen van Kandinsky gehekeld. Bovendien is

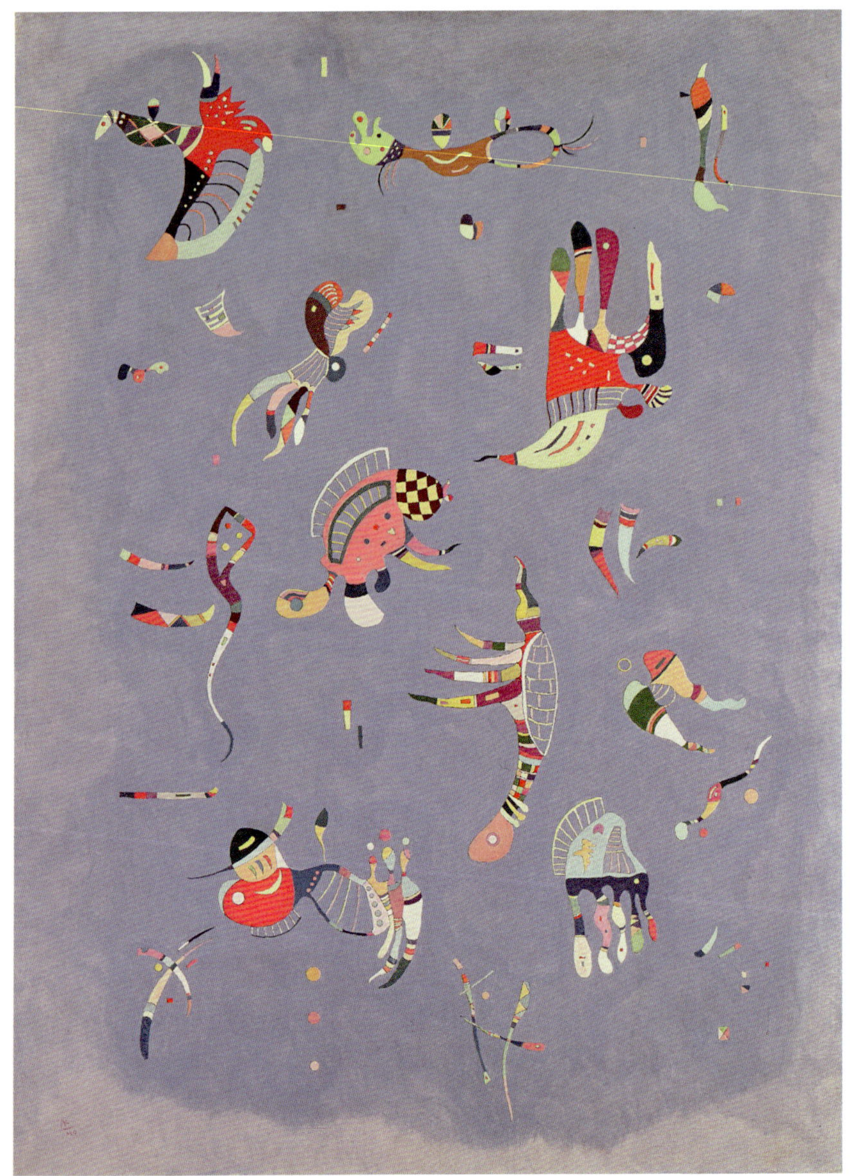

Sky Blue

Bleu de ciel

Himmelblau

Azul de cielo

Blu di cielo

Hemelsblauw

1940, Oil on canvas/Huile sur toile, 100 × 73 cm, Musée National d'Art Moderne, Centre Pompidou, Paris

In the painting "Sky Blue", cheerful-seeming biomorphic figurations are seen floating on a light blue base in an image typical of Kandinsky's work from his time in Paris, during which he was inspired by the images of microorganisms found in books which he had discovered and studied.

Dans le tableau « Bleu de ciel », des figurations biomorphes d'allure plutôt enjouée – typiques de l'univers des formes de Kandinsky dans ses années parisiennes – planent sur un fond azuréen. Le peintre s'est inspiré ici des organismes microscopiques qu'il est alors en train de découvrir et d'étudier dans des livres.

In dem Bild „Himmelblau" schweben auf einem hellblauen Grund heiter wirkende biomorphe Figurationen, die typisch für Kandinskys Formenwelt der Pariser Zeit sind. Dazu ließ er sich von Abbildungen von Kleinstlebewesen inspirieren, die er in Büchern entdeckte und studierte.

En su cuadro "Cielo azul", pueden advertirse figuraciones biomórficas de aspecto alegre flotando sobre una base azul claro en una imagen característica del trabajo de Kandinsky de su época en París, durante la que se inspiró en las imágenes de microorganismos que encontró en los libros que descubrió y estudió.

Nel dipinto Blu di cielo sono ritratte delle figure biomorfe apparentemente allegre che galleggiano su uno sfondo blu chiaro in un'immagine tipica dell'opera di Kandinsky durante il suo soggiorno a Parigi, quando trasse ispirazione dalle immagini di microrganismi presenti in alcuni libri che aveva scoperto e studiato.

In het schilderij Hemelsblauw zweven vrolijk aandoende biomorfe figuren boven een helderblauwe ondergrond. De figuren zijn kenmerkend voor Kandinsky's vormenwereld tijdens zijn Parijse periode, waarin hij zich liet inspireren door afbeeldingen van microben, die hij in boeken was tegengekomen en bestudeerde.

la ciudadanía francesa. En 1940 pasaron tres meses de verano en los Pirineos, donde recibieron la noticia de la muerte de su viejo amigo Paul Klee. La ocupación de Francia por las tropas alemanas forzó su regreso a París. En estos últimos años de guerra Kandinsky sufrió la escasez de materiales y pintaba principalmente en pequeñas cajas de cartón.

Kandinsky murió el 13 de diciembre de 1944 tras sufrir una larga arteriosclerosis y verse debilitado por la gripe.

e sua moglie decisero di prendere la cittadinanza francese. Nel 1940 trascorsero tre mesi estivi nei Pirenei, durante i quali giunse loro notizia della morte del loro amico di lunga data Paul Klee. L'occupazione della Francia da parte delle truppe tedesche li costrinse a tornare a Parigi. Nei suoi ultimi anni durante la guerra Kandinsky soffrì di penuria di materiali e dipinse principalmente su piccole scatole di cartone.

Kandinsky morì il 13 dicembre 1944 dopo aver sofferto per lungo tempo di arteriosclerosi ed essere stato indebolito dall'influenza.

het Duitse paspoort van het echtpaar verlopen, waarop ze besluiten het Franse staatsburgerschap aan te nemen. In 1940 brengen ze de drie zomermaanden door in de Pyreneeën, waar ze het nieuws krijgen dat hun oude vriend Paul Klee is overleden. De Duitse bezetting van Frankrijk dwingt ze om terug te keren. Gedurende de laatste oorlogsjaren schildert Kandinsky wegens gebrek aan materiaal op kleine stukken karton.

Kandinsky lijdt al langere tijd aan arteriosclerose en is verzwakt door een griepaanval; op 13 december 1944 overlijdt de kunstenaar.

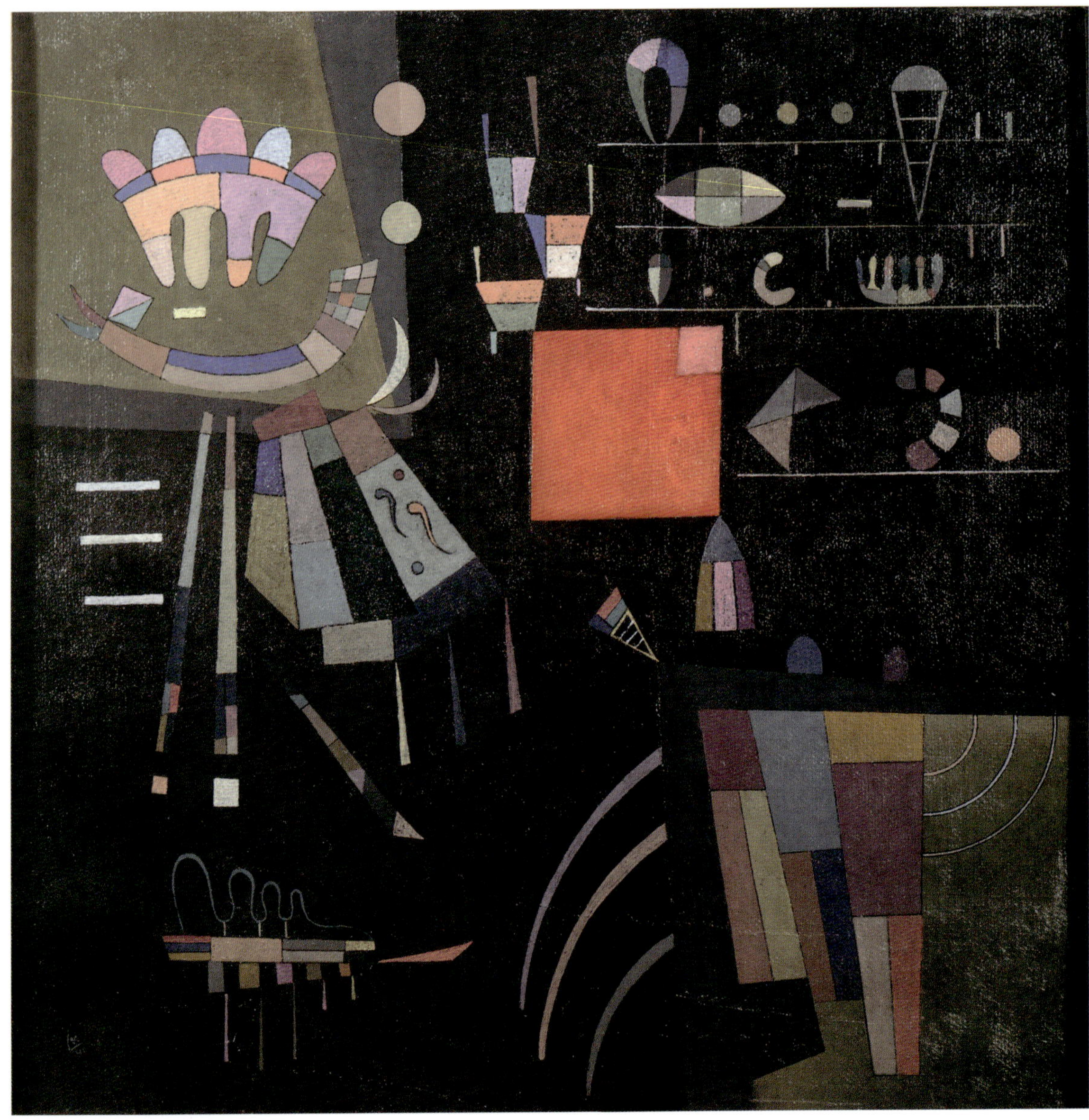

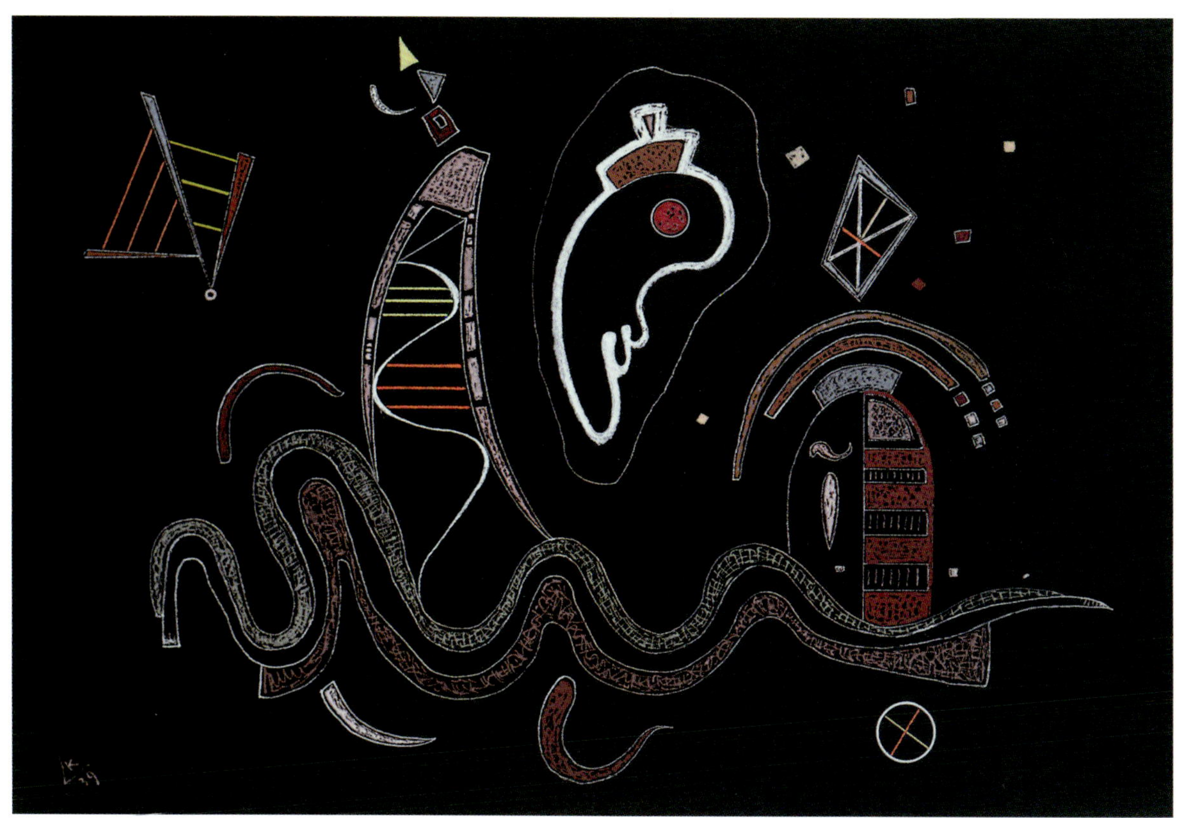

Composition

Composition

Komposition

Composición

Composizione

Compositie

1941, Oil on canvas/Huile sur toile, Private collection

The Entourage

L'Entourage

Begleitung

El entorno de

L'entourage

Gevolg

1939, Gouache on paper/Gouache sur papier, 34 × 49,6 cm, Private collection

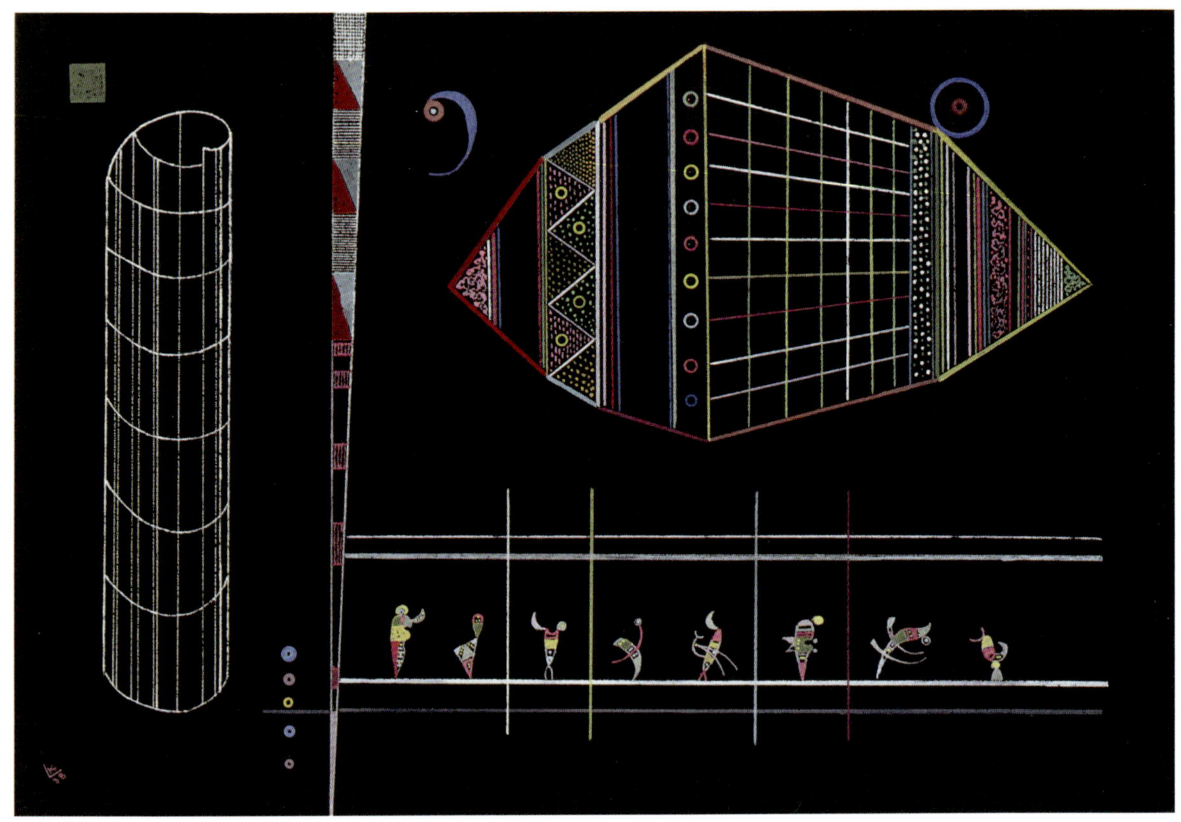

Above
Au dessus
Oben
Por encima de
Sopra
Boven

*1938, Gouache on black paper/Gouache sur papier noir, 34 × 49,6 cm,
Private collection*

Blue Circles
Blaue Kreise (Cercles bleus)
Blaue Kreise
Círculos azules
Cerchi blu
Blauwe cirkels

*1932, Watercolor and gouache on paper/Aquarelle et gouache sur papier,
44 × 44 cm, Private collection*

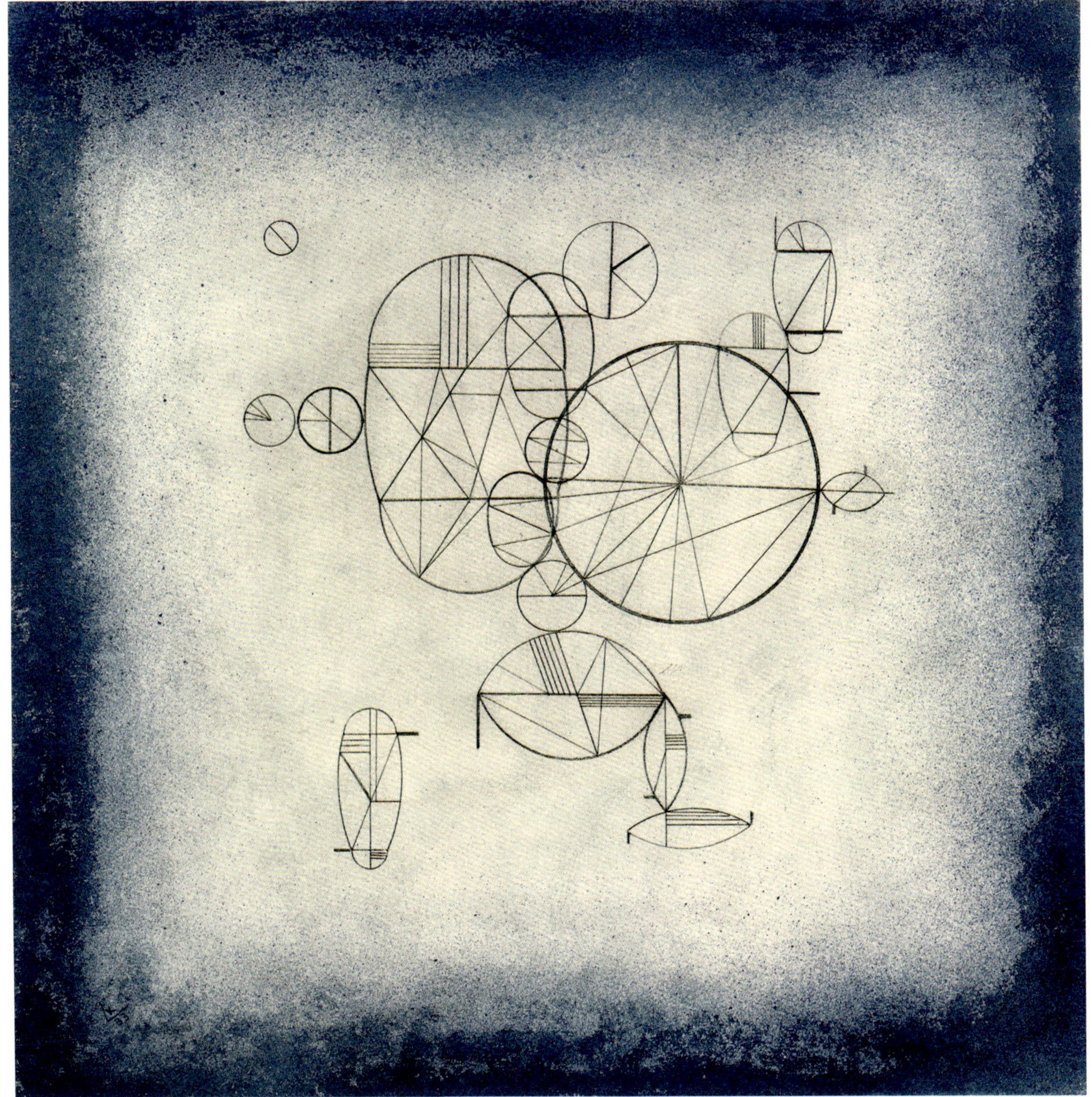

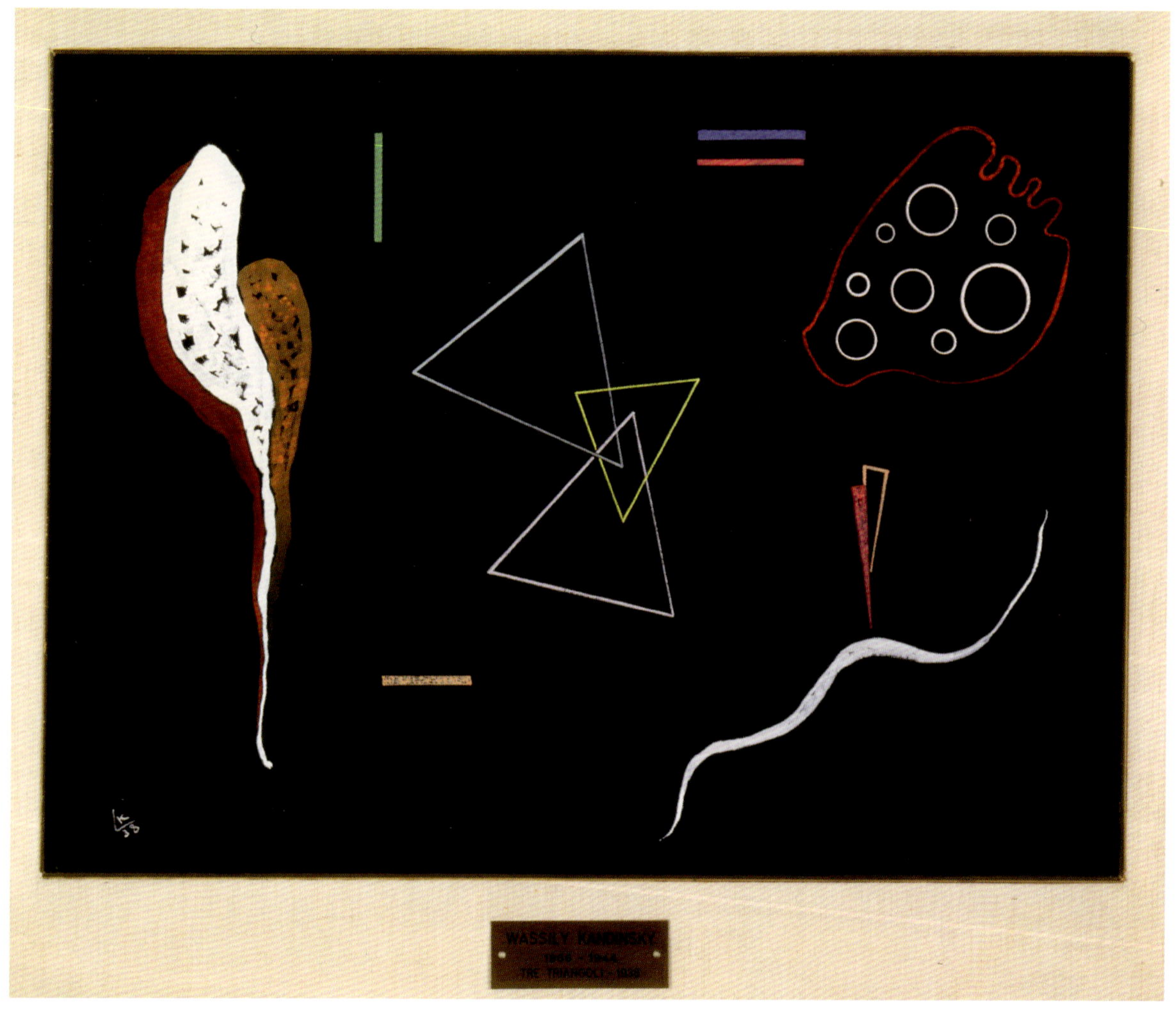

Three Triangles   **Drei Dreiecke**   **Tre triangoli**

Trois triangles   **Tres triángulos**   **Drie driehoeken**

1938, Oil on canvas/Huile sur toile, Museo d'Arte Moderna di Ca' Pesaro, Venice

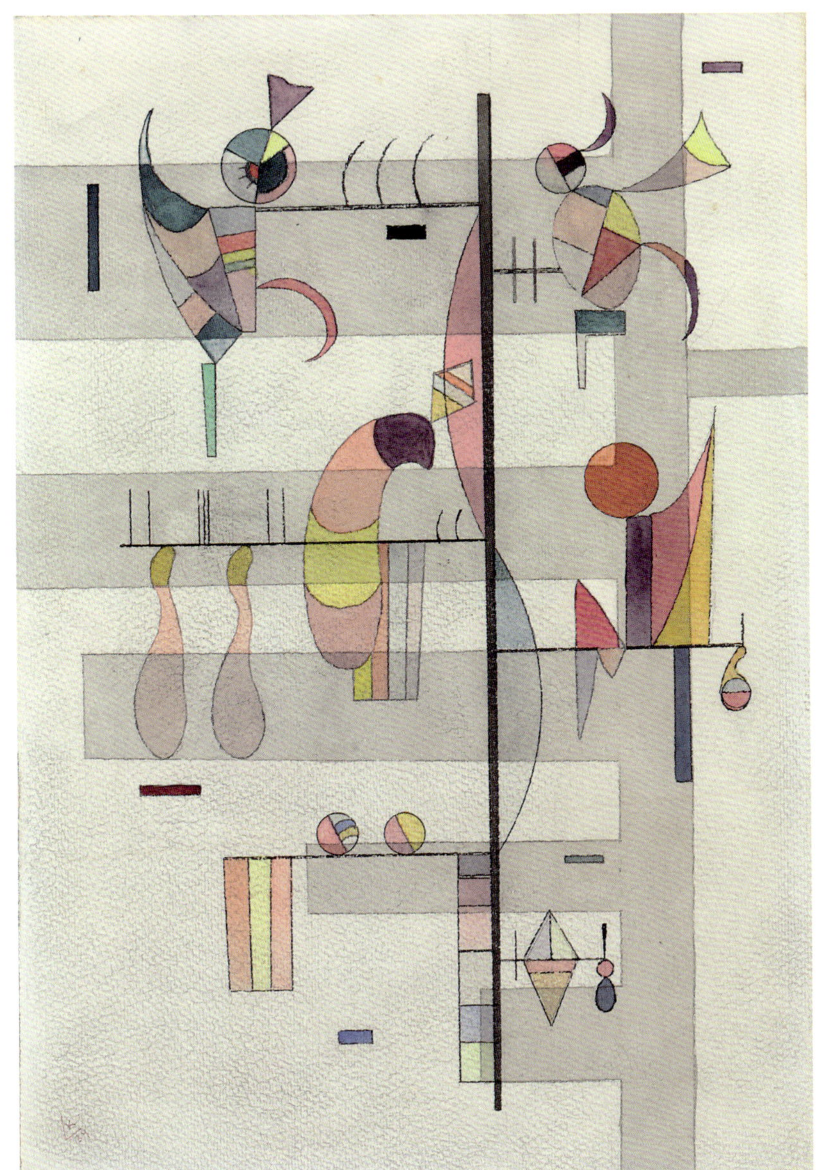

Distribution
Distribution
Verteilung
Distribución
Distribuzione
Verdeling

*1940, Watercolor, ink and pencil on paper/
Aquarelle, encre de Chine et mine de plomb
sur papier, 54,3 × 37,8 cm, Private collection*

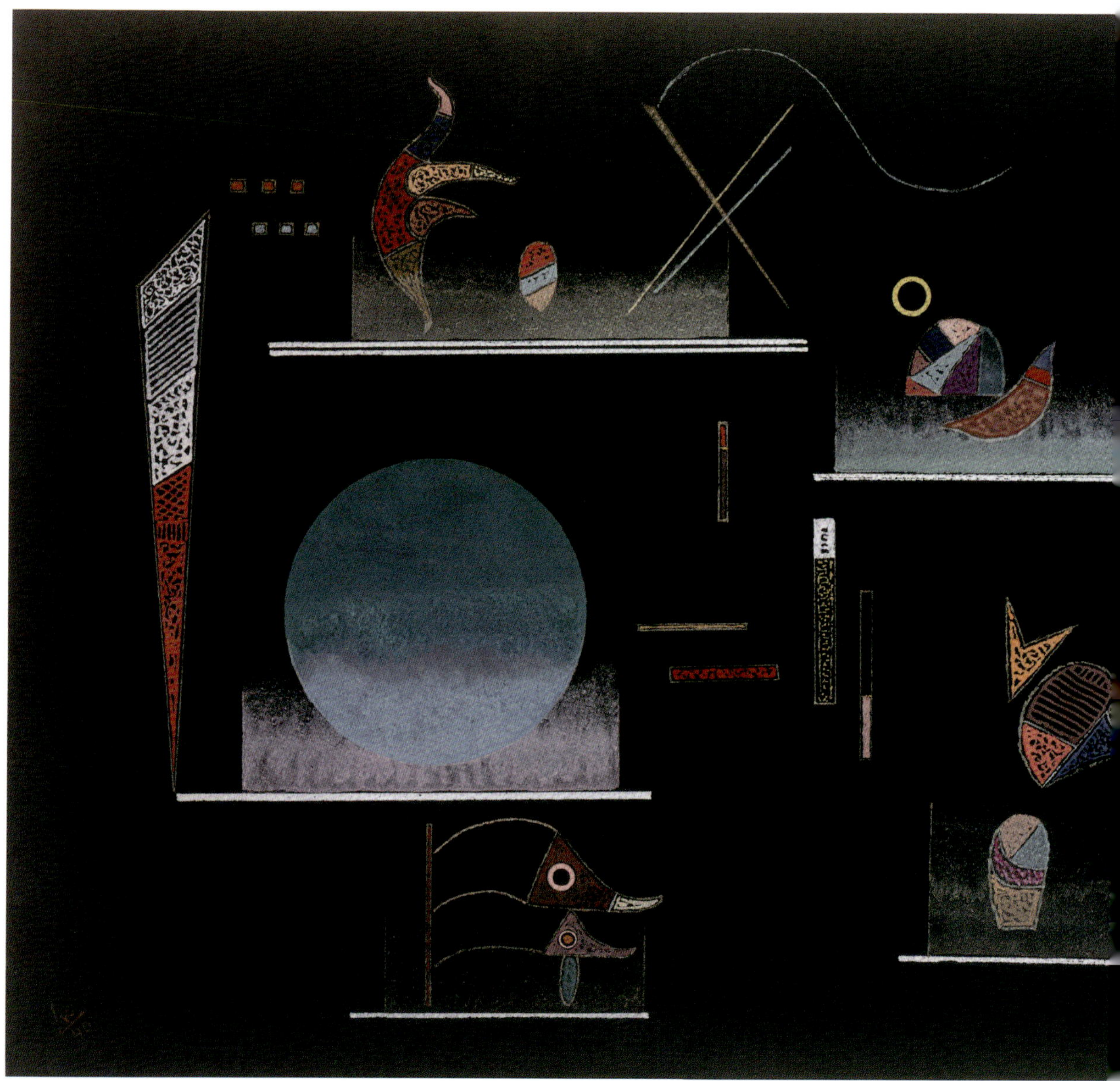

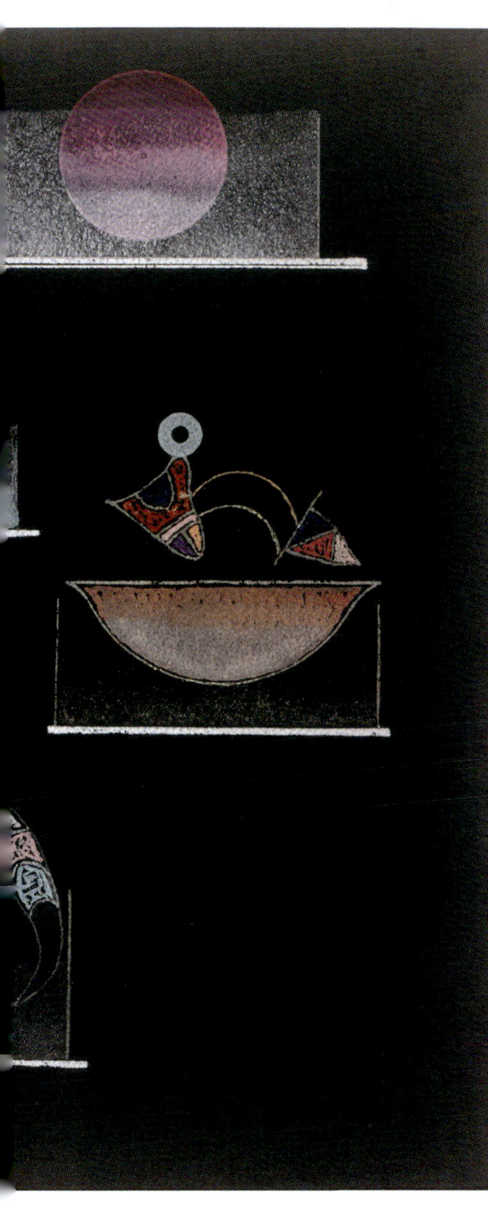

Untitled

Sans titre

Ohne Titel

Sin título

Senza titolo

Zonder titel

1940, Gouache on paper/Gouache sur papier,
32 × 49,5 cm, Private collection

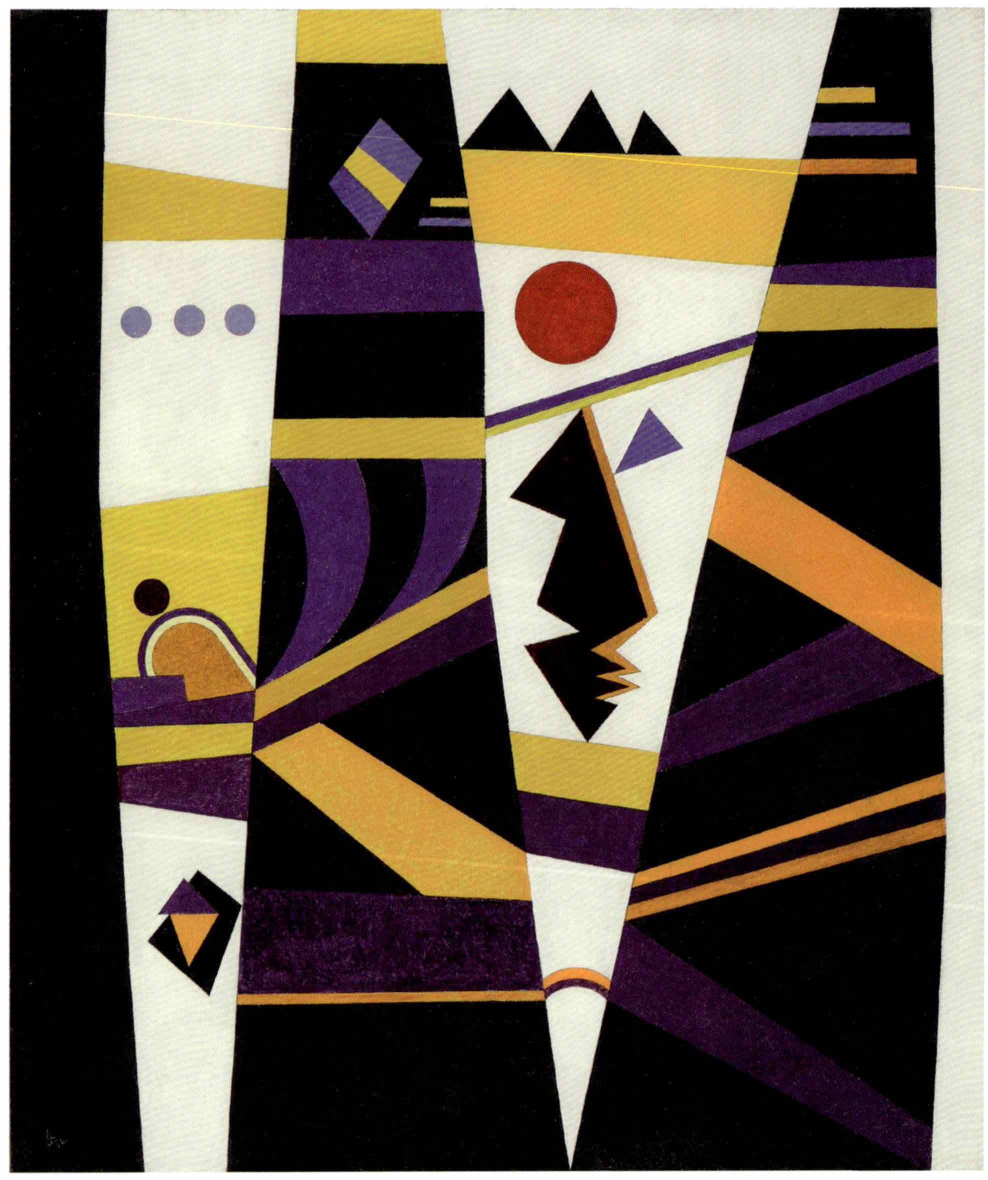

Liaison
Liaison
Bindung
Enlace
Liaison
Verbinding

*1932, Oil on canvas/
Huile sur toile,
70 × 60 cm,
Private collection*

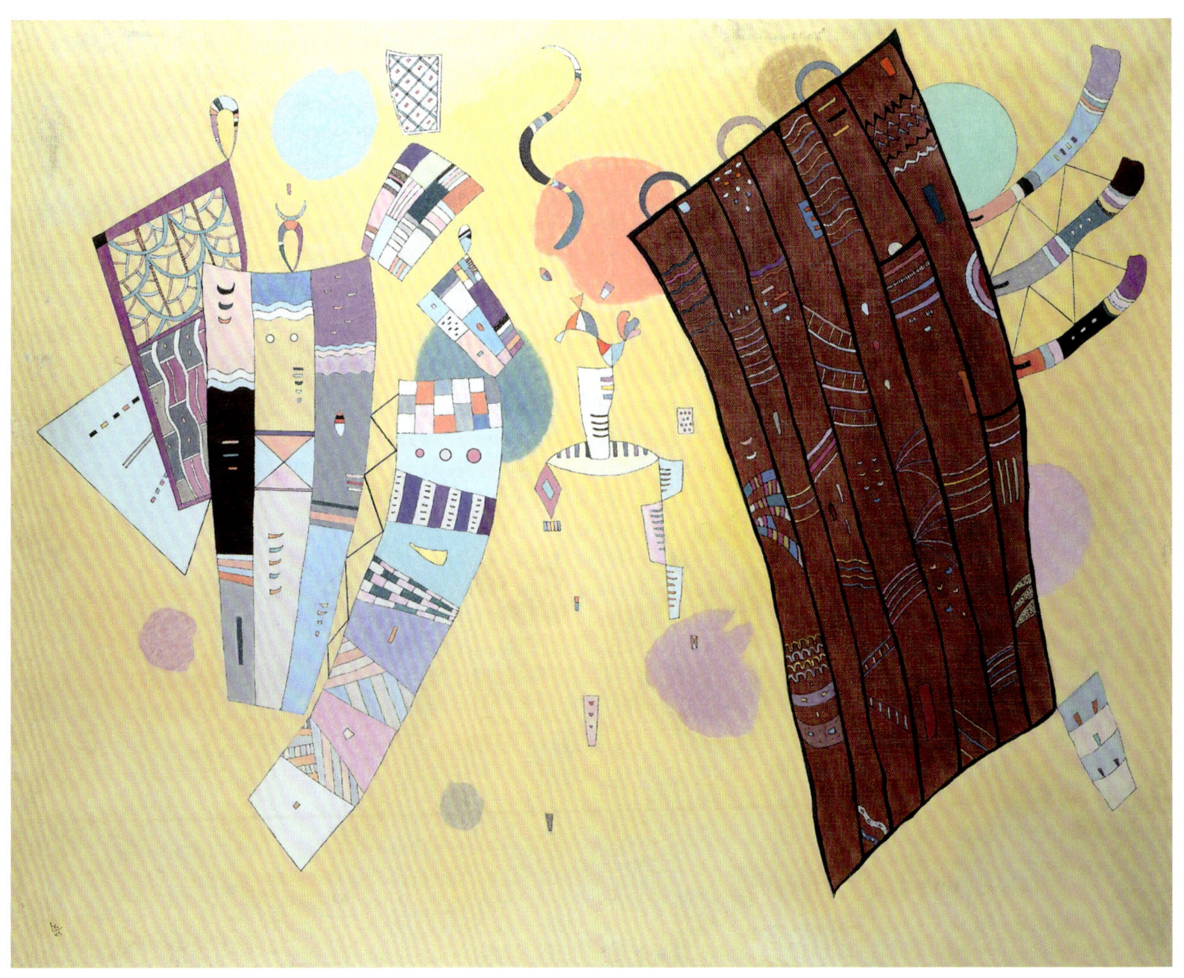

Delicate Tensions **Zarte Spannungen** **Tensioni delicate**

Tensions délicates **Delicadas tensiones** **Tedere spanningen**

1942, Oil on canvas/Huile sur toile, 81 × 100 cm, Private collection

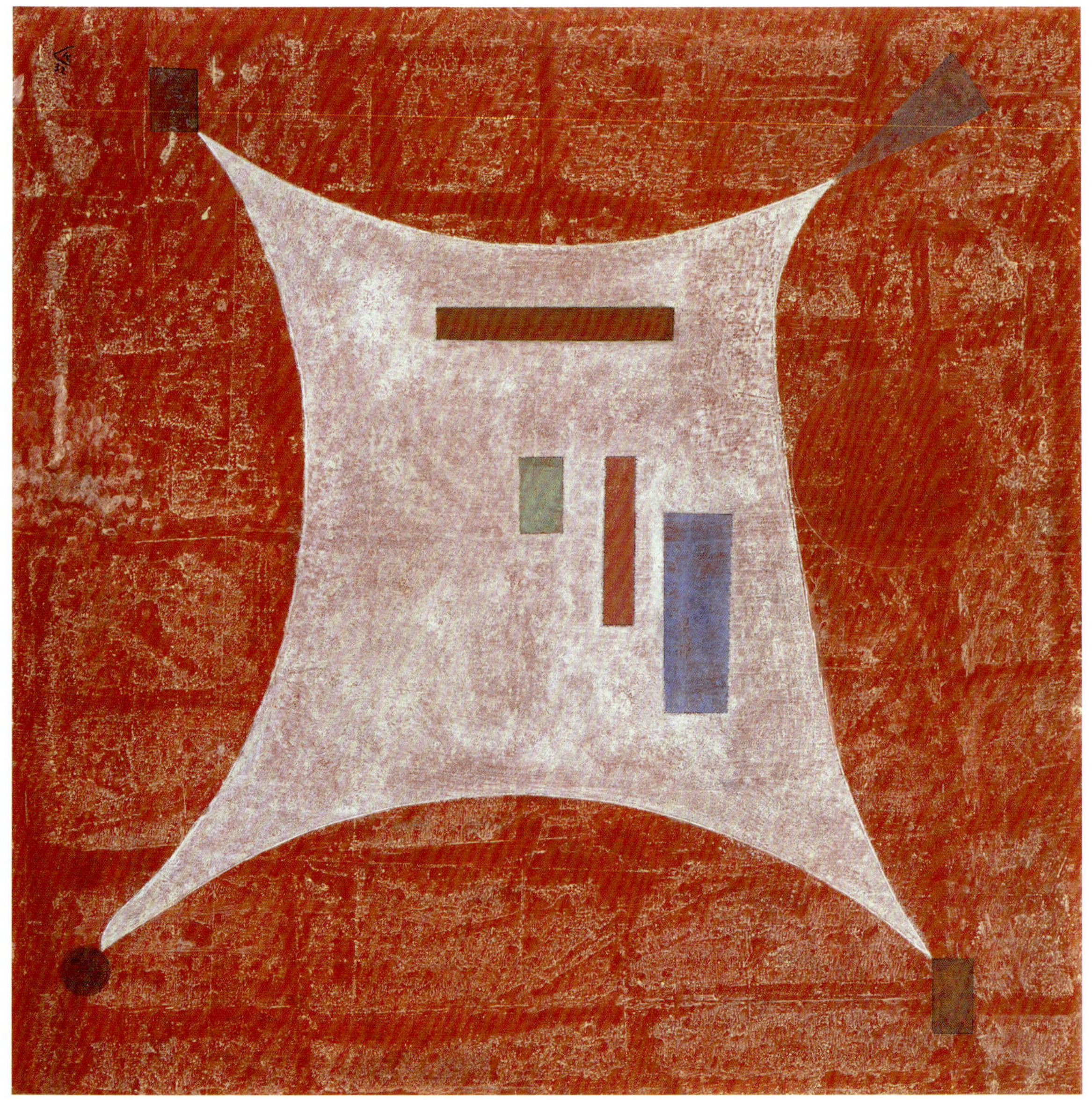

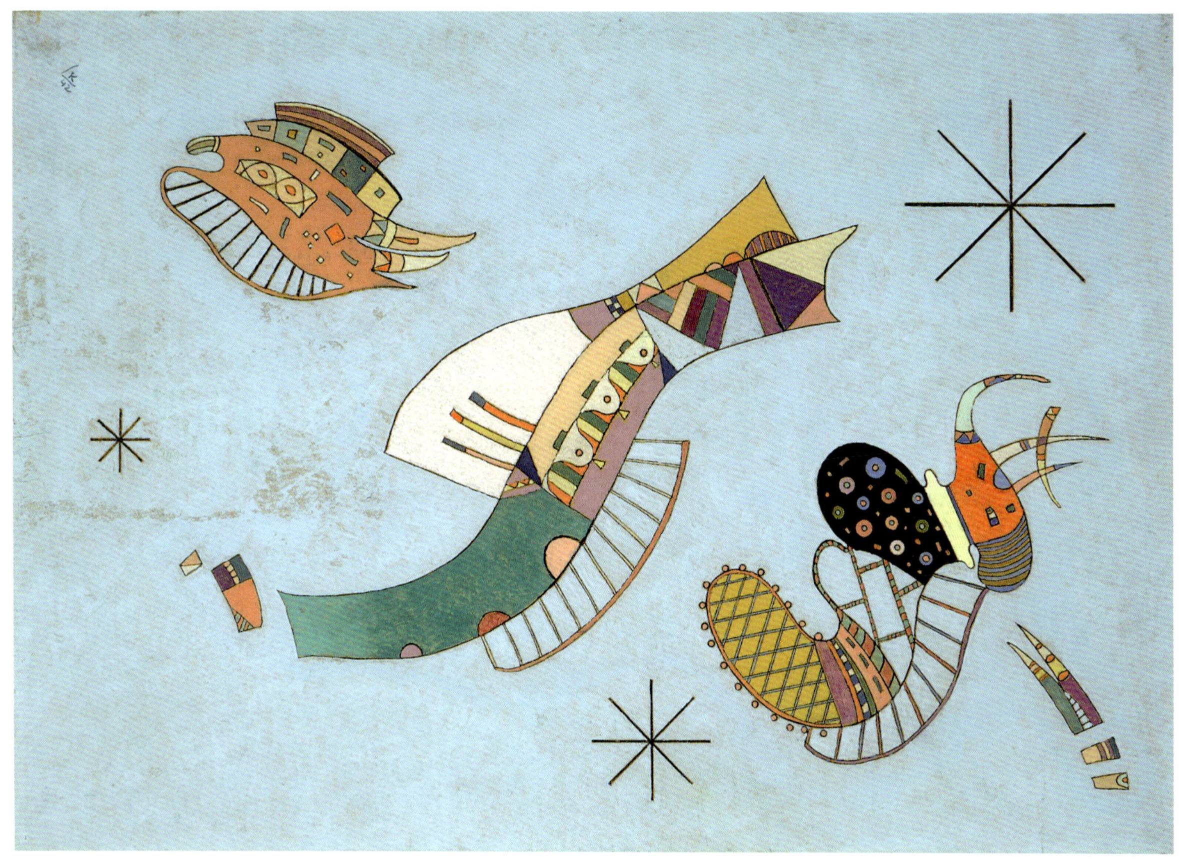

In the Four Corners
Aux quatre coins
In alle vier Ecken
En las cuatro esquinas
I quattro angoli
Naar de vier hoeken
1932, Oil, pen and ink on board/Huile, plume et encre de Chine sur carton, 70 × 70 cm, Private collection

Three Stars
Trois Étoiles
Drei Sterne
Tres estrellas
Tre stelle
Drie sterren
1942, Oil on cardboard/
Huile sur carton, 48,3 × 34,9 cm,
Private collection

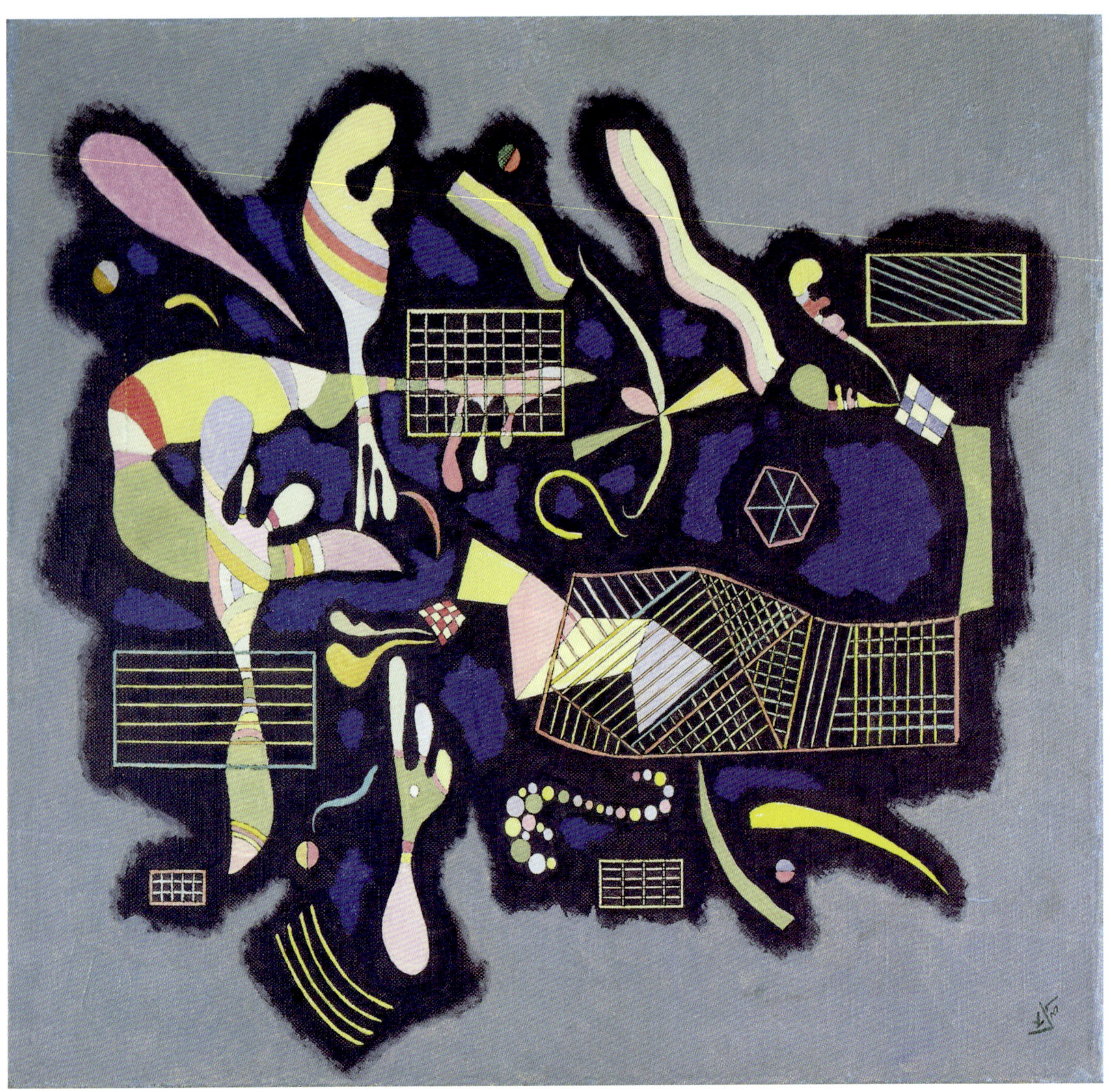

258

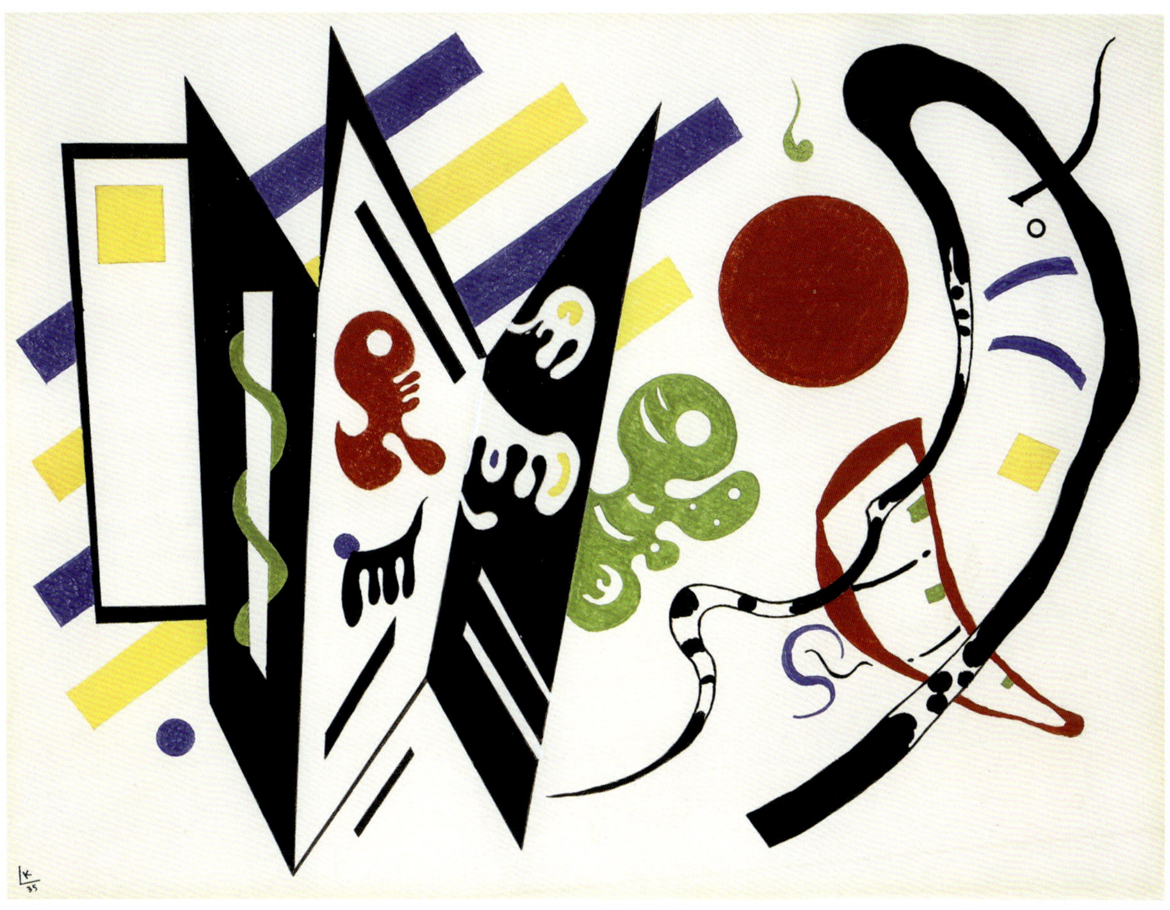

Grills and other

Grilles et autres

Gitter und anderes

Parrillas y otros

Griglie e altro

Rasters en andere

1937, Oil on canvas/Huile sur toile, 48 × 36 cm, Private collection

Reciproque

Réciproque

Reziprok

Reciproque

Reciproque

Wederzijds

1936, Gouache, ink and pencil on paper/Gouache, encre de Chine et mine de plomb sur papier, 50,1 × 65,3 cm, Private collection

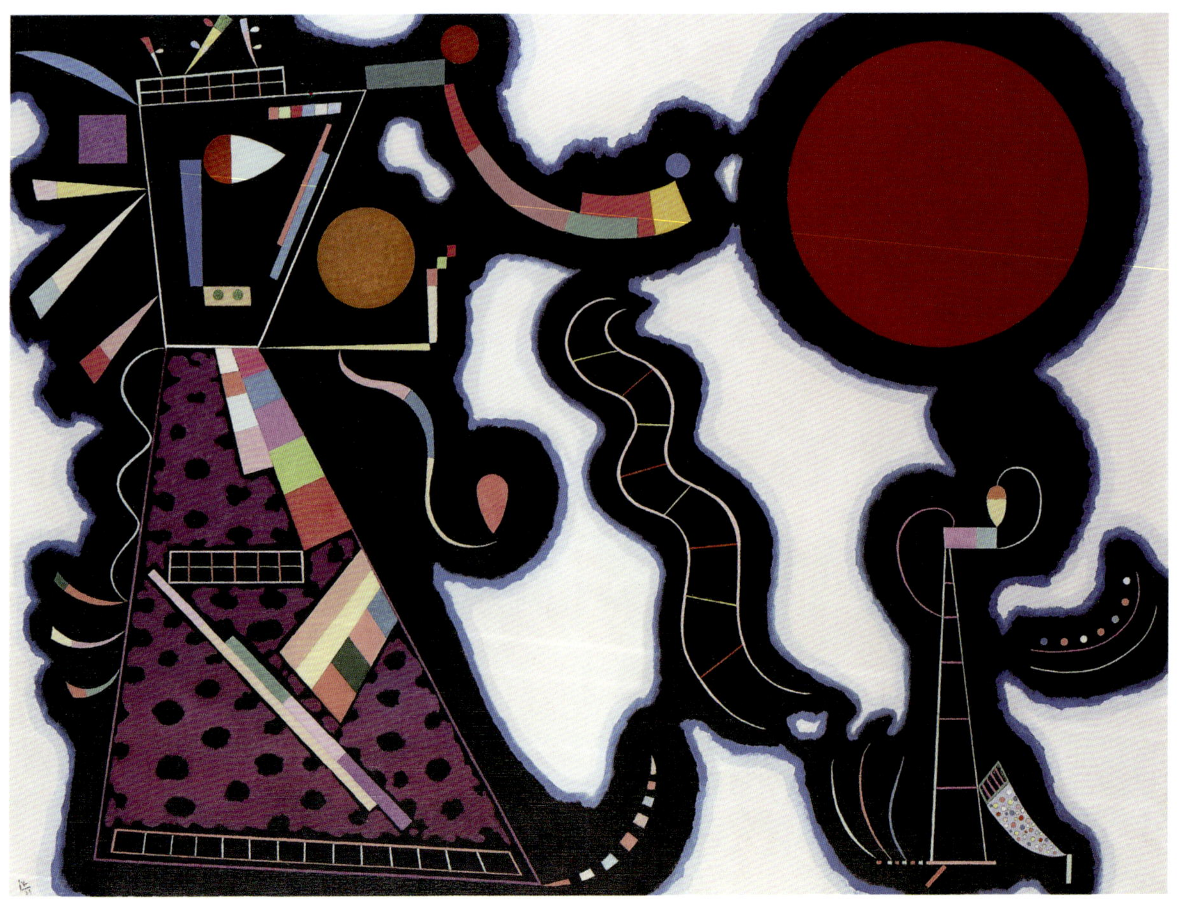

The Red Circle

Le Cercle rouge

Der rote Kreis

El círculo rojo

Il cerchio rosso

De rode cirkel

1939, Oil on canvas/Huile sur toile, 89 × 116 cm, Private collection

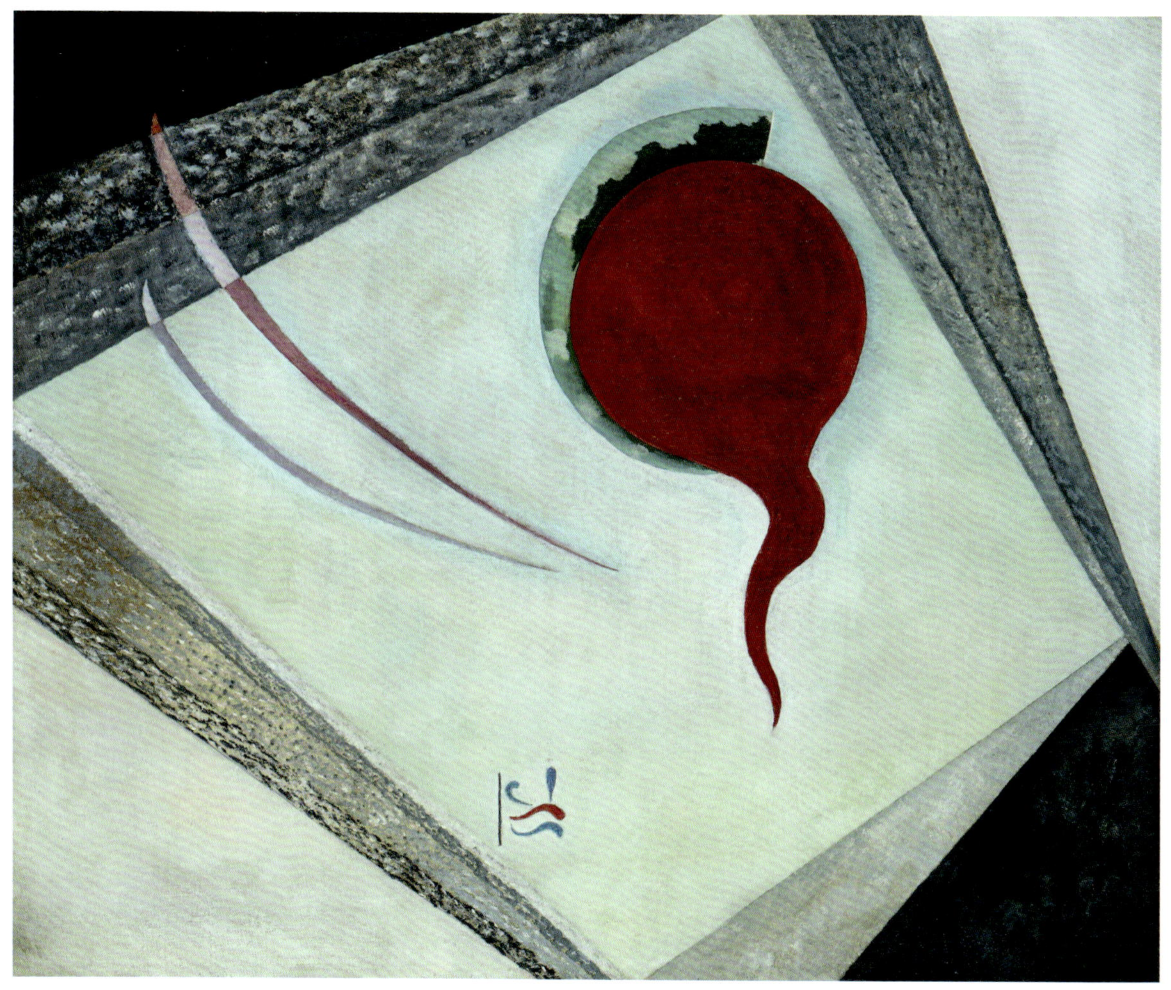

Poids Monte

Poids léger

Leichte Gewichte

Poids Monte

Poids Monte

Lichte gewichten

1935, Oil and tempera on canvas/Huile et tempéra sur toile, 60 × 72,5 cm, Private collection

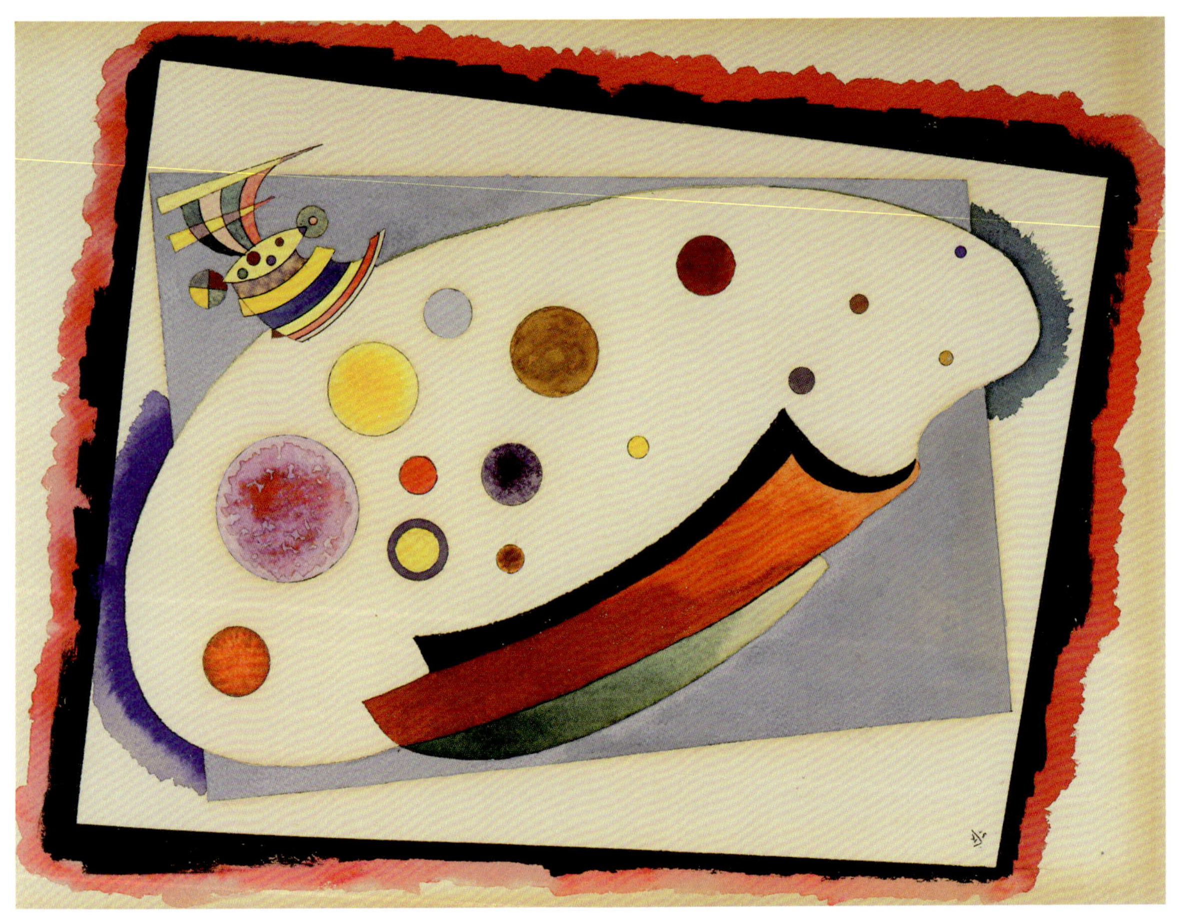

Ovale Anime
Ovale animé
Belebtes Oval
ovale Anime
Ovale Anime
Levendig ovaal
1935, Gouache on paper/Gouache sur papier, 48,2 × 36,5 cm, Private collection

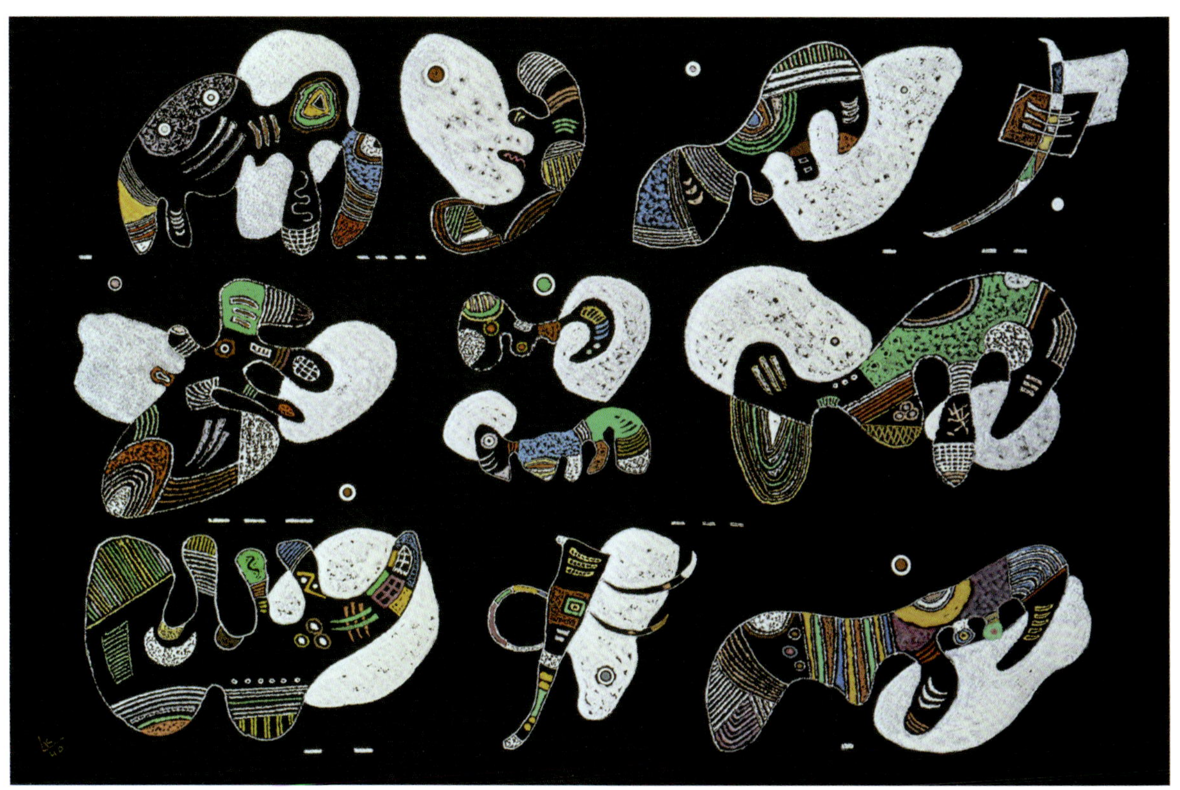

1940, Gouache on black paper/Gouache sur papier noire, 33,5 × 51 cm, Private collection

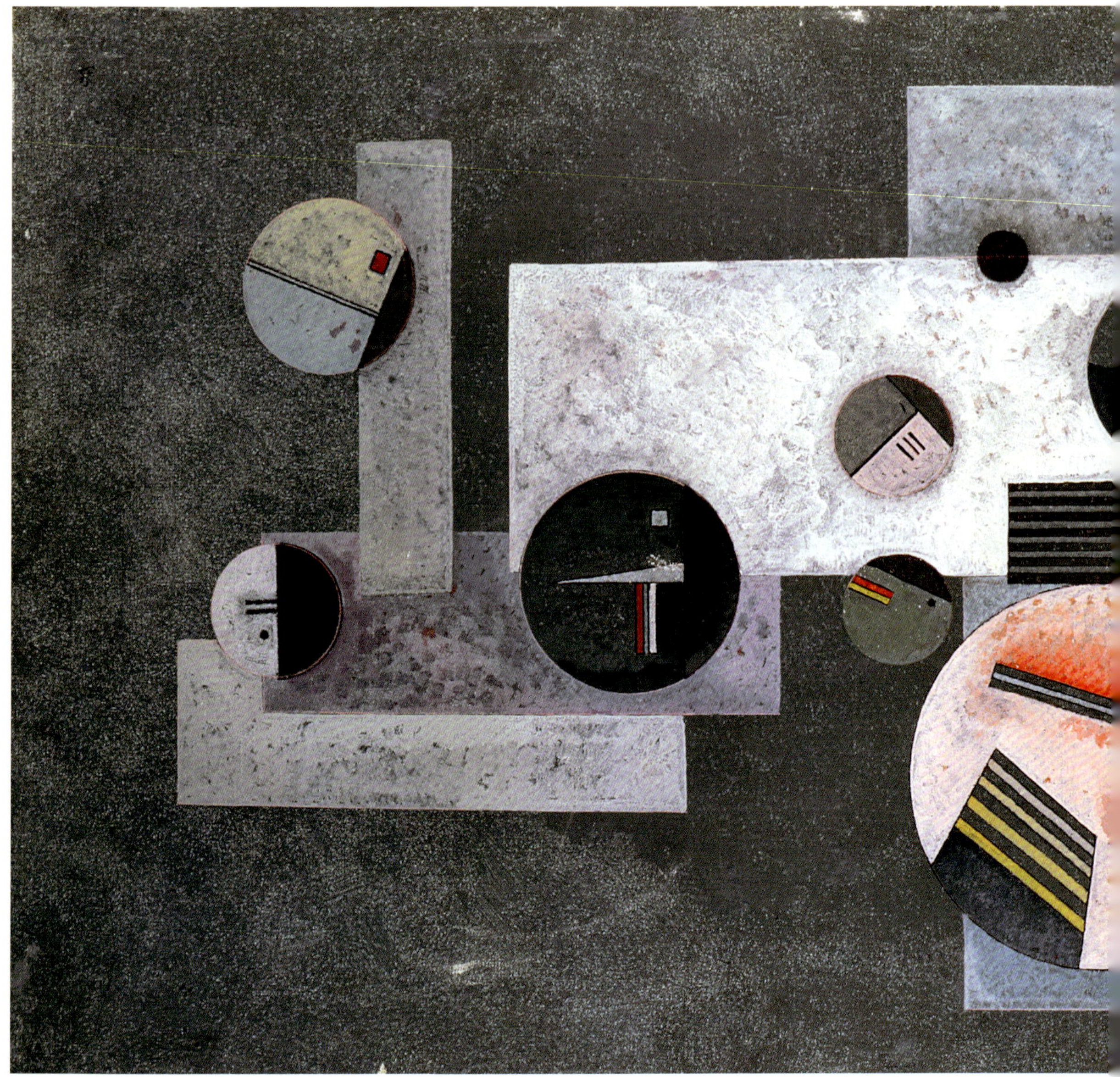

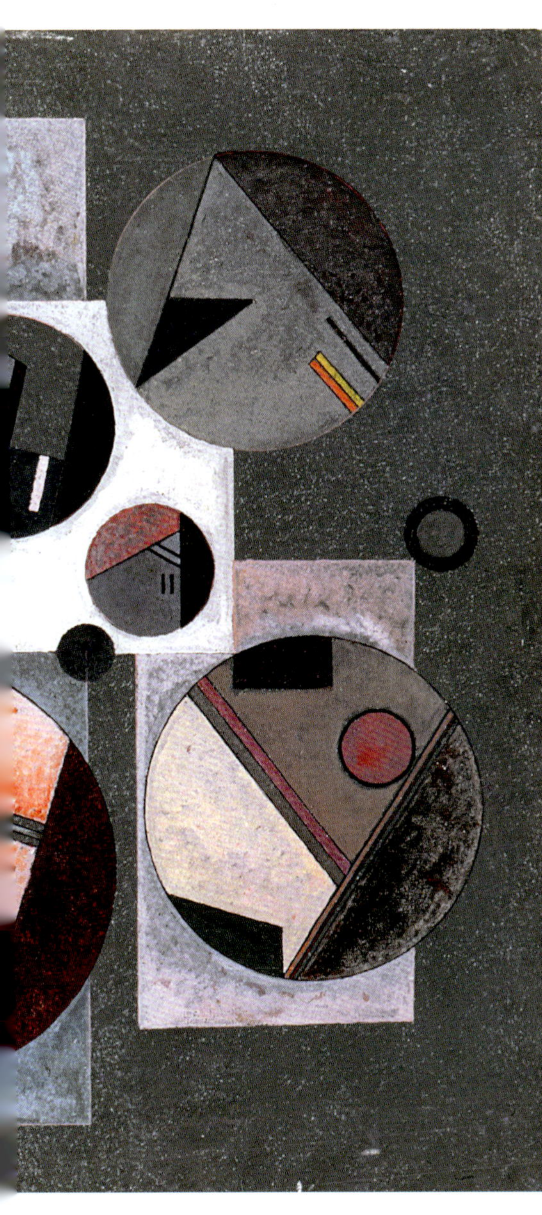

Closed Circles

Cercles fermés

Geschlossene Kreise

Círculos cerrados

Cerchi chiusi

Gesloten cirkels

1933, Oil on canvas/Huile sur toile, 99 × 63 cm, Galerie Maeght, Paris

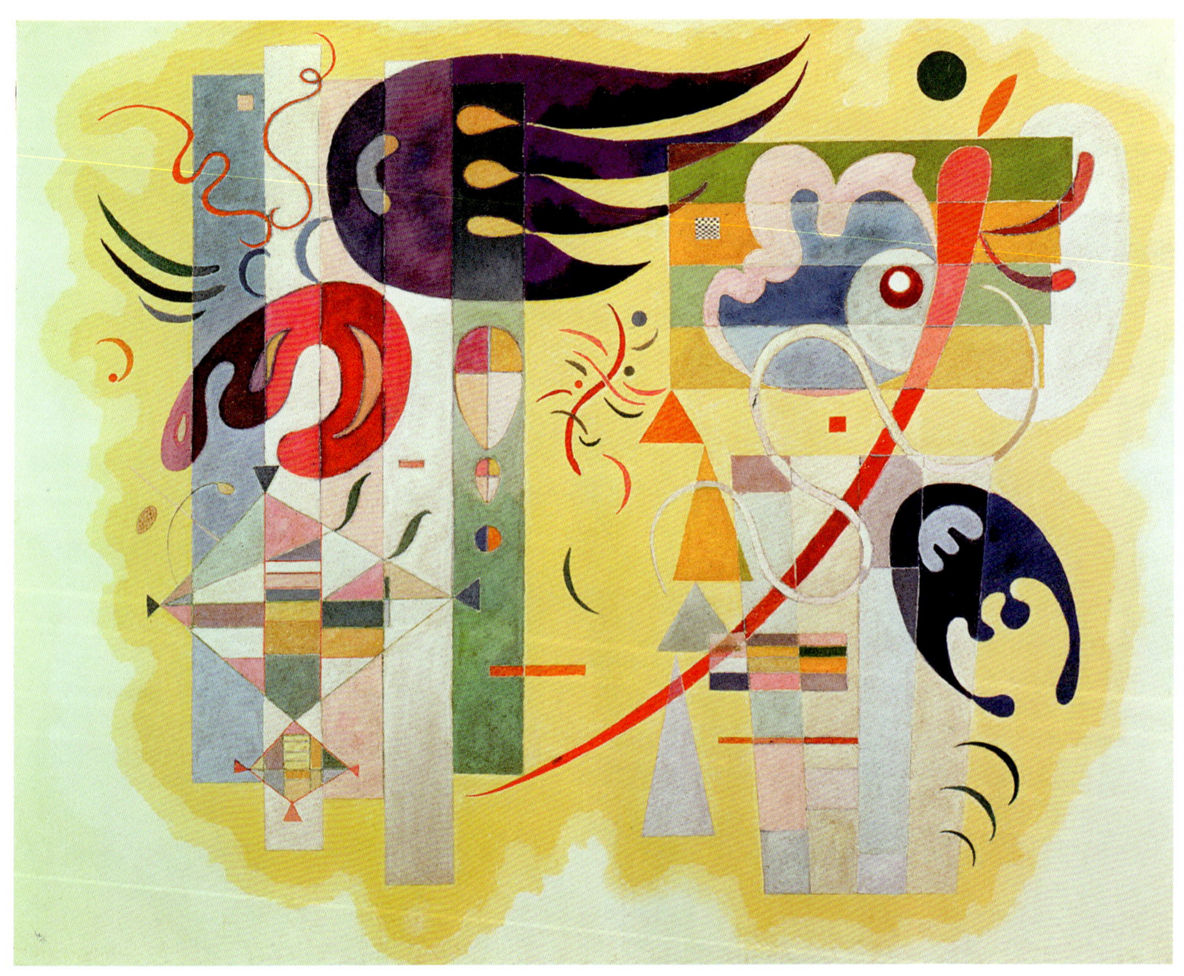

Dominant Violet   **Dominantes Violett**   **Viola dominante**

Videt dominant   **Violeta dominante**   **Dominant paars**

1934, Oil and sand on canvas/Huile et sable sur toile, 130 × 162 cm, Galerie Maeght, Paris

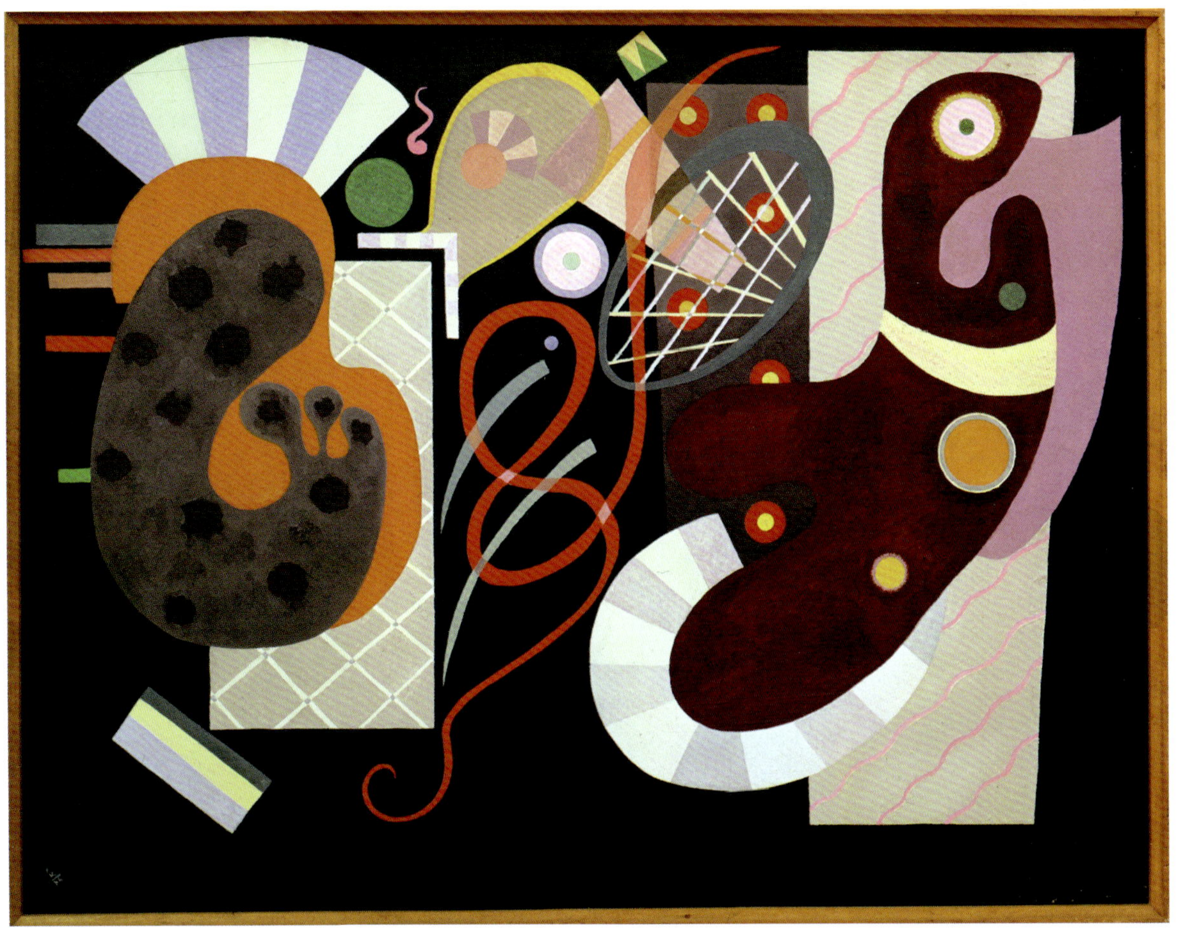

Red Knot
Nœud rouge
Roter Knoten
Nudo rojo
Nodo rosso
Rode knoop
1936, Oil on canvas/Huile sur toile, 89 × 116 cm, Fondation Maeght, Saint-Paul-de-Vence

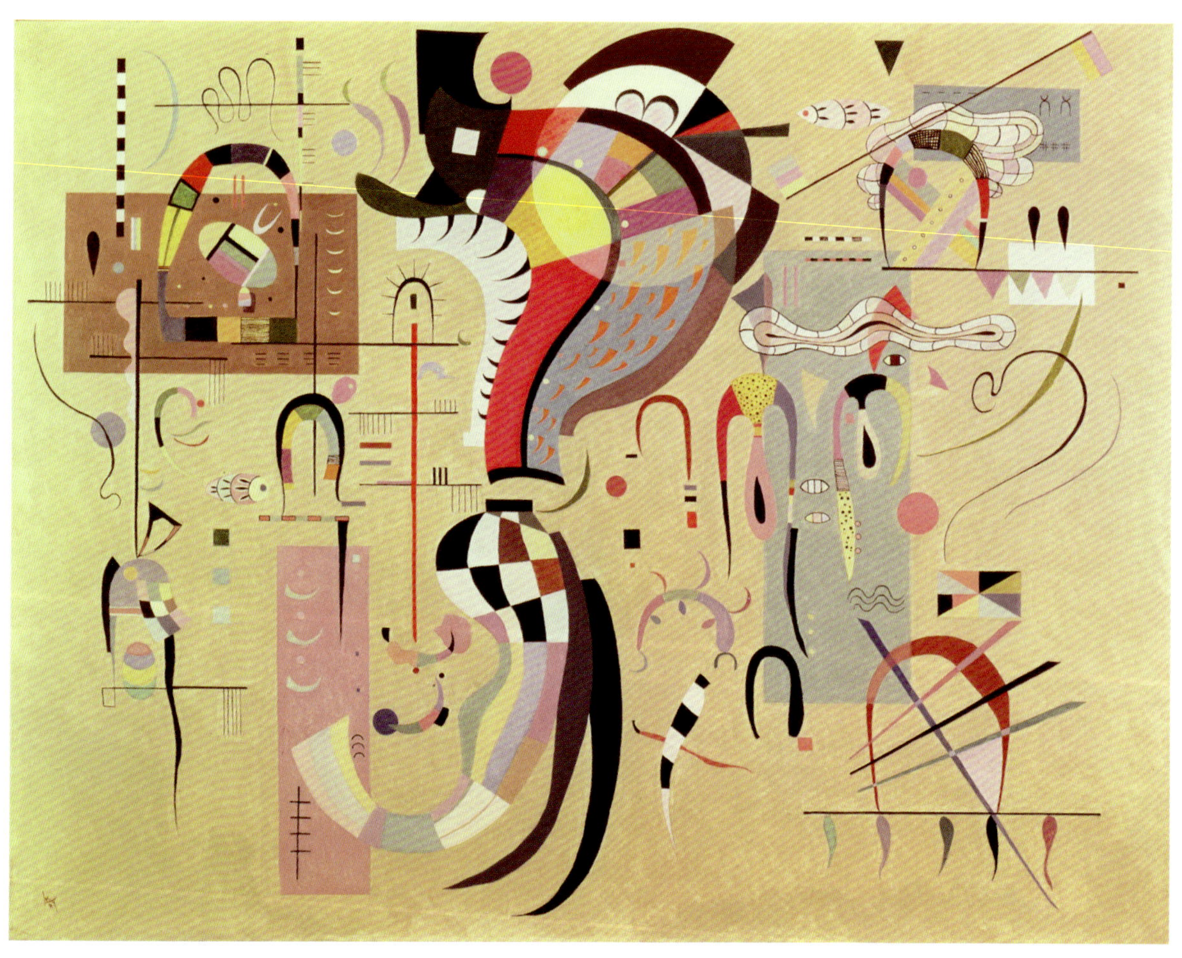

Accompanied Center **Zentrum mit Begleitung** **Centro con accompagnamento**

Centre accompagné **Centro acompañado** **Centrum met gevolg**

1937, Oil on canvas/Huile sur toile, 114 × 146 cm, Galerie Maeght, Paris

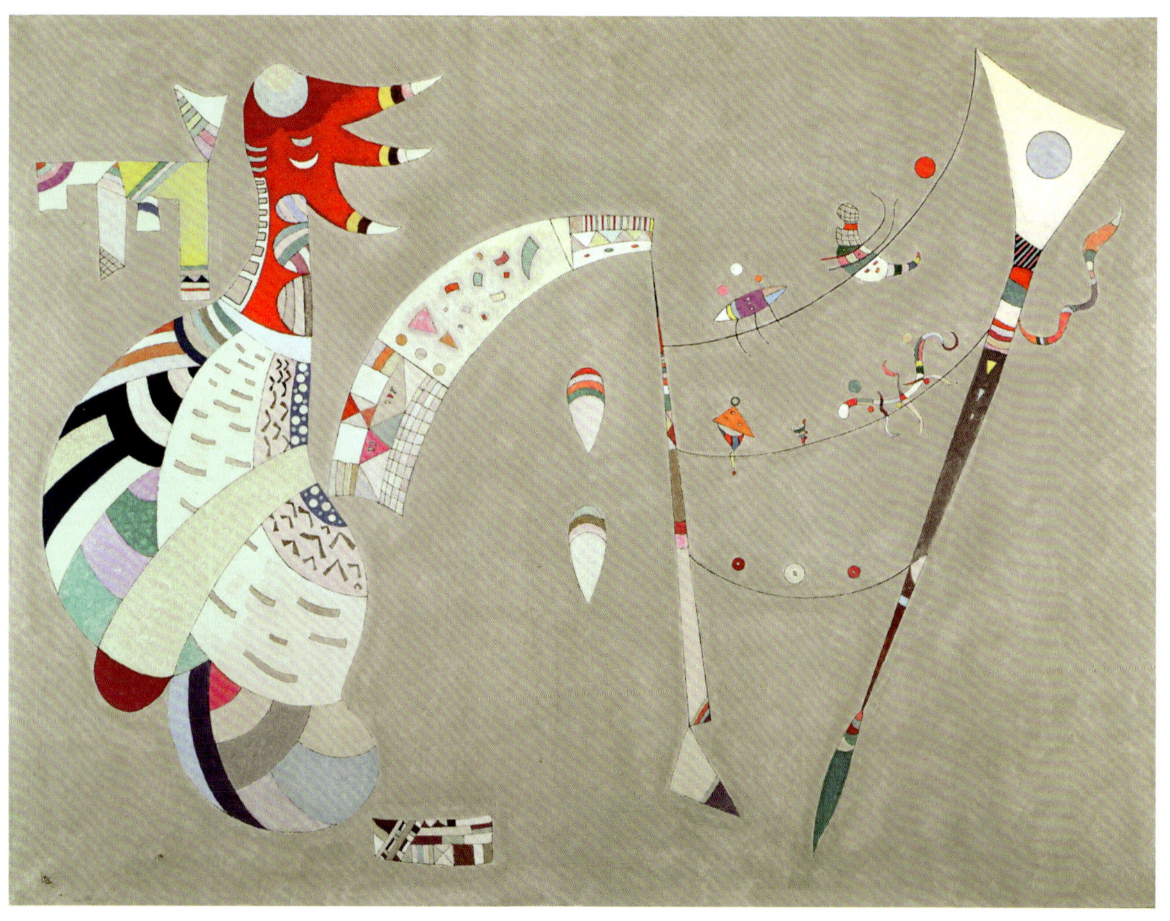

1942, Oil on canvas/Huile sur toile, 89 × 116 cm, Galerie Maeght, Paris

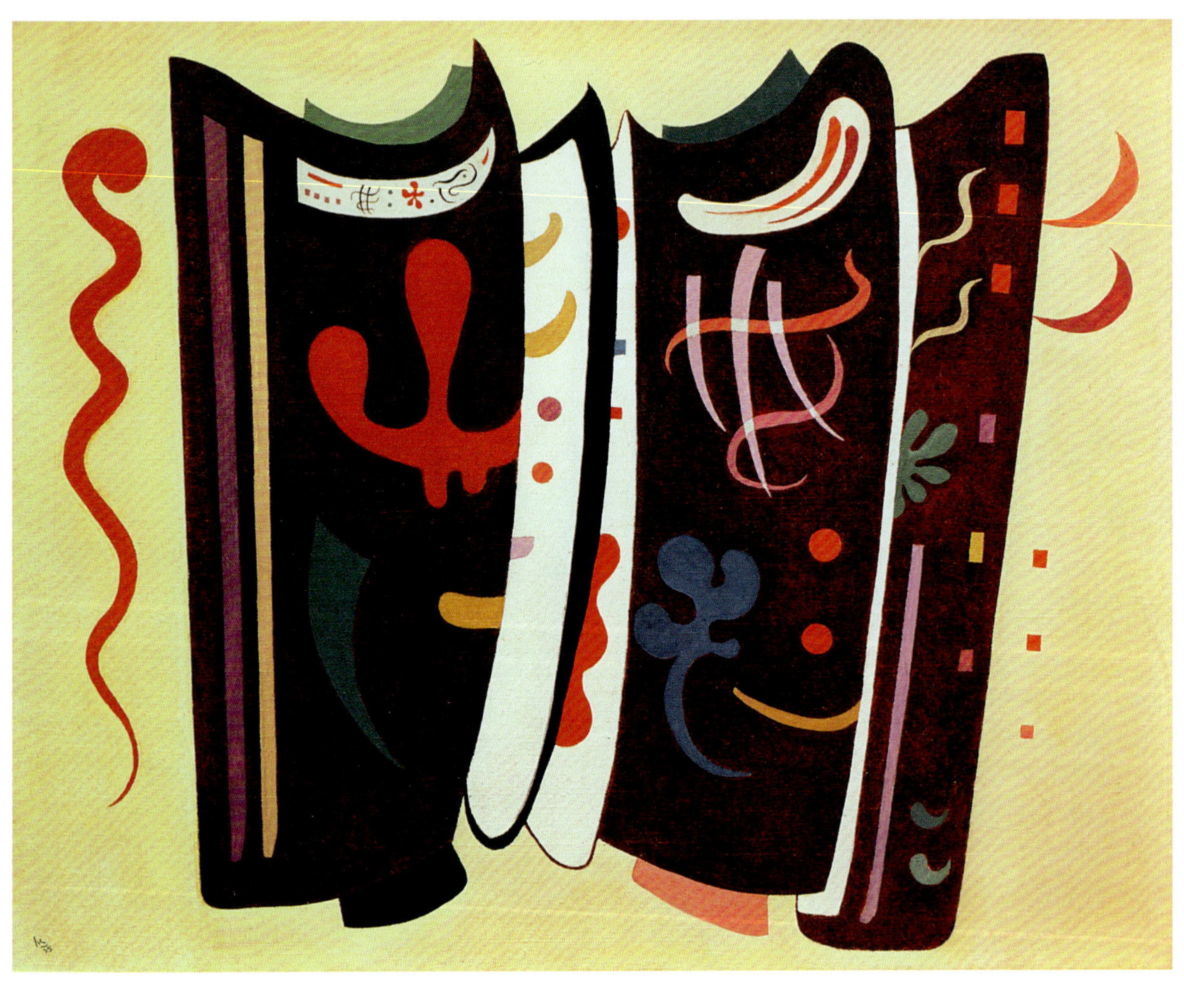

Brown with supplement   **Braun mit Ergänzung**   **Marrone con supplemento**

Marron avec complément   **Marrón con suplemento**   **Bruin met aanvulling**

1935, Oil on cardboard/Huile sur carton, 81 × 100 cm, The Merzbacher collection, Switzerland

270

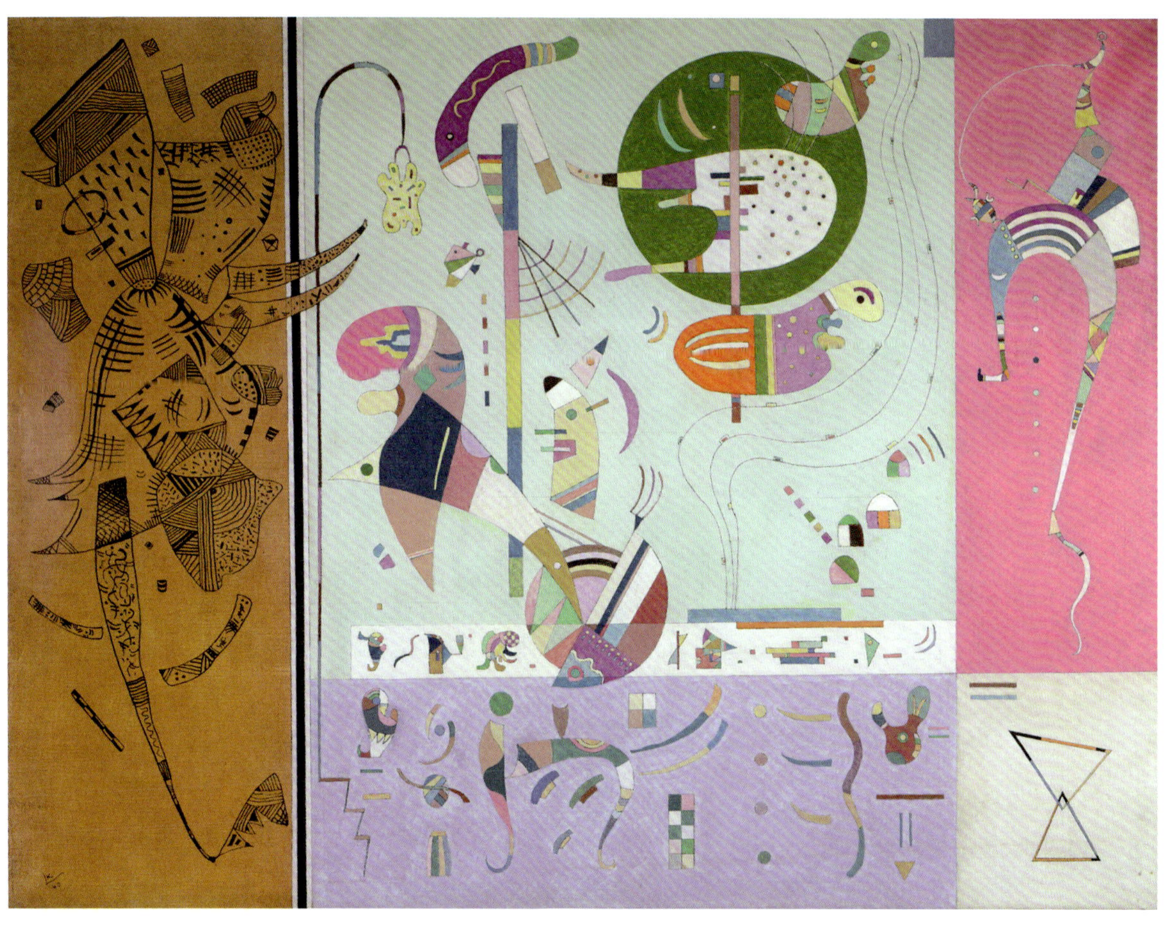

Various parts
Parties diverses
Verschiedene Teile
Partes diversas
Parties diverses
Diverse delen

1940, Oil on canvas/Huile sur toile, 89 × 116 cm,
Städtische Galerie im Lenbachhaus, Munich

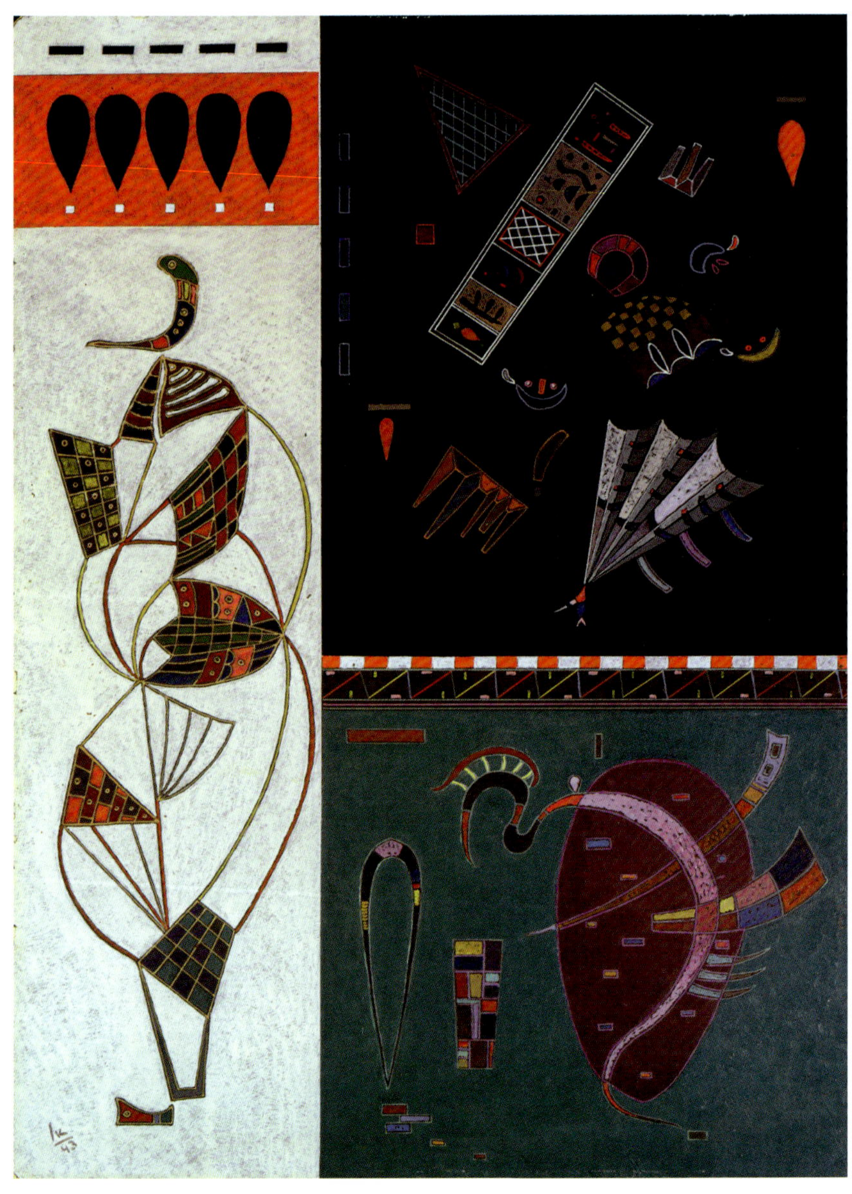

Division Unite
Division réunie
Teilung vereint
División se unen
Division Unite
Deling verenigd

1943, Oil on board/Huile sur carton,
57,8 × 41,9 cm, Private collection

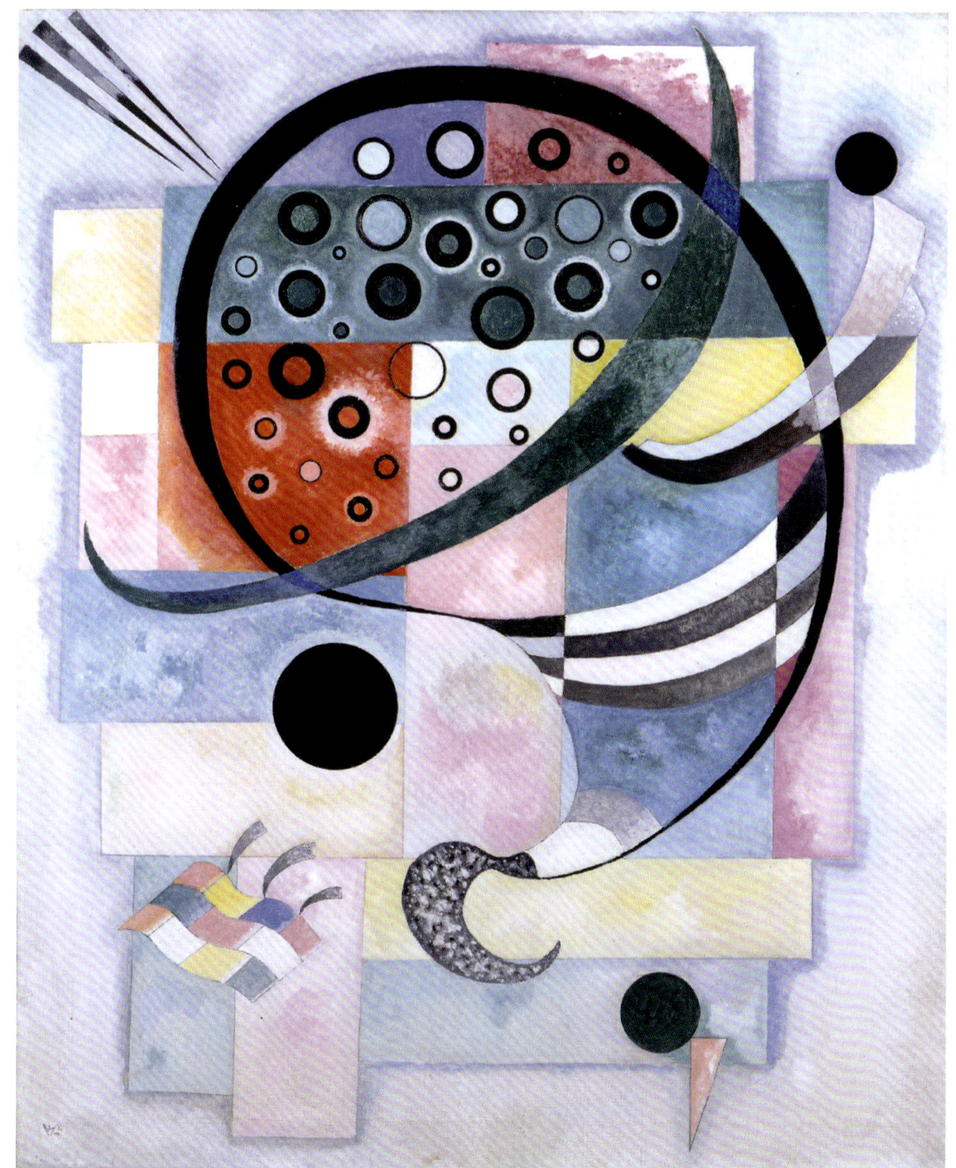

Fixed

Fixé

Fixiert

Fijo

Fisso

Gefixeerd

1935, Oil on canvas/Huile sur toile, 73 × 60 cm, The Israel Museum, Jerusalem

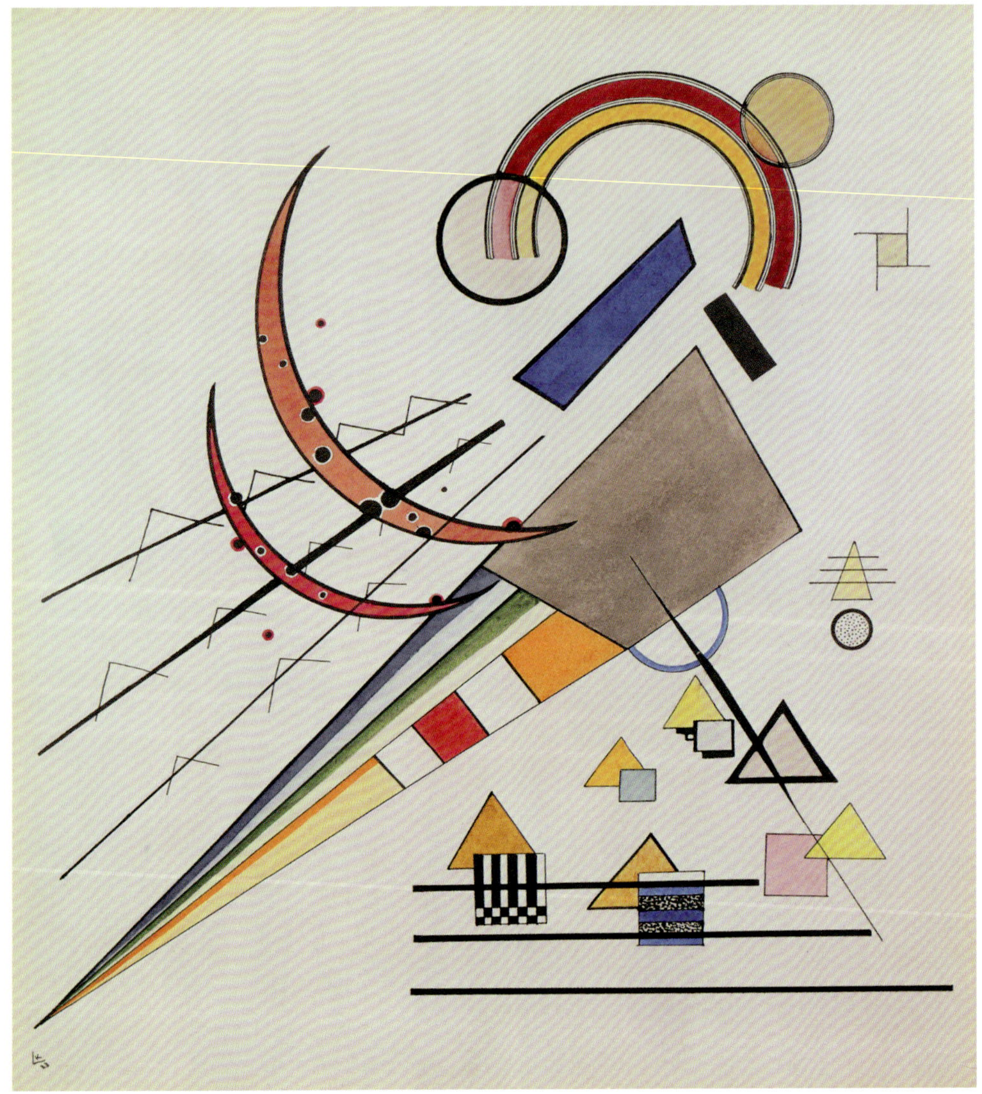

With the Triangle
Avec le triangle
Mit dem Dreieck
Con el triángulo
Con il triangolo
Met de driehoek

1930, Watercolor
and gouache on
paper/Aquarelle et
gouache sur papier,
45,7 × 43 cm,
Private collection

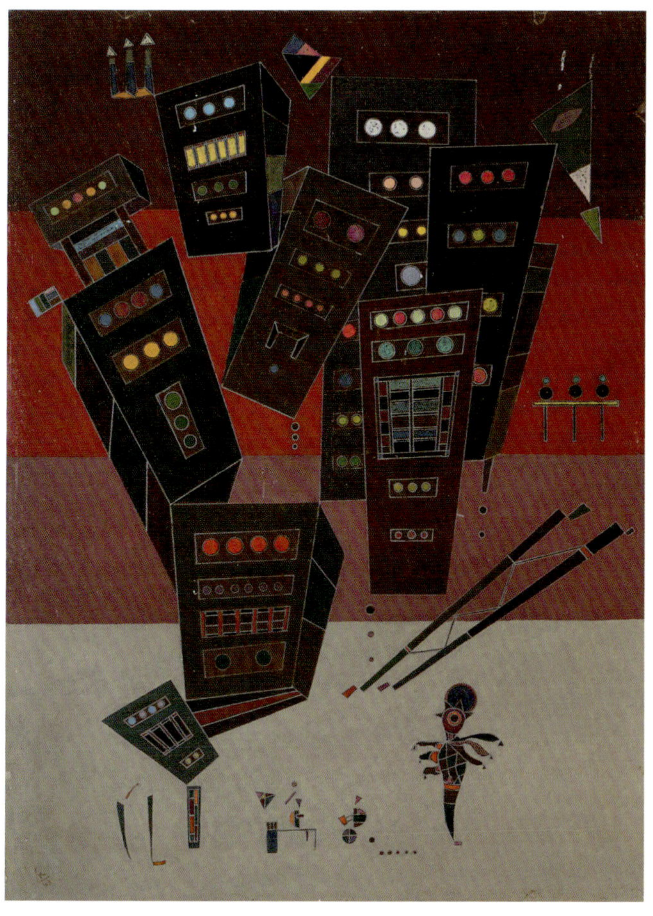

Darkness

Obscurité

Dunkelheit

Oscuridad

Oscurità

Duisternis

1943, Oil on board/Huile sur carton, 58 × 42 cm, Private collection

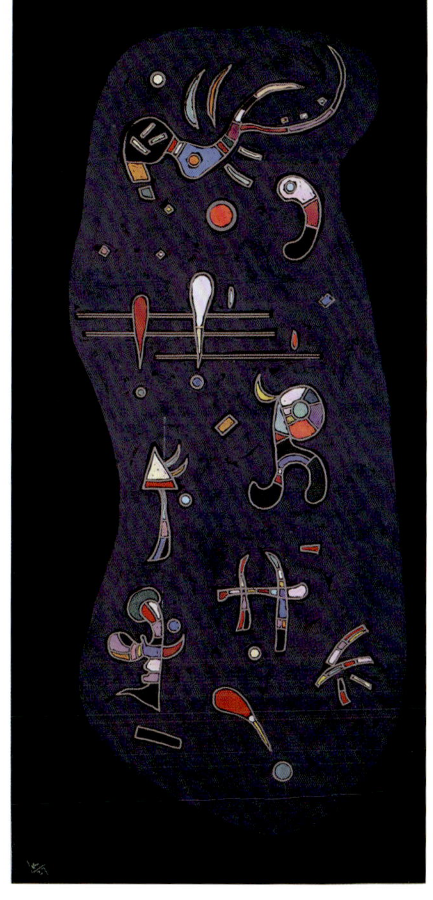

De l'Un a L'Autre

De l'un à l'autre

Von einem zum anderen

De uno a otro

De l'Un a L'Autre

Van het ene naar het andere

1937, Tempera on panel/Tempéra sur bois,
48,5 × 24 cm, Private collection

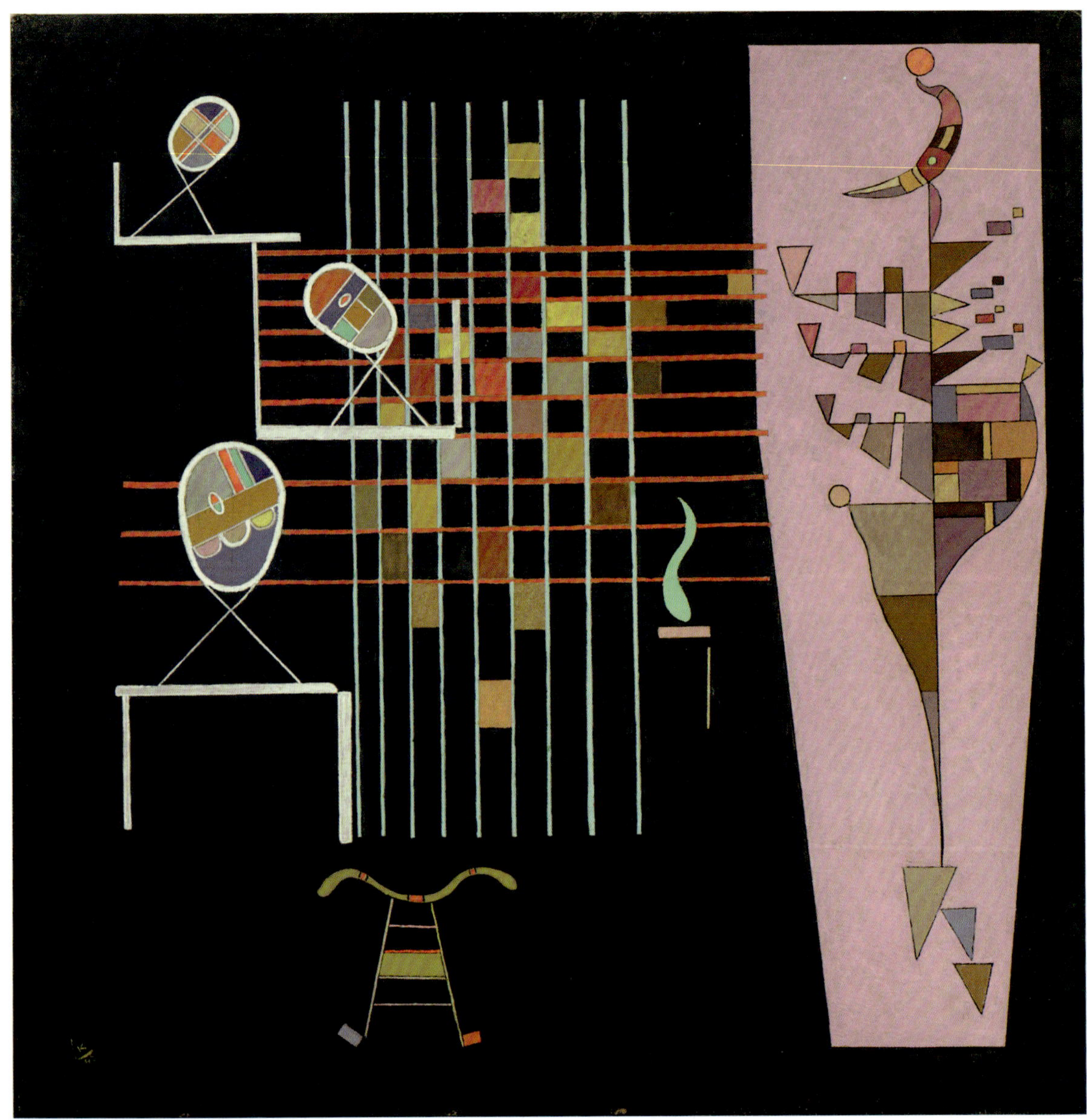

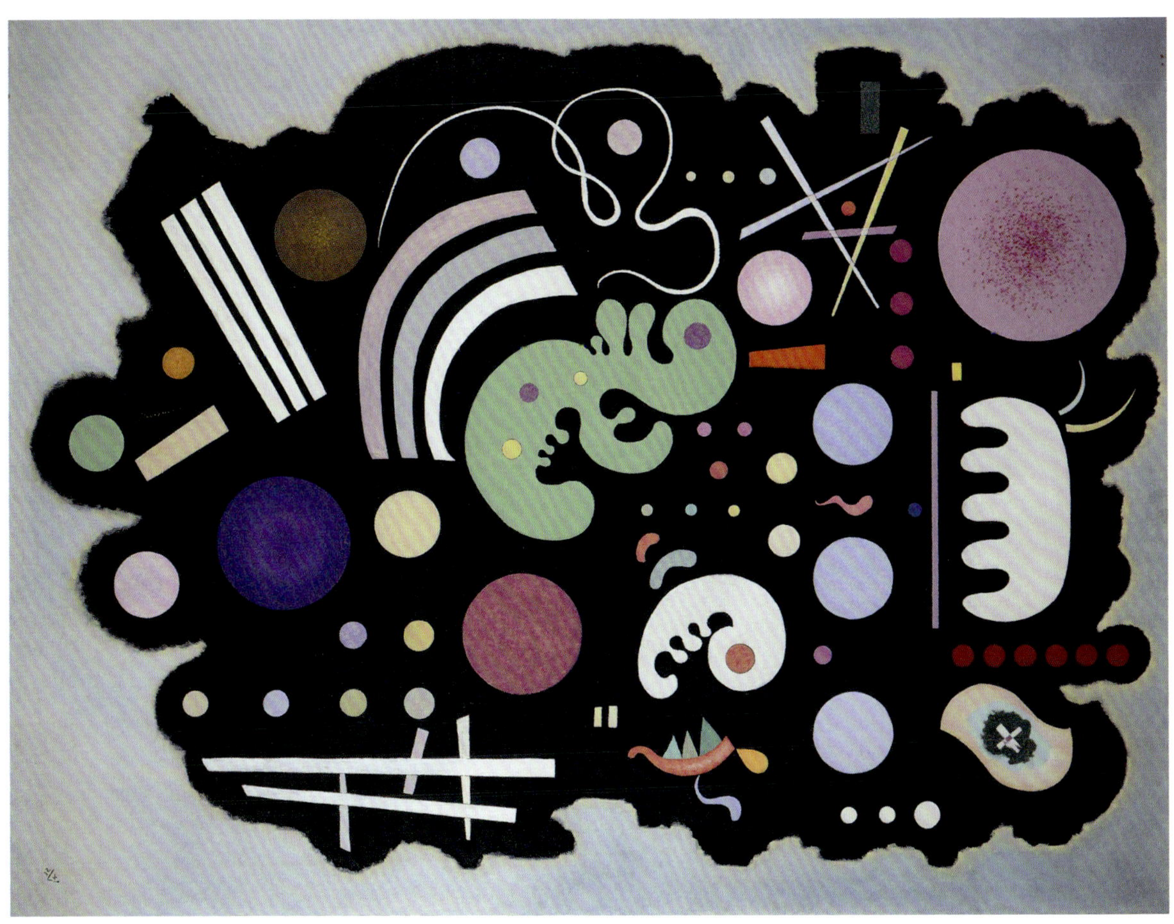

The Three Ovals
Trois ovales
Drei Ovale
Los tres óvalos
I tre ovali
Drie ovalen
1942, Oil on canvas/Huile sur toile, 49 × 49 cm, Private collection

Black Patchwork
Noir bigarré
Schwarzes Flickwerk
Mosaico negro
Patchwork nero
Zwart patchwork
1935, Oil on canvas/Huile sur toile, 116 × 89 cm, Private collection

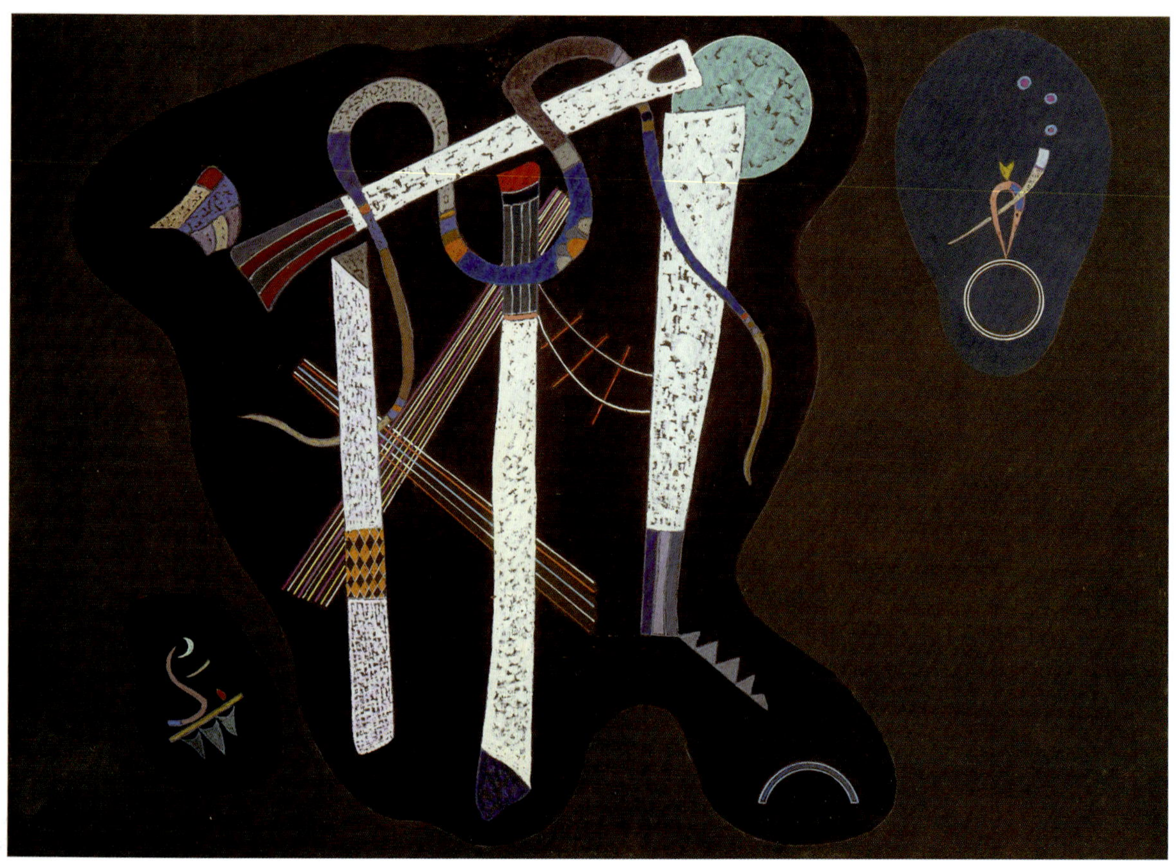

Three Pillars

Trois colonnes

Drei Säulen

Tres pilares

Tre pilastri

Drie zuilen

1943, Oil on board/Huile sur carton, 41,5 × 57,8 cm, Private collection

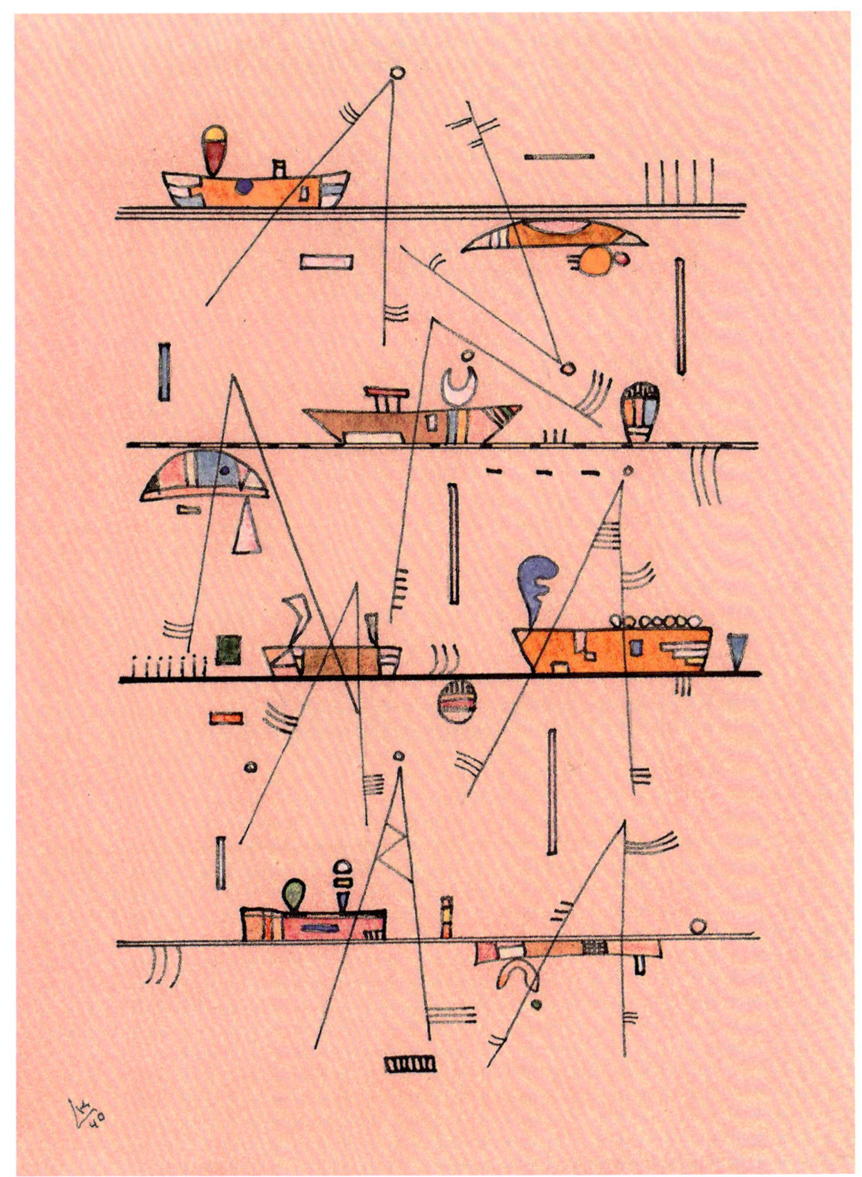

Untitled

Sans titre

Ohne Titel

Sin título

Senza titolo

Zonder titel

1940, Watercolor and ink on paper/
Aquarelle et encre de Chine sur papier,
21,2 × 16 cm, Private collection

Curriculum Vitae

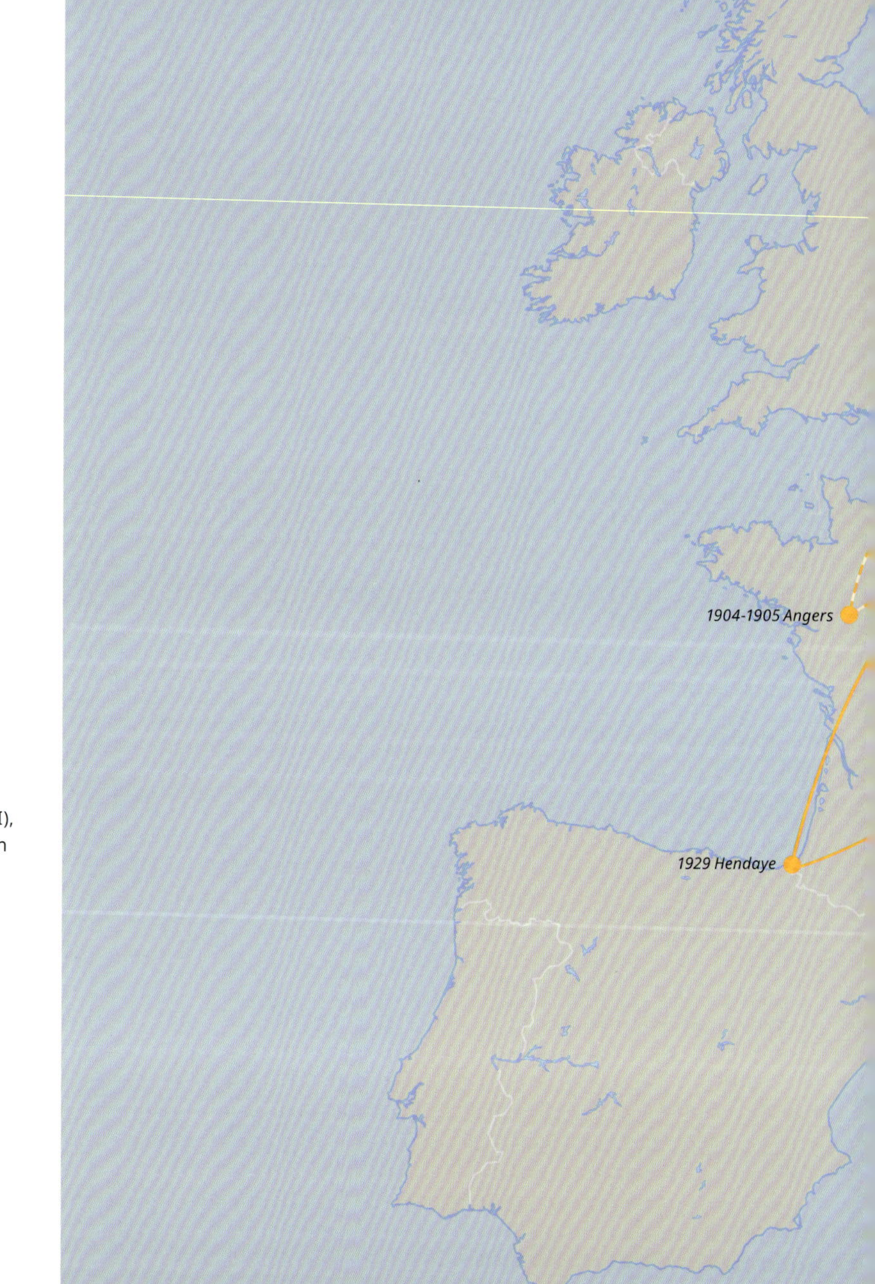

* 4.12.1866 Moscow
1871 Odessa
1885 Moscow
1896 Munich
1904–1905 Travel: Holland, Berlin,
Odessa, Paris, Tunis,
Dresden, Odessa, Rapallo (I),
Sèvres (F), Angers (F), Berlin
1908 Munich and Murnau
1912 Moscow
1913 Berlin
1914 Goldach/Bodensee (CH) –
Moscow
1921 Berlin
1922 Weimar
1925 Dessau
1929 Ostend (B),
Hendaye (F)
1932 Berlin
1933 Neuilly-sur-Seine (F)
†13.12.1944 Neuilly-sur-Seine (F)

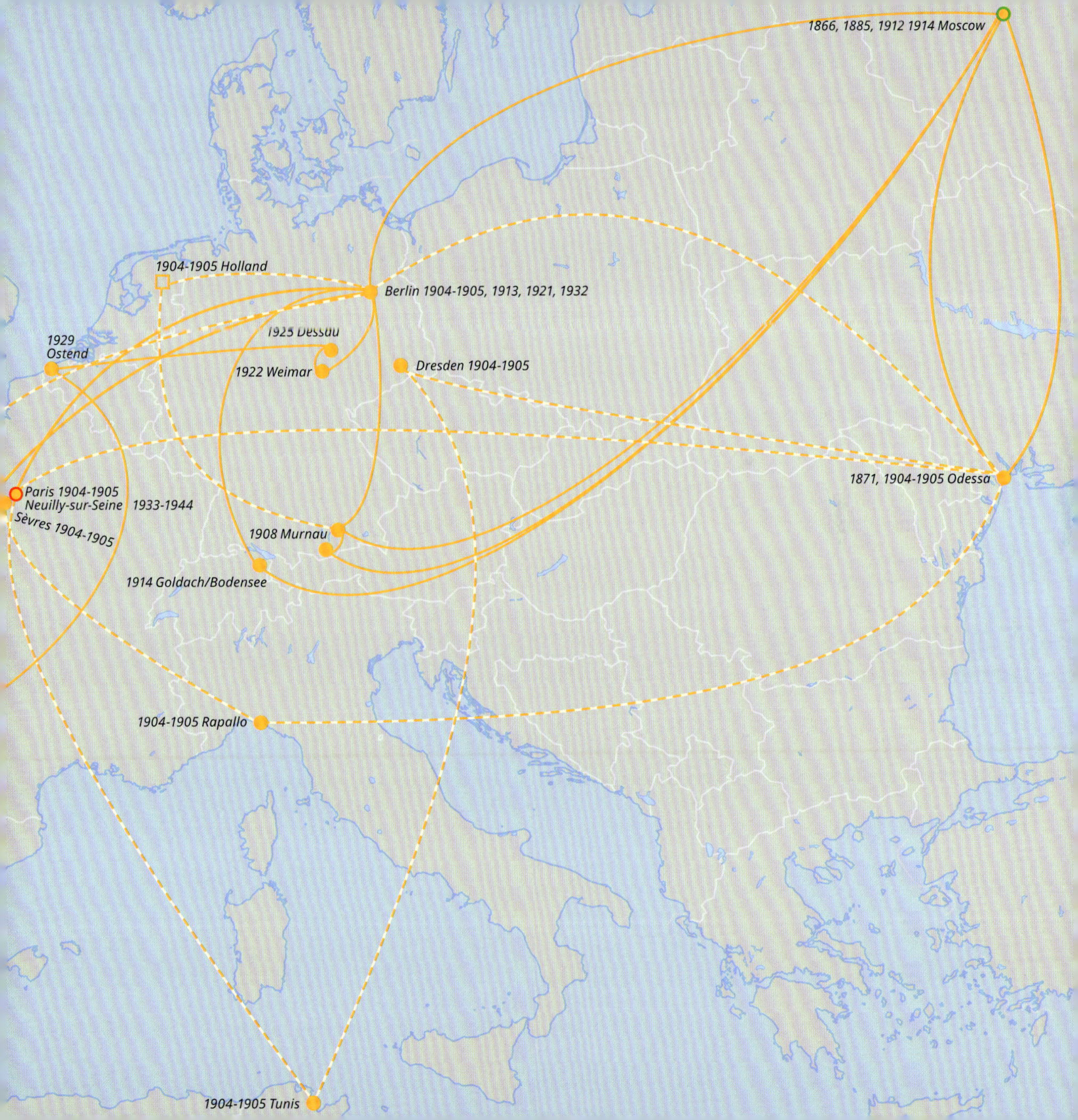

1866, 1885, 1912 1914 Moscow
1904-1905 Holland
Berlin 1904-1905, 1913, 1921, 1932
1929
Ostend
1925 Dessau
1922 Weimar
Dresden 1904-1905
1871, 1904-1905 Odessa
Paris 1904-1905
Neuilly-sur-Seine
Sèvres 1904-1905
1933-1944
1908 Murnau
1914 Goldach/Bodensee
1904-1905 Rapallo
1904-1905 Tunis

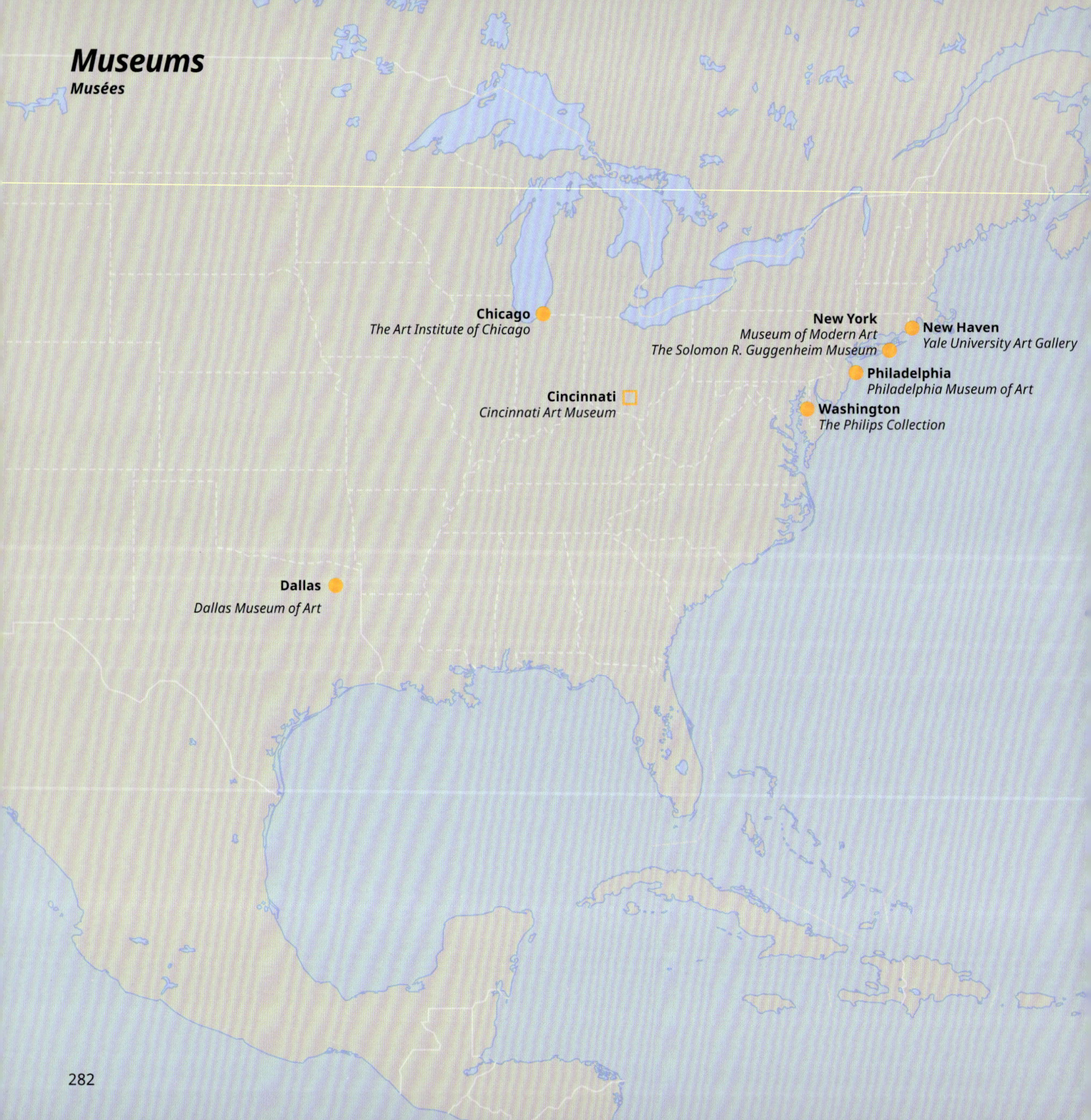
Museums
Musées

Chicago
The Art Institute of Chicago

New York
Museum of Modern Art
The Solomon R. Guggenheim Museum

New Haven
Yale University Art Gallery

Philadelphia
Philadelphia Museum of Art

Cincinnati
Cincinnati Art Museum

Washington
The Philips Collection

Dallas
Dallas Museum of Art

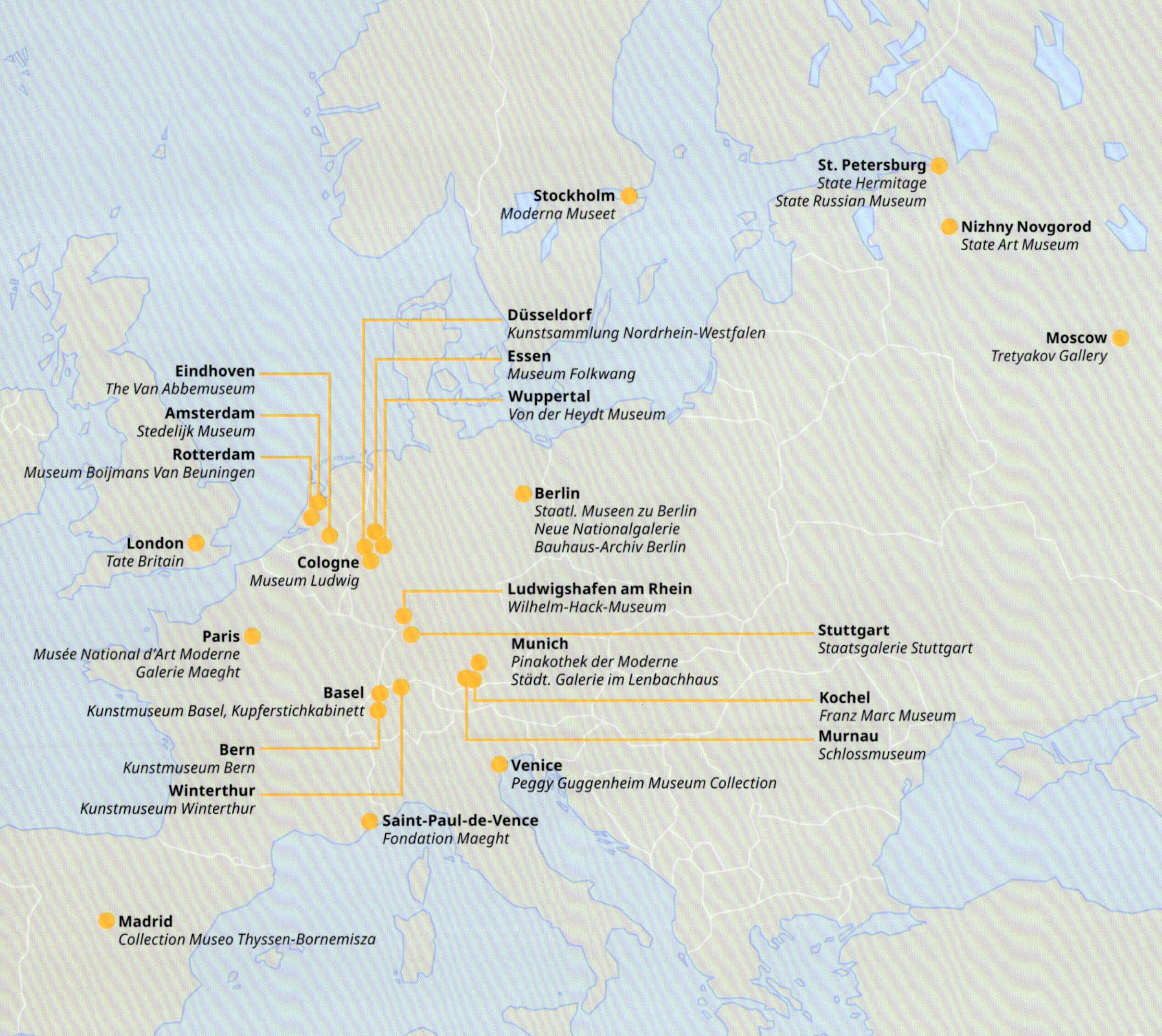

Stockholm
Moderna Museet

St. Petersburg
State Hermitage
State Russian Museum

Nizhny Novgorod
State Art Museum

Moscow
Tretyakov Gallery

Düsseldorf
Kunstsammlung Nordrhein-Westfalen

Essen
Museum Folkwang

Wuppertal
Von der Heydt Museum

Eindhoven
The Van Abbemuseum

Amsterdam
Stedelijk Museum

Rotterdam
Museum Boijmans Van Beuningen

Berlin
Staatl. Museen zu Berlin
Neue Nationalgalerie
Bauhaus-Archiv Berlin

London
Tate Britain

Cologne
Museum Ludwig

Ludwigshafen am Rhein
Wilhelm-Hack-Museum

Paris
Musée National d'Art Moderne
Galerie Maeght

Stuttgart
Staatsgalerie Stuttgart

Munich
Pinakothek der Moderne
Städt. Galerie im Lenbachhaus

Basel
Kunstmuseum Basel, Kupferstichkabinett

Kochel
Franz Marc Museum

Bern
Kunstmuseum Bern

Murnau
Schlossmuseum

Winterthur
Kunstmuseum Winterthur

Venice
Peggy Guggenheim Museum Collection

Saint-Paul-de-Vence
Fondation Maeght

Madrid
Collection Museo Thyssen-Bornemisza

Recommended Literature

Camilla Gray, *The great Experiment: Russian Art 1863–1922*, New York/London 1962

Angelica Zander Rudenstine, *The Guggenheim Museum Collections: Paintings 1880–1945*, New York 1976

John Bowlt, *Russian Art of the Avant-Garde: Theory and Criticism 1902–1934*, New York 1976

Peter Vergo, *The Blue Rider*, New York 1977

Peg Weiss, *Kandinsky in Munich: The Formative Jugendstil Years*, Princeton, N.J. 1979

Rose-Carol Washton-Long, *Kandinsky: The Development of an Abstract Style*, Oxford/New Yok 1980

Vivian Endicott Barnett, *Kandinsky Drawings. Catalogue Raisonné, Vol.1: Individual Drawings*, London 2006

V.E. Barnett, *Kandinsky Drawings. Catalogue Raisonné Vol. 2: Sketchbooks*, London 2007

Littérature recommandée

W. Kandinsky, *Regards sur le passé*, Gabriele Uffet-Picabia, Paris 1946

W. Kandinsky, *Du spirituel dans l'art et dans la peinture en particulier*, Pierre Volboudt, Paris 1969

Christian Derouet/Jessica Boissel, *Kandinsky: oeuvres de Vassily Kandinsky (1866–1944)*, Collections du Musée National d'Art Moderne. Centre Georges Pompidou, Paris 1984

W. Kandinsky, *Ecrits complets*, hrsg.v. Philipp Sers, 3 Bde., Paris 1970-1975

François LeTargat, *Kandinsky*, Paris 1986

Michel Henry, *Voir l'invisible: Sur Kandinsky*, Paris 1988

Annette Vezin, *Kandinsky et le Cavalier Bleu*, Paris 1991

Philippe Sers, *Kandinsky. Philosophie de l'abstraction, l'image métaphysique*, Genf 1995

Literaturempfehlungen
Eigene Schriften:

Über das Geistige in der Kunst, München 1912

Der Blaue Reiter, hrsg. von Wassily Kandinsky und Franz Marc München 1912 (Dokumentarische Neuausgabe von Klaus Lankheit, München und Zürich 1979)

Rückblicke, Der Sturm, Berlin 1913 (Neuabdruck im Verlag Woldemar Klein, Baden-Baden, 1955)

Punkt und Linie zu Fläche. Beitrag zur Analyse der malerischen Elemente. Bauhausbücher 9, München 1926 (Neuauflage Benteli-Verlag, hrsg. von Max Bill, 1969)

Essays über Kunst und Künstler, hrsg. von Max Bill, Stuttgart 1955

Die Gesammelten Schriften Bd.1, hrsg. von Hans K. Roethel und Jelena Hahl-Koch, Benteli-Verlag Bern 1980

Wassily Kandinsky. Die Basis-Bibliothek, mit einer Einführung von Hajo Düchting, Benteli 2016

Werkverzeichnisse:
Hans Konrad Roethel, *Kandinsky. Das graphische Werk*, Köln (Dumont) 1970
Hans Konrad Roethel und Jean K.Benjamin (Hrsg.), *Kandinsky-Werkverzeichnis der Ölgemälde*, Bd.1, 1900–1915, München (Verlag C.H. Beck) 1982
Bd.2, 1916–1944, München 1984
Vivian Endicott Barnett, *Kandinsky-Aquarelle. Catalogue raisonné. Werkverzeichnis der Aquarelle*, Bd.1, 1900–1921, München (Verlag C.H.Beck), 1992; Bd, 1922–1944, München 1994

Ausgewählte Bücher und Kataloge über Kandinsky:
Will Grohmann, *Wassily Kandinsky. Leben und Werk*, Köln 1958, 2. Auflage 1961
Nina Kandinsky, *Kandinsky und ich*, München 1976
Jelena Hahl-Koch (Hrsg.), Arnold Schönberg, *Wassily Kandinsky: Briefe, Bilder, Dokumente einer außergewöhnlichen Begegnung*, Salzburg/Wien 1980
Armin Zweite (Hrsg.), *Kandinsky und München, Begegnungen und Wandlungen 1896–1914*, Städt. Galerie im Lenbachhaus München, München 1982
Clark V.Poling (Hrsg.), *Kandinsky, Russische Zeit und Bauhausjahre 1915–1933*, Bauhaus-Archiv, Museum für Gestaltung, Berlin 1984
Andreas Hünke (Hrsg.), *Der Blaue Reiter. Dokumente einer geistigen Bewegung*, Leipzig 1989
Wassily Kandinsky. *Die erste sowjetische Retrospektive, Gemälde, Zeichnungen und Graphik aus sowjetischen und westlichen Museen*, Schirn-Kunsthalle Frankfurt a.M. 1989
Vivian Endicott Barnett und Armin Zweite (Hrsg.), *Kandinsky. Kleine Freuden. Aquarelle und Zeichnungen*, München 1992

Annegret Hoberg, *Wassily Kandinsky und Gabriele Münter in Murnau und Kochel 1902–1914. Briefe und Erinnerungen*, München 1994
Hajo Düchting, *Wassily Kandinsky 1866–1944. Revolution der Malerei*, Köln 1992
Ulrike Becks-Malorny, *Wassily Kandinsky 1866–1944. Aufbruch zur Abstraktion*, Köln 1993
Magdalena M. Moeller (Hrsg.), *Der frühe Kandinsky 1900–1910*, München 1994
Vivian Endicott Barnett und Helmut Friedel, *Das Bunte Leben. Wassily Kandinsky im Lenbachhaus*, Köln 1995
Helmut Friedel/Annegret Hoberg (Hrsg.), *Der Blaue Reiter im Lenbachhaus München 2000*
Helmut Friedel (Hrsg.), *Kandinsky Absolut Abstrakt*, Kat. Ausst. Städt. Galerie im Lenbachhaus und Kunstbau München, München 2008–2009
Erik Stephan (Hrsg.), *Punkt und Linie zu Fläche. Kandinsky am Bauhaus*, Kat. Ausst. Kunstsammlung Jena 2009
Helmut Friedel/Annegret Hoberg (Hrsg.), *Kandinsky. Das druckgrafische Werk*. Complete Prints, Kat.Ausst. Städt. Galerie im Lenbachhaus und Kunstbau, München 2009